Java® Media APIs: Cross-Platform Imaging, Media, and Visualization

Alejandro Terrazas, John Ostuni, and Michael Barlow

201 West 103rd St., Indianapolis, Indiana, 46290 USA

Java™ Media APIs: Cross-Platform Imaging, Media, and Visualization

Copyright © 2002 by Sams Publishing

International Standard Book Number: 0-672-32094-0

Library of Congress Catalog Card Number: 2001091791

Printed in the United States of America

First Printing: November 2002

04   03   02   4   3   2   1

Trademarks

Warning and Disclaimer

EXECUTIVE EDITOR
Michael Stephens

ACQUISITIONS EDITOR
Carol Ackerman

MANAGING EDITOR
Charlotte Clapp

PROOFREADER
Suzanne Thomas

TECHNICAL EDITOR
Chunyen Lui
Starfire Research

TEAM COORDINATOR
Lynne Williams

MEDIA DEVELOPER
Dan Scherf

INTERIOR DESIGNER
Anne Jones

COVER DESIGNER
Aren Howell

Contents at a Glance

Table of Contents

11   Creating the Virtual World   521

About the Authors

Dr. Alejandro Terrazas is president of VRSciences, a startup company developing VR therapies for the treatment of mental disorders including addiction and age-related memory impairments. The company also conducts research and develops software for simulation and training in virtual urban environments. Alex is an expert in functional brain imaging, neurophysiology and the brain mechanisms of navigation and memory formation in virtual environments. He previously held the position of associate director of the Machine Interface Network Design (MIND) Lab at Michigan State University where he oversaw research in telepresence, virtual environments, and 3D graphics. Dr. Terrazas received his Ph.D. in Cognition and Neural Systems from the University of Arizona.

John Ostuni graduated from Rutgers University with a Ph.D. in Biomedical Engineering. Since that time, he has worked at the National Institutes of Health where he is currently a senior staff scientist in the Warren Grant Magnuson Clinical Center. He has taught various courses in Java and C++, and his current interests are medical image processing and converting research-based software into clinical applications. He currently resides in Maryland with his wife Sandra and his two sons Steven and Anthony.

Dr. Michael Barlow (he prefers simply to be called Spike)is the founding director of the Virtual Environment and Simulation Laboratory (VESL) and a senior lecturer within the School of Computer Science at the University of New South Wales, ADFA (Australian Defence Force Academy).

For the past 15 years, Spike has been an active researcher in the area of media and speech recognition in particular, including a stint of two years in Japan's NTT (Nippon Telegraph and Telephone) Human Interface Laboratories working on Large Vocabulary Continuous Speech Recognition. His other major research areas include virtual environments for scientific visualization and education and multi-agent systems for simulation and modeling.

Spike has taught Java at the university level for several years. He currently teaches courses on OO programming, data structures, multimedia, and virtual environments.

Dedication

To Jane for her guidance and patience through our ten years of marriage.
To Victoria, Enrique, and Rebecca for being such wonderful kids.
To my late best friend, James G. Boyer, who lived and died like James Dean. —Alex Terrazas

To God and to my family. —John Ostuni

For now and then:
To Champ, Zoe-Blowie, and Grantly-Cantly. Life has never been so good!
In loving memory of Billy Leitch, the gentle prankster of my childhood. —Michael Barlow

Acknowledgments

I would like to thank all of the researchers, clinicians, and technologists at NIH for their ideas, help, and friendships. I would like to thank Alex for inviting me to write Chapters 4 through 6 in this book. I would also like to thank all the editors and reviewers, especially Regina Geoghan, for their help in preparing these chapters. I am also grateful to my many students for helping me to organize and refine much of this work. Most importantly, I would like to thank my family for supporting me throughout this book and throughout my career. —John Ostuni

Thanks to the multi-talented Mark Grundy (The Black Duck) for the music recordings used as audio examples in Chapter 7.

My thanks go to my colleagues and workmates at the School of Computer Science, ADFA, who provided both support and a bit of good-natured ribbing. In particular, my thanks go to Peter Morris, who captured and encoded the video samples of Chapter 7 and provided much good advice besides.

Thanks also to Wen Ung for the generous loan of a Webcam with which to test video capture code. Also thanks go to Aaron Mihe, who got my home PC (on which a lot of the text was written) up and running again after my fiddling—yet more proof that programmers shouldn't go near hardware. Finally, to Professor Charles Newton, Head of School, who supported my efforts with the book.

Thanks to Alex for taking me on board with the book. Last, but first in my heart, thanks to my family: Maria, Zoe, and Grant. They supported me in every way and didn't deserve the nights and weekends lost to my authoring. —Michael Barlow

I wish to thank Justin Couch and Alan Hudson of Yumetech for their considerable contributions to the ROAM code, their participation in the Java 3D mailing list and their tireless work on www.j3d.org. The Java 3D community is lucky to have them.

Thanks to Julian Gomez for his friendship and mentoring in 3D graphics.

Thanks to Paul Byrne for his contributions to the ROAM algorithm.

Thanks to Mark Hood for explaining the View Model with such clarity and for helping me so many times in getting various goggles working.

Finally, thanks to my students, Jose Thota, Eric Blackwell and Mike Meyer at Michigan State University who contributed to some of the writing and a lot of the testing of the code in Chapters 11-14 —Alex Terrazas

Tell Us What You Think!

As the reader of this book, *you* are our most important critic and commentator. We value your opinion and want to know what we're doing right, what we could do better, what areas you'd like to see us publish in, and any other words of wisdom you're willing to pass our way.

As an executive editor for Sams Publishing, I welcome your comments. You can fax, e-mail, or write me directly to let me know what you did or didn't like about this book—as well as what we can do to make our books stronger.

Please note that I cannot help you with technical problems related to the topic of this book, and that due to the high volume of mail I receive, I might not be able to reply to every message.

When you write, please be sure to include this book's title and authors' names as well as your name and phone or fax number. I will carefully review your comments and share them with the authors and editors who worked on the book.

Fax: 317-581-4770

E-mail: feedback@samspublishing.com

Mail: Michael Stephens
          Executive Editor
          Sams Publishing
          201 West 103rd Street
          Indianapolis, IN 46290 USA

Visualization, Media, and Imaging on the Java Platform

IN THIS CHAPTER

3D Modeling and Visualization with Java 3D

-Dr. Alejandro Terrazas

Java 3D is an object-oriented, scene-graph–based API for programming interactive 3D content on multiple platforms. Quite a lot of information is in the preceding sentence, so we will spend some time trying to unpack that statement.

Two basic flavors of Java 3D exist: OpenGL and DirectX. Java 3D takes advantage of these lower-level 3D APIs to do rendering; however, it is definitely a mistake to think that Java 3D simply makes bindings to the low-level API. It turns out that calls to OpenGL and DirectX are done through native interface calls, JNI, which are computationally expensive. Therefore, Java 3D performs a large number of optimizations and work in its own renderer before making the precious few calls to the low-level API.

Scene-graph API

One of the most important innovations to occur in 3D graphics programming in the last several years is the development of the scene graph. Two early adoptors of the scene graph are OpenInventor and VRML.

Generally speaking, the scene graph is a formal way to organize your 3D content, and as such it enables a number of optimizations. A full description of the advantages of the scene graph is given in Chapter 10, "3D Graphics, Virtual Reality, and Visualization." For now, consider that the scene graph organizes the data largely along the spatial dimension. Therefore, culling and other spatial optimizations that reduce the number of computations required for rendering a scene can eliminate entire branches of the tree structure.

Another major advantage of the scene graph approach is that the state of various attributes can be handed down to the children within the hierarchy.

Finally, the scene graph is a structure for managing content. The value of this function becomes apparent when developing a large project.

Object-Oriented 3D Graphics

Object-oriented programming is a natural way to think about 3D graphics. It is much preferable (from a content development and management perspective) than thinking about vertices and triangles. Nevertheless, the 3D content has to come from somewhere. Java 3D allows the developer to get down to the level of the vertices or to import pre-built geometry through loaders.

The other advantage to using object-oriented 3D graphics is extensibility. Java 3D provides a rich mechanism for extension. Developers will find themselves using extension time and time again.

Interactive Graphics

As already stated, Java 3D is generally for interactive graphics. Interactive refers to the fact that the user can make changes to the scene in near real-time. In other words, the model exists to be played with, and the user can create a totally novel view of the model by moving the mouse or interacting with the model in some way. Interactive graphics enable visualization and virtual navigation.

Getting the Java 3D API

Java 3D is freely downloadable from the `java.sun.com` Web site. There are a number of options for downloading the software. One of the first questions is whether the user wants OpenGL or DirectX versions. Like other Java APIs, there is a runtime version and an SDK. The runtime is there for any user to download and run Java 3D applets and applications. There is no facility for compiling Java 3D programs in the runtime. To write and compile a Java 3D program, the user will need to download the SDK. The most current version of Java 3D is FCS J3D1.3 v1.3 beta2. The Java 3D download includes a set of utilities that will be used extensively throughout the Java 3D section of the book.

Assuming that you already have Java installed, download and install the Java 3D SDK. The instructions are pretty straightforward. The only real trick is to put the java3d-utils-src.jar in the classpath.

You might also want to download the J3DFly examples. These examples are in addition to the Java 3D examples that come with the download, and they can be found at

`http://java.sun.com/products/java-media/3D/`

The Java Media Framework

-Dr. Michael "Spike" Barlow

The second major section of the book, Chapters 7, 8, and 9, covers time-based media (that is, video and audio) and the JMF—Java Media Framework, a Java API dedicated to the processing of time-based media.

Fundamentally, the JMF is an extension to Java for handling audio and video (audio and video being the two primary forms of time-based media). More rigorously, the JMF API (Java Media Framework Application Programming Interface) is one of the official Java Optional Packages from Sun Microsystems that extends the functionality of the core Java Platform. Included in this group of Optional Packages are others that are covered in the book: Java 3D and *Java Advanced Imaging (JAI)*.

The JMF comprises some 200 odd additional classes pertaining to the handling of time-based media. Handling is used in the broadest sense to include playback, capture, processing, and transmission, for either local media or media from a remote site, and as part of either an applet or application. Among the possibilities the API affords are platform (hardware and OS) independent video conferencing, complete audio and video editing suites, empowering the latest mobile computing such as cellular phones and *PDAs (Personal Digital Assistants)*, and when taken in conjunction with the other media APIs, completely integrated multimedia applications written entirely in Java and running on any platform.

JMF Coverage in the Book

The three chapters in this section of the book follow a progression of simple out-of-the-box utilization of the API to sophisticated usage, such as in combination with other specialized features and APIs of Java. Hence, a linear progression through the material is recommended as the default. However, those of you possessing a familiarity with time-based media or parts of the API might want to skip some of the introductory material.

The structure of the three chapters is as follows:

- Chapter 7, "Time-Based Media and the JMF: An Introduction"—The first chapter of the section on the JMF serves as both an introduction to time-based media in general and to the JMF API. Some of the fundamental concepts and issues for both digital audio and video are introduced. Midway through the chapter is an introduction to the JMF API in terms of its features, promise, central concepts, and main classes.

- Chapter 8, "Controlling and Processing Media with JMF"—This chapter serves as the core chapter of the JMF section, covering the key features of the JMF API. The topics covered include managers, data sources and sinks, multiplexing and demultiplexing, codecs, format conversion, effects, and the capture of media from devices.

- Chapter 9, "RTP and Advanced Time-Based Media Topics"—This chapter covers some of the more advanced features of the JMF API. Chief among these topics is the *Real-Time Transport Protocol (RTP)* support within JMF and the corresponding ability to transmit or receive streaming media such as over the Internet. Also covered are issues such as extending the API and utilizing other APIs in conjunction with JMF.

Obtaining and Installing the JMF

The JMF extends the functionality of the Java platform and is an official Optional Package. As such, it is a free download available from Sun Microsystems' Java site: `http://java.sun.com`. Following the Products & APIs link will present the browser with a wealth of APIs; among them, the JMF can be found under the Optional Packages heading at the bottom of the page.

Alternatively, and more directly, Sun maintains a central Web page regarding the JMF: `http://java.sun.com/products/java-media/jmf/index.html`. You should definitely bookmark this URL: It not only has links for downloading the latest version of the JMF, but it also links to documentation and example programs, as well as the latest JMF-related news.

Sun provides several different versions of the JMF for download. These differ in the OS platform they are intended to run on. The current version, as of the time of writing, is v2.1.1a. At the previously mentioned central site, Sun provides links for a cross-platform Java version, a Windows Performance Pack, and a Solaris SPARC Performance Pack. A link is also provided to Blackdown's JMF implementation for Linux. All versions require JDK 1.1.6 or later for full functionality. Those of you who want to obtain the JMF without possessing the JDK should download and install that first.

Although the cross-platform version is pure byte code and will run on any machine supporting Java, it is recommended that you download and install the OS specific versions that matches your OS. This is because these implementations have been optimized with native code where appropriate, and hence should run faster than the cross-platform version. Thus, those of you who are running Windows 95, 98, or NT should download the Windows Performance Pack, those of you who are running on one of Sun's UNIX machines should download the Solaris SPARC Performance Pack, and those of you who are under Linux should download Blackdown's version of the JMF for Linux. Those of you who are not employing any of these (for example, on a Macintosh) should download the cross-platform version.

Sun provides detailed and specific instructions regarding the download and installation process. Those instructions are tailored to the specific version downloaded. Following the download links will take the browser through those instructions. Thus, specific download and installation instructions are not repeated here. Installation of any version of the JMF is quite simple, consisting of self-installing executables or the equivalent. However, those of you who want detailed installation instructions can find them at `http://java.sun.com/products/java-media/jmf/2.1.1/setup.html`.

Following the installation process, you should check that the JMF is available for usage. One means of checking this is to attempt to run the JMStudio demonstration program that is provided as part of the JMF. Discussed further in Chapter 7, JMStudio is a powerful application that demonstrates many of the capabilities of the JMF, such as playback, capture, and processing. Running JMStudio is as simple as typing `java JMStudio` at your command prompt. If the JMF installed properly, a small JMStudio window will pop up from which the various functions can be selected.

An alternative means of checking whether the JMF installed correctly is to point your browser at `http://java.sun.com/products/java-media/jmf/2.1.1/jmfdiagnostics.html`, Sun's JMF diagnostic page. As part of the installation process, the JMF is made available to your

Web browser so that JMF-based applets can be run. The preceding URL tests this feature. Similarly, `http://java.sun.com/products/java-media/jmf/2.1.1/samples/index.html` contains JMF-based applets that will play movie trailers, providing that the JMF is installed on your machine, and it is arguably a more exciting means of testing the functionality of the newly installed JMF.

Additional JMF-Related Resources

A number of resources pertaining to the JMF are available on the Web. Sun's central JMF page, `http://java.sun.com/products/java-media/jmf/index.html`, acts as a clearing house for many, but not all, of these additional resources.

Two key resources that anyone undertaking serious JMF programming should possess are the API (class) documentation and the Programmer's Guide from Sun. The API documentation is a class-by-class description of the API. The Programmer's Guide is a comprehensive introduction to the API from its authors. Both these documents can be browsed online or downloaded to a user's machine. Both the online and downloadable version of these documents can be found linked from Sun's central JMF page.

Other resources at Sun's site include excellent sample programs, source code for the JMF itself and JMStudio, as well as user guides for JMStudio and JMFRegistry.

Sun maintains a free mailing list: *jmf-interest*, for those wanting to discuss the JMF. The details for subscribing to and posting to the list can be found at the following URL: `http://java.sun.com/products/java-media/jmf/support.html`. (It is also linked from Sun's main JMF site.) Joining the list is highly recommended for those undertaking programming in the JMF—the list is a small but helpful community with relatively low traffic (typically fewer than a dozen messages a day) with Sun engineers periodically monitoring and posting on the list. The list's past archives, found at `http://archives.java.sun.com/archives/jmf-interest.html`, contain a wealth of information.

Finally, it is worth noting that although the JMF comes with many audio and video codecs (the compression schemes that are used for audio and video and which dictate its format), further codecs can be installed. These additional codecs then expand the functionality of the JMF—JMF is then able to handle media of that format. Two popular codecs of note, MPEG-4 and DivX, can be incorporated into the JMF in this manner. IBM, through its AlphaWorks division, has provided an implementation of MPEG-4 for the JMF at `http://www.alphaworks.ibm.com/tech/mpeg-4`. DivX support, currently a popular video format on the Internet because its high compression and good visual quality, can be incorporated into the JMF by downloading the DivX codec from the DivX home page: `http://www.divx.com/`.

Loading and Manipulating Images

-Dr. John Ostuni

Another major section of this book is composed of Chapters 4, 5, and 6. These sections cover loading and manipulating image data. Although Java has always included methods to decode GIF and JPEG images, the ability to read other formats was not available. Also the ability to write formatted images was not available at all. These limitations were removed with the introduction of the Image I/O API in jdk1.4. The Image I/O API provides a pluggable architecture for working with images stored in files and accessed across the network. This API is based on format-specific plug-ins, some of which are contained as part of the Java standard edition whereas others can be downloaded from third parties or written as needed.

Besides loading image data, another difficulty in Java was the limitations in working with image data. Although there were classes to perform image processing, it was difficult to put together a professional image processing application. These limitations were removed with the release of the Java Advanced Imaging API. This API provides the foundation necessary for complex image manipulation, processing, and analysis. The *Java Advanced Imaging (JAI)* API can be thought of as an extension of Java 2D. It was designed so that a user can develop sophisticated and complete image processing applets and applications. It contains more than 80 image processing operations. It is also extensible so that users can add their own operations. It provides support for many different data types and image formats. One more interesting aspect of the JAI API is that for many platforms, native code is included in order to take advantage of any platform specific libraries that might improve image processing speed. At runtime, if the Java interpreter finds the native classes, they will be used. If they are not found, the interpreter will fall back to a pure Java mode.

Image I/O and Image Manipulation Coverage in This Book

The three chapters in this section of the book progress in a logical manner. Chapter 4 covers the standard image I/O and image manipulation prior to the release of jdk1.4 and the Java Advanced Imaging API. Chapter 5 covers the Image I/O API, whereas Chapter 6 covers the Java Advanced Image API.

The structure of the three chapters is as follows:

- Chapter 4, "Immediate Mode Imaging Model"—In this chapter, I will discuss the image I/O and image processing available in the Java 2D API. This chapter covers the basic concepts of an image: how to load and manipulate images.

- Chapter 5, "Image I/O API"—In this chapter, I will not only examine how the Java Image I/O API is used, but also I will devote a significant portion of this chapter to developing new Image I/O plug-ins. All the major features, concepts, and classes are discussed.

- Chapter 6, "Java Advanced Imaging"—In this chapter, I will concentrate on the main JAI classes, specifically why they were developed and how they interact. I will examine all the image processing operations and how they are used. Finally, I will discuss some advanced topics such as a rendered versus renderable layer, remote image processing, and extending the JAI to add your own image processing operations.

Obtaining and Installing the Image I/O API and the Java Advanced Imaging API

Starting with jdk1.4, the Java I/O API is part of the Java standard edition. Thus, there is no need to download it separately.

On the other hand, the Java Advanced Imaging API is not part of the Java standard edition and must be downloaded separately. This can be done at the following URL: `http://java.sun.com/products/java -media/jai/downloads/download.html`. Because there is native code in this API, you will have to choose among a Solaris, Linux, or Windows download. Besides being able to download the JAI API, you can also download demos and a tutorial at this URL.

Additional Resources for the Image I/O and the Java Advanced Imaging APIs

To augment the information found in Chapter 4, refer to the Java 2D home page at `http://java.sun.com/products/java-media/2D/index.html`.

To augment the information found in Chapter 5, refer to the Image I/O home page at `http://java.sun.com/j2se/1.4/docs/guide/imageio/index.html`. This URL contains a description of each of the packages composing the Image I/O API. It also contains a link to a Java Image I/O API Guide.

To augment the information found in Chapter 6, refer to the JAI home page at `http://java.sun.com/products/java-media/jai/index.html`. Another useful URL is the JAI API page at `http://java.sun.com/j2se/1.4/docs/api/index.html`. This page provides all the methods for all the JAI classes, so it makes a great resource when you start programming. You can download a local copy of this API from the JAI Documentation page at `http://java.sun.com/products/java-media/jai/docs/index.html`. This page also contains a JAI programming guide so that you can see examples of Java programs using JAI.

If you still have questions regarding some aspect of the JAI, you can go to the JAI FAQ page at `http://java.sun.com/products/java-media/jai/forDevelopers/jaifaq.html`. Another useful resource is the JAI Interest Group, which provides answers and comments to the questions other members of the group pose. To view an archive of this e-mail, refer to `http://archives.java.sun.com/archives/jai-interest.html`. Finally, if you find some part of the JAI that isn't working as it should, you can refer to the JAI bug pages to either submit a bug report or to see whether it has already been submitted. This page can be found at `http://java.sun.com/products/java-media/jai/jai-bugs.html`.

Summary

The Java Media APIs provide a common platform for developing media, imaging, and visualization applications that are suitable for many platforms and the Internet. One of the particular strengths is having access to the entire Java language as well as the other Java Media APIs.

This book attempts to get the developer up and running with the Java 3D APIs using less complicated heuristic examples augmented by more complex comprehensive examples. There is no way that the entire API could be covered in this text nor any other for that matter. Java 3D is immense and is changing frequently. You will also gain some insight into 3D graphics. From experience, we can say that these are both somewhat difficult topics that can take years to master. However, much of what developers want to produce can be done rapidly with Java 3D.

We wish you well in your use of these exciting technologies. We hope you will enjoy using them as much as we enjoyed writing about them.

2D Graphics and Imaging on the Java Platform: The Java 2D, Java Advanced Imaging, and Java Image I/O APIs

IN THIS PART

Imaging and Graphics on the Java Platform

IN THIS CHAPTER

Java provides a rich platform for writing graphics and imaging applications. This chapter is an overview and roadmap for how to approach writing a graphics or imaging application in Java, and we will develop some of the concepts that will be necessary as you further explore this exciting part of the Java Media APIs.

Evolution of Graphics and Imaging on the Java Platform

Java-based imaging has progressed through three main stages: the AWT model, the Java 2D API extensions to that model, and the *Java Advanced Imaging (JAI)* API extensions to the Java 2D API. All the major parts of Java 2D and JAI can ultimately trace their lineage to the AWT model. That said, the AWT model is fairly simple and will receive attention only as needed to explain Java 2D and JAI concepts. The beginning reader will want to become familiar with a set of core packages, especially `java.awt` and `java.awt.image` and will want to bookmark the following URLs:

> `http://java.sun.com/j2se/1.3/docs/api/java/awt/package-summary.html`
>
> `http://java.sun.com/j2se/1.3/docs/api/java/awt/Image.html`

It should be emphasized at the outset that many imaging and graphics problems can be solved by simply using the Java 2D API. The developer will want to weigh heavily whether it is necessary to use the JAI extensions. A primary reason is that, at present, the JAI API isn't part of the core Java Foundation Classes. The Java 2D API is part of the JFC and is thus supported on all Java platforms since 1.2. Java 2D's being a standard part of the JFC simplifies matters greatly for many basic Internet applications because the user isn't required to set classpaths or download class libraries. Another important reason for choosing Java 2D over JAI is simplicity. Getting a handle on JAI can be challenging, even for experienced image processing programmers.

On the other hand, JAI is truly an advanced imaging API. It is a complete extension to Java 2D and allows for powerful imaging operations such as multiresolution imaging, image tiling, and imaging over a network (explained in Chapter 5, "Image I/O Package"). JAI comes with more than 80 image operators and provides an extension mechanism for developing additional operators. Further, JAI uses a sophisticated imaging model, called the pull model, that enables a number of optimizations and allows so-called *deferred* execution, in which images are processed as needed, thus avoiding unnecessary image computation. Another important aspect of the JAI is the use of native code for many image processing operations.

JAI is suitable for applications such as medical imaging, interactive special effects, and remote sensing applications, just to name a few. My own emphasis is on functional brain imaging and virtual reality. In both of these areas, I see the potential for a lot of exciting applications. Nonetheless, a more mundane aspect of my research involves the design of computerized cognitive tasks, essentially little custom user interfaces that are displayed on the computer screen to study some particular cognitive skill. For the development of these applications, Java 2D is ideal. Given that Java 2D has some reasonably sophisticated image processing capabilities, excellent and complete graphics support, and is included as part of the core JDK 1.2, most developers will want to strongly consider using Java 2D unless compelled to do otherwise.

It is further true that a basic knowledge of Java 2D (at least the imaging aspects of Java 2D) is essential to understanding the JAI. Readers already knowledgeable about things such as the immediate mode rendering model and the difference between rendered and renderable images might want to skip ahead to Chapter 6, "Java Advanced Imaging," where the JAI is described in detail.

Graphics Versus Imaging

At the onset, it is necessary to separate the notions of graphics and imaging. *Graphics* refers to the drawing of two-dimensional geometric shapes and text, whereas *imaging* is reserved to mean the spatial representation of some physical quantity. In the case of digital photography, for example, the physical quantity is light intensity across the rectangular view area of the camera. A *texture* is somewhere in between a graphic and an image in that a texture is typically a programmed pattern that is treated more or less like an image. As an aside, we note that generating images from graphics is straightforward; however, the reverse isn't true. The generation of geometric shapes from images is a fundamental problem in computer vision and image analysis.

Although some overlap will exist between the operations performed on graphics and images, they will, in general, be treated as separate here.

Coordinate Spaces: User Space and Device Space

The critical concept necessary for understanding graphics and imaging on the Java platform is the idea of user space and device space because they will be used extensively in this and other sections of the book.

User space is the coordinate space in which the user operates. At instantiation, the origin of user space is at the top-left corner of the screen with the x coordinate increasing to the right and the y coordinate increasing downward. The user can move, translate, and otherwise change the user space.

2

IMAGING AND
GRAPHICS ON THE
JAVA PLATFORM

NOTE

User space is independent of the space of all output devices.

Device space, on the other hand, is completely dependent on the output device and its drivers. Based on the requirements of the targeted device space, Java 2D will create a transformation of the user space to device space (see Figure 2.1), including a color transformation and a resolution transformation. Thankfully, the application developer doesn't need to make this transformation. Knowing that and how the user space to device space transformation occurs, however, is key for understanding the mechanisms and capabilities of Java-based graphics and imaging. The hypothetical device space in Figure 2.1 has a different size and orientation than the user space in which the graphic (in this case, a plus sign) is drawn. A transformation exists between the two spaces so that everything looks as expected when the graphic is rendered.

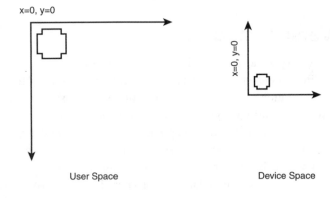

FIGURE 2.1
User space and a hypothetical device space.

So, what's the big deal about user and device space? It comes down to Java's capability to support many devices on many platforms. To reiterate, user space is a generic, *device independent* space to which graphics can be drawn without concern for the ultimate output destination. Device space is *device dependent* and conforms to the specific requirements of the target device. Understanding this difference will serve the reader well during all further discussion.

Finding Out About Device Space

In the vast majority of cases, the programmer doesn't need to worry about device space. However, when you do need to know some details about device spaces and the characteristics of the available devices, the following three classes are invaluable:

- `GraphicsEnvironment`
- `GraphicsDevice`
- `GraphicsConfiguration`

Objects generated by the `GraphicsEnvironment` return a list of all devices on a platform. This list includes the expected printers and video displays, but also lists memory buffers and fonts. Java supports a multimonitor environment that can be important for some imaging and virtual reality applications. More information on this topic is given in Chapter 13, "Working with Input and Output Devices."

Objects instantiated from the `GraphicsDevice` and `GraphicsConfiguration` classes refer to individual devices and configurations, respectively. Note that a single device might have multiple configurations associated with it. Listing 2.1 can be used to query the graphics environment (stored in the examples under GraphicsQuery.java).

LISTING 2.1   GraphicsQuery

```java
import java.awt.*;
import javax.swing.*;
import   java.awt.event.*;
import java.awt.image.*;
import java.applet.Applet;

public class GraphicsQuery extends JApplet {

    public GraphicsQuery() {

        BufferedImage big =
new BufferedImage(200, 200,BufferedImage.TYPE_INT_ARGB);

        GraphicsEnvironment ge =
            GraphicsEnvironment.getLocalGraphicsEnvironment();

        //list all fonts font families on the platform

        System.out.println("****START LISTING FONTS****");

        String[] fonts = ge.getAvailableFontFamilyNames();
        for (int i=0; i < fonts.length; i++) {
            System.out.println("AVAILABLE FONTS; i: " + i +
                            " FONT NAME: " + fonts[i]);
        }

        System.out.println("****STOP LISTING FONTS****");

        GraphicsDevice dscreen = ge.getDefaultScreenDevice();

  System.out.println("DEFAULT SCREEN ID: " +
 dscreen.getIDstring() +  " DEVICE TYPE: " +
 dscreen.getType());
```

LISTING 2.1 Continued

```
    //the following gets an array of screen devices;
//the number is usually one but sometimes many

    GraphicsDevice[] gs = ge.getScreenDevices();
     for (int i = 0; i < gs.length; i++) {
       GraphicsDevice gd = gs[i];
       GraphicsConfiguration[] gc = gd.getConfigurations();

       for (int j=0; j < gc.length; j++) {
         Rectangle gcBounds = gc[j].getBounds();
         System.out.println("SCREEN DEVICE #: " + j +
                            " TYPE: " + gd.getType() +
                            " x bounds: " + gcBounds.x +
                            " y bounds: " + gcBounds.y);
       }
     }
  }

  public static void main(String arg[]) {
      GraphicsQuery gq = new GraphicsQuery();
   }
}
```

What Is Rendering?

Because we will spend a great deal of time talking about rendering, it will be useful to create an operational definition. *Rendering* is the process of making graphics and images objects appear on an output device. An output device is most often the screen, a printer, or a memory area.

Although that sounds pretty simple, the actual implementation is a fairly involved process. Consider the challenge of rendering a simple blue square or other shape to a monitor. A major problem is that the device space of the monitor is likely to be completely different from the user space that the programmer has used for defining the graphics to be output. This is especially true for an application written for the Internet or an intranet where literally hundreds of different monitors will be the output target of a rendering. Additionally, the user might want to print on any number of printers, each with a different resolution and color palette.

As stated earlier, much of this can remain transparent to the programmer because of the user- and device-space paradigm. Ignoring the details, however, will eventually be limiting. It will become important to understand the rendering process in order to develop a robust graphics and imaging application. This knowledge will prove invaluable when moving onto the JAI as well as the Java 3D and JMF portions of this book.

The rendering process is shown schematically in Figure 2.2. The graphics or images to be rendered begin as defined in user space and undergo a series of transformations in the `Graphics2D` object (represented by the large box outlined in black) before being output to the device (that is, printer, file, or screen).

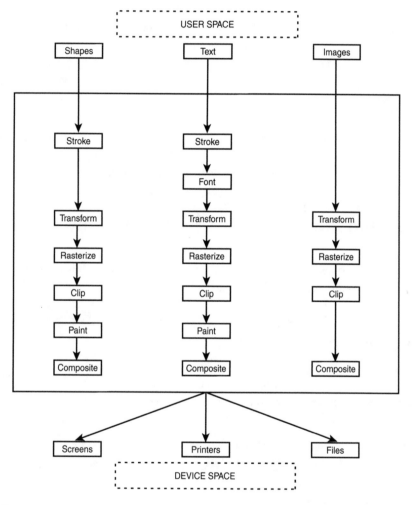

2

IMAGING AND
GRAPHICS ON THE
JAVA PLATFORM

FIGURE 2.2

Rendering steps in Java.

Because this series of steps is so important to our discussion, let's examine it in more detail. Note how we transition from user space to device space as we move through the rendering pipeline.

Determine the Appropriate Rendering Area of the Output Device

This step depends on the graphics object to be rendered. If it is a shape or text, all that is needed is the outline of the shape. The outline is determined by computing a stroke for the shape (basically turning the shape outline into a sequence of primitives). For images, a bounding box is created that surrounds the whole (or parts of the image) to render. Next, the shape or image bounding box is transformed from user space to device space using a set of linear transforms. The proper linear transforms are derived from the manufacturer-supplied drivers of the target device.

Rasterize

Rasterization is the process of turning ideal shapes into a list of pixels. Ultimately, the renderer has to send a stream of values to the output device. A video monitor, for example, scans across the screen, tuning on red, green, or blue guns in sequence. This sequence is determined by rasterization. During the rasterization process, rendering options such as antialiasing and dithering are applied.

Clip the Rendering Operation to Render Only the Desired Parts

After the graphics are transformed to the device space and rasterized, they are clipped. *Clipping* refers to limiting the rendering to particular portions of the output device.

Determine the Colors to Render and Convert to the Device Color Space

Much as it is necessary to apply a transformation to a shape or image in order to make the rendering compatible with the resolution of the target output device, it is also necessary to transform the colors and paints from user space to the palette of device space. This step includes applying transparency values.

By the time the renderer has completed the second step, the graphics objects have entered device space. The color information still is in user space until this step.

To summarize, rendering is the process of taking the graphics or images that are defined in user space and transforming them into the proper description for a particular output device.

Graphics Context

A large part of the process of writing graphics and imaging applications in Java comes down to specifying the desired graphics context for rendering. The *graphics context* refers to a set of attributes that specify the properties for the output rendering. These properties can be as simple as the color used for filling a shape or can be more complex, such as setting the antialiasing for drawing lines. Throughout the next several chapters, pay close attention and make a mental note when changes to the graphics context are made. Most changes to the graphics context are accomplished with methods that begin with set, for example, setPaint() or setColor().

The Basic Recipe for Rendering in Java 2D

A fundamental three-step recipe exists for programming graphics in Java. Get (or modify) the Graphics2D context, create some geometry (or an image), and call a rendering method. The following short code snippet demonstrates this recipe:

```
public void paint(Graphics g) {

//get instance of graphics context
Graphics2D g2d  = (Graphics2D) g;

//modify the graphics context
g2d.setColor(Color.blue);

//call a render method
g2d.fill(new Ellipse2D.Float(5.f,5.f, 40.f, 40.f,);

}
```

Several complete examples are developed in Chapter 3, "Graphics Programming with the Java2D API."

Imaging Fundamentals

A digital image refers to a series of two- or three-dimensional *spatially ordered* digitized samples of some physical quantity. The physical quantity can be practically anything. In digital photography, for example, samples represent light intensity values acquired across the lens. In *positron emission tomography (PET imaging)*, the spatially ordered samples represent the detected level of a radioactive chemical (reflected in the number of so-called annihilation events) that is taken up by the brain or some other organ. In remote sensing, the spatially organized data could represent heat or vegetation density, and so on. The basic key to understanding images is in realizing that the spatially ordered samples are really just a stream of numbers residing in a file or memory.

Consider a simple 4x4 grayscale image (see Figure 2.3). When the data is stored on disk, it typically isn't stored as a 4x4 matrix, but rather it is represented as a list of 16 numbers (4x4=16). The meaning of the order of the numbers must be known if the image is going to be displayed or interpreted in any meaningful way. The most obvious order might be something like every fifth number represents the first element of a new row, for example. The discussion could easily be extended to a 2x2x2 cube. Data for the image is stored in a vector of 16 elements with values increasing consecutively from 1:16. By convention, every fifth element is a shift to a new line.

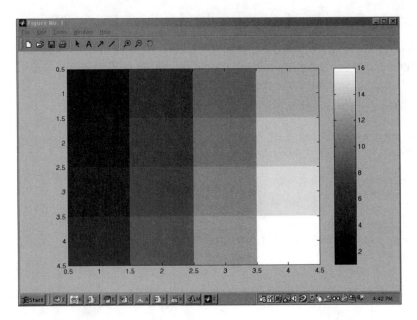

FIGURE 2.3
Simple 4x4 image.

Let's next move on to a real example that will be expanded on in Chapter 4, "Immediate Mode Imaging Model." One common type of brain image is a T2-weighted magnetic resonance image (see Figure 2.4). Each pixel value represents the T2 signal intensity at a particular spatial location in a slice of the brain. All the pixel values are stored sequentially in a file with some header information at the beginning. Because this is a grayscale image, there is a one-to-one correspondence between a number in the file and the value of the pixel. We know the dimension of this image to be 256x256 (because that what's we told the scanner we wanted). We also know that the values are stored in short integers so we can expect 256*256 or a total of 65,536 short (2 bytes) values to be stored in the file (after moving past the slightly annoying header information of 7,904 bytes). It is always useful to calculate the expected file size for these types of projects. The size of this file then is 138,976 bytes—7,904 + (2*65,536). The data is read in with ReadImage.java (see Listing 2.2), stored in a BufferedImage and rendered to the screen.

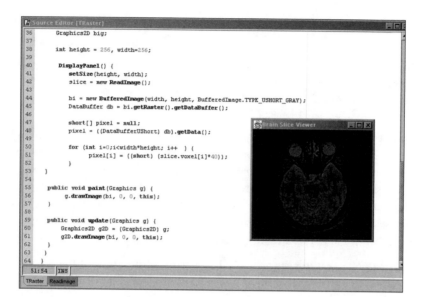

FIGURE 2.4

T2-weighted MRI of the brain.

Listing 2.2 demonstrates the reading of the image data into a one-dimensional array (vector) named voxel:

LISTING 2.2   ReadImage.java

```java
int nvox = 256*256;
try {
DataInputStream vox = new
DataInputStream(newFileInputStream("I.022"));

vox.skip(7904); // skip the annoyingheader
     try {
    for (int i=1;i <= nvox;i++) {
       v = vox.readShort();
     voxel[i] =  v;
    }
} catch (EOFException e) {
   System.out.println("End of file encountered");
}
 } catch (FileNotFoundException e) {
    System.out.println("DataIOTest: " + e);
 } catch (IOException e) {
    System.out.println("DataIOTest: " + e);
 }
}
```

> **NOTE**
>
> This external class is not intended to be run yet and is part of a more comprehensive example that is provided in Chapter 4.

The 256x256 image is stored in a one-dimensional array (that is, vector) with a length of 65,536. Have we lost our information about which pixels are stored where? The answer is no. Every 256th number in our stretched out vector belongs to a new row in our 256x256 2D matrix. You will see this later when the raw data is put in a special data structure known as a Raster and rendered to a BufferedImage. For now, know that the width and height of the image (in this case, 256x256) are specified by the parameters passed to the constructor of our BufferedImage. Thus, the pixels are interpreted correctly.

This emphasizes a point: All images are stored as a series of numbers. If the programmer knows the meaning of the order of numbers, it is possible to read in, display, and otherwise operate on the data representing the image.

Java Images: A Raster and a ColorModel

The previous example is a simple description of what would be referred to as a Raster with a grayscale ColorModel in Java. In other words, the Raster consists of a rectangular array of the pixel values, and the ColorModel contains methods to convert pixel data into colors. Together, they provide the information we need to render the image.

Two pieces make up the Raster: a DataBuffer containing the actual numbers, and a SampleModel, which groups the numbers into pixels. In the Java 2D API, the Sample is the atomic representation of image data. In the case of the grayscale image described previously, one Sample is equivalent to one pixel. However, in the case of color data, there will be multiple Samples for each pixel. For example, in an RGB image, there will be four samples per pixel, one each for red, green, and blue, and one more for the transparency. The data can be stored in a wide variety of orders (for example, all red followed by all blue followed by all green, or alternatively in triplets of RGB, RGB, and so on).

To reiterate an important point, in order to flexibly handle the diversity of file formats and their interpretation, Java 2D uses the SampleModel to interpret the numbers stored in a DataBuffer. The DataBuffer simply holds the image data (the numbers) in storage, but the SampleModel contains the methods for grouping those numbers into pixels.

Individually, a SampleModel and a DataBuffer aren't sufficient to produce an image. Only together can the raw data (stored in the DataBuffer) and the interpretation of that data (the SampleModel) constitute an image.

Whereas the `SampleModel` interprets the `DataBuffer` in terms of pixels, the `ColorModel` interprets the `Raster` (again, `SampleModel` plus `DataBuffer`) in terms of color. Some confusion might follow as to the differences between a `ColorModel` and a `SampleModel`. The difference is as follows: By using a `DataBuffer` and `SampleModel`, it is possible to examine and process the raw values associated with each pixel, but unless the `ColorModel` is specified, there is no way to interpret the pixels into colors. Because of the `SampleModel`, we know what numbers in the `DataBuffer` are associated with each pixel, but we still don't know what they mean in terms of color. An image, then, is fully described by its raw data in the `DataBuffer`, the interpretation of the raw data into pixels via the `SampleModel`, and finally the interpretation of the pixel data into a color space through the `ColorModel`. Without all three of these components, we cannot render raw numbers into an image.

In many cases, the rectangular area represented by the `Raster` will correspond to the entire image; however, the `Raster` can represent *any* rectangular area of the image. Therefore, whereas the space of the `DataBuffer` and `SampleModel` are always defined with an origin of (0,0), the `Raster` itself can be translated from this origin. The `Raster`, therefore contains an X and Y translation. This seemingly esoteric digression will be important when we discuss image tiling and other topics in Chapter 6.

The entire scheme will be discussed in further detail later when we examine the grayscale and color examples in the next several chapters, but it is important for you to pause here and reflect on how an image is represented in Java. To summarize, an image is ultimately made up of numbers; however, a lot of information is needed in order to interpret those numbers. The `DataBuffer` stores the numbers, whereas the `SampleModel` maps the numbers onto pixels. A rectangular array of pixels (`DataBuffer` plus `SampleModel`) is called a `Raster`. After the pixels are organized and interpreted with a `Raster`, the numbers are interpreted further with a `ColorModel`. All these components must be present in order to represent an image in Java.

The Immediate Mode Rendering Model

The AWT imaging model wasn't sufficient for any kind of serious image processing because it didn't provide a mechanism for a persistent memory store of pixel data. In other words, there was no *convenient* way to get to the pixel data. Note that although it is possible to access data through the `grabPixels()` method, operations on this data were quite limited. Easier access to the pixel data was added in Java 2D with the introduction of the immediate mode rendering model. The *immediate mode rendering model* is based on the concept of a buffered image. The class `BufferedImage` represents an area of memory containing pixel data. The ability to use an accessible data buffer enables custom filtering operations such as blurring and sharpening as well as color operations such as color correction and color banding. Buffered imaging is covered in substantially more detail in Chapter 4.

Because a BufferedImage is a Java image in every sense of the word, it must have the three components listed in the preceding Java image description. That is, it must have a DataBuffer, a SampleModel, and a ColorModel.

Rendering Independence: The Renderable and Rendered Imaging Layers

Another important advancement included in the Java 2D API, and one that forms the heart of the JAI, is the ability to do rendering independent imaging operations. The use of rendering independent operations can be quite powerful and is accomplished through classes that implement the Renderable interface. The basic advantage of rendering independence is that image operations can be accomplished without processing the pixel data. This enables a number of important optimizations, not the least of which is a greatly reduced need to render, but also goes a long way toward ensuring optimal quality over all devices. Most of the advanced capabilities that are such an integral part of the JAI are built on the capability of rendering independence.

Many incorrectly equate rendering independence with the related concept of resolution independence, but, strictly speaking, resolution independence is but one part of the more general rendering independence. *Resolution* independence refers to the fact that because a transformation exists between the resolution of the image source and the resolution of the target output device, operations can occur independently of either as long as the final transformation is applied at the end. *Rendering* independence extends this idea beyond resolution to basically all other aspects of the rendering.

It is important to note that it isn't always desirable to operate in a rendering independent fashion. Indeed, one generally has to enter the device dependent world eventually. An important component of the Java 2D and JAI rendering independent model is that a parallel world always exists for performing rendering dependent operations. These two parallel worlds are called the Renderable and Rendered layers. They are intended to work together.

The Renderable layer is the rendering independent layer. As such, a single renderable image can participate in a wide variety of contexts (that is, multiple printers, monitors, and output files). Any operation that produces a Renderable image as output can itself be considered a Renderable source for any other operation. Therefore, a series of Renderable image operations (known as RenderableImageOps) can be set up as an editable chain or graph (Figure 2.5). The design of graphs will be discussed in Chapter 6.

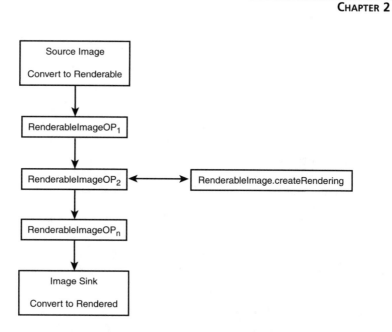

FIGURE 2.5

Rendering graph showing chain of operations in the Renderable Layer.

For now, remember the following: All Renderable images are required to adapt to a rendering context specified through an object instantiated from the RenderContext class. In other words, RenderContext contains the information needed to produce a specific rendering (that is, for a specific context) of an image. This information includes a rendering independent description of the area to be rendered and other information about the rendering context and resolution of the target device. To create a specific rendering, the user instantiates a RenderContext object and calls the createRendering() method of the RenderableImage.

The RenderableImageOps adapts to specific operations through classes implementing the ContextualRenderedImageFactory interface (also known by the acronym CRIF). The CRIF acts as the link between the Renderable and Rendered layers and is passed in during instantiation of the RenderableImageOp. The key idea here is that a single RenderableImageOp is used, but a series of CRIFs are specified to perform the different imaging operations.

The Pull Model

The basic idea of the renderable layer is that the data can be pulled through as needed for rendering, This is the basis for the name pull model that is central to the JAI. This imaging model is also called render on demand or just-in-time rendering.

As the name implies, whenever a rendering is needed, the pixel data can be pulled through the Renderable layer and output in a context dependent manner. Renderable imaging will be covered extensively in Chapter 6.

The consumer-producer model used in the AWT and maintained in Java 2D was also known as a push model because the consumer (or image sink) never requests the image but rather waits for it passively. This approach was good for displaying a few simple images via a Web browser, but is obviously quite limited for image processing. In a pull model, image sources must be able to operate on arbitrary areas of the image data. An `ImageProducer` cannot be used as a source under this regime because it doesn't respond to such requests.

In order to perform network imaging, deferred execution, as well as to enable rendering on demand, JAI went headlong into the pull model. Although the pull model is central to JAI, it doesn't preclude using the `ImageProducer` interface to conform to AWT implementation. But, in general, the user of JAI will want to adapt wholeheartedly to the pull model.

Graphics Capabilities in JAI

You shouldn't be left with the impression that JAI doesn't support graphics. As an extension API, the JAI enables everything that Java 2D does plus a little more. The extra capabilities of the JAI for graphics relate to client-server graphics: use of the pull model for optimization of operations and display (elaborated next), as well as methods for rendering over tiled images and graphics. For the most part, the discussion of graphics programming will be limited to the Java 2D API.

As stated previously, graphics refers to the ability to draw shapes and text. Java 2D offers an extensive set of shapes, including user-specified arbitrary shapes, and a rich set of text capabilities that can be used to make rather stunning output.

Client-Server Imaging

A particularly powerful feature of JAI is its capability to distribute processing across a network. Although the typical application might have no need for this capability, distributed imaging is a powerful weapon for many advanced applications. Examples include telemedicine and online gaming and commerce. The basic idea of client-server imaging involves the use of Java's *Remote Method Invocation (RMI)*. The client instantiates a *stub* object that conveys its methods to the host through serialization (basically, turning your objects into a stream).

Now, imagine that you have a client acting as an image acquisition machine and want to perform a mathematically complex series of image processing operations on that data while the client continues to collect new data. An efficient way to develop such an application would be to specify the operations in a Renderable layer of the graph and delegate this portion of the process to the server. Changes to the image operations could then occur rapidly on the server, and the results could be pulled though the rendering chain to many different clients at the same time. A more detailed description and sample application of client-server imaging is developed on Chapter 6.

Image I/O

Most programmers who have worked with image display and processing will attest to the large amount of time spent dealing with image input and output formats. Fortunately, Java has recently added the Java Image I/O API, which will serve to greatly reduce the amount of time spent programming and implementing Image I/O and will further support networked, disk-based, and direct image reading and writing.

The Image I/O API also supports metadata, that is, image data that are not related to the pixel values themselves but rather represent data about data.

The Image I/O API is the subject of Chapter 5.

Summary

Imaging and graphics on the Java platform has undergone three major changes as it has evolved into its current state. What began as a limited set of methods for displaying images in a browser (the AWT image model) became a robust API for drawing shapes and graphics with some limited imaging capability. The JAI extends Java 2D's graphics and imaging capabilities into a powerful advanced imaging platform for leading edge applications.

A developer wanting to write graphics and imaging applications will have to choose carefully between Java 2D and JAI. The proper choice will depend on whether the limited image processing capabilities of Java 2D are sufficient for the task and whether the application needs to take advantage of the pull imaging model.

Graphics Programming with the Java 2D API

IN THIS CHAPTER

The Java 2D API extends the Java *Advanced Windowing Toolkit (AWT)* to provide classes for professional 2D graphics, text, and imaging. The subject of this chapter is the use of Java 2D for graphics and text. Java 2D imaging is the subject of Chapter 4, "The Immediate Mode Imaging Model."

Keep in mind that, for the most part, all discussion referring to shapes will apply equally to text because for all intents and purposes, text is represented as shapes. Operations such as texture mapping, stroking, and alpha compositing can be applied equally to shapes and text.

The key to using Java 2D for graphics is to understand a simple basic programming paradigm that we will refer to as the Basic Java 2D Recipe.

The Basic Java 2D Recipe

As stated previously, there is a basic three-step recipe for writing a graphics program in Java:

1. Get a graphics context.
2. Set the context.
3. Render something.

Getting the graphics context is pretty straightforward. Cast the Graphics object as a Graphics2D object as follows:

```
public void paint(Graphics g) {
    Graphics2D g2d = (Graphics2D) g;
}
```

The result of making this cast is that the programmer has access to the increased functionality of the methods, classes, and interfaces of the Graphics2D object. These extended capabilities enable the advanced graphics operations described in the next several chapters. The Graphics2D object is covered in detail in the section "Set the Graphics2D Context...."

Step 2 of the recipe, setting the graphics context, is also pretty straightforward once you understand what a graphics context is. For now, let's say that the graphics context is a collection of properties (also known as state attributes) that affect the appearance of the graphics output. The most common example of changing the graphics context is to set the color used for drawing. Most of this chapter deals with changing the myriad state attributes to achieve the desired effect.

The final step in this paradigm is to render something. This refers to the action of outputting graphics to a device. The most obvious graphics output device is a monitor; however, printers, files, and other devices are equally valid output targets for graphics.

Let's examine the recipe in the simplest possible example (see Listing 3.1). In this case, our goal is to draw a square on the screen, as shown in Figure 3.1. Keep in mind, however, that this same recipe can be applied in more complex applications.

LISTING 3.1 BasicRecipeJ2D.java

```
// BasicRecipeJ2D.java
//Part 1 of the recipe, general program setup.

import java.applet.Applet;
import java.awt.*;
import java.awt.event.*;
import java.awt.geom.*;

public class BasicRecipeJ2D extends Frame {

    public BasicRecipeJ2D() {
            //constructor
            super("Java 2D basic recipe");
            this.add(new myCustomCanvas());
            this.setSize(500,500);
            this.show();
            addWindowListener(new WindowEventHandler());
    }


    class WindowEventHandler extends WindowAdapter {
       public void windowClosing(WindowEvent e) {
          System.exit(0);
     }
    }

    public static void main(String[] args) {
     new BasicRecipeJ2D();
    }
}

//Part 2; Java 2D specific-extend the drawing Component -Canvas-
// and override it's paint method.

class myCustomCanvas extends Canvas {

      public void paint(Graphics g) {
         System.out.println("in paint");
```

LISTING 3.1   Continued

```
          // step one of the recipe; cast Graphics object as Graphics2D
          Graphics2D g2d = (Graphics2D) g;

          // step two-set the graphics context
          g2d.setColor(Color.red); //setting context

        //step three-render something
          g2d.fill(new Rectangle2D.Float(200.0f,200.0f,75.0f,75.0f));
      }
}
```

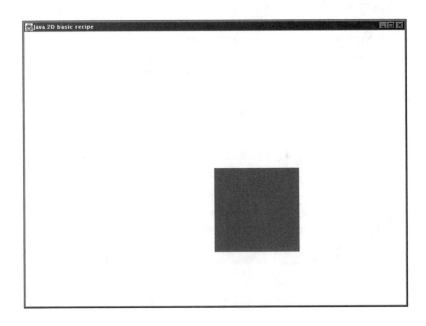

FIGURE 3.1
Output from BasicRecipeJ2D.

By modifying this recipe, it is possible to realize most of the projects you would want to do with Java 2D. Many of the examples that follow will simply modify the paint() method to add whatever functionality is needed.

Because the basic recipe is central to our discussion of Java 2D, let's examine the pieces in more detail.

Part 1 of Listing 3.1 is a basic skeleton for any Java program. The appropriate classes are imported; JFrame is extended and an eventListener is added for exiting the frame. Note that we imported java.awt.geom. This will be necessary to have access to shapes for drawing. The other important thing to notice in part 1 is the following line:

```
this.add(new myCustomCanvas());
```

In this case, we add myCustomCanvas, a class extending Canvas to the main application frame. Note that Canvas extends Component and is the most common graphics component for display of graphics. It should be emphasized that any of the many objects extending Component (such as JButton and JPanel) can be used in the same fashion (see the section "Drawing on Components").

Part 2 of Listing 3.1 is the part of the program that most relates to Java 2D. The Component class Canvas is extended (subclassed), and its paint() method is overridden. This is the fundamental use of Canvas, and you will see this time and time again. Within the overridden paint() method, the three necessary parts of the Java 2D recipe are realized—we get a graphics context by casting the Graphics object as Graphics2D. Steps 2 and 3 of the recipe are then achieved by calling two methods of the Graphics2D object. First, there is a change to the rendering attributes of the Graphics2D object by calling setColor(). Second, a Shape object (in this case, a Rectange2D) is created and drawn using the Graphics2D object's draw() method.

You are encouraged to run the BasicRecipeJ2D now.

Differences Between paint(), repaint(), and update()

After taking a look at the basic recipe, you might have noticed that even though our Java 2D code is contained within the paint() method, we never actually call this method. This underscores an important point that often becomes a source of frustration to the uninitiated. The paint() method is called automatically whenever the window needs to be refreshed. The programmer never calls paint() directly, but instead calls repaint() in order to obtain a rendering. It is repaint() that calls paint(). The rendering is then made at the next convenient time.

It becomes even more confusing when you consider that in actuality, paint() doesn't do all the drawing, another method called update() also participates. The drawing in update() includes an additional step in which the screen is first filled with the Component's foreground color, effectively clearing the screen. The update() method then finally calls the Component's paint() method to output the graphics. There are often cases in which the programmer doesn't want to clear the screen before drawing (see the section "Comprehensive Example: Kspace Visualization" at the end of this chapter). In this case, the programmer will need to override the update() method to eliminate the filling of the background.

As an aside, we note that the statement "The programmer never calls paint() directly" is perhaps a little too strong. Many animation applets do indeed call paint() directly in order to avoid the automatic queing process that results from calling repaint(). These cases tend to be rare and are only recommended in special circumstances.

All Rendering Should Occur in `paint()`

A general rule to follow is that unless there is a compelling reason not to, all drawing for a `Component` should be done in that `Component`'s `paint()` method. In our basic recipe example from Listing 3.1, the `Component` object that we want to draw on is an instance of the class `myCustomCanvas` (which extends `Canvas`).

What might constitute a compelling reason not to place the drawing of objects in the paint method? For most complex applications, the `paint()` method can become unwieldy and should be broken down into smaller methods. Grouping the steps into methods is functionally equivalent to having the code directly in the `paint()` method, so this really isn't a major departure from the rule of doing all drawing in the `paint()` method.

Another case in which you would render outside of `paint()` is when a `BufferedImage` is used. Still, the final rendering occurs in the `paint()` method. This is shown later in PDExamples.java and TexturePaint.java.

Other Methods Similar to `paint()`

Two additional methods are commonly encountered. The `paintAll()` method is often useful and is used in a similar fashion to the `paint()` method except that `paintAll()` will request a `paint()` of the `Component` and all of its subcomponents. For Swing components, `paint()` is often replaced by `paintComponent()` in order to not invoke the `paintChildren()` and `paintBorder()` methods. This is frequently necessary when developing an interface with a custom look and feel.

Set the `Graphics2D` Context...

As mentioned briefly, the graphics context is a collection of state attributes specifying properties of the rendering. State attributes are sometimes also referred to as rendering attributes. Five interfaces and several classes that are part of java.awt package represent these attributes.

The first three interfaces are relevant to most development projects and are listed in Table 3.1. Note that these interfaces are implemented in the set of classes listed in Tables 3.2 and 3.3.

TABLE 3.1   Commonly Used Interfaces Implemented with the `Graphics2D` Context

Interface	Description
Composite	Methods to compose a primitive over the underlying Graphics area.
Paint	Methods to specify rules for generating color patterns. Extends Transparency.
Stroke	Methods to obtain a Shape representing the style of a line.

TABLE 3.2 Classes Implementing the Interfaces

Class	Interface	Description
AlphaComposite	Composite	Implements rules for composite overlays.
Color	Paint	Defines a solid color.
GradientPaint	Paint	Defines a gradient paint pattern.
TexturePaint	Paint	Defines a texture pattern.
BasicStroke	Stroke	Defines shapes to represent a pen style for a line drawing.

Two other interfaces are necessary for certain optimizations but are less commonly used by the programmer. The design of classes that use these interfaces are beyond the scope of this book.

TABLE 3.3 Less Frequently Used Interfaces Necessary for Optimized Context Operations

Interface	Description
CompositeContext	Defines an optimized and encapsulated environment for compositing.
PaintContext	Defines an optimized and encapsulated environment for color pattern generation.

To make a visual effect, the programmer sets rendering attributes of the context according to the desired effect. In the BasicRecipeJ2D example from Listing 3.1, the visual effect we wanted was rather simple—we wanted the square painted red—so we changed the current color (one of many available state attributes) to red by changing the attribute with setColor(Color.Red). Note that the object we passed to the setColor() method is an instance of the Color class (which as shown in Table 3.2, implements the Paint interface).

The methods in Table 3.4 also have complementary methods for getting the current state attributes. The getBackground(), getComposite(), getPaint(), and getStroke() methods will return the corresponding current context attributes.

TABLE 3.4 Commonly Used Graphics2D Methods for Changing the Graphics Context

Method	Description
setBackground()	Sets the background color for the Component.
setComposite()	Sets the compositing rule for subsequent rendering.
setPaint(Paint)	Sets the current paint texture to use for rendering.
setStroke(Stroke)	Sets the stroke style for rendering lines.

3

GRAPHICS PROGRAMMING WITH THE JAVA 2D API

Another important set of attributes, called RenderingHints, allows the programmer to set state attributes for rendering options such antialiasing, dithering, and the interpolation method. The rendering methods will affect the tradeoff between the look of the output versus the speed of rendering. See the following URL for a complete list:

http://java.sun.com/j2se/1.3/docs/api/java/awt/RenderingHints.html

Three other general types of rendering attributes can be set. The first is the font to use for rendering text. Some details of setting the font are covered later. The clipping path and transform, which are changed with the clip() and setTransform() methods, respectively, are covered later.

...and Render Something

After setting the rendering context with any of the previous methods, it is time to complete the recipe and request a rendering of a shape, line, or image. This final step is accomplished with one of several methods contained in the Graphics2D object. For this chapter we will primarily use the draw(), drawLine(),drawString(), and fill() methods, but keep in mind that many other drawing methods exist.

You should examine the Graphics2D documentation at this time:

http://java.sun.com/j2se/1.3/docs/api/java/awt/Graphics2D.html

Rendering on Components

Any object derived from the Component class has a Graphics object that can be used to render graphics onto it. This means that the developer can render high impact graphics on all types of buttons, canvases, and check boxes. Basically, all the user interface objects have an accessible Graphics object that can be cast as a Graphics2D object and used by Java 2D.

Scaling to the Component's Size

So far, the examples have been deficient because they don't take the component size into account when drawing. It is obviously good programming practice to determine the Component's width and height and then scale the drawing accordingly. This can be done by using the Component's getSize() method. Scaling is used in the comprehensive example at the end of this chapter.

As an example of the important concept of drawing on Components, let's go back to our BasicRecipeJ2D program. Here we will replace the inner class, myCustomCanvas, with myCustomButton, an inner class extending JButton. Also, note that we choose to use a GradientPaint object instead of the Color object. Nonetheless, the steps are the same and the result is a custom rendered button.

```
class myCustomButton extends JButton {
    public void paint(Graphics g) {
// step one of the recipe; cast Graphics object as Graphics2D
        Graphics2D g2d = (Graphics2D) g;

        //make a GradientPaint object going
        //from blue to green across from top left to
        //bottom right

        GradientPaint gp = new GradientPaint(0, 0, Color.blue,
                                    this.getSize().width/20,
                                    this.getSize().height/20,
                                    Color.green, true);

        // step two-set the graphics context
        g2d.setPaint(gp); //setting context

        //step three-render something--
            g2d.fill(new Rectangle2D.Float(0.0f,0.0f,75.0f,75.0f));
    } //end paint() method
} //end myCustomButton class
```

Shape Primitives

So far we have only drawn rectangles in our examples, but there are, in fact, nine shape primitives available to us. These shapes are contained almost entirely in the java.awt.geom package and can be used to draw pretty much anything in two dimensions. All shape primitives implement the Shape interface, a set of methods for describing shapes that is part of the java.awt package. In addition, all shape primitives implement the PathIterator object that specifies the outline of the shape. Before explaining the PathIterator interface, we will introduce the shape primitives:

- Arc2D
- Area
- CubicCurve2D
- Ellipse2D
- GeneralPath
- Line2D
- QuadCurve2D
- Rectangle2D
- RoundRectangle2D

This set of primitives can be divided into four categories based on their properties and common lineage.

Rectangle2D, RoundRectangle2D, Arc2D, and Ellipse2D are derived from the abstract class RectangularShape based on the common ability to describe these primitives through a rectangular bounding box.

Line, QuadCurve2D, and CubicCurve2D are line segments described by their two endpoints with the requisite control points.

GeneralPath allows for the specification of a series of points that can be connected with any combination of the straight, cubic, or quadratic line segments. In the next section, GeneralPath is introduced as a general way to understand all geometric shapes.

Finally, Area allows the creation of new shapes through the use of intersection, union, and subtraction of other shapes. Area operations are discussed next.

Note that all the classes mentioned previously are abstract classes; that is, they cannot be instantiated directly but rather are instantiated through a subclass. With the exception of Area and RoundRectangle2D, the classes are actually instantiated using the ending .Float or .Double depending on the desired precision. For example, in the class BasicRecipeJ2D:

```
g2d.draw(new Rectangle2D.Float(0.0f,0.0f,75.0f,75.0f));
g2d.draw(new Rectangle2D.Double(0,0,75,75));
```

For brevity, only GeneralShape and Area are discussed in any detail here. You will find it easy to test other shapes by modifying the BasicRecipe.java application and are encouraged to do so. See the following URL for complete documentation on all geometric shapes:

http://java.sun.com/j2se/1.3/docs/api/java/awt/geom/package-summary.html

Understanding Shapes Through GeneralPath and the PathIterator Interfaces

The GeneralPath Shape and the PathIterator interface together form an important key to understanding most geometric operations in Java 2D including area operations, arbitrary shapes drawing, and hit testing, to name but a few. The challenge is to understand iteration objects, which are individual instances of lines and curves (specifically, quadratic and cubic Bezier splines) that describe the connecting paths encountered as you move (iterates) around the boundary of a geometric object. In other words, imagine yourself standing at the intersection of two lines that are part of a shape. The iteration object is the description you would use to move to the next interaction of the shape; for example "a line from here to 75, 75" or "a quadratic curve to 100, 200 with a control point at 150, 150."

Note the conceptual similarities between a PathIterator and the Shape class GeneralPath. A GeneralPath is a series of curves and lines that is combined to make any arbitrary shape. As such, all geometric shapes, including rectangles and arcs, can be specified the long way; that is, by creating series move and draw commands. For example, Listing 3.2 makes an arbitrary shape that looks like the one shown in Figure 3.2. The method reportGP() at the end of the myCustomCanvas class is used to loop over the PathIterator object derived from the GeneralPath and report the type of current segment as well as the coordinates of each element in the GeneralPath.

LISTING 3.2 PathIteratorEx.java

```
. . .
class myCustomCanvas extends Canvas {
     GeneralPath gp;
   //add a constructor
   public myCustomCanvas() {

} //end of constructor

 public void paint(Graphics g) {

     Graphics2D g2d = (Graphics2D) g;

     g2d.setColor(Color.green); //setting context

     gp = new GeneralPath();
     int cwidth=this.getSize().width;
     int cheight=this.getSize().height;

     gp.moveTo((int)cwidth/2,(int)cheight/2);   //initial starting point
     gp.append(new Rectangle2D.Float((float)cwidth/2,(float)cheight/2,
     ➥ 10.f,10.f),true);
     gp.lineTo((int)cwidth/4,(int)cheight/4);
     gp.lineTo((int)(.9*cwidth),(int)(cheight/4));
     gp.append(new Ellipse2D.Float((float)(.9*cwidth),
                                   (float)(.25*cwidth),
                                   10.f,10.f),true);

     gp.closePath();   //closes path based on most recent moveTo
     g2d.draw(gp);
     reportGP();

} //end of paint

public void reportGP() {
```

3

GRAPHICS
PROGRAMMING WITH
THE JAVA 2D API

LISTING 3.2 Continued

```
System.out.println("**Reporting GeneralPath after repaint**");

//make an empty AffineTransform to pass to PathIterator

AffineTransform at = new AffineTransform();

//note: using non-xformed path

PathIterator pi = gp.getPathIterator(at);
int segnumber=0;
while (pi.isDone() == false) {
  segnumber++;
  System.out.println("**GETTING DATA FOR SEGMENT#: " +
                        segnumber + "**");
  float[] coords = new float[6];

  //the following tells us whether the current segment is:
  // SEG_MOVETO, SEG_LINETO, SEG_QUADTO,
  // SEG_CUBICTO, or  SEG_CLOSE
  //coords will be filled with sequential pairs of x,y coords

  System.out.println("currentSegment type: " +
                        pi.currentSegment(coords));

  for (int j=0;j<6;j++) {
    System.out.println("j: " + j +
                          " coords[j]: " + coords[j] );
  }  //end of for

  pi.next();
} //end while pi.isDone() == false
}
```

You should now attempt to draw different GeneralPaths and observe the corresponding changes in the PathIterator object.

One related class that is often overlooked is the FlatteningPathIterator. The utility of FlatterningPathIterator stems from the fact that whenever any curved shape is rendered, there is an intermediate step in the pipeline for converting curves into straight-line segments (part of the process of rasterization). By specifying a flatness parameter, the application has control over the number of straight-line segments used to approximate curves. The advantage of flattening is that there is a reduced need for resource intensive interpolations to be performed. In many cases, the improvement in performance won't be noticeable; however, in situations in which a great number of curved lines are present, flattening can make a dramatic difference.

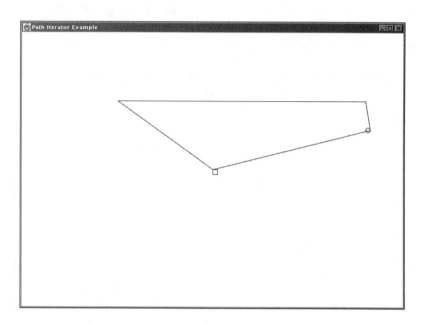

FIGURE 3.2

This shows the screen output from PathIteratorEx.java. When changing the screen size, the GeneralPath *object is changed and* reportGP() *is called.*

Winding Rules and Testing for Containment

A frequent problem encountered in graphics development is testing for containment—that is, determining whether a point or shape is inside another shape. This is obviously critical for operations such as filling, texture mapping, and determining whether the user has clicked on a shape or area. When the shape is simple and has edges that intersect only at the vertices (such as a rectangle or circle) the problem is trivial. In non-trivial cases, however, it becomes necessary to develop an algorithm. Consider the following arbitrary geometric shape (shown in Figure 3.3), in which there is some ambiguity about which points are inside and outside the shape.

There are two common methods for determining if any point is inside a geometric shape. The first, called the *odd-even rule*, is based on drawing a line (ray) from the point to be classified to any point well outside the shape. If the number of edge crossings is odd, the point is inside the shape; otherwise it is not. The second approach is termed the *non-zero winding rule* and likewise determines the number of edge crossings that occur for a ray drawn to a distant point.

However, in the non-zero winding rule scheme, the left to right crossings add to the total number of crossing whereas the right to left crossing subtracts from the total number of crossings. If the sum of left to right and right to left crossing isn't equal to zero, the point is determined to be inside. Figure 3.3 shows an example of applying the two rules. Indeed the odd-even and non-zero winding rules give different answers for the ambiguous area labeled 1.

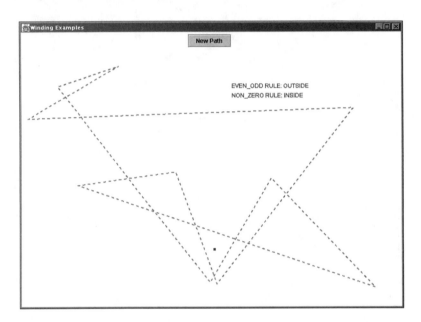

FIGURE 3.3

Form WindingEx showing how winding rules can yield different results in tests for containment.

Listing 3.3 demonstrates winding rules and is another example of using a GeneralPath. The application generates a random GeneralPath each time the New Path button is pushed. The user can then click anywhere inside or outside the shape. The results are often the same for the two methods, but it is a worthwhile exercise to try to predict in which cases they differ.

LISTING 3.3 WindingEx.java

```
. . .
public class WindingEx extends JFrame {

    myCustomCanvas mc;
    JButton newpath;

    public WindingEX() {
        super("Winding Examples");
```

LISTING 3.3 Continued

```
            //layout manager for the frame

            BorderLayout f1 = new BorderLayout();
            Panel uipanel = new Panel();
            newpath = new JButton("New Path");
            uipanel.add(newpath);

            mc = new myCustomCanvas(this);
            mc.setSize(800,600);

            ButtonHandler bhandler = new ButtonHandler(mc);
            MouseHandler mhandler = new MouseHandler(mc);

            newpath.addActionListener(bhandler);

            mc.addMouseListener(mhandler);

            this.getContentPane().setLayout(f1);
            this.getContentPane().add(mc,BorderLayout.CENTER);
            this.getContentPane().add(uipanel,BorderLayout.NORTH);

            this.setSize(800,600);
            this.show();
            addWindowListener(new WindowEventHandler());
    }


    class WindowEventHandler extends WindowAdapter {
       public void windowClosing(WindowEvent e) {
          System.exit(0);
       }
    }

    public static void main(String[] args) {
       new WindingEX();
    }
}


class MouseHandler implements MouseListener {
   myCustomCanvas mc;

. . .

   public void mousePressed(MouseEvent e) {
      mc.drawPoint(e.getX(),e.getY());
```

LISTING 3.3   Continued

```java
    }
}

class ButtonHandler implements ActionListener {

    myCustomCanvas mc;

    public ButtonHandler(myCustomCanvas mc) {
        this.mc = mc;
    }

    public void actionPerformed(ActionEvent e) {
        mc.generateGP();
    }

}

class myCustomCanvas extends Canvas {

        WindingEx wex;
        String insider;
        String even_oddMessage = "Click on a Point";
        String non_zeroMessage = " ";
         Random r;
        GeneralPath gp;

    public myCustomCanvas(WindingEX wex) {
        r = new Random();
        this.wex = wex;
        this.setSize(800,600);

        generateGP();

    }

    public void generateGP() {

        gp = new GeneralPath();
        gp.moveTo(r.nextInt(this.getSize().width),
                r.nextInt(this.getSize().height));
        for (int i=1;i<10;i++) { //choose 10 random points
          gp.lineTo(r.nextInt(this.getSize().width),
                r.nextInt(this.getSize().height));
        }
        gp.closePath();
        gp.drawPoint(r.nextInt(this.getSize().width),
```

LISTING 3.3   Continued

```java
                          r.nextInt(this.getSize().height));
        repaint();
    }

    public void drawPoint(int x, int y) {
        this.x = x;
        this.y = y;

        gp.setWindingRule(GeneralPath.WIND_EVEN_ODD);
        even_oddMessage = "EVEN_ODD RULE: ".concat(isInside(x,y));
        gp.setWindingRule(GeneralPath.WIND_NON_ZERO);
        non_zeroMessage = "NON_ZERO RULE: ".concat(isInside(x,y));

       repaint();
    }

    public String isInside(int x, int y) {

        if (gp.contains(new Point(x,y)))
            insider="INSIDE";
        else
            insider="OUTSIDE";

        return insider;
    }

    public void paint(Graphics g) {

        Graphics2D g2d = (Graphics2D) g;
        g2d.drawString(even_oddMessage,440,80);
        g2d.drawString(non_zeroMessage,440,100);
        g2d.setColor(Color.blue);
        g2d.fill(new Rectangle2D.Double(x,y,5,5));
        // step two-set the graphics context
        g2d.setColor(Color.red); //setting context

        float dash [] = {5.5f};

        BasicStroke stk = new BasicStroke(4.0f,
                                    BasicStroke.CAP_BUTT,
                                    BasicStroke.JOIN_MITER,
                                    10.f, dash, 2.0f);
        g2d.setStroke(stk);

        g2d.draw(gp);
    }
}
```

Basics of Constructive Geometry Using the Area Class

As mentioned at the beginning of this section, constructive area geometry is the making of an arbitrary shape using the intersection, subtraction, or union of other primitives and arbitrary shapes. Simply stated, the goal is to make a new shape from the combination of other shapes. The need for constructive area geometry arises from the fact that drawing an arbitrary shape using line segments and specifying points can be tedious. Often the shape can be drawn using the intersection of just a few shape primitives. Further, it is often easier to change a shape created with constructive area geometry than to respecify the path.

The Area class defines a special shape that supports Boolean operations and is useful in constructive geometry. To make a shape that looks like a Venn diagram, for example, the designer might insert the following into the paint() method of the BasicRecipeJ2D.java class:

```
Area area1 = new Area(new Ellipse2D.Double());
Area area2 = new Area(new Ellipse2D.Double());
Area area3 = new Area(new Ellipse2D.Double());

g2.setColor(Color.blue);
g2.fill(area1);
g2.setColor(Color.green);
g2.fill(area2);

g2.setColor(Color.yellow);
g2.fill(area3);

area1.intersect(area2);
area1.intersect(area3);
setColor(Color.red);
g2.fill(area1);
```

Note that each call of the intersect() method sets the current shape to the result of the operation. Therefore, the intersections accumulate. (That is, area1 first becomes the intersection of itself and area2, and then it becomes the intersection of that result and area3.) The same is true of the subtract(), add(), and exclusiveOr() methods.

Graphics Stroking

The Graphics2D method setStroke() is yet another method for changing the graphics context. We will now examine graphics stroking in greater detail.

Whenever a shape is stroked, it is as if a virtual pen draws an outline around the shape. The virtual pen has a characteristic style defining a set of shape primitives that are combined to make the desired effect. In Java 2D, the pen style is specified in a BasicStroke object.

`BasicStroke` implements the `Stroke` interface and is intended to be used as an argument to the `setStroke()` method of the `Graphics2D` object.

The `BasicStroke` object represents the attributes for line width, endcap, and join style in addition to attributes for specifying different types of dash patterns. Setting the Stroke attributes will affect most of the rendering methods such as `draw()`, `drawArc()`, and so on.

One of the most basic examples of needing to change the `Stroke` attribute is in controlling the line thickness for drawing. Let's once again return to the `BasicRecipeJ2D` class. In this case, we will change the rendering context through the `setStroke()` method. For brevity, only the particular code for changing the context is included.

```
BasicStroke stroke = new BasicStroke(10);
g2d.setStroke(stroke);
```

Another common need is to set a dash pattern for the stroke. In this case, use the `BasicStroke` constructor with six arguments:

```
g2d.setStroke(new BasicStroke(8.0f,
                      BasicStroke.CAP_BUTT,
                      BasicStroke.JOIN_BEVEL,
                      8.0f,
                      new float[] {10.0f, 4.0f},
                      0.0f);
```

Fill Attributes and Painting

Assigning material for painting is done by creating a `Paint` object (specifically, an object implementing the `Paint` interface) and adding it to the `Graphics2D` context with the `setPaint()` method. As you will see next, three general types of `Paint` objects already exist and are easily instantiated. Any of these can readily be used as arguments to `setPaint()`. Before going into these three general types, it is worthwhile to understand the `Paint` interface and how it relates to a second interface, the `PaintContext` interface. An understanding of these two interfaces will be useful when we discuss custom painting later.

The `Paint` interface consists of a unitary method that returns a `PaintContext`:

```
PaintContext createContext(ColorModel cm, Rectangle deviceBounds,
             Recangle2D userBounnds, AffineTransform xform,
             RenderingHints hints);
```

The relationship between `Paint` and `PaintContext` is easily understood if you are comfortable with the concepts of user space and device space described in the introduction to this section.

The `Paint` and `PaintContext` are related in the following way:

The `Paint` object operates in user space. It specifies the way that color patterns are handled by `Graphics2D` operations. The `PaintContext` operates in device space and defines how color patterns are handled by specific devices. Accordingly, `Paint` and `PaintContext` are device dependent and independent, respectively.

Whenever a `Paint` object is instantiated, a `PaintContext` containing (encapsulating) the information necessary for putting color patterns on each output device is automatically set up. The two primary components of a `PaintContext` are a `Raster` (as mentioned previously, a rectangular array of pixel values in device space) and a `ColorModel`.

The `ColorModel`, described briefly in the introduction to this section and covered in detail in Chapter 6, "Java Advanced Imaging," specifies how raw pixel values are interpreted as colors. Again, RGB is the most common `ColorModel` used, but many varieties exist.

The `deviceBounds` and `userBounds` arguments to `Paint`'s `creatContext()` method specify the bounding box of the primitive being rendered in device space and user space, respectively. By placing the appropriate restrictions on the bounds being painted, considerable improvement in runtime can be achieved.

The `AffineTransform` object specifies the transform between user space and device space. Together, `AffineTransform`, `deviceBounds`, and `userBounds` are used to specify the ultimate `Raster` object that is used in device space.

The last argument, `RenderingHints`, is the same class that you saw previously when setting other aspects of the rendering context, and likewise represents a set of options for rendering, particularly those that make a tradeoff of quality and speed. Note that the specific `RenderingHints` that are designated when generating a `PaintContext` are different from those used when describing `Shapes`. Regardless, all rendering hints are grouped together under the same general heading.

Given this background on the `Paint` and `PaintContext` interfaces, we are in a good position to understand the standard `Paint` objects that can be added to the `Graphics2D` context as well as the potential to create our own `Paint` objects in case the standard objects aren't sufficient for a given application.

Preexisting Paint Objects

As mentioned, Java 2D already provides three classes that implement the `Paint` interface. By and large, these three classes are sufficient for most applications.

Solid Color Painting

The simplest `Paint` object (and the object used in all the examples so far) is the `Color` object. There are numerous constructors for the `Color` object; however, some examples of the most commonly used are

```
Color red = new Color.red;   //use the Color.* for predefined colors;

//specify RGB values between 0 and 1;
Color red = new Color(1.f,0.f,0.f);
```

It is also possible to specify an alpha value for transparency.

For example,

```
Color.red = new Color(1.f,0.f,0.f,.5f);
```

Specifies a transparency of .5. Many more options can be specified with the `AlphaComposite` object (see "Transparency and Compositing").

Using your deeper understanding of `Paint` and `PaintContext`, let's examine the steps that occur within a simple solid color paint.

First, a `ColorModel` is created. The `ColorModel` used is most often the `ColorModel` specified in `RenderingHints`. However, a different `ColorModel` from the one specified might occasionally occur because a given device might not use the specified `ColorModel`. Regardless, one way or the other, a device dependent `ColorModel` is selected for rendering.

Second, a `Raster` is generated that contains pixel values for the output device. Remember from Chapter 2, "Imaging and Graphics on the Java Platform," a `Raster` is a rectangular array of pixel values. In this simple case in which a solid color is desired, all pixels of our Raster have the same value. In the case of `GradientPaint` and `TexturePaint` (described next), the pixels have different values. You will see in the GradientPaint example in Listing 3.4 that the `PaintContext`'s `getRaster()` method can be used to get an instance of the `Raster` that we can manipulate in whatever fashion we desire.

Finally, after it is no longer needed, the `PaintContext` object is disposed by calling `System.dispose()`.

Gradient Paints

`GradientPaint` is the second object implementing the `Paint` interface and, like all paint objects, can be added to the `Graphics2D` context with `setPaint()`. A gradient paint is commonly used in practice and represents a transition between two colors. In order to make a `GradientPaint` object, it is necessary to specify the starting and ending points for the transition (see Figures 3.4–3.7), the two colors to use, as well as an optional rule to specify how the paint looks outside the region specified by the starting and ending points. The outer zone can be either *cyclic* (repeats outside the start and endpoints) or *acyclic* (remains at the final value of the gradient outside the start and endpoints).

Listing 3.4 demonstrates the options that can be specified for a GradientPaint.

LISTING 3.4 GradientPaintEx.java

```
. . .
import java.lang.StrictMath;

public class GradientPaintEx extends JFrame {
    myCustomCanvas mc;
    JSlider p1slide, p2slide;
    JRadioButton cyclic_rb, acyclic_rb;

  public GradientPaintEx() {

        super("GradientPaint examples");
        BorderLayout f1 = new BorderLayout();   //layout manager for the frame

        mc = new myCustomCanvas(this);
        mc.setSize(500,500);
. . .
        mc.setPaint(100,200);

        addWindowListener(new WindowEventHandler());
    }


    class WindowEventHandler extends WindowAdapter {
      public void windowClosing(WindowEvent e) {
        System.exit(0);
      }
    }

    public static void main(String[] args) {
      new GradientPaintEx();
    }
}

class SliderListener implements ChangeListener {

    GradientPaintEx gex;
    myCustomCanvas mc;
    int slider_val;

  public SliderListener(GradientPaintEx gex, myCustomCanvas mc) {
        this.gex = gex;
        this.mc = mc;
    }
```

LISTING 3.4   Continued

```java
public void stateChanged(ChangeEvent e) {

  int p1pos = gex.p1slide.getValue();
  int p2pos = gex.p2slide.getValue();

  mc.setPaint(p1pos,p2pos);

 }//End of stateChanged
}//End of SliderListener

class myCustomCanvas extends Canvas {
      GradientPaintEx gex;
      double p1pos, p2pos;
      GradientPaint gpaint;

   public myCustomCanvas(GradientPaintEx gex) {

      this.gex = gex;
   }

  public void setPaint(int p1pos, int p2pos) {
      this.p1pos = (double) p1pos;
      this.p2pos = (double) p2pos;

      boolean cycle = true;
      if (gex.cyclic_rb.isSelected())
         cycle = true;
      else
         cycle = false;
         Point x = new Point2D.Double(p1pos,
                                 this.getSize().height/2),

         Point y = new Point2D.Double(p2pos,
                                 this.getSize().height/2),

         gpaint = new GradientPaint(x, y,
                              Color.red,
                              Color.green,cycle);
      repaint();
   }

   public void update(Graphics g) {
      paint(g);
   }
```

LISTING 3.4   Continued

```java
public void paint(Graphics g) {

    gex.p1slide.setMaximum(this.getSize().width);
    gex.p2slide.setMaximum(this.getSize().width);

    Graphics2D g2d = (Graphics2D) g;

    g2d.setPaint(gpaint); //setting context

    g2d.fill(new Rectangle2D.Double(0,
                                    0,
                                    this.getSize().width,
                                    this.getSize().height));

    g2d.setColor(Color.black);
    BasicStroke stroke = new BasicStroke(4);
    g2d.setStroke(stroke);
    Line2D line1 = new Line2D.Double(p1pos,
                                     0,
                                     p1pos,
                                     this.getSize().height);
    g2d.draw(line1);

    Line2D line2 = new Line2D.Double(p2pos,
                                     0,
                                     p2pos,
                                     this.getSize().height);
    g2d.draw(line2);
    // step two-set the graphics context


    }
}
```

In Figure 3.4, the gradient of a GradientPaint is specified by two points, P1 and P2, together with the colors to use at each point. If a fifth argument, cyclic, is specified, the pattern is repeated outside of the points in cyclic fashion. If acyclic is specified, the full colors prevail in the zones outside the points.

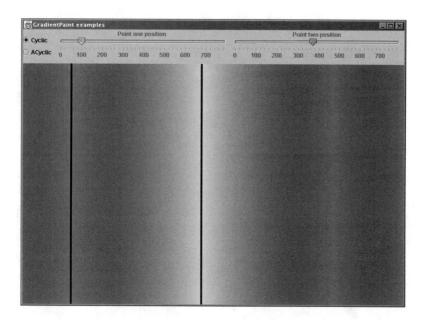

FIGURE 3.4

A cyclic GradientPaint *object with moderate separation of P1 and P2.*

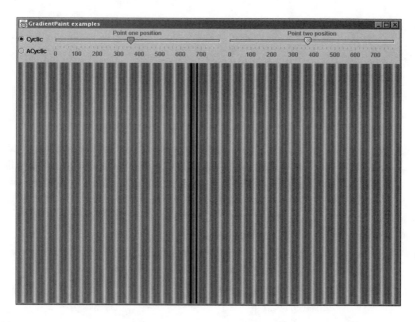

FIGURE 3.5

A cyclic GradientPaint *object with small separation of P1 and P2.*

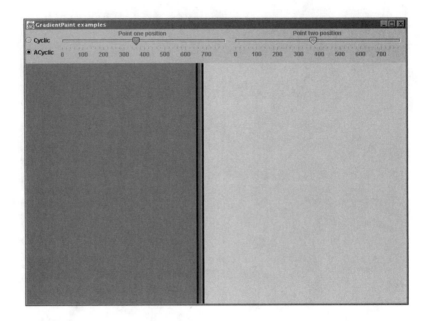

FIGURE 3.6
An acyclic GradientPaint *object with small separation of P1 and P2.*

> **NOTE**
>
> Because the GradientPaint is specified as acyclic, the gradient doesn't repeat past the two points.

Texture Paints

A texture can be specified for the Paint object. Textures will be explained in greater detail in both Chapter 4 and in Part III, "Visualization and Virtual Environments: The Java 3D API," where texture painting is used in the Virtual Shopping Mall example. For now, realize that you must create a BufferedImage object either from an external source or, alternatively, by pro-grammatically filling a BufferedImage using some algorithm. The BufferedImage object is then used as an argument to the constructor of the TexturePaint object. In addition, a Rectangle2D object must be passed that specifies how the texture is replicated across the Component to be painted. The constructor for a TexturePaint object is as follows:

```
public TexturePaint(BufferedImage txtbuffer,
                    Rectangle2D anchor);
```

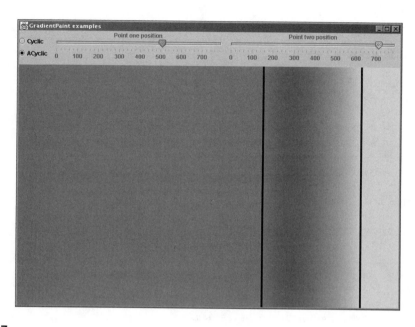

FIGURE 3.7

An acyclic GradientPaint *object with moderate separation of P1 and P2.*

One critical point to keep in mind when using the TexturePaint object is that the size of the BufferedImage should be kept relatively small because the BufferedImage is replicated to fill whatever graphics object is being painted. When the TexturePaint object is instantiated, an anchoring rectangle is specified in user space coordinates. This anchoring rectangle (with its associated BufferedImage) is copied in both x and y directions infinitely across the shape to be rendered.

Listing 3.5 demonstrates the use of a TexturePaint object. In this example, four slider bars are used to control the anchoring rectangle.

LISTING 3.5   TexturePaintEx.java

```
class SliderListener implements ChangeListener {

    TextureEx tex;
    myCustomCanvas mc;

  public SliderListener(TextureEx tex, myCustomCanvas mc) {
        this.tex = tex;
        this.mc = mc;
  }
```

LISTING 3.5 Continued

```
public void stateChanged(ChangeEvent e) {

   int hanchor = tex.hanchor_slide.getValue();
   int vanchor = tex.vanchor_slide.getValue();

   int hsize = tex.hsize_slide.getValue();
   int vsize = tex.vsize_slide.getValue();

   mc.createPaint(hanchor,vanchor,hsize,vsize);
  }//End of stateChanged
 }//End of SliderListener

class myCustomCanvas extends Canvas {

    private String texture = "texture.jpg";
    private TexturePaint tpaint;
    private int texheight, texwidth;
    Rectangle imageRect;
    private int hanchor,vanchor,hsize,vsize;
    Image image;
    TextureEx tex;

    public myCustomCanvas(TextureEx tex) {

        this.tex = tex;
        this.setSize(800,600);
        image = this.getToolkit().getImage(texture);

        MediaTracker mt = new MediaTracker(this);
        mt.addImage(image, 0);
        try {
            mt.waitForID(0);
        } catch (Exception e) {
            System.out.println("exception while loading ..");
        }

        if (image.getHeight(this) == -1) {
            System.out.println("Could not load: " + texture);
        }
        else {
            System.out.println("Loaded: " + texture);
        }

        texheight = image.getHeight(this);
        texwidth = image.getWidth(this);
        //createPaint(0,0,30,30);
```

LISTING 3.5 Continued

```java
        this.setSize(800,600);
    }

    public void createPaint(int hanchor, int vanchor, int hsize, int vsize) {
        this.hanchor = hanchor;
        this.vanchor = vanchor;
        this.hsize = hsize;
        this.vsize = vsize;

        BufferedImage bi =
            new BufferedImage
            ➥(texwidth,texheight,BufferedImage.TYPE_INT_RGB);

        Graphics2D big = bi.createGraphics();
        big.drawImage(image,0,0,this);
        RenderingHints interpHints = new
          RenderingHints(RenderingHints.KEY_INTERPOLATION,
                         RenderingHints.VALUE_INTERPOLATION_BICUBIC);
        big.setRenderingHints(interpHints);

        RenderingHints antialiasHints = new
          RenderingHints(RenderingHints.KEY_ANTIALIASING,
                         RenderingHints.VALUE_ANTIALIAS_ON);
        big.setRenderingHints(antialiasHints);
        Font f1 = new Font("Helvetica", Font.BOLD, 24);
        big.setFont(f1);
        big.setColor(Color.black);

        big.drawString("VRSciences", 125,100);
        big.setColor(Color.white);
        Font f2 = new Font("Helvetica", Font.BOLD, 18);
        big.setFont(f2);
        big.drawString("Cognitive Neuroscience", 75, 120);
        big.drawString("meets", 160, 140);
        big.drawString("Virtual Reality",120, 160);
        big.drawString("www.vrsciences.com", 100, 180);

        imageRect =
            new Rectangle(hanchor,vanchor, hsize, vsize);

        tpaint = new TexturePaint(bi,imageRect);
          repaint();
    }

    public void update(Graphics g) {
        paint(g);
```

3

GRAPHICS PROGRAMMING WITH THE JAVA 2D API

2D Graphics and Imaging on the Java Platform

LISTING 3.5 Continued

```
    }
      public void paint(Graphics g) {

          tex.hsize_slide.setMaximum(this.getSize().width);
          tex.vsize_slide.setMaximum(this.getSize().height);

          tex.hanchor_slide.setMaximum(hsize);
          tex.vanchor_slide.setMaximum(vsize);

          Graphics2D g2d = (Graphics2D) g;

          g2d.setPaint(tpaint); //setting context

          g2d.fill(new Rectangle2D.Float(0.0f,
                                         0.0f,
                                         this.getSize().width,
                                         this.getSize().height));

      }
}
```

Figures 3.8 through 3.10 show the effects of changing some of the setting in `TexturePaintEx.java`.

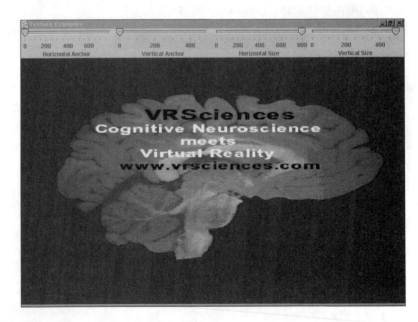

FIGURE 3.8

A screen from `TexturePaintEx` with settings for a large anchoring rectangle.

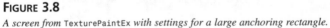

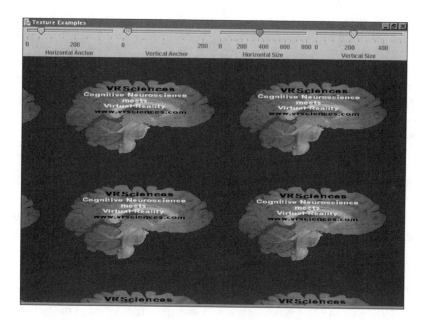

FIGURE 3.9

A screen from TexturePaintEx *with settings for a moderately sized and shifted anchoring rectangle.*

FIGURE 3.10

A screen from TexturePaintEx *with settings for an extremely small anchoring rectangle.*

Making a Custom Paint

Finally, in cases where the three standard Paint objects cannot be used to make the desired effect, you can create a custom paint. This can be fairly challenging. The problem becomes tenable, however, given a proper understanding of the Paint and PaintContext interfaces discussed previously. For expediency, the developer should consider at length the many ways in which transparency and composite overlay can be used with the preexisting Paint classes to accomplish a particular goal.

Creating a custom Paint object is a two-part process. The developer must write at least one implementation of the PaintContext interface and then write an implementation of the Paint interface that uses this custom PaintContext.

The most code intensive part is writing a custom implementation of the PaintContext interface. There are only three different methods in the PaintContext interface. They are as follows:

```
public void dispose();
ColorModel getColorModel();
Raster getRaster(int x, inty, int w, int h );
```

If you are familiar with the Java representation of an image (described in the introduction to this section and in far greater detail in the next chapter), it is clear that we have the makings of an image here. Specifically, there is a Raster and a ColorModel present. Remember that a Raster consists of data (the DataBuffer object) and the methods for interpreting that data (SampleModel).

When creating a custom implementation of PaintContext, it generally isn't necessary to modify the getColorModel() or dispose() methods. Most of the real work occurs in writing the getRaster() method. Overall, this work falls in the domain of image processing. The custom Paint is made by operating on the pixels in the Raster. An example of making a custom Paint object is given in the next chapter.

The last part of the procedure is to implement the custom Paint interface object. As already mentioned, there is only one method in the Paint interface, the createContext() method, who's sole purpose is to return a PaintContext whenever Paint is called. So, for example, if the PaintContext that was made is called myCustomPaintContext, implementing the createContext() method would look like the following:

```
public PaintContext createContext(ColorModel cm,
                    Rectangle deviceBounds,
                    Rectangle2D userBounds,
                    AffineTransform transform,
                    RenderingHints hints) {
    try{
      return new myCustoomPaintContext(args);
    }catch(NoninvertibleTransformException e){
```

```
        e.printStackTrace();
        throw new IllegalArgumentException();
    }
}
```

Transparency and Compositing

Many visually impressive effects can be made using transparency and composite overlay.

Composite attributes are generally set in an `AlphaComposite` object and added to the `Graphics2D` context with the `Graphics2D.setComposite()` method. There is no direct way to instantiate an `AlphaComposite` object. Instead, a so-called factory method, `AlphaComposite.getInstance()`, is called. There are two variations of the `getInstance()` method; the first has one argument specifying the mixing rule to use (discussed next). The second version of the `getInstance()` method has both the argument for specifying the mixing rule as well as an argument specifying the transparency value to use. The transparency value ranges from 0–1 (in floating point) with 0.f being totally opaque and 1.f being totally transparent.

The mixing rules conform to a set of rules formalized by Porter and Duff and hence known as the Porter-Duff compositing rules.[1] A key element for understanding the Porter-Duff rules is to appreciate the difference between the source and destination objects. The *source* refers to the new graphic that is to be rendered over existing graphics, called the *destination*. The process, then, is to first create the destination graphics, build an `AlphaComposite` object with the appropriate rules set, and add it to the attributes of the `Graphics2D` context. The last step is to create the source shape and render it.

The application PDExamples.java is used to demonstrate the Porter-Duff rules. Portions of the class are shown in Listing 3.6. You should run the example and experiment with different rules and transparency values. A sample screen from this program is shown in Figure 3.11.

LISTING 3.6   PDExamples.java

```java
class myCustomCanvas extends Canvas {
    float srcalpha, dstalpha;
    PDExamples2 pd;

    public myCustomCanvas(PDExamples2 pd) {
        this.pd = pd;
    }

    public void paint(Graphics g) {
```

---

[1] *T. Porter and T. Duff, Compositing Digital Images, SIGGRAPH 84, 253–259.*

LISTING 3.6 Continued

```
Graphics2D g2d = (Graphics2D) g;

float xcenter = this.getSize().width/2;
float ycenter = this.getSize().height/2;

float srcalpha = 1-((float)pd.srcalpha.getValue()/100);
float dstalpha = 1-((float)pd.dstalpha.getValue()/100);

Shape dstRectangle = new Rectangle2D.Float(xcenter,
                                           ycenter-110,
                                           80,
                                           300);
Shape srcRectangle = new Rectangle2D.Float(xcenter-110,
                                           ycenter,
                                           300,
                                           80);

   //create a BufferedImage to put destination and source
BufferedImage bi = new BufferedImage(this.getSize().width,
                                     this.getSize().height,
                                     BufferedImage.TYPE_INT_ARGB);
Graphics2D big = bi.createGraphics();

big.setColor(new Color(1.f,0.f,0.f,dstalpha)); //setting context
big.fill(dstRectangle);

  big.setColor(Color.blue);

 //check all radio buttons

 if (pd.clear_rb.isSelected() == true) {
     big.setComposite(AlphaComposite.getInstance
     ➥(AlphaComposite.CLEAR,srcalpha));
 }
 else if (pd.dstin_rb.isSelected() == true) {
     big.setComposite(AlphaComposite.getInstance
     ➥(AlphaComposite.DST_IN,srcalpha));
 }
 else if (pd.dstout_rb.isSelected() == true) {
     big.setComposite(AlphaComposite.getInstance
     ➥(AlphaComposite.DST_OUT,srcalpha));
 }
 else if (pd.dstover_rb.isSelected() == true) {
```

LISTING 3.6   Continued

```
                big.setComposite(AlphaComposite.getInstance
                ➡(AlphaComposite.DST_OVER,srcalpha));
        }
        else if (pd.src_rb.isSelected() == true) {
                big.setComposite(AlphaComposite.getInstance
                ➡(AlphaComposite.SRC,srcalpha));
        }
        else if (pd.srcin_rb.isSelected() == true) {
                big.setComposite(AlphaComposite.getInstance
                ➡(AlphaComposite.SRC_IN,srcalpha));
        }
        else if (pd.srcout_rb.isSelected() == true) {
                big.setComposite(AlphaComposite.getInstance
                ➡(AlphaComposite.SRC_OUT,srcalpha));
        }
        else if (pd.srcover_rb.isSelected() == true) {
                big.setComposite(AlphaComposite.getInstance
                ➡(AlphaComposite.SRC_OVER,srcalpha));
        }

        big.fill(srcRectangle);
        g2d.drawImage(bi, null, 0, 0);


    }
}

class RadioListener implements ActionListener {
    myCustomCanvas mc;

    public RadioListener(myCustomCanvas mc) {
        this.mc = mc;
    }

    public void actionPerformed(ActionEvent e) {
      mc.repaint();
    }
 }

class SliderListener implements ChangeListener {
    myCustomCanvas mc;
```

LISTING 3.6 Continued

```
public SliderListener(myCustomCanvas mc) {
      this.mc = mc;
}

public void stateChanged(ChangeEvent e) {
  mc.repaint();
  }//End of stateChanged
}//End of SliderListener
```

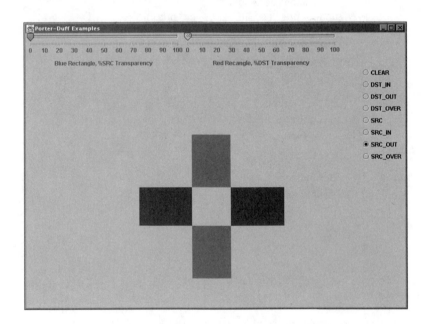

FIGURE 3.11

Output from the PDExample.java demonstrating the SRC_OUT rule with 0 transparency (full opacity).

As in all of our examples so far in this chapter, we created an inner class extending Canvas. Note again the use of the BufferedImage for storing the current graphics, as used in Listing 3.4. This time, the necessity of using the BufferedImage stems from a different reason than needing a BufferedImage for the TexturePaint() constructor. In this case, we need to use the BufferedImage because the destination graphics won't have transparency. Therefore, we create a BufferedImage with transparency to hold our destination graphics and to give them a transparency value.

Also notice that we use a method `paintGraphics()` to set up and fill the `BufferedImage`. Therefore, our `paint()` method is pretty simple; it draws the `BufferedImage` to the `Canvas`.

Text

One of the keys to understanding Java 2D text rendering is to realize that in most ways text can be treated as a shape. As such, most of the methods used on shape primitives can be used on text primitives. However, some special properties of graphics-based text should be considered.

Before diving into these special properties, it is necessary to consider some terminology. The different terms used to describe text, layout, and style largely reflect the different ways primitives are grouped to lay out text.

The overall goal of text layout is to artistically represent symbols (known as *characters*) that have meaning in a particular language. Each character is represented by a set of shape primitives called *glyphs*. Technically, glyphs are made up of little bitmapped images. Often, but not always, a single glyph represents a single character.

To render a character, then, it is necessary to assemble a set of glyphs. This is accomplished through a lookup (mapping) table that specifies the glyphs to use for each particular character. A current standard, and the one used by Java, is Unicode.

A *font* is simply the collection of glyphs needed to make a set of characters with a particular style and size. The collection of glyphs that make up the font known as Helvetica 10 point, for example, will be different from the set of glyphs representing Times New Roman 10 point because of the subtle differences in the way the curves arch, the lines are terminated, and so on. An interesting exercise is to zoom in closely on text with a variety of fonts using any drawing program. It is easy to see the glyphs and subtle differences among the different fonts.

Most of the classes and interfaces discussed in this section are part of the `java.awt.Font` package.

Getting a List of Available Fonts

The first point of divergence concerning shapes and fonts is that each environment doesn't have the same resident fonts. Java has a very useful method for determining the fonts recognized by the system. The `GraphicsEnvironment` object's `getAvailableFontFamilyNames()` method returns an array of strings containing the names of the available fonts on the system. The following code can be put in a Java program to print a list of fonts available. Likewise, the fonts can be added to a Collection object (that is, vector or hash table) for use in user interface selection.

```
GraphicsEnvironment ge =
    GraphicsEnvironment.getLocalGraphicsEnvironment();

    String availablefonts[] =
    ge.getAvailableFontFamilyNames();

    for ( int i = 1; i < availablefonts.length; i++ ) {
        System.out.println(envfonts[i]);
    }
```

Laying Out Text

Before going too deeply into Java 2D's text rendering methods, you should know that most applications can get by with a very simple model of getting an instance of a font, setting the Graphics2D context for that font with the setFont() method, and using the Graphics2D rendering method drawString() to render a string. This is the clear way to go for basic tasks such as labeling the axis of a plot and placing short strings of text on the screen.

That said, Java 2D has some pretty advanced text rendering capabilities, most of which can be realized with the TextLayout class (discussed next). The following introduction will hardly scratch the surface of the different kinds of text processing that are possible with Java 2D, but should provide enough of an introduction so that you can continue. We will focus on a few classes, primarily the TextLayout and AttributedString classes.

Introduction to the TextLayout Class

When producing even the most rudimentary text layout, it is often necessary to combine strings in different styles and control the flow of the text as in a paragraph layout. TextLayout is the essential class for laying sections of text. It is a graphical representation of character data that allows for most of the advanced text capabilities of Java 2D. Table 3.5 lists some of these capabilities.

TABLE 3.5 Text Layout Operations Supported in Java 2D

Layout Operation	Description
International Support	Classes to handle many challenges in producing international text such as right-to-left language. Conforms to Unicode97 standard.
Editing	Editing, carets, cursor positioning, highlighting
Rendering	Justification, text metrics
Paragraph Layout	Use in conjunction with LineBreakMeasurer

After the `TextLayout` object is instantiated, it can be rendered either through its own `draw()` method or through `Graphics2D`'s `drawString()` method. The following code snippet illustrates the basic use of `TextLayout`:

```
FontRenderContext frc = g2d.getFontRenderContext();  //contains measurement
➥info
Font f = new Font("Helvetica",Font.BOLD, 24);
String s = new String("Simple test string");
TextLayout textlayout = new TextLayout(s, f, frc);
Textlayout.draw(g2d, height, width);   //use TextLayout's draw method
```

There are several things to notice in the previous code snippet. First, although we created a `TextLayout` object, we didn't do anything very special with it. In fact, this snippet achieves the same result that we would have realized with the `drawString()` method. The use of `TextLayout` with longer strings is left as an exercise for you. Generally, it is useful to read in longer strings from an external file.

Second, notice that it is necessary to create an instance of `FontRenderContext` to pass to the `TextLayout` constructor. The `FontRenderContext` object contains the basic information important for measuring text (also known as font metrics), including a reference to the mathematical transform necessary to convert points to pixels as well as information about specific rendering attributes that might have been set as such. Rendering attributes include whether antialiasing has been set or fractional metrics are in use. Although all the `TextLayout` constructors require the `FontRenderContext` object to be passed, it isn't necessary to worry too much about `FontRenderContext` for most applications in general.

A final point about the previous code snippet is that once instantiated, the `TextLayout` object is immutable. Therefore, any changes to the text layout (such as changing the string) during program operation will require the creation of a new `TextLayout` object.

Generating an Attributed String for `TextLayout`

As stated previously, we haven't done anything special with our `TextLayout` object. Because it is immutable once it is created anyway, we are pretty limited in our text layout possibilities. The key to using the immutable `TextLayout` object is in generating an `AttributedCharacterIterator` object to pass to the `TextLayout` constructor (or, alternatively, the `Graphics2D` `drawString()` method).

The `AttributedCharacterIterator` is used by `Graphics2D` and `TextLayout` when rendering styled text to walk through the text to be rendered. This is completely analogous to the `PathIterator` object for moving around the boundary of a shape that was demonstrated previously.

A common source of confusion arises because the programmer doesn't specify the details of pairing characters and their attributes. Instead, the pairings are specified in an `AttributedString` object. This step accounts for the majority of the work in laying out the text. The `AttributedCharacterIterator` is then instantiated with the `AttributedString`'s `getIterator()` method.

The following code represents a prototypical example of setting the attributes (colors, sizes, and fonts) of individual characters in a line of text. Step 1 involves instantiating the `AttributedString` object without setting the attributes. We will set the attributes short. Although this is probably the easiest way to proceed, other constructors of `AttributedString` will allow you to set the attributes in the constructor. Regardless, let's instantiate the object and add some attributes:

```
//step one; create the AttributedString object
String text = new String("abcdefghijklmnopqrstuvwxyz");
AttributedString attText = new AttributedString(text);

//step two;add some attributes
attText.addAttribute(TextAttribute.FOREGROUND, Color.black);  //default
attText.addAttribute(TextAttribute.FAMILY, "helvetica"); //helvetica

//step three; change attribute of the third character

for (int i;i<25;i++) {
    attText.addAttribute(TextAttribute.SIZE, (float) 2*i, i, i+1 );
}
```

Remember that the `TextAttribute.FONT` attribute supercedes all other font attributes (for example, the `TextureAttribute.FAMILY` attribute set previously).

Another caveat is that all graphical information returned from a `TextLayout` object's methods is relative to the origin of the `TextLayout`, which is the intersection of the `TextLayout` object's baseline with its left edge. Also, coordinates passed into a `TextLayout` object's methods are assumed to be relative to the `TextLayout` object's origin.

Dozens of attributes can be added. The full list is located at http://java.sun.com/j2se/1.3/docs/api/java/awt/font/TextAttribute.html.

Formatting Paragraph Text

The code from the preceding section represents one way to create a `TextLayout` object and is sufficient for single lines of text. A second class, however, called `LineBreakMeasurer`, also creates a `TextLayout` object but further provides methods to control the line breaks to form blocks of text. `LineBreakMeasurer` is intended for use in laying out paragraphs.

The strategy implemented by LineBreakMeasurer is simply to place as many words on each line as will fit. If a word won't fit in its entirety on a given line, a break is placed before it and it is shifted to the next line. Strategies that use hyphenation or minimize the differences in line length within paragraphs require low-level calls and aren't handled easily with LineBreakMeasurer.

In order to break a paragraph of text into lines, it is necessary to construct a LineBreakMeasurer object for the entire paragraph. Separate segments of the text are obtained using the nextLayout() method, which returns a TextLayout object that fits within the specified width for each line (called the *wrapping width*). When the nextLayout() method reaches the end of the text, it returns Null to indicate that no more segments are available.

Inserting Shapes and Images into Text

It is also possible to embed shapes and even images into a line of text. This is accomplished by adding the TextureAttribute.CHAR_REPLACEMENT attribute with the desired replacement object. For shapes and images, the replacement object needs to be an object of type ShapeGraphicsAttribute or ImageGraphicsAttribute, respectively.

Building a Custom Font

Another somewhat common task is the creation of a custom font based on an existing font. This can be accomplished by passing an existing font name with the desired size and style to the constructor of the Font class. It is also possible to use the deriveFont() method:

```
Font sourceFont = new Font("Helvetica", Font.ITALICS, 12);
Font derivedFont = fontSource.deriveFont(Font.BOLD, 12);
```

Of course, there are much more interesting things you would want to do with a custom font. The deriveFont() method has a number of constructors, including one for using a custom attribute mapping and another for applying affine transforms to fonts. (For information on the AffineTransform class, see the later section "Coordinate Space Transformations.")

Text Hit Testing

The TextLayout class greatly simplifies the task of hit testing in text with three methods, getNextRightHit(), getNextLeftHit(), and hitTestChar(), that each return an instance of TextHitInfo. A TextHitInfo object contains information about the character position within a text model as well as its bias (whether the position is to the right or to the left of the character). You should bear in mind that the offsets contained in TextHitInfo objects are specified relative to the start of the TextLayout object and not to the text used to create the TextLayout.

Clipping

The clipping path is a state attribute that specifies which part of a shape is to be rendered. In order to specify the clipping region, a path (see Listing 3.2 for the definition of a path) is created such that only the parts of the shape within the path are rendered. The clipping region can be specified by any valid Shape (for example, a GeneralPath or Rectangle2D). For example, a simple clipping path could be used in the myCustomRenderer class in our basic java graphics program recipe by adding the following:

```
GeneralPath gp = new GeneralPath();
gp.moveTo((50,50);   //initial starting point
gp.lineTo(30,200);
gp.lineTo(110,140);
gp.lineTo(90,190);
gp.lineTo(300,50);
gp.closePath();

g2.setClip(gp);
g2.setColor(new GradientPaint());
g2.fill(new Rectangle2D.float(0.f,0.f,500.f,500.f);
```

Coordinate Space Transformations

If you wanted to rotate or otherwise transform a graphics object and then redraw it, there would be two obvious ways to go. One way, which is generally impractical, is to transform each point of the graphics object and then render the transformed object. Any reasonably complicated shape would require many hundreds of transforms. The preferred way is to transform the user space, draw on it, and then render the user space to the output device.

```
class myCustomCanvas extends Canvas {

    public void paint(Graphics g) {

        Graphics2D g2d = (Graphics2D) g;
        g2d.setColor(Color.red); //setting context
        Rectangle2D sq1 = new Rectangle2D.Float(0.f,0.f,175.0f,175.0f);
    //translate user space to center
        g2d.translate(this.getSize().width/2, this.getSize().height/2);
        g2d.fill(sq1);
        g2d.rotate(-45);   //rotate user space
        g2d.setColor(Color.blue);
        g2d.fill(sq1);

    }
}
```

In Figure 3.12, a translation of user space and the blue rectangle are filled. Next, the user space is rotated -45 degrees, and the same rectangle is drawn.

FIGURE 3.12
Output from BasicRecipeJ2D.java after adding the preceding code snippet.

Another method available in Java 2D is the `AffineTransformOp`. An *affine* transformation is a linear matrix multiplication to a coordinate space. Many effects can be produced using an affine transformation including rotate, translate, shear, and scale. Indeed, when any graphics are rendered from user space to device space, an affine transformation is used to make the conversion. It isn't necessary to modify the transformation from user to device space, but it is interesting to note that the same method is usable for making transformations within user space. For a quick example, we will rotate the rectangle we created in the `myCustomRenderMethod`.

Techniques for Graphical User Input

Most user interaction problems in 2D consist of determining whether the user clicked on a particular shape or text area and other forms of so-called hit testing. Two methods, `Graphics2D.hit()` and the `Shape.contains()`, are particularly useful for solving shape clicking problems. `Shape.contains()` can be placed in the `mouseEvent` methods such as `mousePressed()` and `mouseClicked()` to test if a particular shape has been selected after the desired mouse event. An example of using the `contains()` method is provided in Listing 3.3.

Graphics2D.hit() can be used in more or less the same fashion; however, it is necessary to pass the hit() method a rectangular area of device space in which to search for the selected object.

Double Buffering

Double buffering is a technique for reducing flicker in animations that at first might seem a little counter intuitive. The problem stems from the fact that when a new animation frame is rendered, it is desirable to first clear the old frame. This causes a flicker to occur. The basic idea of double buffering is to create a virtual screen out of the user's view. At the beginning of this chapter, it was stated that a graphics device could be a screen, printer, file, or memory area. The virtual screen used as the buffer is the primary example of using a memory space as a graphics device. When paint() is called, the clearing and painting of the animation frame can occur on the virtual screen and the resulting rendered image can then be transferred to the real screen immediately upon completion. The cost of double buffering is in memory and CPU consumption. However, this cost is probably unavoidable for complex animations and usually isn't too expensive.

Another application of double buffering is in spirited animations. A sprite is a graphics object that moves over another, usually larger, graphic. The sprite itself can be a series of animated frames, thus allowing, for example, an animation of a small butterfly flitting its wings while flying over a static or dynamic texture. Another name used for sprite animations is cast-based animation, which is derived from the use of sprites as cast members who can move over texture maps. Sprites are commonly used in non-3D gaming applications.

Comprehensive Example: Kspace Visualization

The following is a comprehensive example that will be integrated with some of Java 3D examples from Part III to form one of the integrated examples at the end of the book. It isn't necessary to understand the subject matter to understand the graphics programming; however, some background information is helpful.

Background Information on Kspace

One of the fundamental concepts in magnetic resonance imaging is kspace. It is sometimes said in jest that kspace is a place where no one can hear you scream. Without a doubt, kspace is a tough concept for people learning MRI. However, kspace is a simple extension of the concept of Fourier space that is well known in imaging. For now, suffice it to say that Fourier space and image space are different representations of the same data. It is possible to go back and forth between image space and Fourier space using the forward and inverse Fourier transform. Many image processing routines make direct use of this duality.

What makes MRI different from other imaging modalities is that the data are collected directly in Fourier space by following a time-based trajectory through space. The position in Fourier space is directly related to the gradient across the object being imaged. By changing the gradient over time, many points in kspace can be sampled in a trajectory through Fourier space. Discreet samples are taken at each point until the Fourier space is filled. A backward (inverse) Fourier Transform is then performed to yield the image of the object (in image space).

It turns out that there are numerous (almost infinite ways) to traverse kspace. One such trajectory is called spiral and benefits from improved coverage of kspace per unit time because of the inherent properties of the circle. The spiral kspace trajectory allows for images to be taken in snapshot (20ms) fashion and is used for such leading-edge applications such as imaging of the beating heart or imaging brain activity (functional magnetic resonance imaging). Figure 3.13 shows the final trajectory. Blue dots indicate that all time points up to the current time, whereas red dots indicate the full trajectory. This part of the visualization will be integrated with Java 3D models in the KspaceModeller application developed in Part III of this book.

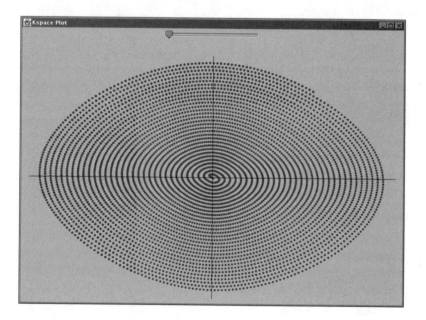

FIGURE 3.13

Final kspace trajectory for KspacePlot.java.

In this example, we will use a slider bar to advance through time and see the current and previously sampled kspace points. The visualization will be made using an actual file that sits on the computer that runs an MRI scanner. We will later expand the number of kspace trajectories we can make, including making programmatic versions that aren't based on real data.

Step 1—The Visualization

First, let's make a skeleton of our external extended Canvas and call it KspaceCanvas. It is in this external class that all our painting will be accomplished. We will begin by painting an x- and y-axis with labels. An important part of this process is determining the height and width of the Canvas (accomplished with the getSize() method).

LISTING 3.7   KspaceCanvas.java—a Custom Canvas for Visualization

```java
import java.awt.*;
import java.awt.geom.*;
import java.awt.image.*;


public class KspaceCanvas extends Canvas {
    int xcenter, ycenter, offsetx, offsety;

    KspaceCanvas() {
     System.out.println("Creating an instance of KspaceCanvas");
    }

    public void drawKspace(int tpoint) {
        System.out.println("drawKspace");
        this.tpoint = tpoint;
        repaint();
    }

    public void paint(Graphics g){

        Graphics2D g2d = (Graphics2D)g;   //always!

         offsetx = (int) this.getSize().width/50;
         offsety = (int) this.getSize().height/50;
         xcenter = (int) this.getSize().width/2;
         ycenter = (int) this.getSize().height/2;

      //call method to paint the x-y axix
        paintAxis(g2d);
    }

     public void paintAxis(Graphics2D g2d) {
        //setup font for axis labeling
        Font f1 = new Font("TimesRoman", Font.BOLD, 14);
        g2d.setFont(f1);
```

LISTING 3.7   Continued

```
    g2d.drawString("Kx",this.getSize().width-(2*offsetx),
                         this.getSize().height/2);

    g2d.drawString("Ky",this.getSize().width/2,offsetx);

    // draw  axis for kspace

    g2d.setColor(Color.black);  //set rendering attribute
    g2d.drawLine(offsetx, ycenter, xcenter-xoffset, ycenter-yoffset);
    g2d.drawLine(xcenter, yoffset, xcenter, ycenter-yoffset);

  }


}
```

Notice the `drawKspace()` method that receives the `int` argument `tpoint`, whose sole function is to set the current timepoint and call `repaint()`. The `tpoint` variable will represent the current timepoint in the kspace trajectory and will run from 0 to 5499. In the next step, we will create a slider bar with an attached listener. In that listener, the `drawKspace()` method will be called with the `tpoint` variable representing the current value of the slider bar.

The other important code for this part occurs in the overridden `paint()` and `paintAxis()` methods. First, in the `paint()` method, we get information necessary for scaling the axis appropriately. We want the x and y centers located half way up the Canvas regardless of size, so we use the `getSize()` method that was briefly described previously.

Step 2—Setting Up the User Interface

This step is fairly easy. We will extend `JFrame` and add two `JPanels`, one to hold the user interface components and another to hold our `Canvas`, as shown in Listing 3.8.

LISTING 3.8   KspaceSpacePlot.java

```
import java.applet.Applet;
import java.awt.*;
import java.awt.event.*;
import javax.vecmath.*;
import javax.swing.*;
import java.awt.BorderLayout;

import java.util.Vector;
```

LISTING 3.8 Continued

```java
import java.awt.GraphicsConfiguration;

public class KspacePlot extends JFrame {

    int kwidth, kheight;

    KspaceData ks;
    KspaceCanvas kspacec;

  public KspacePlot (int initx, int inity) {

    super("Kspace Plot");

    Panel sliderpanel = new Panel();
    JSlider hslider = new JSlider();
    hslider.setMinimum(0);
    hslider.setMaximum(5498);
    hslider.setValue(0);
    hslider.setPreferredSize(new Dimension(300,20));
    sliderpanel.add(hslider);

    BorderLayout f1 = new BorderLayout();
    this.getContentPane().setLayout(f1);
    this.getContentPane().add(sliderpanel, BorderLayout.NORTH);
    ks = new KspaceData();
    kspacec = new KspaceCanvasA();

    this.getContentPane().add(kspacec);
    kspacec.drawKspace(0);
}

public static void main(String[] args) {
    int initialSizex=500;
    int initialSizey=500;

    WindowListener l = new WindowAdapter() {
     public void windowClosing(WindowEvent e)
        {System.exit(0);}
     public void windowClosed(WindowEvent e)
        {System.exit(0);}
     };

    KspacePlot k = new KspacePlot(initialSizex, initialSizey);
    k.addWindowListener(l);
```

LISTING 3.8 Continued

```java
        k.setSize(500,500);
        k.setVisible(true);

    }

}

class SliderListener implements ChangeListener {

    KspaceCanvasA kc;
    int slider_val;

    public SliderListener(KspaceCanvasA kc) {
        this.kc = kc;
    }

  public void stateChanged(ChangeEvent e) {

    JSlider s1 = (JSlider)e.getSource();
    slider_val = s1.getValue();
    System.out.println("Current value of the slider: " + slider_val);
    kc.drawKspace(

}//End of stateChanged
 }//End of SliderListener
//
```

Step 3—Reading the Scanner Trajectory

Because we want to plot an actual trajectory from the scanner, we will read bytes from a file into an array using a `FileInputStream` object. There are a few examples that read raw data in this book and you will find that, in practice, reading bytes is occasionally necessary. It probably isn't necessary to get into the details of this class. The important concept is that two files (kxtrap.flt and kytrap.flt) are read into two public arrays. Maximum and minimum values are computed for each array and stored in public variables. Another public array of time values is calculated based on the number of timepoints. The values stored in these arrays will be made accessible to KspaceCanvas by adding code to the KspaceCanvas constructor in "Step 4—Modifying KspaceCanvas to Plot the Data." Note that this class is external and stored in the file KspaceData.java (see Listing 3.9).

LISTING 3.9   KspaceData.java—an External Class for Reading a Scanner Trajectory

```java
import java.awt.*;
import java.io.*;

class KspaceData {

    int tpoints=5500;

    double Gxcoord[] = new double[tpoints];
    double Gycoord[] = new double[tpoints];
    int time[] = new int[tpoints];

    double Gx, Gy;

    double Gxmax=0.0;
    double Gymax=0.0;
    double Gxmin=0.0;
    double Gymin=0.0;

    KspaceData() {
       readdata();
    }

    public void readdata() {

     try {
            DataInputStream disx =
new DataInputStream(new FileInputStream("kxtrap.flt"));
            DataInputStream disy =
new DataInputStream(new FileInputStream("kytrap.flt"));

             try {
                for (int i=0; i < tpoints-1; i++) {
                    Gx = disx.readFloat();
            Gy = disy.readFloat();

              //find min and max gradient values to determine scaling
                    if (Gx > Gxmax) {
                        Gxmax=Gx;
                    }
                    if (Gy > Gymax) {
                        Gymax=Gy;
                    }
                    if (Gx < Gxmin) {
                        Gxmin=Gx;
                    }
```

LISTING 3.9   Continued

```
                if (Gy < Gymin) {
                    Gymin=Gy;
                }

                Gycoord[i] = Gy;
          Gxcoord[i] = Gx;
            }
            } catch (EOFException e) {
        }
        } catch (FileNotFoundException e) {
           System.out.println("DataIOTest: " + e);
        } catch (IOException e) {
           System.out.println("DataIOTest: " + e);
        }
    }
}
```

Step 4—Modifying `KspaceCanvas` to Plot the Data

Now that we can read the kx and ky files, it is time to plot the data over the axis that we made in step 1.

Add the method `paintData()` just below the `paintAxis()` method in `KspaceCanvas.java`:

```
//method to plot kspace data

public void paintData(Graphics2D g2d) {

    for (int i=1; i<tpoints-2; i++){
    // Scale Gx and Gy between -1 and 1; called Kx and Ky;
    // Multiply Kx and Ky times the width and height
    //of the Canvas in the same step
       Kx[i] = (ks.Kx[i] *this.getSize().width*scalefac;
       Ky[i] = (ks.Ky[i])*this.getSize().height*scalefac;

       g2d.setColor(Color.lightGray);
       g2d.draw(new Ellipse2D.Double(kxcenter + Kx[i],
                                     kycenter + Ky[i],3.0,3.0));
       g2d.setColor(Color.blue);
       g2d.fill(new Ellipse2D.Double(kxcenter + Kx[i],
                                     kycenter + Ky[i],4.0,4.0));

    }

}
```

In addition, we need to instantiate an object from our KspaceData class. In the
KspacePlot.java class, add the following line just above the initial call to the KspaceCanvas
constructor:

```
ks = new KspaceData();
```

We now need to modify the constructor to KspaceCanvas to allow for the passing in the newly
constructed KspaceData object. First change the constructor in KspaceCanvas.java:

```
KspaceCanvas(KspaceData ks) {
    this.ks = ks;
}
```

And, change the initial call to the constructor in KspacePlot.java accordingly to the following:

```
kspacec = new KspaceCanvas(ks);
```

Finally, let's add the call to paintData() right after the call to paintAxis() in the paint()
method of KspaceCanvas:

```
paintData(g2d);
```

After running the program, your screen should resemble Figure 3.8.

Step 5—Overriding the Update Method in KspaceCanvas

You will notice immediately that, although the program is starting to look promising, it is
largely unusable in its present state. The primary problem is that the screen is erased and fully
redrawn every time the slider bar changes.

Remember from before that repaint ends up calling update(), which puts the background color
over the component before the Component's paint() method is called. This is one of the times
when this is undesirable. We must therefore override the update() method and have our program only redraw the points that are new since the last call to repaint(). The following code
segment is inserted into KspaceCanvas.java:

```
public void update(Graphics g) {
    paint(g);
}
```

Step 6—Add RenderingHints to Improve the Rendering

In this final step, we want to make the output look better. This is achieved through adding
RenderingHints to the Graphics2D object. In this case, we want to add antialiasing so that our
data point ellipses (dots) look smoother. We also need to add bicubic spline interpolation so
that the dots line up better. Add the following lines in the paint() method:

```
RenderingHints interpHints =
            new RenderingHints(RenderingHints.KEY_INTERPOLATION,
                               RenderingHints.VALUE_INTERPOLATION_BICUBIC);
g2d.setRenderingHints(interpHints);

RenderingHints antialiasHints =
            new RenderingHints(RenderingHints.KEY_ANTIALIASING,
                               RenderingHints.VALUE_ANTIALIAS_ON);

g2d.setRenderingHints(antialiasHints);
```

You could just as well add this code to the constructor so that the `RenderingHints` aren't created each time `paint()` is called; however, this doesn't provide a substantial difference in performance.

Summary

In this chapter, we covered graphics programming in Java 2D, and you saw that the vast majority of graphics applications in Java 2D follow a basic three step recipe—obtain a `Graphics2D` object, set the context, and render something. You should always consider the relationship between user space and device space when learning advanced features of the platform. The rest is straightforward but does require a knowledge of the vast array of state attributes that can be combined to produce the desired graphics effect as well as how to produce the necessary geometry.

We will next look into buffered imaging and the immediate mode imaging model, which, other than printing, forms the other major part of the Java 2D API.

Immediate Mode Imaging Model

IN THIS CHAPTER

Before discussing the *immediate mode* imaging model, it is important to understand the older, *push* imaging model. It is from the limitations of this model that the immediate mode model was created, just as the limitations of the immediate mode model led to the creation of the *Java advanced imaging (JAI)* API discussed in Chapter 6, "Java Advanced Imaging." But just as the limitations of one model led to the creation of another, each model is built on the functionality of the one before, so understanding the push model is important to understanding the immediate mode model just as understanding the immediate mode model is important to understanding JAI.

As a quick introduction, both the push imaging model and the immediate mode imaging model are part of the Java *Advanced Windowing Toolkit (AWT)* package, although at one time the immediate mode model was part of a separate Java 2D package. (The Java 2D package has since been incorporated into the AWT package.) In the push imaging model, the image data isn't introduced into the imaging pipeline until it is needed; at which time an object called an `ImageProducer` starts pushing the data into this pipeline. On the other end of this pipeline is an `ImageConsumer` that must wait for the data to get pushed to it. In contrast, the immediate mode imaging model makes the image data available in memory immediately after each step in the imaging pipeline.

Push Imaging Model

It is a misconception that the push model was poorly designed and is no longer useful. On the contrary, this model was designed to provide a simple way to load images into Applets and applications. The main advantage of this model is that it can load and display images incrementally as they become available over the network. Another advantage is that by using the push model, your images can be viewed by almost all browsers without the need for plug-ins to replace the browser's *Java virtual machine (JVM)*. The main disadvantage of the push model is that the image data isn't collected into an accessible location, making anything more than simple image processing difficult. A second disadvantage is that the programming interface can be confusing, especially when you encounter it for the first time.

Images

Conventionally, an image can be thought of as a formatted collection of pixel values. In Java programming, this type of thinking can cause confusion. It is better to think of the `java.awt.Image` class as a group of resources and methods that provide a means for transferring and inquiring about a collection of image data and not as the collection itself. For example, let's look at the two code lines typically used to load an image into an Applet:

```
Image anImage = getImage(url);   //java.awt.Applet method
```

and

```
drawImage(anImage, xlocation, ylocation, this);
//java.awt.Graphics method where "this" is an
ImageObserver
```

Note that for an application, the first line can be replaced by

```
Image anImage = Toolkit.getDefaultToolkit().getImage(url);
```

or

```
Image anImage = Toolkit.getDefaultToolkit().getImage(filename);
```

In all cases, the initial step doesn't start loading the image data, but instead instantiates an `Image` object that creates the resources necessary to process the image data. The second method begins the image loading, although the method returns immediately regardless of how much of the image is available to display. The reason for this is so that the executing thread can move on to other tasks while the image data is loading. The actual loading continues in a separate thread, where an object implementing the `java.awt.ImageProducer` interface sends image data to an object implementing the `java.awt.ImageConsumer` interface.

It is of interest to note that the three classes explicitly used to load the image data—that is, `Applet`, `Graphics`, and `Image`—don't implement any of these interfaces. Thus, the separate thread connecting the `ImageProducer` to the `ImageConsumer` is a bit mysterious in this context, although a reference to the `ImageProducer` can be obtained through the `getSource` method of the `Image` class. It should be noted that the `drawImage` method of the `Graphics` class isn't the only method that will start the image data loading. This is true of any method that requires information about the image data, such as the `Image` methods `public int getWidth(ImageObserver)` and `public int getHeight(ImageObserver)`.

An important question at this point is how does the applet know how much data has been transferred to the `ImageConsumer`, where it is available for drawing? This task is left up to an object implementing the `java.awt.ImageObserver` interface. As the flow of data between the `ImageProducer` and the `ImageConsumer` progresses the

```
public boolean imageUpdate(Image img, int infoflags,
                          int x, int y, int width, int height)
```

method of the `ImageObserver` is called. Each time it is called, information is passed to it through an integer value representing a set of flags. This information can describe such things as whether the image width or image height is known, whether additional data bits have been loaded, or whether all the image data has been loaded. The trick to getting all this to work is to note that the `java.awt.Component` class implements the `ImageObserver` interface and, thus, defines this `imageUpdate` method. Therefore, the `Component` class and any descendent of it,

4

IMMEDIATE MODE
IMAGING MODEL

such as the Applet class, is an ImageObserver. So, when you specify this as the ImageObserver, you are actually specifying that the Applet's imageUpdate method gets called when the ImageProducer sends data to the ImageConsumer. The default behavior of the Applet's imageUpdate method is to repaint the Applet whenever new data bits are available.

Listing 4.1 demonstrates the use of the Applet class as an ImageObserver. We have simply replaced the default imageUpdate method with one that is functionally similar, but much more verbose.

LISTING 4.1   ImageLoaderApplet.java

```java
package ch4;

import java.applet.*;
import java.awt.*;
import java.net.*;
import java.awt.image.ImageObserver;

/**
 * ImageLoaderApplet.java -- load and display image specified by imageURL
 */
public class ImageLoaderApplet extends Applet {
    private Image img;
    private String imageURLString = "file:images/peppers.png";

    public void init() {
        URL url;
        try {
            // set imageURL here
            url = new URL(imageURLString);
            img = getImage(url);
        }
        catch (MalformedURLException me) {
            showStatus("Malformed URL: " + me.getMessage());
        }
    }

    /**
     * overloaded method to prevent clearing drawing area
     */
    public void update(Graphics g) {
        paint(g);
    }

    public void paint(Graphics g) {
        g.drawImage(img, 0, 0, this);
    }
```

LISTING 4.1   Continued

```java
/**
 * Verbose version of ImageConsumer's imageUpdate method
 */
public boolean imageUpdate(Image img, int flags,
                           int x, int y, int width, int height) {
    System.out.print("Flag(s): ");
    if ( (flags & ImageObserver.WIDTH) != 0) {
        System.out.print("WIDTH:("+width+") ");
    }

    if ( (flags & ImageObserver.HEIGHT) != 0) {
        System.out.print("HEIGHT:("+height+") ");
    }

    if ( (flags & ImageObserver.PROPERTIES) != 0) {
        System.out.print("PROPERTIES ");
    }

    if ( (flags & ImageObserver.SOMEBITS) != 0) {
        System.out.print("SOMEBITS("+x+","+y+")->(");
        System.out.print(width+","+height+") ");
        repaint();
    }

    if ( (flags & ImageObserver.FRAMEBITS) != 0) {
        System.out.print("FRAMEBITS("+x+","+y+")->(");
        System.out.print(width+","+height+") ");
        repaint();
    }

    if ( (flags & ImageObserver.ALLBITS) != 0) {
        System.out.print("ALLBITS("+x+","+y+")->(");
        System.out.println(width+","+height+") ");
        repaint();
        return false;
    }

    if ( (flags & ImageObserver.ABORT) != 0) {
        System.out.println("ABORT \n");
        return false;
    }

    if ( (flags & ImageObserver.ERROR) != 0) {
        System.out.println("ERROR ");
        return false;
    }
```

LISTING 4.1 Continued

```
        System.out.println();
        return true;
    }
}
```

If you were to run this `Applet` using the appletviewer or another browser with a defined standard output, the output would be similar to the following:

```
Flag(s): WIDTH:(256) HEIGHT:(256)
Flag(s): PROPERTIES
Flag(s): SOMEBITS(0,0)->(256,1)
Flag(s): SOMEBITS(0,1)->(256,1)
Flag(s): SOMEBITS(0,2)->(256,1)
. . .
Flag(s): SOMEBITS(0,253)->(256,1)
Flag(s): SOMEBITS(0,254)->(256,1)
Flag(s): SOMEBITS(0,255)->(256,1)
Flag(s): ALLBITS(0,0)->(256,256)
```

Note that the meaning of the arguments *width* and *height* change according to the set flags. For the `WIDTH`, `HEIGHT`, `FRAMEBITS`, and `ALLBITS` flags, the *width* and *height* represent the image dimensions. For the `SOMEBITS` flag, the *width* and *height* represent the dimensions of the block of data received by the `ImageConsumer`.

Before moving on to `Image` filtering, we will take a quick look at the methods belonging to the `ImageProducers` and the `ImageConsumers`. When you look at the methods of the `ImageProducer`, you can see that the two most important methods involve registering `ImageConsumers` and starting production of `Image` data—that is, `public void addConsumer(ImageConsumer ic)` and `public void startProduction(ImageConsumer ic)`. When you look at the methods of the `ImageConsumer`, you find that they are meant to be called by the `ImageProducer` and that they correspond closely to the flags in the `ImageObserver`'s `imageUpdate` method (see Table 4.1).

TABLE 4.1 Correspondence Between `ImageConsumer` Methods and `ImageObserver` Flags

`ImageConsumer` *Method*	`ImageObserver` *Flag*
setPixels	SOMEBITS
imageComplete	FRAMEBITS, ALLBITS, ABORT, ERROR
setDimensions	WIDTH and HEIGHT
setProperties	PROPERTIES

Thus, the communication between the `ImageProducer`, `ImageConsumer`, and `ImageObserver` is as follows: The `ImageConsumer` registers itself with the `ImageProducer` using the `ImageProducer`'s `addConsumer` method. The `ImageProducer` then starts sending data to this `ImageConsumer` when its `startProduction` method is called. The `ImageProducer` communicates with the `ImageConsumer` by calling one of the `ImageConsumer`'s methods such as `setPixels` or `imageComplete`. The status of the `ImageConsumer` arrives at the `ImageObserver` through the `ImageObserver`'s `imageUpdate` method with the appropriate flags set so that the `ImageObserver` knows what information is available to it with respect to the loading image data.

Filtering

In this context, filtering is defined as an operation that changes the pixel values or the number of pixels represented by an `Image`. The most basic and most common type of filtering is simply scaling.

Image Scaling

The easiest way to perform `Image` scaling is with the `Image` method `Image getScaledInstance(int width, int height, int hints)`, where `width` and `height` represent the dimensions of the new scaled `Image`. You can give one of them the value of `-1` to ensure that the `Image` aspect ratio doesn't change. For example, if the original `Image` dimensions were 256X200 and a `width` and `height` value of `512`, `-1` were used in the `getScaledInstance` method, the new `Image` dimensions would be 512X400.

The `hints` parameter allows you to specify how pixel interpolation should be performed. For example, using the previously mentioned dimensions, the number of pixels in the `Image` increase from 51,200 to 204,800 and the `hints` parameter gives the programmer some options in specifying how these additional 153,600 pixel values are calculated. Basically, the choices refer to either pixel replication or pixel averaging. With the `hints` parameter set to `Image.SCALE_REPLICATE` the new pixel columns and rows introduced will just be copies of existing pixel columns and rows. Similarly, if the `Image` had decreased in size, pixel columns and rows would have just dropped out. The disadvantage of this method is that the resulting `Image` might appear coarse with neighboring pixels exhibiting large differences in values. The advantage to this method is that the `Image` scaling will be performed very quickly. On the other hand, if the `hints` parameter is set to `Image.SCALE_AREA_AVERAGING`, the new pixel values will be linearly related to their neighboring pixels with close pixels contributing more and far pixels contributing less. This method of `Image` scaling takes longer, but it produces smoother image data than simply replicating pixel values. Although the `getScaledInstance` method is a method of the `Image` class, it is the only such method that allows `Image` filtering. For more advanced push model filtering, a subclass of the `java.awt.image.ImageFilter` must be used.

ImageFilter

During simple image drawing, the ImageConsumer can be difficult to find, but there are situations in which it is well defined. For example, you can use an ImageFilter, which is an ImageConsumer, to process image data as it passes from the original ImageProducer to the final ImageConsumer.

In early versions of Java image processing, there wasn't much support for image manipulation because image data was never meant to be collected into an accessible area. Therefore, image manipulation was primarily developed for filtering single pixel values. In other words, as the ImageProducer sent image data to the ImageConsumer, this data could get filtered. But, this filtering was designed to be done asynchronously on a pixel by pixel basis. Thus, easily implemented ImageFilter subclasses were created, which could crop out certain regions of pixels or process individual pixel values (java.awt.image.CropImageFilter and java.awt.image.RGBImageFilter, respectively). But, if you wanted to write a push model filter that replaces each pixel value with the average of itself and its neighbors (simple smoothing filter), things became much more complex. For this latter task, you would have to subclass the ImageFilter directly, which involves fully implementing an ImageConsumer in order to handle the information sent from the ImageProducer. Because this procedure isn't really useful anymore, it won't be covered in this chapter.

The basic idea behind the ImageFilter class and its subclasses is that they are ImageConsumers, which allow them to receive data from an ImageProducer. These filters get wrapped in an ImageProducer (java.awt.Image.FilteredImageSource), which sends out the filtered data (see Figure 4.1). So the original ImageProducer sends out data and the final ImageConsumer receives data unaware that there was one (or more) ImageConsumer/ImageProducer pairs in the pipeline filtering the data. In Figure 4.1, note that ImageFilter is an ImageConsumer, and FilteredImageSource is an ImageProducer. The ImageObserver is told the status of the image loading in the final ImageConsumer through calls to its imageUpdate method.

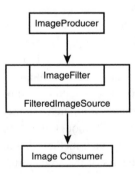

FIGURE 4.1

Push model pixel pipeline showing how asynchronous rendering takes place using ImageFilter/FilteredImageSource *pairs.*

In summary, consider Figure 4.1. When a `Graphics` object calls a `drawImage` method to draw the created `Image`, the `ImageProducer` producing the original image data passes this data to the `ImageFilter`, which acts as an `ImageConsumer`. The `ImageFilter` then filters the data before the `FilteredImageSource`, acting as an `ImageProducer`, passes the data to the final `ImageConsumer`. The `ImageConsumer` then communicates this progress to the `ImageObserver` (the `Applet`) through the `Applet`'s `imageUpdate` method. Although admittedly this seems a bit involved, there isn't much code required. The following code block takes care of most of it with the exception of defining the filter, which we will explore in the next several sections. The only thing that remains to be done is to start the production of the image data and this will occur when the `filteredImage` data is requested.

```
Image originalImage = getImage(url);
ImageFilter if = new ImageFilterSubclass(subclassParameters));
ImageProducer ip = new FilteredImageSource(originalImage.getSource(), if);
Image filteredImage = createImage(ip);    //Component method
```

CropImageFilter

The `CropImageFilter` is a subclass of the `ImageFilter` which allows you to crop the dimensions of an `Image`. To create a `CropImageFilter`, simply specify the x, y value of the top left corner depicting where you want the new `Image` to start and a `width` and `height` value. As the original image data passes through this filter, only the data within this rectangle will be passed through. Of course, the `FilteredImageSource` lets its `ImageConsumer`(s) know the new `Image` dimensions through their `setDimensions` method so that they will be expecting the correct number of pixels. The constructor for the `CropImageFilter` is as follows:

```
ImageFilter if = new CropImageFilter(int x, int y, int width, int height);
```

RGBImageFilter

An `RGBImageFilter` is a subclass of the `ImageFilter` which allows you to change individual pixel values. To create an `RGBImageFilter`, you must extend the `RGBImageFilter` class and overwrite the `public int filter(int x, int y, int rgb)` method, where x and y represent the pixel location and rgb is the pixel's original red, green, and blue color samples packed into a single integer. Likewise, the return value is the pixel's new red, green, and blue color samples packed into an integer. This type of color representation will be discussed further in the section "Pixel Storage and Conversion," so for now it is enough to know that the filtering that takes place in an `RGBImageFilter` can only be performed one pixel at a time using that pixel's color samples and its location.

Because the `public int filterRGB(int x, int y, int rgb)` method is abstract in the `RGBImageFilter`, it must be defined. But, the parameters used to do this filtering are up to the programmer. Thus, the constructor for the `RGBImageFilter` subclass should be passed any necessary filtering parameters. In Listing 4.2, a subclass of the `RGBImageFilter` is defined, which

4

IMMEDIATE MODE
IMAGING MODEL

linearly scales the red, green, and blue components of the image data. For example, the constructor parameters 1.2, 1.0, 1.0 will increase the red component by 20%, but leave the green and blue components unchanged.

LISTING 4.2   ColorComponentScaler.java

```java
package ch4;

import java.awt.*;
import java.awt.image.RGBImageFilter;

/**
 * ColorComponentScaler -- filters an image by multiplier its
 * red, green and blue color components by their given
 * scale factors
 */
public class ColorComponentScaler extends RGBImageFilter {
    private double redMultiplier, greenMultiplier, blueMultiplier;
    private int newRed, newGreen, newBlue;
    private Color color, newColor;

    /**
     * rm = red multiplier
     * gm = green multiplier
     * bm = blue multiplier
     */
    public ColorComponentScaler(double rm, double gm, double bm) {
        canFilterIndexColorModel = true;
        redMultiplier = rm;
        greenMultiplier = gm;
        blueMultiplier = bm;
    }

    private int multColor(int colorComponent, double multiplier) {
        colorComponent = (int)(colorComponent*multiplier);
        if (colorComponent < 0)
            colorComponent = 0;
        else if (colorComponent > 255)
            colorComponent = 255;

        return colorComponent;
    }

    /**
     * split the argb value into its color components,
```

LISTING 4.2 Continued

```
     * multiply each color component by its corresponding scaler factor
     * and pack the components back into a single pixel
     */
    public int filterRGB(int x, int y, int argb) {
        color = new Color(argb);
        newBlue = multColor(color.getBlue(), blueMultiplier);
        newGreen = multColor(color.getGreen(), greenMultiplier);
        newRed = multColor(color.getRed(), redMultiplier);
        newColor = new Color(newRed, newGreen, newBlue);
        return (newColor.getRGB());
    }
}
```

One last point is that the instance variable `canFilterIndexColorModel` specifies whether this filter method can be applied to Images using an `IndexColorModel`. The `IndexColorModel` will be discussed in the later section "Creating and Using ColorModels," but for now it is enough to know that the pixels in some Images don't correspond to color components, but instead to indices of an array (or arrays) where the color components are held. In these cases, you don't want to filter the pixel values, but instead, you should filter the array (or arrays) holding the color components. The `canFilterIndexColorModel` variable gives the `RGBImageFilter` permission to do this.

PixelGrabber/MemoryImageSource

Although you can directly subclass the `ImageFilter` in order to create more complex filters, it is usually simpler to just collect all the data into an array and process it in its entirety before sending it out again. This doesn't allow incremental image rendering, but that isn't always of importance. The `java.awt.image.PixelGrabber` class is used for just this purpose. There are a few different constructors for the `PixelGrabber`, but the one used throughout this book is the following:

```
PixelGrabber(Image img, int x, int y, int w, int h, boolean forceRGB)
```

where x, y, w, and h are provided in case you wanted to obtain some rectangular subset of the image data. If you are interested in the entire Image, make the origin of this rectangle (0, 0) and w and h equal to the width and height of the Image. If the image dimensions are not known, you can grab the entire image by using a value of -1 for both the width and the height along with an origin of 0,0. The last parameter forces the `PixelGrabber` to convert all pixels into the default `ColorModel`. (ColorModels will be discussed in the later section entitled "Creating and Using ColorModels.")

The `PixelGrabber` is an `ImageConsumer` so it can receive image data, but it marks the end of the push model and the beginning of an immediate mode model because the image data is put into an array instead of being passed to another `ImageConsumer`.

> **CAUTION**
>
> It is important to realize that this immediate mode isn't the same as the formal immediate mode that originated as part of the Java2D package. They are similar in that the image data is collected into one accessible area. The Java2D immediate mode imaging model will be discussed in the later section "Immediate Mode Imaging Model."

The way the `PixelGrabber` collects the image data is through the use of its `public boolean grabPixels()` method; for example,

```
PixelGrabber grabber = new PixelGrabber(originalImage, 0, 0, -1, -1, true);
try {
    if (grabber.grabPixels()) {
        int width = grabber.getWidth();
        int height = grabber.getHeight();
        int[] originalPixelArray = (int[])grabber.getPixels();
    }
    else {
        System.err.println("Grabbing Failed");
    }
}
catch (InterruptedException e) {
    System.err.println("PixelGrabbing interrupted");
}
```

When all the image data is together in an array, any type of filtering can be performed as long as it is written to handle an array of integers, where each integer typically represents red, green, and blue color components. Last, the post-filtered data, contained in the original array or a new array, can be given to an `ImageProducer` that will send it to an `ImageConsumer`, thus returning the imaging pipeline back to a push model. The class used to read the image array data and pass it to an `ImageConsumer` is the `java.awt.image.MemoryImageSource` class (see Figure 4.2).

Because the `MemoryImageSource` is an `ImageProducer`, it is typically used with the following `Component` method:

```
Image createImage(ImageProducer producer)
```

as follows:

```
MemoryImageSource mis;
mis = new MemoryImageSource(width, height,
                            newPixelArray, arrayOffset, scanLength);
Image filteredImage = createImage(mis);
```

where `newPixelArray` is the filtered pixel array, `arrayOffset` is the number of bytes prior to the pixel data in the array, and `scanlength` is the number of pixels in each array column. Usually the `scanlength` is the same as the `width`. Once `filteredImage` is created, any use of this `Image` will cause the `ImageProducer` to start sending `Image` data to an `ImageConsumer`.

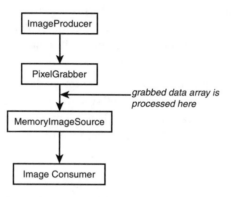

FIGURE 4.2

The push model doesn't adequately describe this figure because the use of the `PixelGrabber` *stops the asynchronous pixel delivery.*

TIP

The data provided by the `PixelGrabber` and passed to the `MemoryImageSource` is unformatted pixel data. This means that if you were to write this data out to a file, it wouldn't be a gif or a jpeg image even if that is how the data originated. The ability to write formatted images to a file didn't originate until the Java Image I/O package, which will be discussed in Chapter 5, "Image I/O API."

One last point is that the `MemoryImageSource` can be used for simple animations. The way this is done is by calling its `public void setAnimation(boolean value)` method immediately after it is instantiated. As an example, consider the `Applet` code in Listing 4.3 in which an image appears correctly, but then fades to black. This is done by starting with a data array filled with the original pixel values, and each time the `paint` method is called, these pixel values are brought closer to zero. Note that this code was provided for four purposes:

- The main reason was the use of the `PixelGrabber` to collect the image data and the `MemoryImageSource` to start up the push model again.

- A second reason was to introduce simple animations.

- The third reason was to introduce the idea that a pixel isn't the smallest unit of interest and usually needs to be broken down into pixel samples representing the different color components. In this case, we are using the default ARGB ColorModel in which each pixel represents a transparency component and three color components: red, green, and blue. In order to separate the samples from the pixel values, you can do bitwise `shifts` and `ands` with the appropriate mask. In general, getting color components from pixels is much more involved, and it will be covered in detail in the later section "Pixel Storage and Conversion."

- The last reason was to introduce handling of 2D image data stored in a 1D image array. Generally, this conversion takes place as follows: pixel at `location(x,y)` = `GrabbedImageArray[x + imageWidth*y]`. This equation describes the situation in which the 2D image data is stored as a 1D array, where the first row of the image data is stored first, the second row next, and so on.

LISTING 4.3   GrabandFade.java

```java
package ch4;

import java.awt.*;
import java.applet.*;
import java.net.*;
import java.awt.image.PixelGrabber;
import java.awt.image.MemoryImageSource;

/**
 * GrabandFade.java -- displays provided image and then slowly
 * fades to black
 */
public class GrabandFade extends Applet {
    private Image originalImage;
    private Image newImage;
    private MemoryImageSource mis;
    private int width;
    private int height;
    private int index = 10;
    private int[] originalPixelArray;
```

LISTING 4.3   Continued

```
    private boolean imageLoaded = false;
    private String imageURLString = "file:images/peppers.png";


    public void init() {
        URL url;
        try {
            // set imageURLString here
            url = new URL(imageURLString);
            originalImage = getImage(url);
        }
        catch (MalformedURLException me) {
            showStatus("Malformed URL: " + me.getMessage());
        }

        /*
         * Create PixelGrabber and use it to fill originalPixelArray with
         * image pixel data.  This array will then by used by the
         * MemoryImageSource.
         */
        try {
            PixelGrabber grabber = new PixelGrabber(originalImage,
                                            0, 0, -1, -1, true);
            if (grabber.grabPixels()) {
                width = grabber.getWidth();
                height = grabber.getHeight();
                originalPixelArray = (int[])grabber.getPixels();

                mis = new MemoryImageSource(width, height,
                                        originalPixelArray,0, width);
                mis.setAnimated(true);
                newImage = createImage(mis);
            }
            else {
                System.err.println("Grabbing Failed");
            }
        }
        catch (InterruptedException ie) {
            System.err.println("Pixel Grabbing Interrupted");
        }
    }

    /**
     * overwrite update method to avoid clearing of drawing area
     */
```

LISTING 4.3   Continued

```java
public void update(Graphics g) {
    paint(g);
}

/**
 * continually draw image, then decrease color components
 * of all pixels contained in the originalPixelArray
 * array until color components are all 0
 */
public void paint(Graphics g) {
    int value;
    int alpha, sourceRed, sourceGreen, sourceBlue;
    if (newImage != null) {
        g.drawImage(newImage, 0, 0, this); // redraw image

        // if image isn't faded to black, continue
        if (imageLoaded == false) {
            imageLoaded = true;
            for (int x=0; x < width; x+=1)
                for (int y=0; y < height; y+=1) {

                    // find the color components
                    value = originalPixelArray[x*height+y];
                    alpha = ( value >> 24) & 0x000000ff;
                    sourceRed =    ( value >> 16) & 0x000000ff;
                    sourceGreen = ( value >> 8) & 0x000000ff;
                    sourceBlue = value & 0x000000ff;

                    // subtract index from each red component
                    if (sourceRed > index) {
                        sourceRed-=index;
                        imageLoaded = false;
                    }
                    else
                        sourceRed = 0;

                    // subtract index from each green component
                    if (sourceGreen > index) {
                        sourceGreen-=index;
                        imageLoaded = false;
                    }
                    else
                        sourceGreen = 0;
```

LISTING 4.3   Continued

```
                    // subtract index from each blue component
                    if (sourceBlue > index) {
                        sourceBlue-=index;
                        imageLoaded = false;
                    }
                    else
                        sourceBlue = 0;

                    /*
                        when we pack new color components into integer
                        we make sure the alpha (transparency) value
                        represents opaque
                    */
                    value = (alpha << 24);
                    value += (sourceRed << 16);
                    value += (sourceGreen << 8);
                    value += sourceBlue;

                    // fill pixel array
                    originalPixelArray[x*height+y] = value;
                }
            mis.newPixels(); //send pixels to ImageConsumer
        }
    }
  }
}
```

Another interesting thing about Listing 4.3 is that if you use the `imageUpdate` method defined in Listing 4.1, the following output appears:

```
Flag(s): WIDTH:(256) HEIGHT:(256)
Flag(s): PROPERTIES
Flag(s): SOMEBITS(0,0)->(256,256)
Flag(s): FRAMEBITS(0,0)->(256,256)
Flag(s): FRAMEBITS(0,0)->(256,256)
Flag(s): FRAMEBITS(0,0)->(256,256)
. . .
Flag(s): FRAMEBITS(0,0)->(256,256)
Flag(s): FRAMEBITS(0,0)->(256,256)
Flag(s): FRAMEBITS(0,0)->(256,256)
Flag(s): ALLBITS(0,0)->(256,256)
```

In comparison with the output from Listing 4.1, there isn't a series of SOMEBITS flags because the PixelGrabber grabbed all the image data before it was needed. Also, because we are now sending a series of frames to the ImageConsumer, the FRAMEBITS flag appears multiple times.

One additional thing to notice in Listing 4.3 is the method called public void update (Graphics g). When repaint() is called (typically by the ImageObserver's imageUpdate method), the method that gets called isn't paint(Graphics g), but update(Graphics g). The default behavior of this method is to first clear the viewing area and then call paint(Graphics g). Often, this clearing of the viewing area results in the animation appearing choppy. To avoid this problem, it is common to override this update method and have it only call the paint method, that is,

```java
public void update(Graphics g) {
        paint(g);
}
```

When doing animations, the only time this update method doesn't need to be overwritten is if you are using a swing component such as a javax.swing.JComponent or a javax.swing.JApplet. The designers of swing decided to overwrite the update method so that it no longer clears the viewing area before calling the paint method.

Double Buffering

As was mentioned in the beginning of this chapter, a java.awt.Image is unlike a conventional image in that it doesn't hold any pixel data. It is usually easier to think of an Image as a class with methods and resources to allow image data to be processed and displayed. With double buffering, an Image takes on another unconventional role: that of a drawing surface. You can obtain a Graphics object of a particular Image and use that object to draw on the Image. For example, using the following block of code:

```java
Image dbimg = someComponent.createImage(512, 512);
Graphics dbgraphics = dbimg.getGraphics();
```

anything that gets drawn using the dbgraphics object will be drawn on the hidden drawing area of Image dbImg.

When this drawing process is completed, you can then draw the Image dbImg onto another drawing surface (such as an Applet's) using code similar to the following:

```java
public void paint(Graphics g) {
        if (dbimg != null)
                g.drawImage(dbimg,0,0,null);
}
```

This technique can be very useful for tasks such as animation in which one frame is being displayed on an Applet while another frame is being invisibly built on an Image. When this hidden frame is completed, it is then displayed on the Applet while another frame can be invisibly built. This allows the transitions that occur during the frame building to be completely hidden from the user.

In Listing 4.4, a circle continually passes over an Image. This is an excellent application to appreciate the role of double buffering and of overloading the update method. If either one of these techniques isn't used, the circle won't appear to be traveling smoothly over the image.

LISTING 4.4   DoubleBufferedImage

```
package ch4;

import java.awt.*;
import java.applet.*;
import java.net.*;

public class DoubleBufferedImage extends Applet {
    private Image dbImage;
    private Image originalImage;
    private int xLocation = 0;
    private int imageWidth, imageHeight;
    private Graphics dbImageGraphics;
    private String imageURLString = "file:images/peppers.png";

    public void init() {
        URL url = null;
        try {
            url = new URL(imageURLString);
        }
        catch (MalformedURLException me) {
            showStatus("Malformed URL: " + me.getMessage());
        }

        originalImage = getImage(url);

        MediaTracker mt = new MediaTracker(this);
        mt.addImage(originalImage, 0);
        try {
            mt.waitForID(0);
        }
        catch (InterruptedException ie) {
        }
```

Listing 4.4 Continued

```java
        //don't need ImageObservers since the Image is already loaded
        imageWidth = originalImage.getWidth(null);
        imageHeight = originalImage.getHeight(null);

        dbImage = this.createImage(imageWidth, imageHeight);
        dbImageGraphics = dbImage.getGraphics();
    }

    public void update(Graphics g) {
        paint(g);
    }

    public void paint(Graphics g) {
        if (xLocation == imageWidth)
            xLocation = 0;

        //anything drawn using the dbImagGraphics object is hidden
        dbImageGraphics.clearRect(0,0,imageWidth, imageHeight);
        dbImageGraphics.drawImage(originalImage, 0, 0, this);
        dbImageGraphics.setColor(Color.red);
        dbImageGraphics.fillOval(xLocation, imageHeight/2, 20, 20);

        //now dbImage's drawing area appears
        g.drawImage(dbImage,0,0,this);

        xLocation ++;
        repaint(10);
    }
}
```

Tip

One very useful class used in this example is the `java.awt.MediaTracker`, which allows you to wait until a particular image or a group of images is loaded before proceeding. A typical usage of this class is as follows:

```java
MediaTracker mt = new MediaTracker(someImageObserver);
mt.addImage(img, id);   //give each Image a possibly non-unique id value
try {
    //wait for all Images referred to by id to completely load
    mt.waitForID(id);
}
catch (InterruptedException ie) {
    //waiting was interrupted
}
```

Pixel Storage and Conversion

Each location in an `Image` is associated with a single pixel, but a pixel isn't the smallest unit of interest. Each pixel contains one or more samples representing the different bands in the `Image`. For example, pixels representing a color image could have samples of red, green, blue or alpha, red, green, blue, where alpha is a measure of transparency not a color component. Similarly, pixels representing a grayscale image might only contain one sample. Another thing that must be considered is output devices. A pixel may represent bands of red, green, and blue, but an output device, such as a printer, might expect bands of cyan, magenta, and yellow. So when working with image data, two required steps are:

1. Extract the samples from a pixel given that pixel's location.
2. Interpret and convert(if necessary) these samples.

These tasks are performed by the `java.awt.image.Raster` and `java.awt.image.ColorModel`, respectively.

Rasters

A `Raster` is made up of two main objects, a `java.awt.image.DataBuffer` and a `java.awt.image.SampleModel`. The `DataBuffer`'s job is the storage of the `Image` pixels, and the `SampleModel`'s job is the understanding of this storage. Thus, the `SampleModel` can get the appropriate pixel samples from the `DataBuffer` given a pixel location. The entire process of converting a pixel location into pixel samples proceeds as follows (see Figure 4.3).

1. A `Raster` is passed a pixel location.
2. It gives this location to its `SampleModel`.
3. The `SampleModel` obtains the correct samples from its corresponding `DataBuffer`.
4. The `SampleModel` then gives these values back to the `Raster` so that they can be passed on for interpretation and conversion.

The `Raster` class provides methods to access the data contained in a `DataBuffer`, whereas a `Raster` subclass, the `WritableRaster`, adds the capability to change this data. One other point regarding `Raster`s is that they do more than simply pass coordinates to the `SampleModel` and return the results. A `Raster` allows image data to be used with an x and/or y offset, whereas a `SampleModel` doesn't (`SampleModel`s always have an origin of 0, 0). In order to find the difference between the `SampleModel`'s origin and the `Raster`'s origin, you can use the `Raster`'s `public int getSampleModelTranslateX()` and `public int getSampleModelTranslateY()` methods. So, in addition to containing a `DataBuffer` and a `SampleModel`, a `Raster` contains a `java.awt.Point` representing its origin.

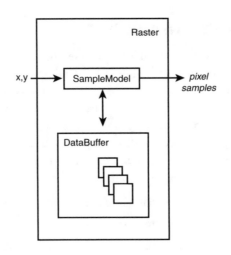

FIGURE 4.3

The Raster*'s* SampleModel *uses its corresponding* DataBuffer *to convert a pixel's location into samples.*

DataBuffers and SampleModels

A DataBuffer stores the pixel data as one or more arrays of some primative data type. For example, with respect to image data containing bands of alpha, red, green, and blue with each band consisting of 1 byte, three common ways to provide storage are as follows:

- SinglePixelPacked technique—Each array element represents all the pixel samples for a particular location. In this case, these packed samples are held in a DataBuffer containing a single array of type integer (see Figure 4.4). This is by far the most common method to store image data. An example of how the different 8 bit components are extracted from a 32 bit integer as well as an example of how they are packed back into an integer can be found in Listing 4.3.

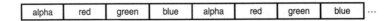

FIGURE 4.4

In this integer array, each element contains all the samples from a single pixel. Each sample uses eight of the integer's 32 bits.

- BandedSample technique—Each array element represents a single sample with all the alpha components in one array, the red components in another array, and likewise, the green and blue components in two other arrays. In this case, the DataBuffer object would contain four arrays of type byte. To find all of the samples for pixel number n, simply take the nth element from each array (see Figure 4.5).

alpha	alpha	alpha	alpha	alpha	alpha
red	red	red	red	red	red
green	green	green	green	green	green
blue	blue	blue	blue	blue	blue

FIGURE 4.5

In the top byte array, each element represents the alpha sample from a different pixel. The red, green, and blue samples are held in three other arrays.

- PixelInterleaved technique—Each array element represents a single sample with interleaved alpha, red, green, and blue components. In this case, the DataBuffer would contain a single array of type byte. To find all of the samples for pixel n, simply take elements 4*n, 4*n+1, 4*n+2 and 4*n+3 (see Figure 4.6).

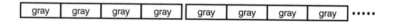

FIGURE 4.6

In this byte array, the different samples alternate within a single array.

There is one more common image storage method, but this one is for single band images (images with a single sample per pixel), such as grayscale images. In the case of this MultiPixelPacked technique, a packed primitive data type holds the pixel sample of more than one pixel (see Figure 4.7).

| gray | gray | gray | gray | gray | gray | gray | gray | ••••• |

FIGURE 4.7

In this packed integer, the gray samples from four different pixels are contained in one packed integer.

Two of the four techniques (SinglePixelPacked and MultiPixelPacked) are *packed* techniques—meaning that each array element represents more than one sample. The other two techniques (Banded and Interleaved) are *component* techniques—meaning that each array element represents one and only one sample.

As you've just seen, there are many different ways to represent pixel color components using arrays. Thus it would be difficult to try and communicate directly with the DataBuffer object. For this reason, SampleModels are used. A SampleModel can be thought of as the *brains* behind the data storage because each one understands the organization of its corresponding DataBuffer. Given an x, y location, it can obtain the corresponding pixel samples from the array or arrays in the DataBuffer without the user having to know anything about the actual data allocation. Different subclasses of the SampleModel class know how to find pixel samples from DataBuffers that use different storage techniques (see Table 4.2).

4

IMMEDIATE MODE IMAGING MODEL

TABLE 4.2 SampleModel Subclasses

SampleModel Subclass	Description
SinglePixelPackedSampleModel	Knows how to obtain pixel samples when the DataBuffer is storing all of a pixel's samples in one array element (refer to Figure 4.4).
ComponentSampleModel	Knows how to obtain pixel samples when the DataBuffer is storing each sample in a separate array element. Parent class of BandedSampleModel and PixelInterleavedSampleModel.
BandedSampleModel	Knows how to obtain pixel samples when the DataBuffer contains separate arrays for each band (refer to Figure 4.5).
PixelInterleavedSampleModel	Knows how to obtain pixel samples when the DataBuffer contains a single array whose elements alternate between the different bands (refer to Figure 4.6)
MultiPixelPackedSampleModel	Knows how to obtain pixel samples when the image data represents a single band and the DataBuffer is storing more than one sample into a single array element (refer to Figure 4.7)

Creating and Using Rasters

The easiest way to create a Raster is to provide a SampleModel, a DataBuffer, and an offset Point to the Raster's createRaster or createWritableRaster static method:

```
static Raster createRaster(SampleModel sm, DataBuffer db, Point location)

static WritableRaster createWritableRaster(SampleModel sm,
                                     DataBuffer db, Point location)
```

As mentioned, this offset Point is used to translate the origin in the Raster because the SampleModel's origin is always (0,0). If you don't want to translate the origin of the Raster, you can simple use null for the offset Point. It should be noted that it is also common to create Rasters without first creating a SampleModel. This is done by using the Raster's, createBandedRaster, createInterleavedRaster, or createPackedRaster methods, which internally create a BandedSampleModel, an InterleavedSampleModel, or either a SinglePixelPackedModel or a MultiPixelPackedSampleModel, respectively.

In Listing 4.3, we used bit operations in order to extract alpha and the red, green, and blue color components from a packed integer. In a sense, we were acting like a

SinglePixelPackedSampleModel because we knew how the data was stored and were able to convert a pixel location into a set of pixel samples; in this case, alpha, red, green, and blue. Under these conditions, this is a reasonable way to obtain these samples (in fact, if you know where and how your data is stored, bitwise operations are the most efficient way to work with pixels), but in general this isn't the most robust way to do this. If you rely on bitwise mathematics, you're forced to understand how your data is stored and more importantly, you won't be able to write generic algorithms for pixel processing. In other words, your pixel processing methods should simply take a Raster or WritableRaster argument without worrying about the SampleModel being used. Inside your methods, you can use these Raster methods for obtaining either individual pixel samples or an array of a pixel's samples:

```
int getSample(int x, int y, int bandNumber)
```

where bandNumber is the number of the band whose sample you want. Usually, 0 = red, 1 = green, 2 = blue, and 3 = alpha.

```
int[] getPixel(int x, int y, int[] iArray)
```

where iArray is an integer array whose size is greater than or equal to the number of samples in the pixel. If this value isn't null, it will also be the returned object. If this value is null, an appropriate array is allocated, filled, and returned. If a WritableRaster is used, the following two methods for setting pixel values are available:

```
void setSample(int x, int y, int bandNumber, int sampleValue)
```

where sampleValue will be the new value of the pixel sample corresponding to band number bandNumber.

```
void setPixel(int x, int y, int[] iArray)
```

where iArray is an integer array holding the pixel's new sample values (one sample per array element). To see how these methods are used, we will redo the earlier GrabandFade example (from Listing 4.3)—this time using DataBuffers, SampleModels, and Rasters (see Listing 4.5).

LISTING 4.5 GrabandFadewithRasters

```
package ch4;

import java.awt.*;
import java.applet.*;
import java.net.*;
import java.awt.image.PixelGrabber;
import java.awt.image.MemoryImageSource;
import java.awt.image.DataBuffer;
import java.awt.image.DataBufferInt;
```

LISTING 4.5   Continued

```java
import java.awt.image.Raster;
import java.awt.image.WritableRaster;
import java.awt.image.SampleModel;
import java.awt.image.SinglePixelPackedSampleModel;


/**
 * GrabandFadewithRasters.java -- displays provided image
 * and then slowly fades to black
 */
public class GrabandFadewithRasters extends Applet {
    private Image originalImage;
    private Image newImage;
    private MemoryImageSource mis;
    private int width;
    private int height;
    private int index = 10;
    private int[] originalPixelArray;
    private boolean imageLoaded = false;
    private WritableRaster raster;
    private String imageURLString = "file:images/peppers.png";

    public void init() {
        URL url;
        try {
            url = new URL(imageURLString);
            originalImage = getImage(url);
        }
        catch (MalformedURLException me) {
            showStatus("Malformed URL: " + me.getMessage());
        }

        try {
            PixelGrabber grabber = new PixelGrabber(originalImage,
                                              0, 0, -1, -1, true);
            if (grabber.grabPixels()) {
                width = grabber.getWidth();
                height = grabber.getHeight();
                originalPixelArray = (int[])grabber.getPixels();

                mis = new MemoryImageSource(width, height,
                                          originalPixelArray,0, width);
                mis.setAnimated(true);
                newImage = createImage(mis);
            }
```

LISTING 4.5   Continued

```
            else {
                System.err.println("Grabbing Failed");
            }
        }
        catch (InterruptedException ie) {
            System.err.println("Pixel Grabbing Interrupted");
        }

        DataBufferInt dbi = new DataBufferInt(originalPixelArray,
                                              width*height);

        int bandmasks[] = {0xff000000,0x00ff0000,0x0000ff00,0x000000ff};
        SampleModel sm;
        sm = new SinglePixelPackedSampleModel(DataBuffer.TYPE_INT,
                                              width, height, bandmasks);

        raster = Raster.createWritableRaster(sm, dbi, null);
    }

    public void update(Graphics g) {
        paint(g);
    }

    public void paint(Graphics g) {
        int value;
        int sourceRed, sourceGreen, sourceBlue;
        if (newImage != null) {
            g.drawImage(newImage, 0, 0, this);
            if (imageLoaded == false) {
                imageLoaded = true;
                for (int x =0; x < width; x+=1)
                    for (int y =0; y < height; y+=1) {
                        value = originalPixelArray[x*height+y];
                        sourceRed = raster.getSample(x,y,1);
                        sourceGreen = raster.getSample(x,y,2);
                        sourceBlue = raster.getSample(x,y,3);

                        if (sourceRed > index) {
                            sourceRed-=index;
                            imageLoaded = false;
                        }
                        else
                            sourceRed = 0;
```

LISTING 4.5 Continued

```
                    if (sourceGreen > index) {
                        sourceGreen-=index;
                        imageLoaded = false;
                    }
                    else
                        sourceGreen = 0;

                    if (sourceBlue > index) {
                        sourceBlue-=index;
                        imageLoaded = false;
                    }
                    else
                        sourceBlue = 0;

                    raster.setSample(x,y,1,sourceRed);
                    raster.setSample(x,y,2,sourceGreen);
                    raster.setSample(x,y,3,sourceBlue);
                }
            mis.newPixels();
        }
    }
  }
}
```

In the previous discussion as well as in Listing 4.3, we only considered a single pixel at a time. In practice, it is more efficient to deal with arrays of pixels, and both the getPixels/setPixels methods and the getSamples/setSamples methods allow you to do this.

Last, there is one other way to get and set pixel data from a Raster and that is with the Raster's getDataElements/setDataElements methods:

```
public Object getDataElements(int x, int y, Object outData)

void setDataElements(int x, int y, Object inData)
```

where outData and inData are references to arrays defined by the Raster's getTransferType method. These getDataElements/setDataElements methods transfer the samples in a form that is dependent upon the type of SampleModel being used (see Table 4.3). For example, in a SinglePixelPackedSampleModel, the pixel samples are held in a packed primitive data type, which is the transfer type. For a MultiPixelPackedSampleModel, the pixel sample is taken out of its packed primitive data type and returned in the smallest data type that can represent it. For ComponentSampleModels, the samples are returned in an array of whatever type held the samples. Because the getDataElement methods return pixel samples differently depending on the underlying `SampleModel`, care must be taken when using them. On the other hand, they are useful for efficiently transferring data between `Raster`'s with similar `SampleModels`, that is,

```
raster1.setDataElements(x, y, raster2.getDataElements(x, y, null))
```

or

```
raster1.setDataElements(x, y, w, h, raster2.getDataElements(x, y, w, h, null))
```

where x and y represent either the pixel location (in the first method) or the origin of the rectangle to be copied (in the second method). Likewise, w and h represent the width and height of this rectangle. As you'll see, these methods are also useful for transferring data between `Rasters` and `ColorModels`.

TABLE 4.3 Raster Transfer Types

Raster's `SampleModel` Class	Raster's Transfer Type
SinglePixelPackedSampleModel	Packed primative data type
MultiPixelPackedSampleModel	Smallest primitive data type that can represent an unpacked sample
ComponentSampleModel	Array of whatever type held the samples

ColorModels

When looking at Listing 4.5, it appears that all the pieces necessary to convert pixels into color components are available, but one thing is still missing. That piece is the `java.awt.image.ColorModel`. The `ColorModel` takes pixel samples returned by the `Raster` and converts them to color components. As you've noticed in the previous examples, there are times when a pixel's samples are identical to the output device's required color components. For example, let's assume that our output device is a color monitor that requires color components of red, green, and blue with each component being an integer value between 0 and 255. If each pixel of our image data contains three samples representing red, green, and blue with each sample being between 0 and 255, a `ColorModel` object isn't necessary. On the other hand, what if the pixel samples are packed into a short integer (16 bits) instead of an integer (32 bits)? Then a reasonable scheme would be for each sample to be represented by 5 bits, allowing 32 possible values per sample. If you tried to use these pixel samples as color components, the image would appear too dark when displayed. In this case, a `ColorModel` is necessary to make the correct conversions.

Because the `ColorModel` is concerned with converting pixel samples to color components and vice versa, it requires two sets of methods: one to convert pixel samples to color components and one to convert color components to pixel samples. These method groups are the getComponents and the getDataElement methods, respectively. (Note that when we talk about color components, we also include alpha when it is relevant.) The two main getComponents methods are as follows:

```
int[] getComponents(Object pixel, int[] components, int offset)
```

```
int[] getComponents(int pixel, int[] components, int offset)
```

In the first method, the pixel parameter is expected to be an array of the ColorModel's transfer type that, for compatibility, should be the same as the Raster's transfer type (refer to Table 4.3). The component parameter will be an integer array that will be used to hold the color components. If this array is non null, a reference to it will also be returned by this method. If the component array is null, an appropriately sized integer array will be allocated and returned. Last, the offset parameter specifies where to begin putting the color components in the component array. The second method is really a special case of the first one. This special case occurs when you are using a ColorModel subclass that expects the pixel samples to be packed into a single integer. As you'll see in the next section, this ColorModel subclass is called a DirectColorModel.

As mentioned, the getDataElement methods convert color components to pixel samples. The two main getDataElement methods are the following (note that the first method is called getDataElements and the second is called getDataElement):

```
Object getDataElements(int[] components, int offset, Object obj)
```

```
int getDataElement(int[] components, int offset)
```

Again, the first method is concerned with arrays of type transfer type, where the components parameter holds the color components, the offset parameter describes where the first color component is in the components array, and the obj parameter will be an array of type transfer type and will hold the pixel samples. If the obj array is non null, a reference to it will be returned. If this array is null, an appropriate array will be allocated and returned. In the second method, the pixel samples will be returned packed into a single integer.

Creating and Using ColorModels

Because the Raster and the ColorModel need to work together, some care is required to make sure that they are compatible. For instance, the number of bands of pixel samples must match the number of components expected by the ColorModel. Also, the transfer type must be compatible. In other words, if the SampleModel is sending four pixel samples packed into a single integer, that is how the ColorModel should expect them (see Table 4.4).

TABLE 4.4 Typical Correspondence Between `SampleModels` and `ColorModels`

SampleModel *Subclass*	ColorModel *Subclass*
SinglePixelPackedSampleModel	DirectColorModel (subclass of abstract PackedColorModel)
BandedSampleModel	ComponentColorModel
InterleavedSampleModel	ComponentColorModel
MultiPixelPackedSampleModel	IndexColorModel

The `DirectColorModel` is used when the image pixels represent red, green, and blue (and possibly alpha) samples; and these samples are packed together into an integer, short integer, or byte. A `ComponentColorModel` is used when each image pixel represents all of its color (and possibly alpha) information as separate samples, and all samples are stored in a separate data element. The `IndexColorModel` is used when the image pixels represent indices into an array containing the actual pixel samples. This is a common technique for grayscale images, which are used with an output device, such as a monitor, that expect pixel samples of red, green, and blue. For example, without indexing, if there are three samples per pixel (red, green, and blue) and each one takes 8 bits, the memory required is 8*3*imageWidth*imageHeight bits. If we are using a grayscale image so that the red, green, and blue samples must be equal, then there are only 256 different combinations of pixel samples that can be used. Thus, a grayscale image only requires 8*width*height bits of memory if each image pixel is a single byte and is used as an index to obtain the red, green, and blue pixel samples from three arrays. Of course, this latter calculation isn't completely accurate because the red, green, and blue arrays must be allocated, which would take up an additional 3*256 bytes.

As an example of the `ColorModel`'s role in interpreting pixel samples, consider Listing 4.6. In this listing, two `DirectColorModels` are created. The first one expects 8-bit pixel samples of red, green, blue, and alpha. The second one expects 5-bit pixel samples of red, green, and blue. In both cases, the red, green, and blue samples are the same, but the normalized color components (color components whose values vary from 0.0 to 1.0) are very different. In other words, the `ColorModels` know the allowable range of the sample values, and they consider the ratio of the sample value to its maximum value.

LISTING 4.6 FindComponents

```
package ch4;

import java.awt.image.DirectColorModel;
public class FindComponents {
    DirectColorModel dcm32;
    DirectColorModel dcm16;
```

LISTING 4.6   Continued

```java
    int[] components;
    float[] componentsf;
    int value32;
    short value16;
    int red8, green8, blue8, alpha8;
    short red5, green5, blue5;

    /**
        FindComponents.java -- prints out normalized color components for two
dif
ferent
     */
    public FindComponents() {
        red8 = red5 = 30;
        green8 = green5 = 20;
        blue8 = blue5 = 10;
        alpha8 = 255;

        dcm32 = new DirectColorModel(32, 0x00ff0000, 0x0000ff00,
                                     0x000000ff, 0xff000000);
        value32 = (alpha8<<24) + (red8<<16) + (green8<<8) + blue8;
        components = dcm32.getComponents(value32, null, 0);
        componentsf = dcm32.getNormalizedComponents(components,0,null,0);
        System.out.println("Normalized components are: ");
        for(int i=0;i<componentsf.length;i++)
            System.out.println("\t"+componentsf[i]);

        dcm16 = new DirectColorModel(16, 0x7c00, 0x3e0, 0x1f);
        value16 = (short)((red5<<10) + (green5<<5) + blue5);
        components = dcm16.getComponents(value16, null, 0);
        componentsf = dcm16.getNormalizedComponents(components,0,null,0);
        System.out.println("Normalized components are: ");
        for(int i=0;i<componentsf.length;i++)
            System.out.println("\t"+componentsf[i]);
    }

    public static void main(String[] args) {
        new FindComponents();
    }
}
```

When run, the output of this listing would be the following:

```
Normalized components are:
        0.11764706
        0.078431375
        0.039215688
        1.0
Normalized components are:
        0.9677419
        0.6451613
        0.32258064
```

ColorSpaces

Another interesting example, which leads us to the concept of color space, is if we are using a printer for our output device. In this situation, the color components might need to be *cyan, magenta, and yellow (CMY)*; in which case, we'll need to convert each pixel into three color components just as we did for the color monitor that needed *red, green, and blue (RGB)* components. So clearly just converting pixels into color components isn't enough: We still need to interpret these components. This interpretation is the job of the java.awt.color.ColorSpace. In other words, the number, order, and interpretation of color components for a ColorModel is specified by its ColorSpace. Thus, given three color components, you would need to look at the ColorModel's ColorSpace in order to understand whether they are CMY, RGB, or something else entirely.

Although there are many different color spaces, in Java the two most important are the sRGB color space and the CIEXYZ color space. All ColorSpaces have methods to convert to and from these two color spaces. The sRGB color space is a proposed standardized RGB color space that all ColorModels use by default. For more information regarding this color space, see http://www.w3.org/pub/WWW/Graphics/Color/sRGB.html. Because most people are familiar with representing colors using red, green, and blue components, this color space is easy to use and work with, although a minor problem with the sRGB color space is that it is possible to lose information if you convert from one color space to another by going through an intermediate sRGB color space. The CIEXYZ color space, on the other hand, can be used to convert between any two color spaces without worrying about lost information. Besides the ideal sRGB and the ideal CIEXYZ, Java provides a few other ideal color spaces such as GRAY.

These color spaces also allow you to convert colors between different ideal colorspaces. The way this conversion is performed is by using profiles. *Profiles* define the transformation between a particular color space and something called a *Profile Connection Space (PCS)*. Each profile describes how to transform a color from its color space to the PCS and vice versa. Therefore, using profiles, you can convert a color in any color space to any other color space

4

IMMEDIATE MODE
IMAGING MODEL

by going through the PCS. Of course, no input or output device is ideal, so if exact color replication is desired, profiles can also be used to transform to and from a non-ideal, device dependent color space. For more information on profiles, see the International Color Consortium
Web site at http://www.color.org.

So to summarize this section, if you are working with red, green, and blue color components,
you can ignore the ColorSpace class most of the time. Similarly, if you are using packed integer ARGB or RGB data, you often don't need to use a Raster because the bit manipulation
isn't that difficult. On the other hand, to create generic, robust code you will need Rasters,
ColorModels, and ColorSpaces, and you will need them to be compatible. As an illustration,
if we augment Figure 4.3, you can see how the output of the Raster interacts with the
ColorModel so that the ColorModel can extract and interpret (via its ColorSpace) the color
components (see Figure 4.8). Later in this chapter, we will introduce the BufferedImage class,
which contains all these objects, thus greatly simplifying the coding of image processing software.

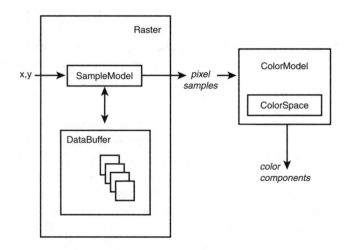

FIGURE 4.8

The Raster's SampleModel *uses its corresponding* DataBuffer *to convert a pixel's location into samples. These samples
get passed to a* ColorModel *for conversion into color components in the appropriate color space.*

Immediate Mode Imaging Model

Because the Image class was primarily set up for asynchronous handling of image data, many
times it cannot easily provide the functionality required for advanced image processing tasks.
For this reason, we've been using PixelGrabbers to collect all the data before processing it.
For simple processing this worked well, but as things became more complex, we required

`Rasters`, `ColorModels`, and a series of other classes necessary for data storage and interpretation. In practice, this extra code not only can make your software more difficult to write and understand, but it can also provide opportunities for software errors to occur. For these reasons, the immediate mode imaging model and its associated classes were developed and introduced in the Java 2D package. Basically, this model provides memory allocation and storage of all image data, thus making it available to the programmer at all times just as if you collected all the pixel data using a `PixelGrabber` in the older push model. Also, there are new classes of predefined image filters that provide much more functionality than the `ImageFilter` subclasses. These filters allow the processing of image data in ways that permit a particular destination pixel to be a function of more than one source pixel. This wasn't easily done in the push model of image processing.

BufferedImages

Unlike its parent (`java.awt.Image`), a `java.awt.image.BufferedImage` allows easy access to the underlying pixel data. This is achieved by having each `BufferedImage` contain both a `Raster` and a `ColorModel`. Therefore, you can obtain the color components of a particular pixel location directly from the `BufferedImage` without having to worry about the underlying detail involving `DataBuffers`, `SampleModels`, and so on.

Note that because it extends the `Image` class, a `BufferedImage` can be used anywhere an `Image` is used (for example, in the `Graphic` classes' `drawImage` methods). On the other hand, the conversion from an `Image` to a `BufferedImage` isn't as simple because a `BufferedImage` contains all the image data. The following list illustrates the required steps (also see Listing 4.7):

1. Make sure that all the image data is loaded.
2. Create a new `BufferedImage` using the `Image` width, height, and image data type (usually `BufferedImage.TYPE_INT_ARGB`).
3. Obtain the `BufferedImage`'s `Graphics2D` object.
4. Using this graphics object, draw the `Image` onto the `BufferedImage` (as done earlier in the double buffering section).

LISTING 4.7   createBufferedImage

```
package ch4;

import java.awt.Graphics;
import java.awt.Label;
import java.awt.Image;
import java.awt.MediaTracker;
import java.awt.image.BufferedImage;
```

4

LISTING 4.7   Continued

```
/**
    BufferedImageConverter.java -- static class containing
    a method to convert a java.awt.image.BufferedImage into
    a java.awt.Image
*/
public final class BufferedImageConverter {

    // default version of createBufferedImage
    static public BufferedImage createBufferedImage(Image imageIn) {
        return createBufferedImage(imageIn,
                                    BufferedImage.TYPE_INT_ARGB);
    }


    static public BufferedImage createBufferedImage(Image imageIn,
                                                    int imageType) {

        //you can use any component here
        Label dummyComponent = new Label();
        MediaTracker mt = new MediaTracker(dummyComponent);
        mt.addImage(imageIn, 0);
        try {
            mt.waitForID(0);
        }
        catch (InterruptedException ie) {
        }
        BufferedImage bufferedImageOut =
            new BufferedImage(imageIn.getWidth(null),
                                imageIn.getHeight(null), imageType);
        Graphics g = bufferedImageOut.getGraphics();
        g.drawImage(imageIn, 0, 0, null);

        return bufferedImageOut;
    }
}
```

Step 2 mentions that the Image type needed to be specified. This is so the correct SampleModel, DataBuffer, and ColorModel subclasses can be used. For example, if a set of image pixels represent ARGB color components packed into a single integer, a DirectColorModel object, a SinglePixelPackedSampleModel object, and a DataBufferInt object will be used (see Table 4.5).

TABLE 4.5   Some Basic `BufferedImage` Types

BufferedImage *Type*	*Description*
TYPE_INT_RGB	8-bit RGB color components packed into an integer (1 pixel/int)
TYPE_INT_ARGB	8-bit ARGB color components packed into an integer (1 pixel/int)
TYPE_BYTE_BINARY	A byte packed binary image (8 pixels/byte)
TYPE_USHORT_555_RGB	5-bit RGB color components packed into an unsigned short (1 pixel/ ushort)
TYPE_BYTE_GRAY	An unsigned byte grayscale image (1 pixel/byte)

For the complete list of image types, see the `BufferedImage` documentation on the Java Web site (`http://java.sun.com/j2se/1.4/docs/api/java/awt/image/BufferedImage.html`).

Filtering

During our earlier discussion of the push imaging model, we described filter classes that could be used for image processing. Some examples of such classes are the `CropImageFilter` and the `RGBImageFilter`. Now that we are discussing the immediate mode imaging model, we will also discuss filter classes. Because of the fact that in the immediate mode imaging model the image data is always available, there are many more types of filters than there are for the push model. For instance, filter classes for performing convolution and geometric transformations are available.

Interpolation

Before image filter classes are discussed, it is important to understand the concept of *interpolation*. To begin, assume that we have a very small (1x3) grayscale image with pixel values of 50, 100, and 150. Next assume that a destination image is set equal to this source image translated a distance equivalent to one third of a pixel horizontally (see Figure 4.9). Now, with respect to the middle destination pixel, the center of the source pixel containing a value of 50 lies two thirds of a pixel away from it and the center of the source pixel with a value of 100 lies one third of a pixel away from it. The question that interpolation attempts to solve is what value do we give this middle destination pixel. One technique would be to simply give it the value of whichever source pixel value was closest (in this case 100). This technique is referred to as *nearest neighbor interpolation*. Another technique would be to come up with a pixel value based on the linear average of all surrounding source pixel values (in this case .333*100 + .666*50 = 83). This technique is referred to as *linear interpolation*. In Figure 4.9, (a) represents the destination pixel values using nearest neighbor interpolation, whereas (b) represents the destination pixel values using bilinear interpolation. In the second case, there is not enough information to calculate a value for the first destination pixel so it is left blank. In Java 2D, the default value for these types of pixels is 0.

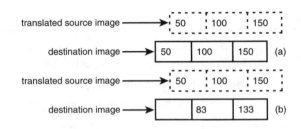

FIGURE 4.9

After a source array of pixel values gets translated, interpolation must be used to estimate the destination pixel values.

Each of these techniques can be useful depending on the situation. Nearest neighbor interpolation is very fast, but tends to appear choppy. Bilinear interpolation (which is linear interpolation in two dimensions) appears smoother, but can increase the image rendering time. For most cases, the increased image quality is worth the extra time required for bilinear interpolation. In the left image of Figure 4.10, nearest neighbor interpolation was performed, whereas in the right image, bilinear interpolation was performed.

TIP

This isn't to say that bilinear interpolation is the best interpolation algorithm available: It is just the best choice out of the given two. In general, bilinear interpolation can cause the destination image to appear blurry.

FIGURE 4.10

A sheared white and black checkerboard. These images were scaled by a factor of 4 in both the x and the y direction for display purposes.

Of course, because we've previously explained that pixel samples are the smallest unit of interest and not pixels, the idea of pixel interpolation can be confusing. What is actually occurring is that all pixel sample bands representing color components are interpolated separately. In other words, if you are using a packed integer representing RGB bands, the value used for interpolation isn't the integer value of the pixel, but instead, the interpolation is done three times, once for each band.

As you'll soon see, many types of image filtering involve interpolation. For these filtering classes, the interpolation type can usually be specified by explicitly stating which type of interpolation to use or by providing an instance of a `java.awt.RenderingHints` object that contains information regarding the preferred interpolation method.

> **TIP**
>
> When using a `RenderingHints` object, the `KEY_INTERPOLATION` hint does have a possible value of `VALUE_INTERPOLATION_BICUBIC`, but the Java 2D filter methods do not support it. The supported choices are `VALUE_INTERPOLATION_NEAREST_NEIGHBOR` and `VALUE_INTERPOLATION_BILINEAR`.

> **TIP**
>
> Most places that require an object of type `RenderingHints` will take a `null` value. This will be interpreted as setting all hints to their default values.

Filtering with Alpha Components

Often, the alpha (transparency) channel is treated as a color component because pixels often have samples representing alpha as well as samples representing color components. In these cases, it is of interest to consider what happens to the alpha channel during image filtering. In many cases, filtering the alpha channel doesn't make sense, such as in the case of color scaling. If you set up a filter to make the color components higher, thus the image brighter, it doesn't mean that you necessarily want the image to be more opaque. In the next few sections when we discuss filters for `BufferedImages` and `Rasters`, we will describe how the alpha channel is handled for each type of filter.

As a quick introduction, filters for `BufferedImages` tend to give alpha special consideration whereas filters for `Rasters` don't. This is because `BufferedImages` contain a `ColorModel` that allows interpretation of the color components, and with a `Raster` no such interpretation is possible. If, for some reason, the special treatment imposed by the `BufferedImage` filter is unwanted, you can filter the `Raster` instead of the `BufferedImage`. The way to obtain the `BufferedImage`'s `Raster` is as follows:

```
public WritableRaster getRaster()
```

BufferedImageOp and RasterOp Interfaces

When performing filtering using the Image class, much of the functionality of the used filter was defined in its parent class (that is, ImageFilter). When performing BufferedImage filtering, much of the functionality of the used filter will be defined by the BufferedImageOp interface. Similarly, when performing Raster filtering, much of the functionality of the used filter will be defined by the RasterOp interface.

In these latter two cases, there can always be a destination object that is separate from the source object. Thus, the filters can use any combination of source pixels to compute destination pixel values, making 2D convolution filters and 2D affine transformation filters possible.

It is of interest to take a closer look at the method that the BufferedImageOp uses to filter BufferedImages (see Figure 4.11):

```
ImageBuffer filter(BufferedImage src, BufferedImage dest)
```

FIGURE 4.11
BufferedImageOp's *filter method.*

This method takes a source BufferedImage and converts it into a destination BufferedImage. Often, the alpha components are not filtered or are filtered differently than the color components. If the source and destination BufferedImages have different ColorModels, a color conversion will automatically occur. The reason this method also returns an ImageBuffer is to provide the added functionality of cascading filters so that the destination of one filter can be the source object for another. If a destination BufferedImage is provided, the returned BufferedImage will simply refer to the destination BufferedImage. If the destination BufferedImage is null, an appropriate BufferedImage will be allocated and returned. This saves the user from having to create the destination BufferedImage in advance. Another feature of classes implementing this interface is that for certain filtering classes, it is possible to have the same BufferedImage object for the source and the destination. This subset of classes is analogous to the set of classes described by the ImageFilter class for use in the push model in that a destination pixel can only be dependent on its original pixel value and its location.

The RasterOp interface is similar to the BufferedImageOp interface except that it allows filtering of Rasters instead of BufferedImages (see Figure 4.12). The method that RasterOp classes use to filter Rasters is the following:

```
WritableRaster filter(Raster src, WritableRaster dest)
```

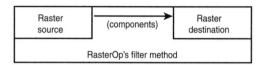

FIGURE 4.12
RasterOp's *filter method.*

This method converts all components from the source Raster into the components for the destination Raster. The alpha component is not given special treatment.

The main difference between filtering BufferedImages and filtering Rasters is that a BufferedImage contains a ColorModel, which allows interpretation of the pixel samples. Therefore, a BufferedImage filter can process the alpha component differently than the color components. With a Raster, all components are treated equally.

The following five classes: AffineTransformOp, RescaleOp, ConvolveOp, LookupOp, and ColorConvertOp all implement both the BufferedImageOp and the RasterOp interfaces; and as we discuss them, we'll point out how they perform both Raster and BufferedImage filtering. The last class we will examine, BandCombineOp, only implements the RasterOp interface, so it can only filter Rasters.

AffineTransformOp

One class that implements both the RasterOp and the BufferedImageOp interfaces is the java.awt.image.AffineTransformOp class. Objects of this class contain an affine transformation (java.awt.geom.AffineTransform) that will either be applied to a source BufferedImage to create a destination BufferedImage or to a source Raster to create a destination Raster.

In order to best explain an affine transformation, it is beneficial to first review two more restrictive groups of transformations; the Euclidean transformation, group and the similarity transformation group. The Euclidean group of transformations is characterized by the fact that distance and area don't change. In other words, if the distance between two points is 5 units, after a Euclidean transformation that distance will still be 5 units regardless of the Euclidean transformation used. Such transformations consist of rotations and translations. The equations representing a 2D Euclidean transformation are as follows:

$$x' = \cos\theta \ x - \sin\theta \ y + t_x$$
$$y' = \sin\theta \ x + \cos\theta \ y + t_y$$

where x, y is the location of the source point, x', y' is the location of this point after the transformation, θ is the rotation angle, t_x is the translation in the horizontal direction, and t_y is the translation in the vertical direction. Note that rotation angles are represented in radians, with the conversion from degrees to radians being

angle in radians = angle in degrees * (Math.PI/180.0)

Similarity transformations extend this group to include global scaling. Under this group of transformations, distance can change, but shape can't. In other words, a square will remain a square after a similarity transformation. The equations representing a 2D similarity transformation are as follows:

$$x' = S(\cos\theta\ x - \sin\theta\ y + t_x)$$
$$y' = S(\sin\theta\ x + \cos\theta\ y + t_y)$$

where S is the global scaling factor.

By increasing the generality of the transformation group once again, you arrive at the group of affine transformations in which shape and area can change, but linearity and parallelism can't. In other words, a line will remain a line after an affine transformation, and two lines that are parallel will remain parallel after an affine transformation. The two addition types of transformation allowed are general scaling and shearing. For example, a transformation that only contains general scaling (as opposed to global scaling where the x and y scale factor are the same) would be as follows:

$$x' = S_x x$$
$$y' = S_y y$$

with S_x and S_y being the two scaling coefficients. Likewise, a transformation that only contains shearing would be as follows:

$$x' = x + Sh_x y$$
$$y' = Sh_y x + y$$

with Sh_x and Sh_y being the two shearing coefficients. An example of a transformation involving shearing components of (.2, 0) is shown in Figure 4.10.

TIP

In Java, the coordinate system's origin is the top left corner with x increasing as you move right and y increasing as you move down.

Thus, the affine transformations contain all the transformations in the Euclidean group(translations, rotations), plus those of the similarity group (global scaling), along with general scaling and shearing. The equations representing a 2D affine transformation are as follows:

$$x' = m_{00}\ x + m_{01}\ y + m_{02}$$
$$y' = m_{10}\ x + m_{11}\ y + m_{12}$$

where m_{rc} is the array element at row r and column c in the selected AffineTransform array.

4

IMMEDIATE MODE
IMAGING MODEL

> **TIP**
>
> Affine transformations are linear transformations so procedures such as image warping cannot be done using the `AffineImageOp` class.

Because an affine transformation is made up of combinations of rotations, translations, scalings, and shearings, the `AffineTransform` class has a series of methods that allow you to specify these transformation groups. For example,

```
//rotate theta radians around the origin
public void rotate (double theta);
```

```
//rotate theta radians around point x,y
public void rotate (double theta, double x, double y);
```

```
//scale by sx in the x direction and sy in the y direction
public void scale (double sx, double sy);
```

```
//translate by tx in the x direction and ty in the y direction
public void translate(double tx, double ty);
```

```
//shear using multipliers of shx and shy
public void shear(double shx, double shy);
```

Note that the initial matrix is set to identity in the `AffineTransform` constructor and each instruction concatenates a new temporary transformation to the stored affine transformation. For this reason, the order of the methods make a difference in the final affine transformation. In other words, the affine transformation created using

```
rotate(.5);
translate(10, 15);
```

will be different from the affine transformation created using

```
translate(10,15)
rotate(.5);
```

In general, there are two ways you can transfer a coordinate space: absolute coordinate system transformations and relative coordinate system transformations. In an absolute coordinate system transformation, the axis and coordinate system remain fixed and everything in it gets transformed. In a relative coordinate system transformation, the axis and coordinate system get transformed and everything in it remains constant with respect to these axes. By default, the `AffineTransform` transformations are done as a relative coordinate system transformation. As an example, let's assume that a rotation was performed followed by a translation along the x axis. In an absolute coordinate system transformation, the translation would be to the right regardless of the preceding rotation because the axes haven't moved. In a relative coordinate system transformation, the x axis moved with the rotation, thus the translation direction is dependent upon the preceding rotation. If this rotation was 90 degrees, a translation along the x axis would be down.

TIP

If it appears as if the `AffineTransformation` is doing your instructions in the reverse order, you are probably designing your instructions for absolute coordinate system transformations.

Last, for the `AffineTransformOp`, the source and destination must be different; otherwise a `IllegalArgumentException` will be thrown.

The constructors for `AffineTransformOp` are as follows:

`AffineTransformOp(AffineTransform xform, int interpolationType)`

`AffineTransformOp(AffineTransform xform, RenderingHints hints)`

where the `interpolationType` can be `AffineTransform.TYPE_BILINEAR` or `AffineTransform.TYPE_NEAREST_NEIGHBOR`.

In Listing 4.8, an affine transformation is created to rotate an image by 45 degrees around the image's center. Because this would normally map some source pixels to points with a negative x or y value, the image will also be translated in both the x and y directions to make sure that the entire image can be represented by the destination `BufferedImage`.

LISTING 4.8   RotateImage45Degrees

```
package ch4;

import java.awt.*;
import javax.swing.*;
import java.awt.image.*;
import java.awt.geom.*;
import java.io.*;

/**
    RotateImage45Degrees.java -
    1. scales an image's dimensions by a factor of two
    2. rotates it 45 degrees around the image center
    3. displays the processed image
 */
```

LISTING 4.8   Continued

```java
public class RotateImage45Degrees extends JFrame {
    private Image inputImage;
    private BufferedImage sourceBI;
    private BufferedImage destinationBI = null;
    private Insets frameInsets;
    private boolean sizeSet = false;

    public RotateImage45Degrees(String imageFile) {
        addNotify();
        frameInsets = getInsets();
        inputImage = Toolkit.getDefaultToolkit().getImage(imageFile);

        MediaTracker mt = new MediaTracker(this);
        mt.addImage(inputImage, 0);
        try {
            mt.waitForID(0);
        }
        catch (InterruptedException ie) {
        }

        sourceBI = new BufferedImage(inputImage.getWidth(null),
                                     inputImage.getHeight(null),
                                     BufferedImage.TYPE_INT_ARGB);

        Graphics2D g = (Graphics2D)sourceBI.getGraphics();
        g.drawImage(inputImage, 0, 0, null);

        AffineTransform at = new AffineTransform();

        // scale image
        at.scale(2.0, 2.0);

        // rotate 45 degrees around image center
        at.rotate(45.0*Math.PI/180.0,
                  sourceBI.getWidth()/2.0,
                  sourceBI.getHeight()/2.0);


        /* translate to make sure the rotation
           doesn't cut off any image data
        */
        AffineTransform translationTransform;
        translationTransform = findTranslation(at, sourceBI);
        at.preConcatenate(translationTransform);
```

4

IMMEDIATE MODE
IMAGING MODEL

LISTING 4.8   Continued

```java
        // instantiate and apply affine transformation filter
        BufferedImageOp bio;
        bio = new AffineTransformOp(at, AffineTransformOp.TYPE_BILINEAR);

        destinationBI = bio.filter(sourceBI, null);

        int frameInsetsHorizontal = frameInsets.right + frameInsets.left;
        int frameInsetsVertical = frameInsets.top + frameInsets.bottom;
        setSize(destinationBI.getWidth() + frameInsetsHorizontal,
                destinationBI.getHeight() + frameInsetsVertical);
        show();
    }


    /*
      find proper translations to keep rotated image
      correctly displayed
    */
    private AffineTransform findTranslation(AffineTransform at,
                                            BufferedImage bi) {
        Point2D p2din, p2dout;

        p2din = new Point2D.Double(0.0,0.0);
        p2dout = at.transform(p2din, null);
        double ytrans = p2dout.getY();

        p2din = new Point2D.Double(0, bi.getHeight());
        p2dout = at.transform(p2din, null);
        double xtrans = p2dout.getX();

        AffineTransform tat = new AffineTransform();
        tat.translate(-xtrans, -ytrans);
        return tat;
    }


    public void paint(Graphics g) {
        if (destinationBI != null)
            g.drawImage(destinationBI,
                        frameInsets.left, frameInsets.top, this);
    }

    public static void main(String[] args) {
        if (args.length!= 1) {
            new RotateImage45Degrees("images/fruits.png");
```

LISTING 4.8   Continued

```
        }
        new RotateImage45Degrees(args[0]);
    }
}
```

With regard to alpha, the alpha component is treated the same as any other component, meaning that the alpha value of the destination pixel is found by interpolating the alpha channel just as the blue component of the destination pixel is found by interpolating the blue channel. Thus, transforming a BufferedImage is identical to transforming a Raster. Last, you cannot use the same source and destination object when filtering.

ConvolveOp

The java.awt.image.ConvolveOp class convolves a kernel with a source image in order to produce a destination image. A kernel can be thought of as a two-dimensional array with an origin. During the convolution, the origin of the array is overlaid on each pixel of the source image. This origin value is multiplied by the pixel value it is over, and all surrounding kernel array values are multiplied by the pixel values that they are over. Finally, all these values are summed together and the resulting number replaces the pixel corresponding to the kernel center. For example, consider the following kernel with an origin at (1, 1):

(1/9) (1/9) (1/9)
(1/9) (1/9) (1/9)
(1/9) (1/9) (1/9)

For each image pixel, its value will be multiplied by (1/9) and each of its neighbors will be multiplied by 1/9. When these values are added together, the original image pixel will be replaced by the average value of itself and its eight neighbors. The effect of this kernel is to cause the destination image to appear like a smoothed version of the input image.

When you are using a convolution algorithm, edge pixels present a difficulty because they don't have all the neighboring pixels that a non-edge pixel does. Under these conditions, convolution algorithms aren't able to function, and some instruction is required as to how these edge pixels should be handled. In one of the ConvolveOp constructors, there is a parameter called edgeConditions, which is an integer. If this value is set to ConvolveOp.EDGE_NO_OP, the edge pixels in the destination object will be identical to those of the source object. If this value is set to ConvolveOp.EDGE_ZERO_FILL, the edge pixels will be set to 0. This latter value is the default.

The two ConvolveOp constructors are as follows:

```
ConvolveOp(Kernel kernel)
ConvolveOp(Kernel kernel, int edgeCondition, RenderingHints hints)
```

With regard to the filtered object, if the source object is a `BufferedImage` with an alpha component, this component isn't convolved separately. Instead, the other color components are multiplied by their corresponding normalized alpha component, and the color components are convolved independently. Finally, the alpha value of the source pixel is divided out of the returned components and given to the destination pixel as its alpha value. If this behavior isn't wanted, you can filter the `BufferedImage`'s `Raster`—in which case, all components—including alpha—are convolved independently. You cannot use the same source and destination object when filtering.

RescaleOp

This class multiplies each pixel sample by a scaling factor before adding an offset to it. Mathematically, this can be expressed as follows:

$$dstSample = (srcSample*scaleFactor) + offset$$

Similar to the `ConvolveOp` class, any value above the maximum allowed value (usually `255`) gets clipped to the maximum value and any value below `0` gets clipped to `0`. You can use the source image as the destination image for this filtering operation. The constructors for this class are as follows:

```
RescaleOp(float scaleFactor, float offset, RenderingHints hints)
```

```
RescaleOp(float[] scaleFactors, float[] offsets, RenderingHints hints)
```

In the first constructor, only a single scale factor can be given, but in the second constructor, any number of scale factors can be given. Table 4.6 illustrates how the choice of constructor and the choice of the object to be filtered effect the destination pixels.

TABLE 4.6   `RescaleOp` Behavior

Object Filtered	Number of scaleFactors	Filtering
BufferedImage	Number of color components	Each color component scaled separately; alpha not changed
BufferedImage	Number of components	Each component scaled separately
BufferedImage	1	Each color component scaled identically; alpha not changed
Raster	Number of components	Each component scaled separately
Raster	1	Each component scaled identically

LookupOp

The `java.awt.image.LookupOp` object provides a means to filter `Rasters` and `BufferedImages` using a *lookup table(LUT)*. In the `LookupOp` class, the LUT is simply an array in which the source pixel samples are treated as array indices. The corresponding destination pixel samples get their values from the array elements. In other words:

```
dstSample = LUTarray[srcSample]
```

A LookupTable contains one or more of these lookup arrays, which allow you to process individual bands differently. The LookupOp class contains a filter method for Rasters and for BufferedImages with slightly different behaviors (see Table 4.7).

TABLE 4.7   LookupOp Behavior

Object Filtered	Number of Bands in LookupTable	Filtering
BufferedImage	Number of color components	Each color component filtered separately; alpha not changed
BufferedImage	Number of components	Each component filtered separately
BufferedImage	1	Each color component filtered identically; alpha not changed
Raster	Number of components	Each component filtered separately
Raster	1	Each component filtered identically

There are two main LookupTable subclasses, ByteLookupTable and ShortLookupTable, where the ByteLookupTable assumes that the current input image's pixel samples all lie between 0–255 inclusive whereas the ShortLookupTable assumes that they lie between 0–66635 inclusive. Last, you can use the same source and destination object when filtering.

ColorConvertOp

The java.awt.image.ColorConvertOp class performs a pixel by pixel color conversion of the image source into the image destination. This is done by converting the pixels from the source image's color space into the destination image's color space. This class has three main constructors that can take zero, one, or two ColorSpaces as parameters. These three constructors are as follows:

```
ColorConvertOp(RenderingHints hints)
ColorConvertOp(ColorSpace cspace, RenderingHints hints)
ColorConvertOp(ColorSpace srcCspace, ColorSpace dstCspace, RenderingHints hints)
```

When this operation is to be performed on BufferedImages, no ColorSpace is necessary in the ColorConvertOp's constructor because the BufferedImages contain ColorModels that already represent a particular ColorSpace. Alternatively, you can provide a single ColorSpace if a null destination BufferedImage is going to be used in the filter method. In this case an appropriate BufferedImage with the provided ColorSpace will be created and returned by the filter method. Unlike BufferedImages, Rasters do not contain ColorModels, so for Raster filtering, two ColorSpace objects must be provided in the ColorConvertOp's constructor. Last, you can use the same source and destination object when filtering.

BandCombineOp

The last filter that we will look at is the java.awt.image.BandCombineOp filter. Unlike the other filters discussed, this filter only implements the RasterOp interface and not the BufferedImageOp interface, meaning that it can only be used to filter Rasters. The purpose of this filter is to perform linear combinations of the Raster bands. In other words, the value of each band in the destination Raster will be found through a linear function of the bands in the source Raster. The constructor for this class is as follows:

BandCombineOp(float[][] matrix, RenderingHints hints)

where the number of rows in the matrix is equal to the number of bands in the destination Raster and the number of columns is either equal to the number of columns in the source Raster or the number of columns in the source Raster plus one. In this latter case, an additional band is created that is always equal to one. For example, consider a BandCombineOp filter that switches the red and blue bands of a Raster containing a red, green, and blue band. That would require the following matrix:

$$
\begin{array}{ll}
[\text{destRedBand}] & [\,0\ \ 0\ \ 1\,] \quad [\text{sourceRedBand}] \\
[\text{destGreenBand}] = [\,0\ \ 1\ \ 0\,] \times [\text{sourceGreenBand}] \\
[\text{destBlueBand}] & [\,1\ \ 0\ \ 0\,] \quad [\text{sourceBlueBand}]
\end{array}
$$

Similarly, a BandCombineOp filter that inverts the green band is as follows:

$$
\begin{array}{ll}
[\text{destRedBand}] & [\,1\ \ 0\ \ 1\ \ 0\,] \quad\ \ [\text{sourceRedBand}] \\
[\text{destGreenBand}] = [\,0\ -1\ \ 0\ \ 255\,] \times [\text{sourceGreenBand}] \\
[\text{destBlueBand}] & [\,0\ \ 0\ \ 1\ \ 0\,] \quad\ \ [\text{sourceBlueBand}\,] \\
& \qquad\qquad\qquad\quad\ [\qquad 1 \qquad]
\end{array}
$$

In this latter example, the number of columns in the array were equal to the number of bands in the Raster + 1. For this reason, an extra band was created with each element being equal to 1. Last, for this filter class, the source Raster and the destination Raster can be the same.

Summary

When we began this chapter by looking at the java.awt.Image class, we noted that the Image class shouldn't be considered a conventional image because it didn't have accessible image data. It, instead, should be thought of as a set of resources that allow the loading and displaying of image data. The Image class is typically used with the push model of image processing in which the object displaying or filtering the image data makes a request to the object producing the image data to start producing. It then waits for this producer to push the data asynchronously to it. The advantage of this method is that the data arrives as it is available so that the drawing or filtering can begin right away without having to wait until all the image data is loaded.

Next, we examined the java.awt.image.BufferedImage class which is a subclass of the Image class. The main differences between the Image and BufferedImage classes is that the BufferedImage contains not only accessible pixel data but also a Raster to extract samples from the pixels and a ColorModel to interpret these samples. The BufferedImage class is typically used with the immediate mode imaging model in which the image data is immediately accessible to any objects that want to use it. This imaging model shouldn't be considered completely separate from the push imaging model because they are usually used together (see Figure 4.13). In other words, the image data gets pushed into the immediate mode model pipeline where it is filtered. The BufferedImage, which is a subclass of Image, can then return the filtered data back into a push model pipeline.

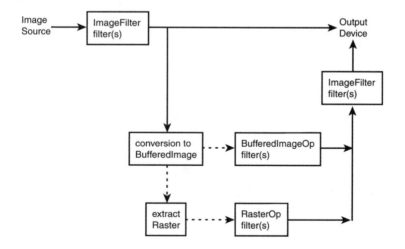

4

IMMEDIATE MODE
IMAGING MODEL

FIGURE 4.13

There are many ways to filter image data in Java using both the push and the immediate mode imaging models.

NOTE

For more information on the topics discussed in this chapter, we recommend that you refer to John Zukowski's *Java AWT Reference* (O'Reilly, 1997) or Jonathon Knudsen's *Java 2D Graphics* (O'Reilly, 1999).

Image I/O API

CHAPTER

5

IN THIS CHAPTER

In Chapter 4, "Immediate Mode Imaging Model," we looked at how an image gets loaded and what to do with it after it is loaded, but there wasn't much discussion regarding what types of images can be loaded. The reason for this is that until the Java Image I/O package was developed, you could only read GIF and JPEG images. Also, until this package was created, you could only write out unformatted pixel values. In this chapter, we'll explore the basics of the Java Image I/O package and how it solved both of these problems.

Two of the more useful aspects of the Image I/O package are its use of plug-ins and metadata. The capability to read and write formatted images is available through plug-ins, which means that at runtime the Java virtual machine (JVM) discovers which image readers/writers are available and what types of image formats they can decode/encode. Metadata is useful in communicating non-pixel information about the input images and output images. In the Image I/O package, the metadata classes are designed to be easily converted into XML DOM trees, enabling the use of the Java XML DOM API when working with this image information.

Image Formats

While the number of image formats is large, there are a few that are well known and commonly used. In this chapter, we will only mention the image formats that are most often associated with Web browsers: GIF, JPEG, and PNG; as well as a sample format called ch5, which we will use for illustrative purposes throughout this chapter.

GIF: Graphics Image Format

The Graphics Image Format (GIF; also referred to as CompuServe GIF format) represents each pixel using 3 bytes, depicting its red, green and blue color components. This format takes all the unique sets of color components within the GIF image(not exceeding 256) and puts them into a color table. This limits the number of colors that can be represented in a GIF image to 256 out of a possible 2^{24} (approximately 16 million). By using this color table, a pixel no longer needs to contain a red, a green, and a blue component, but instead can simply contain an index for the color table. In this way, each pixel can be represented using a single byte instead of 3 bytes. A lossless compression is then performed in order to reduce the image size. Thus, one of the main advantages of the GIF format is that any 256 out of approximately 16 million colors can be represented using images whose size is relatively small. This is an important point when transferring images over a network. Another advantage is that the compression is lossless, so the image quality won't be diminished. Also, one of the 256 colors in the color table can represent a transparent color; meaning that any pixel mapped to this value will appear transparent (alpha value of 0) when displayed. Some additional features are that the GIF image format can represent more than one image, making animation possible, and that it supports interlacing, so that when an image is displayed it immediately appears at a very low resolution and progressively redraws itself until it is at the proper resolution. The main disadvantage of the GIF image format is the range of colors a single image can represent is limited. If one needs more then 256 colors, then another image format must be used.

JPEG

Like the GIF image format, the Joint Photographic Experts Group (JPEG) format represents each pixel using 3 bytes, one each for the red, green, and blue color components. Unlike the GIF format, the JPEG format does not limit the number of colors that can be used in an image. Thus, it must employ another strategy in order to prevent prohibitively large image sizes. This strategy is the use of lossy compression, which can compress an image to a greater degree than lossless compression. Therefore, the main advantage of the JPEG format is that it can represent a large number of colors using relatively small image sizes, whereas a disadvantage is that the uncompressed image may not be of the same quality as the original image. In most cases, this latter point is insignificant because the loss in quality is not visible to the human eye, although there are times when it is apparent. For instance, if there are large regions in an image that are a single color, then the JPEG compression/decompression process might make those regions appear blotchy. Also, sharp changes in contrast might be blurred, as will text (especially fine text). A good thing to remember is that JPEG was designed for photographs, and that is what it does best. So, for real world scenes JPEG should be used, and for artificial scenes, such as logos, GIF should be used.

PNG

The Portable Network Graphics (PNG) image format might potentially replace the GIF image format someday. It has all the advantages of GIF, with the exception of animation. It also supports an alpha channel (GIF only supports alpha values of 0 or 255), and two-dimensional interlacing (GIF's is just horizontal). Also, because the PNG format is open software, there are no patents involved with its use.

ch5 Format

For illustrative purposes a sample image format will be defined and used throughout this chapter for the development of plug-ins. This format will be referred to as the ch5 format, and it will be an 8-bit grayscale format specified by the following pattern:

> 5 (String representing format's magic number)
> Number of Images in Stream (String)
> Image #1 Width (String)
> Image #1 Height (String)
> Image #1 Data (series of pixels, 1 byte/pixel)
> Image #2 Width (String)
> Image #2 Height (String)
> and so on.

In a later section when we discuss metadata, it will be explained that metadata is the collection of non-pixel image information. In this ch5 format, the "Number of Images in Stream" value will be considered part of the image stream's metadata, whereas the "Width" and "Height" values will be considered part of each image's metadata.

Reading and Writing Basics

In the previous chapter we saw that with the Java2D package, input images are converted to Images using the getImage methods of the Applet class and the Toolkit class. In this chapter we'll see that, with the Image I/O package, input images are converted to BufferedImages using the read methods of the javax.imageio.ImageReader class. Generally, more than one ImageReader subclass will be available, so the initial step in reading an image is to choose an ImageReader that can decode the format of the image of interest. This is done by providing information about that image's format to a set of ImageReader service providers (javax.imageio.ImageReaderSpis). This information can be in the following forms:

- Image file suffix
- Image MIME type
- Image format
- Image data

Using the provided information, the ImageReaderSpis respond as to whether their corresponding ImageReader can decode that format or not. One of the ImageReaders whose service provider responds positively will then be chosen to convert the image data into a BufferedImage.

An important point to understand in this arrangement is that the ImageReaders are available through plug-ins. Thus, while some will be part of the Java standard development kit, the rest can be downloaded from third party vendors, freeware, and shareware sites. If no appropriate ImageReader is available, then one can be written, as will be demonstrated in later sections.

The process for writing images is very similar, except in reverse. The available javax.imageio.ImageWriters have service providers that are given information about the potential output image's format, and they respond if they are able to convert the BufferedImage of interest into an output image using this format.

ImageIO

The ImageIO class contains static methods that are mainly used for locating ImageReaders and ImageWriters. For example, if you want to find out which image formats or image MIME types your JVM can currently decode or encode, you can use the following ImageIO methods:

```
static String[] getReaderFormatNames()
static String[] getReaderMIMETypes()
```

```
    static String[] getWriterFormatNames()

    static String[] getWriterMIMETypes()
```

In Listing 5.1 these `ImageIO` methods are used to display the available `ImageReaders` and `ImageWriters` according to image format and MIME type.

LISTING 5.1   RWtypes.java

```java
package ch5.imageio;
import javax.imageio.ImageIO;

/**
* RWtypes.java - a class to display available ImageReaders and
* ImageWriters by image format and MIME type
*/
public class RWtypes {
   public static void main(String[] args) {
       String[] readers, writers;

       System.out.println("For Reading:");
       readers = ImageIO.getReaderFormatNames();
       System.out.println("\tBy format:");
       for (int i=0; i<readers.length;i++)
           System.out.println("\t\t" + readers[i]);

       readers = ImageIO.getReaderMIMETypes();
       System.out.println("\tBy MIME Types:");
       for (int i=0; i<readers.length;i++)
           System.out.println("\t\t" + readers[i]);

       System.out.println("For Writing:");
       writers = ImageIO.getWriterFormatNames();
       System.out.println("\tBy format:");
       for (int i=0; i<writers.length;i++)
           System.out.println("\t\t" + writers[i]);

       writers = ImageIO.getWriterMIMETypes();
       System.out.println("\tBy MIME Types:");
       for (int i=0; i<writers.length;i++)
           System.out.println("\t\t" + writers[i]);
   }
}
```

If you were to run this application, the following output might appear:

```
For Reading:
        By format:
                    png
                    jpeg
                    JPEG
                    gif
                    jpg
                    JPG
        By MIME Types:
                    image/jpeg
                    image/png
                    image/x-png
                    image/gif
For Writing:
        By format:
                    PNG
                    png
                    jpeg
                    JPEG
                    jpg
                    JPG
        By MIME Types:
                    image/jpeg
                    image/png
                    image/x-png
```

TIP

If you are using a version of the Java standard development kit (SDK) prior to 1.4.0, you'll need to have imageio.jar (from the Image I/O package) and crimson.jar (from the JAXP package) somewhere in your classpath.

Thus, without adding additional ImageReader and ImageWriter plug-ins, we are only able to read GIF, JPEG, and PNG images, and we can only write JPEG and PNG images.

NOTE

This output is dependent upon the version of the Java Image I/O package being used. In the early access version of this package, JPEG ImageReaders and ImageWriters are not provided.

While this type of output is useful to examine what kinds of image formats one can decode and encode, a more common concern is that of finding an appropriate `ImageReader` for a given image. This task can also be done by using static methods of the `ImageIO` class (see Figure 5.1). These methods enable one to find an `ImageReader` by specifying an image's format, its MIME type, or its file suffix, as in one of the following:

```
static Iterator getImageReadersByFormatName(String formatName)

static Iterator getImageReadersByMIMEType(String MIMEType)

static Iterator getImageReadersbySuffix(String fileSuffix)
```

Any of the `ImageReaders` contained in the returned `Iterator` can be used to convert the input image into a `BufferedImage`.

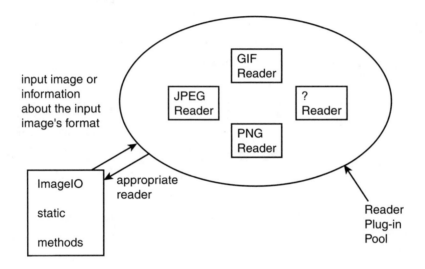

FIGURE 5.1

When given information about an input image, IOImage *static methods are used to discover which of the available* ImageReaders *can decode its format.*

Thus, there are various ways to find an appropriate `ImageReader`, but most of those ways do not involve examining the input stream. This is because the methods relying upon image format, image suffix, and image MIME type are based on assumptions that if given an image with that property, then a particular `ImageReader` can decode it. A more reliable method is to just let the image input stream be examined, or more exactly, the object representing the image input stream (`javax.imageio.stream.ImageInputStream`) be examined, as seen in

```
static Iterator getImageReaders(Object input)
```

where input is usually an `ImageInputStream`.

Some examples of `ImageInputStream` creation are as follows:

```
URL url = new URL(imageURL);
ImageInputStream iis = ImageIO.createImageInputStream(url.openStream());
```

or

```
Socket s = new Socket(imageHost, imagePort);
ImageInputSream iis = ImageIO.createImageInputStream(s.getInputStream());
```

or

```
FileInputStream fis = new FileInputStream(imageFileName);
ImageInputStream iis = ImageIO.createImageInputStream(fis);
```

Lastly, if you already have an `ImageWriter`, you can use it to get a corresponding `ImageReader` (assuming that the plug-in which defined the `ImageWriter` also defined an `ImageReader`), as in

```
static ImageReader getImageReader(ImageWriter writer)
```

> **NOTE**
>
> Most image formats begin with something called a *magic number*, which is the part of the `ImageInputStream` that most `ImageReaderSpis` use to decide whether they can decode an image format.

Many of the `ImageIO` static methods pertaining to `ImageWriters` are analogous to those pertaining to `ImageReaders`, so an `ImageWriter` can be found using any one of the following methods:

```
static Iterator getImageWritersByFormatName(String formatName)
static Iterator getImageWritersByMIMEType(String MIMEType)
static Iterator getImageWritersbySuffix(String fileSuffix)
static ImageWriter getImageWriter(ImageReader reader)
```

One last method to obtain an `ImageWriter`, which is loosely analogous to the

```
static Iterator getImageReaders(Object input)
```

method, is the following:

```
static Iterator getImageWriters(ImageTypeSpecifier type, String format)
```

where the `javax.imageio.ImageTypeSpecifier` class is a convenience class that specifies a `ColorModel`/`SampleModel` combination (in this case, of the `BufferedImage` to be written) and the `format` parameter specifies an output image format.

ImageReader Usage

Although a more detailed discussion of ImageReaders will be provided later in this chapter, it is necessary at this point to understand the basics of how an ImageReader is used. The two main reasons that an application will interact with an ImageReader are:

- To provide it with an input source

- To use it to read the source image(s)

To give the ImageReader an input source, the following method is used:

```
public void setInput(Object input, boolean seekForwardOnly)
```

where the input parameter is usually an ImageInputStream and the seekForwardOnly parameter is used to specify whether an application can go backwards in the input stream. Thus, if an image stream consists of two images and you want to allow the application to read the first image after the second image has been read, the seekForwardOnly parameter would need to be false.

After an image source is defined, the ImageReader can read source images using either of the following two methods:

```
public void read(int imageIndex)
```

or

```
public void read(int imageIndex, ImageReadParam param)
```

where imageIndex is the index of the image that will be read and the param parameter provides control over how this image is to be read. The ImageReadParam class will be discussed in an upcoming section entitled "ImageReadParam," so for now it's enough to know that it can provide functionality such as clipping and subsampling of the input image.

> **NOTE**
>
> There is a field called minIndex in the ImageReader that is initialized to 0. Whenever an imageIndex is passed to the read method, it is checked to make sure it is not less than minIndex. If it is, an IndexOutOfBoundsException is thrown. If imageIndex is an allowable value and seekForwardOnly is true, minIndex takes the value of the last imageIndex. If seekForwardOnly is false, the value of minIndex remains at 0.

Because an image index is involved in image reading, one often needs to know how many images are available from a particular source. This information is obtained using the following ImageReader method:

```
public int getNumImages(boolean allowSearch)
```

where the `allowSearch` parameter specifies whether you want the entire `ImageInputStream` examined to determine the number of available images. In other words, in some image formats, the number of images is immediately available, while in other formats this can only be discovered by searching the entire image input stream. If the `allowSearch` parameter is false, the number of images available will be returned only if it is immediately available. If it's not, then a -1 will be returned. This parameter permits the programmer to specify that finding the number of images is required for the application and, if necessary, it should wait for the entire `ImageInputStream` to be searched before continuing. In many cases the `allowSearch` parameter can be set to false because it is possible to read all the available images without knowing how many there are by simply catching any `IndexOutofBounds` exceptions, illustrated by the following:

```
int imageIndex = 0;
BufferedImage bi;
try {
    while (bi=reader.read(imageIndex++)) {
        /* process image here */
    }
}
catch (IndexOutOfBoundsException exception) {
    // no more images left
}
```

An example of `ImageReader` usage is provided in Listing 5.2. In this listing, an `ImageReader` is found by examining the input image's `ImageInputStream`. This application takes an image URL and uses it to create a `BufferedImage` that is displayed.

LISTING 5.2   displayImage.java

```
package ch5.imageio;

import java.io.*;
import java.util.*;
import java.awt.*;
import java.net.*;
import javax.swing.*;
import java.awt.image.*;
import javax.imageio.ImageIO;
import javax.imageio.ImageReader;
import javax.imageio.IIOException;
import javax.imageio.stream.ImageInputStream;

/**
 * displayImage.java -- displays an image or a series of images contained
 * at the URL provided on the command line.
 */
```

LISTING 5.2   Continued

```java
public class displayImage extends JFrame {
    private BufferedImage bi;
    private Insets insets;
    private ImageReader reader;
    private ImageInputStream iis;
    private URL url;
    private int imageIndex = 0;

    public displayImage(String inputURL) {
        /*
         * The following line looks for plug-ins on the application
         * classpath -- this will be discussed in a later section
         */
        ImageIO.scanForPlugins();

        try {
            url = new URL(inputURL);
        }
        catch (MalformedURLException mue) {
            System.out.print("MalformedURLException: ");
            System.out.println(mue.getMessage());
            System.exit(1);
        }

        try {
            iis = ImageIO.createImageInputStream(url.openStream());
        }
        catch (IIOException ie) {
            System.out.println("IIOException:  " + ie.getMessage());
            System.exit(1);
        }
        catch (IOException ie) {
            System.out.println("IOException:  " + ie.getMessage());
            System.exit(1);
        }

        /*
         * get ImageReaders which can decode the given ImageInputStream
         */
        Iterator readers = ImageIO.getImageReaders(iis);

        /* if there is a set of appropriate ImageReaders, then take
         * the first one
         */
        if(readers.hasNext()) {
```

LISTING 5.2   Continued

```
                reader = (ImageReader)readers.next();
                reader.setInput(iis, true);
            }
        if (reader == null) {
            System.err.print("No Available ImageReader can ");
            System.err.println("decode: " + url);
            System.exit(1);
        }

        addNotify();
        insets = getInsets();

        show();
        showImage();
    }

    /**
     * This method iteratively displays all images in the given
     * ImageInputStream
     */
    private void showImage() {
        imageIndex = 0;

        reader.setInput(iis, true);
        /*
         * read and display all images
         */
        while(true) {
            try {
                bi = reader.read(imageIndex);
                setSize(bi.getWidth()+insets.left+insets.right,
                        bi.getHeight()+insets.top+insets.bottom);
                imageIndex++;
                repaint();
            }
            catch (IOException ie) {
                System.out.println("IIOException " + ie.getMessage());
                System.exit(1);
            }
            catch (IndexOutOfBoundsException iobe) {
                // all of the images have been read
            }
        }
    }
```

LISTING 5.2   Continued

```java
/**
 * simple image paint routine which double buffers display
 */
public void paint(Graphics g) {
    Image buffer;
    Graphics g2d;

    if (bi != null) {
        buffer = createImage(bi.getWidth(), bi.getHeight());
        g2d = buffer.getGraphics();

        /*
         * first clear viewing area
         * then draw image on buffered image
         * then draw buffered image on JFrame
         */
        g2d.clearRect(0, 0, bi.getWidth(), bi.getHeight());
        g2d.drawImage(bi, 0, 0, null);
        g.drawImage(buffer, insets.left, insets.top, null);
    }
}

public static void main(String[] args) {
    if (args.length == 0)
        new displayImage("file:images/fruits.png");
    else
        new displayImage(args[0]);
}
}
```

ImageWriter Usage

When we discussed ImageReader usage, we were primarily interested in its setInput and read methods. For ImageWriter usage, we will discuss the analogous setOutput and write methods.

The most common setOutput method is

```java
public void setOutput(Object output)
```

where output is typically an ImageOutputStream, as in

```java
Socket s = new Socket(imageHost, imagePort);
ImageOutputStream ios = ImageIO.createImageOutputStream(s.getOutputStream());
```

5

IMAGE I/O API

or

```
FileOutputStream fos = new FileOutputStream(imageFileName);
ImageOutputStream ios = ImageIO.createImageOutputStream(fos);
```

The main write method is as follows:

```
public void write(IIOMetadata streamMetadata,
                  IIOImage iioimage,
                  ImageWriteParam param)
```

where the streamMetadata parameter represents the stream metadata to be included in the output stream, and the param parameter provides control over how the output image is written to the output stream. Because both of these topics will be considered later in this chapter, we'll ignore them for now. In practice, these values can be set to null if there is no stream metadata, and/or no special control is required for writing the images to the output stream. The middle parameter, iioimage, is an object of type javax.imageio.IIOImage, which is a container class used for holding the following information:

- The image
- The image's associated thumbnail images, represented as a java.util.List of BufferedImages
- The image's metadata (note that this is different than the stream's metadata, which was a parameter in the write method)

If the output image format does not support thumbnail images or image metadata, these can both be set to null. The constructors for instantiating an IIOImage object are as follows:

```
IIOImage(Raster raster, List thumbnails, IIOMetadata metadata)
```

```
IIOImage(RenderedImage image, List thumbnails, IIOMetadata metadata)
```

Service Provider Interfaces

One obvious question resulting from the previous discussion is how do the ImageIO static methods know which ImageReader(s) can decode the image data? Theoretically, one way this can be done is to have each of the ImageReaders contain a set of methods that would return a list of image formats, file suffixes, and MIME types that it can decode. Another method could take an ImageInputStream and return true or false if the ImageReader can decode it. Using these techniques, it would be up to the plug-in developers to write these methods and therefore provide this information. Although this idea has its merits, there is one problem: In order to find out an ImageReader's functionality, it needs to be registered; and to register each of the ImageReaders, an object of each ImageReader class would need to be instantiated. This would be a waste of time and memory because not all of the ImageReaders will be needed. For this

reason, *service provider interfaces (spi)* are used. Spis are small classes (such as
ImageReaderSpi and ImageWriterSpi) that are used to describe the functionality of larger
classes (such as ImageReader and ImageWriter). Thus, in practice the JVM can instantiate an
object of each ImageReaderSpi, and these objects can be used to decide which ImageReader(s)
can decode an image format. Similarly, the JVM can instantiate an object of each
ImageWriterSpi, and these objects can be used to decide which ImageWriter(s) can encode an
image format.

ImageReaderSpi

Consider Listing 5.3, which implements an ImageReaderSpi. The purpose of this listing is to
illustrate how the ImageReaderSpi passes information about its corresponding ImageReader to
the ImageIO's static methods. Note that the ImageReader that corresponds to this
ImageReaderSpi will be developed in a later section entitled "ImageReadParam."

LISTING 5.3   ch5v1ImageReaderSpi.java

```
package ch5.imageio.plugins;

import java.io.*;
import java.util.*;
import javax.imageio.ImageReader;
import javax.imageio.spi.ImageReaderSpi;
import javax.imageio.stream.ImageInputStream;

/**
 *  Simple, non-functional ImageReaderSpi used to understand how
 *  information regarding format name, suffices and mime types
 *  get passed to ImageIO static methods
 */
public class ch5v1ImageReaderSpi extends ImageReaderSpi {

    static final String[] suffixes = { "ch5", "CH5"};
    static final String[] names = {"ch5"};
    static final String[] MIMETypes = { "image/ch5" };

    static final String version = "0.50";

    static final String readerCN="ch5.imageio.plugins.ch5v1ImageReader";

    static final String vendorName = "Company Name";

    //writerSpiNames
    static final String[] wSN={"ch5.imageio.plugins.ch5v1ImageWriterSpi"};
```

LISTING 5.3   Continued

```java
//StreamMetadataFormatNames and StreamMetadataFormatClassNames
static final boolean supportedStandardStreamMetadataFormat = false;
static final String nativeStreamMFN = null;
static final String nativeStreamMFCN = null;
static final String[] extraStreamMFN = null;
static final String[] extraStreamMFCN = null;

//ImageMetadataFormatNames and ImageMetadataFormatClassNames
static final boolean supportedStandardImageMetadataFormat = false;
static final String nativeImageMFN = null;
static final String nativeImageMFCN = null;
static final String[] extraImageMFN = {null};
static final String[] extraImageMFCN = {null};

public ch5v1ImageReaderSpi() {
super(vendorName,
      version,
      names,
      suffixes,
      MIMETypes,
      readerCN, // reader class name
      STANDARD_INPUT_TYPE,
      wSN, // writer spi names
      supportedStandardStreamMetadataFormat,
      nativeStreamMFN,
      nativeStreamMFCN,
      extraStreamMFN,
      extraStreamMFCN,
      supportedStandardImageMetadataFormat,
      nativeImageMFN,
      nativeImageMFCN,
      extraImageMFN,
      extraImageMFCN);
}

public String getDescription(Locale locale) {
return "Demo ch5 image reader, version " + version;
}

/**
 * We haven't created the corresponding ImageReader class yet,
 * so we'll just return null for now.
 */
```

LISTING 5.3   Continued

```
public ImageReader createReaderInstance(Object extension) {
return new ch5v1ImageReader(this);
}

/**
 * This method gets called when an application wants to see if
 * the input image's format can be decoded by this ImageReader.
 * In this case, we'll simply check the first line of data to
 * see if it is a 5 which is the format type's magic number.
 * Note that we initially make sure the input object is of
 * type ImageInputStream so we know it is compatible with
 * mark and reset methods.
 */
public boolean canDecodeInput(Object input) {
boolean reply = false;

    if (!(input instanceof ImageInputStream))
    return reply;

ImageInputStream iis = (ImageInputStream)input;
iis.mark(); // mark where we are in ImageInputStream
try {
    String magicNumber = iis.readLine().trim();
    iis.reset(); // reset stream back to marked location
    if (magicNumber.equals("5"))
    reply = true;
}
catch (IOException exception) {
}
return reply;
}

/**
 * This method gets called when the set of file suffices is
 * requested by the ImageIO's getImageReadersBySuffix method
 * It doesn't need to be redefined here, but is done for
 * illustrative purposes
 */
public String[] getFileSuffixes() {
return super.getFileSuffixes();
}

/**
 * This method gets called when the set of file mime types is
 * requested by the ImageIO's getImageReadersByMIMEType method
```

LISTING 5.3   Continued

```
 * It doesn't need to be redefined here, but is done for
 * illustrative purposes
 */
public String[] getMIMETypes() {
return super.getMIMETypes();
}

/**
 * This method gets called when the set of format names is
 * requested by the ImageIO's getImageReadersByFormatName method
 * It doesn't need to be redefined here, but is done for
 * illustrative purposes
 */
public String[] getFormatNames() {
return super.getFormatNames();
}
}
```

ImageWriterSpi

In general, the explanation of the `ImageWriterSpi` class is similar to that of the
`ImageReaderSpi` class, except that instead of having a

```
public boolean canDecodeImage(Object source)
```

it has a

```
public boolean canEncodeImage(ImageTypeSpecifier its)
```

where, as previously mentioned, the `ImageTypeSpecifier` class is simply a container class for
holding an image's `ColorModel` and `SampleModel`. Thus, while an `ImageReader` can be chosen
using the input image's suffix, MIME type, format, or by examining the input stream, an
`ImageWriter` can be chosen using the output image's suffix, MIME type, format, or by considering the image's `ColorModel` and `SampleModel` pair. Sample code for an `ImageWriterSpi` is
shown in Listing 5.4. In this listing, all metadata will be given null values. In the final section,
"Final Plug-in Code," it will be redone using metadata.

LISTING 5.4   ch5v1ImageWriterSpi.java

```
package ch5.imageio.plugins;

import java.io.*;
import java.util.*;
import java.awt.image.*;
```

LISTING 5.4   Continued

```java
import javax.imageio.ImageWriter;
import javax.imageio.ImageTypeSpecifier;
import javax.imageio.spi.ImageWriterSpi;
import javax.imageio.stream.ImageInputStream;

/**
 *  Simple, non-functional ImageWriterSpi used to understand how
 *  information regarding format name, suffices and mime types
 *  get passed to ImageIO static methods
 */
public class ch5v1ImageWriterSpi extends ImageWriterSpi {

    static final String[] suffixes = {"ch5", "CH5"};
    static final String[] names = {"ch5"};
    static final String[] MIMETypes = {"image/ch5" };

    static final String version = "0.50";

    static final String writerCN = "ch5.imageio.plugins.ch5v1ImageWriter";

    static final String vendorName = "Company Name";
    static final String[] rdrSpiNames={"ch5.imageio.ch5v1ImageReaderSpi"};

    static final boolean supportsStandardStreamMetadataFormat = false;
    static final String nativeStreamMetadataFormatName = null;
    static final String nativeStreamMetadataFormatClassName = null;
    static final String[] extraStreamMetadataFormatNames = null;
    static final String[] extraStreamMetadataFormatClassNames = null;


    static final boolean supportsStandardImageMetadataFormat = false;
    static final String nativeImageMetadataFormatName = null;
    static final String nativeImageMetadataFormatClassName = null;
    static final String[] extraImageMetadataFormatNames = null;
    static final String[] extraImageMetadataFormatClassNames = null;

    public ch5v1ImageWriterSpi() {
    super(vendorName,
          version,
          names,
          suffixes,
          MIMETypes,
          writerCN, //writer class name
          STANDARD_OUTPUT_TYPE,
          rdrSpiNames, //reader spi names
```

5

IMAGE I/O API

LISTING 5.4   Continued

```java
            supportsStandardStreamMetadataFormat,
            nativeStreamMetadataFormatName,
            nativeStreamMetadataFormatClassName,
            extraStreamMetadataFormatNames,
            extraStreamMetadataFormatClassNames,
            supportsStandardImageMetadataFormat,
            nativeImageMetadataFormatName,
            nativeImageMetadataFormatClassName,
            extraImageMetadataFormatNames,
            extraImageMetadataFormatClassNames);
}

public String getDescription(Locale locale) {
return "Demo ch5 image writer, version " + version;
}


/**
 * We haven't created the corresponding ImageWriter class yet,
 * so we'll just return null for now.
 */
public ImageWriter createWriterInstance(Object extension) {
return new ch5v1ImageWriter(this);
}

/**
 * This method gets called when an application wants to see if
 * the corresponding ImageWriter can encode an image with
 * a ColorModel and SampleModel specified by the ImageTypeSpecifier.
 * For this example, we will only advertise that we can encode
 * gray scale images with 8 bit pixels.
 */
public boolean canEncodeImage(ImageTypeSpecifier its) {
if (its.getBufferedImageType() == BufferedImage.TYPE_BYTE_GRAY)
    return true;
else
    return false;
}

/**
 * This method gets called when the set of file suffices is
 * requested by the ImageIO's getImageWritersBySuffix method
 * It doesn't need to be redefined here, but is done for
 * illustrative purposes
 */
```

LISTING 5.4 Continued

```
public String[] getFileSuffixes() {
return super.getFileSuffixes();
}

/**
 * This method gets called when the set of file mime types is
 * requested by the ImageIO's getImageWritersByMIMEType method
 * It doesn't need to be redefined here, but is done for
 * illustrative purposes
 */
public String[] getMIMETypes() {
return super.getMIMETypes();
}

/**
 * This method gets called when the set of format names is
 * requested by the ImageIO's getImageWritersByFormatName method
 * It doesn't need to be redefined here, but is done for
 * illustrative purposes
 */
public String[] getFormatNames() {
return super.getFormatNames();
}
}
```

Using JAR Files to Specify SPIs

In order for the JVM to discover the `ImageReader` and `ImageWriter` plug-ins, they must be contained in a properly formatted JAR file. Furthermore, the JAR file must contain a META-INF/services directory for listing the service providers contained in that JAR file. For each service provider interface that is implemented by a class stored in this JAR file, a file whose name is the fully qualified class name of the SPI should be placed in the services directory. Inside each of these files should be the fully qualified names of the implementation classes contained in the JAR file (one per line). For example, in Listing 5.3 the SPI is `javax.imageio.spi.ImageReaderSpi`, so that will be the name of a file in the META-INF/services directory. The name of the class implementing this interface is `ch5.imageio.ch5v1ReaderSpi`, so that name will go inside that file. Using Listings 5.1–5.4, the contents of their JAR files would show the following:

```
META-INF/
META-INF/MANIFEST.MF
META-INF/services/
META-INF/services/javax.imageio.spi.ImageReaderSpi
META-INF/services/javax.imageio.spi.ImageWriterSpi
```

```
ch5/
ch5/imageio/
ch5/imageio/RWtypes.class
ch5/imageio/plugins/
ch5/imageio/plugins/ch5v1ImageReaderSpi.class
ch5/imageio/plugins/ch5v1ImageWriterSpi.class
ch5/imageio/displayImage.class
```

If you examine the contents of the file META-
INF/services/javax.imageio.spi.ImageReaderSpi, you will see the text ch5.imageio.plu-
gins.ch5ImageReaderSpi.

TIP

One way to format your JAR file is to create an appropriate services directory, and
then use the following commands:

(for UNIX)

```
jar cf ch5.jar ch5
jar xf ch5.jar META-INF
mv services META-INF/services
rm ch5.jar
jar cfM ch5.jar ch5 META-INF
```

(for DOS)

```
jar cf ch5.jar ch5
jar xf ch5.jar META-INF
move services META-INF\services
del ch5.jar
jar cfM ch5.jar ch5 META-INF
```

The last step in getting the application to acknowledge these SPI classes is to make sure that
this JAR file is located somewhere on the application classpath. If we run Listing 5.1 with this
JAR file located on the application classpath, the new output is as follows:

```
For Reading:
        By format:
                png
                jpeg
                JPEG
                gif
                jpg
                JPG
                ch5
```

```
        By MIME Types:
                image/jpeg
                image/ch5
                image/png
                image/x-png
                image/gif
For Writing:
        By format:
                PNG
                png
                jpeg
                JPEG
                jpg
                JPG
                ch5
        By MIME Types:
                image/jpeg
                image/ch5
                image/png
                image/x-png
```

IIOParam Classes

By default, the ImageReader's read method does not offer much control over how the input image is read. Similarly, neither does the ImageWriter's write method offer much control over how the output image is written. One way to achieve more control in both of these situations is by using an object of the javax.imageio.IIOParam class. This class provides methods for describing how an image stream should be encoded and decoded. The IIOParam class contains one subclass for image reading, and one subclass for image writing. They are javax.imageio.ImageReadParams and javax.imageio.ImageWriteParams, respectively.

ImageReadParam

A javax.imageio.ImageReadParam object can be obtained using the following ImageReader method:

```
public ImageReadParam getDefaultReadParam()
```

After a reference to an ImageReadParam object is obtained, one can then make changes to the state of this object in order to specify how the input image should be read. After the ImageReadParam object is set appropriately, the following ImageReader read method should be used:

```
public BufferedImage read(int imageIndex, ImageReadParam imageReadParam)
```

One of the more common `ImageReadParam` methods used to control image reading is the following:

```
public void setSourceRegion(Rectangle sourceRegion)
```

where the parameter `sourceRegion` represents the image dimensions to be read. Thus, if you wanted to only read the top half of an image, you could use the following:

```
Rectangle rectangle;
rectangle = new Rectangle(imageReader.getImageWidth(imageIndex),
                          imageReader.getImageHeight(imageIndex)/2));
imageReadParam.setSourceRegion(rectangle);
BufferedImage bi = imageReader.read(imageIndex, imageReadParam);
```

Another useful method is `setSourceSubSampling`, which permits you to eliminate all pixels which are not multiples of provided x and y `SubSamplingFactors`. For example, if the `xSubSamplingFactor` is 2 and the `ySubSamplingFactor` is 1, then only columns 0, 2, 4, and so on will be kept.

```
public void setSourceSubsampling(int sourceXSubsampling,
                                 int sourceYSubsampling,
                                 int subsamplingXOffset,
                                 int subsamplingYOffset)
```

Thus, if you wanted to use subsampling to reduce an image size by a factor of 16, you could use the following:

```
imageReadParam.setSourceSubSampling(4, 4, 0, 0);
BufferedImage bi = imageReader.read(imageIndex, imageReadParam);
```

For a user of the Image I/O API, the `ImageReadParam` class is primarily for controlling the reading of input images. On the other hand, if one is a plug-in designer, this class has two other important purposes. Its values are used in the `ImageReader`'s `getDestination` method to instantiate the appropriate sized `BufferedImage`. After this `BufferedImage` has been instantiated the `ImageReadParam` parameters are used to correctly fill the `BufferedImage` in with the input image's data.

In more detail, there is a predefined `ImageReader` method that gets executed in the `read` method. This method returns the `BufferedImage` object in which the decoded input data should be placed. This `getDestination` method is as follows:

```
protected static BufferedImage getDestination(ImageReadParam param,
                                              Iterator imageTypes,
                                              int width, int height)
```

where the `param` parameter is the `ImageReadParam` object that was passed to the `read` method and `imageTypes` is an `Iterator` object containing the set of allowable `ImageTypeSpecifiers` (with the default one first). The `width` and `height` parameters are the true width and height of the input image. Thus, given this information, the `ImageReader`'s `getDestination` method will return a `BufferedImage` of the appropriate size taking into account any clipping and subsampling. This `BufferedImage` must then be filled appropriately using the `ImageReadParam` settings and the input image.

> **NOTE**
>
> If the `ImageReadParam` object's `setDestinationType` method and `setDestination` method are not used, the `BufferedImage` type returned by the `ImageReader`'s `getDestination` method will be the first `ImageTypeSpecifier` specified by the `imageTypes` parameter. Typically, this parameter will represent the return value of the `ImageReader`'s `getImageTypes` method.

In Table 5.1, the results of using the `ImageReadParam`'s `setSourceRegion` and `setSubsampling` methods on the size of the destination `BufferedImage` are shown. As illustrated in this table, the destination image size will be found by first clipping any image regions not common to both the original image region and the defined source region, and then subsampling the resulting area using the formulas

```
new width = (original width + xsubsamplingfactor-1)/xsubsamplingfactor
```

and

```
new height = (original height + ysubsamplingfactor-1)/ysubsamplingfactor
```

TABLE 5.1 `ImageReadParam` Settings Versus Resulting Destination `BufferedImage` Size for a 256 x 256 Input Image

Source Rectangle Dimensions	SubSample x, y Values	Resulting Destination BufferedImage Width, Height
0, 0, 256, 256	1, 1	256, 256
0, 0, 256, 256	2, 3	128, 86
50, 75, 256, 256	1, 1	206, 181
50, 75, 200, 200	2, 3	100, 61

In Listing 5.5, a simple version of an `ImageReader` is shown. The part to note in this listing is that the `ImageReadParam` object dictates the dimensions of the destination `BufferedImage` that is returned from the `ImageReader`'s `getDestination` method. Also note that it is up to the plug-in designer to correctly read in the pixel data and to fill this `BufferedImage` using these `ImageReadParam` values.

LISTING 5.5   ch5v1ImageReader.java

```java
package ch5.imageio.plugins;

import java.io.*;
import java.util.*;
import java.awt.*;
import java.awt.image.*;
import javax.imageio.IIOException;
import javax.imageio.ImageReader;
import javax.imageio.ImageTypeSpecifier;
import javax.imageio.ImageReadParam;
import javax.imageio.metadata.IIOMetadata;
import javax.imageio.spi.ImageReaderSpi;
import javax.imageio.stream.ImageInputStream;

/**
 * ch5v1ImageReader.java -- this class provides the functionality to
 * read an image of format ch5.  This class does not make use of
 * IIOMetadata classes for representing metadata.  A second version of
 * this class will be provided later in this chapter which will
 * correctly represent the metadata
 */
public class ch5v1ImageReader extends ImageReader {
    private ImageInputStream iis;
    private int[] width = null;
    private int[] height = null;
    private int numberImages = -1;


    public ch5v1ImageReader(ImageReaderSpi originatingProvider) {
    super(originatingProvider);
    }

    /**
     * this method returns null for now.  We will revisit it at the
     * end of this chapter after metadata has been discussed.
     */
    public IIOMetadata getStreamMetadata() {
    return null;
    }

    /**
     * this method returns null for now.  We will revisit it at the
     * end of this chapter after metadata has been discussed.
```

LISTING 5.5   Continued

```
    */
    public IIOMetadata getImageMetadata(int imageIndex) {
    return null;
    }

    /**
     * this method sets the input for this ImageReader and also
     * calls the setStreamMetadata method so that the numberImages
     * field is available
     */
    public void setInput(Object object, boolean seekForwardOnly) {
    super.setInput(object, seekForwardOnly);
        if (object == null)
        throw new IllegalArgumentException("input is null");

    if (!(object instanceof ImageInputStream)) {
        String argString = "input not an ImageInputStream";
        throw new IllegalArgumentException(argString);
    }
    iis = (ImageInputStream)object;
    setStreamMetadata(iis);
    }

    /**
     * this method provides suggestions for possible image types that
     * will be used to decode the image specified by index imageIndex.
     * By default, the first image type returned by this method will
     * be the image type of the BufferedImage returned by the
     * ImageReader's getDestination method.  In this case, we are
     * suggesting using an 8 bit grayscale image with no alpha
     * component.
     */
    public Iterator getImageTypes(int imageIndex) {
    java.util.List l = new java.util.ArrayList();;
        int bits = 8;

    /*
     *can convert ch5 format into 8 bit grayscale image with no alpha
     */
        l.add(ImageTypeSpecifier.createGrayscale(bits,
                        DataBuffer.TYPE_BYTE,
                        false));
    return l.iterator();
    }
```

LISTING 5.5 Continued

```java
/**
 * read in the input image specified by index imageIndex using
 * the parameters specified by the ImageReadParam object param
 */
public BufferedImage read(int imageIndex, ImageReadParam param) {

checkIndex(imageIndex);

if (isSeekForwardOnly())
    minIndex = imageIndex;
else
    minIndex = 0;

BufferedImage bimage = null;
    WritableRaster raster = null;

/*
 * this method sets the image metadata so that we can use the
 * getWidth and getHeight methods
 */
setImageMetadata(iis, imageIndex);


int srcWidth = getWidth(imageIndex);
int srcHeight = getHeight(imageIndex);

// initialize values to -1
int dstWidth = -1;
int dstHeight = -1;
int srcRegionWidth = -1;
int srcRegionHeight = -1;
int srcRegionXOffset = -1;
int srcRegionYOffset = -1;
int xSubsamplingFactor = -1;
int ySubsamplingFactor = -1;
    if (param == null)
        param = getDefaultReadParam();

    Iterator imageTypes = getImageTypes(imageIndex);
    try {
    /*
     * get the destination BufferedImage which will
     * be filled using the input image's pixel data
     */
```

LISTING 5.5   Continued

```
        bimage = getDestination(param, imageTypes,
                srcWidth, srcHeight);

/*
 * get Rectangle object which will be used to clip
 * the source image's dimensions.
 */
Rectangle srcRegion = param.getSourceRegion();
if (srcRegion != null) {
srcRegionWidth = (int)srcRegion.getWidth();
srcRegionHeight = (int)srcRegion.getHeight();
srcRegionXOffset = (int)srcRegion.getX();
srcRegionYOffset = (int)srcRegion.getY();

/*
 * correct for overextended source regions
 */
if (srcRegionXOffset + srcRegionWidth > srcWidth)
    dstWidth = srcWidth-srcRegionXOffset;
else
    dstWidth = srcRegionWidth;

if (srcRegionYOffset + srcRegionHeight > srcHeight)
    dstHeight = srcHeight-srcRegionYOffset;
else
    dstHeight = srcRegionHeight;
}
else {
dstWidth = srcWidth;
dstHeight = srcHeight;
srcRegionXOffset = srcRegionYOffset = 0;
}
/*
 * get subsampling factors
 */
xSubsamplingFactor = param.getSourceXSubsampling();
ySubsamplingFactor = param.getSourceYSubsampling();

/**
 * dstWidth and dstHeight should be
 * equal to bimage.getWidth() and bimage.getHeight()
 * after these next two instructions
 */
dstWidth = (dstWidth-1)/xSubsamplingFactor + 1;
```

LISTING 5.5   Continued

```
        dstHeight = (dstHeight-1)/ySubsamplingFactor + 1;
    }
    catch (IIOException e) {
        System.err.println("Can't create destination BufferedImage");
    }
    raster = bimage.getWritableTile(0, 0);


/* using the parameters specified by the ImageReadParam
 * object, read the image image data into the destination
 * BufferedImage
 */
    byte[] srcBuffer = new byte[srcWidth];
    byte[] dstBuffer = new byte[dstWidth];
int jj;
int index;
    try {
    for (int j=0; j<srcHeight; j++) {
    iis.readFully(srcBuffer, 0, srcWidth);

    jj = j - srcRegionYOffset;
    if (jj % ySubsamplingFactor == 0) {
        jj /= ySubsamplingFactor;
        if ((jj >= 0) && (jj < dstHeight)) {
        for (int i=0;i<dstWidth;i++) {
            index = srcRegionXOffset+i*xSubsamplingFactor;
            dstBuffer[i] = srcBuffer[index];
        }
        raster.setDataElements(0, jj, dstWidth,
                      1, dstBuffer);
        }
    }
    }
    }
    catch (IOException e) {
        bimage = null;
    }
    return bimage;
}

/**
 * this method sets the image metadata for the image indexed by
 * index imageIndex.  This method is specific for the ch5 format
 * and thus only sets the image width and image height
 */
```

LISTING 5.5   Continued

```
private void setImageMetadata(ImageInputStream iis,
             int imageIndex) {
try {
    String s;
    s = iis.readLine();
    width[imageIndex] = Integer.parseInt(s.trim());
    s = iis.readLine();
    height[imageIndex] = Integer.parseInt(s);
}
catch (IOException exception) {
}
}


/**
 * this method sets the stream metadata for the images represented
 * by the ImageInputStream iis.  This method is specific for the
 * ch5 format and thus only sets the numberImages field.
 */
private void setStreamMetadata(ImageInputStream iis) {
try {
    String magicNumber = iis.readLine();
    numberImages = Integer.parseInt(iis.readLine().trim());
    width = new int[numberImages];
    height = new int[numberImages];
    for (int i=0;i<numberImages;i++)
    width[i] = height[i] = -1;
}
catch (IOException exception) {
}
}


/**
 * This method can only be used after the stream metadata
 * has been set (which occurs in the setInput method).
 * Else it will return a -1
 */
public int getNumImages(boolean allowSearch) {
return numberImages;
}


/**
 * This method can only be used successfully after the image
 * metadata has been set (which occurs in the setInput method).
 * Else it returns -1
 */
```

LISTING 5.5   Continued

```
public int getHeight(int imageIndex) {
if (height == null)
    return -1;
checkIndex(imageIndex);

return height[imageIndex];
}

/**
 * This method can only be used successfully after the image
 * metadata has been set (which occurs in the setInput method).
 * Else it returns -1
 */
public int getWidth(int imageIndex) {
if (width == null)
    return -1;
checkIndex(imageIndex);

return width[imageIndex];
}

private void checkIndex(int imageIndex) {
if (imageIndex >= numberImages) {
    String argString = "imageIndex >= number of images";
    throw new IndexOutOfBoundsException(argString);
}
if (imageIndex < minIndex) {
    String argString = "imageIndex < minIndex";
    throw new IndexOutOfBoundsException(argString);
}
}
}
}
```

ImageWriteParam

The `javax.imageio.ImageWriteParam` object dictates the dimensions of the output image just
as the `ImageReadParam` dictated the dimensions of the input `BufferedImage`. Also, just as it
was up to the plug-in designer to correctly use the `ImageReadParam` values to clip and subsample the input image to fill a `BufferedImage`, the plug-in designer must use the
`ImageWriteParam` values to correctly clip and subsample the output `BufferedImage` to produce
the correct output image. So just like the `ImageReadParam`, the `ImageWriteParam` has two different roles. One role is to allow the user to specify how an image should be written out and
the other is to provide these values to the `ImageWriter`'s write method.

Besides a `BufferedImage`, an `ImageWriter` might also use a `Raster` for an output image source.

A `ImageWriteParam` object can be obtained using the following `ImageWriter` method:

```
public ImageWriteParam getDefaultWriteParam()
```

After a reference to an `ImageWriteParam` object is obtained, a user then makes changes to the state of this object in order to specify how the output image should be saved. The two most common methods of the `ImageWriteParam` class are the same as for the `ImageReadParam` class, namely

```
public void setSourceRegion(Rectangle sourceRegion)
```

and

```
public void setSourceSubsampling(int sourceXSubsampling,
                                 int sourceYSubsampling,
                                 int subsamplingXOffset,
                                 int subsamplingYOffset)
```

In the end of this chapter, an `ImageWriter` will be presented so that the use of the `ImageWriteParam` object in writing the output image can be better understood.

IIOParamController

Besides obtaining an `IIOParam` (superclass of `ImageReadParam` and `ImageWriteParam`) object and changing its state through method calls, there is another way to control image reading and writing. That way is by using an `javax.imageio.IIOParamController`. An `IIOParamController` is used to set the `IIOParam` object to the correct state by using a controlling class provided by the plug-in, such as

```
ImageReadParam param = reader.getDefaultReadParam();
IIOParamController controller = param.getController();
if (controller != null)
    controller.activate(param);
```

Typically, this controlling class is a graphical user interface (GUI), but it could be any class that implements the following method:

```
public void activate(IIOParam param)
```

Metadata

Corresponding to an image is a set of non-pixel data that represents properties of that image. Some examples are width, height, color table, color space, and so on. Although there are `ImageReader` methods for obtaining the image width and height(such as `getWidth` and `getHeight`), it is not possible to provide a separate method for each piece of metadata that could be contained in an image format. Instead, the `ImageReader` class provides the metadata information collectively using the following two methods:

```
IIOMetadata getImageMetadata(int imageIndex)
```

and

```
IIOMetadata getStreamMetadata()
```

The first method provides the metadata for the image specified by the index `imageIndex`, while the second method provides the metadata that is descriptive of all images contained in a single stream. For example, a single file could hold any number of images that all share a common color table. In this situation, the color table could be described by the stream metadata. Another example is the ch5 format that we are using in this chapter. The number of images is part of the stream metadata and the width and height measures are part of each image's metadata.

XML and XML APIs

Extensible Markup Language (XML) is a language for creating and using markup languages for data storage and organization. The different data elements are delimited through the use of tags. The exact tags are not predefined in XML, but are instead defined by the implementer using XML. For example, the following XML code describes an example of the image metadata for the ch5 format that we've been using in this chapter. This code block shows two elements, `ch5.imageio.ch5image_1.00` and `imageDimensions` with the `imageDimensions` element containing attributes of `imageWidth` and `imageHeight`.

```
<ch5.imageio.ch5image_1.00>
    <imageDimensions imageWidth=256 imageHeight=256>
    </imageDimensions>
</ch5.imageio.chstream_1.00>
```

Within a single XML document, there is one main element in which all other elements are contained. Thus, this main element can be considered a parent element to all other elements within the document. Similarly, each of the elements within an XML file might be considered a parent to any elements they contain as well as to any of their attributes. Using this line of reasoning, it can be useful to consider the XML document as a tree with the main element being the root node of the tree.

There are two main ways for working with XML documents in Java. The first way is through a Simple Parser for XML (SAXP) that treats the XML document like a serial stream of data. This parser generates events whenever anything interesting occurs while a data stream is being parsed. When working with a SAXP parser, you must implement methods to handle the events as they arise. The advantages of using SAXP parsers is that they're fast and they don't require much memory, because they do not store the parsed elements. The second method for working with XML documents is with a Document Object Model (DOM) that stores the entire XML document in a tree format. Instead of generating events, it simply gives an application access to this DOM tree. It's important to note that the DOM tree nodes do not simply contain the elements and attributes, but objects representing elements and attributes. Thus, each of the DOM nodes contain functionality for manipulating this tree. Besides element and attribute node types, there are also node types for document, document type, processing instruction, entity, and so on.

IIOMetadata

`javax.imageio.metadata.IIOMetadata` classes are used to represent metadata while also providing the capability to access this information as a tree of
`javax.imageio.metadata.IIOMetadataNode` objects. The `IIOMetadataNode` class implements the Java DOM `Element` interface (which extends the DOM `Node` interface) so that one can treat stream and image metadata using the XML DOM API. For example, to convert a `IIOMetadata` object into a DOM tree, simply use the following method:

```
public org.w3c.dom.Node getAsTree(String formatName)
```

where `formatName` is the desired metadata format.

When designing `IIOMetadata` classes, designers can create stream and image metadata classes any way they like, although generally the closer a metadata format follows a particular image format, the less able it is to describe any other image formats. Often, there are tradeoffs when designing a metadata format between the number of image formats that it can be used for, and how much information each of these applicable image formats will lose when using this format.

TIP

There is one plug-in–neutral metadata format already defined, and it is called `com.sun.imageio_1.0`. All image formats can be expressed using this format, but many will contain some information that this format cannot express and will be lost. This format has child nodes for chroma, compression, dimension, document, text, tile, and transparency.

Final Plug-in Code

As discussed previously, ImageReaders and ImageWriters may be made known to the JVM through the use of plug-ins. The remainder of the chapter will be devoted to presenting the code listings for the ch5ImageReader and ch5ImageWriter classes, along with their corresponding service provider interfaces and metadata classes.

ch5ImageReader

Listing 5.6 is identical to Listing 5.5, except that the metadata formats have now been defined so the getMetadata and getImageData methods no longer return null.

The way metadata is used in this ImageReader class is that the setInput and read methods obtain the stream and image metadata respectively (see Table 5.2). This metadata is then available to be returned to an application that uses the ImageReader's getStreamMetadata and getImageMetadata methods.

TABLE 5.2   Relationship Between ImageReader Methods and Metadata in the ch5ImageReader Class

ImageReader *Method*	*Effect on Metadata*
setInput	Decodes stream metadata
read	Decodes image metadata
getStreamMetadata	Converts stream metadata to an IIOMetadata object that is returned
getImageMetadata	Converts image metadata to an IIOMetadata object that is returned

LISTING 5.6   ch5ImageReader.java

```
package ch5.imageio.plugins;

import java.io.*;
import java.util.*;
import java.awt.*;
import java.awt.image.*;
import javax.imageio.IIOException;
import javax.imageio.ImageReader;
import javax.imageio.ImageTypeSpecifier;
import javax.imageio.ImageReadParam;
import javax.imageio.metadata.IIOMetadata;
import javax.imageio.spi.ImageReaderSpi;
```

LISTING 5.6   Continued

```java
import javax.imageio.stream.ImageInputStream;
import ch5.imageio.plugins.*;

/**
 * ch5ImageReader.java -- this class provides the functionality to
 * read an image of format ch5.
 */
public class ch5ImageReader extends ImageReader {
    private ImageInputStream iis;
    private ch5ImageMetadata[] imagemd;
    private ch5StreamMetadata streammd;

    public ch5ImageReader(ImageReaderSpi originatingProvider) {
    super(originatingProvider);
    }

    /**
     * return the ch5StreamMetadata object instantiated in
     * the setStreamMetadata method
     */
    public IIOMetadata getStreamMetadata() {
    return streammd;
    }

    /**
     * return the ch5ImageMetadata object instantiated in
     * the setImageMetadata method
     */
    public IIOMetadata getImageMetadata(int imageIndex) {
    return imagemd[imageIndex];
    }

    /**
     * this method sets the input for this ImageReader and also
     * calls the setStreamMetadata method so that the numberImages
     * field is available
     */
    public void setInput(Object object, boolean seekForwardOnly) {
    super.setInput(object, seekForwardOnly);
        if (object == null)
        throw new IllegalArgumentException("input is null");

    if (!(object instanceof ImageInputStream)) {
        String argString = "input not an ImageInputStream";
        throw new IllegalArgumentException(argString);
```

LISTING 5.6   Continued

```java
    }
iis = (ImageInputStream)object;
setStreamMetadata(iis);
}


/**
 * this method provides suggestions for possible image types that
 * will be used to decode the image specified by index imageIndex.
 * By default, the first image type returned by this method will
 * be the image type of the BufferedImage returned by the
 * ImageReader's getDestination method.  In this case, we are
 * suggesting using an 8 bit grayscale image with no alpha
 * component.
 */
public Iterator getImageTypes(int imageIndex) {
java.util.List l = new java.util.ArrayList();;
    int bits = 8;

/*
 * can convert ch5 format into 8 bit grayscale image with no alpha
 */
    l.add(ImageTypeSpecifier.createGrayscale(bits,
                    DataBuffer.TYPE_BYTE,
                    false));
return l.iterator();
}


/**
 * read in the input image specified by index imageIndex using
 * the parameters specified by the ImageReadParam object param
 */
public BufferedImage read(int imageIndex, ImageReadParam param) {

checkIndex(imageIndex);

if (isSeekForwardOnly())
    minIndex = imageIndex;
else
    minIndex = 0;

BufferedImage bimage = null;
    WritableRaster raster = null;
```

Listing 5.6   Continued

```
/*
 * this method sets the image metadata so that we can use the
 * getWidth and getHeight methods
 */
setImageMetadata(iis, imageIndex);

int srcWidth = getWidth(imageIndex);
int srcHeight = getHeight(imageIndex);

// initialize values to -1
int dstWidth = -1;
int dstHeight = -1;
int srcRegionWidth = -1;
int srcRegionHeight = -1;
int srcRegionXOffset = -1;
int srcRegionYOffset = -1;
int xSubsamplingFactor = -1;
int ySubsamplingFactor = -1;
    if (param == null)
        param = getDefaultReadParam();

    Iterator imageTypes = getImageTypes(imageIndex);
    try {
    /*
     * get the destination BufferedImage which will
     * be filled using the input image's pixel data
     */
        bimage = getDestination(param, imageTypes,
                srcWidth, srcHeight);

    /*
     * get Rectangle object which will be used to clip
     * the source image's dimensions.
     */
    Rectangle srcRegion = param.getSourceRegion();
    if (srcRegion != null) {
    srcRegionWidth = (int)srcRegion.getWidth();
    srcRegionHeight = (int)srcRegion.getHeight();
    srcRegionXOffset = (int)srcRegion.getX();
    srcRegionYOffset = (int)srcRegion.getY();

    /*
     * correct for overextended source regions
     */
    if (srcRegionXOffset + srcRegionWidth > srcWidth)
```

5

Image I/O API

LISTING 5.6 Continued

```
            dstWidth = srcWidth-srcRegionXOffset;
        else
            dstWidth = srcRegionWidth;

        if (srcRegionYOffset + srcRegionHeight > srcHeight)
            dstHeight = srcHeight-srcRegionYOffset;
        else
            dstHeight = srcRegionHeight;
        }
        else {
        dstWidth = srcWidth;
        dstHeight = srcHeight;
        srcRegionXOffset = srcRegionYOffset = 0;
        }
        /*
         * get subsampling factors
         */
        xSubsamplingFactor = param.getSourceXSubsampling();
        ySubsamplingFactor = param.getSourceYSubsampling();

        /**
         * dstWidth and dstHeight should be
         * equal to bimage.getWidth() and bimage.getHeight()
         * after these next two instructions
         */
        dstWidth = (dstWidth-1)/xSubsamplingFactor + 1;
        dstHeight = (dstHeight-1)/ySubsamplingFactor + 1;
        }
        catch (IIOException e) {
            System.err.println("Can't create destination BufferedImage");
        }
        raster = bimage.getWritableTile(0, 0);

    /* using the parameters specified by the ImageReadParam
     * object, read the image image data into the destination
     * BufferedImage
     */
        byte[] srcBuffer = new byte[srcWidth];
        byte[] dstBuffer = new byte[dstWidth];
    int jj;
    int index;
        try {
        for (int j=0; j<srcHeight; j++) {
        iis.readFully(srcBuffer, 0, srcWidth);
```

Listing 5.6   Continued

```
        jj = j - srcRegionYOffset;
        if (jj % ySubsamplingFactor == 0) {
            jj /= ySubsamplingFactor;
            if ((jj >= 0) && (jj < dstHeight)) {
            for (int i=0;i<dstWidth;i++) {
                index = srcRegionXOffset+i*xSubsamplingFactor;
                dstBuffer[i] = srcBuffer[index];
            }
            raster.setDataElements(0, jj, dstWidth,
                          1, dstBuffer);
            }
        }
        }
        }
        catch (IOException e) {
            bimage = null;
        }
        return bimage;
    }

/**
 * this method sets the image metadata for the image indexed by
 * index imageIndex.  This method is specific for the ch5 format
 * and thus only sets the image width and image height
 */
private void setImageMetadata(ImageInputStream iis,
              int imageIndex) {
imagemd[imageIndex] = new ch5ImageMetadata();
try {
    String s;
    s = iis.readLine();
    imagemd[imageIndex].imageWidth = Integer.parseInt(s.trim());
    s = iis.readLine();
    imagemd[imageIndex].imageHeight = Integer.parseInt(s.trim());
}
catch (IOException exception) {
}
}

/**
 * this method sets the stream metadata for the images represented
 * by the ImageInputStream iis.  This method is specific for the
 * ch5 format and thus only sets the numberImages field.
 */
private void setStreamMetadata(ImageInputStream iis) {
```

LISTING 5.6   Continued

```java
streammd = new ch5StreamMetadata();
try {
    String magicNumber = iis.readLine();
    int numImages = Integer.parseInt(iis.readLine().trim());
    streammd.numberImages = numImages;
    imagemd = new ch5ImageMetadata[streammd.numberImages];
}
catch (IOException exception) {
}
}


/**
 * This method can only be used after the stream metadata
 * has been set (which occurs in the setInput method).
 * Else it will return a -1
 */
public int getNumImages(boolean allowSearch) {
return streammd.numberImages;
}


/**
 * This method can only be used after the stream metadata
 * has been set (which occurs in the setInput method).
 * Else it will return a -1
 */
public int getHeight(int imageIndex) {
if (imagemd == null)
    return -1;
checkIndex(imageIndex);

return imagemd[imageIndex].imageHeight;
}

/**
 * This method can only be used after the stream metadata
 * has been set (which occurs in the setInput method).
 * Else it will return a -1
 */
public int getWidth(int imageIndex) {
if (imagemd == null)
    return -1;
checkIndex(imageIndex);
```

LISTING 5.6   Continued

```
    return imagemd[imageIndex].imageWidth;
    }

    private void checkIndex(int imageIndex) {
    if (imageIndex >= streammd.numberImages) {
        String argString = "imageIndex >= number of images";
        throw new IndexOutOfBoundsException(argString);
    }
    if (imageIndex < minIndex) {
        String argString = "imageIndex < minIndex";
        throw new IndexOutOfBoundsException(argString);
    }
    }
}
```

ch5ImageWriter

The way metadata is used in this `ImageWriter` class is that the `write` method writes both the stream and image metadata (see Table 5.3 and Listing 5.7). Because the `write` method might be called any number of times for different images, a boolean variable (`StreamMetadataWritten`) is used to ensure that the stream metadata is only written during the initial `write` method call.

The metadata that is being written must be obtained from the application and passed to the `ImageWriter`. The application gets this metadata by instantiating `IIOMetadata` objects for the stream and image metadata (`ch5StreamMetadata` and `ch5ImageMetadata` in this example), and then setting them to the correct state.

TABLE 5.3   Relationship Between `ImageWriter` Methods and Metadata

ImageWriter *Method*	*Effect on Metadata*
Constructor	Passes stream and image metadata into the `ImageWriter`.
write	1. If stream metadata hasn't already been encoded, it encodes stream metadata.
	2. Encodes image metadata.

LISTING 5.7   ch5ImageWriter.java

```
package ch5.imageio.plugins;

import java.io.*;
import java.util.*;
```

5

IMAGE I/O API

LISTING 5.7 Continued

```
import java.awt.*;
import java.awt.image.*;
import org.w3c.dom.*;
import javax.imageio.IIOImage;
import javax.imageio.ImageTypeSpecifier;
import javax.imageio.ImageWriter;
import javax.imageio.ImageWriteParam;
import javax.imageio.metadata.IIOMetadata;
import javax.imageio.metadata.IIOMetadataNode;
import javax.imageio.spi.ImageWriterSpi;
import javax.imageio.stream.ImageInputStream;
import javax.imageio.stream.ImageOutputStream;

/**
 * ch5ImageWriter.java -- this class provides the functionality to
 * write an image of format ch5.
 */
public class ch5ImageWriter extends ImageWriter {
    private ImageOutputStream ios;
    private boolean streamMetadataRead;

    public ch5ImageWriter(ImageWriterSpi originatingProvider) {
     super(originatingProvider);
     streamMetadataRead = false;
    }

    /**
     * this method is used to convert an ImageReader's image metadata
     * which is in a particular format into image metadata that can be
     * used for this ImageWriter.  Primarily this is used for
     * transcoding (format conversion).  This ImageWriter does not
     * support such conversions
     */
    public IIOMetadata convertImageMetadata(IIOMetadata metadata,
                        ImageTypeSpecifier specifier,
                        ImageWriteParam param) {
     return null;
    }

    /**
     * this method is used to convert an ImageReader's stream metadata
     * which is in a particular format into stream metadata that can
     * be used for this ImageWriter.  Primarily this is used for
     * transcoding (format conversion).  This ImageWriter does not
```

LISTING 5.7   Continued

```
 * support such conversions
 */
public IIOMetadata convertStreamMetadata(IIOMetadata metadata,
                        ImageWriteParam param) {
 return null;
}

/**
 * provide default values for the image metadata
 */
public IIOMetadata getDefaultImageMetadata(ImageTypeSpecifier specifier,
                        ImageWriteParam param) {
 ch5ImageMetadata imagemd = new ch5ImageMetadata();
 imagemd.initialize(256, 256);  // default image size
 return imagemd;
}

/**
 * provide default values for the stream metadata
 */
public IIOMetadata getDefaultStreamMetadata(ImageWriteParam param) {
 ch5StreamMetadata streammd = new ch5StreamMetadata();
 streammd.initialize(1);  // default number of images
 return streammd;
}


/**
 * write out the output image specified by index imageIndex using
 * the parameters specified by the ImageWriteParam object param
 */
public void write(IIOMetadata metadata,
          IIOImage iioimage,
          ImageWriteParam param) {
 Node root = null;
 Node dimensionsElementNode = null;
 Raster raster = iioimage.getRaster();

 /*
  * Set stream metadata if it hasn't been set yet
  */
 if (streamMetadataRead == false) {
     root = metadata.getAsTree("ch5.imageio.ch5stream_1.0");
     dimensionsElementNode = root.getFirstChild();
```

5

IMAGE I/O API

LISTING 5.7   Continued

```
        Node numberImagesAttributeNode
= dimensionsElementNode.getAttributes().getNamedItem("numberImages");
        String numberImages = numberImagesAttributeNode.getNodeValue();
        try {
        ios.writeBytes("5\n");
        ios.writeBytes(numberImages+"\n");
        streamMetadataRead = true;
        }
        catch (IOException exception) {
        }
    }

    ch5ImageMetadata imageMetadata = (ch5ImageMetadata)iioimage.getMetadata();
    root = imageMetadata.getAsTree("ch5.imageio.ch5image_1.0");
    dimensionsElementNode = root.getFirstChild();

    Node widthAttributeNode = dimensionsElementNode.getAttributes().
    ➥getNamedItem("imageWidth");
String widthString = widthAttributeNode.getNodeValue();

    Node heightAttributeNode = dimensionsElementNode.getAttributes().
    ➥getNamedItem("imageHeight");
    String heightString = heightAttributeNode.getNodeValue();

    int sourceWidth = Integer.parseInt(widthString);
    int sourceHeight = Integer.parseInt(heightString);
    int destinationWidth = -1;
    int destinationHeight = -1;
    int sourceRegionWidth = -1;
    int sourceRegionHeight = -1;
    int sourceRegionXOffset = -1;
    int sourceRegionYOffset = -1;
    int xSubsamplingFactor = -1;
    int ySubsamplingFactor = -1;

        if (param == null)
            param = getDefaultWriteParam();

    /*
     * get Rectangle object which will be used to clip
     * the source image's dimensions.
     */
    Rectangle sourceRegion = param.getSourceRegion();
    if (sourceRegion != null) {
```

LISTING 5.7   Continued

```
        sourceRegionWidth = (int)sourceRegion.getWidth();
        sourceRegionHeight = (int)sourceRegion.getHeight();
        sourceRegionXOffset = (int)sourceRegion.getX();
        sourceRegionYOffset = (int)sourceRegion.getY();

        /*
         * correct for overextended source regions
         */
        if (sourceRegionXOffset + sourceRegionWidth > sourceWidth)
        destinationWidth = sourceWidth-sourceRegionXOffset;
        else
        destinationWidth = sourceRegionWidth;

        if (sourceRegionYOffset + sourceRegionHeight > sourceHeight)
        destinationHeight = sourceHeight-sourceRegionYOffset;
        else
        destinationHeight = sourceRegionHeight;
    }
    else {
        destinationWidth = sourceWidth;
        destinationHeight = sourceHeight;
        sourceRegionXOffset = sourceRegionYOffset = 0;
    }
    /*
     * get subsampling factors
     */
    xSubsamplingFactor = param.getSourceXSubsampling();
    ySubsamplingFactor = param.getSourceYSubsampling();

    destinationWidth = (destinationWidth-1)/xSubsamplingFactor + 1;
    destinationHeight = (destinationHeight-1)/ySubsamplingFactor + 1;

    byte[] sourceBuffer;
    byte[] destinationBuffer = new byte[destinationWidth];

        try {
        ios.writeBytes(new String(destinationWidth+ "\n"));
        ios.writeBytes(new String(destinationHeight+ "\n"));

        int jj;
        for (int j=0; j<sourceWidth; j++) {
        sourceBuffer= (byte[])raster.getDataElements(0, j, sourceWidth, 1,
        ➥ null);
jj = j - sourceRegionYOffset;
```

LISTING 5.7   Continued

```
            if (jj % ySubsamplingFactor == 0) {
                jj /= ySubsamplingFactor;
                if ((jj >= 0) && (jj < destinationHeight)) {
                for (int i=0;i<destinationWidth;i++)
                    destinationBuffer[i] =
                    ➥sourceBuffer[sourceRegionXOffset+i*xSubsamplingFactor];
                ios.write(destinationBuffer, 0, destinationWidth);
                ios.flush();
                }
            }
            }
        }
        catch (IOException e) {
         System.err.println("IOException: " + e.getMessage());
        }
    }

    public void setOutput(Object output) {
     super.setOutput(output);

        if (output == null)
         throw new IllegalArgumentException("output is null");

     if (!(output instanceof ImageOutputStream))
         throw new IllegalArgumentException("output not an ImageOutputStream");

     ios =  (ImageOutputStream)output;
     streamMetadataRead = false;
    }
}
```

ch5StreamMetadata

This is the class used to hold the stream metadata (see Listing 5.8). For reading, its values are taken from the input stream. For writing, its values must be set by the application. The document type definition (DTD) for this class is the following:

```
<!ELEMENT ch5.imageio.ch5stream_1.00 (imageDimensions)>
<!ATTLIST imageDimensions
   numberImages  CDATA  #REQUIRED
>
```

Clearly, this is a very minimal set of stream metadata used for illustrative purposes. In practice, these classes will be much more complicated.

LISTING 5.8   ch5StreamMetadata.java

```java
package ch5.imageio.plugins;

import java.io.UnsupportedEncodingException;
import java.util.ArrayList;
import java.util.List;
import javax.imageio.ImageTypeSpecifier;
import javax.imageio.metadata.IIOMetadata;
import javax.imageio.metadata.IIOMetadataNode;
import javax.imageio.metadata.IIOMetadataFormat;
import org.w3c.dom.Node;


/**
 * ch5StreamMetadata.java -- holds stream metadata for the ch5 format.
 * The internal tree for holding this metadata is read only
 */
public class ch5StreamMetadata extends IIOMetadata {
    static final String
        nativeMetadataFormatName = "ch5.imageio.ch5stream_1.0";

    static final String[] metadataFormatNames = {
        nativeMetadataFormatName
    };

    public int numberImages;

    public ch5StreamMetadata() {
        super(nativeMetadataFormatName, metadataFormatNames);
        numberImages = -1;
    }

    public boolean isReadOnly() {
        return true;
    }

    /**
     * IIOMetadataFormat objects are meant to describe the structure of
     * metadata returned from the getAsTree method.  In this case,
     * no such description is available
     */
    public IIOMetadataFormat getMetadataFormat(String formatName) {
        if (formatName.equals(nativeMetadataFormatName)) {
            return null;
        } else {
```

LISTING 5.8   Continued

```java
                throw new IllegalArgumentException("Not a recognized format!");
        }
    }

    /**
     * returns the stream metadata in a tree corresponding to the
     * provided formatName
     */
    public Node getAsTree(String formatName) {
        if (formatName.equals(nativeMetadataFormatName)) {
            return getNativeTree();
        } else {
            throw new IllegalArgumentException("Not a recognized format!");
        }
    }

    /**
     * returns the stream metadata in a tree using the following format
     * <!ELEMENT ch5.imageio.ch5stream_1.0 (imageDimensions)>
     * <!ATTLIST imageDimensions
     *      numberImages   CDATA   #REQUIRED
     */
    private Node getNativeTree() {
        IIOMetadataNode node; // scratch node

        IIOMetadataNode root =
            new IIOMetadataNode(nativeMetadataFormatName);

        // Image descriptor
        node = new IIOMetadataNode("imageDimensions");
        node.setAttribute("numberImages", Integer.toString(numberImages));
        root.appendChild(node);

        return root;
    }


    public void setFromTree(String formatName, Node root) {
        throw new IllegalStateException("Metadata is read-only!");
    }

    public void mergeTree(String formatName, Node root) {
        throw new IllegalStateException("Metadata is read-only!");
    }
```

LISTING 5.8   Continued

```
public void reset() {
    throw new IllegalStateException("Metadata is read-only!");
}


/**
 * initialize the stream metadata element numberImages
 */
public void initialize(int numberImages) {
    this.numberImages = numberImages;
}
}
```

ch5ImageMetadata

This is the class used to hold the image metadata (see Listing 5.9). For reading, its values are taken from the input stream. For writing, its values must be set by the application. The DTD for this class is the following:

```
<!ELEMENT ch5.imageio.ch5image_1.0 (imageDimensions)>
<!ATTLIST imageDimensions
    imageWidth    CDATA  #REQUIRED
    imageHeight   CDATA  #REQUIRED
>
```

As was true for the ch5StreamMetadata class, this is a very minimal set of metadata used for illustrative purposes, and in practice these classes will be much more complicated.

LISTING 5.9   ch5ImageMetadata.java

```
package ch5.imageio.plugins;

import java.io.UnsupportedEncodingException;
import java.util.ArrayList;
import java.util.List;
import javax.imageio.ImageTypeSpecifier;
import javax.imageio.metadata.IIOMetadata;
import javax.imageio.metadata.IIOMetadataNode;
import javax.imageio.metadata.IIOMetadataFormat;
import org.w3c.dom.Node;

/**
 * ch5ImageMetadata.java -- holds image metadata for the ch5 format.
 * The internal tree for holding this metadata is read only
```

LISTING 5.9   Continued

```java
*/
public class ch5ImageMetadata extends IIOMetadata {
    static final String
        nativeMetadataFormatName = "ch5.imageio.ch5image_1.0";

    static final String[] metadataFormatNames = {
        nativeMetadataFormatName
    };

    public int imageWidth;
    public int imageHeight;

    public ch5ImageMetadata() {
        super(nativeMetadataFormatName, metadataFormatNames);
        imageWidth = -1;
        imageHeight = -1;
    }

    public boolean isReadOnly() {
        return true;
    }

    /**
     * IIOMetadataFormat objects are meant to describe the structure of
     * metadata returned from the getAsTree method.  In this case,
     * no such description is available
     */
    public IIOMetadataFormat getMetadataFormat(String formatName) {
        if (formatName.equals(nativeMetadataFormatName)) {
            return null;
        } else {
            throw new IllegalArgumentException("Not a recognized format!");
        }
    }

    /**
     * returns the image metadata in a tree corresponding to the
     * provided formatName
     */
    public Node getAsTree(String formatName) {
        if (formatName.equals(nativeMetadataFormatName)) {
            return getNativeTree();
        } else {
```

LISTING 5.9   Continued

```
            throw new IllegalArgumentException("Not a recognized format!");
        }
    }

    /**
     * returns the image metadata in a tree using the following format
     * <!ELEMENT ch5.imageio.ch5image_1.0 (imageDimensions)>
     * <!ATTLIST imageDimensions
     *       imageWidth    CDATA   #REQUIRED
     *       imageHeight   CDATA   #REQUIRED
     */
    private Node getNativeTree() {
        IIOMetadataNode root =
            new IIOMetadataNode(nativeMetadataFormatName);

        IIOMetadataNode node = new IIOMetadataNode("imageDimensions");
        node.setAttribute("imageWidth", Integer.toString(imageWidth));
        node.setAttribute("imageHeight", Integer.toString(imageHeight));
        root.appendChild(node);

        return root;
    }

    public void setFromTree(String formatName, Node root) {
        throw new IllegalStateException("Metadata is read-only!");
    }

    public void mergeTree(String formatName, Node root) {
        throw new IllegalStateException("Metadata is read-only!");
    }

    public void reset() {
        throw new IllegalStateException("Metadata is read-only!");
    }

    /**
     * initialize the image metadata elements width and height
     */
    public void initialize(int width, int height) {
        imageWidth = width;
        imageHeight = height;
    }
}
```

5

IMAGE I/O API

ch5ImageReaderSpi

Listing 5.10 is identical to Listing 5.3, except that the metadata formats have now been defined so non-null values are provided for the metadata-related objects.

LISTING 5.10   ch5ImageReaderSpi.java

```java
package ch5.imageio.plugins;

import java.io.*;
import java.util.*;
import javax.imageio.ImageReader;
import javax.imageio.spi.ImageReaderSpi;
import javax.imageio.stream.ImageInputStream;

/**
 *  Simple, functional ImageReaderSpi used to understand how
 *  information regarding format name, suffices and mime types
 *  get passed to ImageIO static methods
 */
public class ch5ImageReaderSpi extends ImageReaderSpi {

    static final String[] suffixes = {"ch5", "CH5"};
    static final String[] names = {"ch5"};
    static final String[] MIMETypes = {"image/ch5"};

    static final String version = "1.00";
    static final String readerCN = "ch5.imageio.plugins.ch5ImageReader";
    static final String vendorName = "CompanyName";

    //writerSpiNames
    static final String[] wSN={"ch5.imageio.plugins.ch5ImageWriterSpi"};

    //StreamMetadataFormatNames and StreamMetadataFormatClassNames
    static final boolean supportedStandardStreamMetadataFormat = false;
    static final String nativeStreamMFN = "ch5.imageio.ch5stream_1.00";
    static final String nativeStreamMFCN = "ch5.imageio.ch5stream";
    static final String[] extraStreamMFN = null;
    static final String[] extraStreamMFCN = null;

    //ImageMetadataFormatNames and ImageMetadataFormatClassNames
    static final boolean supportedStandardImageMetadataFormat = false;
    static final String nativeImageMFN = "ch5.imageio.ch5image1.00";
    static final String nativeImageMFCN = "ch5.imageio.ch5image";
    static final String[] extraImageMFN = null;
    static final String[] extraImageMFCN = null;
```

LISTING 5.10   Continued

```java
public ch5ImageReaderSpi() {
super(vendorName,
      version,
      names,
      suffixes,
      MIMETypes,
      readerCN, //readerClassName
      STANDARD_INPUT_TYPE,
      wSN, //writerSpiNames
          false,
          nativeStreamMFN,
          nativeStreamMFCN,
          extraStreamMFN,
          extraStreamMFCN,
          false,
          nativeImageMFN,
          nativeImageMFCN,
          extraImageMFN,
          extraImageMFCN);
}

public String getDescription(Locale locale) {
return "Demo ch5 image reader, version " + version;
}

public ImageReader createReaderInstance(Object extension) {
return new ch5ImageReader(this);
}

/**
 * This method gets called when an application wants to see if
 * the input image's format can be decoded by this ImageReader.
 * In this case, we'll simply check the first byte of data to
 * see if its a 5 which is the format type's magic number
 */
public boolean canDecodeInput(Object input) {
boolean reply = false;

ImageInputStream iis = (ImageInputStream)input;
iis.mark(); // mark where we are in ImageInputStream
try {
    String magicNumber = iis.readLine().trim();
    iis.reset(); // reset stream back to marked location
    if (magicNumber.equals("5"))
```

LISTING 5.10 Continued

```
        reply = true;
    }
    catch (IOException exception) {
    }
    return reply;
    }
}
```

ch5ImageWriterSpi

Listing 5.11 is identical to Listing 5.4, except that the metadata formats have now been defined so non-null values are provided for the metadata-related objects.

LISTING 5.11   ch5ImageWriterSpi.java

```
package ch5.imageio.plugins;

import java.io.*;
import java.util.*;
import java.awt.image.BufferedImage;
import javax.imageio.ImageWriter;
import javax.imageio.ImageTypeSpecifier;
import javax.imageio.spi.ImageWriterSpi;
import javax.imageio.stream.ImageInputStream;

/**
 * Simple, functional ImageWriterSpi used to understand how
 * information regarding format name, suffices and mime types
 * get passed to ImageIO static methods
 */
public class ch5ImageWriterSpi extends ImageWriterSpi {

    static final String[] suffixes = {"ch5", "CH5"};
    static final String[] names = {"ch5"};
    static final String[] MIMETypes = {"image/ch5" };

    static final String version = "1.00";
    static final String writerClassName = "ch5.imageio.plugins.ch5ImageWriter";
    static final String vendorName = "Company Name";
    static final String[] readerSpiNames =
    ➥{"ch5.imagio.plugins.ch5ImageReaderSpi"};
    /*
    static final String nativeStreamMetadataFormatName =
    ➥"ch5.imageio.ch5stream_1.0";
```

LISTING 5.11   Continued

```
static final String[] streamMetadataFormatNames =
➥{nativeStreamMetadataFormatName};
static final String nativeImageMetadataFormatName =
➥"ch5.imageio.ch5image_1.0";
static final String[] imageMetadataFormatNames =
➥{nativeImageMetadataFormatName};
*/

static final String nativeStreamMetadataFormatName =
➥"ch5.imageio.ch5stream_1.00";
static final String nativeStreamMetadataFormatClassName =
➥"ch5.imageio.ch5stream";
static final String[] extraStreamMetadataFormatNames = {null};
static final String[] extraStreamMetadataFormatClassNames = {null};

static final String nativeImageMetadataFormatName =
➥"ch5.imageio.ch5image_1.00";
static final String nativeImageMetadataFormatClassName =
➥"ch5.imageio.ch5image";
static final String[] extraImageMetadataFormatNames = {null};
static final String[] extraImageMetadataFormatClassNames = {null};

public ch5ImageWriterSpi() {
super(vendorName,
      version,
      names,
      suffixes,
      MIMETypes,
      writerClassName,
      STANDARD_OUTPUT_TYPE,
      readerSpiNames,
          false,
          nativeStreamMetadataFormatName,
          nativeStreamMetadataFormatClassName,
          extraStreamMetadataFormatNames,
          extraStreamMetadataFormatClassNames,
          false,
          nativeImageMetadataFormatName,
          nativeImageMetadataFormatClassName,
          extraImageMetadataFormatNames,
          extraImageMetadataFormatClassNames);

}
```

5

LISTING 5.11   Continued

```java
public String getDescription(Locale locale) {
return "Demo ch5 image writer, version " + version;
}


public ImageWriter createWriterInstance(Object extension) {
return new ch5ImageWriter(this);
}

/**
 * This method gets called when an application wants to see if
 * the corresponding ImageWriter can encode an image with
 * a ColorModel and SampleModel specified by the ImageTypeSpecifier
 */
public boolean canEncodeImage(ImageTypeSpecifier its) {
if (its.getBufferedImageType() == BufferedImage.TYPE_BYTE_GRAY)
    return true;
else
    return false;
}
}
```

Summary

We began this chapter by looking at the ImageIO class and how its static methods are used to find appropriate ImageReaders and ImageWriters. This was done through the use of service provider classes (ImageReaderSpi and ImageWriterSpi), which are small classes that describe the functionality of their corresponding ImageReaders and ImageWriters. The process of discovering available ImageReaders and ImageWriters is done at runtime through the use of plug-ins so that additional functionality can be added to the Image I/O package at any time. We then described the IIOParam subclasses, ImageReaderParam and ImageWriterParam, which provide control over the reading and writing process. We next considered the IIOMetadata subclasses, which allows the user to access both the stream's metadata and the image's metadata when reading and to provide this metadata when writing. Last, we described how to write your own ImageReader and ImageWriter plug-ins in order to work with your own image formats.

Java Advanced Imaging

IN THIS CHAPTER

Introduction

To begin, let's look at a simple program written using the *Java Advanced Imaging (JAI)* package. This program (shown in Listing 6.1) takes as parameters an image filename and a scale factor. It loads the image, scales its dimensions, and displays the results.

LISTING 6.1   Intro.java

```
package ch6;

import java.awt.*;
import javax.swing.*;
import java.awt.image.renderable.ParameterBlock;
import javax.media.jai.JAI;
import javax.media.jai.RenderedOp;

/**
   Intro.java -- objects of this class perform the following steps:
   1.  reads an image file
   2.  scales the image dimensions using provided scale factor
   3.  displays the result
*/
public class Intro extends JFrame {

    public Intro(String filename, String scaleFactor) {
        ParameterBlock pb;

        /*
          create new ParameterBlock,
          add filename parameter,
          create RenderedOp
        */
        pb = new ParameterBlock();
        pb.add(filename);
        RenderedOp inputRO = JAI.create("fileload", pb);

        /*
          create new ParameterBlock,
          add a source and add a scale parameter,
          create RenderedOp
        */
        pb = new ParameterBlock();
        pb.addSource(inputRO);
        float scale = Float.parseFloat(scaleFactor);
        pb.add(scale); // x dimension scale factor
```

LISTING 6.1 Continued

```
        pb.add(scale); // y dimension scale factor
        RenderedOp scaledRO = JAI.create("scale", pb);

        // display result
        getContentPane().add(new ch6Display(scaledRO));
        pack();
        show();
    }

    public static void main(String[] args) {
        if (args.length != 2)
            System.err.println("Usage:  filename scaleFactor");
        else
            new Intro(args[0], args[1]);
    }
}
```

By examining Listing 6.1, you will notice the pattern that is underlying much of JAI's functionality. That pattern follows these steps:

1. Set up a `ParameterBlock` with the necessary sources and parameters according to the corresponding operation.

2. Call the `JAI` class's static method `create` with the operation name and the `ParameterBlock`.

3. Use the result of this operation as a source for subsequent operations.

Note that this listing and most listings in this chapter make use of the `ch6Display` class defined in Listing 6.2 for displaying images.

LISTING 6.2 ch6Display.java

```
package ch6;

import java.awt.*;
import javax.swing.*;
import java.awt.geom.*;
import java.awt.image.*;

/**
   Very simple class for displaying RenderedImages
 */
public class ch6Display extends JPanel {
    public ch6Display(RenderedImage image) {
```

LISTING 6.2 Continued

```
            super();
            source = image;
            setPreferredSize(new Dimension(source.getWidth(),
                                    source.getHeight()));
    }

    public synchronized void paintComponent(Graphics g) {
        Graphics2D g2d = (Graphics2D)g;

        // account for borders and source image offsets
        Insets insets = getInsets();
        int tx = insets.left - source.getMinX();
        int ty = insets.top  - source.getMinY();

        AffineTransform af;
        af = AffineTransform.getTranslateInstance(tx, ty);

        // Translation moves the entire image within the container
        g2d.drawRenderedImage(source, af);
    }
    protected RenderedImage source = null;
}
```

As you will see in the remainder of this chapter, not only is the Java Advanced Imaging package simple to use, but it also has many useful features not illustrated in this example, such as the ability to

- Go easily back and forth between Java 2D classes and JAI classes.
- Provide resolution independent operations.
- Work on remote images.
- Add your own image processing operators.
- Use float and double data types for pixel values.
- Use native code to increase speed of image processing operations.

In this chapter, we will start off describing underlying concepts such as imaging models. We will then look at some important JAI classes. Then we will look into the different JAI operators that are provided and how they are to be used. Finally, we will look at some more advanced topics such as remote image processing, renderable images, and creating your own image processing operators.

Imaging Models

In the original AWT package, the main class used for image processing is the `java.awt.Image` class. This class doesn't store image data, but it contains methods and resources to allow this data to be displayed and manipulated. The image data is obtained through an `ImageConsumer`, which registers itself with an `ImageProducer`. This `ImageConsumer` instructs the `ImageProducer` to start producing data. It is important to note that the `ImageConsumer` never requests data for a particular pixel location. It just asks that the image production begin, and then processes data as it arrives. This behavior specifies a *push* imaging model, as illustrated in Figure 6.1.

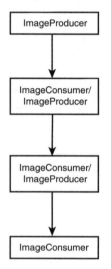

FIGURE 6.1
Java's push imaging model.

In this figure, a request from the final `ImageConsumer` causes the initial `ImageProducer` to begin image production. As the image data is produced it passes through the `ImageConsumer`/ `ImageProducer` pipeline until it is received by the final `ImageConsumer`. In this model, the final `ImageConsumer` might be processing or displaying image data it has received while the initial `ImageProducer` is still producing the rest of the image data. Note that for the `ImageConsumer`/ `ImageProducer` pairs, the `ImageConsumers` are usually `java.awt.image.ImageFilters` and the `ImageProducers` are usually `java.awt.image.FilteredImageSources`.

In the Java2D package, the main class used for image processing is the `java.awt.image.` `BufferedImage` class. Unlike the `Image` class, `BufferedImage` objects provide storage for image data. Whenever a new BufferedImage is created, its image pixels are immediately calculated and made available to any object that requests them. This behavior specifies an *immediate mode* imaging model.

As illustrated in Figure 6.2, the requesting objects are usually BufferedImageOps. When a BufferedImageOp's filter method is called, it creates a new BufferedImage whose data can be used by the next BufferedImageOp. Note that Figure 6.2 is just one example of the Java immediate mode imaging model. An analogous interface called RasterOp performs the same function for Rasters that BufferedImageOps performs for BufferedImages. Thus, this figure could have also been diagrammed using RasterOps and WritableRasters.

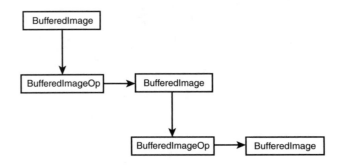

FIGURE 6.2

Java's immediate mode imaging model.

In the JAI package, the main class used for image processing is the javax.media.jai. PlanarImage class. PlanarImage objects don't make their data immediately available, but wait until an object requests it; at which time, all its pixel data is calculated before being passed on. This behavior specifies a new Java imaging model referred to as the *pull* imaging model, as illustrated in Figure 6.3.

In this figure, when the final RenderedImage is requested, its corresponding RenderedOp attempts to create it. To do so, it requests the data from its source RenderedOps, which must then create their RenderedImages. These requests work their way to the original RenderedOp, which will have no image sources and will be able to create its RenderedImage without making any further requests. In each case, only after all its image data is created will a RenderedOp object provide its RenderedImage to the requesting object.

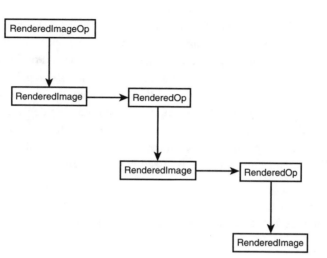

FIGURE 6.3

Java's pull imaging model.

BufferedImage Revisited

In Chapter 4, "The Immediate Mode Imaging Model," the BufferedImage class was described as having a Raster for holding and accessing pixel data and a ColorModel for pixel data interpretation. Further understanding of a BufferedImage's behavior can be obtained by examining the two interfaces it implements: the java.awt.image.RenderedImage and java.awt.image.WritableRenderedImage interfaces. The RenderedImage interface describes the functionality required to provide tiled, read only images in the form of a Raster. The WritableRenderedImage interface describes the additional functionality required to provide tiled, writable images in the form of a WritableRaster, which is a Raster subclass. Thus, a BufferedImage can provide its image data as either a Raster or a WritableRaster.

JAI Image Classes

The javax.media.jai.PlanarImage class is an abstract class that also implements the RenderedImage interface, so any concrete PlanarImage subclass has the capability to provide image data in a Raster to objects requesting its data. The PlanarImage class doesn't implement the WritableRenderedImage interface, but one subclass that does have this functionality is the javax.media.jai.TiledImage class. The TiledImage class is the main class for performing image processing directly on pixel data. Another important PlanarImage subclass is the javax.media.jai.RenderedOp class. This class doesn't implement the WritableRenderedImage interface, but does provide methods for data creation through a set of operators.

Thus, a `TiledImage` object allows you to edit the pixel data yourself, whereas a `RenderedOp` object edits the pixel data for you according to its corresponding operator. We will examine these three classes in detail starting with the `PlanarImage`. At the end of this chapter, we will examine two other `PlanarImage` subclasses: `RenderableOp` and `ImageOp`. The `RenderableOp` class performs a function similar to the `RenderedOp` class except that it is meant to be used with rendering independent `RenderableImages` instead of rendering dependent `RenderedImages`. This distinction will be made clearer when `RenderableOps` are discussed. The final subclass, `ImageOp`, is used to carry out the operations specified in the `RenderedOp` and `RenderableOp` objects. This class will be discussed in the "Extending JAI" section.

PlanarImage

In order to better understand the `PlanarImage` class, we will discuss the following topics:

- Image layout
- Properties
- Sources
- Tiles

Image Layout

A `PlanarImage` contains an object of class `javax.media.jai.ImageLayout`, which is used to hold information describing the image dimensions (minimumXValue, minimumYValue, width, height), information describing pixel access (`SampleModel`), information describing pixel interpretation (`ColorModel`), and information describing the tile grid layout (tileGridXOffset, tileGridYOffset, tileWidth, tileHeight). The `PlanarImage` class contains accessor methods so that these values can be read without going through the contained `ImageLayout` object.

Properties

`PlanarImages` not only contain pixel data, but they also contain a set of properties. These properties are often referred to as the image's metadata (see Chapter 5, "Image I/O Package," for more information on metadata). Typical properties for a new `PlanarImage` are the following: `image_min_x_coord`, `image_min_y_coord`, `image_width`, and `image_height`. However, depending on the image's initial format, the number and type of initial properties can vary. As will be discussed when describing the set of statistical operators, some operations can add to this property list. For example, the `"mean"` operation provides a property called *mean* that provides the average value of each of the image's bands. The value of any property can be found as follows:

```
public Object getProperty(String name)
```

where the return value must be cast into the correct class, that is,

```
double[] meanValuesForEachBand = (double [])planarImage.getProperty("mean");
```

You can also add properties to a `PlanarImage`, which is a convenient way to keep created metadata with its corresponding image. This is done using the following `PlanarImage` method:

```
void setProperty(java.lang.String name, java.lang.Object value)
```

Sources and Sinks

With any image, there can be one or more images that were used to derive it. For example, if *imageA* and *imageB* were added to create *imageC*, *imageA* and *imageB* could be considered *imageC*'s source images. In JAI, a `PlanarImage` object keeps a reference to its sources and because its sources are also `PlanarImages`, they keep references to their sources. Thus, a `PlanarImage` represents much more than a single image: It is part of a graph describing the history of its creation. For this reason, a `PlanarImage` is often considered part of a *directed acyclic graph (DAG)* that is a graph in which the connection between nodes is uni-directional and once you travel from one node to another, there is no way to get back again. In these JAI DAGs, each `PlanarImage` is considered a node and the reference from one `PlanarImage` to another is considered a graph edge (see Figure 6.4).

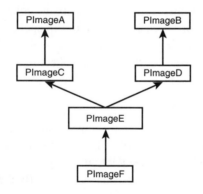

FIGURE 6.4
A reference to PImageF actually contains information about all `PlanarImages` used to create it.

A `PlanarImage`'s sources can be found using one of the following methods:

```
public java.util.Vector getSources()
public PlanarImage getSourceImage(int index)
```

The latter one is often used in conjunction with the following `PlanarImage` method:

```
public int getNumSources()
```

> **CAUTION**
>
> Images and BufferedImages contain a getSource method, but this method is very different from the getSources method that was just discussed. The getSource method provides a reference to an ImageProducer for use with the push imaging model.

A PlanarImage also has *sinks*, which refer to the PlanarImages that the PlanarImage helped create. The use of sinks isn't completely analogous to the use of sources because of the way JAI defines *reachable nodes*. This definition is important because a node that isn't considered reachable is available to be garbage collected. The definition states that any node in a DAG that has an external reference is reachable and any node that is a source to a node with an external reference is reachable. Any other node in the DAG is unreachable and can be garbage collected.

For example, referring back to Figure 6.4, if there were a reference to PImageF, all nodes in that DAG would be reachable and none would be garbage collected. On the other hand, if there were no external references to PImageF and there was an external reference to PImageE instead, PImageF would be unreachable and would eventually be garbage collected. What makes this confusing is that if PImageF hasn't been garbage collected, using PImageE's getSinks method can provide an external reference to PImageF; at which point it becomes reachable. Therefore, the difficulty of working with sinks is that depending on the DAG's external references and the efficiency of the garbage collector, a PlanarImage's sinks might or might not exist.

Tiles

Tiles are rectangular segments of a Raster that allow you to process or display particular regions of an image instead of trying to work with the entire image at once. This is very useful for large images that might not fit completely into memory. All image tiles have the same width and height, so they divide the Raster into a rectangular grid. By default, a tile has the same dimensions as its corresponding image, meaning that its Raster is composed of a single tile.

> **NOTE**
>
> Tiles can lie outside the bounds of a Raster; in which case, those pixel values are considered undefined.

A tile contains the same pixel bands as its associated Raster and is used to access that Raster's data. One way to access this data is through the public Raster getTile(int x, int y) method, which will return the tile associated with tile index x, y. Because the returned object is a `Raster` and not a `WritableRaster`, this method can be used to get tiles for read-only purposes. The ability to provide changeable `Raster` data isn't part of the `PlanarImage` class, but is available in its `TiledImage` subclass. As will be described in the following section, the `TiledImage` class provides management of the writable tiles so that if more then one object has a reference to the same writable tile, the `TiledImage` object can be used to inform them all if a change is made to that data.

TiledImage

The `javax.media.jai.TiledImage` class is JAI's closest analogy to the `BufferedImage` class. You can roughly think of it as taking a `BufferedImage` and adding the necessary functionality to allow it to be used in the JAI package. The three constructors for `TiledImages` are as follows:

```
TiledImage(int minX, int minY, int width, int height,
        int tileGridXOffset, int tileGridYOffset,
        java.awt.image.SampleModel tileSampleModel,
        java.awt.image.ColorModel colorModel)

TiledImage(java.awt.image.RenderedImage source,
        boolean areBuffersShared)

TiledImage(java.awt.image.RenderedImage source,
        int tileWidth, int tileHeight)
```

where the first constructor creates a `TiledImage` from the provided parts, whereas the second and third constructors create `TiledImages` using a `RenderedImage` to supply these parts. The second constructor provides the added functionality of being able to share the data in the `RenderedImage`, whereas the third constructor allows you to retile this data as it is being copied. For examples of how these constructors are used, the first constructor is demonstrated in Listing 6.14 and the second and third constructors are demonstrated in Listing 6.3.

The `TiledImage` class implements both the `RenderedImage` and `WritableRenderedImage` interfaces so that it can provide read-only and writable tiles. To obtain read-only tiles, use the same method that was discussed for `PlanarImage`, namely `getRaster`. In order to edit tiles, one of the following three ways should be used.

The first way is through the `public WritableRaster getWritableRaster(int x, int y)` method, which returns a `WritableRaster` so that you can edit individual pixels or samples using methods previously discussed in Chapter 4, namely `setPixel`, `setPixels`, `setDataElements`, `setSample`, and `setSamples` methods. All these methods are declared in the `WritableRenderedImage` interface.

When using the `getWritableTile` method, care must be taken whenever the data contained in one of the tiles is changed. This is because the `getWritableTile` method doesn't make a copy of the Raster's data, so all objects that call getWritableTile using the same tile index will obtain a reference to the same writable tile. The best way to ensure that each of these objects is aware of any changes is for each object interested in a particular writable tile to register itself with the TiledImage object. Then through the use of appropriate events, each of these objects can be kept informed about any changes to that tile. The next section will describe this process in more detail.

A second way to edit tile data is to use one of the following TiledImage methods to overwrite all or part of the tile data using a Raster:

```
public void setData(Raster r)
public void setData(Raster r, Roi roi)
```

In the first method, all regions of the TiledImage data that overlap the provided Raster will be set to the Raster's data values. All regions of the TiledImage outside the Raster's bounds will be unchanged. In the second setData method, a javax.media.jai.ROI (region of interest) object is provided. A ROI object is a single band image which contains a threshold value. All ROI pixels greater than or equal to this threshold value are considered *on* and all ROI pixels less than this threshold value are considered *off*. The way the ROI object is used in this setData method is that it is overlaid on top of the provided Raster. Then only the Raster pixels that correspond to *on* ROI pixels will be used to set the tile data. Thus, if the *on* ROI pixels make up a circle, only the tiled data corresponding to that circle will be set. All tiled data outside of that circle will be unchanged.

The last way to edit Raster data is to simply use the TiledImage's public Graphics2D createGraphics() method to obtain a Graphics2D object that can be used for drawing directly on the WritableRaster.

TiledImage Events

Because any number of objects can have an interest in a particular tile, there needs to be some mechanism for finding out if this tile's data has changed. This can be done by having these objects register themselves as java.awt.image.TileObservers using the TiledImage's addTileObserver method. In order to become a TileObserver, you must implement the java.awt.image.TileObserver interface and define the

```
public void tileUpdate(WritableRenderedImage source,
                       int tileX, int tileY, boolean willBeWritable)
```

method. Then whenever a tile is about to be updated or released, this information is sent to the TileObserver using the tile index (tileX, tileY) and a willBeWritable variable, which specifies whether that tile is about to be updated (willBeWritable == true) or if it is about to be released (willBeWritable == false). Each TiledImage object uses its getWritableTile method and its releaseWritableTile method to decide when to send out tile update events.

Basically, each `getWritableTile` call adds an external reference to a tile, and each `releaseWritableTile` call removes an external reference from a tile. Thus, a tile is considered "about to be updated" when it goes from a state in which no object has an external reference to it as a writable tile to a state in which an object has called `getWritableTile` for that tile.

Similarly, a tile is considered "about to be released" when it goes from a state in which at least one object has an external reference to it as a writable tile to a state in which the last object that has such a reference releases it by calling `releaseWritableTile`. Note that the `TiledImage`'s `setData` method initially calls the `getWritableTile` method for each affected tile before it changes the pixel data and then calls the `releaseWritableTile` method for each tiles when it is done. Thus, if there are no other external references to the tile of interest, the `setData` method will generate two tile update events. This can be demonstrated in Listing 6.3, which uses both the `getWritableTile` method and the `setData` method to change the `TileImage` data. One last point is that using a `Graphics2D` object to write on a `TiledImage` will also generate tile update events for all affected tiles.

NOTE

Throughout this section we talk about `TileObserver` events, but this is done only for descriptive purposes. There is no actual `java.awt.Event` sent to the `TileObservers`.

LISTING 6.3   `TileTester.java`

```java
package ch6;

import java.awt.*;
import java.awt.image.*;
import javax.swing.*;
import javax.media.jai.*;
import javax.media.jai.widget.*;

public class TileTester extends JFrame implements TileObserver {

    /**
       TileTester.java - takes two images of the same size and uses
       tiles from the first image to edit tiles in the second image.
    */
    public TileTester(String filename1, String filename2) {
        RenderedOp inputRO1 = JAI.create("fileload", filename1);
        RenderedOp inputRO2 = JAI.create("fileload", filename2);
        if ( (inputRO1.getWidth() != inputRO2.getWidth()) ||
             (inputRO1.getHeight() != inputRO2.getHeight()) ) {
```

LISTING 6.3   Continued

```java
        System.err.print("Images must have same dimensions ");
        System.err.println("for this example to run properly");
        System.exit(1);
    }

    /*
        Create two TiledImages, one for each RenderedOp.

        We are specifying the tile size as half the
        width and height of the source RenderedOps

        Thus, each TiledImage will have 4 tiles,
        tile(0,0), tile(0,1), tile(1,0) and tile(1,1);
    */
    TiledImage ti1 = new TiledImage(inputRO1,
                                    inputRO1.getWidth()/2,
                                    inputRO1.getHeight()/2);
    TiledImage ti2 = new TiledImage(inputRO2,
                                    inputRO2.getWidth()/2,
                                    inputRO2.getHeight()/2);

    //addTileObserver for the 2nd TiledImage
    ti2.addTileObserver(this);

    //ti2copy will copy data from ti2's DataBuffer
    TiledImage ti2copy = new TiledImage(ti2, false);

    //ti2share will share ti2's DataBuffer
    TiledImage ti2share = new TiledImage(ti2, true);

    /*
        Force rendering of ti2copy and ti2share.
        Rendering either will cause ti2 to be rendered.
        Displaying them will also cause them to be rendered,
        but it happens in a separate thread.  This way we
        have more control.
    */
    Raster[] tmpR;
    tmpR = ti2copy.getTiles(); // render ti2copy
    tmpR = ti2share.getTiles(); // render ti2share

    // now display the TiledImage
    getContentPane().setLayout(new GridLayout(2,2));
    getContentPane().add(new ch6Display(ti1));
```

LISTING 6.3   Continued

```
        getContentPane().add(new ch6Display(ti2));
        getContentPane().add(new ch6Display(ti2copy));
        getContentPane().add(new ch6Display(ti2share));

        pack();
        show();

        /*
          take tile(0,0) from TiledImage ti1 and use it to replace
          tile(0,0) in TiledImage ti2.

          This will only effect ti2 and ti2share, not ti2copy.

          Also, the setData method will cause ti2 to generate two tile
          update events.  One for when tile with index 0,0 is about to
          become writable and one when it is about to be released.

          Both of which happen implicitly since there are no calls to
          getWritableTile or releaseWritableTile
        */

        Raster r00 = ti1.getTile(0,0);
        ti2.setData(r00);
        repaint();

        /*
          copy tile(1,1) from TiledImage t1 and use it to
          replace tile(1,1) in ti2.
          Again ti2 generates two tile update events.
          Both of these happen explicitly;
          one when getWritableTile is called and one
          when releaseWritableTile is called
        */
        Raster ri11 = ti1.getTile(1,1);
        WritableRaster wr = ti2.getWritableTile(1,1);
        wr.setRect(0,0,ri11);
        ti2.releaseWritableTile(1,1);
        repaint();
    }

    /*
      this method gets called to handle any tile update events
    */
    public void tileUpdate(WritableRenderedImage source,
```

LISTING 6.3 Continued

```
                          int tileX,
                          int tileY,
                          boolean willBeWritable) {
        System.out.println("Tile("+tileX+","+tileY+")");
        if (willBeWritable)
            System.out.println(" is writable");
        else
            System.out.println(" is not writable");
    }

    /**
        input should be two filenames representing equal sized images
    */
    static public void main(String[] args) {
        if (args.length != 2)
            System.err.println("Usage: TileTester filename1 filename2 ");
        else
            new TileTester(args[0], args[1]);
    }
}
```

The output of Listing 6.3 will be as follows:

```
Tile(0,0) is writable
Tile(0,0) is not writable
Tile(1,1) is writable
Tile(1,1) is not writable
```

RenderedOp

Another important `PlanarImage` subclass is the `javax.media.jai.RenderedOp` class. The objects of this class store information necessary to carry out image processing operations. This information consists of an operation name, a `java.awt.image.renderable.ParameterBlock` (containing sources and parameters), and a `java.awt.RenderingHints` object, which provide hints for how the `RenderedOp` object should perform its image rendering. Each one of these items will be described in detail later in this section.

Because a `PlanarImage` contains a reference to each of its source `PlanarImage`'s, a `RenderedOp` object contains a reference to each of its source `PlanarImages` (which could be `RenderedOp` object or another `PlanarImage` subclass), thus `RenderedOp` objects can be viewed as a DAG just as `PlanarImage` objects were (refer to Figure 6.4 and Figure 6.5). What is interesting about a DAG consisting of `RenderedOp` objects is that a particular `RenderedOp` object can describe the complete set of image processing operations, source images, and parameters necessary to derive its `RenderedImage` from the original source images.

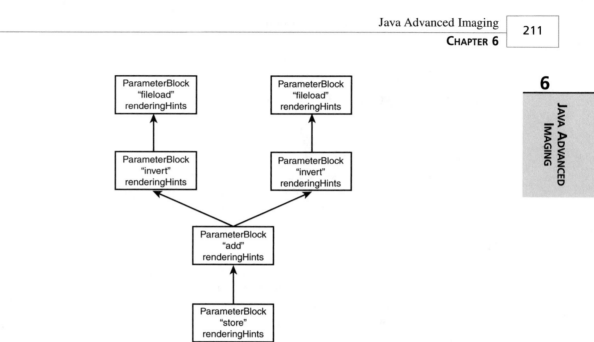

FIGURE 6.5

Being part of a DAG, the bottom RenderedOp *contains all the information necessary to load two images, invert them, add them together, and store them.*

When it is time for the final RenderedOp in the RenderedOp DAG to be rendered, it pulls the data from its sources, which in turn, pulls the data from their sources, and so on. Thus, in order for one RenderedOp node to be rendered, all the preceding RenderedOps must be rendered. Of course, if a RenderedOp has already been rendered, it will not be rerendered unless a source or a parameter is changed. (See the "RenderingChangeEvents" section for more information on how changing parameters and sources can cause a RenderedImage to be rerendered.)

When a RenderedOp is rendered, it creates a RenderedImage. This rendering usually occurs in one of two ways: with an explicit call to its getRendering method or by an implicit call to this method. This latter situation occurs whenever an object tries to use the RenderedImage data or tries to find out information regarding some of the RenderedImage's metadata, such as image width or image height. Another way a rendering can be performed is by using the createRendering method. This method creates a rendering without marking the RenderedOp node as being rendered. The importance of this classification will be described in the "RenderingChangeEvents" section. Before this can be discussed, we first need to examine the different parts of a RenderedOp: the operation, the parameter block, and the rendering hints.

Operations

With respect to RenderedOps, an operation is simply a String specifying how to create a destination RenderedImage. Some examples of valid operations are add, addConst, and invert, where the first operation adds two source images, the second operation adds a source image to an array of constants (one constant per image band), and the last operation inverts a source image.

Each allowable operator corresponds to a class implementing the javax.media.jai.OperationDescriptor interface. Each of these classes describes how their corresponding operation works. They also describe the number of source objects and the number and types of parameters they require. For example, operator descriptor classes for the previously listed operations are javax.media.jai.AddDescriptor, javax.media.jai.AddConstDescriptor, and javax.media.jai.InvertDescriptor. OperationDescriptor classes will be covered more completely in the later section entitled "Extending JAI."

Another class that will be discussed in the "Extending JAI" section is the javax.media.jai.OperationRegistry. All allowable operations must be registered in order for them to be used. In Listing 6.4, the OperationRegistry object is used to display the set of registered operations.

LISTING 6.4   ListRegistry.java

```
package ch6;

import javax.media.jai.JAI;
import javax.media.jai.OperationRegistry;
import javax.media.jai.RegistryMode;

/**
   lists all allowable JAI operations
 */
public class ListRegistry {
    public ListRegistry() {
        or = JAI.getDefaultInstance().getOperationRegistry();
        String[] modeNames = RegistryMode.getModeNames();
        String[] descriptorNames;

        for (int i=0;i<modeNames.length;i++) {
            System.out.println("For registry mode: " + modeNames[i]);

            descriptorNames = or.getDescriptorNames(modeNames[i]);
            for (int j=0;j<descriptorNames.length;j++) {
                System.out.print("\tRegistered Operator: ");
                System.out.println(descriptorNames[j]);
            }
        }
    }
```

LISTING 6.4   Continued

```
    public static void main(String[] args) {
        new ListRegistry();
    }

    private OperationRegistry or;
}
```

ParameterBlock

The `java.awt.image.renderable.ParameterBlock` class is used to encapsulate information regarding sources and parameters necessary for a particular operation to be carried out. For example, for an add operation, the corresponding `ParameterBlock` would need to contain two sources. For the `addConst` operation, it would need to contain one source and one array of constants (one for each band), and for the `invert` operation, a single source is all that is required. To place a `PlanarImage` source in a `ParameterBlock` one can use the `ParameterBlock`'s `addSource` method, and to place a parameter in a `ParameterBlock` one can use its add method. For example, a `ParameterBlock` that could be used for an `addConst` operation is as follows:

```
ParameterBlock pb = new ParameterBlock()
pb.addSource(planarImageSource);
pb.add(constantDoubleArray);
```

One last note regarding `ParameterBlocks` is that once a `ParameterBlock` is created it can be changed using one of the `ParameterBlock`'s set or `setSource` methods. For example, to reuse the preceding `ParameterBlock` to perform an `addConst` operation on another source image, simply use

```
setSource(newPlanarImageSource, 0); //where 0 refers to the source index
```

As will be discussed in the "RenderingChangeEvents" section, changing a `ParameterBlock` contained within a `RenderedOp` causes the parts of the DAG dependent on that `ParameterBlock` to change. So by simply changing a contained `ParameterBlock`, not only will its associated operation be carried out again, but all operations dependent on the created `RenderedImage` will be redone.

RenderingHints

As described in Chapter 3, "Graphics Programming with the Java2D API," and Chapter 4, "The Immediate Mode Imaging Model", the `java.awt.RenderingHints` class provides hints for use when creating a `RenderedImage`. All these hints have default values, so a `null` can be used whenever a `RenderingHints` object is expected. These default values are considered the global set of rendering hints. Whenever a `RenderedOp` is created using the JAI's `create` method, a non-null or local set of rendering hints can be passed to it in order to override one or more global rendering hints.

At the end of this chapter, when we discuss `RenderableImages`, you will see that a single set of local rendering hints can be provided to the final `RenderableOp` in a `RenderableOp` DAG, and that set will be combined with the global set and used for all operations in that DAG. This is unlike a `RenderedOp` DAG in which every node can have its own set of local rendering hints.

RenderingChangeEvents

When a `RenderedOp` is rendered using the `getRendering` method (either implicitly or explicitly) it is marked as being rendered. After this occurs, any time it gets rerendered it sends out a `javax.media.jai.RenderingChangeEvent` event to any object that had registered itself as being interested in these events. Because the `RenderingChangeEvent` is a subclass of the `java.beans.PropertyChangeEvent`, any object interested in receiving `RenderingChangeEvents` can implement the `PropertyChangeListener` interface and register themselves as such using the `PlanarImage`'s `addPropertyListener` method.

An interesting aspect of the `RenderedOp` class is that whenever a `RenderedOp` node is created, it registers itself as a `PropertyChangeListener` for all of its immediate source nodes. This way, whenever one of these source nodes gets rerendered, it can also rerender itself. In the same manner, if any node in the `RenderedOp` DAG gets rerendered, all the following `RenderedOp` nodes will rerender themselves. The question now is: what can make a `RenderedOp` node rerender itself in order to start this process? The answer is any change in its operation, or its `ParameterBlock` object or its `RenderingHints` object. Thus, if in Figure 6.5, you change the filename contained in a `ParameterBlock` in one of the top `RenderedOp` nodes, that `RenderedOp` and all the dependent `RenderOp` nodes will rerender their images, causing the final `RenderedImage` to change.

> ## CAUTION
>
> If you want to change either a source or a parameter in a `ParameterBlock`, you should go through the `RenderedOp`'s `setSource` or `setParameter` methods. These methods get passed to the underlying `ParameterBlock` where they take effect. Changes to the original `ParameterBlock` do not have any effect in the DAG because they are cloned for use by the `RenderedOp` object.

An example of this situation appears in Listing 6.5. In this listing, a `PlanarImage` is created, rotated, and displayed. The name of the file to be loaded is then changed in the initial `ParameterBlock`, causing the corresponding `RenderedOp` to rerender its image. This `RenderedOp` sends out a `RenderingChangeEvent` so the next `RenderedOp` also rerenders its image. When run, Listing 6.5 displays the image corresponding to the first filename adjacent to a rotated version of this image. After a delay of two seconds, both images change to depict the change in the name of the file to be loaded.

LISTING 6.5   RenderingChangeEventTest.java

```java
package ch6;

import java.awt.*;
import java.io.*;
import java.util.*;
import javax.swing.*;
import java.awt.image.renderable.ParameterBlock;
import java.awt.image.RenderedImage;
import javax.media.jai.JAI;
import javax.media.jai.PlanarImage;
import javax.media.jai.RenderedOp;


/**
   RenderingChangeEventTest.java -- objects of this class
   1.  create a RenderedOp by loading filename1
   2.  create a 2nd RenderedOp representing rotation
       of the first RenderedOp
   3.  renders and displays both RenderedOps
   4.  changes the input filename used in the 1st RenderedOp
       to filename2 which generates a RenderingChangeEvent causing
       the rotated image to change.
*/
public class RenderingChangeEventTest extends JFrame {

    public RenderingChangeEventTest(String filename1, String filename2) {
        this.filename2 = filename2;
        RenderedOp inputRO = JAI.create("fileload", filename1);
        RenderedOp rotatedRO = createRotatedImage(inputRO);

        /*
          Force rotatedRO to be rendered.  This is not usually needed,
          but for this example we need the rotatedRO object's rendering
          to be done before the rotation angle is changed.
        */
        RenderedImage tmp = (PlanarImage)rotatedRO.getRendering();

        // display original and rotated
        getContentPane().setLayout(new GridLayout(1,2));
        getContentPane().add(new ch6Display(inputRO));
        getContentPane().add(new ch6Display(rotatedRO));
        pack();
        show();
```

LISTING 6.5   Continued

```java
        // wait 2 seconds so images don't change to quickly
        try{
            Thread.sleep(2000);
        }
        catch(InterruptedException ie) {
        }

        changeFilename(rotatedRO);

        // redisplay images
        repaint();
    }

    /**
        Returns a RenderedOp representing a rotated
        version of RenderedOp toBeRotatedRO
    */
    private RenderedOp createRotatedImage(RenderedOp toBeRotatedRO) {
        float angle = (float)((45.0/180.0)*Math.PI); //45 degree rotation

        ParameterBlock param;
        param =   new ParameterBlock();
        param.addSource(toBeRotatedRO);
        param.add(new Float(toBeRotatedRO.getWidth()/2));
        param.add(new Float(toBeRotatedRO.getHeight()/2));
        param.add(new Float(angle));
        RenderedOp ro = JAI.create("rotate", param);

        return ro;
    }

    /**
        1.  go to the RenderedOp's source image
        2.  change the filename parameter in its ParameterBlock
        3.  this will generate a RenderingChangeEvent which will
        cause the rotatedRO RenderedOp to rerender its images
    */
    private void changeFilename(RenderedOp toBeChangedRO) {
        //get source RenderedOp
        RenderedOp tmpRO = (RenderedOp)toBeChangedRO.getSourceImage(0);
        tmpRO.setParameter(filename2, 0);
    }
```

LISTING 6.5 Continued

```
public static void main(String[] args) {
    if (args.length != 2)
        System.err.println("Usage:  filename1 filename2");
    else
        new RenderingChangeEventTest(args[0], args[1]);
}
String filename2;
}
```

The JAI Class

The JAI class primarily contains a set of methods to create RenderedOp objects given an operation, a ParameterBlock object, and a RenderingHints object (refer to Listing 6.1). Its most common method is the static create method, that is,

```
static public RenderedOp create(String operationName,
                                ParameterBlock param,
                                RenderingHints renderingHints)
```

or if the RenderingHints object is null (meaning that default values should be used), you can use

```
static public RenderedOp create(String operationName,
                                ParameterBlock param)
```

There are also a large number of other JAI create methods that allow you to perform an operation without using a ParameterBlock. In all listings in this chapter, ParameterBlocks will be used in the JAI's create methods, but, in practice, it is common to see method calls such as JAI.create("Fileload", filename) for loading an image file.

> **NOTE**
>
> The case of the operator isn't significant, so the operations add, Add, and ADD are treated identically.

There is another set of methods called createRenderable, which act similar to the create methods, but create a RenderableOp instead of a RenderedOp. The RenderableOp class will be discussed in a later section entitled "RenderedOps Versus RenderableOps". One last point is that when the JAI's create method is used, numerous verifications occur with regard to the provided ParameterBlock and the operation String. For instance, the number of sources are checked as well as the number, types, and values of the parameters.

Operators

In the previous discussion, the operation to be performed must be one of the operations registered with the JAI package (refer to Listing 6.4). In Tables 6.1 to 6.12, the different operators are presented. In these tables, the format of the necessary `ParameterBlock` is provided along with a short description of each operator.

> **TIP**
>
> For more information about a particular operator, look at the documentation for its descriptor class. For instance, the add operator's descriptor class will be called `javax.media.jai.operator.AddDescriptor`.

Before examining these tables, a few points need to be made.

Use of Constant Arrays

In many cases, the parameters provided to a `ParameterBlock` object are arrays; for example in the `Clamp` operator, the two parameters are double arrays specifying a set of low values and a set of high values. These are specified as an array instead of as a simple data value to give the user the ability to process each of the image bands differently. The way this is done is that if the number of elements in the array is equal to or greater than the number of image bands, the array value that will be used for a particular band will be `constantArray[bandNumber]`. On the other hand, if the number of array elements is less than the number of image bands, the array value that will be used for each band will be `constantArray[0]` and all bands will be treated equally. Thus, the constant array value used to process each band is as follows:

```
if (constantArray.length >= dstNumBands)
    value = constantArray[bandNumber];
else
    value = constantArray[0];
```

Parameter Object Types and Default Values

In the JAI API documentation, the operators are listed as requiring `Object` parameters. For example, whenever an integer array is needed, instead of `int[]`, it will be listed as `Integer[]`. In all cases, you can use either, so we decided to use the primitive data types for simplicity. Also, many of the parameters required for an operation have default values. In order to use a default value, you can just use `null` for that parameter value. In the upcoming tables, default values will be listed when available.

Clamping

In general, the output of all operators are clamped according to the data type of the destination image. In other words, each data type has a minimum and maximum allowable value. Any destination value higher than the maximum value will be set to the maximum value and any destination value lower than the minimum value will be set to the minimum value.

> **NOTE**
>
> Images composed of data types float or double are clamped at 0.0, 1.0.

Also, the output of all operators are rounded if the destination data type isn't float or double.

Samples

As discussed in Chapter 4, a pixel isn't the smallest element of an image. Each pixel is composed of one or more samples in which each sample corresponds to a particular image band. Thus an image with three bands (possible red, green, and blue) will have three samples per pixel. Most of the JAI operators work directly on samples although they are often described as operating on pixels. For example, when it is said that the Invert operator inverts pixels, it actually inverts each sample in each pixel.

Operation Groupings

As will be discussed in the "Extending JAI" section, a natural operator grouping exists based on the OpImage subclass that the operator implementation extends. Although this grouping is functionally useful, we have chosen different operator groupings in order to present smaller, more descriptive groups.

Pixel Operators

Associated with each pixel is a location. Pixel operators iteratively go through all pixel locations in a PlanarImage and carry out some type of computation. These computations are performed independently on each location without considering any other pixel locations within that PlanarImage. These operations can be grouped into two categories: single source pixel operators and multisource pixel operators.

Single Source Pixel Operators

Single source pixel operators calculate destination pixel values directly from the corresponding pixel value in a source image. A more mathematical form is *destination[c][r][b] = function(source[c][r][b])*, where c is the column number, r is the row number, and b is the band number. These operations can be further broken down into one group that requires no parameters such as Absolute, Exp, Format, Invert, Log, and Not (see Table 6.1) and one group that does require parameters such as Clamp, ColorConvert, Lookup, Rescale, and Threshold (see Table 6.2).

TABLE 6.1   Summary of Single Source Pixel Operators Which Require No Parameters

Operator	Parameter Block Format/Description
Absolute	addSource(PlanarImage pi);
	The Absolute operator computes the absolute value of all pixels in pi.
Format	addSource(PlanarImage pi);
	add(int datatype);
	The Format operator reformats an image by casting each of its data samples to a different data type, where datatype can be one of the following:
	DataBuffer.TYPE_BYTE (default value), DataBuffer.TYPE_SHORT, DataBuffer.TYPE_USHORT, DataBuffer.TYPE_INT, DataBuffer.TYPE_FLOAT, or DataBuffer.TYPE_DOUBLE)
	See Listing 6.12 for an example of this operator.
Exp	addSource(PlanarImage pi);
	The Exp operator computes the exponential of all pixels in pi.
Invert	addSource(PlanarImage pi);
	The Invert operator computes the inverse of all pixels in pi. If pi's datatype is signed, a sample's inverse is the negation of the sample's value. If pi's datatype is unsigned, the sample's inverse is the maximum value of that datatype minus the sample's value.
Log	addSource(PlanarImage pi);
	The Log operator computes the natural log of all pixels in pi.
Not	addSource(PlanarImage pi);
	The Not operator performs bitwise logical NOT on all pixels in pi.

Table 6.2 provides a list of the single source pixel operators requiring one or more parameters. Be sure to refer to the previous section "Use of Constant Arrays" to understand how the operators use the array parameters. Unless otherwise noted, the parameters don't have default values.

TABLE 6.2   Summary of Single Source Pixel Operators that Require One or More Parameters

Operator	Parameter Block Format/Description
Clamp	addSource(PlanarImage pi);
	add(double[] low);
	add(double[] high);
	The Clamp operator sets any pixel in pi under the value specified by low to low and any pixel in pi over the value specified by high to high. All other pixel values are unchanged.

TABLE 6.2 Continued

Operator	Parameter Block Format/Description
ColorConvert	`addSource(PlanarImage pi);`
	`add(ColorModel cm);`
	The `ColorConvert` operator converts each pixel in `pi` to the colorspace specified by `cm`.
Lookup	`addSource(PlanarImage pi);`
	`add(LookupTableJAI table);`
	The `Lookup` operator uses the lookup table `table` to transform pixel values in `pi`. This operation uses a `javax.media.jai.LookupTableJAI` object, which contains both a lookup table and an offset value.
	If `table` contains as many elements or more elements than the source image has bands, the destination values will be
	`tmp = source[c][r][b] - offset[b];`
	`destination[c][r][b] = lookup[b][tmp],`
	where c = column number, r = row number, and b = band number.
	If `table` has less elements than the source image has bands, the destination values will be
	`tmp = source[c][r][b] - offset[0];`
	`destination[c][r][b] = lookup[0][tmp]`
Rescale	`addSource(PlanarImage pi);`
	`add(double[] constants);`
	`add(double[] offsets);`
	The `Rescale` operator multiplies each pixel in `pi` by `constants` before adding `offsets`.
	If the `constants` and `offsets` array have as many elements or more elements than the source image has bands, the destination values will be
	`tmp = source[c][r][b]*scale[b]`
	`destination[c][r][b] = tmp + offset[b],`
	where c = column number, r = row number, and b = band number.
	If the `constants` and `offsets` array have less elements than the source image has bands, the destination values will be
	`tmp = source[c][r][b]*scale[0]`
	`destination[c][r][b] = tmp + offset[0]`

Table 6.2   Continued

Operator	Parameter Block Format/Description
Threshold	addSource(PlanarImage pi);
	add(double[] low);
	add(double[] high);
	add(double[] constants);
	The Threshold operator maps all pixel values in pi that fall within the inclusive limits specified by low and high to constants. Any pixel value that lies outside of this range will be unchanged.

Multiple Source Pixel Operators

Multiple source pixel operators calculate a destination pixel value directly from the corresponding pixel values of more than one source. Mathematically, using two sources, this can be expressed as follows: `destination[c][r][b] = function(source1[c][r][b], source2[c][r][b])`, where c is the column number, r is the row number, and b is the band number. This group of operators can be broken down into two groups. The first group uses multiple image sources and no parameters, and the second group uses a single source image and a constant array parameter. In these operators, this constant array acts like a second image source.

Examples of the first group of operators are `Add`, `AddCollection`, `And`, `Divide`, `DivideComplex`, `Max`, `Min`, `Multiply`, `MultiplyComplex`, `Or`, `Subtract`, and `Xor` (see Table 6.3). Note that `AddCollection` is the only operator that allows more than two sources. Examples of the second group of operators are `AddConst`, `AndConst`, `DivideByConst`, `DivideIntoConst`, `MultiplyConst`, `OrConst`, `SubtractConst`, `SubtractFromConst`, and `XorConst` (see Table 6.4).

In Table 6.3 there are two operations involving complex data, that is, `DivideComplex` and `MultiplyComplex`. A complex image is simply a `PlanarImage` with an even number of bands in which the odd-numbered bands (first, third, and so on) will be interpreted as making up the real part of the image, whereas the even-numbered bands (second, fourth, and so on) will be interpreted as making up the imaginary part of the image.

Table 6.3   Summary of Multiple Source Pixel Operators that Require No Parameters

Operator	Parameter Block Format/Description
Add	addSource(PlanarImage pi1);
	addSource(PlanarImage pi2);
	The Add operator adds corresponding pixels in pi1 and pi2.
AddCollection	addSource(CollectionImage ci);
	The AddCollection operator adds corresponding pixels in all images contained in ci.

TABLE 6.3   Continued

Operator	Parameter Block Format/Description
And	addSource(PlanarImage pi1);
	addSource(PlanarImage pi2);
	The And operator performs logical AND on corresponding pixels in pi1 and pi2.
Divide	addSource(PlanarImage pi1);
	addSource(PlanarImage pi2);
	The Divide operator divides pixels in pi1 by corresponding pixels in pi2.
DivideComplex	addSource(PlanarImage pi1);
	addSource(PlanarImage pi2);
	The DivideComplex operator divides complex pixels in pi1 by corresponding complex pixels in pi2.
Max	addSource(PlanarImage pi1);
	addSource(PlanarImage pi2);
	The Max operator finds the maximum value of corresponding pixels in pi1 and pi2.
Min	addSource(PlanarImage pi1);
	addSource(PlanarImage pi2);
	The Min operator finds the minimum value of corresponding pixels in pi1 and pi2.
Multiply	addSource(PlanarImage pi1);
	addSource(PlanarImage pi2);
	The Multiply operator multiplies corresponding pixels in pi1 and pi2.
MultiplyComplex	addSource(PlanarImage pi1);
	addSource(PlanarImage pi2);
	The MultiplyComplex operator multiplies corresponding complex pixels in pi1 and pi2.
Or	addSource(PlanarImage pi1);
	addSource(PlanarImage pi2);
	The Or operator computes the logical OR of corresponding pixels in pi1 and pi2.
Subtract	addSource(PlanarImage pi1);
	addSource(PlanarImage pi2);
	The Subtract operator subtracts pixels in pi2 from corresponding pixels in pi1.

TABLE 6.3   Continued

Operator	Parameter Block Format/Description
Xor	addSource(PlanarImage pi1);
	addSource(PlanarImage pi2);
	The Xor operator computes the XOR value of corresponding pixels in pi1 and pi2.

In Table 6.4, each `ParameterBlock` contains a single image source and a constant array that can be considered a second image source. Be sure to refer to the preceding section "Use of Constant Arrays" to understand how the operators use the array parameters.

TABLE 6.4   Summary of Multiple Source Pixel Operators in Which One Source Is Derived from a Constant Array

Operator	Parameter Block Format/Description
AddConst	addSource(PlanarImage pi);
	add(double[] constants);
	The AddConst operator adds constants to each pixel in pi.
AndConst	addSource(PlanarImage pi);
	add(int[] constants);
	The AndConst operator performs logical AND between constants and pixels in pi.
DivideByConst	addSource(PlanarImage pi);
	add(double[] constants);
	The DivideByConst operator divides each pixel in pi by constants.
DivideIntoConst	addSource(PlanarImage pi);
	add(double[] constants);
	The DivideIntoConst operator divides constants by pixels in pi.
MultiplyConst	addSource(PlanarImage pi);
	add(double[] constants);
	The MultiplyConst operator multiplies constants to each pixel in pi.
OrConst	addSource(PlanarImage pi);
	add(int[] constants);
	The OrConst operator performs a logical OR between constants and each pixel in pi.

TABLE 6.4   Continued

Operator	Parameter Block Format/Description

SubtractConst	addSource(PlanarImage pi);
	
	add(double[] constants);
	
	The SubtractConst operator subtracts constants from each pixel in pi.

SubtractFromConst	addSource(PlanarImage pi);
	
	add(double[] constants);
	
	The SubtractFromConst operator subtracts each pixel in pi from constants.

XorConst	addSource(PlanarImage pi);
	
	add(int[] constants);
	
	The XorConst operator performs logical XOR between constants and each pixel in pi.

Other Pixel Operators

The pixel operators that don't fit in any of the previous groups are presented here. They are the BandCombine, BandSelect, Composite, Constant, MatchCDF, Overlay, Pattern and Piecewise operators (see Table 6.5). Because of the complexity of these operators, examples of many of them are provided following this table. Unless otherwise noted, the parameters don't have default values.

TABLE 6.5   Summary of Other Pixel Operators

Operator	Parameter Block Format/Description

BandCombine	addSource(PlanarImage pi);
	
	add(double[][] matrix);
	
	The BandCombine operator linearly combines the bands in pi according to the matrix array. The number of columns in matrix represent the number of bands in pi plus one. The number of rows in matrix represent the number of bands in the destination image. This operator is similar to the java.awt.Image.BandCombineOp described in Chapter 4 (see Listing 6.6).

BandSelect	addSource(PlanarImage pi);
	
	add(int[] bandIndices);
	
	The BandSelect operator copies bands in pi to the destination image in the order specified by bandIndices (see Listing 6.7).

TABLE 6.5   Continued

Operator	Parameter Block Format/Description
Composite	`addSource(PlanarImage pi1);`
	`addSource(PlanarImage pi2);`
	`add(PlanarImage alpha1);`
	`add(PlanarImage alpha2);`
	`add(Boolean alphaPremultiplied);`
	`add(Integer destAlpha);`
	The Composite operator combines corresponding pixels in `pi1` and `pi2` using the alpha values provided in `alpha1` and `alpha2`. `destAlpha` describes whether the destination image should have an alpha band and if so, whether it should be the first band or the last. Possible values for `destAlpha` are
	`CompositeDescriptor.NO_DESTINATION_ALPHA`
	`CompositeDescriptor.DESTINATION_ALPHA_FIRST`
	`CompositeDescriptor.DESTINATION_ALPHA_LAST`
	Default values are `alpha2 = null` (opaque); `alphaPremultiplied = false`; `destAlpha = CompositeDescriptor.NO_DESTINATION_ALPHA` (see Listing 6.8).
Constant	`add(Float width);`
	`add(Float height);`
	`add(Number[] constants);`
	The Constant operator creates a new image of size `width`, `height` where each pixel is set equal to `constants` (see Listing 6.9).
MatchCDF	`addSource(PlanarImage pi);`
	`add(float[][] CDF);`
	The MatchCDF operator attempts to make `pi`'s cumulative density function (CDF) match the provided CDF. The format of CDF is as follows:
	`CDF[numberOfBands][numberOfBinsInBand]` where, for a particular band, each subsequent CDF value must be nonnegative and nondecreasing. The final value for each band must be 1.0.
Overlay	`addSource(PlanarImage pi1);`
	`addSource(PlanarImage pi2);`
	The Overlay operator covers pixels on `pi1` with pixels from `pi2` wherever the bounds of the two source images intersect.

TABLE 6.5   Continued

Operator	Parameter Block Format/Description
Pattern	`add(int width);`
	`add(int height);`
	`add(Raster pattern);`
	The `Pattern` operator creates a destination image of dimensions (`width`, `height`) made up of a repeated pattern specified by `pattern`. The tile dimensions in the destination image will be the dimensions of `pattern`.
Piecewise	`addSource(PlanarImage pi);`
	`add(float[][][] breakPoints);`
	The `Piecewise` operator performs a piecewise linear mapping of pixel values in `pi`, where `breakPoints` is defined as `breakPoints[numBands][2][numBreakPoints]`.
	When the array's second index is equal to 0, the `breakPoints` array represents a list of possible source sample values. When this array index is equal to 1, the `breakPoints` array represents a list of possible destination sample values. Thus, the `breakPoints` array maps a set of source sample values to a set of destination sample values. Any source sample value that isn't contained in the set of source sample values will have its destination value computed using the closest source values that do exist in this set along with their corresponding destination values (see Listing 6.9).

NOTE

Listings 6.6 through 6.9 are not standalone applications, but are methods belonging to an application named `OtherPointOperatorsTester.java`.

In Listing 6.6, an example of a method using the `"BandCombine"` operator is shown. Assuming that an image has three color components and is using an RGB color space, the general equation for a particular band in the destination image is

```
x*sourceRedComponent + y*sourceGreenComponent + z*sourceBlueComponent + t
```

where *x*,*y*,*z*, and *t* are variables. Thus a band in the destination image is created by linearly combining bands in a source image plus adding an offset. Using `"BandCombine"` operator, the *x*,*y*,*z*, and *t* variables are contained in a two-dimensional double array.

LISTING 6.6   bandCombine Method of `OtherPointOperatorsTester.java`

```
/**
    BandCombine operation in which the destination band components are;
    destinationRedComponent = 255 - sourceRedComponent
    destinationGreenComponent = sourceBlueComponent;
    destinationBlueComponent = sourceGreenComponent;.
*/
public PlanarImage bandCombine(PlanarImage pi) {
    double[][] matrix = {
        { -1.0D,  0.0D, 0.0D, 255.0D },
        { 0.0D,   0.0D, 1.0D, 0.0D },
        { 0.0D,   1.0D, 0.0D, 0.0D },
    };
    ParameterBlock param =  new ParameterBlock();
    param.addSource(pi);
    param.add(matrix);
    return JAI.create("BandCombine", param);
}
```

In Listing 6.7, an example of a method using the `"BandSelect"` operation is shown. Assuming that the source bands are contained in an array called `sourceBandArray` and the destination bands are contained in an array called `destinationBandArray`, the general equation for a particular band is

```
destinationBand[bandNumber] = sourceBand[bandSelectArray[bandNumber]]
```

where `bandSelectArray` is a single dimensional `int` array with as many elements as there are bands in the destination image.

LISTING 6.7   bandSelect Method of `OtherPointOperatorsTester.java`

```
/**
    BandSelect method used to reverse the second and third bands
    Thus, if the initial band order is red, green, blue
    the destination band order will be red, blue, green
  */
public PlanarImage bandSelect(PlanarImage pi) {
    int[] array = {0, 2, 1};

    ParameterBlock param =  new ParameterBlock();
    param.addSource(pi);
    param.add(array);
    return JAI.create("BandSelect", param);
}
```

In Listing 6.8, an example of a method using the "Composite" operation is shown.

LISTING 6.8 Composite Method of OtherPointOperatorsTester.java

```
/**
       performs compositing of PlanarImages pi1 and pi2 using
       normalized alpha values of .5 for pi1 and normalized alpha
       values of 1.0 (opaque) for pi2.  Thus, the destination pixels
       will be made up of equal parts of pi1 and pi2.
    */

    public PlanarImage composite(PlanarImage pi1, PlanarImage pi2) {
        byte alpha1Value = (byte)128;   //normalized value of .5
        byte alpha2Value = (byte)256;   //normalized value of 1.0

        ParameterBlock param =  new ParameterBlock();
        param.addSource(pi1);
        param.addSource(pi2);
        param.add(makeAlpha(pi1.getWidth(), pi1.getHeight(),
                            alpha1Value, alpha1Value, alpha1Value));
        param.add(makeAlpha(pi2.getWidth(), pi2.getHeight(),
                            alpha2Value, alpha2Value, alpha2Value));
        param.add(new Boolean(false));
        param.add(CompositeDescriptor.NO_DESTINATION_ALPHA);

        return JAI.create("Composite", param);
    }


    /**
       returns a PlanarImage containing 3 bands with samples being of
       type byte.  All sample in band0 will be set to alpha0, all
       samples in band1 will be set to alpha1 and all samples in band2
       will be set to alpha2.

    */
    private PlanarImage makeAlpha(float width, float height,
                                   byte alpha0, byte alpha1, byte alpha2) {
        byte[] alphaValues;

        alphaValues = new byte[3];
        alphaValues[0] = alpha0; //alpha value for 1st band
        alphaValues[1] = alpha1; //alpha value for 2nd band
        alphaValues[2] = alpha2; //alpha value for 3rd band

        ParameterBlock param =  new ParameterBlock();
        param.add(width);
```

LISTING 6.8   Continued

```
        param.add(height);
        param.add(alphaValues);
        RenderedOp ro = JAI.create("Constant", param);
        return ro;
    }
```

The `"Composite"` operator combines two source `PlanarImages` in such a way that by taking into account each pixel's corresponding alpha (transparency) values, the two images appear together (see Figure 6.6).

FIGURE 6.6
Composite operation.

Alpha values are supplied by interpreting the pixel values of two other `PlanarImages` as the alpha values for the two source images. In Listing 6.8, in order to create these alpha `PlanarImages`, a method using the `"Constant"` operation is used.

For more details on how this compositing is performed, let

>   pi1Value = sample value of PlanarImage1
>   pi2Value = sample value of PlanerImage2
>   pi1Alpha = normalized alpha value for PlanarImage1
>   pi2Alpha = normalized alpha value for PlanarImage2

(where normalized alpha values range from 0.0, 1.0).

The `"Porter-Duff over"` composite rule (which is the composite rule used) can then be defined as

>   destinationValue = pi1Value*pi1Alpha + (1-pi1Alpha)*(pi2Value*pi2Alpha)

In Figure 6.6, the left and middle images are the source images. The last image is the result of the composite operator applied to these two source images. In this operation, all pixels in the first source image were given a normalized alpha value of .5, whereas all pixels in the second source image were given an alpha value of 1.0. Thus, the destination image represents each of the two source images equally.

In Listing 6.9, an example of a method using the `"Piecewise"` operator is shown.

LISTING 6.9   piecewise Method of OtherPointOperatorsTester.java

```java
/**
    performs piecewise linear mapping of a PlanarImage with 3 bands
    In this example:
    all values under 50 will become 100
    all values over 200 will become 255
    all other values becomes linearly interpolated between the two, i.e.,
    100 + (value-50)*(255-100)/(200-50)
*/
public PlanarImage piecewise(PlanarImage pi) {
    float[][][] breakPoints = new float[3][2][2];
    breakPoints[0][0][0] = 50;
    breakPoints[0][1][0] = 100;
    breakPoints[0][0][1] = 200;
    breakPoints[0][1][1] = 255;

    breakPoints[1][0][0] = 50;
    breakPoints[1][1][0] = 100;
    breakPoints[1][0][1] = 200;
    breakPoints[1][1][1] = 255;

    breakPoints[2][0][0] = 50;
    breakPoints[2][1][0] = 100;
    breakPoints[2][0][1] = 200;
    breakPoints[2][1][1] = 255;

    ParameterBlock param =  new ParameterBlock();
    param.addSource(pi);
    param.add(breakPoints);

    return JAI.create("Piecewise", param);
}
```

This operator requires a three-dimensional float array often called `breakPoints`. The format of this array is as follows:

```java
float breakPoints[numBands][2][numBreakPoints]
```

In order to understand this operator, it is best to think of this array as two separate arrays; that is, sourceBreakPoints and destinationBreakPoints where

```
sourceBreakPoints[bandNumber][breakPoints] =
breakPoints[bandNumber][0][breakPoint]
```

and

```
destinationBreakPoints[bandNumber][breakPoints] =
breakPoints[bandNumber][1][breakPoint]
```

Thus, this operator maps the values in the sourceBreakPoints array into the values in the destinationBreakPoints array.

For the sourceBreakPoints and the destinationBreakPoints arrays, each subsequent break point must have a higher value than the one before it. For example for a single band image, the source breakpoints could be {2, 4, 6, 8} and the destination breakpoints could be {1, 4, 12, 20}.

The purpose of these arrays is to map source pixel values into destination pixel values. If a source pixel value corresponds to a source breakpoint, its destination pixel value will simply be the corresponding destination breakpoint value. If a source pixel value falls between two breakpoints, its destination pixel value will be linearly computed according to the two closest source breakpoints and their corresponding destination breakpoints. For example, using the source and destination breakpoints listed previously, any source pixel value less than or equal to 2 will have a destination pixel value of 1. Any source pixel value of 2 or 3 will have a destination pixel value of

```
1+ (value-2)*(4-1)/(4-2)
```

Any source pixel value of 4 or 5 will have a destination pixel value of

```
4+(value-4)*(12-4)/(6-4)
```

Any source pixel value of 6 or 7 will have a destination pixel value of

```
12+(value-6)*(20-12)/(8-6)
```

Any source pixel value of 8 or above will have a destination pixel value of 20.

Area Operators

Unlike point operators, when computing the value of a destination pixel, area operators generally need to use more than a single pixel within a source image. For example, a smoothing filter can compute a destination pixel's value by averaging its corresponding source pixel with a region containing that source pixel's neighbors. The listed area operators are Border, BoxFilter, Convolve, Crop, and Median Filter. Because of the confusion that often occurs between borders and a related concept of border extenders, a section titled "Creating Borders and Border Extenders" immediately follows Table 6.6 that discusses these concepts.

TABLE 6.6   Summary of Area Operators

Operator	*Parameter Block Format/Description*
Border	addSource(PlanarImage pi);
	add(int leftBorderSize);
	add(int rightBorderSize);
	add(int topBorderSize);
	add(int bottomBorderSize);
	add(BorderExtender extenderType);
	The Border operator puts a border around the source image pi. The extenderType describes which type of border to use. This choice is usually specified by using BorderExtender.createInstance(int type), where type is one of the following:
	BorderExtender.BORDER_COPY
	BorderExtender.BORDER_ZERO
	BorderExtender.BORDER_REFLECT
	BorderExtender.BORDER_WRAP
	Alternatively, the extenderType can be specified through
	new BorderExtenderConstant(double[] constant)
	(see Listing 6.10)
BoxFilter	addSource(PlanerImage pi);
	add(int boxWidth);
	add(int boxHeight);
	add(int boxXOrigin);
	add(int boxYOrigin);
	The BoxFilter operator convolves pi with a box kernel with dimensions of boxWidth, boxHeight and a center located at boxXOrigin, boxYOrigin. Each element of the box filter has a weight equal to 1/(boxWidth*boxHeight).
Convolve	addSource(PlanarImage pi);
	add(KernelJAI kernel);
	The Convolve operator convolves pi with kernel kernel, where this kernelJAI object contains the kernel's shape, origin, and element values.

TABLE 6.6 Continued

Operator	Parameter Block Format/Description
Crop	`addSource(PlanarImage pi);`
	`add(int xOrigin);`
	`add(int yOrigin);`
	`add(int width);`
	`add(int height);`
	The `Crop` operator crops `pi` using a rectangle with an origin at xOrigin, yOrigin and dimensions of width, height.
GradientMagnitude	`addSource(PlanarImage pi);`
	`add(KernelJAI kernel1);`
	`add(KernelJAI kernel2);`
	The `GradientMagnitute` operator computes the magnitude of the two values found by implementing convolution using kernel1 and kernel2 independently.
MedianFilter	`addSource(PlanarImage pi);`
	`add(int maskShape);`
	`add(int maskSize);`
	The `MedianFilter` operator performs median filtering of `pi` using a mask of size maskSize and a shape of one of the following:
	`MedianFilterDescriptor.MEDIAN_MASK_SQUARE,`
	`MedianFilterDescriptor.MEDIAN_MASK_PLUS`
	`MedianFilterDescriptor.MEDIAN_MASK_X`
	`MedianFilterDescriptor.MEDIAN_MASK_SQUARE_SEPARABLE`
	where this latter mask shape uses a square mask, but instead of computing the median of all pixels in the square, it first computes a median value for each row and then computes the median of the calculated row medians.

Creating Borders and Border Extenders

There are two ways to provide pixel data at locations past an image's natural boundaries. The first way is through the `Border` operation as described in Table 6.6. This method creates a border around an image by extending the image dimensions and filling the border area as specified: copy, constant, reflect, wrap, or zero.

- copy—Border pixels replicate values of edge and corner pixels.
- constant—Border pixels are set to provided constant values.

- reflect—Border appears as a reflection of the image.
- wrap—Border appears as a reproduction of the image.
- zero—Border pixels are all set to 0.

Listing 6.10 illustrates how the different border descriptors are used (see Figure 6.7).

LISTING 6.10   BorderTester.java

```java
package ch6;

import java.awt.*;
import javax.swing.*;
import java.io.*;
import java.awt.image.renderable.ParameterBlock;
import javax.media.jai.JAI;
import javax.media.jai.BorderExtender;
import javax.media.jai.BorderExtenderConstant;
import javax.media.jai.RenderedOp;
import javax.media.jai.RenderedImageList;

/**
   BorderTester -- this class illustrates the 5 different border types
 */

public class BorderTester extends JFrame {
    public BorderTester(String filename) {
        setTitle("ch6.BorderTester");

        int borderThickness = 20;
        int extenderType;
        ParameterBlock param;
        RenderedOp sourceImage = JAI.create("fileload", filename);

        param =  new ParameterBlock();
        param.addSource(sourceImage);
        param.add(borderThickness);
        param.add(borderThickness);
        param.add(borderThickness);
        param.add(borderThickness);

        extenderType = BorderExtender.BORDER_COPY;
        param.add(BorderExtender.createInstance(extenderType));
        RenderedOp bdrCopy = JAI.create("border", param);

        extenderType = BorderExtender.BORDER_ZERO;
        param.set(BorderExtender.createInstance(extenderType), 4);
        RenderedOp bdrZero = JAI.create("border", param);
```

LISTING 6.10   Continued

```
extenderType = BorderExtender.BORDER_REFLECT;
param.set(BorderExtender.createInstance(extenderType), 4);
RenderedOp bdrReflect = JAI.create("border", param);

extenderType = BorderExtender.BORDER_WRAP;
param.set(BorderExtender.createInstance(extenderType), 4);
RenderedOp bdrWrap = JAI.create("border", param);

double[] constantValues = {128.0, 128.0, 128.0}; //gray border
param.set(new BorderExtenderConstant(constantValues), 4);
RenderedOp bdrConstant = JAI.create("border", param);


getContentPane().setBackground(Color.white);
getContentPane().setLayout(new GridLayout(2,3));
getContentPane().add(new ch6Display(sourceImage));
getContentPane().add(new ch6Display(bdrCopy));
getContentPane().add(new ch6Display(bdrZero));
getContentPane().add(new ch6Display(bdrReflect));
getContentPane().add(new ch6Display(bdrWrap));
getContentPane().add(new ch6Display(bdrConstant));

/*
   add a little extra space so viewer can
   distinguish between the different images
*/
Insets insets = getInsets();
int xSize = 3*(sourceImage.getWidth()+80);
xSize += insets.left+insets.right;
int ySize = 2*(sourceImage.getHeight()+80);
ySize += insets.top+insets.bottom;
setSize(xSize, ySize);

show();
}

public static void main(String[] args) {
    if (args.length != 1)
        System.err.println("Usage:  BorderTester imageFileName");
    else
        new BorderTester(args[0]);
}
}
```

FIGURE 6.7

Border operations.

In Figure 6.7, the top left image is the source image. In the following images (presented in order from top row to the bottom row), the following border types are illustrated: copy, zero, reflect, wrap, and constant.

The main purpose of the `Border` operator is to extend the image dimensions for visual purposes. By mistake, it is often used so that when an operation requires pixel values past the normal image dimensions, they are available. This situation is very common for some of the area operators such as `Convolution`, `BoxFilter`, and `MedianFilter`. The reason this type of image extension should not be done is that once you use the `Border` operator, the created border becomes part of the image. Thus, it will be processed by all subsequent operators and will appear when displayed. A better way to provide these additional pixel values is to use a border extender instead of a border.

Like a border, a border extender provides pixel values to operators that require values beyond the dimensions of an image. Unlike a border, border extenders are otherwise invisible. Thus, they don't extend the dimensions of the image, they don't get processed by other operators, and they don't appear when the image is displayed. In Figure 6.8 the first column depicts an original source image, the source image with a border extender and the source image with a border of width 10 pixels on each side. The second column depicts these three images filtered using a 19x19 box filter with an origin at (10, 10). Note that the images in this figure were created using Listing 6.11.

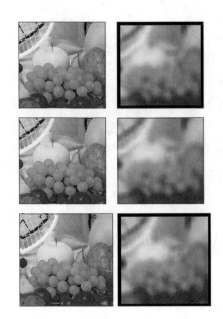

FIGURE 6.8

Borders versus border extenders.

An important thing to remember about border extenders is that they aren't operators, but are rendering hints. Thus they are used in a rendering by creating a rendering hints key/value pair with the key being JAI.KEY_BORDER_EXTENDER and the value being a java.media.jai.BorderExtender object. This key/value pair is then added to a RenderingHints object, that is,

```
BorderExtender extender;
extender = BorderExtender.createInstance(BorderExtender.BORDER_ZERO);
RenderingHints.Key extenderKey = JAI.KEY_BORDER_EXTENDER;
RenderingHints renderHints = new RenderingHints(extenderKey, extender);
```

This RenderingHints object can than be passed to a created RenderedOp in the JAI's create method. Listing 6.11 provides an example of the use of both borders and border extenders. This application produced the image shown in Figure 6.8.

LISTING 6.11   BordersAndBorderExtenders.java

```
package ch6;

import java.awt.*;
import javax.swing.*;
import java.io.*;
import java.awt.image.renderable.ParameterBlock;
```

LISTING 6.11   Continued

```java
import javax.media.jai.JAI;
import javax.media.jai.PlanarImage;
import javax.media.jai.BorderExtender;
import javax.media.jai.BorderExtenderConstant;
import javax.media.jai.RenderedOp;
import javax.media.jai.RenderedImageList;

/**
   BordersAndBorderExtenders -- this class illustrates box filtering
   using border extenders and using borders
 */
public class BordersAndBorderExtenders extends JFrame {

    public BordersAndBorderExtenders(String filename) {
        setTitle("ch6.BordersAndBorderExtenders");

        int extenderType = BorderExtender.BORDER_REFLECT;
        BorderExtender extender;
        extender = BorderExtender.createInstance(extenderType);

        RenderingHints.Key extenderKey = JAI.KEY_BORDER_EXTENDER;

        RenderingHints renderHints;
        renderHints = new RenderingHints(extenderKey, extender);

        RenderedOp sourceImage = loadImageFile(filename);
        RenderedOp filteredImage = filter(sourceImage);
        RenderedOp sourceImageWithExtender;
        sourceImageWithExtender = loadImageFile(filename, renderHints);
        RenderedOp filteredImageWithExtender;
        filteredImageWithExtender = filter(sourceImage, renderHints);

        // create image with black border of width 10 pixels on each side
        RenderedOp sourceImageWithBorder;
        sourceImageWithBorder = createBorderedImage(sourceImage, 10);
        RenderedOp filteredImageWithBorder;
        filteredImageWithBorder = filter(sourceImageWithBorder);


        getContentPane().setBackground(Color.white);
        getContentPane().setLayout(new GridLayout(3,2));
        getContentPane().add(new ch6Display(sourceImage));
        getContentPane().add(new ch6Display(filteredImage));
```

LISTING 6.11   Continued

```
        getContentPane().add(new ch6Display(sourceImageWithExtender));
        getContentPane().add(new ch6Display(filteredImageWithExtender));

        getContentPane().add(new ch6Display(sourceImageWithBorder));
        getContentPane().add(new ch6Display(filteredImageWithBorder));



        printSize(sourceImage, "sourceImage");
        printSize(sourceImage, "filteredImage");
        printSize(sourceImageWithExtender, "sourceImageWithExtender");
        printSize(filteredImageWithExtender, "filteredImageWithExtender");
        printSize(sourceImageWithBorder, "sourceImageWithBorder");
        printSize(filteredImageWithBorder, "filteredImageWithBorder");

        /*
           add a little extra space so viewer can
           distinguish between the different images
        */
        Insets insets = getInsets();
        int xsize = 2*(sourceImage.getWidth()+40);
        xsize += (insets.left+insets.right);
        int ysize = 3*(sourceImage.getHeight()+40);
        ysize += (insets.top+insets.bottom);
        setSize(xsize, ysize);
        show();
    }

    private void printSize(PlanarImage pi, String name) {
        System.out.print("Size of " + name + " is ");
        System.out.println(pi.getWidth() + ", " + pi.getHeight());
    }

    private RenderedOp loadImageFile(String filename) {
        ParameterBlock pb = new ParameterBlock();
        pb.add(filename);
        return JAI.create("fileload", pb);
    }

    private RenderedOp loadImageFile(String filename,
                                     RenderingHints rh) {
        ParameterBlock pb = new ParameterBlock();
        pb.add(filename);
        return JAI.create("fileload", pb, rh);
    }
```

LISTING 6.11   Continued

```java
    private RenderedOp createBorderedImage(PlanarImage pi,
                                           int length) {
        ParameterBlock borderParams =  new ParameterBlock();
        borderParams.addSource(pi);
        borderParams.add(new Integer(length));
        borderParams.add(new Integer(length));
        borderParams.add(new Integer(length));
        borderParams.add(new Integer(length));
        int extenderType = BorderExtender.BORDER_REFLECT;
        borderParams.add(BorderExtender.createInstance(extenderType));

        return JAI.create("Border", borderParams);
    }


    /**
       filter using a 19x19 box filter with an origin of 10,10
    */
    private RenderedOp filter(PlanarImage pi) {
        ParameterBlock param = new ParameterBlock();
        param.addSource(pi);
        param.add(19);
        param.add(19);
        param.add(10);
        param.add(10);
        return JAI.create("Boxfilter", param);
    }

    private RenderedOp filter(PlanarImage pi, RenderingHints rh) {
        ParameterBlock param = new ParameterBlock();
        param.addSource(pi);
        param.add(19);
        param.add(19);
        param.add(10);
        param.add(10);
        return JAI.create("Boxfilter", param, rh);
    }

    public static void main(String[] args) {
        if (args.length != 1) {
            System.err.print("USAGE: ");
            System.err.println("BordersAndBorderExtenders imageFilename");
        }
        else
            new BordersAndBorderExtenders(args[0]);
    }
}
```

The typical output for Listing 6.11 is the following:

```
Size of sourceImage is 256, 256
Size of filteredImage is 256, 256
Size of sourceImageWithExtender is 256, 256
Size of filteredImageWithExtender is 256, 256
Size of sourceImageWithBorder is 276, 276
Size of filteredImageWithBorder is 276, 276
```

Note that the border extenders didn't increase the image dimensions.

Geometric Operators

Geometric operators calculate destination pixel values by spatially transforming a destination image. In other words, each location in a destination image is transformed into a location in a source image. Because these new pixel locations might not correspond to integer values, interpolation must be used in order to derive an appropriate value for that location using the surrounding source pixel values. That calculated value will then be applied to the original destination pixel location. (For more information regarding interpolation, see Chapter 4.)

Because of this need for interpolation, most of the geometric operators require an interpolation type to be specified. This is done by instantiating a subclass of the javax.media.jai.Interpolation class. The possible subclasses are the javax.media.jai.Nearest (the default value), javax.media.jai.Bilinear, javax.media.jai.Bicubic, and javax.media.jai.Bicubic2 for nearest neighbor, bilinear, and two different types of bicubic polynomial interpolation, respectively.

For many of these geometric operations, there will be times when the operator requires image data that isn't available. For example, a translation of 20 pixels in the x direction will leave 20 columns in the destination image not containing data from that source image. One way to control what pixel values are placed in these columns is to specify a border extender as described in the previous section. The geometric operators are Affine, Rotate, Scale, Shear, Translate, Transpose and Warp (see Table 6.7).

It is important to note a discrepancy between the previous discussion and the operator descriptions in Table 6.7. As is commonly done, the operators are described as applying some type of transformation to a source image. What actually occurs is that the inverse transformation is applied to the destination image. This is done in order to obtain destination pixel values in the manner just described.

TABLE 6.7   Summary of Geometric Operators

Operator	*Parameter Block Format/Description*

Affine	addSource(PlanarImage pi);
	
	add(java.awt.geom.AffineTransform transform);
	
	add(javax.media.jai.Interpolation type);
	
	The Affine operator performs the affine transformation described by transform to source image pi.

Rotate	addSource(PlanarImage pi);
	
	add(float XOrigin);
	
	add(float YOrigin);
	
	add(float rotation);
	
	add(javax.media.jai.Interpolation type);
	
	The Rotate operator performs a rotation of rotation radians around point (xOrigin, yOrigin) of pi.

Scale	addSource(PlanarImage pi);
	
	add(float xScaleFactor);
	
	add(float yScaleFactor);
	
	add(float xTranslation);
	
	add(float yTranslation);
	
	add(javax.media.jai.Interpolation type);
	
	The Scale operator performs resizing and translating of source image pi, where
	
	destinationXLocation = sourceXLocation*xScaleFactor + xTranslation
	
	DestinationYLocation = sourceYLocation*yScaleFactor + yTranslation

Shear	addSource(PlanarImage pi);
	
	add(float shear);
	
	add(javax.media.jai.operator.ShearDir direction);
	
	add(float xTranslation);
	
	add(float yTranslation);
	
	add(javax.media.jai.Interpolation type);
	
	The Shear operator performs shearing on the source image pi, where direction must be one of the following values:
	
	ShearDescriptor.SHEAR_HORIZONTAL or ShearDescriptor.SHEAR_VERTICAL
	
	The shear equations are as follows:
	
	For a direction of SHEAR_HORIZONTAL:

TABLE 6.7   Continued

Operator	Parameter Block Format/Description
	destinationXLocation = sourceXLocation + xTranslation + shear*sourceYLocation
	destinationYLocation = sourceYLocation;
	For a direction of `SHEAR_VERTICAL`:
	destinationXLocation = sourceXLocation;
	destinationYLocation = sourceYLocation + yTranslation + shear*sourceXLocation
Translate	addSource(PlanarImage pi);
	add(float xTrans);
	add(float yTrans);
	add(javax.media.jai.Interpolation type);
	The `Translate` operator translates pi by xTrans in the x direction and yTrans in the y direction.
Transpose	addSource(PlanarImage pi);
	add(javax.media.jai.operator.TransposeType type);
	The `Transpose` operator transposes pi using one of the following values:
	`TransposeDescriptor.FLIP_VERTICAL`, `TransposeDescriptor.FLIP_HORIZONTAL`, `TransposeDescriptor.FLIP_DIAGONAL`, `TransposeDescriptor.FLIP_ANTIDIAGONAL`, `TransposeDescriptor.ROTATE_90`, `TransposeDescriptor.ROTATE_180`, `TransposeDescriptor.ROTATE_270`
Warp	addSource(PlanarImage pi);
	add(java.media.jai.WARP warp);
	add(javax.media.jai.Interpolation type);
	The `Warp` operator defines a warping of the source image pi. Possible concrete classes for warp are `javax.media.jai.WarpGrid`, which contains a mapping of rectilinear points on the destination image to the source image pi; `javax.media.jai.WarpQuadratic`, which maps destination pixels to the source image pi through a pair of quadratic bivariate polynomial functions; and javax.media.jai.WarpPerspective, which uses a javax.media.jai.Perspective transformation to map destination pixels into the source image pi.

Color Quantization Operators

Two operators, ErrorDiffusion and OrderedDither, are used for situations in which the output device cannot represent the colors contained in the image. For example, a monitor might be limited to only displaying 256 colors, whereas a JPEG image might have thousands of different colors that need to be represented (see Table 6.8).

TABLE 6.8   Summary of Quantization Operators

Operator	Parameter Block Format/Description
ErrorDiffusion	addSource(PlanarImage pi);
	add(LookupTableJAI table);
	add(javax.media.jai.KernelJAI kernel);
	The ErrorDiffusion operator finds the closest available pixel value from the lookup table, table. It then calculates how different the actual pixel value is from the found pixel value and applies a portion of this difference to the pixel under it and the pixel to the right of it in order to make this difference appear less noticeable. For example, a pink pixel might be effectively replaced by a red one if white is added to its neighboring pixel values.
	The default kernel value is
	KernelJAI.ERROR_FILTER_FLOYD_STEINBERG
OrderedDither	addSource(PlanarImage pi);
	add(javax.media.jai.ColorCube cube);
	add(javax.media.jai.KernelJAI dithermask);
	The OrderedDither operator finds the closest available pixel value from the provided ColorCube. It then adds some pseudo-randomness in the found color table index by using the provided dither mask.
	The default value for cube is ColorCube.BYTE_496 and the default value for dithermask is KernelJAI.DITHER_MASK_443.

Statistical Operators

Statistical operators are unique because they don't change any of the pixel values in the source image (see Table 6.9). Their only effect is to add one or more properties to a PlanarImage. For example, the Extrema operator adds a property called "minimum", which represents the minimum value in each band; a property called "maximum", which represents the maximum value in each band; and a property called "extrema", which represents both the minimum and maximum values in each band. Thus, this line of code:

```
double[] minValuesForEachBand = (double [])planarImage.getProperty("minimum");
```

has the same affect as these two lines:

```
double[][] extrema = (double[][])planarImage.getProperty("extrema");
double[] minValuesForEachBand = extrema[0];
```

TABLE 6.9   Summary of Statistical Operators

Operator	Parameter Block Format/Description
Extrema	addSource(PlanarImage pi);
	add(javax.media.jai.ROI roi);
	add(int xPeriod);
	add(int yPeriod);
	The Extrema operator computes the minimum and maximum of each band in pi using x and y sampling periods of xPeriod and yPeriod over the regions specified by roi. This operator adds the following properties: double[] minimum, double[] maximum, and double[][]extrema where minimum = extrema[0] and maximum = extrema[1]. The default value of roi is null, which means that the entire image will be processed. Also, the default values for xPeriod and yPeriod are 1.
Histogram	addSource(PlanarImage pi);
	add(javax.media.jai.ROI roi);
	add(int xPeriod);
	add(int yPeriod);
	add(int[] numBins);
	add(double[] lowValue);
	add(double[] highValue);
	The Histogram operator computes a histogram of each band of pi using x and y sampling periods of xPeriod and yPeriod over the regions specified by roi. The histogram will have numBins bins and will only contain those pixel values that are greater than or equal to lowValue and less than or equal to highValue. This operator adds a property called "histogram" of class javax.media.jai.Histogram. The default value for roi is null, which means that the entire image will be processed. The default values for xPeriod and yPeriod are 1, the default value for numBins is {256}, and the default values for lowValue and highValue are {0.0} and {256.0}, respectively.

TABLE 6.9   Continued

Operator	Parameter Block Format/Description
Mean	addSource(PlanarImage pi);
	add(javax.media.jai.ROI roi);
	add(int xPeriod);
	add(int yPeriod);
	The Mean operator finds the mean value of each band in pi using x and y sampling periods of xPeriod and yPeriod over the region specified by roi. This operator adds a property called "mean" of type double[]. The default value for roi is null, which means that the entire image will be processed and the default values for xPeriod and yPeriod are 1.

Frequency Operators

In this section, we will examine the operators for converted to and from the frequency domain as well as some other operators that are useful for frequency domain filtering. These operators are the Conjugate, DCT, DFT, IDCT, IDFT, ImageFunction, Magnitude, MagnitudeSquared, PeriodicShift, Phase, and PolarToComplex operators (see Table 6.10). Prior to this examination, we first need to take a closer look at complex images.

As previously discussed, a complex image is similar to a regular image except that it has two components: a real component and an imaginary component. Thus, a gray scale complex image requires two bands to represent it and an RGB complex image requires six bands. For this reason, in any operator that converts from the spatial domain to the frequency domain (dct and dft), the number of bands in the returned image will be twice that of the source image. Likewise, in any operator converting from the frequency domain to the space domain (idct and idft), the number of bands in the returned image will be half that of the source image.

TABLE 6.10   Summary of Frequency Operators

Operator	Parameter Block Format/Description
Conjugate	addSource(PlanarImage pi);
	The Conjugate operator computes the complex conjugate of pi.
DCT	addSource(PlanarImage pi);
	The DCT operator computes the discrete cosine transform of pi.
DFT	addSource(PlanarImage pi);
	add(int scalingType);
	add(int dataNature);

TABLE 6.10   Continued

Operator	Parameter Block Format/Description
	The DFT operator computes the discrete Fourier transform of pi, where scalingType must be one of the following:
	DFTDescriptor.SCALING_NONE, DFTDescriptor.SCALING_UNITARY, or DFTDescriptor.SCALING_DIMENSIONS
	and dataNature must be one of the following:
	DFTDescriptor.REAL_TO_COMPLEX, DFTDescriptor.COMPLEX_TO_COMPLEX, or DFTDescriptor.COMPLEX_TO_REAL.
IDCT	addSource(PlanarImage pi);
	The IDCT operator computes the inverse discrete cosine transform of complex image pi.
IDFT	addSource(PlanarImage pi);
	add(int scalingType);
	add(int dataNature);
	The IDFT operator computes the inverse discrete Fourier transform of complex image pi, where scalingType must be one of the following:
	DFTDescriptor.SCALING_NONE, DFTDescriptor.SCALING_UNITARY, or DFTDescriptor.SCALING_DIMENSIONS
	and dataNature must be one of the following:
	DFTDescriptor.REAL_TO_COMPLEX, DFTDescriptor.COMPLEX_TO_COMPLEX, or DFTDescriptor.COMPLEX_TO_REAL
ImageFunction	addSource(PlanarImage pi);
	add(int width);
	add(int height);
	add(float xscale);
	add(float yscale);
	add(float xTrans);
	add(float yTrans);
	The ImageFunction operator sends the pixels in pi to the ImageFunction function by calling the ImageFunction's getData method. The actual data locations passed to this function will be
	xScale*(Xlocation - xTrans)
	yScale*(YLocation - yTrans)
	where xLocation, yLocation are the pixel's locations in pi. Default values for xscale and yscale are 1.0, and the default values for xTrans and yTrans are 0.0.

TABLE 6.10 Continued

Operator	Parameter Block Format/Description
Magnitude	addSource(PlanarImage pi);
	The Magnitude operator finds the magnitude of each pixel in the complex image pi.
MagnitudeSquared	addSource(PlanarImage pi);
	The MagnitudeSquared operator finds the squared magnitude of each pixel in the complex image pi.
PeriodicShift	addSource(PlanarImage pi);
	add(int xShift);
	add(int yShift);
	The PeriodicShift operator computes the periodic translation of the complex image pi.
Phase	addSource(PlanarImage pi);
	The Phase operator computes the phase angle of each pixel in the complex image pi.
PolarToComplex	addSource(PlanarImage pi);
	The PolarToComplex operator computes a complex image from a magnitude and phase image represented by pi.

An example of many of these operators can be found in Listing 6.12. In this listing, the DFT of a source image is computed and the resulting complex image is processed for display purposes (see Figure 6.9).

LISTING 6.12 DFTTester

```
package ch6;

import java.awt.*;
import javax.swing.*;
import java.io.*;
import javax.media.jai.JAI;
import javax.media.jai.operator.DFTDescriptor;
import javax.media.jai.KernelJAI;
import javax.media.jai.RenderedOp;
import javax.media.jai.RenderedImageList;
import java.awt.image.renderable.ParameterBlock;
```

LISTING 6.12 Continued

```
/**
    DFTTester -- displays the provided image along side its DFT
*/
public class DFTTester extends JFrame {

    public DFTTester(String filename) {
        setTitle("DFT Tester");
        RenderedOp inputImage = loadImage(filename);
        RenderedOp dftComplexImage = computeDFT(inputImage);
        RenderedOp dftMagnitudeImage = computeMagnitudes(dftComplexImage);
        RenderedOp dftLogImage = computeLogImage(dftMagnitudeImage);
        RenderedOp formattedLogImage = formatForDisplay(dftLogImage);

        getContentPane().setLayout(new GridLayout(1,2));
        getContentPane().add(new ch6Display(inputImage));
        getContentPane().add(new ch6Display(formattedLogImage));

        pack();
        show();
    }

    private RenderedOp loadImage(String filename) {
        ParameterBlock param = new ParameterBlock();
        param.add(filename);
        return JAI.create("Fileload", param);
    }

    /**
        perform Discrete Fourier Transform
    */
    private RenderedOp computeDFT(RenderedOp ro) {
        ParameterBlock param =  new ParameterBlock();
        param.addSource(ro);
        param.add(DFTDescriptor.SCALING_NONE);
        param.add(DFTDescriptor.REAL_TO_COMPLEX);
        return JAI.create("DFT", param);
    }

    /**
        computes the magnitude image from a supplied complex image.
        The number of bands will be decreased by 2
    */
    private RenderedOp computeMagnitudes(RenderedOp ro) {
        ParameterBlock param =  new ParameterBlock();
        param.addSource(ro);
```

LISTING 6.12   Continued

```java
        return JAI.create("Magnitude", param);
    }

    /**
       performs log(pixelValue+1)
    */
    private RenderedOp computeLogImage(RenderedOp ro) {
        ParameterBlock param;

        param =  new ParameterBlock();
        param.addSource(ro);
        double[] constant = {1.0};
        param.add(constant);
        RenderedOp tmp = JAI.create("addConst", param);

        param =  new ParameterBlock();
        param.addSource(tmp);
        return JAI.create("log", param);
    }


    /**
       1. scales input image so that the maximum value is 255
       2. shifts scaled image so DC frequency is in center
       3. formats shifted image to a datatype of byte
    */
    private RenderedOp formatForDisplay(RenderedOp ro) {
        ParameterBlock param;

        param=  new ParameterBlock();
        param.addSource(ro);
        param.add(null);
        param.add(1);
        param.add(1);
        RenderedOp statsImage = JAI.create("Extrema", param);
        double[] maximum = (double[]) statsImage.getProperty("maximum");

        param = new ParameterBlock();
        param.addSource(ro);
        double[] scale = {255.0/maximum[0]};
        param.add(scale);
        double[] offset = {0.0};
        param.add(offset);
        RenderedOp rescaledImage = JAI.create("Rescale", param);
```

LISTING 6.12   Continued

```
            param = new ParameterBlock();
            param.addSource(rescaledImage);
            param.add(new Integer(rescaledImage.getWidth()/2));
            param.add(new Integer(rescaledImage.getHeight()/2));
            RenderedOp shiftedImage = JAI.create("PeriodicShift", param);

            param = new ParameterBlock();
            param.addSource(shiftedImage);
            param.add(java.awt.image.DataBuffer.TYPE_BYTE);
            return JAI.create("format", param);
    }

    public static void main(String[] args) {
        if (args.length != 1)
            System.err.println("USAGE:  DFTTester filename");
        else
            new DFTTester(args[0]);
    }
}
```

FIGURE 6.9
Illustration of output from the DFTTester.java *application shown in Listing 6.12.*

JAI IO

One of the most useful aspects of JAI is the ability to easily read and write image data. Images can be loaded into a PlanarImage if they are contained in a formatted image file, a nonformatted image file, or a BufferedImage. Likewise, the data contained in a PlanarImage can be written into a file as either formatted or unformatted data or the PlanarImage can be converted into a BufferedImage.

File Operator

There are an assortment of operators for reading a specific image format such as BMP, GIF, FPX, JPEG, PNG, PNM, and TIFF (see Table 6.11).

> **NOTE**
>
> The IO for JAI is built on the Image IO package discussed in Chapter 5, so there shouldn't be a discrepancy between the file formats the Image IO package can decode/encode and the file formats the JAI package can decode/encode.

In Table 6.11, the list of IO operators is presented. Note that many of them allow optional encoder or decoder objects in order to provide more control over reading and writing images of specific formats.

TABLE 6.11 Summary of File Operators

Operator	*Parameter Block Format/Description*
AWTImage	add(java.awt.Image image); The AWTImage operator converts a java.awt.Image into a PlanarImage.
BMP	add(com.sun.media.jai.codec.SeekableStream stream); The BMP operator decodes the bmp image contained in stream.

Encode	addSource(PlanarImage pi);
	
	add(java.io.OutputStream stream);
	
	add(String format);
	
	add(com.sun.media.jai.codec.ImageEncodeParam param);
	
	The Encode operator encodes pi onto stream using given format and encoding parameters. The default value for format is "tiff", and the default value for param is null.

FileLoad	add(String filename);
	
	add(com.sun.media.jai.codec.ImageDecodeParam param);
	
	add(boolean checkFileLocally);
	
	The FileLoad operator decodes the image contained in file filename using the given decoding parameters. The image format isn't specified. When loading remote files, checkFileLocally should be set to false; otherwise, an IllegalArgumentException will be thrown when the file isn't found on the local file system. The default value for param is null, and the default value for checkFileLocally is true.

TABLE 6.11   Continued

Operator	Parameter Block Format/Description
FileStore	`addSource(PlanarImage pi);`
	`add(String filename);`
	`add(String format);`
	`add(com.sun.media.jai.codec.ImageEncodeParam param);`
	The FileStore operator encodes pi into file filename using given format and encoding parameters. The default value for format is "tiff" and the default value for param is null.
FPX	`add(com.sun.media.jai.codec.SeekableStream stream);`
	`add(com.sun.media.jai.codec.FPXDecodeParam param);`
	The FPX operator decodes the fpx image contained in stream. The default value of param is null.
GIF	`add(com.sun.media.jai.codec.SeekableStream stream);`
	The GIF operator decodes the gif image contained in stream.
IIP	`add(String url);`
	`add(int[] subImages);`
	`add(float filter);`
	`add(float contrast);`
	`add(Rectangle2D.Float sourceROI);`
	`add(AffineTransform transform);`
	`add(float aspectRatio);`
	`add(Rectangle2DFloat destROI);`
	`add(int rotation);`
	`add(String mirrorAxis);`
	`add(ICC_Profile iccprofile);`
	`add(int jpegquality);`
	`add(int jpegtable);`
	The IIP operator creates a java.awt.image.RenderedImage or a java.awt.image.renderable.RenderableImage based on the data received from the Internet Imaging Protocol (IIP) server. It can optionally apply a sequence of operations to the created image. Refer to the IIP specifications found at http://www.digitalimaging.org for more complete information on this operator.

TABLE 6.11   Continued

Operator	Parameter Block Format/Description

IIPResolution	`add(String url);`
	`add(int resolution);`
	`add(int subImage);`
	
	The `IIPResolution` operator requests from the IIP server an image located at `url` with a resolution level of `resolution`. It then creates a `java.awt.image.RenderedImage` based on the data received from the server. The default value for `resolution` is `IIPResolutionDescriptor.MAX_RESOLUTION`, and the default value for `subImage` is `0`.

JPEG	`add(com.sun.media.jai.codec.SeekableStream stream);` The `JPEG` operator decodes the jpeg image contained in `stream`.

PNG	`add(com.sun.media.jai.codec.SeekableStream stream);`
	`add(com.sun.media.jai.codec.PNGDecodeParam param);`
	
	The `PNG` operator decodes png images contained in `stream`. The default value of `param` is `null`.

PNM	`add(com.sun.media.jai.codec.SeekableStream stream);`
	`add(com.sun.media.jai.codec.PNGDecodeParam param);`
	
	The `PNM` operator decodes the pnm image contained in `stream`. The default value of `param` is `null`.

Stream	`add(com.sun.media.jai.codec.SeekableStream stream);`
	`add(com.sun.media.jai.codec.ImageDecodeParam param);`
	
	The `Stream` operator decodes the image contained in `stream`. The image format isn't specified. The default value of `param` is `null`.

TIFF	`add(com.sun.media.jai.codec.SeekableStream stream);`
	`add(com.sun.media.jai.codec.TIFFDecodeParam param);`
	`add(int page);`
	
	The `TIFF` operator decodes page `page` of the tiff image contained in `stream`. The default value of `param` is `null`, and the default value of `page` is `0`.

URL	`add(java.net.URL url);`
	`add(com.sun.media.jai.codec.ImageDecodeParam param);`
	
	The `URL` operator decodes the image contained in `url`. The image format isn't specified. The default value of `param` is `null`.

There are also three main operators for reading images without specifying an image format. They are the FileLoad, Stream, and URL operators. These operators examine the image bytes to decode the image format and then call the appropriate operator—that is, TIFF, GIF, and so on. Listing 6.13 shows all three operators being used to read the same image data. Writing format-ted image data is done by using the FileStore and Encode operators, which write out image data of a specified format to a file or to a stream, respectively.

LISTING 6.13   ImageLoadTester

```java
package ch6;

import java.awt.*;
import java.awt.image.*;
import javax.swing.*;
import java.io.*;
import java.net.*;
import java.awt.image.renderable.ParameterBlock;
import javax.media.jai.RenderedOp;
import javax.media.jai.JAI;
import com.sun.media.jai.codec.SeekableStream;

/**
    ImageLoadTester -- loads an image using the JAI class' create method.
    This method uses 3 different operator names to load the image
    in 3 different manners, namely "stream", "fileload" and "url"

    It then prints out the properties of the loaded image
 */
public class ImageLoadTester extends JFrame {

    public ImageLoadTester(String filename) {
        SeekableStream stream = null;
        URL url = null;

        try {
            url = new URL("file:"+filename);
            stream = SeekableStream.wrapInputStream(url.openStream(),
                                                    false);
        }
        catch (IOException ioe) {
            System.err.println("IOException: " + ioe.getMessage());
        }
```

LISTING 6.13   Continued

```
        params = new ParameterBlock();
        params.add(stream);
        RenderedOp streamImage = JAI.create("stream", params);

        params = new ParameterBlock();
        params.add(filename);
        RenderedOp fileImage = JAI.create("fileload", params);

        params = new ParameterBlock();
        params.add(url);
        RenderedOp urlImage = JAI.create("url", params);

        //Display Image Properties
        String[] props = streamImage.getPropertyNames();
        for (int i=0;i<props.length;i++) {
            System.out.print("Property: " + props[i] + ", ");
            System.out.println(streamImage.getProperty(props[i]));
        }

        getContentPane().setLayout(new GridLayout(1, 3));
        getContentPane().add(new ch6Display(streamImage));
        getContentPane().add(new ch6Display(fileImage));
        getContentPane().add(new ch6Display(urlImage));

        pack();
        show();
    }

    public static void main(String[] args) {
        if (args.length != 1)
            System.err.println("USAGE:  ImageLoadTester filename");
        else
            new ImageLoadTester(args[0]);
    }
    private ParameterBlock params;
}
```

Reading Unformatted Images

If there is no defined format for an image or the JAI decoders cannot decode the image's format, you'll need to convert the raw pixel data into a PlanarImage yourself. Listing 6.14 illustrates how to read in a series of tiles concatenated into a single image. A common situation in medical imaging occurs when a series of slices are concatenated into a single image file. In this listing, the tiles are assumed to be composed of a single band containing float data.

LISTING 6.14   FloatViewer

```java
package ch6;

import javax.media.jai.*;
import java.awt.*;
import java.awt.color.*;
import java.awt.image.*;
import java.awt.image.renderable.*;
import javax.swing.*;
import java.io.*;

/**
   FloatViewer.java - reads a image file composes of float values,
   scales it for display purposes and displays it.

   This image file can be composed of any number of different images
   as long as they are the same dimensions (referred to as tileWidth
   and tileHeight);
*/
public class FloatViewer extends JFrame {
    public FloatViewer(String filename, String tileWidth,
                       String tileHeight) {
        File f = new File(filename);
        if ( !(f.exists()) ) {
            System.err.println("File: " + filename + " does not exist ");
            System.exit(1);
        }
        this.tileWidth = Integer.parseInt(tileWidth);
        this.tileHeight = Integer.parseInt(tileHeight);

        float[][] dataArray = getData(f);
        PlanarImage inputImage = getTiledImage(dataArray);

        double scaleFactor = findScale(inputImage);
        ParameterBlock pb = new ParameterBlock();
        pb.addSource(inputImage);
        pb.add(new double[] {1.0/scaleFactor});
        pb.add(new double[] {0.0});

        RenderedOp scaledImage = JAI.create("rescale", pb);
        getContentPane().setLayout(new BorderLayout());
        getContentPane().add(new JScrollPane(new ch6Display(scaledImage)),
                             BorderLayout.CENTER);
```

LISTING 6.14   Continued

```java
        show();
        pack();
}

/**
   provides a scale factor for displaying the image data.
*/
private double findScale(PlanarImage pi) {
    ParameterBlock pb = new ParameterBlock();
    pb.addSource(pi);
    PlanarImage pi2 = JAI.create("extrema", pb);
    double[] maximum = (double[])pi2.getProperty("maximum");
    double maxValue = maximum[0];
    return maxValue/2.0;
}

/**
   reads the image data from the file and stores it in an
   array of javax.media.jai.DataBufferFloat elements
   with each tile being stored in a
   separate javax.media.jai.DataBufferFloat element.
*/
private float[][] getData(File file) {
    numberFloats = (int)(file.length()/4); //4 bytes per float
    numberFloatsPerTile = tileWidth*tileHeight;
    numberTiles = numberFloats/numberFloatsPerTile;

    float[][] floatArray = null;
    floatArray = new float[numberTiles][numberFloats];

    try {
        FileInputStream fis = new FileInputStream(file);
        BufferedInputStream bis;
        bis = new BufferedInputStream(fis, numberFloatsPerTile*4);
        DataInputStream dis = new DataInputStream(bis);
        for (int i=0;i<numberTiles;i++) {
            for (int j=0;j<numberFloatsPerTile;j++)
                floatArray[i][j] = dis.readFloat();
        }
        dis.close();
    }
    catch (IOException ioe) {
        System.err.println("IO Exception: " + ioe.getMessage());
        System.exit(1);
```

LISTING 6.14   Continued

```
        }
        return floatArray;
    }

    /**
       creates a TiledImage from an array of
       javax.media.jai.DataBufferFloats
    */
    private PlanarImage getTiledImage(float[][] dataArray) {
        int numberHorizontalTiles;
        int numberVerticalTiles;

        // calculate number of tiles per column and per row
        double tmp = Math.sqrt((double)numberTiles);
        numberVerticalTiles = (int)tmp;
        numberHorizontalTiles = numberTiles/numberVerticalTiles;
        while (numberHorizontalTiles*numberVerticalTiles < numberTiles)
            numberHorizontalTiles++;

        imageWidth = numberHorizontalTiles*tileWidth;
        imageHeight = numberVerticalTiles*tileHeight;

        SampleModel inputImageSM;
        int dt = DataBuffer.TYPE_FLOAT;
        inputImageSM = RasterFactory.createBandedSampleModel(dt,
                                                    tileWidth,
                                                    tileHeight,
                                                    1);

        ColorModel inputImageCM;
        inputImageCM = PlanarImage.createColorModel(inputImageSM);

        /*
           create TiledImage -- note that the tile dimensions come from
           the SampleModel
        */
        TiledImage ti = new TiledImage(0, 0,
                                        imageWidth, imageHeight,
                                        0, 0,
                                        inputImageSM,
                                        inputImageCM);
```

LISTING 6.14 Continued

```java
        // now load the data into the TiledImage
        WritableRaster wr;
        int index = 0;
        for (int j=0;j<numberVerticalTiles;j++)
            for (int i=0;i<numberHorizontalTiles;i++)
                if (index < numberTiles) {
                    wr = ti.getWritableTile(i, j);
                    wr.setPixels(i*tileWidth, j*tileHeight,
                                 tileWidth, tileHeight,
                                 dataArray[index]);
                    index++;
                }
        return ti;
    }


    static public void main(String[] args) {
        if (args.length != 3) {
            System.err.print("USAGE:  FloatViewer ");
            System.err.println("floatImageFile tileWidth tileHeight");
        }
        else
            new FloatViewer(args[0], args[1], args[2]);
    }

    private int numberFloats;
    private int numberTiles;
    private int numberFloatsPerTile;
    private int tileWidth;
    private int tileHeight;
    private int imageWidth;
    private int imageHeight;
}
```

CAUTION

Running Listing 6.14 might cause an `OutOfMemoryError` error to occur. The easiest way to avoid this is to increase the amount of memory allocated to the JVM. In order to do this, use something like the following:

```
java -Xms32m -Xmx128m classFilename
```

This increases the initial memory allocation from 4 megabytes to 32 megabytes and the maximum memory allocation from 16 megabytes to 128 megabytes.

Converting to and from Images and Buffered Images

As we have previously discussed, some of the functionality contained within the `PlanarImage` class is available in a `BufferedImage`, although usually to a lesser extent. Other `PlanarImage` features don't exist in the `BufferedImage` at all. Thus, you need to perform some type of conversion on a `BufferedImage` in order to use it with the JAI package. To do this, convert the `BufferedImage` to a `RenderedImageAdapter` class using the following constructor:

```
public RenderedImageAdapter(RenderedImage src)
```

Because the `RenderedImageAdapter` class is a subclass of the `PlanarImage` class, it can be used wherever the `PlanarImage` class is expected. (Basically it is a `PlanarImage` with no sources.) When creating a `RenderedImageAdapter` in this manner, the data from the `BufferedImage` is copied so subsequent changes to the `BufferedImage` won't affect the `RenderedImageAdapter`.

> **NOTE**
>
> Because both a `BufferedImage` and a `PlanarImage` implement the `RenderedImage` interface, they can both be referred to as a `RenderedImages`. The `RenderedImageAdaptor` is "idempotent" however, meaning that a `BufferedImage` will be converted to a `PlanarImage`, but a `PlanarImage` will be unchanged.

To go from a `PlanarImage` to a `BufferedImage`, you can simply use the `PlanarImage`'s `getAsBufferedImage` method, which returns a copy of the `PlanarImage`'s data contained in a `BufferedImage`.

In some cases, you will have a `java.awt.Image` object that needs to be converted into a `PlanarImage`. In this case you can use the `AWTImage` operator mentioned in Table 6.11.

Advanced Topics

What follows are some advanced topics that we are unable to cover to the extent that they deserve. We have provided enough information to allow you to understand the basics of each topic. We have also provided code samples so that you'll be able to experiment with these features without having to worry about getting things set up and running.

RenderedOps Versus RenderableOps

In some situations a `RenderedOp` is created without knowing how its `RenderedImage` is going to be used. For example, it could be displayed on a low resolution monitor or a high resolution printer. Similarly, it could be displayed as a thumbnail image or it could be scaled to fit a user specified region. The user could specify that it be rendered with an emphasis on speed or an emphasis on quality. For these reasons, it might make sense to wait until all the relevant rendering information is decided before any rendering hints are set. When working with RenderedOps, this isn't possible because the RenderingHints objects are contained in the RenderedOp object and must be available when the RenderedOp is instantiated. For this reason, the RenderableOp layer was developed.

Unlike a RenderedOp, a RenderableOp doesn't contain a RenderingHints because it isn't capable of creating a RenderedImage directly. Instead, after all the rendering hints have been decided, you can pass the RenderingHints to a RenderableOp, which then uses it to create a RenderedOp. The RenderedOp then makes the RenderedImage, which is returned. Although there are RenderableOp methods to create a rendering, this rendering is done in two steps using an intermediate RenderedOp.

One way to think about the relationship between RenderedOps and RenderableOps is that the RenderableOp DAGs are templates to create RenderedOp DAGs. This relationship is similar to that of a class and an object. A single class can be used to form many objects which, depending on the values of their instance variables, can act very differently. Similarly, a RenderableOp can be used to create many RenderedOps which, depending on the values of their RenderingHints, can act very differently.

When a RenderableOp is rendered, it is usually through its

```
public RenderedImage createScaledRendering(int width,
                                           int height,
                                           RenderContext rc)
```

method. After this method is called, the RenderableOp checks whether its sources are rendered. If not, it requests that they become rendered, and this request makes its way up the RenderableOp DAG in the same way that a rendering request makes its way up a RenderedOp DAG. Thus, both RenderedOps and RenderableOps operate in the pull imaging mode. The main difference is that the RenderableOp DAG creates a RenderedOp DAG to produce the final RenderedImage and, of course, a RenderedOp DAG creates the RenderedImage itself.

One last operator that needs to be discussed is the Renderable operator. This operator takes a RenderedImage source, such as a RenderedOp, and converts it into a RenderableOp for use in a RenderableOp DAG (see Table 6.12).

TABLE 6.12   The Renderable Operator

Operator	Parameter Block Format/Description
Renderable	addSource(PlanarImage pi);
	add(RenderedOp downSampler);

TABLE 6.12   Continued

Operator	Parameter Block Format/Description
	`add(int maxLowResDim);`
	`add(float minX);`
	`add(float minY);`
	`add(float height);`
	The `Renderable` operator produces a `RenderableImage` from a `RenderedImage` source, `pi`. The default value for `downSampler` is `null`, the default value for `maxLowResDim` is `64`, the default values for `minX` and `minY` are `0.0`, and the default value for `height` is `1.0`.

Listing 6.15 provides an example of the "`Renderable`" operator. In this example, an image is loaded from a file, inverted and rotated using a `RenderableOp` DAG. It is then displayed two times, once as a small image with an emphasis on rendering speed and once as a larger image with an emphasis on rendering quality.

LISTING 6.15   RenderableImageTester

```
package ch6;

import java.awt.*;
import javax.swing.*;
import java.awt.image.renderable.ParameterBlock;
import java.awt.image.RenderedImage;
import javax.media.jai.JAI;
import javax.media.jai.PlanarImage;
import javax.media.jai.RenderedOp;
import javax.media.jai.RenderableOp;

/**
    RenderableImageTester.java -- objects of this class
    3.  create a RenderableOp by loading image contained in filename
    4.  create a 2nd RenderableOp representing the rotation
        of the first RenderableOp
    5.  displays the final RenderedOp
    6.  displays the RenderableOp according to desired image width and
        height and rendering hints
*/
public class RenderableImageTester extends JFrame {
    public RenderableImageTester(String filename) {
        int xScale, yScale;
```

LISTING 6.15   Continued

```
RenderedOp imageSource = readInputFile(filename);
RenderableOp renderableInput = getRenderable(imageSource);
RenderableOp invertedRenderable;
invertedRenderable = createRenderableInverted(renderableInput);
RenderableOp rotatedRenderable;
rotatedRenderable = createRenderableRotated(invertedRenderable);


RenderingHints rh;
rh = new RenderingHints(RenderingHints.KEY_RENDERING,
                        RenderingHints.VALUE_RENDER_SPEED);

xScale = imageSource.getWidth()/2;
yScale = imageSource.getHeight()/2;

RenderedImage smallRendered;
smallRendered = rotatedRenderable.createScaledRendering(xScale,
                                                        yScale,
                                                        rh);

rh = new RenderingHints(RenderingHints.KEY_RENDERING,
                        RenderingHints.VALUE_RENDER_QUALITY);
xScale = imageSource.getWidth()*2;
yScale = imageSource.getHeight()*2;

RenderedImage largeRendered;
largeRendered = rotatedRenderable.createScaledRendering(xScale,
                                                        yScale,
                                                        rh);
getContentPane().setLayout(new GridLayout(1,2));
getContentPane().add(new ch6Display(smallRendered));
getContentPane().add(new ch6Display(largeRendered));

pack();
show();
}

private RenderedOp readInputFile(String filename) {
    ParameterBlock pb = new ParameterBlock();
    pb.add(filename);
    return JAI.create("fileload", pb);
}
```

LISTING 6.15   Continued

```java
private RenderableOp getRenderable(RenderedOp ro) {
    ParameterBlock pb = new ParameterBlock();
    pb.addSource(ro);
    pb.add(null);
    pb.add(null);
    pb.add(null);
    pb.add(null);
    pb.add(null);
    return JAI.createRenderable("renderable", pb);
}


/**
   Returns a RenderableOp representing a inverted
   version of RenderableOp toBeInverted
*/
private RenderableOp createRenderableInverted(RenderableOp inputro) {
    ParameterBlock param;
    param =   new ParameterBlock();
    param.addSource(inputro);
    RenderableOp ro = JAI.createRenderable("Invert", param);

    return ro;
}


/**
   Returns a RenderableOp representing a rotated
   version of RenderableOp toBeRotatedRO
*/
private RenderableOp createRenderableRotated(RenderableOp inputro) {
    float angle = (float)((45.0/180.0)*Math.PI); //45 degree rotation

    ParameterBlock param;
    param =   new ParameterBlock();
    param.addSource(inputro);
    param.add(new Float(inputro.getWidth()/2));
    param.add(new Float(inputro.getHeight()/2));
    param.add(new Float(angle));
    RenderableOp ro = JAI.createRenderable("Rotate", param);

    return ro;
}
```

LISTING 6.15 Continued

```
public static void main(String[] args) {
    if (args.length != 1)
        System.err.println("Usage:  filename");
    else
        new RenderableImageTester(args[0]);
    }
}
```

Client/Server Imaging

In jdk1.2, Java introduced support for *remote method invocation (RMI)*, which allows you to run a JVM on two different machines and have objects running in one JVM call methods on objects running on another JVM. This can be useful in situations in which there is a reason for running a method on a different computer; for instance it might have a faster CPU, a database, or special files. In JAI, Java not only continues its support for RMI, but also has greatly simplified working with remote images.

The basic idea behind RMI is that a client appears to make a method call on a remote object, but actually makes a method call on something called a *stub* object. This stub object serializes all the method parameters and brings them over to the remote machine where they are placed into the remote machines local memory. The remote object then performs the specified method using these local objects and provides a return object to the stub. (This return object could be a thrown exception.) The stub serializes this return object and brings it back to the client machine where it is placed into local memory. If it is an exception, it is rethrown in the space of the original method call. Thus, in summary, both the client and the server are performing local operations, but the stub object provides the appropriate data transfer, data packaging, and data unpackaging so that it appears as if the client is actually calling a remote method.

TIP

The process of serializing and packaging parameters is usually referred to as *parameter marshalling.*

One obstacle to implementing this type of system is that for it to work, the stub object needs to be instantiated on the remote server and retrieved by the client when it is needed. Thus, the client must know where to get this stub object. This is done by having the server registering its stub object with an rmi registry. The rmi registry is an application provided as part of the standard jdk. The rmi registry runs on the server using a known port (1099 is the default) so that the client knows how to find it.

In basic Java RMI, the programmer must create the client application, the remote classes, and the remote server application containing the code to register the stub object(s) with the rmi registry. In JAI, you only need to write the client application. After starting the rmi registry, you simply need to start the predefined JAI remote class (java.media.jai.JAIRMIImageServer), which registers predefined remote classes with the rmi registry. Two examples of setting up the JAIRMIImageServer are shown below.

For UNIX:

```
#!/bin/sh

CLASSPATH=
rmiregistry &

JAI=/usr/java/jre/lib/ext

CLASSPATH=$JAI/jai_core.jar:$JAI/jai_codec.jar:$JAI/mlibwrapper_jai.jar

java -Djava.rmi.server.codebase="file:$JAI/jai_core.jar file:$JAI/jai_codec.jar
file:$JAI/mlibwrapper_jai.jar"\
   -Djava.rmi.server.useCodebaseOnly=false\
   -Djava.security.policy==file:$PWD/policy\
   com.sun.media.jai.rmi.JAIRMIImageServer
```

FOR WINDOWS:

```
SET CLASSPATH=
start rmiregistry

SET JAI=/usr/java/jre/lib/ext
SET CLASSPATH=%JAI%\jai_core.jar;%JAI%\jai_codec.jar;%JAI%\mlibwrapper_jai.jar

java -Djava.rmi.server.codebase="file:%JAI%\jai_core.jar
file:%JAI%\jai_codec.ja
r" -Djava.rmi.server.useCodebaseOnly=false -
Djava.security.policy=file:%JAI%\pol
icy  com.sun.media.jai.rmi.JAIRMIImageServer
```

CAUTION

When the rmi registry is started, the current directory is examined to see whether it contains any class files. This is a very common problem with setting up remote servers. Make sure that no classfiles are in the directory where the rmiregistry is started and make sure that no classfiles are on the classpath (that is, clear the classpath).

When writing the remote client application, you specify that you are working with remote objects by using the remote subclasses of `PlanarImage` and `RenderedOp`, namely `RemoteImage` and `RemoteRenderedOp`, respectively.

In Listing 6.16, a client application is provided. This application simply takes as input the name of the remote server and a file located on that server. It then accesses that file through the `JAIRMIImageServer` and displays it.

LISTING 6.16   RemoteTester

```
package ch6;

import java.awt.*;
import javax.swing.*;
import java.awt.image.renderable.ParameterBlock;
import javax.media.jai.remote.RemoteJAI;
import javax.media.jai.remote.RemoteRenderedOp;
/**
   RemoteTester.java -- takes as parameters a remote host and a
   filename.  It then reads and displays the image contained in this
   remote file.
*/
public class RemoteTester extends JFrame {

    public RemoteTester(String serverName, String fileName) {
        ParameterBlock pb;
        String protocolName = "jairmi";
        RemoteJAI rc = new RemoteJAI(protocolName, serverName);

        // Create the operations to load the images from files.
        pb = new ParameterBlock();
        pb.add(fileName);
        pb.add(null);
        pb.add(Boolean.FALSE);
        RemoteRenderedOp remoteImage = rc.create("fileload", pb, null);

        getContentPane().add(new ch6Display(remoteImage));

        pack();
        show();
    }

    public static void main(String[] args) {
        if (args.length == 2)
            new RemoteTester(args[0], args[1]);
```

LISTING 6.16   Continued

```
        else
            System.err.println("Usage:  RemoteTester serverName fileName");
    }
}
```

RMI Security

Remote imaging is potentially very dangerous because you must ensure that no unwanted users acquire any of your image data. You also need to ensure that a remote client doesn't do any damage to the files on the server machine. For this reason, the JAIRMIImageServer requires the user to specify a policy file when it is started. This is Java's way of making sure that the server only has the permissions that you specify.

The following policy file will provide the client application all possible permissions and might be helpful in getting your application up and running. It should be used for development purposes only.

```
grant {
    // Allow everything for now
        permission java.security.AllPermission;
    };
```

A better policy file to use for the previous example is as follows:

```
grant {
  permission java.net.SocketPermission "*:1024-",
          "listen, resolve, accept, connect, listen, resolve";
  permission java.io.FilePermission "/usr/java/jre/lib/ext/-", "read";
  permission java.io.FilePermission "remoteImages/-", "read";
};
```

where the first two permissions are necessary for the JAIRMIImageServer to function properly and the last permission is to allow the client to read images contained in a directory called "remoteImages."

Extending JAI

The most successful image processing packages are those that are built on a strong foundation, supply the most common operators, and provide a means for users to add their own operators. JAI does all three things. In this section, the process of adding new operators in JAI will be discussed. The steps are as follows:

1. Provide an operator descriptor.
2. Create a RIF or a CRIF.

3. Create an OpImage.

4. Register the new operator.

In order to describe this process, we will develop an operator called the `CheckAlignment` operator. In many fields such as medical imaging, it is common to combine two images in order to detect abnormalities that couldn't easily be detectable in a single image. Before this can be done, it is important to make sure that the two images are aligned. One way to do this is to create a new image composed of squares, where the pixel values in the squares alternate between the two source images. This operator will take as input two source images and an integer specifying the square dimension.

OperatorDescriptors

The first thing that needs to be done when you are writing a new operator is to provide a description of it using a class that implements the `java.media.jai.OperatorDescriptor` interface. This interface describes the functionality necessary to provide information about the new operator such as operation name, number of sources, number of parameters, types and ranges of parameters, and so on. In order to make this task easier, the `java.media.jai.OperatorDescriptorImpl` class which implements this interface and contains default behaviors for many of the methods is available. Thus, the easiest way to create a new `OperatorDescriptor` is to extend the `OperatorDescriptorImpl` class and define a constructor as shown in Listing 6.17.

LISTING 6.17   `CheckAlignmentDescriptor`

```
package ch6.checkalignment;

import javax.media.jai.OperationDescriptorImpl;
import javax.media.jai.registry.RenderedRegistryMode;

public class CheckAlignmentDescriptor extends OperationDescriptorImpl {
    private static final String[] paramNames = {"samplingPeriod"};
    private static final Object[] paramDefaults = {new Integer(1)};
    private static final Class[] paramClasses = {Integer.class};
    private static final int numSources = 2;
    private static final String[] supportedModes = {"rendered"};
    private static final Object[] validParamValues = {
        new javax.media.jai.util.Range(Integer.class,
                                       new Integer(1),
                                       new Integer(Integer.MAX_VALUE))
            };


    private static final String[][] resources = {
        {"GlobalName", "CheckAlignment"},
```

LISTING 6.17   Continued

```
        {"LocalName", "CheckAlignment"},
        {"Vender", "MyCompanyName"},
        {"Description", "Provides Visual Alignment Check of Two Images"},
        {"DocURL", "none"},
        {"Version", "Beta"},
    };

    public CheckAlignmentDescriptor() {
        super(resources,
                supportedModes,
                numSources,
                paramNames,
                paramClasses,
                paramDefaults,
                validParamValues);
    }
}
```

RIFS and CRIFS

After the descriptor is written, you must create a class implementing either the `java.awt.image.renderable.RenderedImageFactory` class or the `java.awt.image.renderable.ContextualRenderedImageFactory` class. The `RenderedImageFactory` (RIF for short) interface is for use with `RenderedImages`, and the `ContextualRenderedImageFactory` (CRIF for short) is for use with `RenderableImages`. However, a CRIF (which is a subclass of RIF) can also support `RenderedImages`. Because our operator will only be used with `RenderedImages`, we will only implement a RIF.

The main method that must be defined in any class implementing the RIF interface is the

```
public RenderedImage create(ParameterBlock paramBlock,
                            RenderingHints rh)
```

method, which is used for rendering `RenderedOps` (see Listing 6.18). The main methods that must be defined in any class implementing the CRIF interface is the previous `create` method along with the additional

```
public RenderedImage create(RenderContext renderContext,
                            ParameterBlock paramBlock)
```

method, which is used for rendering `RenderableOps`.

LISTING 6.18   CheckAlignmentRIF.java

```java
package ch6.checkalignment;

import java.awt.image.RenderedImage;
import java.awt.image.renderable.ParameterBlock;
import java.awt.image.renderable.RenderedImageFactory;
import java.awt.RenderingHints;
import javax.media.jai.ImageLayout;

public class CheckAlignmentRIF implements RenderedImageFactory {
    public CheckAlignmentRIF() {}

    public RenderedImage create(ParameterBlock paramBlock,
                                RenderingHints renderingHints) {

        RenderedImage source1 = paramBlock.getRenderedSource(0);
        RenderedImage source2 = paramBlock.getRenderedSource(1);
        int samplingPeriod = paramBlock.getIntParameter(0);
        ImageLayout layout = null;
        return new CheckAlignmentOpImage(source1,
                                         source2,
                                         samplingPeriod,
                                         layout,
                                         renderingHints,
                                         false);

    }
}
```

OpImages

The third thing that needs to be done is to implement your operator using a javax.media.jai. OpImage, which is the base class for all image operators. Image operations can be divided into different categories based on the OpImage subclass they extend. Each of these subclasses has a particular set of characteristics which allow them to easily perform certain image processing tasks. The subclasses are shown in Table 6.13.

TABLE 6.13   OpImage Subclasses

OpImage subclass	Brief Description
AreaOpImage	A destination pixel at location x, y is computed using a single source pixel at location x, y and a fixed region around that source pixel.
GeometricOpImage	A destination pixel is computed using a geometric transformation of the source pixels.

TABLE 6.13   Continued

OpImage subclass	Brief Description
PointOpImage	A destination pixel at location x, y is computed using a single source pixel at location x, y.
SourcelessOpImage	Destination pixels are computed without using source pixels.
StatisticsOpImage	No destination pixels are computed. Instead, statistical measures are computed on the source image.
UntiledOpImage	A computed destination image will consist of a single tile equal in size to the image bounds.

For our CheckAlignment operator we will implement a PointOpImage because we are operating on each pixel independently (see Listing 6.19).

LISTING 6.19   CheckAlignmentOpImage

```
package ch6.checkalignment;

import javax.media.jai.ImageLayout;
import javax.media.jai.PointOpImage;
import java.awt.image.RenderedImage;
import java.awt.image.Raster;
import java.awt.image.WritableRaster;

public class CheckAlignmentOpImage extends PointOpImage {

    public CheckAlignmentOpImage(RenderedImage s1,
                                 RenderedImage s2,
                                 int sp,
                                 ImageLayout layout,
                                 java.util.Map configuration,
                                 boolean cobbleSources) {

        super(s1, s2, layout, configuration, cobbleSources);
        source1 = s1;
        source2 = s2;
        samplingPeriod = sp;
    }

    public Raster computeTile(int x, int y) {
        Raster r1 = source1.getTile(x, y);
        Raster r2 = source2.getTile(x, y);
```

LISTING 6.19   Continued

```
            int xBounds = r1.getWidth();
            if (r2.getWidth() < xBounds)
                xBounds = r2.getWidth();
            int yBounds = r1.getHeight();
            if (r2.getHeight() < yBounds)
                yBounds = r2.getHeight();

            WritableRaster wr;
            wr = r1.createCompatibleWritableRaster(xBounds, yBounds);

            int tmpi;
            int tmpj;
            for (int i=0;i<wr.getWidth();i++)
                for (int j=0;j<wr.getHeight();j++) {
                    tmpi = i/samplingPeriod;
                    tmpj = j/samplingPeriod;
                    if ((tmpi % 2 == 0) && (tmpj %2 == 0))
                        wr.setDataElements(i,j,r2.getDataElements(i,j,null));
                    else if ((tmpi % 2 != 0) && (tmpj %2 != 0))
                        wr.setDataElements(i,j,r2.getDataElements(i,j,null));
                    else
                        wr.setDataElements(i,j,r1.getDataElements(i,j,null));
                }
            return wr;
    }

    private RenderedImage source1, source2;
    private int samplingPeriod;
}
```

JAI Registry

The last step in creating an operator is registering the new operator with the JAI registry. The easiest way to do this is to register it in the application. The downside to this is that only applications that add this addition code will be able to use the new operator (see Listing 6.20). It is also possible to make your operator a permanent part of the registry—in which case it is available to all applications on that platform.

LISTING 6.20   CheckAlignmentTester

```
package ch6;

import java.awt.*;
import java.awt.geom.*;
```

LISTING 6.20   Continued

```java
import java.awt.image.*;
import javax.swing.*;
import javax.media.jai.JAI;
import javax.media.jai.RenderedOp;
import javax.media.jai.OperationRegistry;
import javax.media.jai.registry.RIFRegistry;
import java.awt.image.renderable.RenderedImageFactory;
import java.awt.image.renderable.ParameterBlock;
import ch6.checkalignment.*;

public class CheckAlignmentTester extends JFrame{

    /*
      The following static block registers the "CheckAlignment" operator
      with the JAI registry
    */
    static {
        OperationRegistry or;
        or = JAI.getDefaultInstance().getOperationRegistry();
        or.registerDescriptor(new CheckAlignmentDescriptor());
        RenderedImageFactory rif = new CheckAlignmentRIF();
        RIFRegistry.register(or, "CheckAlignment", "ch6example", rif);
    }

    public CheckAlignmentTester(String fileName1,
                                String fileName2,
                                String samplingPeriod) {
        pb = new ParameterBlock();
        pb.add(fileName1);
        RenderedOp sourceImage1 = JAI.create("fileload", pb);
        pb.set(fileName2,0);
        RenderedOp sourceImage2 = JAI.create("fileload", pb);

        pb = new ParameterBlock();
        pb.addSource(sourceImage1);
        pb.addSource(sourceImage2);
        pb.add(Integer.parseInt(samplingPeriod));
        RenderedOp destinationImage = JAI.create("CheckAlignment", pb);

        getContentPane().add(new ch6Display(destinationImage));

        pack();
        show();
    }
```

LISTING 6.20   Continued

```java
    public static void main(String[] args) {
        if (args.length != 3) {
            System.err.print("Usage:  CheckAlignment ");
            System.err.println("filename1 filename2 samplingPeriod");
        }
        else
            new CheckAlignmentTester(args[0], args[1], args[2]);
    }
    private ParameterBlock pb;
}
```

FIGURE 6.10
Illustration of output from the `CheckAlignmentTester` *application shown in Listing 6.20.*

In one image, a single blue square lies in a white background and in the second image a single red square lies in a white background. As you can see, these two colored squares are not perfectly aligned because the resulting image is not a perfect checkerboard.

Native Acceleration

In order to improve the computation speed of image processing applications, the JAI comes with both Java code and native code for many platforms. If the JVM finds the native code, then that will be used. If the native code is not available, the Java code will be used. Thus, the JAI package is able to provide optimized implementations for different platforms that can take advantage of each platform's capabilities. You can find the difference between the native implementation and the Java implementation for a particular application by simply removing the native code libraries. For instance, on a Solaris SPARC platform, they will be located in the Java home directly under jre/lib/sparc. You will know you are using only the Java code when you see the following message: `"Could not load mediaLib accelerator wrapper classes. Continuing in pure Java mode"`.

You will find that the time difference is highly dependent on your application. For the FloatViewer application in Listing 6.14, you won't see any difference. For the DFTTester application in Listing 6.12, you may see a 25 percent decrease in computation time.

Summary

We began this chapter by looking at the PlanarImage class and two of its subclasses: the RenderedOp and the TiledImage. You saw that the PlanarImage is the main JAI class for working with images. It contains a reference to all of its source images, which allows it to be part of Directed Acyclic Graph (DAG). These DAGS allow changes to a particular image to work their way down to the final rendered image. They also allow the JAI to operate in the pull imaging mode, where rendering requests make their way up the DAG.

We described how the TiledImage class was used primarily for situations in which you need to work with a WritableRaster and how the RenderedOp class was used primarily for processing a source image given an operation name. The majority of this chapter was then spent listing and describing the different operators. Finally we looked at some advanced features such as the renderable layer, remote imaging, and writing your own image operators.

Time-Based Media: The Java Media Framework

IN THIS PART

Time-Based Media and the JMF: An Introduction

IN THIS CHAPTER

This section of the book covers time-based media (that is, video and audio) and the *JMF (Java Media Framework)*—a Java API dedicated to the processing of time-based media.

The section is broken into three chapters—this one, Chapter 8, "Processing Media with JMF," and Chapter 9, "RTP and Advanced JMF Topics"—that follow a progression of simple out of the box utilizations of the API to sophisticated usage such as in combination with other specialized features and APIs of Java. Hence, a linear progression through the material is recommended as the default. However, those of you possessing familiarity with time-based media or parts of the API might want to skip some of the introductory material.

In particular the structure of the three chapters is as follows:

> Chapter 7, "Time Based Media and the JMF: An Introduction," serves as both an introduction to time-based media in general and to the JMF API. In particular, some of the fundamental concepts and issues for both digital audio and video are introduced. Midway through the chapter, that is followed by an introduction to the JMF API in terms of its features, promise, central concepts, and main classes.

> Chapter 8, "Processing Media with JMF," serves as the core chapter of Part II, "Time-Based Media: The Java Media Framework and Java Sound," covering the key features of the JMF API. The topics include managers, data sources and sinks, multiplexing and demultiplexing, codecs, format conversion, effects, and capture of media from devices.

> Chapter 9, "RTP and Advanced JMF Topics," covers some of the more advanced features of the JMF API. Chief among these covered topics is the *RTP (Real-Time Transport Protocol)* support within JMF and the corresponding ability to transmit or receive streaming media such as over the Internet. Also covered are issues such as extending the API and utilizing other APIs in conjunction with JMF.

This chapter serves as a general overview of time-based media followed by an introduction to the JMF API. The area of time-based media is not only a broad and involved topic, but also one that is continually changing as new approaches, formats, and standards are introduced. The first section introduces time-based media as well as some of its key concepts and considerations—particularly those with a direct bearing on the JMF API. Those of you who want a more detailed coverage of time-based media are directed to the plenitude of material in book form as well as on the Web.

Midway through the chapter, the JMF API is introduced. The main features and potential of the API are illustrated. Next is a more detailed introduction that covers the main classes of the API, programming approaches to using the API, and the central concept of time before concluding with an example applet that shows how simple using the API can be.

Time-Based Media

The term *media* possesses a number of meanings and connotations to most people: from modern print and broadcast press to the inclusion of terms such as multimedia.

Time-based media, from the perspective of the JMF API and Java, is broadly defined as any data that varies in a meaningful manner with respect to time.

Implicitly, two further properties are understood to be possessed by time-based media:

- The data is intended for presentation (perhaps not immediately but at some, possibly future, stage) to a human being. With current technologies, that is understood to be through vision or hearing.
- The data is in a digital format. Typically this involves capturing (digitizing) analogue (real-world) data such as from a microphone. Alternatively, the media might inherently be digital such as speech synthesized by a computer.

Thus, time-based media is generally understood to be video, audio, or a combination of both.

Both categories, audio and video, can be subdivided into naturally captured media (for example, microphone or video camera) and synthetically produced media (for example, 3D animation sequences). However, the boundaries between natural and synthesized media aren't clear, becoming less so daily. Even naturally captured media is subject to post-capture processing such as to enhance or add features that weren't in the original. (The movie industry practice of blue screening to merge matte painted backgrounds with film of actors recorded in a studio is a classic example of this.) Figure 7.1 shows this breakdown of the types of time-based media. Indeed, the blurring of the distinction between natural and synthetic media is almost a direct result of the fact that after the media is digitized (if that was even necessary), it can be processed in any manner imaginable. In the most general sense of processing that includes capturing, presenting, transmitting, as well as converting, compressing, and so on, controlling and processing time-based media is exactly what the JMF is intended for.

Typical examples of time-based media include TV broadcasts, the data captured from a microphone or video camera attached to a PC, an MP3 file on a hard disk, a video conference across the Internet, and webcasts.

Throughout this and the following chapters, time-based might be dropped from the term media. Such usage indicates time-based media as previously defined, and not any other meaning ascribable to the word media.

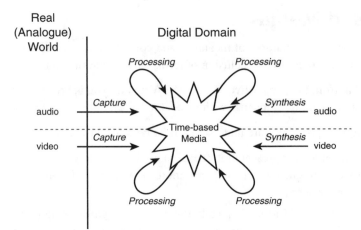

FIGURE 7.1

Origins and types of time-based media.

Time-Based Media on a Computer

In the past decade, there has been a revolution in terms of access to and in particular generation of time-based media, most notably digital media. Previously, only large production companies in the form of movie studios, TV and radio stations, and other such specialists, were capable of producing high-quality media. Correspondingly, dedicated devices or venues were required to present such media for an audience: a TV set for TV broadcasts, a radio for radio broadcasts, and a cinema for movies.

Changes in computing, both in terms of technology and penetration of daily life, have fundamentally altered the paradigm from production only by specialists and presentation only on dedicated devices to production by anyone (with a computer) and a very versatile presentation option (the computer).

The technological advances that have driven this change include the ongoing and significant increases in both processor power and storage capacity of the PC, together with improvements in networking and telecommunication. These hardware advances have gone hand-in-hand with software developments that have made it possible to harness the greater power afforded by the average PC. Advances in processor power have meant that the various compressed formats used to store video and audio could be processed in real time. Thus, a PC could be used to present and even save the media. Advances in storage capacity, as first witnessed by the advent of the CD-ROM as a standard peripheral, increasingly large (in terms of storage capacity) hard disks, and more recently the *DVD (digital versatile disc)* have meant that inherently large media files can be stored on a PC. Correspondingly, network advances have meant that it is now possible, and commonplace, to access media stored or generated remotely.

Socially, the computer has transitioned from being seen as a specialist device for computation and calculation to a general-purpose household item with wide applicability in many areas—not the least of which is communication. This is particularly illustrated by the *World Wide Web (WWW)* in which users not only see it as commonplace to surf the Net (pulling in content from all over the world), but also increasingly expect or demand that the content be dynamic and entertaining—often with time-based media! The JMF was designed, at least in part, with this purpose in mind, and is centrally placed: Java has been a key-enabler of the Web and in particular Web-interactivity since its earliest days—JMF further enhances the Web support power of Java.

Bandwidth, Compression, and Codecs

Time-based media, in its raw form suitable for presentation through speakers or on a display, is particularly large—high in bandwidth. That poses a particular challenge in the area of storing (for example, on a hard disk) and transmitting (for example, over a modem) media and introduces the idea of compression.

The following sections on audio and video go into further detail, but for a moment consider the size of a typical three-minute audio track on a music CD, bearing in mind that raw video is even more demanding (often about 100 times more).

The raw audio format is known as *PCM (Pulse Code Modulation)*. CD audio is particularly high quality: It covers the entire range of human hearing (which ranges up to about 20KHz: twenty thousand hertz). With such accuracy in representation, most people cannot discern the difference between the original and the stored signal. To achieve that detailed representation, 44,100 samples are taken each second for each of the left and right audio channels. Each sample is 16 bits (two bytes: a range of some 65,536 possible values). That equates to 176,400 bytes or 1,411,200 bits of information per second. For the three-minute piece of music, that equates to 31,752,000 bytes (over 30 megabytes) of information.

A modern PC's hard disk will soon fill with a few hundred such audio files. More significant and sobering is the transfer rate required to stream that audio data across a network so that it can be played in real-time: over one million bits per second. Contrasting that with a 56K modem(peak performance not reaching 56,000 bits per second) that most home users have as their means of connecting to the Internet, it can be seen that compromises are necessary: the required transfer rate exceeds that possible by a factor greater than 20 times.

The need for compression is obvious. Although the particulars of modern compression algorithms are complicated, the fundamentals of all approaches are the same. The media is kept in a compressed format while being stored or transmitted. The media is decompressed only immediately prior to presentation or if required for processing (for example, to add an effect).

The components that perform this task of compression and decompression are known as *codecs (COmpression/DECompression)* and can work in hardware or software. For each audio and video, there is a range of codecs that vary in their compression capabilities: the quality of the resulting media, amount of processing required, and the support they receive from the major companies working in the multimedia arena.

Most codecs are *lossy*, meaning that they don't perfectly preserve the original media: Some quality of the original media is lost when it is compressed and is thereafter unrecoverable. Although this is unfortunate, appropriate design of the codec can result in some or most of the losses not being perceptible to a human audience. Examples of such losses might be the blurring of straight edges (for example, text) in a video image or the addition of a slight buzz to the audio. Regardless of the undesirability of these losses in quality, no known lossless codecs are capable of achieving anywhere near the compression necessary for streaming high quality audio and video over a typical (home) user of today's connection to the wider network.

All codecs employ one or more of the following three general strategies in order to achieve significant compression:

> Spatial redundancy—These schemes exploit repetition within the current frame (sample) of data. Although not applicable for audio encoding in which each frame is a single value, significant savings can be made for typical video images. Most images have regions of a solid color—backgrounds such as a blue sky, the beige walls of a house, or individual subject elements such as a white refrigerator or a solid-color shirt. Basically, such schemes can be thought of as recording the recurring color and the region of the image that it ranges over, rather than keeping multiple copies (one for each pixel that composes the solid color block) of the same thing.

> Temporal redundancy—These schemes exploit the fact that the difference between successive video frames or successive audio samples is generally small relative to the size of the frame or sample itself). Rather than transmit or store a completely new frame or sample, only the difference from the previous sample needs to be stored or transmitted. For both audio and video, this approach is generally very effective. Although there are instances, such as a new scene in a video, in which that isn't true. A strong example of the benefits of such approaches include video of a news anchorperson: Most of the image is static, and only relatively minor changes occur from frame to frame—the anchorperson's head and facial movements. Even far more dynamic video (for example, a football match) still has considerable static (from frame to frame) regions, and significant savings are still achieved. Similarly, most sound—whether speech, music, or noise—is tightly constrained in a temporal sense. Temporal encoding based schemes pose challenges for non-linear editing. (A frame is defined in terms of its predecessor, but what if that predecessor is removed or, even more challenging, altered?) Such schemes tend to degrade in compression performance and quality over a long period time. For both reasons, these

schemes periodically (for example, once per second) transmit a completely new frame (known as a key-frame).

Features of human perception—The human visual and auditory systems have particular idiosyncrasies that might be exploited. These include non-linearity across the spectrum being perceived as well as more complex phenomenon such as masking. Visually, humans distinguish some regions of the color spectrum less keenly, whereas in the auditory domain, human perception strongly emphasizes the lower frequency (deeper) components of a sound at the expense of those higher frequency components. Clever coding schemes can exploit these coarser regions of perception and dedicate fewer resources to their representation. Strategies based on human perception differ fundamentally to the two pervious schemes because they are based on subjective rather than objective measures and results.

Figure 7.2 shows the concept of spatial compression, whereas Figure 7.3 shows temporal compression. Figure 7.4 shows the non-linearity of human perception in the auditory domain: the range of human hearing (in Hertz on the horizontal axis) is shown against the perceptually critical bands (bark) found through psychoacoustic experiments. Such known relationships can be exploited by audio compression schemes.

Regions (blocks) of solid color in the image that could be spatially compressed

Figure 7.2

Spatial compression opportunities.

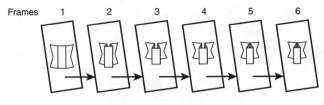

Successive frames in an image.

FIGURE 7.3

Temporal compression could be used to record only the differences from the previous frame.

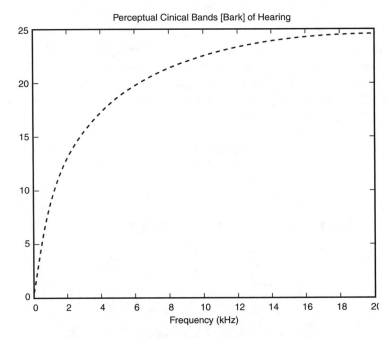

FIGURE 7.4

Perceptually critical bands (bark) of human hearing matched against the frequency range of human hearing.

Format, Content Type, and Standards

The codec used to encode and decode a media stream defines its format. Thus the format of a media stream describes the actual low-level structure of the stream of data. Examples of formats include cinepak, H.263, and MPEG-1 in the video domain and Mu-Law, ADPCM, and MPEG-1 in the audio domain.

Sitting atop a media's format, and often being confused with it, is known as the *content type* or sometimes the *architecture* of the media. The content type serves as a type of super-structure allowing the specification of codecs and other details such as file structure of the total API. Examples of content types include such well-known names as AVI, QuickTime, MPEG, and WAV.

As an illustration of the distinction between media format and content type, it is worth noting that most content types support multiple possible formats. Thus the QuickTime content type can employ Cinepak, H.261, and RGB video formats (among others), whereas the WAV (Wave) content type might be A-law, DVI ADPCM, or U-Law (among others). Hence an alternative model is to see the various content types as *media containers*; each can hold media in a number of different formats.

An obvious question, given the apparent profusion of formats and content types, is where are the standards? Why are there so many formats and content types, and are they all really necessary?

International standards do exist in the form of the various MPEG versions. (It's currently at three, although the latest version is known as MPEG-4 because no MPEG-3 standard exists.) MPEG stands for the Motion Picture Expert Group and is a joint committee of the *ISO (International Standards Organization)* and *IEC (International Electrotechnical Commission)*. These standards are of very high quality: well designed and with high compression. However, because of a number of interrelated factors that include commercial interests, differences in technology, historic developments, as well as differing requirements from formats, these standards are yet to dominate the entirety of the audio and video fields.

Perhaps the most important reason that various formats exist is that each is designed with a different purpose in mind. Although some are clearly better than others (particularly older formats) in a number of dimensions, none dominate in all aspects. The most important aspects of differentiation are degree of compression, quality of the resulting media, and processing requirements. These three aspects aren't mutually exclusive, but are competing factors: For instance, higher compressions are likely to require greater processing and result in more loss of quality. Various formats (codecs) weight these factors differently, resulting in formats with diverse strengths and weaknesses. It becomes clear then that there is no single best format; the best can only be defined in terms of the constraints and requirements of a particular application.

On the other hand, the different content types are chiefly attributable to commercial and historical developments. Some content types such as QuickTime and AVI, although now almost cross-platform standards, were traditionally associated with a particular PC platform: the Macintosh in the case of QuickTime and the Windows PC in the case of AVI. The advent of the WWW and more powerful PCs have seen a second generation of content type such as RealMedia (RealAudio/RealVideo), which is specifically targeted at streaming media across the Internet.

Tracks and Multiplexing/Demultiplexing

Time-based media often consists of more than one channel of data. Each of these channels is known as a *track*. Examples include the left and right channels for traditional stereo audio or the audio and video track on an AVI movie. Recent standards, such as the MPEG-4 content type, support the concept of a multitude of tracks composing a single media object.

Each track within a media object has its own format. For instance, the AVI movie could possess a video track in *MJPG (Motion JPEG)* format and an audio track in *ADPCM (Adaptive Differential Pulse Code Modulation)* format. The media object, however, has a single content type (in our example, AVI). Such multitrack media are known as *multiplexed*.

Creation of multiplexed media involves combining multiple tracks of data, a process known as *multiplexing*. For instance, the audio track captured from a microphone would be multiplexed with the video track captured from a video camera in order to create a movie object. Similarly, the processing of existing media might result in further multiplexing as additional tracks (for instance, a text track of subtitles for a movie) are added to the media.

The corollary operation of separating individual tracks from a multitrack media object is known as *demultiplexing*. This is necessary prior to presentation of the media so that each track can have the appropriate codec applied for decompression and the resulting raw media sent to the correct output device (for example, speakers for audio track, display for the video track).

If processing of a media object is required, the appropriate tracks would need to be demultiplexed so that they could be treated in isolation, processed (such as to add an effect), and then multiplexed back into the media object. This processing can also result in the generation of new tracks, which then need to be multiplexed into the media object. An example of this might be adding subtitles to a movie: the audio track is demultiplexed and processed automatically by a speech recognizer to generate a transcription as a new track. That new track is then multiplexed back in with the original video and audio.

Figures 7.5, 7.6, and 7.7 show the various roles of multiplexing and demultiplexing in media creation, processing, and presentation.

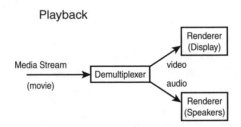

FIGURE 7.5

Role of demultiplexer in playback of media.

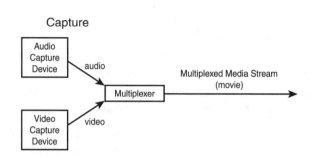

FIGURE 7.6
Role of multiplexer in capture of media.

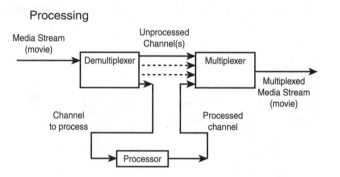

FIGURE 7.7
Role of demultiplexer and multiplexer in the processing of media.

Streaming

The origins of time-based media on the computer lie in applications where media was stored on devices such as a CD-ROM and played from that local source. These forms of applications are still commonplace and important. They were enabled by emerging technologies, such as higher storage capacity devices in the form of CD-ROMs; similarly, Internet technology (combined with increasing computing power) has led to challenging new areas of application for time-based media.

True streaming (also called *real-time streaming*) of media is the transfer and presentation, as it arrives, of media from a remote site (in the typical case, across the Internet). Examples of such streaming of media can be found in the numerous webcasts that have proliferated on the Web, including numerous radio stations and national TV broadcasters such as the BBC.

A hybrid form of streaming known as progressive streaming also exists, which is less technically challenging than true streaming and quite common on the Web today. *Progressive streaming* is employed where it is expected or known that the bandwidth requirements of the media (in order to play in real-time) exceed the available bandwidth for transfer. With progressive streaming, the media is downloaded to your system's hard disk. However, the rate of transfer and portion downloaded is monitored. When the estimated (based on current transfer rate) time to complete the transfer drops below the time required to play the entire media, play is begun. This ensures that play of the media is begun as soon as possible while guaranteeing (as long as transfer rate doesn't drop) that the presentation will be continuous.

In this *passive* reception aspect, streaming, in its end result, is little different from the already familiar forms of radio and TV. The aspect that really empowers the potential of streaming is that media creation (not just reception) is possible for each user. This enables new levels of communication between users when audio and video can be streamed between sites in real-time. The "killer application" of this technology is the video conference: all participants in the conference stream audio and video of themselves to all other participants while simultaneously receiving and playing or viewing the streams received from other participants. Figure 7.8 shows a typical video conferencing scenario.

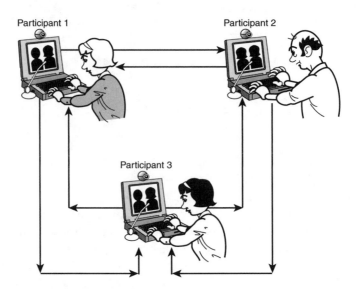

FIGURE 7.8

Typical video conferencing scenario.

Streaming affords considerable technical challenges, many of which still haven't been overcome adequately. Not the least of these challenges is the already discussed bandwidth requirements for time-based media. Streaming across the low-bandwidth connections to the Internet possessed by today's typical user—a 56K modem—can be achieved only by the application of the most extreme compression codecs, resulting in severe quality loss (typically a few pixilated

Time-Based Media and the JMF: An Introduction

CHAPTER 7

293

7

TIME-BASED MEDIA
AND THE JMF:
AN INTRODUCTION

or blurred frames per second). The situation is less extreme for audio but still not perfect. The situation is only exacerbated by the fact that simultaneous, bi-directional streaming is required for applications such as video conferencing: both sites transmitting and receiving media simultaneously.

The challenges don't stop simply at bandwidth limitations but more generally stem from data transmission across a network, typically a *Wide Area Network (WAN)* such as the Web. The data that forms the media stream, typically in fixed sized packets, suffers a delay, known as *latency*, between its transmission and receipt. That latency can and typically does vary between packets as network load and other conditions change. Not only does this pose a problem for the timely presentation of the media, but also the latency might vary so much between packets that they are received out of order whereas others might simply be lost (never received) or corrupted. Both ends of the media stream, the transmitter and receiver (or source and sink), have no control over these conditions when operating across a network such as the Internet. Transmission using appropriate protocols for communications such as *RTP (Real-time Transfer Protocol)* and *RTCP (RTP Control Protocol)* can aid the monitoring and, hence, detection of and possible compensation for such network induced problems. However it cannot fix them.

Processing Media

The great advantage of possessing media in a digital format is that it opens endless possibilities. No longer is media simply captured and then stored or transmitted prior to presentation. After it has been captured (or generated), it becomes digital data that might be processed in any number of ways including filtering, adding effects, being compressed or decompressed, as well as being combined with other media. Figure 7.9 shows the traditional analogue approach to media capture, editing, and transmission. Figure 7.10 shows the digital approach and the additional opportunities it affords.

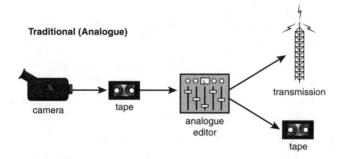

Traditional (Analogue)

camera   tape   analogue editor   transmission   tape

FIGURE 7.9

Traditional analogue approach to media capture, editing, and transmission.

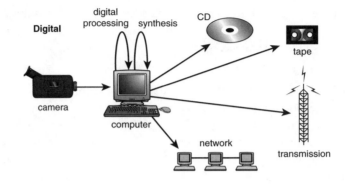

FIGURE 7.10
Digital approach to media capture, processing, and distribution.

Traditionally, the act of processing media is known as editing, or alternatively post production. With the advent of digital media, this became known as *Non-Linear Editing (NLE)*. The media could be edited (for example, composited) at an arbitrary location (time) along its length rather than be constrained to linearly editing (from start to finish) the media due to representation and storage restrictions (for example, on a tape).

However, both the terms editing (whether linear or non-linear) and post production have a strong association with direct human manipulation of the media. Typically, video and audio editing software such as Adobe's Premiere, Ulead's Media Studio, Sonic Foundry's Sound Forge, or Goldwave is used by a person to manually segment, splice, transform, and so on the media. Editing then is a subset of processing because processing not only includes direct human control of the operation, but also includes automated processing entirely under software control. Direct software processing of media without the need for human intervention opens a host of exciting possibilities and new applications: for instance, automatic subtitling, motion tracking, and image enhancement.

The following list defines some of the more common audio and video processing (editing) operations that are carried out:

Capture—Recording audio or video content directly in a digital format. Alternatively, transferring it from an analogue medium (for example, VCR) into a digital form.

Compositing—Blending two media objects together to combine them. It is the same technique as Superimposing. Examples include adding captions to a video sequence.

Cropping—Removing a portion of the media. This term is typically used for audio content.

Fading In/Out—Smoothing the transition between two different images or sounds to convey a sense of continuity. It is a common form of Transition.

Filter—Using this dedicated tool to modify either video or audio by adding an effect. Audio might be filtered to remove noise at a particular frequency band, whereas a motion-blur filter might be applied to video for effect.

Logging—Viewing the original media material and determining the sections that will be employed in the project being constructed.

Morphing—Transforming one image into another across time by mapping features of one image to another. Typical examples include morphing one person's face to another's.

Printing—Saving a video object from the computer back to a more traditional format such as a VCR or camcorder.

Resampling—Changing the sample frequency for some audio. Typically done as a means of reducing the size of the object by resampling to a lower frequency (*downsampling*).

Superimposing—Laying one media object over the top of the other in order to combine them. For instance, the image of actors in a studio can be superimposed over an outdoor backdrop.

Transition—Moving between two dissimilar video images or audio samples rather than simply juxtaposing them. Examples include fading, wiping, and scrolling.

Audio Primer

Sound occurs because of a vibration of molecules that arrives at our ears as a wave. Typically the molecules vibrating are air, but sound also propagates through other mediums including liquids and solids.

The rate at which the molecules vibrate determines the *pitch* of the sound, whereas the amount (amplitude) of vibration determines the *volume*. The rate of vibration is known as the *frequency* and is measured in hertz. One hertz represents one complete cycle or vibration per second. A person with unimpaired hearing is able to perceive sound from around 20Hz to around 20KHz (20,000 Hertz). However, human perception isn't evenly distributed across that frequency range: Far more attention or emphasis is given to the lower frequency range that, perhaps not surprisingly, matches the frequency contained in human speech. Transforming the frequency scale to a log representation provides a reasonable first approximation of the "weight" given to different frequencies by our hearing system. Figure 7.4 (shown earlier) shows the perceptually critical bands of hearing.

Nearly every sound, with the exception of pure tones generated musically or automatically, is a complex amalgam of vibrations at different frequencies. It is the sum of these individual vibrations and their amplitudes (strengths or volumes) that make up the sound. Thus, not only can a sound be described, but also composed or generated by detailing the individual frequencies (and their amplitudes) that compose it. Similarly, a sound can be altered by changing the frequency or amplitude of one or more of the pure tones that compose it. This type of functionality is available in some of the more sophisticated audio studio applications.

Normal sounds such as speech, music, and much of what we consider noise (for example, traffic or office sounds) aren't static and unvarying but constantly changing in their component frequency and amplitude characteristics. Indeed it is that fundamental time varying property that allows us to generate speech as a sequence of sounds (*phonemes*) and music as a sequence of notes.

Sound, arriving as it does, is inherently an analogue quantity. Digitization is the process of transforming an analogue sound into a digital representation. Dedicated hardware, such as a PC's soundcard, is required to perform this task of analogue-to-digital (A-to-D) conversion as well as the inverse digital-to-analogue (D-to-A) conversion when a digital sound is to be presented (sent to speakers).

In performing digitization, two choices must be made, which both significantly impact the quality of the recorded (in the computer) sound and the size of the resulting media object (file if it is saved or conversely bandwidth required if it is being transmitted). These are the sampling frequency and the quantization level.

The first choice is the *sampling rate* (frequency)—the number of times per second that the sound will be captured (turned into a number). It is vital for the sound to be sampled frequently enough to capture its ever-changing nature and the frequency of the individual components of each sound. The Nyquist Theorem exactly describes this relationship between sampling frequency and frequency of the signal being captured. If a signal is being sampled at frequency f_n, only signals up to $f_n/2$ will be accurately represented. For instance, the sampling rate used for audio CDs is 44.1KHz (44,100 Hertz), meaning that all sounds up to 22.05KHz will be reliably captured: quite sufficient for the human ear. However if a lower sampling rate is used (as is often done), the higher frequency components of the sound won't be represented correctly. For instance, if sampling at 11,025Hz (a submultiple of 44.1KHz that is often used), nothing above 5.5KHz would be correctly represented. Not only could this result in the loss of an important part of the sound, but also it tends to adversely affect perceptions of naturalness because nearly all sounds have resonances that extend into the higher frequencies.

Signal frequencies above the Nyquist frequency (half sampling rate) aren't lost but folded back into the lower frequency domain in a process similar to taking the modulus of a number. This is known as *aliasing*. It is a familiar visual phenomenon with the rotors on helicopters and planes, and even the spokes on wheels, appearing to be stationary or going backward on film (the interaction of the frequency of the rotation of the rotor, blade, or spoke and the much lower sampling frequency at which the film was shot). Such an outcome will result in significant corruption of the signal, manifesting as a hiss or other noise, if there were strong signals above the Nyquist frequency. For this reason, low-pass filters are normally used to eliminate these high frequency components prior to sampling.

The second choice in the digitization process is the quantization level: the number of bits used to represent each sample. The greater the number of bits employed, the better dynamic range or sound resolution that occurs because of being able to more accurately define the amplitude at that point in time. The choice of an adequate number of bits (for example, 16 that is used in CD audio) will ensure that quieter passages aren't lost. Too few bits make the audio signal sound fuzzy such as through a poor telephone.

Choices of sampling rate and quantization not only affect the quality of the resulting audio, but also directly determine the bandwidth (size) of that audio object. This is a very important factor when considering streaming audio over a network with a bandwidth limitation. The following formula illustrates the relationship whereas Table 7.1 shows the bandwidth for one second of audio at some of the more common sampling rate and quantization level combinations:

Bits per Second = # Channels x Sampling rate x quantization level

TABLE 7.1 Bandwidth Requirements for Audio at Different Sampling Rates and Quantization Levels

GuidelineExamples of Quality	Sampling Rate	Quantization Level	Number of Channels	Kilobytes/ Second
CD Audio	44.1KHz	16	2 (stereo)	176.4
FM Radio	22.05KHz	16	2 (stereo)	88.2
Stereo 1 - Acceptable	11.025KHz	16	2 (stereo)	44.1
AM Radio	11.025KHz	16	1 (mono)	22.05
Stereo 2 - Grainy	11.025KHz	8	2 (stereo)	22.05
Old hand-held game machine	11.025KHz	8	1 (mono)	11.025

Clearly, a choice of lower sampling rates, quantization levels, and the number of channels can significantly reduce bandwidth requirements, but at the expense of a potentially significant reduction in quality. Some of the most commonly employed codecs (compression schemes) for audio coding will be discussed in the next section. These audio codecs can significantly reduce the bandwidth requirements.

Speech and Music

The two most commonly processed forms of audio data are speech and music, each of which has its own unique characteristics.

Speech is produced by the human vocal apparatus in which placement of the articulators—the lips, tongue, jaw, and velum (soft palate that includes the uvula)—form the shape of the passage through which air flows. The shape of this passage determines its resonant frequencies and hence the sound produced from the lips as air escapes.

One property of speech sounds lends itself well to compression—most of the signal's energy is concentrated in a frequency range from 100Hz to under 5KHz (varies depending on the sound and speaker). This isn't to say that higher frequency components to the sound don't exist because they certainly do. Rather, most of the information that people use to determine the sound as well as other information such as speaker gender and identity can be found in this region. This can be exploited by sampling at a frequency to capture the vital information, but not to preserve the total sound. Although the digitized speech might not sound exactly like the original, most of the vital information will still be preserved, and at a considerable bandwidth saving. For example, speech sampled at 11KHz is still easily intelligible.

Music is such an encompassing category, being dependent on the form of music and type of instruments used, that it is difficult to make generalizations about its properties. However, music is far more likely to cover a wider frequency range than speech and, hence, suffer more from sampling at lower frequencies.

Figure 7.11 shows the time waveform of a short passage of a speech, "The JMF; an API for Handling Time-based Media," from an adult male in the top plot, as well the first cords of "Smoke on the Water" played on an electric guitar in the bottom plot.

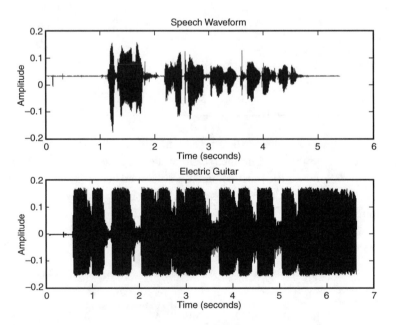

FIGURE 7.11

Contrast between two sound waveforms.

An alternative form of encoding music is known as *MIDI* (pronounced "mid-ee") for *Musical Instruments Digital Interface*. This is a digital format for recording the instruments and notes that are being played in a piece of music—not the sounds themselves. As such, it is an extremely compact format when contrasted with digitized sound. On the down side, MIDI doesn't guarantee the same level of fidelity in reproduction that sampling can—it is dependent on the quality of the playback instrument (often a computer soundcard but originally synthesizers and other such instruments) in its capability to use its voices (different sampled or synthesized instruments) to reproduce the sound appropriately.

Content Types, Formats, and Codecs

The origins of the three major audio content types are associated with a particular computer platform—Wave (WAV) from the Windows platform, AIFF from the Macintosh platform, and AU from Unix. All three have grown in parallel such that they roughly provide similar functionality in terms of supported formats. The JMF provides support for all three as well as MIDI, GSM, and the various MPEG schemes.

Until recently, the dominant codecs in the audio arena have had their origins in the telecommunication area, being codecs for compressing speech over telephone lines. Among this group are codecs such as ADPCM, A-Law, and U-Law. A common approach among such codecs is known as *companding*. The basis of companding is to use a non-linear quantization scale: fewer bits are allocated to the higher values (somewhat analogous to transforming to the log domain).

New codecs have appeared based on perceptual compression and designed for music (more challenging than speech). The MPEG schemes are the best known of these. In particular, MP3 (MPEG Layer 3, not MPEG-3 because such an entity doesn't exist) is famous because of its use to encode music on the Internet. The MPEG compression scheme is frequency domain based. Sound is transformed into a number of (for example, 32) frequency channel values. The frequency dependence of the threshold of hearing (minimum volume for a sound to be heard) is combined with masking effects (loud sounds at one frequency raise the hearing threshold for other frequencies) so that the minimum number of bits are used to encode each channel and hide quantization noise. The MP3 scheme is well known for achieving roughly a 10:1 compression while also maintaining a (perceptually) high quality.

The following lists some of the better-known audio codecs:

ADPCM (Adaptive Differential Pulse Code Modulation)—A temporal based compression scheme that looks at the difference between successive samples. The scheme is further strengthened (but complicated) by predicting what the next sample should be and transmitting or storing only the difference between the predicted and actual difference. A non-linear scheme is employed to record this value. ADPCM is supported by the JMF.

A-Law—A companding compression scheme, A-Law is a standard from the ITU that is closely related to G7.11 (U-Law), and used in those countries where U-Law isn't found. Based on the compression of speech over phone lines, it is able to reduce 12-bit samples to 8-bit quantization. A-Law is supported by the JMF.

G.711 (U-Law)—A companding compression scheme, G7.11 is an ITU standard employed in Japan and North America, as well as being used commonly on the Web and by Sun and NeXT machines. It is related to the A-Law scheme. G.711 compression is supported by the JMF.

GSM—An international standard for mobile digital telephones, GSM is based on linear predictive coding: the prediction of future samples based on (a weighted sum of) those that have already been seen. The scheme achieves significant compression but at a noticeable loss of quality. GSM is supported by the JMF.

MPEG Layer I, II, and III—From the MPEG-1 and MPEG-2 standards, the three layers represent an increasingly (from 1 to 3) sophisticated compression scheme based on perception (see the previous discussion). Layer I corresponds to a data rate of 192Kbps, Layer II a data rate of 128Kbps, and Layer III (MP3: the most famous and widely used) corresponds to an upper-bound on data rate of 64Kbps. The JMF supports all three layers.

RealAudio—From Real Networks and famous because of its widespread exposure and usage on the Internet. RealAudio is a codec designed to support the real-time streaming of audio. RealAudio is a proprietary codec.

To illustrate the differences in terms of degree of compression and audio quality between different codecs, the book's Web site (www.samspublishing.com) has a number of versions of the same audio sample. The audio sample is a short piece in four segments. The first segment is a speech from an adult male speaker of Australian English and serves as an introduction. The three remaining segments are all instrumental music. The first musical piece is an organ playing a few bars of "California Dreaming." The second musical piece is a guitar playing a few, well known, bars of "Smoke on the Water." The third and final musical piece is a five second segment of a Didgeridoo being played: a traditional woodwind instrument of the Australian Aborigine. The same original audio sample has been transcoded using a number of different codecs so that they can be contrasted. The name of each file identifies the codec, sampling rate, and quantization level used:

<codec>_<sampling rate>_<quantisation>.<content_type>

For instance, GSM_8_16.wav is a Wave file encoded using GSM at 8KHz sampling and a quantization level of 16 bits. Sampling rates that aren't exact multiples of one thousand (for example, 22.05KHz and 11.025KHz) are rounded as such for the purposes of filenames only. Thus, Linear_22_16.wav is a Wave file with linear encoding sampled at 22.05KHz with 16-bit quantization.

Video Primer

Persistence of vision is the name of the phenomenon that enables humans to see a succession of still frames, projected at sufficient speed, as a smooth moving picture. Both video and animation rely on this property of the human visual system. The fusion frequency is the rate at which the frames must be projected in order for them to "fuse" into a perceptually continuous stream. The particular frequency varies between individuals (and the amount of motion between frames) with around 40 frames per second ensuring a flicker-free perception of smooth motion. However persistence of vision isn't a binary (all-or-nothing) effect: lower frame rates still convey the illusion of motion, although with worse flicker and jerkiness as the frame rate drops. However, anything below about 10 frames per second is perceived for what it really is: a succession of still frames.

The roots of video lie in the television industry and its various standards, although some of the limitations that shaped television standards, such as the low screen refresh rates of televisions, no longer hold for modern computer-based technology. The three analogue broadcast standards are known as *NTSC (National Television Systems Committee)* used in the United States and Japan, *PAL (Phase Alternating Line)* used in Europe and Australia, and *SECAM (Sequential Couleur Avec Memoire)* used in France. Although the particular horizontal and vertical resolutions, as well as frame rate, differ somewhat among the three standards, all follow a similar approach for encoding the signal. Because of bandwidth considerations at the time (some concerns clearly don't change), each frame is divided into two fields, one consisting of the even lines in the frame, and the other consisting of the odd lines. These are transmitted in succession, and the frame is composed by interlacing the fields.

On the other hand, each frame in a raw (digital) video sequence is a separate and complete image. These raw frames are invariably kept as *bitmaps*—an image composed of a number of picture elements (*pixels*). The number of pixels is defined by the horizontal and vertical resolution of the image. The more pixels there are, the more sharp, clear, and detailed the image is. Each pixel records the color intensities at that point of the image. Color might be recorded as *RGB (Red, Green, Blue)* or Luminance/Chrominance values. Regardless, a number of bits are employed to represent that color value at each pixel. The more bits employed, the truer the colors of the resulting image. A far more complete discussion of 2D images can be found in Chapter 10, "3D Graphics, Virtual Reality, and Visualization."

Just as for audio, choices of number of frames per second and quantization not only affect the quality of the resulting video, but also directly determine the bandwidth (size) of that video object. This is a very important factor when considering storing video or even more constraining, streaming over a network. The following formula illustrates the relationship while Table 7.2 shows the bandwidth for one second of video at some of the more common frame rate and quantization level combinations.

Bits per Second = Frame rate x Horizontal Resolution

```
x Vertical Resolution x Bits per Pixel
```

TABLE 7.2   Bandwidth Requirements for Video at Different Resolutions, Frame Rates, and Color Quantization Levels

Typical Example	Frame Rate	Horizontal Resolution	Vertical Resolution	Bits per Pixel	Kilobytes/ Second
NTSC	~30	640	480	24	27,000
PAL	25	768	576	24	32,400
"Quarter Screen" TV	24	320	240	24	5,400
Video Conference 1	12	320	240	16	1,800
Video Conference 2	12	160	120	16	450

Contrasting Table 7.2 with Table 7.1, it can be seen just how greedy video is with regard to bandwidth. Even the lowest quality settings from Table 7.2—something that would result in little more than a very small image of low quality in one corner of the screen—consumes nearly three times the bandwidth of CD quality audio. To achieve (current) television quality video, a bandwidth over 150 times greater than that required by an audio CD is required. Compression is an absolute necessity for video if it is to be used with today's computers and networks.

Content Types, Formats, and Codecs

Two content types (architectures) have long dominated the video arena, becoming de facto standards. These are QuickTime and AVI. Although originally associated with a single platform (the Macintosh for QuickTime, and Windows PC for AVI), they are now cross-platform. Each supports a number of video (and audio) codecs within its architecture: in fact chiefly the same ones. Both of these content types are strongly supported in the JMF.

A third significant, but far more recent, name in the video content type area is RealVideo. Both a content type and format, RealVideo from Real Networks is targeted at streaming of video over networks, and has become the Web leader in this area.

Unlike audio, which is far less demanding of bandwidth, significant compression is required in order to play video on a computer, including from a CD-ROM. For this reason, the area of video codecs has and continues to receive considerable attention and effort from international bodies, the private sector, and academia. An example of this ongoing development is the relatively recent release of the MPEG-4 standard.

Invariably the codecs in common usage at the moment are lossy. Most are based on a block compression scheme in which the individual frame image is subdivided into a number of fixed-sized blocks. A common size for such blocks is eight-by-eight pixels. Two techniques are commonly used to compress these square blocks—*Vector Quantization (VQ)* and *Discrete Cosine Transforms (DCT)*. The full details of each approach are beyond the scope of this book.

However, VQ builds a codebook of different possible blocks—similar to color swatches. Each image block is then encoded (quantized) as the number of the codebook element that it most resembles (is closest to). On the other hand, those schemes using DCT transform each block into the frequency domain (the DCT is analogous to the Fourier transform). Savings (compression) can then be made by utilizing fewer bits to represent higher frequency components because these are known not to contribute as significantly to the perceptual quality of an image.

A number of codecs are asymmetric, taking different amounts of time to compress versus decompress the same stream. In all cases, the compression takes longer. This is due to the nature of the task—compression is simply more time-consuming because of all the calculations required—and partly due to design choices. It is generally assumed that the equipment dedicated to compressing video might be specialized and powerful, whereas playback might have to occur across a range of equipment. Under such an assumption, easing the task of decompression at the expense of compression is a good choice.

Some of the better known video codecs are as follows:

Cinepak—A very common format spanning multiple PC platforms (originally designed for Apple's QuickTime) and even game consoles. Cinepak is perhaps the most popular means currently employed to encode video in multimedia applications. Cinepak employs temporal and spatial compression in a lossy scheme that uses VQ and blocks. The scheme is intended for software implementation with compression, taking considerably more time than decompression. Cinepak performs well with video that contains substantial motion, but can have problems with static images. The Cinepak codec is supported in the JMF 2.1.1.

DivX—An open-source codec based on the MPEG-4 (see later) standard, DivX is gaining wide popularity on the Internet because of its free availability for most platforms and the quality of its compression.

H.261—An international standard targeted at the video-conferencing area with bandwidths in the 16-48 kilobytes-per-second range, H.261 is a lossy scheme using block DCT and motion compensation. It has some similarity to MPEG-1, which it predates. The H.261 codec is supported in the JMF 2.1.1.

H.263—Another international standard and an advance on H.261, H.263 is also designed for video conferencing applications at low bit rates. Its compression algorithms are superior to H.261 (block based DCT), and it should be used in preference to that standard when bandwidth is critical. The H.263 codec is supported by the JMF.

Indeo—A codec from Intel, Indeo is now available on a number of platforms. Indeo employs both spatial and temporal compression in a lossy scheme that uses VQ and blocks. Indeo takes longer to compress than decompress video. Indeo v32 and v50 are supported by JMF 2.1.1.

MJPG—Motion-JPEG is a scheme directly based on the *JPEG (Joint Picture Experts Group)* approach of compressing individual still images. MJPG employs spatial compression only, considering each frame in isolation. This is not optimal in a compression sense, but it does make stream editing easier. The scheme is widely used by video capture cards. The approach is lossy and based on a block-oriented DCT. The MJPG standard is supported in JMF 2.1.1.

MPEG-1—The first standard issued by the Motion Picture Expert Group, MPEG-1 is a lossy scheme employing spatial compression and a more sophisticated (than Cinepak, for instance) temporal compression system. MPEG-1 is the standard on which the Video CD is based. The scheme is lossy and uses DCT for block-oriented compression. MPEG-1 was designed (in 1988) to be carried out in hardware (particularly compression), although modern PC systems are more than capable of decoding MPEG-1 in real-time and can also perform compression (with acceptable delays). MPEG-1 is supported in JMF 2.1.1.

MPEG-2—An extension of the MPEG-1 standard to take it from 30 frames per second to 60 frames per second of high quality video and used in applications requiring such quality (for example, broadcast transmissions over satellite). MPEG-2 is the standard on which products such as Digital Television set-top boxes and the DVD are based. Initially (the standard was ratified in 1994), MPEG-2 required specialized hardware, particularly for the compression side. However, all modern PC systems are capable of rendering MPEG-2 in real-time and can perform compression with acceptable delays.

MPEG-4—The latest international standard from the MPEG team, MPEG-4 is more than a video compression scheme. The video compression scheme holds much promise, yielding high-quality images at low bit rates, and is closely related to the H.263 standard. MPEG-4 follows the MPEG family of codecs approach of block-based DCT compression. MPEG-4 is supported in JMF-2.1.1 via extensions provided by IBM. These are discussed in Chapter 9.

RealVideo—A proprietary codec from Real Networks, RealVideo is currently probably the most commonly found codec on the Web for streaming video. One of the features of RealVideo is that several different versions of a movie can be provided in order to match the bandwidth limitations of different users (for example, T1 versus cable modem versus 28.8Kbps version).

Sorensen—A software codec, the same as Indeo and Cinepak, the Sorensen codec employs spatial and temporal compression in a lossy scheme based on vector quantization of blocks. A newer codec than Indeo and Cinepak, Sorensen employs a more sophisticated temporal compression scheme that includes motion compensation, and can therefore achieve better results.

To illustrate the differences in terms of degree of compression and artifacting (losses or artifacts in the images because of the compression scheme) between different codecs, the book's Web site (www.samspublishing.com) has a number of versions of the same video. The video is

Time-Based Media and the JMF: An Introduction

CHAPTER 7

305

7

TIME-BASED MEDIA
AND THE JMF:
AN INTRODUCTION

a short piece in three segments. The first segment is a "talking head"—a static shot of me talking to the camera. The second segment is outdoor and dynamic—me riding a bicycle within camera range; whereas the third segment is a short synthetic (generated, not captured with a camera) sequence. The same original video has been transcoded using a number of different codecs so that they can be contrasted. Figure 7.12 shows four images from the video, where each image is from a different encoding: the top-left panel is Cinepak, the top right is IV32, bottom left is RGB, and bottom right is motion JPEG. Each version differs because of the codec used to compress it. However, the static screen shot shouldn't be used as the basis of comparison because of artifacts of the screen capture.

FIGURE 7.12
JMStudio playing four versions of the same sample file.

The name of each file identifies the codec and screen resolution found in that sample.

    <codec>_<horizontal>x<verticaln>.<content_type>

For instance, the file `MJPG_320x240.mov` is a QuickTime (.mov) file encoded with Motion JPEG at a resolution of 320×240.

What Is the JMF?

Fundamentally, the JMF is an extension to Java for handling audio and video. More rigorously, the *JMF API (Java Media Framework Application Programming Interface)* is one of the Official Java optional APIs that extends the functionality of the core Java Platform. Included in this group of optional APIs, freely available from Sun, are others such as Java 3D and *Java Advanced Imaging (JAI)*.

JMF, as its name implies, is a collection of classes to enable the processing of (time-based) media objects. Sun Microsystems' JMF 2.1.1 Programmer's Documentation introduces the JMF as

Java Media Framework (JMF) provides a unified architecture and messaging protocol for managing the acquisition, processing, and delivery of time-based media data. JMF is designed to support most standard media content types, such as AIFF, AU, AVI, GSM, MIDI, MPEG, QuickTime, RMF, and WAV.

Sun's main JMF page has the following to say of the API:

The Java Media Framework API (JMF) enables audio, video and other time-based media to be added to Java applications and applets. This optional API, which can capture, play-back, stream and transcode multiple media formats, extends the multimedia capabilities on the J2SE platform, and gives multimedia developers a powerful toolkit to develop scalable, cross-platform technology.

Thus, the JMF is a collection of classes aimed at extending the Java Platform in the areas of video and audio processing, whether locally or across a network, and for both applets and applications.

Features of the JMF API

Amongst the key features of the API are

- Platform independence. There is a reference implementation that will run anywhere Java runs.
- Integrated and uniform handling of Audio and Video as media objects.
- Support for a significant number of the major audio and video content types and codecs.
- Playback of media.
- Saving of media (to a file).
- Capture of media from devices such as cameras and microphones.
- Receipt of media streams transmitted across the network.
- Transmission of media streams (across the network).
- Multiplexing/Demultiplexing (combining and splitting) of media.
- Transcoding (altering to a different format) media.
- A unified processing framework that supports all operations on media (for example, effects) as processing.
- Extensibility to support further formats and plug-ins.
- Seamless integration with the existing Java API.

The Promise of JMF

Enumerating the features of JMF provides a rather bland view of the API. Only after the potential applications implemented using the JMF are considered can the true possibilities become clear.

Among the exciting possibilities, are the following:

- Video conferencing across a range of platforms and networks
- A complete video and audio editing suite
- Empowering the latest mobile computing such as cellular phones and *PDAs (Personal Digital Assistants)*
- Integrated multimedia applications entirely in Java and hence running on any platform

Video conferencing is often considered a "killer app," bringing together a number of technologies in order to allow people to visually and verbally communicate in real-time. The availability of a video conferencing system of reasonable quality and independent of both hardware (particular cameras, microphones, hardware codecs) and software (particular operating systems) constraints would likely have a major impact in the conduct of both business and private life. The JMF, and Java more broadly, is a framework in which that can be achieved. The challenge remains bandwidth; but newer codecs (all of which can be incorporated into the JMF) and network services continue to whittle away at this hurdle.

The strength of the JMF lies not so much in the functionality of the API itself but in the broader context of the complete Java platform. This brings not only portability but also seamless integration with a number of other APIs and suites. For instance, a complete video and audio editing suite could be developed by using the JMF for handling the raw media, in combination with Java's AWT and Swing sets for presenting a GUI, and the JAI (Java Advanced Imaging) API for performing a number of the (video) effects.

Similarly, Java is a perfect solution in the consumer and embedded technologies area such as mobile phones, personal digital assistants, and TV-set-top boxes (for example, digital television set top boxes). Indeed one of the design goals of Java was to meet the security and portability demands of such a range of devices. The Java Micro Edition and related technologies deliver on that need. The advent of the next generation of these devices has seen the availability of increased processing power coupled with the demand for more sophisticated interfaces and content. The JMF is perfectly suited for these needs and is already being used to, among other things, stream video to the latest mobile phones.

With that said, it is worth remembering that the JMF is in its adolescence right now and, not being fully mature, it has some shortcomings. In particular a number of formats, including the important MPEG-2 and MPEG-4 standards, currently aren't part of the JMF distribution. That is expected to be addressed in the next JMF release, and Sun representatives have said that they have a continuing dedication to supporting the latest open standards.

Another catch for the unwary JMF programmer is that the JMF is a separate download and not part of the standard Java platform—a vanilla *JVM (Java Virtual Machine)* isn't capable of running a JMF program. This has implications for those people wanting to write applets using features of the JMF. To ensure that the widest audience can run them, the author must provide either instructions for downloading and installing the JMF (a difficult task for many users) or an automated mechanism for installing the necessary subset of the JMF classes.

Java and Time Based Media: A Short History

Although the Java platform (standard edition) is a powerful tool for many applications, including some aspects of multimedia, its support of time-based media has never been strong. Until recently (SDK1.3), the only class within the core Java platform that dealt directly with time-based media was AudioClip, a relatively simple class that supported the loading and play of (Sun) AU audio files, and little else.

The Java Media Framework was designed to extend the functionality of Java into the arena of time-based media. It has gone through two major versions with the current release number being v2.1.1.

JMF v1.0 was known as the Java Media Player and provided playback functionality. Two reference implementations were released: one for Windows and one for Solaris. Version 1.1 was a platform independent (or Pure Java) release. Version 1 of the JMF API was developed by Sun Microsystems, Silicon Graphics, Inc., and Intel Corporation.

JMF 2.0 dramatically extended the capabilities of JMF 1.0 by adding streaming, multiplexing and demultiplexing, media capture, transcoding, a unified processing framework, and an extensible plug-in design. It was designed by Sun Microsystems and IBM. Three implementations of JMF2.0 were released: a Pure Java Reference version, as well as an optimized version for Windows and one for Solaris. Version 2.1 of the API added support for Linux as well as increasing support for various streaming video servers. Version 2.1.1, current as of the time of writing, has improved the RTP API as well as added support for the H.263 codec.

Media Formats and Content Types Supported by JMF

The JMF provides support for a number of the most important and popular content types and formats in both the audio and video arenas. In the area of content types, that includes names such as QuickTime, AVI, Wave, and MPEG. In the area of formats or codecs, that includes MPEG (for example, MP3), U-law, Cinepak, MJPG, and H.263. Further, as witnessed by the history of the various versions of JMF, that support has continued to increase (for example, H.263 added in the most recent version).The two most important formats currently absent from the JMF are MPEG-2 and MPEG-4. These are significant omissions! However the JMF development team at Sun has set support for these two formats as its highest priority. As such, it is expected that support for MPEG-2 and MPEG-4 will be found in the next major release of the JMF.

Time-Based Media and the JMF: An Introduction

CHAPTER 7

309

7

TIME-BASED MEDIA
AND THE JMF:
AN INTRODUCTION

That broad coverage of content types and formats allows the JMF not only to claim platform and format independence, but also to provide new opportunities to programmers. Programmers can select the appropriate format for the task at hand and even transcode between formats as needed.

In the area of protocols, the JMF supports the file, http, ftp, and rtp protocols.

Tables 7.3 and 7.4 show the media format and content type support of the current version (v2.1.1) of the JMF. Table 7.3 shows support for audio content types, and Table 7.4 shows support for video content types. There are three implementations of JMF2.1.1: the cross-platform (Cross) pure Java version, the Solaris (Sol) performance version, and the Windows (Win) performance version. They differ slightly in their support of formats. Most formats supported by the JMF can be both read (decoded) and write (encoded); however, in some cases that isn't true. Hence these tables have entries that list content type, format, which implementations can decode that format, and which implementations can encode it.

TABLE 7.3   Audio Content Types and Formats (Codecs) Supported by the JMF 2.1.1 Implementations

Content Type	Format	Decode/Read	Encode/Write
AIFF (.aiff)	8-bit mono/stereo linear	Cross, Sol, Win	Cross, Sol, Win
	16-bit mono/stereo linear	Cross, Sol, Win	Cross, Sol, Win
	G.711 (U-law)	Cross, Sol, Win	Cross, Sol, Win
	A-law	Cross, Sol, Win	
	IMA4 ADPCM	Cross, Sol, Win	Cross, Sol, Win
GSM (.gsm)	GSM mono audio	Cross, Sol, Win	Cross, Sol, Win
MIDI (.mid)	Type 1 & 2 MIDI	Sol, Win	
MPEG Layer II Audio (.mp2)	MPEG layer 1,2 audio	Cross, Sol, Win	Sol, Win
MPEG Layer III Audio (.mp3)	MPEG layer 1, 2 or 3 audio	Cross, Sol, Win	Sol, Win
Sun Audio (.au)	8-bit mono/stereo linear	Cross, Sol, Win	Cross, Sol, Win
	16-bit mono/stereo linear	Cross, Sol, Win	Cross, Sol, Win
	G.711 (U-law)	Cross, Sol, Win	Cross, Sol, Win
	A-law	Cross, Sol, Win	
Wave (.wav)	8-bit mono/stereo linear	Cross, Sol, Win	Cross, Sol, Win
	16-bit mono/stereo linear	Cross, Sol, Win	Cross, Sol, Win
	G.711 (U-law)	Cross, Sol, Win	Cross, Sol, Win

Table 7.3   Continued

Content Type	Format	Decode/Read	Encode/Write
	A-law	Cross, Sol, Win	
	GSM mono	Cross, Sol, Win	Cross, Sol, Win
	DVI ADPCM	Cross, Sol, Win	Cross, Sol, Win
	MS ADPCM	Cross, Sol, Win	
	ACM	Win	Win

Table 7.4   Video Content Types and Formats (Codecs) Supported by the JMF 2.1.1 Implementations

Content Type	Format	Decode/Read	Encode/Write
AVI (.avi)	Audio: 8-bit mono/stereo linear	Cross, Sol, Win	Cross, Sol, Win
	Audio: 16-bit mono/stereo linear	Cross, Sol, Win	Cross, Sol, Win
	Audio: DVI ADPCM compressed	Cross, Sol, Win	Cross, Sol, Win
	Audio: G711 (U-law)	Cross, Sol, Win	Cross, Sol, Win
	Audio: A-law	Cross, Sol, Win	
	Audio: GSM mono	Cross, Sol, Win	Cross, Sol, Win
	Audio: ACM	Win	Win
	Video: Cinepak	Cross, Sol, Win	Sol
	Video: JPEG (411,		
422, 111)	Cross, Sol, Win	Sol, Win	
	Video: RGB	Cross, Sol, Win	Cross, Sol, Win
	Video: YUV	Cross, Sol, Win	Cross, Sol, Win
	Video: VCM	Win	Win
Flash (.swf, .spl)	Macromedia Flash 2	Cross, Sol, Win	
HotMedia (.mvr)	IBM HotMedia	Cross, Sol, Win	
MPEG-1 Video (.mpg)	Multiplexed System stream	Sol, Win	
	Video-only stream	Sol, Win	
MPEG-4 Video		IBM	IBM
QuickTime (.mov)	Audio: 8-bit mono/stereo linear	Cross, Sol, Win	Cross, Sol, Win
	Audio:16-bit mono/stereo linear	Cross, Sol, Win	Cross, Sol, Win

TABLE 7.4   Continued

Content Type	Format	Decode/Read	Encode/Write
	Audio: G711 (U-law)	Cross, Sol, Win	Cross, Sol, Win
	Audio: A-law	Cross, Sol, Win	
	Audio: GSM mono	Cross, Sol, Win	Cross, Sol, Win
	Audio: IMA4 ADPCM	Cross, Sol, Win	Cross, Sol, Win
	Video: Cinepak	Cross, Sol, Win	Sol
	Video: H.261	Sol, Win	
	Video: H.263	Cross, Sol, Win	Sol, Win
	Video: JPEG (411, 422, 111)	Cross, Sol, Win	Sol, Win
	Video: RGB	Cross, Sol, Win	Cross, Sol, Win

An additional feature of JMF 2.0 and later is that it is user extensible in the area of protocols, content type, and formats supported. A number of Interfaces are supplied, which users can implement with their own classes. The multiformat support of JMF should continue to grow, not only through the releases of Sun, but also through third party and individual development.

Chapter 8 includes a sample class that queries the JMF Manager class in order to determine the types of media supported for the particular version of JMF and the platform it is running on. That and Sun's JMF site can be used to determine the level of support for various media offered by the JMF.

Levels of Usage of the JMF API

The JMF affords the user a range of programming opportunities. These extend from using the JMF without ever writing a single line of code (using JMFStudio), through simple player programming as found in the example at the end of this chapter, all the way to extending the capabilities of the JMF by adding new formats, effects, or codecs (as discussed in Chapter 9).

This has two implications. First, it is possible to take a minimalist approach in learning the JMF: learning only the necessary features for the application required while still achieving the desired effect. Second, it is possible to learn the JMF in layers—starting with the easier concepts and applications and slowly delving into the underlying structure and complexity as and when it becomes desirable.

This part's chapters follow an approach of moving from a simple to a more complicated utilization of the API. The following subsections identify some of the most common levels of utilization that occur, though typically an individual's usage and knowledge don't correspond exactly to any of the following four categories.

Out of the Box with `JMStudio`

As a demonstration of the capabilities inherent in the JMF API, Sun has included an application known as `JMStudio` (Java Media Studio) in the JMF 2.1.1 bundle. The class file is found with all the classes from the JMF API in the file jmf.jar. Running the application is as simple as `java JMStudio`.

Despite its innocuous appearance (see Figure 7.13), `JMStudio` is a powerful application that supports playback, capture, transmission, and transcoding. In these later aspects of capture, transmission, and transcoding, it far exceeds the capabilities of free players, although as noted previously the JMF doesn't support all possible video and audio formats. (In particular, the important formats of RealMedia, Sorensen, and divX aren't to be found, whereas MPEG-2 and MPEG-4 are expected to appear in the next release.)

FIGURE 7.13

The innocuous appearing, yet extremely versatile, `JMStudio` *application that comes as part of the JMF 2.1.1 distribution.*

A complete discussion of `JMStudio` is beyond the scope of this part. Sun maintains documentation on the application at `http://www.java.sun.com/products/java-media/jmf/2.1.1/jmstudio/jmstudio.html`. Although `JMStudio` is chiefly a proof of concept, it is worth enumerating the functionality it provides because it is often more convenient to use `JMStudio` to perform a task (such as transcode between two formats) than write a one-off piece of code to carry out the same thing.

The features of `JMStudio` include

- Support for multiple content types (architectures) and codecs.
- Play audio and video.
  - From local file
  - From URL
  - From an RTP stream
- Capture audio or video from devices connected to computer.
- Export (transcode) media to a file.
- Transmit media via RTP.
- View the plugins (and progress there of) currently processing a media object.

In addition to all the functionality listed previously, this last feature is particularly useful for those wanting to learn about the API itself. By invoking the PlugIn Viewer, it is possible to see the individual objects chained together to form the processing, as well as observe such statistics as the frame rate and size. Figure 7.14 shows the PlugIn Viewer as a QuickTime video (encoded with the Cinepak codec) is decoded for play.

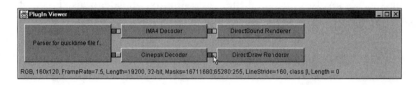

FIGURE 7.14
JMF's PlugIn Viewer in action.

Those only wanting to use the JMF indirectly through `JMStudio` will likely have sufficient knowledge by reading this chapter. However, reading the main portions of at least the following chapter will convey a far deeper understanding of how the JMF API works.

Simple Players

One of the common usages of the JMF is to incorporate audio or video play into an applet or application. As you will see with the example at the end of this chapter, that is a relatively painless and straightforward task. JMF provides a centralized manager from which can be obtained a player capable of dealing with a particular media object (content type and format). The player operates under a similar model to that of a modern VCR/DVD player: It can be started and stopped, as well as having its rate of play changed.

Programming at this level requires an understanding of the key concepts of the JMF (such as its model of time) together with the knowledge of some of the central classes in the API.

Those wanting to program the JMF at this level will likely only need to consult this and the earlier portions of the Chapter 8. However the deeper the knowledge of the API, the more subtle and complete control can be exercised over any players created. Further, if streaming capabilities are required, the first half of Chapter 9 will also need to be consulted.

Processing: Getting Under the Hood

The JMF provides powerful features for processing time-based media, including multiplexing, demultiplexing, transcoding, saving to a file, and so on. Although many users of the JMF will start off initially satisfied with simpler player applications, it is likely that a significant portion will move into these areas of more sophistication.

Processing is the topic of Chapter 8, and hence it serves as core material for those wanting to utilize the JMF in this manner. In addition, it is likely that most of the material covered in Chapter 9 will also be relevant to users with such applications in mind.

Extending the API, and Interfacing with Other APIs

The most sophisticated levels of usage of the JMF fall into two categories. The first category involves extending the API. The JMF is designed to be extensible so that users can write their own codecs, formats, effects, and so on and thus expand the JMF to suit their needs and constraints. This level of programming requires a strong familiarity with the API as well as the specialized knowledge concerning the feature being added. It is one of the topics covered in Chapter 9.

The second category involves employing the JMF as part of a larger, integrated application in which the processing can be chained or synchronized. An example of such an application includes feeding a JMF video into a Java 3D virtual world. Such applications have great potential, but require the programmer to have familiarity with all the APIs concerned. This synergy between APIs is covered in part (from a JMF perspective) in Chapter 9, and is the topic of Chapter 14, "Integrating Across the Java Media API."

Programming Paradigms When Using JMF

JMF based applets and applications tend to require particular programming approaches that other general calculation programs don't usually possess. This section addresses those approaches.

The JMF deals with time-based media. That requires not only a sophisticated model of time, but also support for the idiosyncratic and asynchronous behavior of a range of hardware devices and networks. Different capture devices might take considerably different times to become ready, network streams might drop out, and file systems might become full through saving large media files. All these eventualities and many, many more should be dealt with robustly and appropriately by a well-written JMF program.

Event Driven

Event-driven programming lies at the heart of most JMF programs. Graphical user interfaces programmed in the AWT or Swing set must wait and respond to user actions (for example, a button press) that occur asynchronously (that is, the program has no knowledge of when they'll occur). Also, a JMF program that is playing or processing must wait and respond to the various timing events and actions arising from a player or processor.

Those of you who aren't familiar with the concepts and practice of event-driven programming should consider acquiring such practice before delving too deeply into the JMF API. Such knowledge is necessary because of the central role of events in controlling the API.

The later section within this chapter dealing with time and the next chapter cover the major listener interfaces and events of the API. However, it is extremely typical to see lines like those found in Listing 7.1 in a JMF program.

LISTING 7.1   Skeleton Example of the Type of Event Driven Programming Used in Conjunction with the JMF

```
public class MyJMFProgram implements ControllerListener {
:
:
  player.addControllerListener(this);
:
:
public synchronized void controllerUpdate(ControllerEvent e) {
:
}
}
```

Such a class is listening to, and will be sent events from, the player object.

Threading

The devices responsible for controlling and transporting time-based media (for example, networks, renderers, and capture devices) are asynchronous. As in many applications, when this is combined with the control of multiple streams, channels, tracks, or sources and destinations of media, it is necessary to delegate control of individual items to separate threads so that the whole program won't suffer a bottleneck or be brought to an unresponsive halt by a single recalcitrant subtask.

Java provides strong and fundamental support for threads through the Thread class and Runnable interface. User classes that are to run as threads can either extend Thread or implement Runnable. Because of Java's single inheritance, it is often better for a class to implement Runnable (which only consists of the single run() method) than the subclass Thread.

An application employing threads tends to consist of a main, controller program that creates the threads for the individual tasks and both monitors and communicates with them as necessary. The classes that are to act as the threads must possess a run() method. This is started when the thread is started, and the thread is alive only while the method hasn't returned.

A threaded program usually possesses code similar to that found in Listing 7.2.

LISTING 7.2   Typical Structure of Code Starting Up a New Thread

```
// Need to create a thread to handle a sub-task. First create
// a new instance of the class that will do the work. Then
// pass that object to the Thread constructor. Finally, start
// up the thread.

MyThreadedController controlObj = new MyThreadedController(…);
Thread theThread = new Thread(controlObj);
theThread.start();
```

Exceptions

Exceptions in Java represent unusual, abnormal, and unexpected results that halt the normal flow of program execution. For JMF programs, exceptions are a very real possibility that a well-written and robust program must be capable of dealing with or at least exiting gracefully and with the maximum amount of information for the user. Examples of such exceptions within the context of a JMF program include the inability to create a player or processor for the media object specified, a number of time related exceptions (for example, trying to invoke a method on a processor that isn't yet in a state to support that action), as well as IO exceptions (for example, attempting to open a file that doesn't exist).

Hence, it is common to find a number of try {...} catch { ...} blocks in a program, whereby the code that could potentially throw an exception is enclosed in the try block; whereas the one or more catch blocks contain code for dealing with the exceptions that might arise. If you are unfamiliar with exceptions and the mechanism for handling them, refer to a general Java textbook or reference. A typical example of this type of processing is found in Listing 7.3.

LISTING 7.3   Typical Usage of try{ }, catch{ } Blocks to Deal with Thrown Exceptions

```
try {
  Player player = Manager.createPlayer(locator);
}
catch (NoPlayerException e) {
  System.err.println("Unable to create a player for…" + e);
}
```

URLs and Networks

One of the important features of Java is the integration of network support into the heart of the language. That theme of integrating networking support extends to the JMF, where for instance it is not only possible to play a file across the network, but also it is relatively simple. One central class of the API is the MediaLocator, which specifies the location of a media object and is closely related to Java Platform's URL class.

Integration of networking features into the JMF extends into support for *RTP (Real-time Transport Protocol)*, the communication protocol employed to stream media across networks. That topic is covered in Chapter 9.

Structure of the API

The JMF API (v2.1.1) comprises a total of 209 classes, of which 85 are interfaces, divided among 11 APIs.

In Java, APIs serve both to group related classes while also acting as a means of controlling the visibility of the attributes and methods of those classes. In order to employ a class that is the member of an API, it, or the entire API, must be imported.

The 11 APIs that comprise the JMF, together with their domain, are listed as follows:

- javax.media—The main, top-level API comprising most of the classes and also most of the important ones such as Time, Manager, Processor, and Player.

- javax.media.bean.playerbean—A collection of seven classes that provide Java Bean encapsulation for a Player. MediaPlayer is the most important class in the API.

- javax.media.control—An API comprised of 18 Interfaces defining the different types of controls. Examples include FrameRateControl and FormatControl.

- javax.media.datasink—An API of one interface and three events defining a listener for datasink events.

- javax.media.format—An important API of 10 classes (one of which is an exception) defining the different formats that JMF is capable of processing. Examples of the classes include AudioFormat and H263Format.

- javax.media.protocol—An important API of 25 classes (15 being interfaces) providing support for communication with datasources and capture devices. Among the important classes included in this API are DataSource and CaptureDevice.

- javax.media.renderer—An API of two interfaces defining a renderer (for video content).

- javax.media.rtp—The top-level of the three APIs dealing with *RTP (Real-time Transport Protocol)* it comprises 26 classes (most interfaces) dealing with streaming content with RTP.

- javax.media.rtp.event—An API of 23 events that might result when using RTP.

- javax.media.rtp.rtcp—An API of five classes (four being interfaces) defining usage of *RTCP (RTP Control Protocol)* within the JMF.

- javax.media.util—An API of two highly useful classes: BufferToImage and ImageToBuffer for converting between JMF buffers and AWT images.

Similar to all the Java APIs, and indeed the larger APIs within the core Java Platform, it takes considerable time to gain a thorough familiarity with the entire structure of the API. However, each class and interface in the API has been created for a purpose, and time spent studying the API isn't wasted, and indeed can save considerable effort or frustration.

Further, if this and the following chapters on the JMF don't mention a particular class or functionality within JMF, it doesn't mean that such a class doesn't exist within the API. In three chapters, it is impossible to cover all 209 classes in the API while also providing sufficient coverage of the most important aspects of the API. When in doubt and no JMF-related resource appears to have an answer, one of the first places to start should be with the JMF API Specification: `http://java.sun.com/products/java-media/jmf/2.1.1/apidocs/`.

Key Classes in the API

Although all classes in the API have a role to play, some are more central than others. These central classes can be found again and again in JMF programs and provide the backbone of those programs.

The next chapter discusses each of the classes in depth. However the following list serves as a reference to many of those backbone classes and what roles they serve in programs, without becoming overly cluttered with details.

`AudioFormat`—Information about an audio format including sampling rate and quantization level.

`CaptureDevice`—Interface defining behavior that all capture devices (for example, cameras) must possess.

`CaptureDeviceInfo`—Information about a particular capture device, including the formats supported.

`CaptureDeviceManager`—Manager aware of all the capture devices on the system and capable of providing information about them or, for example, a list that supports a particular format.

`Clock`—Interface defining JMF's fundamental time model. Key classes such as `Players` and `Processors` implement this interface.

`Codec`—Interface supporting the processing of media data from one format into (typically) another.

`Controller`—Interface built on `Clock` that defines the five states of stopped time (see the next section).

`ControllerListener`—Interface defining a listener for `Controller` generated events. Because `Controllers` include `Players` and `Processors`, this is a vital interface that is implemented somewhere in just about every JMF program.

`Controls`—An interface specifying a means of obtaining a control for an object.

DataSink—Interface for accepting data and rendering it to some source such as a file.

DataSource—Class providing a simple protocol for managing media arriving from a particular source (for example, a file).

Demultiplexer—Interface defining a processing unit that accepts a single input stream and outputs the demultiplexed tracks that composed the stream.

Effect—An interface defining a media processing unit that accepts a buffer of data, processes it in some way (but doesn't change its format), and outputs the processed buffer. The Effect interface supports many types of processing.

FileTypeDescriptor—Defines the different content type (architectures) supported.

Format—An abstraction of the format of a media object without all the encoding specific details.

Manager—Central manager or access point for obtaining resources such as Players, Processors, DataSources, and DataSinks.

MediaEvent—A Parent event class for all media events (for example, ControllerEvent).

MediaLocator—A means of specifying the location of media content. Used in the creation of players and data sources and sinks.

Multiplexer—A processing unit that accepts multiple input tracks and interleaves them to produce a single output container format.

Participant—A participant in an RTP session: a sender or receiver.

Player—An object for rendering (playing) and controlling (for example, stopping, changing rate of play) a media object.

PlugIn—An interface defining a generic plug-in that processes media data in some manner.

Processor—An extension to the Player interface, the Processor defines an object capable of processing and controlling a media object.

PullDataSource—A media source from which the data must be pulled (for example, a file).

PushDataSource—A media source from which the data is streaming (for example, an RTP session).

Time—An object that defines time to nanosecond precision.

TimeBase—A constantly ticking source of time.

VideoFormat—Format information about video data including frame rate.

Time—A Central Concept

Not surprisingly, after all it is called time-based media, time is a key concept in the JMF. Thus it is important that programmers who employ the API have a good understanding of the model of time that JMF uses.

JMF provides a layered model of time. At the bottom-most layer exists an exact representation of an instant in time at the nanosecond level. The next layers support the concept of a constantly ticking source of time: a clock. The highest layers support abstractions of time as being started or stopped and being in one of a number of potential states. These layers allow a programmer to exercise timing control (for example, alter play rate) as well as keep track of time-based processes at the level appropriate for the task. In particular, the abstracted higher-level models of time, as being one of a number of states, are particularly important for most JMF programs.

This section broadly discusses the high-level, abstract models of time because these are the most important in gaining a conceptual understanding of the functioning of a JMF program. The next chapter contains a far more detailed discussion of the time model of the JMF and the classes that support that model.

Controlling the processing (for example, playing or transcoding) of time-based media might, at first glance, appear to be either a process that is started (ongoing or happening) or stopped (yet to begin or finished). Certainly that division between started and stopped is true. However, initiating control is generally not instantaneous; indeed, it can be quite time-consuming. Resources generally need to be gathered. For instance, a file might need to be read, a socket opened, or a buffer filled. For this reason, the JMF divides stopped time into five exclusive states. In that way, JMF programs are better capable of managing the asynchronous and perhaps lengthy preparation tasks involved in handling time-based media. Figure 7.15 shows those five states and their relationships to one another.

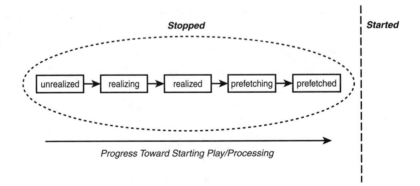

FIGURE 7.15

The five (stopped) states a Controller *transitions goes through before it is ready to start.*

These five states represent the life cycle of a media Controller (for example, Player) from creation to being ready to start. Transitions that forward toward a Prefetched (ready to start)

Time-Based Media and the JMF: An Introduction
CHAPTER 7
321

7
TIME-BASED MEDIA
AND THE JMF:
AN INTRODUCTION

...eas errors or other events might lead to a transition in the ...ight be informed of state changes by adding themselves ...anner, a program can initiate operations as well as ...those operations move through their various stages.

...ide stopped time are

...is been created but hasn't even begun to perform its task by ...ontrollers start in this state.

...acquiring information about the resources it needs to func- ...ıld result in the controller becoming Realized, although the

... gathered information about all the resources it needs to ...likely to have acquired all those resources necessary, which ...exclusive system resource (for example, grabbing a hard- ...teady state; it is moved past when the controller has

...is performing start-up processing such as filling buffers or ...es. This is a transition state that should result in the controller ...becoming Prefetched, although the time taken is unknown.

Prefetched—The controller has acquired all necessary resources, performed all prestartup processing, and is ready to be started.

Bare Bones Player Applet—A First Applet Using JMF

This final section introduces a simple bare bones applet that illustrates how simply features of the JMF can be used.

BBPApplet (Bare Bones Player Applet) is an applet that will play a single media object. The name of the media object (file) is specified as a parameter in the HTML file (within the applet tag) that contains the applet. The applet is written in a minimalist fashion: Only those necessary features of the JMF are employed, and nothing fancy is done with regard to GUI design. Subsequent examples in the next chapter will be more sophisticated.

Listing 7.4 is the source of the applet, which can also be found on the book's companion Web site (www.samspublishing.com). What should be clear is how small the applet is: It consists of just two methods, each of fewer than a dozen lines. Yet the result is an applet capable of playing any number of a range of different video and audio formats while also giving the user direct control over that playback through a control panel. Figure 7.16 shows the applet in action playing a synthetically generated video. Also shown are the Media Properties and PlugIn Viewer windows that were raised through the BBPApplet's controls.

LISTING 7.4   BBPApplet (Bare Bones Player Applet)

```
/******************************************************************
* A "Bare Bones" Player Applet (BBP Applet) that will play
* the media object indicated in the "media2Play" property
* of the Applet tag.
*
*<p>The applet demonstrates the relative ease with which
* the JMF can be employed, particularly for playing. The
* applet is a minimal player, placing the controls for the
* player and the visual component for the played object
* within the Applet. The object plays once, but can be
* controlled by the user through the control panel provided.
*
*<p>The tag for the Applet should look something like:
*
* <!-- Sample HTML
* <applet code="BBPApplet.class" width=300 height=400>
* <param name="media2Play" value="myVideo.mpg">
* </applet>
* -->
*
*@author Spike Barlow
******************************************************************/

import java.applet.*;
import java.awt.*;
import java.awt.event.*;
import java.net.*;
import java.io.*;
import java.util.*;
import javax.media.*;
public class BBPApplet extends Applet implements ControllerListener {

    /*****************************************
    * Object to play the media. Only attribute
    * that the Applet really needs.
    *****************************************/
    protected Player    player;

    /*****************************************
    * The name of the media to be played.
    *****************************************/
    protected String    nameOfMedia2Play;

    /******************************************
    * Name of the Property field within the
```

LISTING 7.4   Continued

```
    * applet tag indicating the name of the media
    * to play.
    ***********************************************/
    private static final String   MEDIA_NAME_PROPERTY = "media2Play";

    /***********************************************
    * Object describing the location of the media to
    * be played.
    ************************************************/
    protected MediaLocator      locator;



/******************************************************************
* Initialise the applet by attempting to create and start a
* Player object capable of playing the media specified in the
* applet tag.
******************************************************************/
public void init() {

    setLayout(new BorderLayout());
    setBackground(Color.lightGray);
    try {
        nameOfMedia2Play = (new URL(getDocumentBase(),
                            getParameter(MEDIA_NAME_PROPERTY)
                            )).toExternalForm();
        locator = new MediaLocator(nameOfMedia2Play);
        player = Manager.createPlayer(locator);
        player.addControllerListener(this);
        player.start();
    }
    catch (Exception e) {
        throw new Error("Couldn't initialise BBPApplet: "
                + e.getMessage());
    }
}



/******************************************************************
* Respond to ControllerEvents from the Player that was created.
* For the bare bones player the only event of import is the
* RealizeCompleteEvent. At that stage the visual component and
* controller for the Player can finally be obtained and thus
* displayed.
```

LISTING 7.4 Continued

```
******************************************************************/
public synchronized void controllerUpdate(ControllerEvent e) {

    if (e instanceof RealizeCompleteEvent) {
        add(player.getVisualComponent(),"North");
        add(player.getControlPanelComponent(),"South");
        validate();
    }

}

}
```

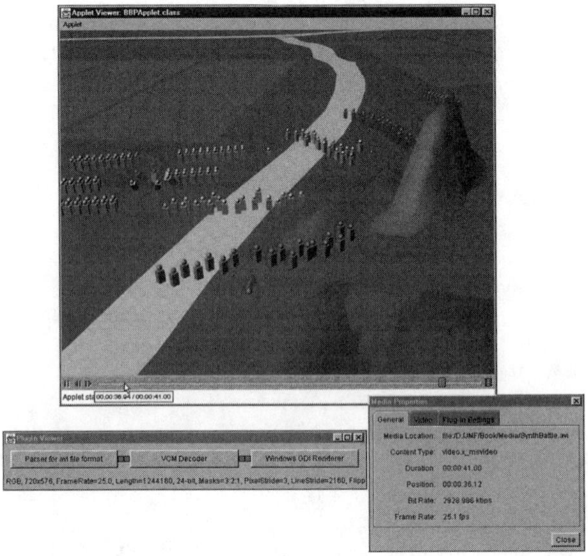

FIGURE 7.16
The BBPApplet (Bare Bones Player Applet) playing a synthetically generated video.

Several objects from the JMF API are employed in the applet. Chief among these is the Player object *player*. It is the only real attribute that the applet must possess because both methods need to refer to it. In order to create the Player object, a MediaLocator object *locator* is constructed from the user-specified filename that contains the media to be played. After that object is constructed, it is passed to the Manager class so that the Player can be created.

Several features typical of JMF programming can be found in this small example. The applet employs event-driven programming in order to determine when the Player is realized, and thus when a visual component and control panel for that Player can be obtained. Further, try/catch blocks are used to enclose the code in the init() method that could conceivably throw an exception, although for this short example nothing clever is done about an exception.

The fundamental algorithm of the applet can be written as follows:

1. Obtain the name of media file to play (using the parameter/property tag).
2. Convert filename to a MediaLocator object.
3. Create a Player object for the MediaLocator.
4. Listen to the Player object for events.
5. Start the Player object.
6. Wait for the Player object to become realized.
7. At the time of realization:

    •Obtain the Player object's visual component and place at top of applet.

    •Obtain the Player object's control component and place at bottom of applet.

Steps 1–5 all occur within the init() method, which is called when the applet is initialized. Step 6 is an expression of the event-driven nature of the program: There is no loop waiting or checking for realization to occur. Rather, it will be signaled by an event generated by the player. Step 7 occurs within the controllerUpdate() method, which is called when the Player object generates an event. If that event is a RealizeCompleteEvent, the Player object's components are obtained and added to the applet.

Two particulars of Listing 7.4 are worth further explanation. First, the initial line inside the try block of the init() method chains several steps together that result in a fully qualified name for the media object to play. As a first step in that process the value of the applet property that specifies the name of the file is obtained. That is combined with the *document base* of the applet, typically the same directory in which the applet is found, to produce a URL (object) that is then transformed back to a String (suitable for the MediaLocator constructor). Second, a layout manager—BorderLayout—is employed to ensure reasonable positioning of the controls and display on the screen. This allows the visual component of the player to be added to the top of the applet, whereas the controls are added to the bottom.

It is worth noting that a more complete example would likely override such methods as start() and stop() in order to control or free resources (that is, the Player object) as appropriate. Further, detecting and responding to the other types of events generated by the Player object could be used to provide additional functionality (for instance, looping play).

7

TIME-BASED MEDIA
AND THE JMF:
AN INTRODUCTION

Summary

This chapter serves as an introduction to time-based media and the *Java Media Framework (JMF)*, setting the stage for the next two chapters, which delve into the details of the JMF API.

The first half of the chapter provides a general and broad introduction to the concepts and practice of time-based media. The common features of all time-based media are covered before audio and video are addressed separately. A recurring theme is the high bandwidth demands of time-based media and hence the needs for compression. The alternatives in content types (architectures) and codecs for both audio and video were discussed.

The second half of the chapter introduces the JMF API. The potential of and support provided by the API is broached first. That is followed by an overview of the different levels of complexity at which the JMF can be employed together with common programming approaches when using the API. Finally, the key classes of the API are surveyed along with a synopsis of the JMF model of time. The chapter concludes with a short applet that plays media files, showing how simple it can be to write JMF programs.

Controlling and Processing Media with JMF

IN THIS CHAPTER

This chapter covers control of time-based media with the *JMF (Java Media Framework)* API. It serves as the core chapter of three chapters that cover time-based media: Chapter 7, "Time-Based Media and the JMF: An Introduction," serves as an introduction, and Chapter 9, "RTP and Advanced Time-Based Media Topics," covers advanced and specialized topics.

In the context of this chapter, control is used in the broadest sense to cover all actions concerning time-based media. That encompassing definition includes what is traditionally considered processing: decoding, encoding, transcoding (decoding from one format and encoding as another), effects, filters, multiplexing, and demultiplexing, as well as sourcing the data itself: capturing, reading from a file, and outputting (presentation or saving).

In fact, the fundamental approach to control can be seen as falling into three steps:

1. Source the media.

2. Process the media.

3. Output the media.

Figure 8.1 shows these three steps in control.

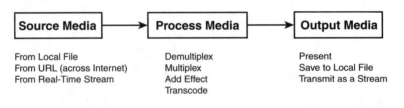

FIGURE 8.1

Three steps in control of media with the JMF.

This control can be chained: The output of one control stage can serve as the input to another. For instance, one control segment might secure a movie streaming across the Internet and demultiplex it into separate audio and video tracks that are saved to separate files. A second control module might then take that output audio data and add a reverb effect to one segment before multiplexing it back with the video track and saving the resulting movie.

Step 2, processing, can be an involved multistaged action, perhaps involving effects, codecs, multiplexers, and demultiplexers. Figure 8.2 is a schematic diagram showing multistage processing and chaining of control.

The chapter falls into three broad modules, each consisting of the following sections:

• Major steps and classes with roles in the control chain

• Processing

• Media Capture

Chaining Control

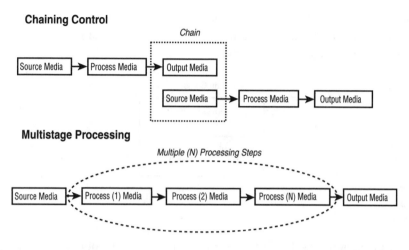

Multistage Processing

FIGURE 8.2

Chaining the processing of media.

The first module is a grab bag of topics covering the approach used by JMF in achieving control over media and is a necessary prelude to the details of the later modules. In particular, it includes a more detailed discussion of the JMF model of time (than that presented in the previous chapter) and an introduction to the key manager classes, as well as discussions of Controls, DataSources, and DataSinks.

The second module concerns processing and begins with a discussion of the expanded stop-time categories that the JMF employs for processing. The topics of the earlier sections of the chapter are then illustrated with a number of processing examples (such as transcoding).

The final module covers the topic of media capture—sampling audio or video directly from devices attached to the computer.

Detailed Time Model

As discussed in Chapter 7, the JMF employs a layered approach to its representation of time. At the low-level end of the time model are classes for representing time to nanosecond accuracy. At the high-level end of the model, the JMF sees controllers as being in one of a number of states that are transitioned between under program control.

Low-Level Time: `Time` and `TimeBase` Classes

Two classes, `Time` and `SystemTimeBase`, and one interface, `TimeBase`, detail the JMF's low-level model of time.

At the bottom of the hierarchy and also perhaps the most fundamental is the `Time` class. A `Time` object represents a particular instant in time to one nanosecond accuracy. Figure 8.3 shows the `Time` class's constructors and public methods.

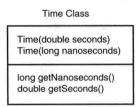

Time Class

Time(double seconds)
Time(long nanoseconds)

long getNanoseconds()
double getSeconds()

FIGURE 8.3

The Time *class.*

`Time` objects are often returned by methods used to query the temporal status of another object; for instance, the amount of elapsed play time on some media.

Similarly, `Time` objects can be employed to alter the temporal properties of an object. For instance, to specify a particular point in time from which to start playback of media, a `Time` object might be employed as follows:

1. Construct a `Time` object with a value, specified in seconds or nanoseconds, as the offset from the start of the media at which play should commence.

2. Pass that object to the `Player` object's `setMediaTime()` method.

The `Time` class also possesses a special constant `TIME_UNKNOWN`. This constant finds applications in contexts in which an object might be asked the duration of the media it is associated with, but its length hasn't, or cannot, be ascertained.

The `Time` class specifies a single instant in time, whereas time-based media, by its nature, is dynamic and time varying. JMF's support for ticking (at 1 nanosecond per tick) time comes in the form of the `TimeBase` interface. The `TimeBase` interface is an important one, and one that is implemented by a number of important classes. (More accurately, it is subsumed in other key interfaces such as `Controller` and `Player`, which extend the interface.) The `TimeBase` interface defines only two methods, both of which are used to query the current time of the `TimeBase` object. The `getTime()` method returns a `Time` object. An alternate means of obtaining the same information is the `getNanoseconds()` method, which returns a long. There is no provision in a `TimeBase` for altering time: It can only be queried regarding its current state.

As a default implementation of the `TimeBase` interface, JMF provides the class `SystemTimeBase`. `SystemTimeBase` has a single empty constructor and only the two methods defined in the `TimeBase` interface. Alternatively, the system time base can be obtained through the `Manager` class's `getSystemTimeBase()` method.

The `Clock` Interface

Those classes that implement the `TimeBase` interface provide a constantly ticking, unalterable source of time. However, controlling media means providing control over the temporal properties of that media: being able to start or stop the media at arbitrary locations as well as control its rate (for example, fast forward or rewind on a player). The `Clock` interface is the means by which that is achieved, and it is implemented by objects that support the JMF model of time.

In many ways, the `Clock` interface is pivotal both as the cement between the low-level and high-level time models and as a core interface of the API. The `Controller`, `Player`, and `Processor` interfaces, all central to the functionality of the JMF, extend `Clock`.

`Clock`s are typically associated with a media object. Indeed, control over media such as playing or processing entails having a `Clock` associated with that media. (Because `Controller`, `Player`, and `Processor` interfaces extend `Clock`, the `Player` or `Processor` object is also the clock.) A `Clock` serves as both the timekeeper for its media and also a means of altering and adjusting the time of that media. The time a clock keeps is known as the *media time*.

Clocks achieve their dual task of monitoring and altering the time flow of their associated media by employing a `TimeBase`. As noted, `TimeBase` objects represent constantly ticking and unalterable time. Therefore, the `Clock` provides a remapping or transform from the `TimeBase` time to that associated with the media. This is a simple linear transform requiring three parameters: the rate (for example, of play), the media start time, and the time base start time. From these, the media time can be determined as follows:

```
media_time = media_start_time + rate x (time_base_time -
➥time_base_start_time)
```

The meanings of the previous terms are as follows:

Media time—The media's own position in time. For instance, if an audio clip was one minute in length, its media time would range between 0 and 60 seconds.

Media start time—The offset within the media from which play is started. If play starts from the beginning of the media, this value is `0`. If it was started seven and a half seconds in, this value would be `7.5`.

Rate—The rate of time passage for the media. A rate of 1 represents normal forward passage (for example, play), whereas a value of `-5` would represent a fast rewind.

Time base time—The time of the `TimeBase` object that the `Clock` incorporates. This starts ticking (increasing) as soon as the `Clock` object is created and never stops.

Time base start time—The time of the `TimeBase` object at which the `Clock` is started and synchronized with the `TimeBase`. For instance, the `Clock` might be started 3.2 seconds after the `Clock` was created (and hence the `TimeBase` was also created and started ticking). Hence, the time base start time would be 3.2 seconds.

A Clock is in one of two possible states: Started or Stopped. A clock is started by making the syncStart() method call. The syncStart() method accepts a single argument being the time base start time from which the Clock should be started. Once the Clock's TimeBase object reaches that time, the clock will synchronize with the TimeBase and enter the Started state. This mechanism allows a Clock to be set to start at some future time (or at the current time by passing the syncStart() method the Clock's own TimeBase object's current time). Any changes to the media (start) time and rate must be performed before a Clock enters the Started state. Attempting to use the methods that carry out these operations on a Clock in the Started state will result in a ClockStartedError being thrown. Thus, the usual steps in starting a clock are

1. Stop the clock if it is currently started.
2. Set the media (start) time of the Clock.
3. Set the rate of the Clock.
4. syncStart() the Clock.

A Clock's initial state is Stopped. After a clock is Started, it can be stopped in one of two ways. It can either be stopped immediately with the stop() method, or a media stop time can be set: Once the media time reaches (or if it has already exceeded) that time, the Clock will stop.

Finally, it is worth noting that it is possible to synchronize two or more Clocks by setting them to use the same TimeBase object. The Clock interface exposes methods for getting and setting the TimeBase object associated with the clock.

Figure 8.4 shows all the methods of the Clock interface. Besides those already discussed, often used methods are getMediaTime() and getMediaNanoseconds(). For instance, these might be called repeatedly as media is being played in order to provide some feedback on elapsed time for the viewer. Similarly, setRate() and setMediaTime() are used to provide user control in playback scenarios, but might only be called on a stopped clock.

Clock Interface

```
long getMediaNanoseconds()
Time getMediaTime()
float getRate()
Time getStopTime()
Time getSynchTime()
TimeBase getTimeBase()
Time mapToTimeBase(Time t)
void setMediaTime(Time now)
float setRate(float factor)
void setStopTime(Time stopTime)
void stop()
Void synchStart(Time at)
```

FIGURE 8.4

The Clock interface.

High Level Time: The `Controller` Interface

The `Controller` interface directly extends `Clock` in three areas:

- Extends the concept of `Stopped` into a number of states concerning resource allocation, so that time-consuming process can be better tracked and controlled.
- Provides an event mechanism by which the states can be tracked.
- Provides a mechanism by which objects providing further control over the controller can be obtained.

It is on top of the interface that the commonly used `Player`—which is used in the last example in Chapter 7—and `Processor` interfaces sit.

As we explained in the previous chapter, achieving the state where the control, processing, or play of media can be started isn't an instantaneous operation. Resources need to be gathered in order to support that control. Tasks involved in resource gathering include opening files for reading, filling buffers, or gaining exclusive control of hardware devices (for example, a hardware decoder). This point is illustrated in the next subsection in which the time taken to gather resources so that a video can be played is shown.

The `Controller` interface subdivides the `Stopped` category of `Clock` into five stages that reflect the state of preparedness of the `Controller`: how close it is to being capable of being started. Those five states, in order of least prepared through prepared to start, are

Unrealized—A `Controller` that has been created but hasn't undertaken any resource gathering.

Realizing—A transition state reflecting the fact that the `Controller` is gathering information about the resources needed for its task, as well gathering resources themselves.

Realized—A steady state reflecting a `Controller` that has gathered all the nonexclusive resources needed for a task.

Prefetching—A transition state reflecting the fact that the `Controller` is gathering all resources needed for its task that weren't obtained in the realizing state. Typically this means acquiring exclusive usage resources such as hardware.

Prefetched—The `Controller` has acquired all necessary resources, performed all pre-startup processing, and is ready to be started.

The `Controller` interface provides program control for the movement between these states via a set of methods. Similarly, the `Controller` interface allows for program monitoring of those transitions via an event system. Objects can implement the `ControllerListener` interface and thus be sent events as the `Controller` transitions between the various states. Figure 8.5 shows the methods and associated transitions between states. Figure 8.6 shows the events that are generated as a `Controller` transitions between its states.

8

CONTROLLING AND PROCESSING MEDIA WITH JMF

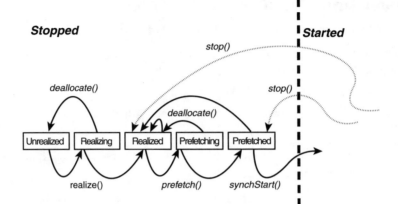

FIGURE 8.5

`Controller` *methods that cause state transitions.*

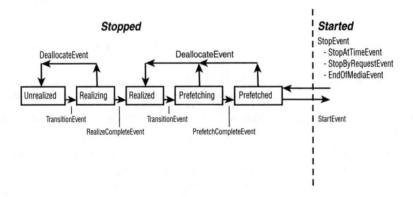

FIGURE 8.6

`Events` *generated as a* `Controller` *transitions between states.*

As shown in Figure 8.5, a `Controller` has five methods for controlling transition between states. The forward motion methods are `realize()`, `prefetch()`, and `synchStart()` (from the `Clock` interface) for moving the `Controller` into a more prepared, and finally `Started`, state. They are *asynchronous*—they return immediately, but the engendered action generally takes some time to complete. When the transition is complete (or interrupted by a `stop()` or other such call), an event is posted. The reverse direction methods are `stop()` and `deallocate()`.

These are *synchronous* methods. `stop()` is used to stop a started `Controller`. The `Controller` transitions to `Prefetched` (or in some cases where resources must be relinquished: `Realized`) and might subsequently be restarted. `deallocate()` frees the resources consumed by a `Controller` and should be used for that purpose (for example, in the `stop()` method of an applet). `deallocate()` cannot be called on a `Started Controller`; it must be stopped first. `deallocate()` returns a `Controller` to the `Realized` state if it is in that state or greater (a state closer to `Started`); otherwise, the `Controller` returns to `Unrealized`.

A `Controller` posts events about its state changes. Those objects wanting to be informed about `Controller` events must implement the `ControllerListener` interface. The `ControllerListener` interface consists of a single method:

```
public synchronized void controllerUpdate(ControllerEvent e)
```

Objects communicate their desire to be sent a `Controller`ís events by calling that `Controller`ís `addControllerListener()` method.

The events posted by a `Controller` fall into one of four categories:

- Life cycle transitions
- Method acknowledgements
- Status change information
- Error notification

The `TransitionEvent`, or a subclass such as `EndOfMediaEvent`, is a `Controller`'s means of reporting state changes. The method acknowledgement events `RealizeCompleteEvent`, `PrefetchCompleteEvent`, `StartEvent`, `DeallocateEvent`, and `StopByRequestEvent` are used to communicate the fulfillment of the corresponding methods—for example, `realize()`—called on the `Controller`. There are three status change events: `RateChangeEvent`, `StopTimeChangeEvent`, and `MediaTimeSetEvent` that inform the listener of changes in rate, stop time, and when a new media time is set. Errors fall under the `ControllerErrorEvent` class and include `ResourceUnavailableEvent`, `DataLostErrorEvent`, and `InternalErrorEvent`. Other errors are thrown as exceptions. For instance, attempting to `syncStart()` a `Controller` before it achieves the `Prefetched` state will result in a `NotPrefetchedError` being thrown.

Figure 8.7 shows all the methods and constants of `Controller` that aren't inherited from the `Clock` or `Duration` interfaces. Among the important methods of the interface not discussed previously are `close()`, `getStartLatency()`, `getControl()`, and `getControls()`. `close()` is used to release all resources and cease all activity associated with a `Controller`. The `Controller` can no longer be employed (its methods called) after it has been closed. The `getStartLatency()` method returns an estimate of the amount of time required in a worst-case scenario before the first frame of data will be presented. It is used to provide an estimate for syncStart() calls. The estimate is more accurate if the Controller is in the Prefetched state. The getControl() and getControls() methods provide a means for obtaining Control objects. These can be used to alter the behavior of the Controller. Controls and Controllers are two different things despite their unfortunate similarity in name. Controls are discussed in a subsequent section.

Controller Interface

```
Time LATENCY_UNKNOWN
Int Unrealized
Int Realizing
Int Realized
int Prefetcing
int Prefetched
int Started
```

```
Void addControllerListener(ControllerListener listener)
void close()
void deallocate()
Control getControl(String aspect2Control)
Control[] getControls();
Time getStartLatency()
int getState()
int getTargetState()
void prefetch()
void realize()
void removeControllerListener(ControllerListener listener)
```

FIGURE 8.7

The Controller *interface.*

Timing a Player

In order to illustrate the concepts covered in this section and the inter-relationship between the high- and low-level models of time that the JMF supports, the simple player applet BBPApplet from the previous chapter was modified slightly.

The modification consisted of time-stamping and printing every Controller event that was received by the applet. This provides a map through time of the course of the player from the instant it is started, until the time the media being played (an mpeg video) finishes.

The modification itself is simple, and rather than reproducing the code of the entire applet again, only the changes made will be discussed. A SystemTimeBase object was constructed immediately prior to the Player being started. Each time the controllerUpdate() method was entered, the `SystemTimeBase` object was queried as to the time, and that value plus the event that was received were printed to the screen. The three steps were

1. Where other attributes such as Player are declared, declare an additional attribute—an object of type `SystemTimeBase`.

   ```
   // The object to be used to timestamp Controller events.
   protected SystemTimeBase    timer;
   ```

2. Immediately prior to the `player.start()` asynchronous call, create the `SystemTimeBase` object in the `init()` method. From that instant forward, the timer will continue to tick with (potentially) nanosecond accuracy.

   ```
   timer = new SystemTimeBase();
   player.start();
   ```

3. In the `controllerUpdate()` method, immediately query the timer object as to its time, and print that (converted into seconds) and the event that was received.

   ```
   // Print the time the event was received, together with the event,
   // to the screen.
   System.out.println(""+(double)timer.getNanoseconds()/Time.ONE_SECOND
       + ": " + e);
   ```

The timing data output when the applet played an mpeg video somewhat over two minutes in length is reproduced in Listing 8.1. Each Controller event received by the class (generated by the Player) has been time stamped and output. The events occur in chronological order with a timestamp (in seconds) being the first piece of information on the line, that being followed by the event itself. Figure 8.8 shows the state transitions through time, distilling the most important information.

8

CONTROLLING AND
PROCESSING
MEDIA WITH JMF

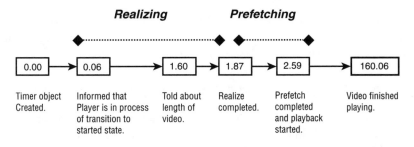

FIGURE 8.8
Timeline for the events a `Player` *received when presenting a video.*

LISTING 8.1   Timing information output by the modified BBPApplet (Bare Bones Player Applet)

```
0.06: javax.media.TransitionEvent[source=com.sun.media.content.video.mpeg.Handle
r@275d39,previous=Unrealized,current=Realizing,target=Started]

1.6: javax.media.DurationUpdateEvent[source=com.sun.media.content.video.
mpeg.Handler@275d39,duration=javax.media.Time@10fe28
1.87: javax.media.RealizeCompleteEvent[source=com.sun.media.content.video.mpeg.H
andler@275d39,previous=Realizing,current=Realized,target=Started]

2.59: javax.media.TransitionEvent[source=com.sun.media.content.video.mpeg.Handle
r@275d39,previous=Realized,current=Prefetching,target=Started]

2.59: javax.media.PrefetchCompleteEvent[source=com.sun.media.content.video.mpeg.
Handler@275d39,previous=Prefetching,current=Prefetched,target=Started]

2.59: javax.media.StartEvent[source=com.sun.media.content.video.mpeg.Handler@275
d39,previous=Prefetched,current=Started,target=Started,mediaTime=javax.media.Tim
e@36e39f,timeBaseTime=javax.media.Time@19dc16]

160.06: javax.media.EndOfMediaEvent[source=com.sun.media.content.video.mpeg.Hand
ler@275d39,previous=Started,current=Prefetched,target=Prefetched,mediaTime=javax
.media.Time@60a26f]

160.06: javax.media.DurationUpdateEvent[source=com.sun.media.content.video.mpeg.
Handler@275d39,duration=javax.media.Time@484a05
```

What is clear from the output and figure is that the steps in preparing to play media are lengthy, particularly from the perspective of a computer that executes millions of instructions per second. The realizing step took over a second and a half, whereas the prefetch step required nearly three quarters of a second, all for media stored locally on the hard disk.

The Control and Processing Chains

Four key classes play central roles in all JMF control and processing. These four classes form links in a chain who's first element is always a source of media. Depending on the particular task that media is then handled (such as playing or processing), that handling might be the end result itself (such as a Player); or the handling might result in a new data source or even a persistent media object (for example, a new media file).

Figure 8.9 shows the key classes involved in playing media. The media is sourced through a `DataSource` object. That is used to create a `Player` object, which renders the media to the appropriate hardware devices.

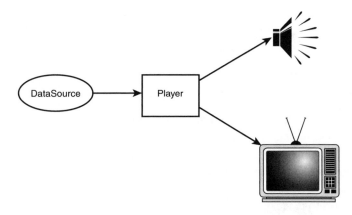

FIGURE 8.9

Playing media with the JMF: The media is sourced through a `DataSource` *and played with a* `Player`.

Figure 8.10 shows the key classes involved in processing media. As with the playing of media, the first step in processing is sourcing the media through a `DataSource` object. That is then processed—an encompassing term that includes multiplexing/demultiplexing, effects, and transcoding. The result of the processing is another `DataSource`. Illustrating that processing can be chained, the `DataSource` produced by a first stage of processing can serve as the input `DataSource` for a second round of processing. Similarly, processing could be performed and the results fed to a `Player` object for final rendering (display).

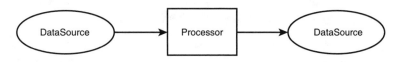

FIGURE 8.10

Employing a `Processor`*: Input arrives from a* `DataSource` *and the* `Processor` *produces a* `DataSource` *as the result of its processing.*

Figure 8.11 shows the key classes concerned when time-based media is to be produced that exists past the termination of the JMF program that produced it. As in all cases, the original

8

CONTROLLING AND PROCESSING MEDIA WITH JMF

media is sourced through a `DataSource` object. That is then typically processed, such as transcoding to a different format, to produce a new `DataSource`. A `DataSink` for that second `DataSource` is obtained so that the media can be preserved (for example, written to a file).

FIGURE 8.11

Employing a `DataSink` *to output data. The* `DataSource` *produced by a* `Processor` *serves as the input to the* `DataSink`.

The `Player`, `Processor`, `DataSource`, and `DataSink` classes are all `MediaHandlers`. Both the `MediaHandler` interface and the four classes are discussed in their own sections later in this chapter. The means of obtaining instances of these classes under the JMF is centralized through a manager class, which is discussed next.

Managing the Complexity

As graphically illustrated in the previous chapter, time-based media is a broad category encompassing not only different types of media (for example, audio and video), but also different content types (for example, QuickTime and AVI), and different formats for compression (for example, MPEG and Cinepak). This leads to a plethora of diverse media that differ at the conceptual level (visual or aural) down to the bit sequence by which they are encoded. Further complexity is added by the multitude of hardware devices from which media can be captured, and to which it can be rendered.

On the other hand, the goal of the JMF is to present a uniform, platform independent interface to controlling, processing, capturing, and rendering media. That means, for example, a single program to play media regardless of particulars of its encoding; *not* a different program for each type (category x content_type x encoding_scheme) of media.

The JMF successfully resolves these two conflicting items by providing four manager classes who's prime role is to track the numerous classes required to support media handling, while shielding the user from that complexity through the provision of a simple and consistent interface. Effectively, the managers act as brokers or intermediaries between user code and the necessarily complex functionality provided by the JMF. This provides user code with a simple, abstracted model; freeing it of unwanted complexity. Figure 8.12 illustrates that conceptual role of the managers. The `BBPApplet` (Bare Bones Player Applet) from Chapter 7, "Time-based Media and the JMF: An Introduction," provides a good example of this abstraction afforded by the managers. The applet simply requests that the manager create an object (`Player`) capable of playing the media it has indicated. The manager responds with an object suitable for the task. The actual object provided will depend on the content type and format of the media in question. However, from the applet's perspective there is simply a Player object which will do the task. The manager hid all the details of finding and constructing an instance of the appropriate class.

Player Interface

```
void addComtroller(Controller toBeControlled)
Component getControlPanelComponent()
GainControl getGainControl()
Component getVisualComponent()
void removeController(Controller noLogerToBeControlled)
void start()
```

FIGURE 8.12

Role of manager classes (for example, Manager*) as registry and shield for user code from the necessary complexity of classes in order to support the multitude of media formats.*

The JMF has four manager classes—each with the word Manager in their name, appropriately enough. Each of these classes exposes a number of static methods through which they provide their service. The four classes are as follows:

Manager—The central management class from which Players, Processors, DataSources, and DataSinks are obtained. This manager is discussed in the next subsection.

CaptureDeviceManager—Manager encapsulating knowledge of the capture devices (for example, sound or video capture cards) attached to the machine. This manager is discussed toward the end of the chapter.

PackageManager—A manager providing knowledge of and control over the packages that contribute to JMF's functionality. This manager is discussed in Chapter 9, "RTP and Advanced Time-Based Media Topics."

PlugInManager—A manager encapsulating knowledge of installed plug-ins, as well as a means of registering new ones. The JMF model of a plug-in incorporates multiplexers, demultiplexers, codecs, effects, and renderers. This manager is discussed in Chapter 9.

Although there are empty constructors for all except the Manager class, all methods exposed by the managers are static: They are invoked using the class name, and don't need an instance of the class constructed before they can be invoked.

Hence, for instance, to obtain information about a particular named CaptureDevice, the code should be written as follows:

```
String    deviceName = "...";   // Set to the actual name of the device
CaptureDeviceInfo captureDInfo = CaptureDeviceManager.getDevice(deviceName);
```

rather than

```
String deviceName="...";   // Set to the actual name of the device
CaptureDeviceManager captureDManager = new CaptureDeviceManager();
CaptureDeviceInfo captureDInfo = captureDManager.getDevice(deviceName);
```

8

CONTROLLING AND
PROCESSING
MEDIA WITH JMF

The Manager Class

The Manager class is the single most important manager class, and arguably the most important class in the JMF given its role in creation of Players, Processors, DataSinks, and DataSources.

Figure 8.13 shows the methods of the Manager class. As can be seen, Manager possesses methods for the creation of DataSources, DataSinks, Players, and Processors. It has already been noted in the previous section that these four classes play the primary roles in the control and processing of media. Given their significance, the importance of Manager as the sole agent of their creation shouldn't be underestimated.

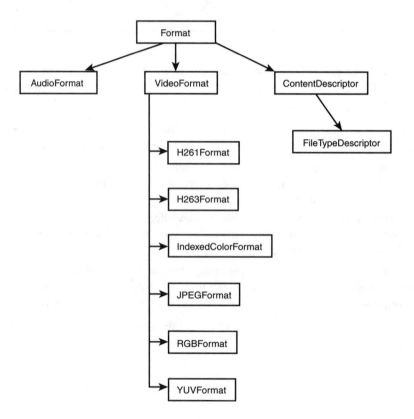

FIGURE 8.13
The Manager *class.*

Although subsequent sections discuss the Player, Processor, DataSource, and DataSink classes, their creation through the Manager class is discussed here.

Creating a `Player`

Objects implementing the `Player` interface are used in controlling the playback of media. The `Manager` class provides six methods for the creation of a `Player`: Three create an `Unrealized` `Player`: `createPlayer()`, whereas the other three create a `Realized` (that is, already partially resourced and more along the path to being ready to start) `Player`: `createRealizedPlayer()`.

The three `createRealizedPlayer()` versions are provided as a means to accelerate the creation of a `Player`. The method calls blocks (that is, the next line of code doesn't execute until the `Player` is `Realized`). This has the advantage that the `Realized` event doesn't need to be listened for by the invoker of the method (and hence methods such as `getVisualComponent()` can be called as the next line).

The three versions of `Player` creation methods (whether for an `Unrealized` or `Realized` `Player`) accept either a `MediaLocator`, `URL`, or `DataSource` as the single parameter. The steps in creating a `Player` that the `Manager` follows are as follows:

1. Convert the `URL` to a `MediaLocator` (if `URL` based method is used).
2. Create a `DataSource` for the `MediaLocator` (if `DataSource` based method isn't used).
3. Obtain the `Player` that can handle the `DataSource`.
4. Attach the `DataSource` to the `Player`.
5. Return the `Player` object.

The `URL` and `MediaLocator` based creation methods are the more commonly used because they correspond to the typical scenario in which a `Player` is employed: The media is in some location (for example, a file) and needs only to be played. On the other hand, the `DataSource` based method is useful when playing is the end result of a chain that involved other processing (that produced a `DataSource`) as earlier steps.

Thus the typical usage of `Manager` to create a `Player` is as follows:

```
MediaLocator locator = new MediaLocator(...);    // Specify media location;
Player player = Manager.createPlayer(locator);
```

Alternatively, a `Realized` `Player` could be created with the `createRealizedPlayer()` method as follows:

```
MediaLocator = new MediaLocator(...);    // Specify the media location;
Player player = Manager.createRealizedPlayer(locator);
```

In creating a `Player` object, `Manager` follows a set algorithm of searching through the various `Player` classes looking for one capable of handling the content type that the `DataSource` (constructed as an earlier part of the process if the `DataSource` wasn't supplied to the method) specifies. The process is simple linear iteration through the list of constructed classnames until one is found capable of handling the media.

If Manager cannot create a Player, it might throw an IOException (that is, file doesn't exist), a NoPlayerException (that is, a content-type that the JMF does not handle), or in the case of the createRealizedPlayer() methods, a CannotRealizeException (that is, couldn't obtain the resources necessary).

Players will be discussed further in a subsequent section.

Creating a Processor

Objects implementing the Processor interface are used in controlling the processing of media. The Manager class provides four methods for the creation of a Processor: Three create an Unrealized Processor: createProcessor() , whereas the final method creates a Realized (that is, already partially resourced and more along the path to being ready to start) Processor: createRealizedProcessor().

The createRealizedProcessor() method is provided as a means of accelerating the creation of a Processor. The method call blocks (that is, the next line of code doesn't execute until the Processor is Realized). This has the advantage that the Realized event doesn't need to be listened for by the invoker of the method. The createRealizedProcessor() method accepts a single parameter that is a ProcessorModel which fully specifies the input or output format of the media; thus the processing to be performed.

The three variants of createProcessor() have the same form as for Player creation: accepting either a MediaLocator, URL, or DataSource as the single parameter. Similarly, the Manager follows the same process in creation of a Processor as it does in the creation of a Player:

1. Convert the URL to a MediaLocator (if URL based method is used).
2. Create a DataSource for the MediaLocator (if DataSource based method isn't used).
3. Obtain the Processor that can handle the DataSource.
4. Attach the DataSource to the Processor.
5. Return the Processor object.

The URL and MediaLocator based creation methods should be used in the case where the processing is the first step in the chain of control. Alternatively, if it is a subsequent step (for example, chained processing) the DataSource based method should be used.

Thus the typical usage of Manager to create a Processor is as follows:

```
MediaLocator locator = new MediaLocator(...);    // Specify media location;
Processor processor = Manager.createProcessor(locator);
```

Alternatively, a Realized Processor could be created with the createRealizedProcessor() method as

```
//Specify the model for processing
ProcessorModel model = new ProcessorModel(...);
// Create the processor
Processor processor = Manager.createRealizedProcessor(model);
```

In creating a `Processor` object, `Manager` follows a set algorithm of searching through the various `Processor` classes that correspond to the same approach as that used for `Player` creation.

If `Manager` cannot create a `Processor`, it might throw an `IOException` (that is, file doesn't exist), a `NoProcessorException` (that is, a content-type that the JMF doesn't handle), or in the case of the `createRealizedProcessor()` methods, a `CannotRealizeException` (that is, couldn't obtain the resources necessary).

`Processors` will be discussed further in a subsequent section.

Creating a `DataSource`

`DataSources` are the means by which `Players`, `Processors`, or `DataSinks` obtain their data. Creation of a `Player`, `Processor`, or `DataSink` always involves a `DataSource`; whether provided explicitly to the creation method (as in the creation of a `DataSink`), or created as part of the larger process (as in the creation of a `Player` where a `MediaLocator` is provided). Details of `DataSources` are fully discussed in a subsequent section.

There are two methods for creating a `DataSource` from a location specification (URL or `MediaLocator`) using `createDataSource()`. There are also two methods for creating specialized `DataSources`: merging `DataSource` (one that combines two or more `DataSources`) with `createMergingDataSource()` and creating a cloneable `DataSource` (one that can be cloned to be processed or played by different systems simultaneously) with `createCloneableDataSource()`.

Listing 8.2 shows a number of the `DataSource` creation methods being used in a hypothetical scenario in which two `DataSources` are created, one is cloned (so it can be dual processed), and then the two sources are combined.

LISTING 8.2 Hypothetical `DataSources` Scenario

```
MediaLocator firstLocation = new MediaLocator(...);     //Location of 1st media
MediaLocator secondLocation = new MediaLocator(...);    // Location of 2nd media
try {
  // Create the two datasources.
  DataSource firstSrc = Manager.createDataSource(firstLocation);
  DataSource secondSrc = Manager.createDataSource(secondLocation);
  // Create cloneable version of 2nd src, then clone it.
  DataSource cloneableSrc = Manager.createCloneableDataSource(secondSrc);
  DataSource cloneA = cloneableSrc.createClone();
  // Create a merged DataSource combining the 1st and 2nd  DataSources.
```

LISTING 8.2   Continued

```
    DataSource srcArray = new DataSource[2];
    srcArray[0] = firstSrc;
    srcArray[1] = cloneA;
    DataSourced mergedSrcs = Manager.createdMergingDataSource(srcArray);
}
```

DataSources are identified by the protocol they support. In creation of a DataSource, the Manager class follows a similar approach as that employed for Player and Processor creation. A list of classes supporting the protocol specified (by the URL or MediaLocator) is compiled and that list is linearly searched until a class capable of sourcing the media is found.

Failure to create a DataSource from a URL or MediaLocator will result in the method throwing an IOException or NoDataSourceException. Failure to create a merging DataSource will result in an IncompatibleSourceException being thrown.

Creating a DataSink

DataSinks are used to take the media from a DataSource and render it to a particular location (for instance, a file). The Manager class provides a single method, createDataSink(), for the creation of a DataSink. The method accepts two parameters—a DataSource from which the media is sourced, and a MediaLocator that specifies the destination location.

The steps that the Manager class follows when creating a DataSource instance are similar to those used in the creation of a DataSource—with the protocol of the MediaLocator used to compile a list of DataSink classes that support the protocol. That list is then searched in order to find an appropriate class for which an instance can be created.

Failure to create a DataSink will result in a NoDataSink exception being thrown.

DataSinks are discussed in a later section of this chapter. However as an example of their usage, Listing 8.3 shows a portion (the object creation) of the process in which a DataSink could be used to create a copy of a media file. (Obviously it would be far more efficient to simply copy the file using the operating system commands.)

LISTING 8.3   Some of the Major Steps in Using a DataSink Object

```
String     origin = "file:...";
String     destination = "file:...";
MediaLocator     originLocation = new MediaLocator(origin);
MediaLocator     destinationLocation = new MediaLocator(destination);
Processor     p = Manager.createRealizedProcessor(null);
DataSource     src = p.getDataOutput();
DataSink     dest = Manager.createDataSink(src,destinationLocation);
:          :
```

Querying the Manager

Besides the methods for creating Players, Processors, DataSources, and DataSinks, the Manager class provides a number of information methods—methods that provide information about the configuration and support of the installed version of the JMF.

These information methods are the various get*() methods:

getHint()—Obtains information about hints provided to JMF.

getCacheDirectory()—Determines what directory the JMF uses for temporary storage.

getDataSourceList()—Determines what DataSource classes support a particular protocol.

getHandlerClassList()—Determines what Player classes support a particular content type.

getProcessorClassList()—Determines what Processor classes support a particular content type.

The getHint() method should be passed one of the constants defined in the Manager class (for example, CACHING) and returns the setting for that as an instance of Object.

The getCacheDirectory() method has no parameters and returns a String.

The three get*List() methods getDataSourceList(), getHandlerClassList(), and getProcessorClassList() each accept a String specifying the content type or protocol for which support is being queried. The methods return a Vector. The elements of the Vector are Strings, and those Strings are the fully qualified names of the classes that provide that support.

Listing 8.4 is an application ManagerQuery, which employs the information gathering methods of Manager in order to provide the user with details about the JMF. In running the program, users can query JMF as to its support (Players, Processors, or DataSources) for different formats and protocols. Alternatively, a complete picture can be produced by not specifying any particular formats or protocols: In this case all classes supporting all known formats are listed. The application can be found on the book's companion Web site. Similarly, a graphical application GUIManagerQuery, based on ManagerQuery, is available from the book's companion Web site. It provides the same functionality as ManagerQuery but with a graphical user interface.

LISTING 8.4   The ManagerQuery Application Used to Discover Details About JMF

```
/******************************************************************
* ManagerQuery - Query the manager class about the configuration and
* support of the installed JMF version. ManagerQuery is a text-based
* application that provides a report on the support of the JMF for
```

LISTING 8.4 Continued

```
* Players, Processors and DataSinks.
*
* Without any command-line arguments ManagerQuery prints a complete
* (LONG) list of Player, Processor, and DataSource classes that
* support the various formats, protocols, and content types.
*
* Alternatively it is possible to provide command-line arguments
* specifying the format or protocol for which support is to be
* checked. The means of calling is as follows:
*    java ManagerQuery [ [-h|-p|-d] support1 support2 ... supportN]
* The -h flag specifies handlers (Players) only.
* The -p flag specifies Processors only.
* The -d flag specifies DataSources only.
* Leaving off the flag defaults behaviour to checking for Players
* only.
*
* For instance:
*    java ManagerQuery -h mp3 ulaw
* would list the classes capable of Playing the MP3 (MPEG, Layer 3)
* and U-Law formats (codecs).
*
* ManagerQuery always prints the version of JMF, caching directory,
* and hints prior to any other output.
*
* @author Spike Barlow
***************************************************************/
import javax.media.*;
import javax.media.protocol.*;
import javax.media.format.*;
import java.util.*;

public class ManagerQuery {
    /////////////////////////////////////////////////////
    // Constants to facilitate selection of the
    // approprite get*List() method.
    /////////////////////////////////////////////////////
    public static final int HANDLERS = 1;
    public static final int PROCESSORS = 2;
    public static final int DATASOURCES = 3;
    /////////////////////////////////////////////////////
    // Array containing all the content types that JMF2.1.1
    // supports. This is used when the user provides no
    // command-line arguments in order to generate a
    // complete list of support for all the content types.
    /////////////////////////////////////////////////////
```

LISTING 8.4 Continued

```
  private static final String[] CONTENTS = {ContentDescriptor.CONTENT_UNKNOWN,
      ContentDescriptor.MIXED, ContentDescriptor.RAW,
ContentDescriptor.RAW_RTP, FileTypeDescriptor.AIFF,
FileTypeDescriptor.BASIC_AUDIO, FileTypeDescriptor.GSM,
      FileTypeDescriptor.MIDI, FileTypeDescriptor.MPEG,
FileTypeDescriptor.MPEG_AUDIO, FileTypeDescriptor.MSVIDEO,
FileTypeDescriptor.QUICKTIME, FileTypeDescriptor.RMF,
FileTypeDescriptor.VIVO, FileTypeDescriptor.WAVE,
      VideoFormat.CINEPAK, VideoFormat.H261, VideoFormat.H263,
VideoFormat.H261_RTP, VideoFormat.H263_RTP,
VideoFormat.INDEO32, VideoFormat.INDEO41, VideoFormat.INDEO50,
      VideoFormat.IRGB, VideoFormat.JPEG, VideoFormat.JPEG_RTP,
VideoFormat.MJPEGA,  VideoFormat.MJPEGB, VideoFormat.MJPG,
VideoFormat.MPEG_RTP, VideoFormat.RGB, VideoFormat.RLE, VideoFormat.SMC,
VideoFormat.YUV, AudioFormat.ALAW,
      AudioFormat.DOLBYAC3, AudioFormat.DVI, AudioFormat.DVI_RTP,
AudioFormat.G723, AudioFormat.G723_RTP, AudioFormat.G728,
AudioFormat.G728_RTP, AudioFormat.G729, AudioFormat.G729_RTP,
AudioFormat.G729A, AudioFormat.G729A_RTP, AudioFormat.GSM,
      AudioFormat.GSM_MS, AudioFormat.GSM_RTP, AudioFormat.IMA4,
AudioFormat.IMA4_MS, AudioFormat.LINEAR, AudioFormat.MAC3,
AudioFormat.MAC6, AudioFormat.MPEG, AudioFormat.MPEG_RTP,
AudioFormat.MPEGLAYER3, AudioFormat.MSADPCM,
AudioFormat.MSNAUDIO, AudioFormat.MSRT24,
AudioFormat.TRUESPEECH, AudioFormat.ULAW, AudioFormat.ULAW_RTP,
AudioFormat.VOXWAREAC10, AudioFormat.VOXWAREAC16,
AudioFormat.VOXWAREAC20, AudioFormat.VOXWAREAC8,
AudioFormat.VOXWAREMETASOUND, AudioFormat.VOXWAREMETAVOICE,
AudioFormat.VOXWARERT29H, AudioFormat.VOXWARETQ40,
      AudioFormat.VOXWARETQ60, AudioFormat.VOXWAREVR12,
AudioFormat.VOXWAREVR18};
  ////////////////////////////////////
  // The protocols that JMF supports.
  ////////////////////////////////////
  private static final String[] PROTOCOLS = { "ftp", "file", "rtp",
"http"};


/***************************************************************
* Return a String being a list of all hints settings.
***************************************************************/
public static String getHints() {

  return "\tSecurity: " + Manager.getHint(Manager.MAX_SECURITY) +
     "\n\tCaching: " + Manager.getHint(Manager.CACHING) +
```

LISTING 8.4   Continued

```
      "\n\tLightweight Renderer: " +
Manager.getHint(Manager.LIGHTWEIGHT_RENDERER) +
      "\n\tPlug-in Player: " +
Manager.getHint(Manager.PLUGIN_PLAYER);
}


/***********************************************************************
* Produce a list of all classes that support the content types or
* protocols passed to the method. The list is returned as a formatted
* String, while the 2nd parameter (which) specifies whether it is
* Player (Handler), Processor, or DataSource classes.
***********************************************************************/
public static String getHandlersOrProcessors(String[] contents,
int which) {
  String  str="";
  Vector  classes;
  int     NUM_PER_LINE = 1;
  String  LEADING = "\t     ";
  String  SEPARATOR = "   ";

  if (contents==null)
    return null;

  //////////////////////////////////////////////////////////////////
  // Generate a separate list for each content-type/protocol
  //specified.
  //////////////////////////////////////////////////////////////////
  for (int i=0;i<contents.length;i++) {
    str=str + "\t" + contents[i] + ":\n";
    if (which==HANDLERS)
      classes = Manager.getHandlerClassList(contents[i]);
    else if (which==PROCESSORS)
      classes = Manager.getProcessorClassList(contents[i]);
    else
      classes = Manager.getDataSourceList(contents[i]);
    if (classes==null)
      str = str + "\t     <None>\n";
    else
      str = str + formatVectorStrings(classes,LEADING,NUM_PER_LINE,
                  SEPARATOR);
  }
```

LISTING 8.4   Continued

```
  return str;
}


/***********************************************************************
 * Get a list of all Handler (Player) classes that support each of the
 * formats (content types).
 ***********************************************************************/
public static String getHandlers() {

  return getHandlersOrProcessors(CONTENTS,HANDLERS);
}


/***********************************************************************
 * Get a list of all Processor classes that support each of the
 * formats (content types).
 ***********************************************************************/
public static String getProcessors() {
  return getHandlersOrProcessors(CONTENTS,PROCESSORS);
}


/***********************************************************************
 * Get a list of all DataSources classes that support each of the
 * protocols.
 ***********************************************************************/

public static String getDataSources() {
  return getHandlersOrProcessors(PROTOCOLS,DATASOURCES);
}

/***********************************************************************
 * Format the Vector of Strings returned by the get*List() methods
 * into a single String. A simple formatting method.
 ***********************************************************************/
public static String formatVectorStrings(Vector vec, String leading,
int count, String separator) {
  String  str=leading;

  for (int i=0;i<vec.size();i++) {
    str = str + (String)vec.elementAt(i);
    if ((i+1)==vec.size())
      str = str + "\n";
```

LISTING 8.4   Continued

```
      else if ((i+1)%count==0)
        str = str + "\n" + leading;
      else
        str = str + separator;
    }
    return str;
  }


  /*************************************************************
   * Produce a list showing total support (i.e., Player,
   * Processors, and DataSinks) for all content types and
   * protocols.
   *************************************************************/
  public static void printTotalList() {
    System.out.println("\nPlayer Handler Classes:");
    System.out.println(getHandlers());
    System.out.println("\nProcessor Class List:");
    System.out.println(getProcessors());
    System.out.println("\nDataSink Class List: ");
    System.out.println(getDataSources());
  }


  /*******************************************************************
   * Main method. Produce a version and hints report. Then if no command
   * line arguments produce a total class list report. Otherwise process
   * the command line arguments and produce a report on their basis.
   *******************************************************************/
  public static void main(String args[]) {

    System.out.println("JMF: " + Manager.getVersion());
    String cacheArea = Manager.getCacheDirectory();
    if (cacheArea==null)
      System.out.println("No cache directory specified.");
    else
      System.out.println("Cache Directory: " + cacheArea);
    System.out.println("Hints:");
    System.out.println(getHints());

    // No command-line arguments. Make a total report.
    if (args==null || args.length==0)
      printTotalList();
    else {
```

LISTING 8.4 Continued

```
// Command-line. Process flags and then support to be
// queried upon in order to generate appropriate report.
String  header="";
int     whichCategory = 0;
String[]  interested;
int     i;
int     start;
if (args[0].equalsIgnoreCase("-h")) {
  header = "\nPlayer Handler Classes: ";
  whichCategory = HANDLERS;
}
else if (args[0].equalsIgnoreCase("-p")) {
  header = "\nProcessor Class List:";
  whichCategory = PROCESSORS;
}
else if (args[0].equalsIgnoreCase("-d")) {
  header = "\nDataSink Class List: ";
  whichCategory = DATASOURCES;
}
if (whichCategory==0) {
  whichCategory = HANDLERS;
  header = "\nPlayer Handler Classes: ";
  interested = new String[args.length];
  start = 0;
}
else {
  interested = new String[args.length-1];
  start = 1;
}
for (i=start;i<args.length;i++)
  interested[i-start] = args[i];
System.out.println(header);
System.out.println(getHandlersOrProcessors(interested,whichCategory));
  }
}
}
```

In order to specify a particular query, the formats or protocols in question are provided as command-line arguments to the application. An initial flag specifier supports Processors (-p), DataSources (-d), or Players (handlers, hence -h), which are being examined. Failure to specify a flag is interpreted as being a query about Players, whereas a lack of any command-line arguments is interpreted as a query about Player, Processor, and DataSource support for all formats and protocols. Listing 8.5 shows two runs of the program. The first in which Processor classes supporting the mpg (MPEG) and avi (AVI) content types are listed. The second in which handlers (Players) classes supporting http (Hypertext Transfer Protocol) are listed.

LISTING 8.5   Two Runs of the ManagerQuery Application Show How It Can Be Employed and the Output Produced

```
D:\JMF\Book\Code>java ManagerQuery -p mpg avi
JMF: 2.1.1
Cache Directory: C:\WINDOWS\TEMP
Hints:
        Security: false
        Caching: true
        Lightweight Renderer: false
        Plug-in Player: false

Processor Class List:
        mpg:
            media.processor.mpg.Handler
            javax.media.processor.mpg.Handler
            com.sun.media.processor.mpg.Handler
            com.ibm.media.processor.mpg.Handler
        avi:
            media.processor.avi.Handler
            javax.media.processor.avi.Handler
            com.sun.media.processor.avi.Handler
            com.ibm.media.processor.avi.Handler

D:\JMF\Book\Code>java ManagerQuery -h http
JMF: 2.1.1
Cache Directory: C:\WINDOWS\TEMP
Hints:
        Security: false
        Caching: true
        Lightweight Renderer: false
        Plug-in Player: false

Player Handler Classes:
        http:
            media.content.http.Handler
            javax.media.content.http.Handler
            com.sun.media.content.http.Handler
            com.ibm.media.content.http.Handler
```

It's All About Control

The various objects provided by the JMF such as Players, Processors, DataSources, DataSinks, and plug-ins have complex and configurable behavior. For instance, it is desirable to allow the frame that a Player starts playing from to be set, or the bit rate for a codec to be specified. The JMF provides a uniform model for controlling the behavior of objects through the Control interface.

Many JMF objects expose Control objects through accessor (get) methods. These can be obtained and used to alter the behavior of the associated objects. Indeed, there is an interface known as Controls that many objects implement as a uniform means of providing Control objects that specify their behavior.

Hence the standard approach in tailoring a Processor, Player, DataSource, or DataSink to match a particular need is as follows:

1. Create the Player, Processor, DataSource, or DataSink.
2. Obtain the Control object appropriate to the behavior to be configured.
3. Use methods on Control object to configure the behavior.
4. Use the original Player, Processor, DataSource, or DataSink.

Because of some unfortunate naming choice for classes and interfaces in the JMF, the following classes bear similar names: Control, Controls (x2), and Controller, as well as a package known as control. It is worth taking this opportunity to delineate the differences among these confusingly named classes:

Control—An interface describing an object that can be used to control the behavior of a JMF object such as a Player or Processor. The Control interface is discussed in this section. It is extended to a number of specialized Control Interfaces, such as FramePositioningControl.

Controller—An interface upon which Player and Processor are built and which is intimately associated with the timing model of the JMF. The Controller interface was discussed in an earlier section of this chapter.

Controls (javax.media.Controls and javax.media.protocol.Controls)—An interface implemented by objects that provide a uniform mechanism for obtaining their Control objects(s).

javax.media.control—A package within the JMF API that contains 18 interfaces that extend the basic Control interface. Examples include FramePositioningControl, TrackControl, and FormatControl.

The Control interface itself is particularly simple, possessing a single method only, with the real control functionality being specified in the various 18 Control interfaces that extend

Control in the JMF API. Each of those interfaces has a specific functionality as detailed by its name and methods. Instances of these interfaces are the means of configuring the behavior of the object from which they were obtained. The following list quickly summarizes each of them:

BitRateControl—A control for specifying and querying the bit rate settings, such as the encoding bit rate for a compressor (codec).

BufferControl—A control for querying and specifying buffer thresholds and sizes.

FormatControl—A control for querying the format support as well as setting the format for the associated object.

FrameGrabbingControl—A control for enabling the grabbing of still video frames from a video stream.

FramePositioningControl—A control to allow the precise positioning of a video stream as either a frame number of time (from start).

FrameProcessingControl—A control to specify the parameters employed in frame processing.

FrameRateControl—A means of querying as well as setting the frame rate.

H261Control—A control for specifying the parameters of the H.261 video codec.

H263Control—A control for specifying the parameters of the H.263 video codec.

KeyFrameControl—A control for specifying or querying the KeyFrame interval: the interval between transmission of complete (keyframes) rather than delta frames in codecs (such as mpeg) that use temporal based compression.

MonitorControl—A control for specifying the degree of monitoring (viewing or listening to) of media as it is captured.

MpegAudioControl—A control for specifying the parameters of MPEG Audio encoding.

PacketSizeControl—A control for specifying the packet size parameters.

PortControl—A control to access the input and output ports of a device (such as a capture device).

QualityControl—A control for specifying the parameters of quality (higher quality generally comes at the expense of higher processing demands).

SilenceSuppressionControl—A control for specifying the parameters of silence suppression. Silence suppression is an audio compression scheme whereby silent passages aren't transmitted.

StreamWriterControl—A control by which the maximum size for an output stream (for example, DataSink or Multiplexer) can be set as well as the size queried.

TrackControl—A control to query, manipulate, and control the data of individual media tracks in a Processor.

Each of these Control interfaces can be found in the javax.media.control package, which necessitates the import of that package if they are to be employed.

As mentioned previously, each interface possesses methods specific to its functionality. Some are simple such as FrameGrabbingControl with its single method grabFrame() that returns a Buffer object; others such as MpegAudioControl have more than a dozen methods plus associated constants. However, most interfaces are small, with 3–5 methods, and quite easy to understand.

Visual Control for the User

Time-based media, as defined in the Chapter 7, is intended for presentation to a human being. It is natural, then, to provide the viewer or listener with maximum control over that experience. To that end, many Control objects have an associated visual Component. That Component can be obtained and added to the graphical user interface provided for the user. Actions upon the Component result in method calls on the associated Control object that hence alter the behavior of the associated Player, Processor, DataSource, or DataSink.

The Control interface that is the superclass of the previous 18 possesses a single method, getControlComponent(), that returns an AWT Component—a graphical component that can be added to a graphical user interface and through which the user can directly and intuitively set the control parameters.

However, not all Controls have an associated graphical Component. Those that don't have a Component return null to the getControlComponent() method call. Thus code using the method should check to ensure that a non-null reference was returned before attempting to add the Component to an AWT Container (for example, Applet, Frame, or Panel). Adding a null Component to a Container will result in an exception being thrown.

Getting Control Objects

There are two methods by which Control objects can be obtained. These methods, getControl(), and getControls() are defined in the Controls interface. The Controls interface is extended by many important interfaces including DataSink, Codec, Renderer, and the various pull and push data and buffer streams. Other important classes such as Controller (that is, the superclass of Player and Processor) also provide the two methods.

The getControl() method is used to obtain a single Control object. The method is passed the complete name of the Control class as a String and returns an object implementing that interface. The fully qualified name of the class must be passed, thus listing the package "path" to the class. Then the method returns an object of class Control, necessitating it to be cast to the type of Control before its methods can be employed. For example,

```
BitRateControl bitControl = (BitRateControl)
processor.getControl("javax.media.control.BitRateControl");
```

The second means of obtaining `Control` objects is through the `getControls()` method. The method accepts no arguments and returns (supposedly) all the `Control` objects, as an array, associated with the object on which `getControls()` was called. Look at the following example:

```
Control[] allControls = player.getControls();
```

As an example of the `Control` objects associated with a `Player`, Listing 8.6 shows the `Control` objects obtained from the `Player` used in the `BBPApplet` example of Chapter 7. The `getControls()` method of the `Player` object (actually inherited from `Controller`) was called once the `Player` was realized and the objects returned were printed.

LISTING 8.6 The 11 Control Objects Obtained on a Particular `Player` Object when `getControls()` Was Called

```
11 controls for a Player @ REALIZED:
1: com.ibm.media.codec.video.mpeg.MpegVideo
2: com.sun.media.codec.video.colorspace.YUVToRGB
3: com.sun.media.renderer.video.DDRenderer
4: com.sun.media.renderer.audio.DirectAudioRenderer$MCA
5: com.sun.media.renderer.audio.AudioRenderer$BC
6: com.sun.media.PlaybackEngine$BitRateA
7: com.sun.media.PlaybackEngine$1
8: com.sun.media.controls.FramePositioningAdapter
9: com.sun.media.BasicJMD
10: com.sun.media.PlaybackEngine$PlayerTControl
11: com.sun.media.PlaybackEngine$PlayerTControl
```

It is worth noting several points in connection with Listing 8.6. First, the `11 controls` case corresponds to the `Manager` being instructed to create `Players` that support plug-ins for demultiplexing, codecs, and so on. In the case where the created `Player` wasn't plug-in enabled, only three `Controls` were obtained. Enabling plug-in based `Players` was achieved as follows:

```
Manager.setHint(Manager.PLUGIN_PLAYER,new Boolean(true));
```

Second, all the `Controls` returned by the previous call are from the Sun and IBM packages (com.sun.media and com.ibm.media) and hence aren't documented in the API. Further, only the `BasicJMD` `Control` had a visual component, that being the PlugIn Viewer. That combination of undocumented classes plus lack of visual components makes the `getControls()` approach of exerting control not particularly helpful and next to useless, at least in this case.

However, it appears that controller's `getControls()` method doesn't actually return all possible `Control` objects for a `Player`. As noted previously, rather than asking for all `Control` objects, it is possible to ask for them by name. When that was done, it was possible to obtain a number of `Control` objects including `FrameRateControl` and `FrameGrabbingControl` among others as follows:

```
FrameGrabbingControl frameControl = (FrameGrabbingControl)
player.getControl("javax.media.control.FrameGrabbingControl");
```

As in the previous case, these `Controls` were only available when the `Manager`'s `PLUGIN_PLAYER` hint had been set to `true`.

Thus, the surest and safest means of obtaining the appropriate `Control` objects and using them is with the following algorithm:

```
If using a Player
        Set Manager's PLUGIN_PLAYER hint to true prior to creating the Player
For each Controller needed
        Get it by name (full class name to getControl() method).
        If object returned not null
                "Use it"
                If want to provide direct user control
                        Call getControlComponent() on Controller object
                        If object returned is not null
                                Add that to GUI
                else
                                Implement own GUI interface
```

Sourcing Media and Media `Format`

Controlling and handling media always begins with its sourcing and is achieved by specifying its location, protocol, and format. With that information, the media stream can be obtained and the appropriate `Controller` (for example, `Player` or `Processor`) or `DataSink` instances can be created (see the earlier section on the `Manager` class).

Hence, the first significant step in media control is creating a `DataSource` object, although sometimes this isn't done explicitly by the user but implicitly by the `Manager` class.

`DataSource` isn't the only class with relevance to this vital first stage. Several other classes are involved in the sourcing of media:

> `MediaLocator`—Specifies the location and protocol for the media. Closely related to the `URL` class. Needed to create a `DataSource`.
>
> `Manager`—Creates a `DataSource` either explicitly or implicitly (for example, when a `Player` or `Processor` is created).
>
> `DataSource`—A manager for media transfer. Required to create `Players`, `Processors`, or `DataSinks`. One of the most central classes in the whole JMF.

SourceStream—A stream of data. SourceStreams are managed by DataSources. A number of subclasses of SourceStream depend on whether the stream is push or pull and the format is low level.

Format—An abstraction of the format of media. This class is extended by the more specialized classes ContentDescriptor, FileTypeDescriptor, AudioFormat, and VideoFormat. Each SourceStream of a DataSource has an associated ContentDescriptor (Format).

Figure 8.14 shows the relationships between these classes, with DataSource cast as the central participant because of its significance in the creation of Players or Processors.

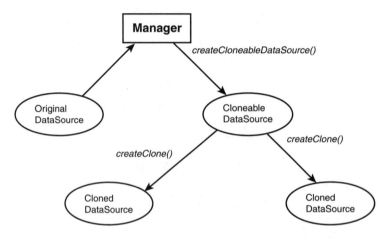

FIGURE 8.14
The relationship of other data description classes to that of DataSource.

DataSource

Media processed by the JMF can be a video file on the local file system, an audio track on CD, a videoconference streaming across the Internet, or a range of other possibilities. All these are instances of media sources, and the JMF provides a uniform means of describing them and managing their transfer via the DataSource class.

The DataSource class provides an abstracted, simple model of the media that can then be employed as part of the processing or control chain: creation of a Player, Processor, or DataSink by the Manager class involves the prior creation of a DataSource (either by the caller, or implicitly as part of the creation process).

DataSources can be seen as managing the transfer of media content. Their creation requires the specification of a protocol and a location from which the media can be obtained. With that specification, the Manager class follows an iterative process of finding a DataSource class that supports the protocol and data format.

DataSource instances manage media transfer by managing one or more SourceStreams—the media streams.

A key feature of all DataSources is that they cannot be reused. For instance, a DataSource used by a Player cannot later be used by a Processor.

From a user's perspective, a DataSource object is generally rather passive. Not only is it often created as a (again, from the user's perspective) by-product of creating a Player or Processor, but also it isn't common to use the methods on a DataSource object because these are invoked by the associated Player or Processor. Figure 8.15 shows the methods of DataSource.

DataSource Class

DataSource()   DataSource(MediaLocator location)
void connect()   void disconnect(0   String getContentType()   MediaLocator getLocator()   void initCheck()   void setLocator(MediaLocator location)   void start()   void stop()

FIGURE 8.15

The DataSource *class.*

Although it is possible to construct a DataSource directly with one of its two constructors, it is next to worthless because the base DataSource provides no functionality. Only those subclasses constructed by Manager provide the required abilities. Hence, the Manager class should be used to create DataSources. As discussed in the earlier section on the Manager, there is an overloaded createDataSource() method of Manager—it accepts either a URL or a MediaLocator and returns a DataSource. There are also two methods of Manager for creating specialist DataSources—merging and cloneable. These will be discussed shortly.

The key methods of the class are connect(), disconnect(), start(), and stop(). As their names imply, the connect() and disconnect() methods open (or close) a connection to the media source that was specified by the MediaLocator used to create the DataSource. Similarly start() initiates a data transfer whereas stop() halts it.

DataSources can be classified on two axes—one axis being how data transfer is initiated (push or pull) and the other being the unit of transfer (raw bytes of a Buffer object). Pull

DataSources have the transfer initiated and controlled by the client. Examples of these protocols include http (Hypertext Transfer Protocol), ftp (File Transfer Protocol), and file. Push DataSources have the transfer controlled by the server. Examples of push media include broadcast media, Web casts (multicasts), and video on demand. Two categories for each of the two axes leads to four subclasses of DataSource: PullDataSource, PullBufferDataSource, PushDataSource, and PushBufferDataSource. Each subclass extends DataSource by providing a getStreams() method that returns an array of the appropriate SourceStream (for example, PullSourceStream for a PullDataSource). Clearly, the type of DataSource dictates the type of operations that can be supported on it, whereas a video obtained from a file can be replayed, played in reverse, or positioned. The same isn't true for a broadcast video.

Cloneable and Merged DataSources

Two special DataSources, cloneable and merged, are created through the Manager class (see the earlier section on the Manager). Not surprisingly, the cloneable DataSource can be cloned so that, for instance, multiple versions of the same media stream can be processed simultaneously. The DataSource returned by Manager's createCloneableDataSource() has an additional method createClone(). After a DataSource has been cloned, the original (not cloneable) version shouldn't be employed. Figure 8.16 shows the process of creating and using a cloneable DataSource.

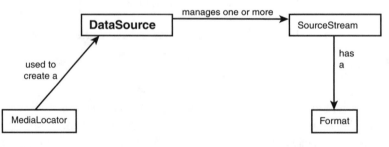

FIGURE 8.16
Steps involved in cloning a DataSource *object.*

On the other hand, the merged data source is simply the combination of two or more DataSources. Manager's createMergingDataSource() is passed an array of DataSources and returns a single DataSource that is their merged combination. All DataSources in the array must be of the same type (for example, all PullBufferDataSources); otherwise, an IncompatibleSourceException will be thrown.

MediaLocator

The MediaLocator class is the JMF's means of describing the location of media. Closely related to the Java Platform's URL class, a MediaLocator can be constructed from a String (for example, `MediaLocator ml = new MediaLocator("file://media/example.mov")` or from a URL.

`MediaLocator` objects serve little purpose other than providing the necessary information—the media's location and protocol—for the construction of a `DataSink`, `Player`, or `Processor`. The object possess five accessor style methods:

`getProtocol()`—Returns a `String` such as `"http"`

`getRemainder()`—Returns a `String` that is all except the protocol

`getURL()`—Returns a URL object

`toExternalForm()`—Returns a `String` representation suitable for constructing a `MediaLocator`

`toString()`—Returns a `String` version suitable for printing

SourceStream and Buffer

A `SourceStream` abstracts a single (source) stream of media data. Each `DataSource` manages one or more `SourceStream` objects.

`SourceStream`s represent a lower level of detail than many JMF programs interact with directly. For the greater portion of JMF applications, the `DataSource` class provides sufficient detail with the desired abstraction from the complexity and detail of the underlying data.

Just as for `DataSource`, the `SourceStream` interface is extended by four interfaces that classify the method of transfer initiation (pull or push), and the unit of transfer (raw data or buffer): `PullBufferStream`, `PullSourceStream`, `PushBufferStream`, and `PushSourceStream`.

The `SourceStream` interface specifies three methods as well as the two methods resulting from the extension of `Controls`. The three methods are as follows:

`endOfStream()`—a Boolean method that returns `true` if the end of stream has been reached

`getContentDescriptor()`—Returns the `ContentDescriptor` (format) for the stream

`getContentLength()`—Returns the length of the stream in bytes (or `SourceStream.LENGTH_UNKNOWN` if it cannot be ascertained)

The two additional methods are the `getControl()` and `getControls()` methods of the `Controls` interface. All the subinterfaces provide a `read()` method for actually transferring data.

As seen with both the `DataSource` and `DataStream` classes, objects of these two types can either be raw data or buffered. The `Buffer` class is the JMF representation of these buffers or containers that transfer data from one processing stage to the next in a `Player` or `Processor`, or between a buffer source stream and its handler.

The `Buffer` object not only carries the media data, but also metadata such as the media format, timestamps, length, and other header information.

The `Buffer` class is pivotal in allowing the JMF to be combined with other Java APIs such as *JAI (Java Advanced Imaging)* because the JMF provides methods to convert between `Buffer` objects and AWT `Image` objects. This combination of APIs and deliberate low-level processing of media data are the two chief reasons for employing a `Buffer` class: Most JMF applications don't need to delve to this level of detail.

The `Buffer` class itself is complex with a large number of fields (most constants) and methods. Among the more important methods are `getData()`, `getHeader()`, `getLength()`, `getFormat()`, and `getSequenceNumber()`. The `Buffer` class will be discussed further in Chapter 9.

Format

The `Format` class is provided as the means of describing the format of media in an abstract sense: `Format` objects carry no information about encoding specific or timing specific information.

The `Format` class is extended by three more specific classes: `AudioFormat`, `VideoFormat`, and `ContentDescriptor`. The `VideoFormat` class itself is extended by a number of codec specific classes (for example, `H263Format`, `YUVFormat`). Similarly, the `ContentDescriptor` class is extended by the `FileDescriptor` class. Figure 8.17 shows the hierarchy of relationships between the `Format` classes, whereas the list that follows the figure indicates the chief purpose of each of the classes.

`Format` is an abstraction of an exact media format. It is the superclass of all other format classes.

- `AudioFormat`—Format information specific to audio media such as number of channels, sampling rates, or quantization level.
- `ContentDescriptor`—Format information about media data containers: raw, raw RTP, and mixed.

    `FileTypeDescriptor`—Fundamentally an enumeration (listing) of all content types that are file based (for example, QuickTime, AVI, Wave, and so on).

- `VideoFormat`—An enumeration of the various video formats (codecs) supported by JMF (for example, motion JPEG, run-length encoding, and YUV) as well as video parameters such as frame rate and encoding type.

    `H261Format`—Format information specific to the H261 codec

    `H263Format`—Format information specific to the H263 codec

    `IndexedColorFormat`—Format information specific to the indexed color codec

JPEGFormat—Format information specific to the JPEG codec and decimation schemes

RGBFormat—Format information specific to the RGB codec

YUVFormat—Format information specific to the YUV codec

Manager Class

```
static int CACHING
static int LIGHTWEIGHT_RENDERER
static int MAX_SECURITY
static int PLUGIN_PLAYER
static String UNKNOWN_CONTENT_NAME
```

```
static DataSource createCloneableDataSource(DataSource source)
static DataSink createDataSink(DataSource source, MediaLocator destination)
static DataSource createDataSource(MediaLocator source)
static DataSource createDataSource(URL source)
static DataSource createMergingDataSource(DataSource[] sources)
static Player createPlayer(DataSource source)
static Player createPlayer(MediaLocator source)
static Player createPlayer(URL source)
static Processor createProcessor(DataSource source)
static Processor createProcessor(MediaLocator source)
static Processor createProcessor(URL source)
static Player createRealizedPlayer(DataSource source)
static Player createRealizedPlayer(MediaLocator source)
static Player createRealizedPlayer(URL source)
static Processor createRealizedProcessor(ProcessorModel model)
static String getCacheDirectory()
static Vector getDataSourceList(String protocolName)
static Vector getHandlerClassList(String contentName)
static Object getHint(int hint)
static Vector getProcessorClassList(String contentName)
static TimeBase getSystemTimeBase()
static String getVersion()
static voidsetHint(int hint, Object value)
```

8

CONTROLLING AND
PROCESSING
MEDIA WITH JMF

FIGURE 8.17

The class hierarchy stemming from the Format *class.*

Each SourceStream (managed by a DataSource) has an associated ContentDescriptor that can be obtained with the getContentDescriptor() method of SourceStream. Similarly, each Buffer object has an associated Format that can be obtained with the getFormat() method.

As with SourceStreams, many JMF programs providing significant functionality remain blissfully free of the details inherent in the various Format classes. The ManagerQuery application from earlier in the chapter employs the various constants (static final attributes) of the Format classes in order to generate a comprehensive list of all formats supported by the JMF.

The most important methods of the Format class are getDataType(), which returns a Class that is the type of data (for example, a byte array); getEncoding(), which returns a String uniquely identifying the encoding; and `matches()`, which is a `boolean` method accepting another `Format` and returning `true` if they match.

MediaHandler

`MediaHandler` is the centralized interface for objects that read and control media delivered from a `DataSource` object. Interfaces that extend `MediaHandler` include `Player`, `Processor`, `DataSink`, and `Demultiplexer`, which are all key classes commonly used in JMF programs.

The `MediaHandler` interface consists of a single method `setSource()`. The method accepts a `DataSource` and associates or links that `DataSource` with the object in question: that is the location in which the data to be handled will be obtained.

The creation of `Players`, `Processors`, or `DataSinks` by the `Manager` class requires a `DataSource` that the `Manager` needs to create as a prestep if it isn't supplied with a `DataSource` as part of the call. Part of the creation process by the `Manager` class is the invocation of the `setSource()` method on the `Player`, `Processor`, or `DataSink`. That is why the method generally isn't called from user code. Indeed, the `setSource()` method can throw either an `IOException` or `IncompatibleSourceException`. The presence or lack of an exception is how the `Manager` class searches the list of possible candidate classes until one that supports a particular `DataSource` (and hence media format) is found.

Playing Media

One of the most common uses of the JMF is for playing media: audio or video. As already illustrated in the previous chapter with `BBPApplet`, playing media with the JMF is a relatively simple process because of the abstraction from format details provided by the JMF.

The JMF provides the `Player` class for playing media. `Player` creation is achieved through the `Manager` class, as described in a previous section, by specifying the location of the media. A `Player` object provides methods and additional associated objects (`Control` objects) for controlling the playback: starting and stopping, setting the rate of play, and so on. Indeed the Player class exposes graphical (AWT) `Components` for control and visualization of the playback. These can be added directly to a GUI, preventing the need for the user to construct a large number of GUI components and linking those to actions (methods) on the `Player` object.

Player Interface

A `Player` is a `MediaHandler` object for controlling and rendering media. It is the chief class within the JMF for combined handling and rendering and provides an abstracted, high-level model of the process to user code that separates it from lower-level considerations such as the format of the media tracks. Hence, code employing a `Player` sees a single object with the same methods and attributes, regardless of the particulars of the media being played.

The `Player` interface directly extends that of `Controller`. Thus, a `Player` not only provides all the methods detailed for a `Controller`, but also supports the five-state model of stopped time (Unrealized, Realizing, Realized, Prefetching, Prefetched) of `Controller`. Understanding the `Player` interface requires an understanding of the `Controller` interface. However only the extensions of `Player` to the `Controller` interface will be discussed here; readers needing to reacquaint themselves with the features of `Controller` should revisit the first section of this chapter.

Creation of a `Player` (with the exception of the `MediaPlayer` Bean, which is discussed in the next subsection) is achieved through the central `Manager` class. As discussed in the earlier section on the `Manager`, there are six methods for creating a `Player`; three for creating an Unrealized `Player` and three for creating a Realized `Player`. A `Player` can be created on the basis of a `URL`, `MediaLocator`, or `DataSource`. The following code fragment is typical of `Player` creation:

```
String mediaName = "ftp://ftp.cs.adfa.edu.au/media/someExample.wav";
MediaLocator locator = new MediaLocator(mediaName);
Player thePlayer = Manager.createPlayer(locator);
```

Keeping track of the status and maintaining control of a `Player` is achieved through the same mechanism as that for `Controller` discussed earlier. Objects can implement the `ControllerListener` interface and be added as listeners to the `Player`. The `Player` posts events (discussed in the `Controller` section of the chapter) indicating state transitions (for example, Realizing to Realized), errors, and other relevant media events (for example, end of media reached, duration of media now known).

A number of the methods of `Player`, most inherited from `Controller`, exert direct control over the state of a `Player`. Others can alter the state as a side effect. The following list shows those methods:

`realize()`—Moves the `Player` from Unrealized to Realized. Asynchronous (returns immediately).

`prefetch()`—Moves the `Player` from Realized to Prefetched. Asynchronous (returns immediately).

`start()`—Moves the `Player` from whatever state it is in currently to Started. The `Player` will transition through any intermediary states and send notice of such transitions to any listeners. Asynchronous (returns immediately).

`stop()`—Moves the `Player` from Started state back to either (depending on the type of media being played) Prefetched or Realized. Synchronous (returns only after `Player` is actually stopped).

deallocate()—Deallocates the resources acquired by the Player and moves it to the Realized state (if at least Realized at the time of call) or to Unrealized (if in Realizing or Unrealized at time of call). Synchronous.

close()—Closes down the Player totally. It will post a ControllerClosedEvent. The behavior of any further calls on the Player is unspecified: The Player shouldn't be used after it is closed. Synchronous.

setStopTime()—Sets the media time at which it will stop. When the media reaches that time, the Player will act as though stop() was called. Asynchronous (returns immediately and stops play when time reaches that specified).

setMediaTime()—Changes the media's current time. This can result in a state transition. For instance, a started Player might return to Prefetching while it refills buffers for the new location in the stream. Asynchronous (in that any state changes triggered aren't waited for).

setRate()—Sets the rate of playback. Can result in a state change on a started Player for similar reasons to those for setMediaTime(). Asynchronous (in that any state changes triggered aren't waited for).

As you can see, many (of the most important) methods are asynchronous, returning to the caller immediately but before any state transitions can occur. This is particular true of starting a Player: Gathering the resources necessary to play media can be a time-consuming process.

This in turn illustrates the need to listen to a Player: User code must listen to the events generated by a Player so that it can determine, for example, when to place control components on the screen or when to show (and remove) download progress bars.

The Player class extends Controller with the addition of six methods as shown in Figure 8.18. One method is extremely useful and commonly employed. The start() method will transition a Player object through all intermediary stopped states, regardless of starting state (for example, Unrealized), to Started. This is the most common way to start a Player because it lifts the burden of calculating an appropriate synchronization time to be passed to the syncStart() methods. State transitions are still reported to all ControllerListener's listening to the Player. Thus it is still possible to initiate appropriate actions (for example, obtain control and visual Components) as the Player passes through the appropriate states.

Two other methods of Player, getControlPanelComponent() and getVisualComponent(), find high usage. These are used to obtain AWT Components suitable for controlling and displaying the output (playback) of the Player, respectively. These methods are only valid on a Player that is in a Realized, or higher (closer to Started) state. Calling them on an Unrealized player will result in a NotRealizedError exception being thrown. Hence, it is necessary to listen to the Player's events to ascertain when these Components can safely be obtained. Further, the methods return null if there isn't a valid Component, such as is the case with a visual Component for purely audio media. The user should always check that the returned object isn't null before it is used (generally added to a GUI).

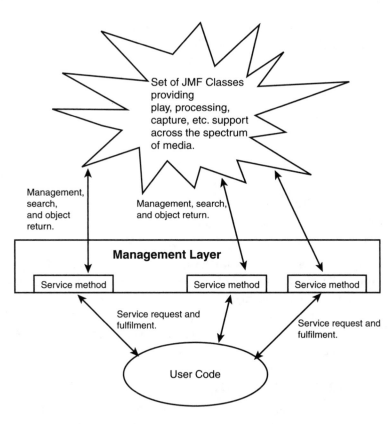

FIGURE 8.18

The Player *interface.*

Finally, the GainControl object obtained with getGainControl() can be used to control the gain (volume) of playback. The addController() and removeController() methods are provided for cases in which a single Player controls the synchronized handling (generally other Players) of multiple media. This is discussed briefly in a subsequent subsection.

The MediaPlayer Bean

The JMF directly exposes one class that implements the Player interface: MediaPlayer. MediaPlayer is a fully featured JMF Player encapsulated as a Java Bean.

Playing media with the MediaPlayer Bean is quite simple and painless because not only are various methods provided for configuring the behavior of the Bean, but it also handles the transition from playing one media to another when a different location is set. Set the PlayerOfMedia example application in the following section for user code to deal with that issue.

The following code fragment shows how simple setting up and starting a `MediaPlayer` can be. In this case, the fragment sets the `MediaPlayer` to play the media in videos/example1.mov once.

```
Player mp = new MediaPlayer();
mp.setLoop(false);
mp.setMediaLocation("file://videos.example1.mov");
mp.start();
```

Controlling Multiple `Players`/`Controllers`

It is possible through the `addController()` and `removeController()` methods of `Player` to employ a single `Player` object to manage a number of `Controllers`. This is an approach that allows playback (or indeed processing) among a number of `Players` to be synchronized by being driven by a single `Player`.

There are a number of details and caveats to the approach, and users considering such synchronization should carefully read the `Player` class specification, which includes a lengthy discussion of this topic. However, the fundamental model of the approach is that `Controllers` added to a `Player` fall under the control of that `Player`. Method calls on the `Player` are also made on the added `Controllers`, and events from the `Controllers` can propagate back to those listening to the `Player` object.

Application: Player of Media

This subsection discusses an example application, `PlayerOfMedia`, that illustrates a number of the features of the `Controller`, `Player`, and other classes already discussed.

As its name indicates, `PlayerOfMedia` is an application capable of rendering time-based media. Through a simple menu system, the user might select to open (for play) any media. He might then enter the URL of the media or browse the local filesystem to select a file. If the application is unable to create a `Player` for the media, the user is informed via a pop-up dialog box. Otherwise, the application adds the appropriate visual and control components to the GUI, resizing itself appropriately, and hands control to the user (through the control component). When the end of the media is reached, play restarts from the beginning.

In terms of core functionality, the ability to play media, `PlayerOfMedia`, isn't dissimilar to the `BBPApplet` example from Chapter 7. However, `PlayerOfMedia` provides further features in its ability for users to specify the actual media they want played. That requires the handling of not only arbitrary media, but also more importantly graceful handling of errors or exceptions as well as resource management. If a new `Player` object is created, the old `Player` object (if one exists) and its associated resources must be freed up.

Listing 8.7 shows the source of the application, which can also be found on the book's companion Web site. It is worth noting that the greater portion of the code doesn't concern the JMF per se, but rather the graphical user interface (simple as it is) that the program provides. The creation of menus and dialog boxes is one of the main reasons for the size of the code. Figure 8.19 shows the application as the user is playing one media (a video) and about to replace it with another (a WAVE file of didgeridoo play).

FIGURE 8.19

The `PlayerOfMedia` *GUI application running and displaying a video while the user is about to open a different media file.*

The two methods, `createAPlayer()` and `controllerUpdate()`, directly concern the JMF. The `createAPlayer()` method is responsible for creating a new `Player` and moving it to the `Realized` state. It is passed a `String`, which is the name and location of the media to be played. However, before a new `Player` can be created, the method ascertains if there is an existing Player object. If so, it is stopped and any resources it had acquired are freed with the `close()` call. Similarly, the old `Player` is no longer listened to (events generated from it won't be received). A `MediaLocator` is constructed and passed to the `Manager` class in order to create the new `Player`. Any resulting exceptions are caught and the user informed. Otherwise, if the process of creation was successful, the application starts listening to the new `Player` as well as directing it to become `Realized`.

The `controllerUpdate()` method is required for any class that implements the `ControllerListener` interface and is where nearly all the control of the `Player` object occurs. The method is called with events generated by the currently listened to `Player` object. These typically represent state transition events, such as from `Realizing` to `Realized`, but can also include errors or information about the duration of the media. The method reacts to the particular type of event received and acts accordingly, which perhaps alters its user interface, moves the `Player` along to the next appropriate state, or even posts an error message. In particular, a `RealizeComplete` event means that visual and control `Components` can be obtained for the new `Player` object. Any old `Components` (from the previous `Player`) or download progress bars should first be discarded; then the new ones should be obtained and added to the GUI. Reaching the end of play (signaled by an `EndOfMedia` event) is dealt with by setting the media's own time to zero (back to the start) and restarting the `Player`.

LISTING 8.7 The `PlayerOfMedia` GUI application that Allows the User to Select the Media He Wants to Play

```java
import java.awt.*;
import java.awt.event.*;
import javax.media.*;
import javax.media.protocol.*;
import javax.media.control.*;
import java.io.*;
/******************************************************************
* A Graphical application allowing the user to choose the media
* they wish to play.
* PlayerOfMedia presents a Dialog in which the user may enter
* the URL of the media to play, or select a file from the local
* system.
*
* @author Spike Barlow
******************************************************************/
public class PlayerOfMedia extends Frame implements ActionListener,
        ControllerListener {

    /** Location of the media. */
    MediaLocator  locator;

    /** Player for the media */
    Player        player;

    /** Dialog for user to select media to play. */
    Dialog        selectionDialog;

    /** Buttons on user dialog box. */
    Button        cancel,
                  open,
                  choose;

    /** Field for user to enter media filename */
    TextField     mediaName;
```

LISTING 8.7   Continued

```
/** The menus */
MenuBar      bar;
Menu         fileMenu;
/** Dialog for informing user of errors. */
Dialog       errorDialog;
Label        errorLabel;
Button       ok;

/** Graphical component for controlling player. */
Component    controlComponent;

/** Graphical component showing what isbeing played. */
Component    visualComponent;

/** Graphical component to show download progress. */
Component    progressBar;

/** Sizes to ensure Frame is correctly sized. */
Dimension    controlSize;
Dimension    visualSize;
int          menuHeight = 50;

/** Directory user last played a file from. */
String       lastDirectory = null;

/** Flags indicating conditions for resizing the Frame. */
protected static final int  VISUAL = 1;
protected static final int  PROGRESS = 2;


/***************************************************************
* Construct a PlayerOfMedia. The Frame will have the default
* title of "Player of Media". All initial actions on the
* PlayerOfMedia object are initiated through its menu
* (or shortcut key).
***************************************************************/
PlayerOfMedia() { this("Player of Media"); }

/***************************************************************
* Construct a PlayerOfMedia. The Frame will have the title
* supplied by the user. All initial actions on the
* PlayerOfMedia object are initiated through its menu
* (or shortcut key).
```

LISTING 8.7   Continued

```
******************************************************************/
PlayerOfMedia(String name) {

  super(name);
  //////////////////////////////////////////////////////////
  // Setup the menu system: a "File" menu with Open and Quit.
  //////////////////////////////////////////////////////////
  bar = new MenuBar();
  fileMenu = new Menu("File");
  MenuItem openMI = new MenuItem("Open...",
new MenuShortcut(KeyEvent.VK_O));
  openMI.setActionCommand("OPEN");
  openMI.addActionListener(this);
  fileMenu.add(openMI);
  MenuItem quitMI = new MenuItem("Quit",
new MenuShortcut(KeyEvent.VK_Q));
  quitMI.addActionListener(this);
  quitMI.setActionCommand("QUIT");
  fileMenu.add(quitMI);
  bar.add(fileMenu);
  setMenuBar(bar);


  ////////////////////////////////////////////////////
  // Layout the frame, its position on screen, and ensure
  // window closes are dealt with properly, including
  // relinquishing the resources of any Player.
  ////////////////////////////////////////////////////
  setLayout(new BorderLayout());
  setLocation(100,100);
  addWindowListener(new WindowAdapter() {
    public void windowClosing(WindowEvent e) {
      if (player!=null) { player.stop(); player.close();}
      System.exit(0); } });


  ////////////////////////////////////////////////////
  // Build the Dialog box by which the user can select
  // the media to play.
  ////////////////////////////////////////////////////
  selectionDialog = new Dialog(this,"Media Selection");
  Panel pan = new Panel();
  pan.setLayout(new GridBagLayout());
  GridBagConstraints gbc = new GridBagConstraints();
  mediaName =new TextField(40);
  gbc.gridx = 0; gbc.gridy = 0; gbc.gridwidth=2;
```

LISTING 8.7   Continued

```
pan.add(mediaName,gbc);
choose = new Button("Choose File...");
gbc.ipadx = 10; gbc.ipady = 10;
gbc.gridx = 2; gbc.gridwidth= 1; pan.add(choose,gbc);
choose.addActionListener(this);
open = new Button("Open");
gbc.gridy = 1; gbc.gridx = 1; pan.add(open,gbc);
open.addActionListener(this);
cancel = new Button("Cancel");
gbc.gridx = 2; pan.add(cancel,gbc);
cancel.addActionListener(this);
selectionDialog.add(pan);
selectionDialog.pack();
selectionDialog.setLocation(200,200);

//////////////////////////////////////////////////
// Build the error Dialog box by which the user can
// be informed of any errors or problems.
//////////////////////////////////////////////////
errorDialog = new Dialog(this,"Error",true);
errorLabel = new Label("");
errorDialog.add(errorLabel,"North");
ok = new Button("OK");
ok.addActionListener(this);
errorDialog.add(ok,"South");
errorDialog.pack();
errorDialog.setLocation(150,300);

Manager.setHint(Manager.PLUGIN_PLAYER,new Boolean(true));
}

/***********************************************************
* React to menu selections (quit or open) or one of the
* the buttons on the dialog boxes.
***********************************************************/
public void actionPerformed(ActionEvent e) {

  if (e.getSource() instanceof MenuItem) {
    //////////////////////////////////////////////////
    // Quit and free up any player acquired resources.
    //////////////////////////////////////////////////
    if (e.getActionCommand().equalsIgnoreCase("QUIT")) {
      if (player!=null) {
        player.stop();
```

LISTING 8.7   Continued

```java
      player.close();
    }
    System.exit(0);
  }
  ///////////////////////////////////////////////////////
  // User to open/play media. Show the selection dialog box.
  ///////////////////////////////////////////////////////
  else if (e.getActionCommand().equalsIgnoreCase("OPEN")) {
    selectionDialog.show();
  }
}
///////////////////////
// One of the Buttons.
///////////////////////
else {
  ///////////////////////////////////////////////////////////
  // User to browse the local file system. Popup a file dialog.
  ///////////////////////////////////////////////////////////
  if (e.getSource()==choose) {
    FileDialog choice = new FileDialog(this,
"Media File Choice",FileDialog.LOAD);
    if (lastDirectory!=null)
      choice.setDirectory(lastDirectory);
    choice.show();
    String selection = choice.getFile();
    if (selection!=null) {
      lastDirectory = choice.getDirectory();
      mediaName.setText("file://"+ choice.getDirectory() +
selection);
    }
  }
  /////////////////////////////////////////////////
  // User chooses to cancel opening of new media.
  /////////////////////////////////////////////////
  else if (e.getSource()==cancel) {
    selectionDialog.hide();
  }
  ///////////////////////////////////////////////////////
  // User has selected the name of the media. Attempt to
  // create a Player.
  ///////////////////////////////////////////////////////
  else if (e.getSource()==open) {
    selectionDialog.hide();
    createAPlayer(mediaName.getText());
  }
```

LISTING 8.7 Continued

```
      /////////////////////////////////////////
      // User has seen error message. Now hide it.
      /////////////////////////////////////////
      else if (e.getSource()==ok)
        errorDialog.hide();
    }
  }


  /*******************************************************************
   * Attempt to create a Player for the media who's name is passed
   * the the method. If successful the object will listen to the
   * new Player and start it towards Realized.
   *******************************************************************/
  protected void createAPlayer(String nameOfMedia) {

    ///////////////////////////////////////////////////////////
    // If an existing player then stop listening to it and free
    // up its resources.
    ///////////////////////////////////////////////////////////
    if (player!=null) {
      System.out.println("Stopping and closing previous player");
      player.removeControllerListener(this);
      player.stop();
      player.close();
    }


    ///////////////////////////////////////////////////////////
    // Use Manager class to create Player from a MediaLocator.
    // If exceptions are thrown then inform user and recover
    // (go no further).
    ///////////////////////////////////////////////////////////
    locator = new MediaLocator(nameOfMedia);
    try {
      System.out.println("Creating player");
      player = Manager.createPlayer(locator);
    }
    catch (IOException ioe) {
      errorDialog("Can't open " + nameOfMedia);
      return;
    }
    catch (NoPlayerException npe) {
      errorDialog("No player available for " + nameOfMedia);
      return;
    }
```

LISTING 8.7   Continued

```java
/////////////////////////////////////////////////////////////
// Player created successfully. Start listening to it and
// realize it.
/////////////////////////////////////////////////////////////
player.addControllerListener(this);
System.out.println("Attempting to realize player");
player.realize();
}


/**************************************************************
 * Popup a dialog box informing the user of some error. The
 * passed argument isthe text of the message.
 **************************************************************/
protected void errorDialog(String errorMessage) {

  errorLabel.setText(errorMessage);
  errorDialog.pack();
  errorDialog.show();
}


/**************************************************************
 * Resize the Frame (window) due to the addition or removal of
 * Components.
 **************************************************************/
protected void resize(int mode) {
  /////////////////////////////////////////
  // Player's display and controls in frame.
  /////////////////////////////////////////
  if (mode==VISUAL) {
    int maxWidth = (int)Math.max(controlSize.width,visualSize.width);
    setSize(maxWidth,
controlSize.height+visualSize.height+menuHeight);
  }
  ////////////////////////////////
  // Progress bar (only) in frame.
  ////////////////////////////////
  else if (mode==PROGRESS) {
    Dimension progressSize = progressBar.getPreferredSize();
    setSize(progressSize.width,progressSize.height+menuHeight);
  }
  validate();
}
```

LISTING 8.7 Continued

```
/*****************************************************************
* React to events from the player so as to drive the presentation
* or catch any exceptions.
*****************************************************************/
public synchronized void controllerUpdate(ControllerEvent e) {

  /////////////////////////////////////
  // Events from a "dead" player. Ignore.
  /////////////////////////////////////
  if (player==null)
    return;

  /////////////////////////////////////////////////////////////////
  // Player has reached realized state. Need to tidy up any
  // download or visual components from previous player. Then
  // obtain visual and control components for the player,add
  // them to the screen and resize window appropriately.
  /////////////////////////////////////////////////////////////////
  if (e instanceof RealizeCompleteEvent) {
    /////////////////////////////////////////////////
    // Remove any inappropriate Components from display.
    /////////////////////////////////////////////////
    if (progressBar!=null) {
      remove(progressBar);
      progressBar = null;
    }
    if (controlComponent!=null) {
      remove(controlComponent);
      validate();
    }
    if (visualComponent!=null) {
      remove(visualComponent);
      validate();
    }
    /////////////////////////////////////////////////
    // Add control and visual components for new player to
    // display.
    /////////////////////////////////////////////////
    controlComponent = player.getControlPanelComponent();
    if (controlComponent!=null) {
      controlSize = controlComponent.getPreferredSize();
      add(controlComponent,"Center");
    }
    else
```

LISTING 8.7   Continued

```java
        controlSize = new Dimension(0,0);
      visualComponent = player.getVisualComponent();
      if (visualComponent!=null) {
        visualSize = visualComponent.getPreferredSize();
        add(visualComponent,"North");
      }
      else
        visualSize = new Dimension(0,0);
      //////////////////////////////////////////////////////////
      // Resize frame for new components and move to prefetched.
      //////////////////////////////////////////////////////////
      resize(VISUAL);
      System.out.println("Player is now pre-fetching");
      player.prefetch();
    }
    //////////////////////////////////////////////////////////
    // Provide user with a progress bar for "lengthy" downloads.
    //////////////////////////////////////////////////////////
    else if (e instanceof CachingControlEvent &&
  player.getState() <= Player.Realizing && progressBar==null) {
      CachingControlEvent cce = (CachingControlEvent)e;
      progressBar = cce.getCachingControl().getControlComponent();
      if (progressBar!=null) {
        add(progressBar,"Center");
        resize(PROGRESS);
      }
    }
    /////////////////////////////////////////////////////
    // Player initialisation complete. Start it up.
    /////////////////////////////////////////////////////
    else if (e instanceof PrefetchCompleteEvent) {
      System.out.println("Pre-fetching complete, now starting");
      player.start();
    }
    /////////////////////////////////////////////////////
    // Reached end of media. Start over from the beginning.
    /////////////////////////////////////////////////////
    else if (e instanceof EndOfMediaEvent) {
      player.setMediaTime(new Time(0));
      System.out.println("End of Media - restarting");
      player.start();
    }
    //////////////////////////////////////////////////////////
    // Some form of error. Free up all resources associated with
```

LISTING 8.7   Continued

```
    // the player, don't listen to it anymore, and inform the
    // user.
    ////////////////////////////////////////////////////////////////
    else if (e instanceof ControllerErrorEvent) {
      player.removeControllerListener(this); ·
      player.stop();
      player.close();
      errorDialog("Controller Error, abandoning media");
    }

  }


  /*******************************************************************
   * Create a PlayerOfMedia object and pop it up on the screen for the
   * user to interact with.
   *******************************************************************/
  public static void main(String[] args) {

    PlayerOfMedia  ourPlayer = new PlayerOfMedia();
    ourPlayer.pack();
    ourPlayer.setSize(200,100);
    ourPlayer.show();
  }
}
```

Playing Media with a Processor

One of the desirable extensions to the PlayerOfMedia application would be for it to provide a number of statistics about the media it is playing: frame rate, size, duration, content type, and codec. However, using a Player, most of that information simply isn't available because a Player provides no control over any of the processing that it performs on the media, nor over how it renders the media itself. The very abstraction that makes it relatively simple to write programs that play media also makes it impossible to determine much information about the media being played.

An alternative to using a Player object to play (render) media is to use a Processor object. Processor objects are discussed in detail in a later section of this chapter. Details aside, a Processor is really just a specialized type of Player that allows control over the processing that is performed on the input media stream. The output of a Processor is either a DataSource or it is rendered (played).

In order to force a `Processor` to render the media rather than outputting it, `Processor`'s `setContentDescriptor()` method should be passed `null`. This will be revisited in the `Processor` section, but passing the `null` reference implies *do not create an output DataSource* (that is, render the media).

`Processors` provide all the user interface control features of `Players` as well as the ability to access the individual tracks that compose the `DataSource`. Through this mechanism, their formats can be ascertained and such a report generated. The subsequent example `MediaStatistics` shows how such a report can be ascertained. A program to play media that also reported statistics on the media would then employ a `Processor` (rather than `Player`) and combine the features of `PlayerOfMedia` and `MediaStatistics`.

Conserving Media

It is often desirable to keep a permanent copy of media by saving it to a file. The media is then available for subsequent playback, processing, or broadcast. The original media to be saved might be captured from a microphone or camera, the result of some processing (such as transcoding), or a broadcast streaming across the network. In JMF, all these instances are represented as `DataSources`, and the class used to save media is known as a `DataSink`. Figure 8.20 shows these possible applications of a `DataSink`.

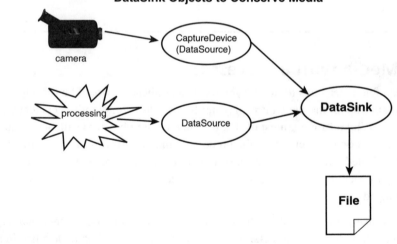

FIGURE 8.20

Uses of a DataSink object to save media to a file.

DataSink

The DataSink interface specifies an object that accepts media from a DataSource and renders it to some destination. Most commonly, that destination is a local file, but it could equally be writing or broadcasting across the network. Hence DataSinks are important objects, and are often seen in JMF programs.

As discussed earlier, a DataSink object is created through the Manager class with the static createDataSink() method. The method expects two parameters: the DataSource to which the DataSink will be connected and a MediaLocator specifying the destination that is the sink. The Manager class returns a DataSink object or throws a NoDataSinkException if it was unable to create the DataSink. The following code fragment shows the typical creation process:

```
DataSource source;
MediaLocator destination;
DataSink sink;
:            :
// Code that would see source and destination with valid values
:            :
try { sink = Manager.createDataSink(source,destination); }
catch (NoDataSinkException nde) { // Do something }
```

Figure 8.21 shows the methods of DataSink (excluding those inherited from MediaHandler and Controls which DataSink extends). Transfer is managed through the open(), start(), stop(), and close() methods. The open() method opens a connection to the destination (specified by the MediaLocator when the DataSource was created). The method might throw an IOException or a SecurityException (for example, not allowed to write to file system when an applet). After an output connection has been established with open(), transfer can be initiated with the start() method. This method also might throw an IOException. Transfer is halted with the stop() method (which can throw an IOException), whereas all resources are freed and the connection closed down with the close() method.

DataSink Interface

```
void addDataSinkListener(DataSinkListener listener)
void close()
String getContentType()
MediaLocator getOutputLocator()
void open()
void removeDataSinkListener(DataSinkListener listener)
void setOutputLocator(MediaLocator location)
void start()
void stop()
```

FIGURE 8.21

The DataSink interface.

DataSink objects generated DataSinkEvent events and can be listened to by those classes that implement DataSinkListener. The methods associated with events are addDataSinkListener() and removeDataSinkListener(). These events generated by DataSink objects are discussed in the next subsection.

setOutputLocator() and getOutputLocator(), as their names imply, are used as a means of specifying or obtaining the output MediaLocator—where the DataSink writes its output. The setOutputLocator() method is rarely used by user programs because this action is performed by the Manager class as part of the DataSink creation process. It is an error (an error is thrown) to call the method more than once. The getContentType() method returns a String specifying the content type of the media that is being consumed by the DataSink.

Employing a DataSink usually follows a number of simple steps:

1. Create the DataSink (from a DataSource).

2. Listen for events from the DataSink.

3. open() and start() the DataSink.

4. When the transfer is complete (for example, end of media reached), stop() and close() the DataSink.

DataSink Events

DataSink objects generate DataSinkEvent events in order to communicate the status of the DataSink. DataSinkEvent objects have two subclasses that indicate the two types of events a DataSink generates: DataSinkErrorEvent and EndOfStreamEvent. As should be evident from their names, these events either indicate an error with the DataSink (DataSinkErrorEvent) or the DataSource feeding the DataSink has signaled an end-of-stream (no more data).

Those objects wanting to receive events from a DataSink must implement the DataSinkListener interface. The interface consists of a single method:

```
void dataSinkUpdate(DataSinkEvent e)
```

Listing 8.8 shows a typical use of a DataSink object (sink) to preserve media coming from a DataSource object (source). Note the use of an anonymous class to listen to events generated by the DataSink and close it when the end of media stream has been detected. The anonymous listener class also performs error detection.

LISTING 8.8 Use of a DataSink and Its Event Handling

```
DataSource    source;              // Assumed to already exist.
DataSink    sink;
MediaLocator    destinationLocation = ...;  // Create destination appropriately
```

LISTING 8.8   Continued

```
try { sink = Manager.createDataSink(source,destinationLocation); }
catch (NoDataSinkException nde) {
  // Print an appropriate error message then rethrow exception
  throw nde;
}
sink.addDataSinkListener(new DataSinkListener() {
    public void dataSinkUpdate(DataSinkEvent e) {
      if (e instanceof EndOfStreamEvent) {
        sink.close();          // Will also stop the sink first
        source.disconnect();
      }
      else if (e instanceof DataSinkErrorEvent) {
        if (sink!=null)
          sink.close();
        if (source!=null)
          source.disconnect();
      }
    }    // End of dataSinkUpdate() method
  });    // End of addDataSinkListener() method
```

PlugIns

PlugIns are a powerful feature of the JMF that allow fine control over the processing of media. Fundamentally, as shown by Figure 8.22, the PlugIn model breaks processing into five component stages that can be chained together.

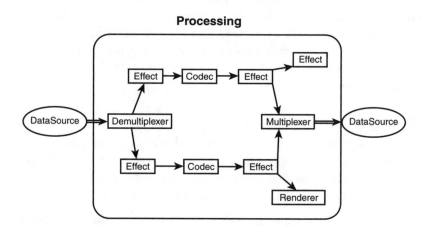

FIGURE 8.22

Position of the various PlugIns in the processing chain.

The components that correspond to each of these five stages are

> `Demultiplexer`—Splits media into its constituent tracks
>
> `Codec`—Compresses or decompresses a media track
>
> `Effect`—Performs special effects processing on a media track; a generic category for any form of manipulation of the media data
>
> `Renderer`—Plays (renders) a media track such as video to the screen or audio to speakers
>
> `Multiplexer`—Combines media tacks into a single media stream

These forms of processing are discussed in greater detail, but independent of the JMF, in the previous chapter.

`Processors` (discussed in the next section) that support `TrackControls` allow the specification and order of the `PlugIns`. The `PlugIns`' order will operate on the individual tracks that compose a media item. Thus, the `PlugIn` model provides a programmer with fine control over the processing performed on media. Indeed, as discussed in Chapter 9, programmers can write their own classes that implement the various `PlugIn` interfaces.

One hindrance is worth mentioning here: It isn't mandatory that `PlugIns` be supported in all JMF implementations. Although the current implementations of version 2.1.1 (Sun reference, Windows performance, Solaris Performance, and Linux performance) all support `PlugIns`, it is possible that some future implementation might not. As an example, this could be the case with a JMF implementation for mobile computing (that is, mobile phones and PDAs) in which resource constraints are tight.

As shown in Figure 8.23, the `PlugIn` interface is relatively simple. All key functionality lies in the `Demultiplexer`, `Codec`, `Effect`, `Renderer`, and `Multiplexer` interfaces that extend `PlugIn`. Hence, a `PlugIn` is a generic processing unit that accepts media in a particular format and processes or presents that data. The `open()` and `close()` methods serve to prepare or terminate the `PlugIn` activity and acquire or free the resources required by the `PlugIn`, respectively. The `reset()` method resets the state of the `PlugIn`, whereas `getName()` returns a human-readable `String` defining the name of the `PlugIn`.

PlugInManager

Given the potential plethora of `PlugIns`, it isn't surprising that the JMF provides a manager class, `PlugInManager`, for maintaining a register of all `PlugIns` that can be both queried and altered. Figure 8.24 shows the methods and class variables of `PlugInManager`. As for the other manager classes, all methods are static (invoked using the class name).

`PlugInManager` finds particular use in those situations in which the list of `PlugIns` is being altered. It will be discussed more in Chapter 9, which deals with, among other things, extending the functionality of the JMF.

PlugIn Interface

static int BUFFER_PROCESSED_FAILED
static int BUFFER_PROCESSED_OK
static int INPUT_BUFFER_NOT_CONSUMED
static int OUTPUT_BUFFER_NOT_FILLED
static int PLUGIN_TERMINATED
void close()
String getName()
void open()
void reset()

FIGURE 8.23

The PlugIn *interface.*

PlugInManager Class

static int CODEC
static int DEMULTIPLEXER
static int EFFECT
static int MULTIPLEXER
static int RENDERER
static boolean addPlugIn(String name, Format[] in, Format[] out, int type)
static void commit()
static Vector getPlugInList(Formats(String name, int type)
static Format[] getSupportedInputFormats(String name, int type)
static Format[] getSupportedOutputFormats(String name, int type)
static boolean removePlugIn(String name, int type)
static void setPlugInList(Vector list, int type)

8

CONTROLLING AND
PROCESSING
MEDIA WITH JMF

FIGURE 8.24

The PlugInManager *class.*

PlugInManager can also be used to query what PlugIns are available. The getPlugInList()
method returns a Vector of PlugIns that are of a particular type (for example,
PlugInManager.CODEC), support a particular input format, and produce a particular output format. Alternatively, given a particular PlugIn, the getSupportedInputFormats() and
getSupportedOutputFormats() methods can be employed to discover what Formats the plug-
in in question supports.

Demultiplexer

The first PlugIn in any processing chain is a Demultiplexer. Its task is to separate a media
stream into its individual tracks. Hence, it has a single input and multiple (the number of
tracks) outputs.

The Demultiplexer plug-in extends the PlugIn, MediaHandler, and Duration interfaces; in addition, it defines the methods as shown in Figure 8.25.

Demultiplexer Interface

```
time getDuration()
Time getMediaTime()
ContentDescriptor[] getSupportedInputContentDescriptors()
Track[] getTracks()
boolean isPositionable()
boolean isRandomAccess()
Time setPosition(Time where, int rounding)
void start()
void stop()
```

FIGURE 8.25

The Demultiplexer *interface.*

The single most important method of the interface is getTracks(), which returns an array of Track objects. This method might either throw a BadHeaderException (if the header information in the media is incomplete or inappropriate) or an IOException. The start() method must be called before Track's readFrame() method will be called on any of the Tracks returned by getTracks(). The stop() method should be called when no further Frames are to be read.

The interface also provides a number of informative methods: Among these is getSupportedInputContentDescriptors(), which returns an array of ContentDescriptor objects that are supported by the demultiplexer.

Codec

A Codec is a PlugIn that performs processing on an input Buffer and produces an output Buffer. This is a surprisingly broad definition because a codec is typically understood to be a compressor or decompressor: a processing unit that converts from one format to another. However, the JMF Codec interface is more encompassing: Any form of processing from input Buffer to output Buffer falls under the category of Codec (although see the next subsection on Effects).

Codec extends the PlugIn interface and thus includes all its methods. Figure 8.26 shows the methods of Codec itself. Codecs work in one of two modes known as frame based and stream based. Frame-based codecs can handle data of any size: Each processing call results in the consumption of the input Buffer and the production of an output Buffer. Stream based Codecs don't have the same synchronization between input and output Buffers. Each processing call might result in only a portion of the input Buffer being consumed (processed). Alternatively, an output Buffer might not be produced after each processing call.

Codec Interface

```
Format[] getSupportedInputFormats()
Format[] getSupportedOutputFormats()
int process(Buffer in, Buffer out)
Format setInputFormat(Format inFormat)
Format setOutputFormat(Format outFormat)
```

FIGURE 8.26
The Codec *interface.*

The key method of the class is process(), which accepts an input Buffer and returns an output Buffer as a parameter. The supported input and output Formats of a Codec can be queried, whereas the particular Formats to be employed for input and output can also be set through the methods of the class.

Effect

The Effect interface is an empty interface that extends Codec: It represents objects that process media data in Buffers but don't alter its Format. For instance, an audio Effect might add reverb to a media track of a particular, or a number of, format(s).

Hence, the Effect interface possesses all the methods of Codec, but no others.

Renderer

The Renderer interface defines a processing unit that renders (plays) a single track of media to a predefined device such as the display or speakers. Being a final link in the processing chain, it has a single input and no outputs.

Figure 8.27 shows the methods of Renderer. The single most important method is process(), which is provided with a Buffer that must be rendered. The start() method initiates the rendering process, whereas stop() halts it. The Formats supported by a Renderer can be queried, whereas the particular Format to use in order to render can be set through the appropriate methods.

Renderer Interface

```
Format[] getSupportedInputFormats()
int process(Buffer toRender)
Format setInputFormat(Format inFormat)
void start()
void stop()
```

FIGURE 8.27
The Renderer *interface.*

8

CONTROLLING AND
PROCESSING
MEDIA WITH JMF

Multiplexer

The `Multiplexer` interfaces define a processing unit that combines one or more (typically more) media tracks into a single output content type (`ContentDescriptor`). The interleaved tracks are available as an output `DataSource` object.

Figure 8.28 shows the methods that the `Multiplexer` interface adds to `PlugIn`. Although, as with other `PlugIns`, the `process()` method is central, several other methods are also vital to achieve any multiplexing task. The `process()` method is provided with a `Buffer` that corresponds to a particular track number. Setting up a `Multiplexer` requires informing the `Multiplexer` of the number of tracks (using the `setNumTracks()` method) and the format of each of those tracks (using the `setInputFormat()` method), as well as specifying the required output content type (using the `setContentDescriptor()` method). The resulting `DataSource` is obtained with the `getDataOutput()` method.

Multiplexer Interface

```
DataSource getDataOutput()
Format[] getSupportedInputFormats()
ContentDescriptor[] getSupportedOutputContentDescriptors(Format[] inputs)
int process(Buffer inBuffer, int TrackNumber)
ContentDescriptor setContentDescriptor(ContentDescriptor outputDescriptor)
Format setInputFormat(Format trackFormat, int trackNumber)
in setNumTracks(int numTracks)
```

FIGURE 8.28

The Multiplexer *interface.*

The following psuedo-code shows the typical steps involved in using a `Multiplexer`.

```
Set the output ContentDescriptor
Set the number of tracks
For each track
        Set its format
while there is more data to multiplex
        for each track
                Process that track's current Buffer
Get the output DataSource
```

Processing Media

In the context of the JMF, processing is a broad and encompassing term that includes all manipulation of time-based media. Examples of processing include compressing and decompressing; transcoding, changing between compression formats and adding digital effects; demultiplexing, splitting the media into tracks; multiplexing, combining tracks into a single stream; and rendering, playing back media. It shouldn't be surprising that these examples match the five plug-in categories discussed in the previous section: PlugIns are processing units within the processing chain.

Processing lies at the heart of all programs written to handle media. Although sourcing media with DataSource and MediaLocator objects is a necessity, and perhaps DataSink objects will also be used, processing is the reason for or purpose of the programming. Even playing media, a very common form of JMF program, falls under the umbrella of processing because to play media is to render it.

Not surprisingly then, understanding the JMF model of processing is a necessity for anyone who intends to carry out any significant JMF based programming. At the core of processing sits the Processor class, which will be discussed next. However, the Processor class extends Player, which extends Controller, which extends Clock—all topics covered earlier in the chapter. Similarly, controlling tasks such as transcoding or multiplexing requires knowledge of the JMF classes employed to represent format (both content type and track). Hence to understand processing fully requires understanding not only this section but also the earlier half of the chapter in which these various topics and classes were covered, primarily as preparation to understand processing.

Processor Timescale

Extending Controller as it does indirectly by extending Player, which extends Controller, the Processor class has a similar model of time. Time is stopped or started. But in recognition of the fact that transitioning from stopped to started isn't instantaneous, requiring significant resource acquisition (as it often does), stopped time is subdivided into a number of states. These states reflect the preparedness (or lack thereof) of the Controller to start.

The Controller interface divides stopped time into five states which, in order of least prepared (to start) to prepared are known as Unrealized, Realizing, Realized, Prefetching, and Prefetched.

Because of the nature of processing and, in particular, the need to determine the format of the tracks that compose the media, as well as to specify the processing that will occur on those tracks, the Processor class subdivides stopped time into seven states. The two additional states, known as Configuring and Configured, are added between the Unrealized and Realized states. That leads to a sequence as follows: Unrealized, Configuring, Configured, Realizing, Realized, Prefetching, Prefetched.

A brief summary of each of those states is as follows:

Unrealized—A Processor that has been created but hasn't undertaken any resource gathering.

Configuring—A transition state reflecting the fact that the input (to the Processor) DataSource is being analyzed as to its format and that of its individual tracks.

Configured—A steady-state reflecting a Processor that has successfully gathered format information about the input DataSource. It is in this state that a Processor should be programmed with its processing task.

Realizing—A transition state reflecting the fact that the Processor is gathering information about the resources needed for its task, as well as gathering resources themselves.

Realized—A steady-state reflecting a Processor that has gathered all the non-exclusive resources needed for a task.

Prefetching—A transition state reflecting the fact that the Processor is gathering all resources needed for its task that weren't obtained in the realizing state. Typically, this means acquiring exclusive usage resources such as hardware.

Prefetched—The Processor has acquired all necessary resources, performed all pre-startup processing, and is ready to be started.

Figure 8.29 shows the seven states and their relationship in terms of preparedness to start. The next section details the methods for transitioning between the states as well as the events that a Processor generates as it makes those transitions.

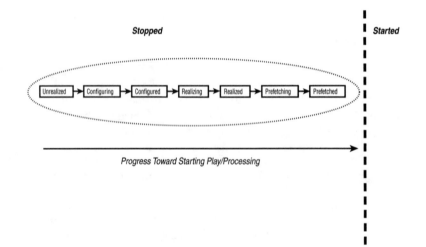

FIGURE 8.29

The seven states of a Processor *as they measure how prepared a* Processor *is to start.*

The addition of the Configuring and Configured states reflects querying the DataSource about its format and that of its constituent tracks. This not only provides finer granularity of stopped time, but also provides the particular instant in which the processor can be programmed. A Processor must be programmed (configured) for what processing it will undertake before it transitions to Realizing because that reflects commitment to a particular type of processing. A

Processor cannot be programmed to the task it will undertake until all relevant information about the source media has been obtained. Hence, the Configured state is the only time at which a Processor can be programmed.

Processor Interface

A Processor is a MediaHandler object that extends the Player interface. In many ways, Processor follows a similar abstracted-from-media-details approach as that of Player. Given a particular set of requirements (in this case, processing media as opposed to simply playing it), a suitable Processor object can be obtained by way of the Manager class. From the user-code perspective, this object looks the same as all other Processor objects, possessing the same set of methods. This uniformity of interface, regardless of media particulars, leads to versatile programs capable of processing multiple types of media.

However, media particulars are also where the Processor differs significantly, in a creation sense, from Player. What is entailed in *playing* media is well understood and requires little specification beyond the media to be played. However, *processing* is far broader, indeed all but infinite, in variability (for instance, consider different digital effects). The potential with the type of processing that can be performed requires a far tighter prescription from the user at the time of Processor configuration so that the desired form of processing can be achieved. In a nutshell, creating and configuring a Processor is far more complicated than the equivalent task for a Player. The means of Processor creation and configuration, both important and involved, are detailed in a separate subsection.

Figure 8.30 shows the six methods of Processor that are above and beyond those inherited from Player. Three of the methods are vital in the programming of a Processor—configure(), getTrackControls(), and setContentDescriptor(). Two are general information or accessor methods—getContentDescriptor() and getSupportedContentDescriptors(). One, getDataOutput(), is the means of obtaining the output or result of the processing that was performed.

Processor Interface

```
void configure()
ContentDescriptor() getContentDescriptor()
DataSource getDataOutput()
ContentDescriptor[] get SupportedContentDescriptors()
TrackControl[] getTrackControls()
contendDescriptor setContentDescriptor(ContentDescriptor outputDescriptor)
```

FIGURE 8.30

The Processor interface.

The `configure()` method asynchronously brings a `Processor` to the Configured state. As discussed in the next subsection, this is a vital step in programming a `Processor`. Only when a `Processor` is in the Configured state can it be programmed for the processing it will carry out.

The `setContentDescriptor()` method sets the `ContentDescriptor` of the `DataSource` that the `Processor` outputs. A content type such as AVI, QUICKTIME, or WAVE of the processor's output is set using this method. A content type is also known as *meta-format* or *media container*. The method returns the actual `ContentDescriptor` that was set, which might be the closest matching `ContentDescriptor` supported by the `Processor`. The method might also return `null` if no `ContentDescriptor` could be set, as well as throwing a `NotConfiguredError` exception if the `Processor` is either Unrealized or Configuring.

The `getTrackControls()` method returns an array of `TrackControl` objects—one for each track in the `DataSource` that is being processed. As described in the next subsection, the `TrackControl` objects can then be employed to program the processing that is performed on the associated track of media. The method throws a `NotConfiguredError` exception if the `Processor` isn't at least Configured at the time of calling.

`Processors` produce a `DataSource` as the result of the processing they perform. That `DataSource` can be used as the input to a subsequent `Processor` or `Player`. The `getDataOutput()` method is the means of obtaining the `DataSource` that a `Processor` produces. The method throws a `NotRealizedError` exception if the `Processor` isn't at least Realized at the time of invocation.

The `getContentDescriptor()` method returns the currently set `ContentDescriptor` that will be used for the output of the processor. The `getSupportedContentDescriptors()` returns an array of all `ContentDescriptors` that the `Processor` can output. Both methods throw a `NotConfiguredError` exception if the `Processor` isn't at least Configured at the time of calling.

A number of the methods of `Processor`, most inherited from Controller or Player, exert direct control over the state of a `Processor`. Others can alter the state as a side effect. The following list shows those methods:

> `configure()`—Moves the `Processor` from Unrealized to Realized. This is a key step in `Processor` management because the Configured stage is the only time that a `Processor` can be programmed as to its task.
>
> `realize()`—Moves the `Processor` from either Unrealized or Configured to Realized. Asynchronous (returns immediately). Generally, `realize()` should only be called after the `Processor` has reached Configured and has been programmed as to its task.
>
> `prefetch()`—Moves the `Processor` from Realized to Prefetched. Asynchronous (returns immediately).

start()—Moves the Processor from its current state to Started. The Processor will transition through any intermediary states and send notice of such transitions to any listeners. As for the realize() method, start() should only be called after a processor has been programmed. Asynchronous (returns immediately).

stop()—Moves the Processor from the Started state back to either Prefetched or Realized, depending on the type of media being processed and the processing task. Synchronous (returns only after Processor is actually stopped).

deallocate()—Deallocates the resources acquired by the Processor and moves it to the Realized state (if at least Realized at the time of call) or to Unrealized (if in Realizing or Unrealized state at time of call). Synchronous.

close()—Closes down the Processor totally. It will post a ControllerClosedEvent. The behavior of any further calls on the Processor is unspecified: the Processor shouldn't be used after it is closed. Synchronous.

setStopTime()—Sets the media time at which it will stop. When the media reaches that time, the Processor will act as though stop() was called. Asynchronous (returns immediately and stops play when time reaches that specified).

setMediaTime()—Changes the media's current time. This might result in a state transition. For instance, a started Processor might return to Prefetching while it refills buffers for the new location in the stream. Asynchronous (in that any state changes triggered aren't waited for).

setRate()—Sets the rate of processing. It might result in a state change on a started Processor for similar reasons to those for setMediaTime(). As for the Player interface, there is no guarantee that a Processor will support any rate other than 1.0. If a requested rate isn't supported, the closest matching rate is set. Asynchronous (in that any state changes triggered aren't waited for).

Figure 8.31 shows the states of a Processor with the methods that force transitions between those states. Figure 8.32 shows the events that a Processor generates as it transitions between states.

Creating and Programming Processors

The key initialization step for a Processor isn't simply its creation but its programming. The specific task that it must perform needs to be defined prior to Processor realization because realization, and the prefetching that follows, involves obtaining the resources necessary to perform the task. However, programming a Processor requires the prior knowledge of the format of the media that will be processed. This apparent dilemma is resolved through the extended model of stopped time provided by Processor: The Configured state provides the opportunity at which the format of the input media is known but prior to the realizing (resource gathering) step.

8

CONTROLLING AND
PROCESSING
MEDIA WITH JMF

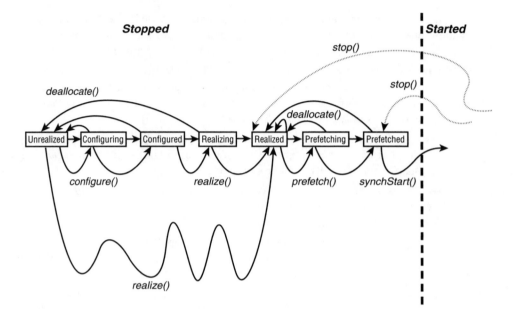

FIGURE 8.31

Methods of Processor *that trigger state changes.*

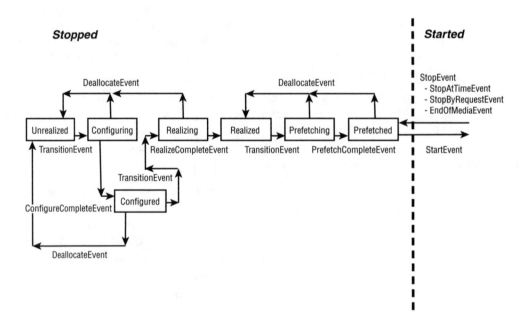

FIGURE 8.32

Events *generated when a* Processor *transitions between states.*

The JMF provides two primary approaches by which the task of a Processor can be programmed. One, perhaps simpler, approach is to encapsulate all necessary processing as a ProcessorModel object and have the Manager class create a Processor object that will perform exactly that task. The second, arguably more complex but certainly more versatile, approach is to have the Manager class create a Processor but leave programming entirely under user control. The user code must bring the Processor to the Configured state and then use methods and objects such as TrackControls to define the task of the Processor. With that completed, the Processor can be moved through to Started.

The Manager class provides four methods for creating a Processor. Three createProcessor() methods accept the specification of the input media (as a DataSource, URL, or MediaLocator) and return an unrealized Processor. It is the user's responsibility to bring that Processor to the Configured state (with the configure() method), carry out the programming, and then start the Processor. The three createProcessor() methods can throw IOException and NoProcessorException exceptions.

The alternative means of creating a Processor is with Manager's createRealizedProcessor() method. The method accepts a ProcessorModel object that describes all processing requirements—the input and output formats as well as the individual tracks. The method is synchronous (blocking)—it won't return until the Processor is realized. This can make programming considerably easier. As for the other Processor creation methods of Manager, createRealizedProcessor() can throw both IOException and NoProcessorException. It can also throw a CannotRealizeException.

ProcessorModel

The simplest way to program a Processor is with a ProcessorModel object at the time of the Processor's creation using Manager's createRealizedProcessor() method. The ProcessorModel object encapsulates all the processing that the Processor is to perform. In particular, it specifies the input media, the required output content type, and the format of each track of the output.

The task of using a ProcessorModel to obtain an appropriate Processor is relatively simple:

1. Construct the objects needed by the ProcessorModel constructor (for example, DataSource and Format objects).

2. Construct the ProcessorModel.

3. Use Manager's createRealizedProcessor() method to obtain an appropriate Processor.

Figure 8.33 shows the constructors and methods of ProcessorModel. As you can see, the methods of ProcessorModel are simply information queries about the object's attributes. The chief role of the class is to encapsulate all necessary information about the processing task to be performed. Hence the class constructors are the most important elements of the class.

ProcessorModel Class

```
ProcessorModel()
ProcessorModel(DataSource source, Format[] formats, ContentDescriptor outputType)
ProcessorModel(Format[] formats, ContentDescriptor outputType)
ProcessorModel(MediaLocator sourceLocator, Format[] formats, ContentDescriptor
outputType)
```

```
ContentDescriptor getContentDescriptor()
DataSource getInputDataSource()
MediaLocator getInputLocator()
Format getOutputFormat(int trackIndex)
int getTrackCount(int availableTrackCount)
boolean isFormatAcceptable(int trackNum, Format QueryFormat)
```

FIGURE 8.33

The ProcessorModel *class.*

There are four constructors, although the no-argument constructor is simply a placeholder. The two most commonly used constructors accept either a MediaLocator or DataSource as the specification of the input to the Processor. That is then followed by an array of Format objects—each element of that array specifying the desired format for the particular track. The final argument is a ContentDescriptor specifying the output content type (media container or meta-format). The fourth constructor accepts no specification of the input media: only output track formats and content type. This constructor is used for capturing media (finding a capture device that will meet the output demands of such a processor).

Listing 8.9 shows the use of a ProcessorModel in the apparent transcoding of a movie. A MediaLocator is created specifying the source media, an output content type of MSVIDEO (AVI) is created, and formats are specified for the two tracks: Cinepak for the video and Linear for the audio. Those objects are used to construct a ProcessorModel, which in turn is employed in the creation of a Processor.

LISTING 8.9 Use of a ProcessorModel Object in the Apparent Transcoding of a Movie

```
// Construct objects needed to make ProcessorModel
MediaLocator src = new MediaLocator(
"file://d:\\jmf\\book\\media\\videoexample\\iv50_320x240.mov");
formats = new Format[2];
formats[0] = new VideoFormat(VideoFormat.CINEPAK);
formats[1] = new AudioFormat(AudioFormat.LINEAR);
```

LISTING 8.9   Continued

```
container = new FileTypeDescriptor(FileTypeDescriptor.MSVIDEO);
// Construct the ProcessorModel
ProcessorModel model = new ProcessorModel(src,formats,container);
// Create the realized Processor using the ProcessorModel
Processor p = Manager.createRealizedProcessor(model);
```

The one drawback of the `ProcessorModel` approach to `Processor` programming is that fine control is removed from the user's hands. In particular, the user has no say over how the processing is performed in terms of what classes are employed. The user cannot specify which `PlugIns` to employ, and this is a particular drawback in two areas. First, it means that no `Effect` processing can be performed through a `ProcessorModel` because a `ProcessorModel` is only aware of output formats, not manipulations within a format. Second, it might be desirable to perform processing as a chain of `PlugIns` more complex than `Demultiplexer`, `Codec`, and `Multiplexer`. This is where the second approach to programming a `Processor`, through its `TrackControl` objects, comes into its own.

TrackControl

The second means of programming the processing task for a `Processor` is directly through the `TrackControl` interface that corresponds to each track composing the media to be processed. The approach is somewhat more involved than using a `ProcessorModel` but is far more flexible, allowing the user to specify codec chains and renderers to be applied to individual tracks—something not possible with the `ProcessorModel` approach.

The basic algorithm for pursuing the `TrackControl` based approach to programming a `Processor` is as follows:

```
Create a Processor through the Manager class
Bring the Processor to the Configured state using configure()
Set the required ContentDescriptor on the Processor which specifies the content
  type of the media that will be produced
Obtain the TrackControls of the Processor
For each TrackControl
        Set the required output Format
        If codecs/effects are to be used for the track
                Set the TrackControl's codec chain
        If the track is to be rendered
                Set the TrackControl's renderer
Start the processor
```

`TrackControl` is an interface that extends both the `FormatControl` and `Controls` interfaces. Figure 8.34 shows the methods of `TrackControl` plus those inherited from `FormatControl` (an interface not discussed to date). In terms of programming a Processor, the most important methods are setEnabled(), setFormat(), setCodecChain(), and setRenderer().

TrackControl (including FormatControl) Interface

```
Format getFormat()
Format[] getSuppportedFormats()
boolean isEnabled()
void setEnabled(boolean state)
Format setFormat(Format desiredFormat)
void setCodecChain(Codec[] chainOfCodecs)
void setRenderer(Renderer toRender)
```

FIGURE 8.34

The TrackControl *interface.*

The setEnabled() method is used to determine whether a track will be processed. Passing the setEnabled() method a value of false means that the track won't be processed and won't be output by the Processor.

The setFormat() method is passed a Format object specifying the desired output Format that the Processor will produce for that track. The method returns the Format that was actually set (the closest matching Format if the requested Format wasn't supported), or null if no Format could be set.

The setCodecChain() method is passed an array of Codec PlugIns that are to be applied to the track as a chain—that is, in the order they are found in the array. This is a powerful mechanism to exactly controlling the order of compression/decompression and effect processing upon each track. It is important to note that the Effect PlugIn is a subclass of Codec, so these can also be passed as elements of the array. The method might throw an UnSupportedPlugInException or a NotConfiguredError exception.

The setRenderer() method is used to specify the Renderer PlugIn that is to play a particular track. By default, Processors don't render the tracks that they are processing but rather only produce an output DataSource.

It is worth mentioning that the TrackControl interface extends Controls; thus it is possible to obtain the Control objects associated with the track. Among these will be Control objects for any codecs being employed. Thus, it is possible to control the particulars of the compression/decompression on a per-track basis by employing such Control objects.

Listing 8.10 shows the programming of a Processor to perform the same task as the one in Listing 8.9. However, in this case, the Processor is programmed through the TrackControl approach ProcessorModel. As you can see, the setup cost for simple transcoding—what both pieces of code are doing—is higher with the TrackControl approach. What isn't being shown in the fragment is the versatility offered in terms of specifying a codec chain or renderer for each track.

LISTING 8.10   Programming of a `Processor` Through the `TrackControls` Approach

```
MediaLocator src = new MediaLocator(
"file://d:\\jmf\\book\\media\\videoexample\\iv50_320x240.mov");
Processor p = Manager.createProcessor(src);
p.addControllerListener(this);
p.configure();
:
:
public void synchronized controllerUpdate(ControllerEvent e) {

if (e instanceof ConfigureCompleteEvent) {
  p.setContentDescriptor(new
        FileTypeDescriptor(FileTypeDescriptor.MSVIDEO));
  TrackControl[] controls = processor.getTrackControls();
  for (int i=0;i<controls.length;i++) {
    if (controls[i].getFormat() instanceof VideoFormat)
      controls[i].setFormat(new VideoFormat(VideoFormat.CINEPAK));
    else
      controls[i].setFormat(new AudioFormat(AudioFormat.LINEAR));
  }
  p.start();
}
else if (e instanceof …) { ...}
```

Utility Class: `MediaStatistics`

This subsection discusses a utility class, `MediaStatistics`, who's source can be found in Listing 8.11 as well as on the book's companion Web site. `MediaStatistics` employs a `Processor` in order to acquire information about the format of the individual tracks that compose a media object. A derivative graphical application `GUIMediaStatistics`, which provides the same functionality but with a graphical user interface, can also be found at the book's companion Web site.

The class itself illustrates a number of the features and classes of JMF that have been discussed in the chapter to date: `Processor` and `Format` classes, `Controller` events, and the asynchronous time model of the JMF.

A `MediaStatistics` object is constructed by providing the name and location (a `String` suitable for constructing a `MediaLocator`) of the media in question. A `Processor` is created for that media and brought to the Configured state. At that stage, the `Format` of the individual tracks can be obtained and reported on.

The class also contains a `main()` method so that it can run as a standalone application. Any command-line options are treated as media names: A `MediaStatistics` object is constructed and used to generate a report on the format of the tracks of the media. Listing 8.12 shows a run of the application for an MPEG video file. Users should note (as in the example) that the media name must consist of both the protocol (file:// if a local file) and the location of the media (the fully qualified pathname if a local file).

Several features of the class are worth noting. Because discovering the format of tracks requires a Configured `Processor`, the format information might not be available immediately. To deal with this, the class keeps track of its own state as well as providing methods such as `getState()` and `isKnown()` (which returns `true` when the formats are finally known) so that the user can check when a report is available. Alternatively, and more powerfully, the class could generate its own events and send those to listener classes. Although not difficult to implement, it would obscure the main purpose of the example and hence is omitted.

Two constructors are provided; one returns instantly but makes no guarantees that the format information is available. The second constructor blocks until the format information is known or a prescribed timeout period has transpired. This has the advantage that the user code employing `MediaStatistics` won't need to wait an unknown period before querying about formats.

The `MediaStatistics` object keeps track of its own state by catching any exceptions that occur in the `Processor` creation as well as listening to the `Processor`. Listening to the `Processor` in this instance is far simpler than for `Players` or more sophisticated `Processors`. Only the `ConfigureCompleteEvent` is of interest; in which case, the `TrackControls` should be obtained as a means of obtaining the `Format` objects for each track. The resources tied up in the `Processor` can then also be released.

The class contains a number of information (accessor) methods including

`getNumTracks()`—Gets the number of tracks possessed by the media

`getState()`—Determines the state of the object

`getReport()`—Gets a `String` detailing the format of all tracks

`getTrackFormat()`—Returns the `Format` object for the specified track number

`isAudioTrack()` and `isVideoTrack()`—Return `true` if the specified track number is an audio or video track

`isKnown()`—Returns `true` if the format information is known (if the object's state is KNOWN).

LISTING 8.11   The `MediaStatistics` Application that Produces Statistics About the
Particular Format of Media

```java
import javax.media.*;
import javax.media.control.*;
import javax.media.format.*;


/**********************************************************************
 * A Class to determine statistics about the tracks that compose
 * a media object. Given the name (URL/location) of media a
 * Processor is constructed and brought to the Configured state.
 * At that stage its TrackControls are obtained as a means of
 * discovering the Formats of the individual tracks.
 *
 * Because reaching Configured can take time, the MediaStatistics
 * object keeps track of its own state and provides methods for
 * determining that state. Only when it reaches the KNOWN state
 * can statistics be obtained. Similarly there are 2 constructors:
 * one creating a Processor and starting it toward Configured but
 * returning immediately. The other is a blocking constructor, it
 * won't return until the Processor reaches Configured or the
 * specified time-out expires. This has the advantage that the
 * object can be used immediately (rather than polling it to
 * determine when it enters the KNOWN state).
 *
 * The chief information gathering method is getReport() which
 * returns a String reporting on the Format of all tracks of
 * the media. Alternatively the Format of individual tracks can
 * also be ascertained.
 *
 * @author Spike Barlow
 **********************************************************************/
public class MediaStatistics implements ControllerListener {

    /** State: Yet to create the Processor. */
    public static final int NOT_CREATED = 0;

    /** State: Unable to create the Processor. */
    public static final int FAILED = -1;

    /** State: Processor is Configuring. */
    public static final int CONFIGURING = 1;

    /** State: Details of media are Known. */
    public static final int KNOWN = 2;
```

LISTING 8.11   Continued

```java
/** Number of tracks is Unknown. */
public static final int UNKNOWN = Integer.MIN_VALUE;

/** Period in milliseconds to sleep for before
* rechecking if reached KNOWN state. */
protected  static final int WAIT_INTERVAL = 20;

/** Number of tracks possessed by the media. */
protected int            numTracks = UNKNOWN;

/** Formats of the individual tracks. */
protected Format[]       trackFormats;

/** Processor needed to ascertain track information. */
protected Processor      processor;

/** State that the object is currently in. A reflection
* of the state the Processor is in. */
protected int            state = NOT_CREATED;

/** The name of the media on which stats are being compiled. */
protected String         nameOfMedia;

/*****************************************************************
* Construct a MediaStatistics object for the media with the
* passed name. This is a blocking constructor. It returns
* only when it is possible to obtain the track statistics or
* when the specified time-out period (in milliseconds) has
* transpired.
*****************************************************************/
MediaStatistics(String mediaName, int timeOutInMilliseconds) {

  nameOfMedia = mediaName;
  // Construct the Processor
  try {
    MediaLocator locator = new MediaLocator(mediaName);
    processor = Manager.createProcessor(locator);
  }
  // Any exception is a failure.
  catch (Exception e) {
    state = FAILED;
    return;
  }
  // Listen to and start configuration of the Processor.
```

LISTING 8.11   Continued

```
  processor.addControllerListener(this);
  state = CONFIGURING;
  processor.configure();
  ///////////////////////////////////////////////////////
  // Wait till the Processor reaches configured (the object
  // reaches KNOWN) or the specified time-out interval has
  // transpired, by looping, sleeping,and rechecking.
  ///////////////////////////////////////////////////////
  if (timeOutInMilliseconds>0) {
    int waitTime = 0;
    while (waitTime<timeOutInMilliseconds && !isKnown()) {
      try { Thread.sleep(WAIT_INTERVAL); }
      catch (InterruptedException ie) { }
      waitTime += WAIT_INTERVAL;
    }
  }
}


/******************************************************************
 * Construct a MediaStatistics object for the media with the
 * passed name. This is not a blocking constructor: it returns
 * immediately. Thus calling getReport() immediately may result
 * in "Still parsing media" report. The isKnown() method should
 * be used to check for this condition.
 ******************************************************************/
MediaStatistics(String mediaName) {
  this(mediaName,-1);
}


/******************************************************************
 * Respond to events from the Porcessor. In particular the
 * ConfigureComplete event is the only one of interest. In this
 * case obtain the TrackControls anduse these to obtain the
 * Formats of each track. Also modify the state and close down
 * the Processor (free up its resources).
 ******************************************************************/
public synchronized void controllerUpdate(ControllerEvent e) {

  if (e instanceof ConfigureCompleteEvent) {
    TrackControl[] controls = processor.getTrackControls();
    // As long as there are TrackControls, get each track's format.
    if (controls.length!=0) {
      numTracks = controls.length;
      trackFormats = new Format[controls.length];
      for (int i=0;i<controls.length;i++) {
```

LISTING 8.11   Continued

```java
        trackFormats[i] = controls[i].getFormat();
   }
    state = KNOWN;
  }
  else {
    state = FAILED;
  }
  // Close down the Processor.
  processor.removeControllerListener(this);
  processor.close();
  processor = null;
  }
}


/****************************************************************
 * Determine what state the object is in. Returns one of the
 * class constants such as KNOWN, FAILED or CONFIGURING.
 ****************************************************************/
public int getState() {
  return state;
}


/****************************************************************
 * Determine the number of tracks possessed by the media. If
 * that is unknown, either due to the processor creation
 * failing or because the processor is not yet Configured then
 * the class constant UNKNOWN is returned.
 ****************************************************************/
public int getNumTracks() {
  return numTracks;
}

/****************************************************************
 * Obtain the Format for the specified track number. If the
 * track doesn't exist, or it has yet to be determined how
 * many tracks the media possesses, null is returned.
 ****************************************************************/
public Format getTrackFormat(int track) {

  if (track<0 || track>=numTracks)
    return null;
```

LISTING 8.11   Continued

```java
  return trackFormats[track];
}


/****************************************************************
 * Is the object in the KNOWN state? The KNOWN state reflects
 * the fact that information is known about the number and
 * Format of the tracks. The method can be used to ascertain
 * whether a report is available (meaningful) or not.
 ****************************************************************/
public boolean isKnown() {
  return state==KNOWN;
}



/****************************************************************
 * Returns true if the specified track number is an audio track.
 * If the track doesn't exist, the number of tracks is yet
 * unknown, or it isn't audio then false is returned.
 ****************************************************************/
public boolean isAudioTrack(int track) {

  if (track<0 || track>=numTracks)
    return false;
  return trackFormats[track] instanceof AudioFormat;
}


/****************************************************************
 * Returns true if the specified track number is a video track.
 * If the track doesn't exist, the number of tracks is yet
 * unknown, or it isn't video then false is returned.
 ****************************************************************/
public boolean isVideoTrack(int track) {

  if (track<0 || track>=numTracks)
    return false;
  return trackFormats[track] instanceof VideoFormat;
}



/****************************************************************
 * Returns a report, as a String, detailing thenumber and format
 * of the individual tracks that compose the media that this
 * object obtained statistics for. If the object is not in the
 * KNOWN state then the report is a simple String, indicating
```

LISTING 8.11   Continued

```
 * this.
 ******************************************************************/
public String getReport() {
  String  mess;

  if (state==FAILED)
    return "Unable to Handle Media " + nameOfMedia;
  else if (state==CONFIGURING)
    return "Still Parsing Media " + nameOfMedia;
  else if (state==KNOWN) {
    if (numTracks==1)
      mess = nameOfMedia + ": 1 Track\n";
    else
      mess = nameOfMedia + ": " + numTracks + " Tracks\n";
    for (int i=0;i<numTracks;i++) {
      if (trackFormats[i] instanceof AudioFormat)
        mess += "\t"+(i+1)+" [Audio]: ";
      else if (trackFormats[i] instanceof VideoFormat)
        mess += "\t"+(i+1)+" [Video]: ";
      else
        mess += "\t"+(i+1)+" [Unknown]: ";
      mess += trackFormats[i].toString() + "\n";
    }
    return mess;
  }
  else
    return "Unknown State in Processing " + nameOfMedia;
}


/****************************************************************
 * Simple main method to exercise the class. Takes command
 * line arguments and constructs MediaStatistics objects for
 * them, before generating a report on them.
 ****************************************************************/
public static void main(String[] args) {

  MediaStatistics[] stats = new MediaStatistics[args.length];

  for (int i=0;i<args.length;i++) {
    stats[i] = new MediaStatistics(args[i],200);
    System.out.println(stats[i].getReport());
    stats[i] = null;
  }
```

LISTING 8.11 Continued

```
  System.exit(0);
}
}
```

LISTING 8.12 Output of a Run of the MediaStatistics Program on a Particular MPEG
Movie File

```
C:\Spike\JMF\Code>java MediaStatistics file://d:\media\badday.mpeg
file://d:\media\badday.mpeg: 2 Tracks
        1 [Video]: MPEG, 176x120, FrameRate=29.9, Length=31680
        2 [Audio]: mpegaudio, 44100.0 Hz, 16-bit, Mono, LittleEndian,
                Signed, 4000.0 frame rate,  FrameSize=16384 bits
```

Utility Class: `Location2Location`

This subsection discusses a utility class, Location2Location, found in Listing 8.13 as well as
on the book's companion Web site. Location2Location is a class that both transcodes media
to a different format and saves/writes the resulting media to a new location.

In order to perform its task, Location2Location combines many of the most important classes
and features of the JMF, and is the most comprehensive example of the JMF features to date in
the book. Key classes involved include Processor, Manager, DataSource, DataSink,
ProcessorModel, and MediaLocator; whereas the event-driven asynchronous nature of the
JMF is illustrated through the class implementing ControllerListener while also using an
anonymous class to listen for events from the DataSink object.

The class is employed through the mechanism of the user constructing a Location2Location
object that specifies the origin and destination of the media (either Strings or
MediaLocators), the desired format for the individual tracks that compose the media (an array
of Formats), and the content type (ContentDescriptor) for the resulting media container.
Construction automatically initiates the transcoding portion of the task, whereas transfer to the
new destination is achieved by calling the transfer() method.

The transcoding tasks—transforming the format of the media—is achieved via the processor
class, whereas the writing to a new location is achieved through a DataSink. The Processor
object is created through the specification of a ProcessorModel that includes the Format specification for the individual tracks as well as the content type (ContentDescriptor) of the resulting container (for example, Quicktime or AVI).

The DataSink is constructed using the DataSource that is the output of the Processor together
with the user specified destination.

8

CONTROLLING AND
PROCESSING
MEDIA WITH JMF

Both the `Processor` and `DataSink` perform their respective tasks (transcoding and rendering to a destination) asynchronously. The class illustrates means of dealing with this pervasive feature of the JMF. The class listens for events from both the `Processor` and `DataSink` and maintains its own internal model of its current state. This is exposed to the user through a number of class constants and a method `getState()`, which is used to query the current state. Further, the `transfer()` method can be invoked asynchronously, which will return immediately, but the user will need to check periodically for when the process is complete. It can also be invoked synchronously, which will block until the process completes. An even better solution would be for `Location2Location` to generate its own events and allow classes to register themselves as listeners for those events. Such an approach isn't difficult to implement, but requires the writing of an additional interface (the `Listener` interface) and class (the `Event` class) as well as the code to maintain the list of listeners. We feel that this further detail would obscure the purpose of the example, which is to illustrate features of the JMF.

LISTING 8.13   The `Location2Location` Utility Class Capable of Transferring and Transcoding Media

```
import javax.media.*;
import javax.media.datasink.*;
import javax.media.protocol.*;

/*******************************************************************
 * Transfer media from one location to another carrying out the
 * specified transcoding (track formats and content type) at the
 * same time.
 *<p>Users specify a source and destination location, the
 * Formats (to be realised) of the individual tracks, and a
 * ContentDescriptor (content type) for output.
 *<p>A Processor is created to perform and transcoding and its
 * output DataSource is employed to construct a DataSink in
 * order to complete the transfer.
 *<p>The most important method of the class is transfer() as
 * this opens and starts the DataSink. The constructor builds
 * both the Processor (which is starts) and the DataSink.
 *<p>The object keeps track of its own state, which can be queried
 * with the getState() method. Defined constants are FAILED,
 * TRANSLATING, TRANSFERRING, and FINISHED. The process is
 * asychronous: transcoding largish movies can take a long time.
 * The calling code should make allowances for that.
 *******************************************************************/
public class Location2Location implements ControllerListener {

    /** Output of the Processor: the transcoded media. */
    protected DataSource  source;
```

LISTING 8.13 Continued

```java
/** Sink used to "write" out the transcoded media. */
protected DataSink   sink;

/** Processor used to transcode the media. */
protected Processor processor;

/** Model used in constructing the processor, and which
 * specifies track formats and output content type */
protected ProcessorModel   model;

/** State the object is in. */
protected int    state;

/** Location that the media will be "written" to. */
protected MediaLocator   sinkLocation;

/** The rate of translation. */
protected float translationRate;

/** Process has failed. */
public static final int FAILED = 0;

/** Processor is working but not finished. DataSink is yet
 * to start. */
public static final int TRANSLATING = 1;

/** DataSink has started but not finished. */
public static final int TRANSFERRING = 3;

/** Transcoding and transfer is complete. */
public static final int FINISHED = 4;

/** String names for each of the states. More user friendly */
private static final String[] STATE_NAMES = {
  "Failed", "Translating", "<UNUSED>", "Transferring",
  "Finished"};

/** Period (in milliseconds) between checks for the blocking
 * transfer method. */
public static final int WAIT_PERIOD = 50;

/** Wait an "indefinite" period of time for the transfer
 * method to complete. i.e., pass to transfer() if the
 * user wishes to block till the process is complete,
```

LISTING 8.13   Continued

```
 * regardless of how long it will take. */
public static final int INDEFINITE = Integer.MAX_VALUE;

/**********************************************************************
 * Construct a transfer/transcode object that transfers media from
 * sourceLocation to destinationLocation, transcoding the tracks as
 * specified by the outputFormats. The output media is to have a
 * content type of outputContainer and the process should (if
 * possible) run at the passed rate.
 **********************************************************************/
Location2Location(MediaLocator sourceLocation,
    MediaLocator destinationLocation, Format[] outputFormats,
    ContentDescriptor outputContainer, double rate) {

  /////////////////////////////////////////////
  // Construct the processor for the transcoding
  /////////////////////////////////////////////
  state = TRANSLATING;
  sinkLocation = destinationLocation;
  try {
    if (sourceLocation==null)
      model = new ProcessorModel(outputFormats,outputContainer);
    else
      model = new ProcessorModel(sourceLocation,
                    outputFormats,outputContainer);
    processor = Manager.createRealizedProcessor(model);
  }
  catch (Exception e) {
    state = FAILED;
    return;
  }

  translationRate = processor.setRate((float)Math.abs(rate));
  processor.addControllerListener(this);

  ////////////////////////////////////////////////////////////////
  // Construct the DataSink and employ an anonymous class as
  // a DataSink listener in order that the end of transfer
  // (completion of task) can be detected.
  ////////////////////////////////////////////////////////////////
  source = processor.getDataOutput();
  try {
    sink = Manager.createDataSink(source,sinkLocation);
  }
```

LISTING 8.13   Continued

```java
    catch (Exception sinkException) {
      state = FAILED;
      processor.removeControllerListener(this);
      processor.close();
      processor = null;
      return;
    }
    sink.addDataSinkListener(new DataSinkListener() {
        public void dataSinkUpdate(DataSinkEvent e) {
          if (e instanceof EndOfStreamEvent) {
            sink.close();
            source.disconnect();
            if (state!=FAILED)
              state = FINISHED;
          }
          else if (e instanceof DataSinkErrorEvent) {
            if (sink!=null)
              sink.close();
            if (source!=null)
              source.disconnect();
            state = FAILED;
          }
        }
    });
    // Start the transcoding
    processor.start();
  }


  /****************************************************************
   * Alternate constructor: source and destination specified as
   * Strings, and no rate provided (hence rate of 1.0)
   ****************************************************************/
  Location2Location(String sourceName, String destinationName,
      Format[] outputFormats, ContentDescriptor outputContainer) {

    this(new MediaLocator(sourceName), new MediaLocator(destinationName),
      outputFormats, outputContainer);
  }


  /****************************************************************
   * Alternate constructor: No rate specified therefore rate of 1.0
   ****************************************************************/
```

LISTING 8.13   Continued

```java
Location2Location(MediaLocator sourceLocation,
    MediaLocator destinationLocation, Format[] outputFormats,
    ContentDescriptor outputContainer) {

  this(sourceLocation,destinationLocation,outputFormats,outputContainer,1.0f);
}


/****************************************************************
 * Alternate constructor: source and destination specified as
 * Strings.
 ****************************************************************/
Location2Location(String sourceName, String destinationName,
    Format[] outputFormats, ContentDescriptor outputContainer,
    double rate) {

  this(new MediaLocator(sourceName), new MediaLocator(destinationName),
    outputFormats, outputContainer, rate);
}


/****************************************************************
 * Respond to events from the Processor performing the transcoding.
 * If its task is completed (end of media) close it down. If there
 * is an error close it down and mark the process as FAILED.
 ****************************************************************/
public synchronized void controllerUpdate(ControllerEvent e) {

  if (state==FAILED)
    return;

  // Transcoding complete.
  if (e instanceof StopEvent) {
    processor.removeControllerListener(this);
    processor.close();
    if (state==TRANSLATING)
      state = TRANSFERRING;
  }
  // Transcoding failed.
  else if (e instanceof ControllerErrorEvent) {
    processor.removeControllerListener(this);
    processor.close();
```

LISTING 8.13   Continued

```
    state = FAILED;
  }
}



/*************************************************************
 * Initiate the transfer through a DataSink to the destination
 * and wait (block) until the process is complete (or failed)
 * or the supplied number of milliseconds timeout has passed.
 * The method returns the total amount of time it blocked.
 *************************************************************/
public int transfer(int timeOut) {

  // Can't initiate: Processor already failed to transcode
  ///////////////////////////////////////////////////////
  if (state==FAILED)
    return -1;

  // Start the DataSink
  ////////////////////////
  try {
    sink.open();
    sink.start();
   }
  catch (Exception e) {
    state = FAILED;
    return -1;
  }
  if (state==TRANSLATING)
    state = TRANSFERRING;
  if (timeOut<=0)
    return timeOut;

  // Wait till the process is complete, failed, or the
  // prescribed time has passed.
  ///////////////////////////////////////////////////////
  int waited = 0;
  while (state!=FAILED && state!=FINISHED && waited<timeOut) {
    try { Thread.sleep(WAIT_PERIOD); }
    catch (InterruptedException ie) { }
    waited += WAIT_PERIOD;
  }
```

LISTING 8.13   Continued

```java
    return waited;
}


/*****************************************************
 * Initiate the transfer through a DataSink to the
 * destination but return immediately to the caller.
 *****************************************************/
public void transfer() {

    transfer(-1);
}


/*****************************************************
 * Determine the object's current state. Returns one
 * of the class constants.
 *****************************************************/
public int getState() {

    return state;
}


/*****************************************************
 * Returns the object's state as a String. A more
 * user friendly version of getState().
 *****************************************************/
public String getStateName() {

    return STATE_NAMES[state];
}


/*****************************************************
 * Obtain the rate being used for the process. This
 * is often 1, despite what the user may have supplied
 * as Clocks (hence Processors) don't have to support
 * any other rate than 1 (and will default to that).
 *****************************************************/
public float getRate() {

    return translationRate;
}


/*****************************************************
```

LISTING 8.13   Continued

```
 * Set the time at which media processing will stop.
 * Specification is in media time. This means only
 * the first "when" amount of the media will be
 * transferred.
 ****************************************************/
public void setStopTime(Time when) {

  if (processor!=null)
    processor.setStopTime(when);
}


/****************************************************
 * Stop the processing and hence transfer. This
 * gives user control over the duration of a
 * transfer. It could be started with the transfer()
 * call and after a specified period stop() could
 * be called.
 ****************************************************/
public void stop() {

  if (processor!=null)
    processor.stop();
}
}
```

As a means of illustrating how the Location2Location class might be employed, the simple example StaticTranscode found in Listing 8.14 is provided. The class provides no user inter-action, performing the same task each time. That task is to transcode two media files into two others. The first media is a short piece of audio (someone playing an electric guitar) that is transcoded from linear, wave format into MP3. The second media is a movie consisting of both audio (GSM format) and video (Indeo 5.0 format) in a Quicktime meta-format, which is transcoded into AVI meta-format with linear audio and Cinepak video. Users wanting to per-form transcoding could use StaticTranscode as a starting template, modifying filenames and formats appropriately. Alternatively, for one-off tasks, JMStudio could be used interactively.

As you can see by viewing the source, employing the Location2Location class requires the prior construction of Format and ContentDescriptor objects that detail the format for the transcoding that will occur.

StaticTranscode is a trivial example, simply illustrating how Location2Location might be used. However it is relatively easy to write applications that build on top of the functionality provided by Location2Location. For example, an audio ripper (or its inverse)—a program that converts CD audio to MP3—could easily be written so that given a directory, it processes all files found there and converts them into MP3.

Listing 8.14   The `StaticTranscode` Class, a Simple Example of How the `Location2Location` Class Might Be Employed

```
import javax.media.*;
import javax.media.protocol.*;
import javax.media.format.*;

/*****************************************************************
* Simple example to show the Location2Location class in action.
* The Location2Location class transfer media from one location to
* another performing any requested tanscoding (format changes)
* at the same time.
*
* The class is used twice. Once to transform a short wave audio
* file of an electric guitar (guitar.wav) into MP3 format.
* The second example converts of Quicktime version of the example
* video from chapter 7, encoded with the Indeo 5.o codec and
* GSM audio into an AVI version with Cinepak codec for the video
* and linear encoding for the audio.
*****************************************************************/
public class StaticTranscode {

public static void main(String[] args) {
   String   src;
   String   dest;
   Format[]  formats;
   ContentDescriptor container;
   int      waited;
   Location2Location dupe;

   ///////////////////////////////////////////////////////////////
   // Transcode a wave audio file into an MP3 file, transferring it
   // to a new location (dest) at the same time.
   ///////////////////////////////////////////////////////////////
   src = "file://d:\\jmf\\book\\media\\guitar.wav";
   dest = "file://d:\\jmf\\book\\media\\guitar.mp3";
   formats = new Format[1];
   formats[0] = new AudioFormat(AudioFormat.MPEGLAYER3);
   container = new FileTypeDescriptor(FileTypeDescriptor.MPEG_AUDIO);

   dupe = new Location2Location(src,dest,formats,container);
   System.out.println("After creation, state = " + dupe.getStateName());
```

LISTING 8.14 Continued

```
waited = dupe.transfer(10000);
System.out.println("Waited " + waited + " milliseconds. State is"
+ " now " +dupe.getStateName());


/////////////////////////////////////////////////////////////////
// Transcode a Quicktime version of a movie into an AVI version.
// The video codec is altered from Indeo5.0 to Cinepak,the audio
// track is transcoded from GSM to linear, and is result is saved
// as a file "qaz.avi".
/////////////////////////////////////////////////////////////////
src = "file://d:\\jmf\\book\\media\\videoexample\\iv50_320x240.mov";
dest = "file://d:\\jmf\\book\\media\\qaz.avi";
formats = new Format[2];
formats[0] = new VideoFormat(VideoFormat.CINEPAK);
formats[1] = new AudioFormat(AudioFormat.LINEAR);
container = new FileTypeDescriptor(FileTypeDescriptor.MSVIDEO);
dupe = new Location2Location(src,dest,formats,container,5.0f);
System.out.println("After creation, state = " + dupe.getStateName());
waited = dupe.transfer(Location2Location.INDEFINITE);
int state = dupe.getState();
System.out.println("Waited " + (waited/1000) + " seconds. State is"
    + " now " +dupe.getStateName() + ", rate was " + dupe.getRate());
System.exit(0);
}
}
```

The output of `StaticTranscode` is shown in Listing 8.15. As you can see, the audio file, 6.5 seconds in length, took just over 2.5 seconds to transcode and save. On the other hand, the movie of less than 1 minute (57 seconds) took more than 10 minutes to transcode and save. This was on a Pentium IV system with 256MB of RAM. Clearly these processes can take a long time to complete. Furthermore, the actual time required varies depending on other factors such as system load at the time. Running the same program again saw variations of as much as 20% in time to complete.

LISTING 8.15 Output of the `StaticTranscode` Program Showing Time Needed to Transcode and Sink the Media

```
After creation, state = 1
Waited 2660 milliseconds. State is now 4
After creation, state = 1
Waited 618 seconds. State is now 4, rate was 1.0
```

Media Capture

One of the more exciting aspects of the JMF, particularly when combined with transmission over a network as discussed in Chapter 9, is the ability to capture media directly from devices attached to the computer. The stereotypical examples of these devices are microphones, video cameras, and video capture boards.

Thus it is possible to directly record sound or video through the appropriate hardware connected to the PC and either save that to a file, play it back, process and transcode it, or even transmit it.

The JMF model of media capture sees the capture device as a DataSource. With the appropriate initialization steps, detailed later, media capture falls within the precincts of playing or processing media: When a DataSource has been found, it can be handled in any way.

Several classes have a role to play in media capture. They are as follows:

> CaptureDeviceManager—Manages the central registry of capture devices known to the JMF. Provides a means for querying and updating that registry as well as a means of obtaining a particular capture device's information (CaptureDeviceInfo).

> CaptureDeviceInfo—Information about a particular capture device, including the Formats it supports. Most importantly, it has a MediaLocator describing the device from which a DataSource can be created (hence the media obtained).

> CaptureDevice—A further specialization of the DataSource produced by a capture device to include appropriate methods for control of the device and its output.

The process of media capture via the JMF tends to proceed as follows:

1. Obtain a CaptureDeviceInfo object for the device from which media will be captured (typically obtained by querying CaptureDeviceManager).

2. Get the CaptureDeviceInfo's MediaLocator.

3. Create a DataSource from the MediaLocator.

4. Create a Player or Processor using the Manager class and the DataSource from the previous step.

5. Perform any necessary configuration or programming (for example, Processor programming or creation of DataSink).

6. Start the Player or Processor.

The following subsections provide more details of the process and classes involved.

JMFRegistry and JMStudio

It is worth mentioning that the two utilities, JMFRegistry and JMStudio that come as part of the JMF 2.1.1 distribution, provide direct control over and information regarding capture.

The JMFRegistry application provides, among other features, the ability to query what capture devices are available on a system. Among the most important information that JMFRegistry provides is the name of the device as it is known to the JMF. This is the name by which the user can obtain that device from the DeviceManager. Similarly, if a new capture device is added to a system, the JMFRegistry can be used to update the list of capture devices known to the JMF. The JMFRegistry is simply invoked as Java JMFRegistry at the command prompt.

Media capture can be performed directly through the JMStudio application. This is often convenient as an alternative to writing code for one-off capture of audio and video. Capture is performed through the Capture option on the File menu, which presents all known capture devices. Such media can also be exported (saved).

CaptureDeviceManager

The CaptureDeviceManager class is the first stop in writing JMF code that captures media. This is because the class is the means by which the chain that leads to a DataSource coming from a capture device is started. The CaptureDeviceManager can return a DeviceInfo object corresponding to a named capture device or all devices that support a particular Format.

Figure 8.35 shows the methods of CaptureDeviceManager. Similar to the other manager classes, all methods are static (invoked using the classname). Of the five methods, three—addDevice(), removeDevice(), and commit()—are concerned with updating JMF's knowledge of connected capture devices. Although the methods provide automatic (program) control over the addition or removal of a device, the same operations can be performed easily through the JMRegistry application.

8

CONTROLLING AND
PROCESSING
MEDIA WITH JMF

CaptureDeviceManager Class

```
static boolean addDevice(DeviceInfo newDeviceInfo)
static void commit()
static CaptureDeviceInfo getDevice(String deviceName)
static Vector getDeviceList(Format mustSupport)
static boolean removeDevice(DeviceInfo toRemove)
```

FIGURE 8.35
The CaptureDeviceManager *class.*

The getDevice() and getDeviceList() methods are the two key methods of the class in terms of initiating a capture task. Given the name of a capture device as a String, getDevice() returns a CaptureDeviceInfo object that matches the device. CaptureDevices have names such as "vfw:Logitech USB Video Camera:0" or "DirectSoundCapture", and must be known to the user. The method returns `null` if the matching capture device couldn't be found.

The alternative means of initiating capture is to specify the desired `Format` of the captured data and find a capture device that can produce data in that format. This capability is provided through the `getDeviceList()` method. The method returns a `Vector` of `CaptureDeviceInfo` objects that support the `Format` in question. Passing a `null` `Format` object to the method results in it returning a `CaptureDeviceInfo` object for all capture devices known. This feature is used by the simple `ListCaptureDevices` application found in Listing 8.15, as well as on the book's companion Web site. The application simply prints a list of all capture devices on the system that the JMF is aware of.

LISTING 8.15 The `ListCaptureDevices` Application that Lists All Capture Devices on the Current Machine

```java
import javax.media.*;
import java.util.*;

/****************************************************************
 * Simple application to list all capture devices currently
 * known to the JMF. The CaptureDeviceManager is queried as to
 * known devices and its output printed to the screen.
 *
 * @author Michael (Spike) Barlow
 ****************************************************************/
public class ListCaptureDevices {

public static void main(String[] args) {

    ////////////////////////////////////////////////////////////
    // Query CaptureDeviceManager about ANY capture devices (null
    // format)
    Vector info = CaptureDeviceManager.getDeviceList(null);
    if (info==null)
      System.out.println("No Capture devices known to JMF");
    else {
      System.out.println("The following " + info.size() +
                " capture devices are known to the JMF");
      for (int i=0;i<info.size();i++)
        System.out.println("\t"+(CaptureDeviceInfo)info.elementAt(i));
    }
  }
}
```

CaptureDeviceInfo

The CaptureDeviceInfo class is the JMF mechanism for describing a capture device. It encapsulates the device's name, supported Formats, and a unique MediaLocator that can be used to source the data the device produces. Figure 8.36 shows the methods of the class.

CaptureDeviceInfo Class

```
CaptureDeviceInfo()
CaptureDeviceInfo(String name, MediaLocator locator, fomat[] supported)

boolean equals(Object obj)
Format[] getFormats()
MediaLocator getLocator()
String getName()
String toString()
```

FIGURE 8.36
The CaptureDeviceInfo *class.*

Although the class has constructors, these are for those third-party developers who are extending the JMF by writing drivers for a new device. The chief means of obtaining a CaptureDeviceInfo object is through the CaptureDeviceManager class with either the getDevice() or getDeviceList() methods.

The key method of CaptureDeviceInfo is getLocator(), which returns a MediaLocator for the device in question. Through the Manager class, that MediaLocator can then be used to create a DataSource—the data being captured by the device.

CaptureDevice

The CaptureDevice interface is a specialization of a DataSource that includes appropriate capture device functionality. This interface isn't typically employed by the programmer because its functionality is covered by the Processor or Player that is handling the captured media. However, the interface does provide the ability to control the Format of individual streams originating from the device as well as controls for starting, stopping, connecting, and disconnecting.

Audio or Video Capture with the SimpleRecorder Application

As an illustration of the process of audio or video capture, the SimpleRecorder application in Listing 8.16 (also on the book's companion Web site) is provided.

LISTING 8.16   The `SimpleRecorder` Application Illustrating the Media Capture Process

```java
import javax.media.*;
import javax.media.format.*;
import javax.media.protocol.*;
import java.util.*;

/**********************************************************************
 * A simple application to allow users to capture audio or video
 * through devices connected to the PC. Via command-line arguments
 * the user specifies whether audio (-a) or video (-v) capture,
 * the duration of the capture (-d) in seconds, and the file to
 * write the media to (-f).
 *
 * The application would be far more useful and versatile if it
 * provided control over the formats of the audio and video
 * captured as well as the content type of the output.
 *
 * The class searches for capture devices that support the
 * particular default track formats: linear for audio and
 * Cinepak for video. As a fall-back two device names are
 * hard-coded into the application as an example of how to
 * obtain DeviceInfo when a device's name is known. The user may
 * force the application to use these names by using the -k
 * (known devices) flag.
 *
 * The class is static but employs the earlier Location2Location
 * example to perform all the Processor and DataSink related work.
 * Thus the application chiefly involves CaptureDevice related
 * operations.
 *
 * @author Michael (Spike) Barlow
 **********************************************************************/
public class SimpleRecorder {

//////////////////////////////////////////////////////////////
// Names for the audio and video capture devices on the
// author's system. These will vary system to system but are
// only used as a fallback.
//////////////////////////////////////////////////////////////
private static final String AUDIO_DEVICE_NAME = "DirectSoundCapture";
private static final String VIDEO_DEVICE_NAME =
                            "vfw:Microsoft WDM Image Capture:0";

//////////////////////////////////////////////////////////////
// Default names for the files to write the output to for
```

LISTING 8.16 Continued

```
// the case where they are not supplie by the user.
//////////////////////////////////////////////////////////
private static final String DEFAULT_AUDIO_NAME =
                                "file://./captured.wav";
private static final String DEFAULT_VIDEO_NAME =
                                "file://./captured.avi";


/////////////////////////////////////////////
// Type of capture requested by the user.
/////////////////////////////////////////////
private static final String AUDIO = "audio";
private static final String VIDEO = "video";
private static final String BOTH = "audio and video";


//////////////////////////////////////////////////////////////////////
// The only audio and video formats that the particular application
// supports. A better program would allow user selection of formats
// but would grow past the small example size.
//////////////////////////////////////////////////////////////////////
private static final Format AUDIO_FORMAT =
                  new AudioFormat(AudioFormat.LINEAR);
private static final Format VIDEO_FORMAT =
                  new VideoFormat(VideoFormat.CINEPAK);


public static void main(String[] args) {

  ///////////////////////////////////////////////////////
  // Object to handle the processing and sinking of the
  // data captured from the device.
  ///////////////////////////////////////////////////////
  Location2Location capture;

  ///////////////////////////////////
  // Audio and video capture devices.
  ///////////////////////////////////
  CaptureDeviceInfo audioDevice = null;
  CaptureDeviceInfo videoDevice = null;

  ///////////////////////////////////////////////////////////
  // Capture device's "location" plus the name and location of
  // the destination.
  ///////////////////////////////////////////////////////////
  MediaLocator      captureLocation = null;
```

Listing 8.16   Continued

```
MediaLocator        destinationLocation;
String              destinationName = null;


//////////////////////////////////////////////////////////////
// Formats the Processor (in Location2Location) must match.
//////////////////////////////////////////////////////////////
Format[]            formats = new Format[1];


/////////////////////////////////////////////////
// Content type for an audio or video capture.
/////////////////////////////////////////////////
ContentDescriptor audioContainer = new
                ContentDescriptor(FileTypeDescriptor.WAVE);
ContentDescriptor videoContainer = new
                ContentDescriptor(FileTypeDescriptor.MSVIDEO);
ContentDescriptor container = null;


//////////////////////////////////////////////////////////////////
// Duration of recording (in seconds) and period to wait afterwards
//////////////////////////////////////////////////////////////////
double              duration = 10;
int                 waitFor = 0;


//////////////////////////
// Audio or video capture?
//////////////////////////
String              selected = AUDIO;


/////////////////////////////////////////////////////////
// All devices that support the format in question.
// A means of "ensuring" the program works on different
// machines with different capture devices.
/////////////////////////////////////////////////////////
Vector              devices;


/////////////////////////////////////////////////////////
// Whether to search for capture devices that support the
// format or use the devices whos names are already
// known to the application.
/////////////////////////////////////////////////////////
boolean             useKnownDevices = false;



/////////////////////////////////////////////////////////
// Process the command-line options as to audio or video,
```

LISTING 8.16   Continued

```java
// duration, and file to save to.
/////////////////////////////////////////////////////
for (int i=0;i<args.length;i++) {
  if (args[i].equals("-d")) {
    try { duration = (new Double(args[++i])).doubleValue(); }
    catch(NumberFormatException e) { }
  }
  else if (args[i].equals("-w")) {
    try { waitFor = Integer.parseInt(args[++i]); }
         catch(NumberFormatException e) { }
  }
  else if (args[i].equals("-a")) {
    selected = AUDIO;
  }
  else if (args[i].equals("-v")) {
    selected = VIDEO;
  }
  else if (args[i].equals("-b")) {
    selected = BOTH;
  }
  else if (args[i].equals("-f")) {
    destinationName = args[++i];
  }
  else if (args[i].equals("-k")) {
    useKnownDevices = true;
  }
  else if (args[i].equals("-h")) {
    System.out.println("Call as java SimpleRecorder [-a | -v | -b]"
       + " [-d duration] [-f file] [-k] [-w wait]");
    System.out.println("\t-a\tAudio\n\t-v\tVideo\n\t-b\tBoth "
       + "audio and video (system dependent)");
    System.out.println("\t-d\trecording Duration (seconds)");
    System.out.println("\t-f\tFile to save to\n\t-k\tuse Known"
       + " device names (don't search for devices)");
    System.out.println("\t-w\tWait the specified time (seconds)"
       + " before abandoning capture");
    System.out.println("Defaults: 10 seconds, audio, and "
      +"captured.wav or captured.avi, 4x recording duration wait");
    System.exit(0);
  }
}


/////////////////////////////////////////////////////////////////
// Perform setup for audio capture. Includes finding a suitable
```

LISTING 8.16   Continued

```java
// device, obatining its MediaLocator and setting the content
// type.
/////////////////////////////////////////////////////////////
if (selected.equals(AUDIO)) {
  devices = CaptureDeviceManager.getDeviceList(AUDIO_FORMAT);
  if (devices.size()>0 && !useKnownDevices)
    audioDevice = (CaptureDeviceInfo)devices.elementAt(0);
  else
    audioDevice =
        CaptureDeviceManager.getDevice(AUDIO_DEVICE_NAME);
  if (audioDevice==null) {
    System.out.println("Can't find suitable audio " +
        "device. Exiting");
    System.exit(1);
  }
  captureLocation = audioDevice.getLocator();
  formats[0] = AUDIO_FORMAT;
  if (destinationName==null)
    destinationName = DEFAULT_AUDIO_NAME;
  container = audioContainer;
}
/////////////////////////////////////////////////////////////
// Perform setup for video capture. Includes finding a suitable
// device, obatining its MediaLocator and setting the content
// type.
/////////////////////////////////////////////////////////////
else if (selected.equals(VIDEO)) {
  devices = CaptureDeviceManager.getDeviceList(VIDEO_FORMAT);
  if (devices.size()>0 && !useKnownDevices)
    videoDevice = (CaptureDeviceInfo)devices.elementAt(0);
  else
    videoDevice =
        CaptureDeviceManager.getDevice(VIDEO_DEVICE_NAME);
  if (videoDevice==null) {
    System.out.println("Can't find suitable video "
        + "device. Exiting");
    System.exit(1);
  }
  captureLocation = videoDevice.getLocator();
  formats[0] = VIDEO_FORMAT;
  if (destinationName==null)
    destinationName = DEFAULT_VIDEO_NAME;
  container = videoContainer;
}
```

LISTING 8.16 Continued

```
else if (selected.equals(BOTH)) {
  captureLocation = null;
  formats = new Format[2];
  formats[0] = AUDIO_FORMAT;
  formats[1] = VIDEO_FORMAT;
  container = videoContainer;
  if (destinationName==null)
    destinationName = DEFAULT_VIDEO_NAME;
}

//////////////////////////////////////////////////////////////////
// Perform all the necessary Processor and DataSink preparation via
// the Location2Location class.
//////////////////////////////////////////////////////////////////
destinationLocation = new MediaLocator(destinationName);
System.out.println("Configuring for capture. Please wait.");
capture = new Location2Location(captureLocation,
                  destinationLocation,formats,container,1.0);

//////////////////////////////////////////////////////////////////
// Start the recording and tell the user. Specify the length of the
// recording. Then wait around for up to 4-times the duration of
// recording (can take longer to sink/write the data so should wait
// a bit incase).
//////////////////////////////////////////////////////////////////
System.out.println("Started recording " + duration +
        " seconds of " + selected + " ...");
capture.setStopTime(new Time(duration));
if (waitFor==0)
  waitFor = (int)(4000*duration);
else
  waitFor *= 1000;
int waited = capture.transfer(waitFor);

//////////////////////////////////////////////////////////////
// Report on the success (or otherwise) of the recording.
//////////////////////////////////////////////////////////////
int state = capture.getState();
if (state==Location2Location.FINISHED)
  System.out.println(selected + " capture successful " +
    "in approximately " + ((int)((waited+500)/1000)) +
    " seconds. Data written to " + destinationName);
else if (state==Location2Location.FAILED)
  System.out.println(selected + " capture failed " +
```

LISTING 8.16   Continued

```
        "after approximately " + ((int)((waited+500)/1000)) +
        " seconds");
    else {
      System.out.println(selected + " capture still ongoing " +
        "after approximately " + ((int)((waited+500)/1000)) +
        " seconds");
      System.out.println("Process likely to have failed");
    }


    System.exit(0);
  }
}
```

The application allows the user to record audio or video (or simultaneous audio and video if the system supports it) from devices attached to the machine. Via command-line arguments, the user can specify audio (-a) or video (-v) capture, duration, and other settings. Listing 8.17 shows the help output of the program. Thus, for instance, to capture 20 seconds of video and save the output to a file 20seconds.avi, the program would be invoked as *java SimpleRecorder –v –d 20 –f file://20seconds.avi*. The application is restricted as to media output format—linear for audio and Cinepak for video—and content type—Wave for audio and AVI for video— simply to keep the example small. A more thorough and useful application would provide the user with the means of specifying the formats.

LISTING 8.17   The Help Output of the `SimpleRecorder` Application Showing Its Various Options

```
D:\JMF\Book\Code>java SimpleRecorder -h
Call as java SimpleRecorder [-a | -v | -b] [-d duration] [-f file]
  [-k] [-w wait]
          -a       Audio
          -v       Video
          -b       Both audio and video (system dependent)
          -d       recording Duration (seconds)
          -f       File to save to
          -k       use Known device names (don't search for devices)
          -w       Wait the specified time (seconds) before abandoning capture
Defaults: 10 seconds, audio, and captured.wav or captured.avi,
  4x recording duration wait
```

The application builds on the earlier `Location2Location` utility class example that took media in one location, transcoded it, and output it to another. Thus the `SimpleRecorder` class consists chiefly of the capture device related elements of the process (as well as user-interface), whereas all `Processor` and `DataSink` related work is dealt with by the `Location2Location` class.

Capture device setup is performed (regardless of audio or video) by querying the `CaptureDeviceManager` to obtain a list of devices that support the format in question. As a fallback position, hard-coded device names are also provided and can be used directly. You might want to use the earlier `ListCaptureDevices` application to ascertain what devices are available upon your machine and alter the source of `SimpleRecorder` (at the top of the class) where the device names are hard-coded. From the resulting `CaptureDeviceInfo` object, a `MediaLocator` can be obtained. Along with the necessary format information, this is sufficient to construct a `Location2Location` object that will perform the data transcoding and sinking.

Recording for a specified duration only is achieved through the `Location2Location` object's `setStopTime()` method. That sets the media stop time on the `Processor` object. This is necessary because microphone and video camera devices are push data sources—they will continue to supply data indefinitely. By setting the `Processor`'s stop time, it will automatically stop when the media time reaches that specified. That is detected by the `DataSink` of `Location2Location`, which subsequently closes itself.

As a final point, it is worth noting that capturing simultaneous audio and video is supported by `SimpleRecorder`, but it is system dependent on whether it will function correctly. (Does the system have a capture device that can provide audio and video?) One of the `ProcessorModel` constructors accepts specification of the output (an array of `Formats` and a `ContentDescriptor`) but no specification of the input `DataSource`. In this case, the JMF searches for a capture device(s) that can support those required formats. The `Location2Location` class is written in such a way that if it receives a null `MediaLocator` as a specification of the media source (to its constructor), it uses this second (no source information) constructor for `ProcessorModel`.

Summary

This chapter is the second of three that cover the control and processing of time-based media using the JMF. It is the core chapter on the JMF, covering the paradigms of control and processing of media both through illustration and discussion of the classes involved in the process. Chapter 7 serves as a general introduction to media and the JMF, whereas Chapter 9 covers the more specialized topics of streaming media and extending the JMF.

This chapter falls into three broad modules or meta-sections. The first module serves as the building block or framework on which understanding of the JMF is built as well as on which the processing and media capture approaches sit. This module covers key concepts of the JMF including the asynchronous `Controller` model of time and state, the central registry role of the manager classes, and the means of sourcing and sinking (outputting) media through the `DataSource` and `DataSink` classes.

The second module concerns the play and processing of media via the `Player` and `Processor` classes. Creation of these two classes is discussed as well as the very important concept of programming a `Processor` in order for it to achieve the desired task. `PlugIns` and their role in the processing chain are also discussed, and the module is illustrated with several examples.

The final module concerns capture of media via devices attached to the computer such as cameras or microphones. The relevant classes representing capture devices are discussed and where they fit within the processing framework already discussed. The module concludes with an illustrative example that shows how capture can be performed, and which utilizes one of the earlier examples.

RTP and Advanced Time-Based Media Topics

IN THIS CHAPTER

This is the third of three chapters concerning time-based media (typically sound and video) and Java (chiefly the *JMF: Java Media Framework*). Although the previous two chapters present an introduction to, and then details of, the JMF, this chapter covers more advanced topics in the field of time-based media processing in Java.

The greater portion of the chapter concerns the JMF in two areas. The first area is that of real-time streaming of media in the JMF via *RTP (Real-Time Transport Protocol)*. This enables applications such as video-conferencing or Web broadcasts to be written using the JMF. The section discusses the basics of RTP before covering the JMF classes that provide the necessary support. The second area concerns extending the JMF by implementing one or more of the various interfaces that are the true core of the JMF. Finally, indications of how the JMF can be connected to other Java APIs or platform features and classes are given.

However, a portion of the chapter doesn't concern the JMF at all, but other Java APIs concerned with time-based media. In particular, Java Sound—a core (as of Java 1.3) platform API dealing with sampled and MIDI sound—is briefly addressed. Integrating the JMF with other Java APIs also is covered before the chapter concludes by examining the future of the JMF.

What's RTP?

RTP is the Real-Time Transport Protocol, an Internet standard for the transport of real-time data (such as audio or video). RTP is defined by the Audio-Video Transport Working Group (AVT Working Group) of the Internet Engineering Task Force (IETF). The IETF (http://www.ietf.org) is an open community concerned with the evolution of the Internet and part of the larger Internet Society (ISOC), a professional membership society that oversees the issues that affect the Internet.

Given RTP's pedigree, which is designed by the Audio-Video Transport Working Group of arguably the Internet's chief standards body, it shouldn't be surprising at all that Sun has adopted RTP as the mechanism for streaming media within the JMF. Thus, to write applications such as video conferencing or even a player of broadcast media in the JMF requires the use of the RTP. But what is RTP, and where does it fit in the scheme of things? Those readers wanting to skip the details and simply write streaming media applications without knowledge of the JMF can do so for a time. As with much of the JMF, the user is provided with a very abstract model that shields him from much of the detail. In that case, readers should move through to the next section concerning RTP and the JMF. However, for those doing anything significant in the area of streaming media, it is likely that the material in this section will need to be visited at some time in the future.

RTP is described by an *RFC (Request for Comments)* of the IETF: RFC1889 (http://www. ietf.org/rfc/rfc1889.txt). Despite the innocuous name, RTP as described by the RFC is a standard that has been in its current form since early 1996 and is thus stable. The abstract of the RFC describes RTP as follows:

> RTP provides end-to-end network transport functions suitable for applications transmitting real-time data, such as audio, video, or simulation data, over multicast or unicast network services.

The introduction section of the document states:

> Applications typically run RTP on top of UDP to make use of its multiplexing and checksum services; both protocols contribute parts of the transport protocol functionality.

The services provided by the RTP include the identification of content type (that is, type and format of media) within a data packet, packet numbering, packet time stamping, and the ability to synchronize media streams from different sources. These are a minimal set of services that might be expected from a protocol providing media transport. Given that data might be delayed for different intervals, be corrupted, or be lost, it is possible for data packets to arrive out of order, not arrive, or that streams synchronized at the source site (for example, captured audio and video in a video-conference) arrive out of synch at the destination. Numbering, time stamps, and identification of content type provide the means for the detection of these problems and the ability for them to be rectified. However higher-level services such as connection negotiation or quality-of-service guarantees aren't part of RTP. RTP was designed to be lean and make the minimal demands on the bandwidth over which the media is being transported. This means that such services aren't the domain of the RTP.

IP and UDP

Figure 9.1 shows the typical case involving streaming media via the RTP, and the lower-level level protocols upon which it sits. Although RTP doesn't require *UDP (User Datagram Protocol)*, it is by far the most common protocol atop which RTP is implemented.

```
┌─────────────────────────────────────────┐
│       Streaming Media Applicatioons      │
├─────────────────────────────────────────┤
│       RTCP (RTP Control Protocol)        │
│ ........................................ │
│    RTP (Real-time Transport Protocol)    │
├─────────────────────────────────────────┤
│      UDP (User Datagram Protocol)        │
├─────────────────────────────────────────┤
│          IP (Internet Protocol)          │
└─────────────────────────────────────────┘
```

FIGURE 9.1

Most common layering of RTP atop UDP/IP to provide media streaming capabilities.

IP (Internet Protocol), which is more commonly heard as part of TCP/IP (Transmission Control Protocol atop Internet Protocol), is a low-level protocol by which most hosts on the Internet communicate with one another. It is a means by which hosts and routers ensure that data packets travel from source to destination host while hiding the details of the transmission medium. A number of protocols are built atop IP.

UDP is a lightweight communication protocol for the transportation of data packets. Inherently packet oriented, UDP is a low overhead protocol (as opposed to say TCP) because of the restricted services it provides. No guarantee is made of packet delivery; UDP provides effectively blind transmission of data. This means that packets can be lost, corrupted, or out-of-order, and one or both ends of the communication channel could be unaware of the fact. Hence, it isn't uncommon for higher-level protocols to be built atop UDP in order to capitalize on its efficiency while building in the possibility of error checking and recovery. RTP is such a protocol.

RTP and RTCP

RTP is augmented by a control protocol—*RTCP (RTP Control Protocol)*. The purpose of RTCP is to provide information about the quality of service of an RTP connection by identifying the participants and relevant information about each. Such information is sent by each participant and includes the number of packets received (if receiving) and sent (if sending), and other timing (clock) and synchronization information. The same RFC (`http://www/ietf.org/rfc/rfc1889.txt`) that describes RTP also describes RTCP.

All RTP packets are composed of two parts: a fixed header and the associated payload. The header includes a payload type (type of media), sequence number (packet number within the media sequence), time stamp, synchronization source, and contributing source (where the media originated from). The header can range in size from 12 bytes (the most common case of media originating from a single source) to 72 bytes (media originating from 16 different sources). The payload is the media data itself.

RTCP packets are compound (consisting of at least two, one of which is always a Source Description), but fall into one of five different types:

> Sender Report—Produced by those who have been sending packets recently. A Sender Report includes the total number of packets and bytes sent as well as synchronization (timing) information.

> Receiver's Report—Produced by those who have been receiving packets recently. Participants send a Receiver's Report packet for each participant they are receiving data from. Information includes number of packets lost, highest (packet) sequence number received, and a timestamp that can be used by the sender to estimate the lag/latency between sender and receiver.

Source Description—Description of the source of the report in canonical name; also possibly other information such as e-mail addresses or physical locations.

Bye—Sent by a participant who is leaving the session. Might include the reason for leaving.

Application Specific—A means for applications to define their own messaging across RTCP.

RTP Applications

RTP applications can be divided into clients, those that passively receive, and servers, those that actively transmit. Some, such as video-conferencing software, are both clients and servers—transmitting and receiving data.

The following terminology describes RTP as used by RTP applications:

RTP Session—An association between a group of applications, all communicating via RTP. A session is identified by a network address and a pair of ports—one for the RTP packets and one for the RTCP packets. Each media type has its own session. Hence for any number of applications participating in the stereotypical video conference (involving both audio and video), it will consist of two sessions—one for audio and one for video.

RTP Participant—An application taking part in an RTP Session.

RTP Port—An integer number used to differentiate between different applications on the same machine. Many common network services have a port associated with them.

Unicast, Multi-Unicast, Broadcast, and Multicast

IP supports a number of addressing schemes: unicast, broadcast, and multicast. The type of addressing scheme is indicated by the IP address of a packet. The three modes can be used in conjunction with RTP (and the JMF).

Unicast, also known as point-to-point, is by far the most common addressing scheme in use on the Internet today, and it describes the transmission of a packet (from a source) to a single address. Figure 9.2 is a schematic of this addressing scheme. In a time-based media context, this approach would be the most sensible for a simple two-person Internet phone scenario— two people transmitting directly to each other.

Multi-unicast is a simple expansion of unicast in that the transmitter sends duplicates of packets to a number of hosts, not just one. In multi-unicast, the packets are duplicated, so it has none of the bandwidth advantages of the multicast approach. Figure 9.3 is a schematic of this scheme. In Figure 9.3's scenario, the transmitter's data is duplicated and sent as two separate streams to the two recipients. A video-conferencing application between three or four participants might use multi-unicast: Each participant would know the address of the other members involved and transmit (audio and video streams) directly to each of those addresses.

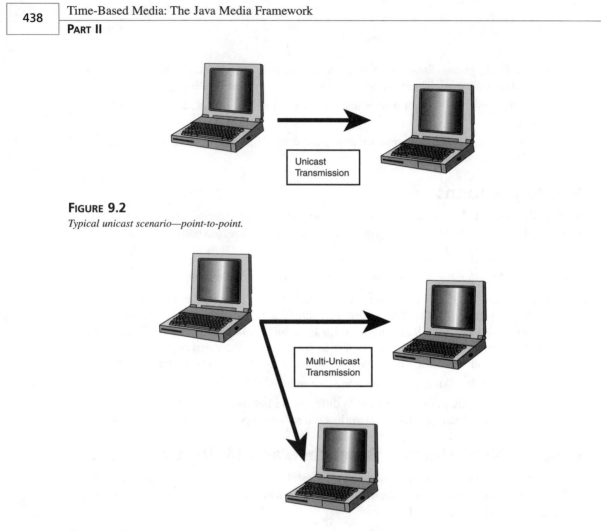

FIGURE 9.2

Typical unicast scenario—point-to-point.

FIGURE 9.3

A multi-unicast scenario with two recipients.

Broadcast describes the transmission of packets to all hosts on a particular subnet. Although it offers bandwidth savings (packets are not duplicated till necessary), it is limited by the constraint of a single subnet. Figure 9.4 is a schematic of this approach to addressing. As an example, broadcast might be used within an organization to send a video to all machines.

Multicast describes the most sophisticated and versatile means of addressing: one that is also of particular significance for many time-based media applications. Multicast is a receiver-centric scheme. The transmitter sends to a single address—that of a multicast session. Receivers join a session by indicating they want to listen to the address associated with a session. The network infrastructure (the routers) is then responsible for delivering data to all receivers (listeners). Figure 9.5 is a schematic of the approach. In this scenario, the transmitter sends to a multicast address. Receivers indicate that they want to listen to that address, and the network infrastructure (routers) is responsible for delivering the data.

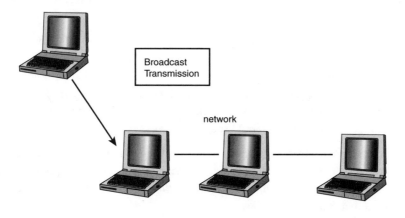

FIGURE 9.4

Typical Broadcast transmission—the data is sent to all machines on a particular subnet.

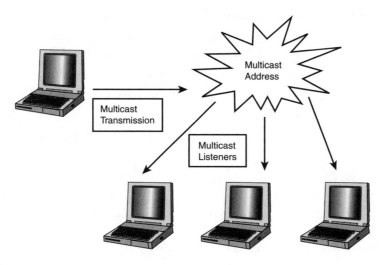

FIGURE 9.5

Typical multicast transmission scenario.

Multicasting is of particular significance to applications such as multi-participant video-conferencing for at least two reasons. First, each participant isn't required to maintain an up-to-date list of other participants—a difficult task because participants come and go for various reasons. Each participant simply transmits and listens to the session address. Second, a multicast scheme means that data packets aren't duplicated until necessary, implying considerable potential bandwidth savings. Only when the route to listeners to a session diverges are the packets duplicated. This is all supported by the network.

Certain network addresses, namely those in the range 224.0.0.0 to 239.255.255.255, are assigned by IANA (Internet Assigned Numbers Authority) for multicast applications. Addresses within that range are further subdivided into various assigned purposes. For instance, the addresses from 224.2.0.0 to 224.2.127.253 (inclusive) are currently assigned for multimedia conference calls. The complete list of multicast assigned numbers can be found at `http://www.iana.org/assignments/multicast-addresses`.

Multicasting is a complex topic, particularly in terms of how the routing is achieved. That is further complicated by the fact that not all older routers are capable of supporting multicast packets. To this end, *MBONE (the Internet Multicast Backbone)* was created as a group of networks and routers that supported multicast.

RTP with the JMF

Three packages within the JMF are concerned with RTP. They are

> `javax.media.rtp`—The top-level of the three packages dealing with RTP. It comprises 26 classes (most interfaces) dealing with streaming content with RTP.
>
> `javax.media.rtp.event`—A package of 23 events that might result when using RTP.
>
> `javax.media.rtp.rtcp`—A package of five classes (four of which are interfaces) defining usage of RTCP within the JMF.

Those applications employing the RTP directly will likely need to import classes from all three packages.

It is worth mentioning that as for `PlugIns` (discussed in Chapter 8), it isn't required that a JMF implementation support or provide the classes found in the preceding three packages. All current implementations of 2.1.1 (reference, Windows, Solaris, Linux) do so. However, it is possible that some future implementation of the JMF—possibly intended for a low-powered embedded system—won't support the RTP related classes.

One key aspect to understand about the RTP related classes of the JMF are that they are extensions to the JMF. They don't replace or supplant the core functionality of the JMF as found in the Player, Processor, `DataSource`, `DataSink`, and `Manager` (among others) classes. These remain unchanged and still lie at the heart of media handling. They fulfil the same role regardless of whether the media is streamed over the Internet or from the local filesystem.

In other words, a JMF program that plays RTP media will still employ a `Player` object obtained through the `Manager` class, as discussed in Chapter 8. Similarly, a JMF program transcoding RTP data it received (from a remote participant in an RTP session) to another format for saving to a local file will still use a `Processor`, `DataSource`, and `DataSink` object. A video-conferencing application will still use `CaptureDeviceInfo`, `Processor`, and `DataSource` objects (amongst others).

Indeed, as discussed in a following subsection, it is possible to play, process, and in general handle media originating from or destined for transport via RTP without employing a single class from the above three packages.

RTP Content Types and Formats

The full gamut of content types (media containers) and formats offered by the JMF aren't available for RTP. In the case of RTP, the choices are far more limited. Those users wanting to use RTP (in particular to transmit over RTP) must be aware of their choices and use only an RTP supported format and content type.

In the area of content type, although there are more than a dozen different `ContentDescriptors` (such as Wave, AVI, GSM, and QuickTime) within the JMF, there is only one for RTP media: `ContentDescriptor.RAW_RTP`. Thus the creation of a `ContentDescriptor` object for RTP always has the following form:

```
ContentDescriptor rtpContainer = new
        ContentDescriptor(ContentDescriptor.RAW_RTP);
```

The JMF support for the format of RTP data is also limited. Although it is possible for the user to extend the JMF by implementing the appropriate interfaces and thus adding further RTP-conversant codecs, the JMF currently provides four standard RTP-specific audio formats and three standard RTP-specific video formats.

The audio formats are known as

- `ULAW_RTP`
- `GSM_RTP`
- `DVI_RTP`
- `G723_RTP`

Whereas the video formats are known as

- `JPEG_RTP`
- `H261_RTP`
- `H263_RTP`

As their names imply, these formats use exactly the same compression schemes as their non-RTP versions. Thus a `JPEG_RTP` stream has been compressed with a JPEG codec. Construction of RTP-specific `Format` objects follows the same form as that for non-streaming media. For instance, use the following code to construct a `Format` object for RTP video data compressed with the H263 codec:

```
Format streamedVideoFormat = new Format(Format.H263_RTP);
```

Handling RTP Data Without RTP Classes

It is completely possible to play or process RTP originating or destined data without employing any of the classes found in `javax.media.rtp` or its two sub-packages. This is attributed to the versatility of the `Manager` and `MediaLocator` classes. Certain restrictions are inherent in this approach: In particular, only the first media stream in a session is available for processing or playing, and there is no means of monitoring the session itself.

Undoubtedly the simplest means of handling RTP data is through Sun's demonstration `JMStudio`. Although it doesn't provide a means for monitoring an RTP session (that requires coding as discussed in the following subsections), it is very simple to both play streaming media and to transmit it. The Open RTP Session option of the File menu allows the play of RTP transmitted data. The user simply enters the IP address and port to which the data is being sent. Similarly, the Transmit option of the File menu provides the user with a mechanism for transmitting either captured (from devices attached to the machine) audio, video, or media in a file over RTP. Thus, it is possible to carry out a video conference using the JMF, but without writing a line of code. Each user would run several instances of `JMStudio` simultaneously on his machine: one instance to capture and transmit his audio and video and another two instances for playing the other participant's media—one for audio and one for video.

Alternatively, it is possible to write code for handling RTP data, but without using the RTP-related classes of the JMF. It is quite possible to create a `MediaLocator` object for an RTP stream. This can then be used with `Manager`'s various create methods, namely `createProcessor()`, `createPlayer()`, `createDataSource()`, and `createDataSink()` in order to obtain the appropriate object for handling the RTP data.

In these cases, the `MediaLocator` constructor is passed a `String` of the form:

```
"rtp://address:port[:ssrc]/content-type/[ttl]"
```

address is an IP address, *port* is an integer port number, and *content-type* is a string such as video or audio. The *SSRC (Synchronizing Source)* and *TTL (Time to Live)* fields are optional. By default, SSRC is the originator of the media, and TTL, being the maximum number of router hops the packets can experience before they are not propagated, is 1.

The resulting MediaLocator object (assuming that it is non-null) can then be used in the appropriate create() method of Manager. For instance, the following code fragment is part of the creation of a Player to handle video data being broadcast to a multicast session with the address 224.123.111.101 and using port 4044:

```
try {
  MediaLocator rtpLocation = new
            MediaLocator("rtp://224.123.111.101:4044/video/");
  Player player = Manager.createPlayer(rtpLocation);
  Player.realize();
  :
```

Indeed, several of the example utility classes from the previous chapter can be used without alteration to transmit or play RTP data. The PlayerOfMedia GUI application is capable of playing streaming media just as it is capable of playing media from the local file system. In the dialog box provided, the user simply enters a suitable RTP locator string, such as the one found in the preceding example, and a player will be created for the media.

The MediaStatistics utility that reports on the format of a specified media can equally report on an RTP stream.

The Location2Location utility that takes media from one specified location, performs any prescribed transcoding, and then sinks the media to another specified location can be used to handle RTP data in a number of ways. The input location might specify an RTP stream; in which case, that received stream could be transcoded and then saved to a file, for instance. If the output location specifies an RTP stream, Location2Location acts as a transmitter, streaming media out using the specified address. If both input and output locations describe RTP streams, Location2Location acts as a kind of re-transmitter: receiving a stream, possibly performing some transcoding, and retransmitting that transcoded stream.

Even the SimpleRecorder application, which captures audio or video from devices (that is, microphones, Webcams, and so on) attached to the machine, could be modified in a quite straightforward manner so that it transmits the captured data as an RTP stream. Half of the capability already exists in that SimpleRecorder allows the user to specify the destination of the captured media with the -f flag. However, the program is currently hard-coded as to content type (Wave and AVI) and formats that it uses for audio (Linear) and video (Cinepak). If this was altered so that it supported the RTP content type and formats, SimpleRecorder could transmit its captured media in a format that it could be played by another application (for example, PlayerOfMedia).

Using the RTP Classes of JMF

Given the previous section's discussion of handling streaming RTP media without the RTP classes of the JMF, it might appear that the RTP classes are superfluous at best. As with other

9

RTP AND
ADVANCED
TIME-BASED
MEDIA TOPICS

matters concerning the JMF, it is a matter of the level of control and sophistication of the required application. Playing, sending, and transcoding a stream are all possible without recourse to the RTP-related classes of the JMF. However, user control is limited to functionality within those spheres.

Among the abilities provided by the RTP-specific classes are the following:

- Managing sessions, participants, and media streams (for example, starting, finishing, adding, and so on)
- Monitoring (through listener interfaces) of RTP events (for example, new participants joining the session)
- Gathering and generating statistics (for example, quality of connection)

In particular, the first and second set of capabilities are highly desirable for applications such as a multiway video-conferencing application in which participants can arrive and leave at different times, employ different coding schemes, and have different qualities of connection to the other participants. Automating control for these scenarios almost requires an automated system that can monitor and respond to the dynamic events across the lifetime of the session.

The central class in an implementation handling RTP data, and explicitly acknowledging that fact in order to maximize control is the RTPManager. As shown in Figures 9.6 (playback of media stream) and 9.7 (transmission of captured video), an RTPManager object effectively acts as an intermediary or shield between the JMF objects handling the media (for example, Player, or Processor) and the protocol and session details.

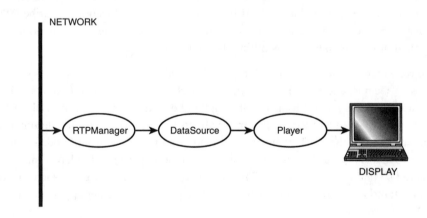

FIGURE 9.6

RTPManager *as intermediary when receiving streaming media.*

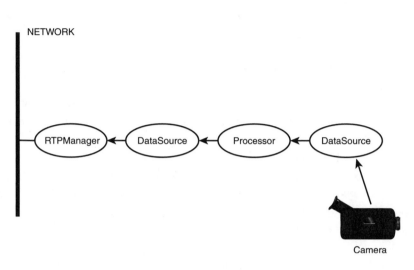

NETWORK

RTPManager ← DataSource ← Processor ← DataSource

Camera

FIGURE 9.7

RTPmanager *as intermediary in the transmission of captured media.*

RTPManager is a new class as of JMF 2.1.1 and supersedes the depreciated SessionManager
interface. Older examples can still be found that use SessionManager rather than RTPManager.
RTPManager provides a uniform interface and method set regardless of whether a unicast,
multi-unicast, or multicast session is being managed—something that SessionManager didn't
provide.

However, RTPManager isn't the only class of relevance to handle RTP sessions. The following
list summarizes the most important:

    InetAddress—Java's representation of an internet address. Part of the java.net package.
    Needed to create session addresses.

    LocalParticipant—The participant (listed next) that is also local to the machine. There
    is only one LocalParticipant: The rest are all remote.

    Participant—An application sending or receiving streams within the session.

    ReceiveStream—An interface representing a received stream of data within an RTP ses-
    sion. Each received stream in a session is represented by a separate ReceiveStream
    object.

    ReceiveStreamListener—An interface that a class can implement in order to receive
    events associated with a ReceiveStream (such as timeouts, byes, a new stream, and
    so on).

    RemoteListener—An interface that a class can implement in order to be informed about
    events generated by remote participants in a session (for example, the availability of
    sender or receiver reports or a name space collision).

9

RTP AND
ADVANCED
TIME-BASED
MEDIA TOPICS

RemoteParticipant—A participant in an RTP session that isn't on the same host (not local) as the RTPManager.

RTPControl—An interface allowing the control of an RTP DataSource object as well as a means of obtaining statistics about said DataSource.

RTPManager—A central class in managing an RTP session: an RTPManager object exists for each RTP session. Capable of creating sessions, streams, adding new participants, and so on.

RTPStream—Superclass of SendStream and ReceiveStream.

SendStream—An interface representing a sent (sending) stream of data within an RTP session. Each sending stream in a session is represented by a separate SendStream object.

SendStreamListener—An interface that a class can implement in order to receive events associated with a SendStream (such as timeouts, payload changes, byes, a new stream, and so on).

SessionAddress—The encapsulation of an RTP session's address as an InetAddress and associated port(s). These objects represent the unicast or multicast addresses associated with participants in the session.

SessionListener—An interface that a class can implement in order to be informed of session wide (that is, not specific to a particular stream) events such as name collisions or the addition of a new participant.

RTPManager

As previously stated, the RTPManager class plays the central role in the management of an RTP session. Unlike the key management classes of the core JMF—such as Manager or CaptureDeviceManager, which are static classes—RTPManager is an abstract class. Instances of the class are created with the static newInstance() method, and each RTP session has its own associated RTPManager object. The following line of code shows the creation of an RTPManager object:

```
RTPManager sessionController = RTPManager.newInstance();
```

Managing an RTP session in which transmission is involved via an RTPManager object typically proceeds as follows:

1. Create an RTPManager object.

2. Initialize the RTPManager with the local host's address (or the multicast address if it is a multicast session).

3. For all targets to be sent to

   a. Create the target address as a SessionAddress.

   b. Add that SessionAddress as a target of the RTPManager.

4. Create a `SendStream` through the `RTPManager` for the `DataSource` to be output. `DataSource` must have appropriate format and content type—one supported for RTP.

5. Set up any listeners (for example, `SessionListener` or `SendStreamListener`).

6. Start the `SendStream`.

7. When the session is finished, perform the following:

   a. For each of the targets that were being sent to, remove them as targets of the `RTPManager` object.

   b. Dispose of the `RTPManager`.

Listing 9.1 and Listing 9.2 show the use of `RTPManager` to control an RTP session. In Listing 9.1, the video image captured from an appropriate device is multicast to two targets with the specified IP and port addresses. In Listing 9.2, a movie, stored as a file, has its video track multicast to a specified address. Neither are complete applications or classes, but they show the major steps in configuring the manager and starting the session.

Both listings share a number of common features that illustrate the basics of RTP session management. The listings differ chiefly in the configuration of the processor—one transmits H263 formatted video captured from a device, whereas the other transmits JPEG video transcoded from a file—and the setting of target addresses for the `RTPManager` object. For the unicast session, the `RTPManager` is initialized with the address of the host machine and has targets specified as the addresses of the machines (plus ports) to be transmitted to. On the other hand, for a multicast session, the `RTPManager` is both initialized with the multicast address and has its single target specified as that address.

LISTING 9.1   An `RTPManager` Object Handles a Multi-Unicast Session—Broadcasting Video Using H263 Format

```
//////////////////////////////////////////////////////////////////////////////
// Need to capture video and output it as H263 RTP stream. Thus need a
// Processor, which needs a ProcessorModel that specifies ContentDescriptor,
// formats and datasource (in this case implicit to be a capture device that
// can supply the format).
//////////////////////////////////////////////////////////////////////////////
ContentDescriptor rtpContainer = new
                    ContentDescriptor(ContentDescriptor.RAW_RTP);
VideoFormat rtpH263 = new VideoFormat(VideoFormat.H263_RTP);
Format[] formats = {rtpH263};
ProcessorModel captureNTranscodeModel = new
                    ProcessorModel(formats, rtpContainer);
```

LISTING 9.1   Continued

```
Processor captureNTranscodeProcessor =
                    Manager.createRealizedProcessor(captureNTranscodeModel);

///////////////////////////////////////////////////////////////////////////
// Listen to the Processor and also obtain its output DataSource so it
// can be used to create a SendStream.
///////////////////////////////////////////////////////////////////////////
captureNTranscodeProcessor.addControllerListener(this);
DataSource source = captureNTranscodeProcessor.getDataOutput();

///////////////////////////////////////////////////////////////////////////
// Create the RTPManager to handle the session, then initialise it by
// providing the address of the local machine (with whatever port
// is available.
///////////////////////////////////////////////////////////////////////////
RTPManager managerOfSession = RTPManager.newInstance();
SessionAddress hostAddress = new SessionAddress();
managerOfSession.initialise(hostAddress);

///////////////////////////////////////////////////////////////////////////
// Create addresses for the two recipients and add them as targets for
//   the RTPManager. Note that these are arbitrary addresses and a user
// would substitute the known (IP) address of their recipient(s).
///////////////////////////////////////////////////////////////////////////
InetAddress firstTargetIP = InetAddress.getByName("175.216.12.3");
SessionAddress firstTargetAddress = new SessionAddress(firstTargetIP,3000);
managerOfSession.addTarget(firstTargetAddress);

InetAddress secondTargetIP = InetAddress.getByName("131.236.21.177");
SessionAddress secondTargetAddress = new SessionAddress(secondTargetIP,3220);
managerOfSession.addTarget(secondTargetAddress);

///////////////////////////////////////////////////////////////////////////
// Listen for all types of events that might occur in relation to this
// session. This would require that the class possess the
// appropriate listener methods (not found in this code fragment).
///////////////////////////////////////////////////////////////////////////
managerOfSession.addSessionListener(this);
managerOfSession.addRemoteListener(this);
managerOfSession.addSendStreamListener(this);

///////////////////////////////////////////////////////////////////////////
// Create and start the stream of video data. The stream is created from the
// Processor's output DataSource, with the 1 argument to createSendStream
```

LISTING 9.1   Continued

```
// specifying that the first track (there should only be 1 for the DataSource
// anyway) be used as the stream.
////////////////////////////////////////////////////////////////////////
SendStream videoStream2Send = managerOfSession.createSendStream(source,1);
videoStream2Send.start();


////////////////////////////////////////////////////////////////////////
// When the transmission is over the targets should be removed (informed)
// and the resources acquired by the RTPManager released (via the
// dispose() call. Hence this fragment of code would be found in another
// portion of the class, such as in response to the user
// pressing a "Stop Transmission" button.
////////////////////////////////////////////////////////////////////////
managerOfSession.removeSessionListener(this);
managerOfSession.removeRemoteListener(this);
managerOfSession.removeSendStreamListener(this);
managerOfSession.removeTargets("Transmission Finished");
managerOfSession.dispose();
captureNTranscodeProcessor.stop();
captureNTranscodeProcessor.close();
```

LISTING 9.2   An RTPmanager Object Handles a Multicast Session—Multicasting a Movie Track to a Particular Address

```
////////////////////////////////////////////////////////////////////////
// Need to transcode a file and transmit as JPEG RTP stream. Thus need a
//  Processor, which needs a ProcessorModel that specifies ContentDescriptor,
// formats and also the location of the media (in a file) to transmit.
////////////////////////////////////////////////////////////////////////
MediaLocator fileLocation = new
                    MediaLocator(file://D:\\jmf\\book\\media\\ex1.mov");
ContentDescriptor rtpContainer = new
                    ContentDescriptor(ContentDescriptor.RAW_RTP);
VideoFormat rtpJPEG = new VideoFormat(VideoFormat.JPEG_RTP);
Format[] formats = {rtpJPEG};
ProcessorModel transcodeModel =  new
                        ProcessorModel(fileLocation, formats, rtpContainer);
Processor transcodeProcessor =  Manager.createRealizedProcessor(transcodeModel);


////////////////////////////////////////////////////////////////////////
// Listen to the Processor and also obtain its output DataSource so it
```

LISTING 9.2   Continued

```
// can be used to create a SendStream.
//////////////////////////////////////////////////////////////////
transcodeProcessor.addControllerListener(this);
DataSource source = transcodeProcessor.getDataOutput();


//////////////////////////////////////////////////////////////////////////
// Create the RTPManager to handle the session. As it is a multicast session the
// multicast session address is used both as the target and to initialise the
// manager. In this case the IP address 224.123.109.101 with ports 4056 and 4057
// has arbitrarily been selected as the multicast session address.
//////////////////////////////////////////////////////////////////////////
RTPManager managerOfSession = RTPManager.newInstance();

InetAddress multicastIP = InetAddress.getByName("224.123.109.101");
SessionAddress multicastAddress = new SessionAddress(multicastIP,4056);
managerOfSession.initialize(multicastAddress);
managerOfSession.addTarget(multicastAddress);


//////////////////////////////////////////////////////////////////////////
// Listen for all types of events that might occur in relation to this
// session. This would require that the class possess the appropriate listener
// methods (not found in this code fragment).
//////////////////////////////////////////////////////////////////////////
managerOfSession.addSessionListener(this);
managerOfSession.addRemoteListener(this);
managerOfSession.addSendStreamListener(this);


//////////////////////////////////////////////////////////////////////////
// Create and start the stream of video data. The stream is created from the
// Processor's output DataSource, with the 1 argument to createSendStream
// specifying that the first track (there should only be 1 for the DataSource
// anyway) be used as the stream.
//////////////////////////////////////////////////////////////////////////
SendStream videoStream2Send = managerOfSession.createSendStream(source,1);
videoStream2Send.start();


//////////////////////////////////////////////////////////////////////////
// When the transmission is over the target should be removed (informed) and the
// resources acquired by the RTPManager released (via the dispose() call). Hence
// this fragment of code would be found in another portion of the class, such as
// in response to a StopEvent from the Processor
//////////////////////////////////////////////////////////////////////////
managerOfSession.removeSessionListener(this);
```

LISTING 9.2   Continued

```
managerOfSession.removeRemoteListener(this);
managerOfSession.removeSendStreamListener(this);
managerOfSession.removeTarget(multicastAddress, "File Finished");
managerOfSession.dispose();
transcodeProcessor.stop();
transcodeProcessor.close();
```

Figure 9.8 shows the methods of RTPManager. As has already been stated and shown in Listings 9.1 and 9.2, RTPManager objects are created via the static newInstance() method.

RTPManager Class

```
void addFormat(Format format, int payload)
void addReceiveStreamListener(ReceiveStreamListener listener)
void addRemoteListener(RemoteListener listener)
void addSendStreamListener(SendStreamListener listener)
void addSessionListener(SessionListener listener)
void addTarget(SessionAddress targetAddress)
SendStream createSendStream(DataSource source, int trackIndex)
Vector getActiveParticipants()
Vector getAllParticipants()
GlobalReceptionStats getGlobalReceptionStats()
GlobalTransmissionStats getGlobalTransmissionStats()
LocalParticipant getLocalParticipant()
Vector getPassiveParticipants()
Vector getReceiveStreams()
Vector getRemoteParticipants()
Vector getRTPManagerList()
Vector getSendStreams()
void initialize(RTPConnector connector)
void initialize(SessionAddress localAddress)
void initialize(SessionAddress[] localAddresses,
        SourceDescription[] sourceDescription, double rtcpBandwidthFraction,
        double rtcpSenderBandwidthFraction, EncryptionInfo encryptionInfo)
static RTPManager newInstance()
void removeReceiveStreamListener(ReceiveStreamListener listener);
void removeRemoteListener(RemoteListener listener)
void removeSendStreamListener(SendStreamListener listener)
void removeSessionListener(SessionListener listener)
void removeTarget(SessionAddress targetAddress, String reason)
void removeTargets(String reason);
```

FIGURE 9.8

The RTPManager *class.*

After an RTPManager object has been obtained and the appropriate pre-configuration performed (such as obtaining a multicast or unicast address as well as a DataSource object), the RTPManager should be initialized with the initialize() method. As its name implies, the method initializes the session. It can only be called once. It can throw either an IOException or an `InvalidSessionAddressException`. There are three versions of the method. The most commonly used version accepts a `SessionAddress`, which is the address of the local host and the associated data and control ports for the session. If a `null SessionAddress` is passed, a default local address will be chosen. If the `RTPManager` subsequently specifies a multicast session address as a target, the local address specified with `initialize()` is ignored. The multi-argument version of `initialize()` allows finer control in terms of the percentage of bandwidth consumed by RTCP traffic and even the encryption (if any) employed. The third version accepts an `RTPConnector` object, which is used when RTP isn't travelling over UDP.

The `addTarget()` method is used to specify the target of an RTP session. For transmission, this target is an IP address and port pair to be transmitted to. For receipt, this target is an IP address port pair to be listened to. The method is passed a `SessionAddress` object that specifies the IP address and port. The method can throw either an `InvalidSessionAddressException` or an `IOException`.

The `addTarget()` method effectively opens a session, causing RTCP reports to be generated as well as appropriate `SessionEvents`. The method should only be called after the associated `RTPManager` object has been initialized, and before the creation of any streams on a session.

Multi-unicast sessions—one host transmitting the same media to more than one recipient, where that transmission is specifically directed to each recipient—are supported by the mechanism of making multiple `addTarget()` calls. For instance, if there were four recipients, four `addTarget()` calls would be made; each one using a `SessionAddress` object that specified the receiving application's address.

Just as targets can be added to a session, they can be removed either individually with `removeTarget()` or en masse with `removeTargets()`. Typically, these methods are employed as an RTP session is being terminated. Although `removeTarget()` might also be used mid-session in a multi-unicast scenario to stop transmission to an address that is no longer participating or perhaps reachable. Both methods accept a `String` argument, which is the reason that the local participant has quit the session. This is transported via RTCP. The `removeTarget()` method has as its first argument a `SessionAddress` object that matches a current target of the session. The method might throw an `InvalidSessionAddressException`.

The `dispose()` method should be called at the end of all RTP sessions. It releases all resources that the `RTPManager` object has acquired during its existence and prepares the object for garbage collection.

`RTPManager` objects manage streams of data that fall into two categories: `SendStreams` for media transmission and `ReceiveStreams` for media receipt. `SendStream` objects are created with the `createSendStream()` method. `ReceiveStream` objects are created automatically as a new stream is received. They can be obtained through the `NewReceiveStreamEvent` (see the next subsection), or all current ReceiveStream objects can be obtained with the getReceiveStreams() method of RTPManager.

The createSendStream() method creates a new SendStream from an existing DataSource object (such as the output of a Processor). This is a necessary and vital step if data is to be sent in an RTP session. The method accepts two arguments—the DataSource and a track (or stream) index. The track index parameter specifies which track (stream) of the DataSource to use in creating the SendStream. The first track has an index of 1, the second track has an index of 2, and so on. Although an index of 0 that specifies an RTP mixer operation is desired, all tracks of the DataSource should be mixed as a single stream. The method can throw an UnsupportedFormatException or an IOException.

The getReceiveStreams() method returns a Vector, where each element of the Vector is a ReceiveStream that the RTPManager has created as the result of detecting a new source of RTP data. There is generally less call to use this method because the newly created ReceiveStream objects can be obtained through methods of the event that informs of their creation (see next subsection). Obtaining a ReceiveStream object allows its associated DataSource to be obtained and hence a Processor, Player, or DataSink created for that received media.

Listeners—ReceiveStreamListener, RemoteListener, SendStreamListener, and SessionListener—associated with the RTP session managed by the RTPManager object are added and removed through a set of add and remove methods of the RTPManager object. Listeners are vital in providing the monitoring and control capabilities of the RTP session. There are four methods for adding a listener: addReceiveStreamListener(), addRemoteListener(), addSendStreamListener(), and addSessionListener(). Listeners are usually added once an RTPManager object has been initialized. Correspondingly, there are four methods for removing listeners from an RTP session: removeReceiveStreamListener(), removeRemoteListener(), removeSendStreamListener(), and removeSessionListener(). Listeners are usually removed at the end of an RTP session. RTP events and their associated listeners are discussed in greater detail in the following subsection.

The JMF represents participants in an RTP session by Participant objects— LocalParticipant and RemoteParticipant. An RTPManager object has several methods for determining the participants in the session it is managing. Those methods are

getActiveParticipants()—Those transmitting in the session

getAllParticipants()—All participants

getLocalParticipant()—The host participant who is also managing the session

getPassiveParticipants()—Those participating but not transmitting data

getRemoteParticipants()—All participants other than the local one

All methods except `getLocalParticipant()`, which returns a `LocalParticipant` object, return a `Vector` of `Participant` objects.

The final group of methods belonging to `RTPManager` pertain to session statistics. As their names indicate, the methods `getGlobalReceptionStats()` and `getGlobalTransmissionStats()` provide a means of obtaining transmission and reception statistics for the session. Session statistics are discussed further in a subsequent subsection.

RTP Events and Listeners

Four super classes of events, and their corresponding listeners, are defined with the JMF. They are

`SessionEvent/SessionListener`—Events that pertain to the session as a whole, such as a new Participant joining

`SendStreamEvent/SendStreamListener`—Changes in the streams that are being transmitted including a new stream, or a stream stopping

`ReceiveStreamEvent/ReceiveStreamListener`—Changes in the streams that are being received including a new stream, or a stream timing out

`RemoteEvent/RemoteListener`—Events that pertain to RTCP messages such as a new receiver or sender report being received

Each of the four events have subclasses that specialize in the information provided. For instance `SessionEvent` has two subclasses: `NewParticipantEvent`, and `LocalCollisionEvent`. All four events share the same parent class, `RTPEvent`, which is a subclass of `MediaEvent`. All events are found in the `javax.media.rtp.event` package.

RTP listeners—`SessionListener, SendStreamListener, ReceiveStreamListener`, and `RemoteListener`—are associated with an RTP session by means of the `RTPManager` object that is managing the session. The `RTPManager` class possesses four methods for adding and four methods for removing listeners—one for each type of listener. For instance, to add a `ReceiveStreamListener` for the session that the `RTPManager` object is managing, that object's `addReceiveStreamListener()` method is called.

All four listener interfaces—`SessionListener, SendStreamListener, ReceiveStreamListener`, and `RemoteListener`—define a single method `update()` that accepts an event of the type associated with the listener. That is, the `SessionListener` interface defines a single method `update(SessionEvent e)`, and so on for the other three with their events.

`SessionListener` objects receive two classes of events through their `update()` methods. The first is a `NewParticipantEvent`, indicating that a new participant has joined the session. The second one is a `LocalCollisionEvent`, indicating that the local host's SSRC has collided (is the same as) with that of another participant.

SendStreamListener objects receive five classes of events through their update() methods. A NewSendStreamEvent indicates that the local participant has just created a new SendStream. An ActiveSendStreamEvent indicates that data transfer has begun from the DataSource used to create the SendStream. An InactiveSendStreamEvent indicates that data transfer from the DataSource used to create the SendStream has stopped. A LocalPayloadChangeEvent indicates that the format of the SendStream has changed. A StreamClosedEvent indicates that the SendStream has closed. Listing 9.3 illustrates how an anonymous SendStreamListener class might terminate an RTP session when it detects that the stream being transmitted in the session is exhausted.

LISTING 9.3 An Anonymous SendStreamListener Terminates an RTP Session After Transmitted Data Is Exhausted

```
DataSource source = processor.getDataOutput();
RTPManager managerOfSession = RTPManager.newInstance();
SessionAddress hostAddress = new SessionAddress();
managerOfSession.initialise(hostAddress);

managerOfSession.addTarget(target1);
SendStream stream2Send =  managerOfSession.createSendStream(source,1);
managerOfSession.addSendStreamListener(new SendStreamListener() {
    public void update(SendStreamEvent e) {
        if (e instanceof InactiveSendStreamEvent) {
            managerOfSession.removeSendStreamListener(this);
            managerOfSession.removeTarget(target1,"Data Source exhausted");
            processor.close();
            managerOfSession.dispose();
        }
    }
}});
stream2Send.start();
```

ReceiveStreamListener objects receive seven classes of events through their update() methods. A NewReceiveStreamEvent indicates that the RTPManager object has just created a new ReceiveStream object for a new data source. An ActiveReceiveStreamEvent indicates that data transfer has begun. An InactiveReceiveStreamEvent indicates that data transfer has stopped. A TimeoutEvent indicates that data transfer has timed out. A RemotePlayloadChangeEvent indicates that the format of a stream has changed. In a StreamMappedEvent, the originating participant is discovered for an existing stream with a previously unknown origin. An ApplicationEvent indicates that a special RTCP application specific packet has been received.

The NewReceiveStreamEvent is particularly important because this is the means by which new streams, transmitted by a remote participant, are discovered. The newly received SendStream can then be obtained with the getReceiveStream() method (inherited from ReceiveStreamEvent). RTPStream's (the superclass of ReceiveStream) getDataSource() could then be used to obtain a DataSource object for the stream. With that DataSource, a Player, Processor, or DataSink object could then be created to handle the stream as desired. Listing 9.4 shows one way in which a newly received media stream might be handled through the creation of a Player object. The listing shows the use of an anonymous ReceiveStreamListener class that reacts to NewReceiveStreamsEvents by creating a realized Player object.

LISTING 9.4   A ReceiveStreamListener Creates a New Player Object in Response to a New Stream Being Received

```
Player player;
SessionAddress destination = new SessionAddress(…);
RTPManager managerOfSession = RTPManager.newInstance();
managerOfSession.addReceiveStreamListener(new ReceiveStreamListener() {
  public void update(ReceiveStreamEvent e) {
    if (e instanceof NewReceiveStreamEvent) {
      ReceiveStream received = e.getReceiveStream();
      if (received==null)
        return;
      DataSource source = received.getDataSource();
      if (source==null)
        return;
      player = Manager.createRealizedPlayer(source);
     // etc. such as listening to the Player, getting itws Components, etc.
    }
}});
SessionAddress hostAddress = new SessionAddress();
managerOfSession.initialise(hostAddress);
managerOfSeesion.setTarget(destination);
```

RemoteListener objects receive three classes of events through their update() method. A ReceiverReportEvent indicates that a ReceiverReport RTCP packet has been received. A SenderReportEvent indicates that a SenderReport RTCP packet has been received. A RemoteCollisionEvent indicates that two particpants' SSRC have collided (are the same).

RTP Streams

The JMF represents streams of data within an RTP session as RTPStream objects. RTPStream is an interface extended by two further interfaces—ReceiveStream for a stream of data being transmitted by and received from another participant, and SendStream for a stream that the current application (participant) is sending. Both types of RTPStream objects are associated with an RTP session and managed by an RTPManager object.

SendStream objects are created by an RTPManager object's createSendStream() method from a DataSource object. On the other hand, ReceiveStream objects are created automatically by an RTPManager object when a new stream of data is received by the manager.

SendStream objects are created by a broadcasting participant in an RTP session. After a SendStream has been created, it can be started with the start() method of the object. Starting s SendStream means that data will be transmitted over the network. Typically, transmitting programs then ignore the SendStream object until the transmission is completed—at which time, the object's close() method is called. Closing a SendStream frees all resources associated with that stream; hence, the method should always be called after the stream is no longer required. It is also possible to temporarily pause transmission of a stream by calling stop() on the SendStream object associated with that stream. This will also result in the DataSource that feeds the stream being stopped (via its stop() method). Hence data isn't lost simply because stop() was called.

ReceiveStream objects are created automatically by the RTPManager object managing a particular RTP session when a new stream of data is detected. User programs typically obtain ReceiveStream by calling the getReceiveStream() method of the NewReceiveStreamEvent that was posted to all ReceiveStreamListeners for the current session. Alternatively, RTPManager provides a method getReceiveStreams() that supplies all ReceiveStream objects being managed.

However, the ReceiveStream object is really an intermediary step in handling the received media. JMF media handlers such as Processors and Players, as well as other important objects such as DataSinks, all require a DataSource for their creation via the key Manager class. RTPStream has a method getDataSource() for obtaining the DataSource associated with a stream (whether ReceiveStream or SendStream). Hence, the standard approach when a new ReceiveStream is detected is to first obtain the ReceiveStream itself from the event and then use the stream to obtain the associated DataSource. That DataSource can then be employed to create the appropriate media handler or class. For instance, if the media was to be recorded, a DataSink would be created for that DataSource.

SessionAddress and InetAddress

RTP sessions are associated with one or, in the case of a multi-unicast session, multiple addresses. Those address(es) represent the participants within a session or the multicast address used for the session. For an RTP session, an address must consist of both an IP address and a port number. In fact, two are needed—one for data and one for control—but the control port defaults to be one greater than the data port if it isn't supplied. The JMF employs the SessionAddress class to represent an RTP address, whereas the InetAddress class of java.net (core platform) represents an IP address.

An InetAddress object is Java's standard means of representing an IP address (that is, usually a machine on the Internet). Hence an InetAddress object is used as a stepping stone in the construction of a SessionAddress object.

The InetAddress class doesn't possess a constructor but rather three static methods from which an InetAddress object can be obtained. Those are getLocalHost(), which returns the InetAddress object for the machine on which the program is running; getByName(), which passes a String representing a machine, (for instance "131.236.20.1" returns an InetAddress object for that named); and getAllByName(), which also accepts a String as an address name and returns an array of valid InetAddress objects for that name. Because RTP sessions are initialized with the local machine's address via RTPManager's initialize(), InetAddress.getLocalHost() is found commonly in JMF programs using RTP. Similarly, RTP broadcasting requires a specification of the address to broadcast to, so InetAddress.getByName() is also found commonly in JMF programs using RTP. Listing 9.5 shows both these methods being used.

SessionAddress objects are the JMF's means of specifying the addresses within an RTP session. In particular, SessionAddress objects are required to initialize an RTPManager, as well as set the (transmission) targets of that manager.

SessionAddress objects represent both an IP address and ports for data and control transmission. There are a number of constructors including no arguments (no functionality): an InetAddress and int data port (the most commonly used), two InetAddress and int port pairs (one for data and one for control), and one constructor that accepts an InetAddress, int data port, and int Time to Live. The most commonly used constructor for a SessionAddress object accepts an InetAddress, the data address, and an int port number—the port on which data is transmitted. The control port number defaults to one higher than the data port.

Listing 9.5 shows the initialization phase of an RTP session in which a stream of data will be sent from the local machine to that with the IP address "145.201.33.9" on port 3000. It shows the construction of two SessionAddress objects—one to initialize the session and one as the target of the session.

LISTING 9.5   Initialization Phase of an RTP Session

```
try {
  RTPManager managerOfSession = RTPManager.newInstance();
  managerOfSession.initialize(new
          SessionAddress(InetAddress.getLocalHost(),3000));
  managerOfSession.setTarget(new
          SessionAddress(InetAddress.getByName("145.201.33.9"),3000));
}
```

Participants

Participants within an RTP session—those receiving or transmitting streams of data—are represented by `Participant` objects within the JMF. The `RTPManager` object for a session keeps track of the participants within a session and provides methods for obtaining them:

Method	Participant Session Type
getActiveParticipants()	Transmitting
getPassiveParticipants()	Receiving only
getLocalParticipant()	Local
getRemoteParticipants()	Remote
getAllParticipants()	All participants

The `Participant` interface is extended by both `LocalParticipant` and `RemoteParticipant`. These subinterfaces are really placeholders though. They don't add any significant methods and, by their names, simply identify the participant types.

Knowing a participant in a session having a `Participant` object, it is possible to obtain `RTPStream` objects that represent all streams that the participant is transmitting. It is also possible to obtain all the most recent RTCP reports for that participant. These are the two most common uses of `Participant` objects—as a means to obtain the streams they are transmitting or as a means to obtain their most recent reports.

`Participant`'s `getStreams()` method returns a `Vector` of all streams that the participant is sending. If none are being sent by that participant, an empty `Vector` is returned. `Participant`'s `getReports()` method returns a `Vector` of `RTCPReport` objects. Those objects represent the most recent report for each stream the participant is sending or receiving.

Statistics

An important task when managing an RTP session is keeping track of the quality of the connection being experienced by all participants. Particularly clever management might, for instance, adjust the payload in response to changes in the network. If it becomes burdened, the frame rate or resolution might be dropped temporarily.

The RTCP provides a basic mechanism for this kind of monitoring through participants issuing periodic reports. In the JMF, RTCP reports are represented by the Report interface and its associated Feedback interface. Report objects are associated with a single participant and a stream they are transmitting or receiving. Session wide statistics are available as GlobalReceptionStats and GlobalTransmissionStats objects from the RTPManager object responsible for a session.

Report objects can be obtained for a Participant with the getReports() method, as well as from an RTPStream object with getSenderReport(). Report objects possess a getFeedbackReports() method that returns a Vector of Feedback objects. Feedback objects provide methods for determining the number of packets lost, inter-arrival jitter, and other properties of the stream (see the JMF API for full details). The Report interface is subclassed into SenderReport and ReceiverReport. ReceiverReport is an empty interface, but SenderReport provides a number of methods for determining sender specific properties such as timestamps and byte counts.

Less specific but generally more useful are the global statistics provided by an RTPManager object for the session it is managing. These global statistics come in the form of GlobalReceptionStats and GlobalTransmissionStats objects and are obtained with the getGlobalReceptionStats() and getGlobalTransmissionStats() methods, respectively.

A GlobalReceptionStats object provides a number of methods for determining the reception quality for the entire session. These include the number of packets that failed to be transmitted, the number of bad packets received, and the number of local collisions. The JMF API provides a complete listing. A GlobalTransmissionStats object provides six methods for determining the transmission quality of an entire session. These include knowing the total number of bytes sent, number of failed transmissions, and number of local and remote collisions.

The manager of an RTP session can use these objects to maintain a profile of the session it is managing. Report objects are generated at regular intervals and have associated events so that it is easy to keep track of their arrival. However, the choice of what to do with the available statistics is still in the jurisdiction of the user's code. Simply present them to the local participant (for example, as part of their GUI) so that they are aware of the session state, or carry out dynamic adjustment of the session in response to the statistics.

Receiving and Transmitting Streams with RTPManager

As detailed in an earlier subsection, RTPManager plays the key central role in controlling an RTP session. It oversees the session in a number of ways: specifying the session address(es), creating streams for transmission, and providing a means for specifying listeners to the various events the session generates.

The earlier subsection on RTPManager provides the rough outlines of an algorithm when RTPManager is being used to transmit data. The corresponding generic and minimum algorithm for the reception (only) case is as follows:

1. Create an RTPManager object.

2. Initialize the RTPManager with the local host's address (or the multicast address if it is a multicast session).

3. For the target address on which transmissions will be received:

   a. Create the target address as a SessionAddress.

   b. Add that SessionAddress as a target of the RTPManager.

4. Set up any listeners (for example, SessionListener or SendStreamListener). You must have a ReceiveStreamListener to detect new streams created by other participants.

5. While the session isn't finished (however finished is defined), react to any receive stream events. For a new receive stream, perform the following:

   a. Get the ReceiveStream

   b. Get its DataSource

   c. Handle the stream (such as creating a Player, Processor, or DataSink, setting up GUI controls for it, adding appropriate listeners, and so on)

6. Dispose of the RTPManager object.

For the often used example of an audio-video conference in which two or more parties participate using a single multicast session address, the approach is a combination of both the receive and transmit cases:

1. Create an RTPManager object.

2. Create a SessionAddress to represent the multi-cast session address.

3. Initialize the RTPManager with the multicast SessionAddress.

4. Set the target of the RTPManager to be the multicast address also.

5. Set up any listeners (for example, SessionListener or SendStreamListener). You must have a ReceiveStreamListener to detect new streams created by other participants.

6. For all streams to send (for example, an audio and a video stream):

   a. Obtain the DataSource (with appropriate format and content type: one supported for RTP).

   b. Create a SendStream object (through the RTPManager) for the DataSource.

9

RTP AND
ADVANCED
TIME-BASED
MEDIA TOPICS

      c. Start that `SendStream`.

      d. Add a `SendStreamListener` (if appropriate).

7. While the session isn't finished (however finished is defined):

      a. React to any receive stream events. For a new receive stream, perform the following:

         Get the `ReceiveStream`.

         Get its `DataSource`.

         Handle the stream (such as creating a `Player`, `Processor`, or `DataSink`, setting up GUI controls for it, adding appropriate listeners, and so on).

      b. React to any send stream events. For an inactive send stream, close and dispose of the `SendStream`.

8. While the session isn't finished (however finished is defined), react to any receive stream events. For a new receive stream, perform the following:

      a.   Get the `ReceiveStream`.

      b. Get its `DataSource`.

      c. Handle the stream (such as creating a `Player`, `Processor`, or `DataSink`, setting up GUI controls for it, adding appropriate listeners, and so on).

9. Dispose of the `RTPManager` object.

For both these algorithms, the `while` loops are a linear approximation of an event-driven program. The code doesn't poll for receive-stream or send-stream events, but simply adds itself as a listener for those events.

It is also feasible for a single program to employ several RTP sessions, and hence `RTPManager` objects, simultaneously. This isn't an uncommon technique used for managing multiple transmissions. For instance, video could be on one session, and audio could be on a separate session.

Sun's excellent `AVTransmit2` and `AVReceive2`, found on the JMF solutions site currently at `http://java.sun.com/products/java-media/jmf/2.1.1/solutions` follow such an approach. `AVTransmit2` is intended for transmitting on one or more RTP sessions, whereas `AVReceive2` is intended for receiving (where receipt entails the playing) of one or more streams on one or more sessions. Potentially, both employ multiple RTP sessions and hence multiple `RTPManager` objects. They are a good next step for those wanting to further understand RTP-based streaming. Indeed, not only can they be used out of the bag for AV conference, but they also serve as a good starting point for the reader wanting to implement his own specialized RTP-based application.

Cloning and Merging for Transmission

In two broadcast RTP scenarios, it is necessary to manipulate the DataSource that forms the basis of a SendStream before the SendStream object is created with the RTPManager object responsible for the RTP session.

In some multi-RTP session scenarios, the same media is being sent directly to different recipients as separate streams. For instance, a three-way AV transmission might be structured so that each pair of participants uses a different session—each participant is then transmitting the same data in two different sessions. In the JMF, a DataSource is single use. For instance, the same DataSource cannot be processed with a Processor and then played with a Player—although the output DataSource of the Processor could be played. This is true for SendStream creation also: A single DataSource can only be used to create a single SendStream. If multiple sessions are to employ the same DataSource to create SendStream objects, the original DataSource must be transformed into a cloneable DataSource and clones created for each SendStream to be created. The following listing is an example of when a DataSource is being used in two different sessions that are managed by two RTPManagers: manager1 and manager2.

```
RTPManager manager1 = RTPManager.newInstance();
RTPManager manager2 = RTPManager.newInstance();
DataSource source = Manager.createDataSource("file://example.wav");
     :          :          :
DataSource cloneable = Manager.createCloneableDataSource(source);
DataSource firstClone = cloneable.createClone();
SendStream firstStream = manager1.createSendStream(firstClone,1);
firstStream.start();
DataSource secondClone = cloneable.createClone();
SendStream secondStream = manager2.createSendStream(secondClone,1);
secondStream.start();
```

On the other hand, if data from separate sources (DataSource objects) is to be transmitted as a single stream, it is necessary to merge those DataSources into a single source before the associated SendStream is created. Also, when the SendStream object is created from the merged DataSource, the second parameter to createSendStream() should be the value of 0, indicating that all tracks (streams) of the DataSource should be mixed.

Buffering, Packet Size, and Jitter

Jitter is the phenomenon sometimes experienced when playing streaming media that isn't consistent in transmission rate (network delays) and reliability (packet loss). Jitter manifests as momentary pauses, drop outs, or jumps in the received (rendered) media.

The most useful technique in a receiver's arsenal is to use a buffer—a pool of data into which arriving media is added and from which media is taken to be rendered. The buffer acts to improve transmission inconsistencies, smoothing out differences in transmission rate. The larger a buffer, the greater the jitter that can be smoothed but also the longer the lag between receipt and rendering. For instance, a buffer size of 5 seconds implies that data currently being rendered was actually received 5 seconds ago. Large buffer sizes tend to adversely affect interactivity (for example, carrying out a conversation in which everything is delayed by a few extra seconds). Clearly there is a payoff or balance between smoothing jitter and loss of timely rendering of the data.

Another factor in the equation is the size of the packets transmitted. Larger packets use bandwidth more efficiently because less bandwidth is dedicated to packet headers. However the loss or damage of a large packet is more costly (and perhaps more likely) than that of a small packet in terms of the perceived quality of the media delivered. Losing a few milliseconds of speech might not even be noticed; on the other hand, one-half second lost could even affect comprehension of what was being said.

Both buffer size and packet size can be altered by JMF programs using RTP. There are few solid guidelines as to ideal values for each—they are both highly reliant on the particular scenario (bandwidth availability, network reliability, type of media being sent, and so on).

Receiving programs can alter the size of their buffer through the use of a `BufferControl` object. `BufferControl` is a `Control` interface and can be obtained for a `ReceiveStream` by first obtaining that `ReceiveStream` object's `DataSource` (using the `getDataSource()` method). The `DataSource`, which implements the `Controls` interface, can then be used to obtain the `BufferControl` object (using the `getControl()` method). `BufferControl` consists of six methods—the most important of which is `setBufferLength()`. This method accepts a single parameter of type long, being the length of the buffer in milliseconds.

Transmitting programs can alter the size of the packets they are transmitting if they can obtain a `PacketSizeControl` object for the transmission. `PacketSizeControl` is a `Control` object, but not all `Codecs` (`Processors`) expose `PacketSizeControl` objects through their `getControl()`/`getControls()` methods. The `PacketSizeControl` interface consists of two methods: `getPacketSize()` and `setPacketSize()`. The packet size is expressed as an int and is the maximum packet size output by the encoder.

Extending the JMF

Although the JMF provides support for an impressive number of formats (codecs), content types, and protocols, its coverage isn't complete. Although Sun's JMF team has pledged to support new open standard codecs and other similar advances in the area of time-based media, there will continue to be gaps between the coverage of the distributed JMF and the totality of time-based media. Several reasons for this difference are as follows:

Lag—Newer standards (for example, MPEG-4) can take some time to be implemented efficiency, tested fully, and brought into the JMF stable.

Proprietary—JMF is a free, open-standard with several complete implementations. The JMF couldn't be free and truly platform independent if it were encumbered by proprietary formats that have restrictions imposed on their use (for example, a fee per use of a particular codec).

Specialization—The JMF team at Sun has only limited resources, whereas the time-based media area is very large and continually advancing. Implementing more commonly used formats will clearly have higher priority than specialist niche formats, implying that specialist formats can take considerable time to appear.

Fortunately, the JMF is purposely built to be extended by users. Users can write their own codecs, multiplexers, demultiplexers, players, data sources, effects, and so on. These can then be seamlessly incorporated into the infrastructure that the JMF provides. They are then automatically (that is, through the central manager classes) available for subsequent usage.

Hence, for instance, an online community employing a particular form of time-based media might (over time) implement a `Codec`, `Multiplexer`, `Demultiplexer`, `Renderer`, and `DataSource` in support of that new format. These could then be seamlessly integrated into the JMF (and indeed distributed to the wider JMF-using community so that users also have automatic support for the new type of media), allowing full playing and processing of the media. Alternatively, a company might sell an AV conferencing system that incorporates custom hardware for compression and decompression but who's software side is implemented in the JMF. By writing custom `Player` and `Processor` (or `PlugIn`) classes, the company can use the JMF infrastructure and paradigm of `DataSources`, `Players`, and `Processors`. However those custom classes would ensure that the system employs the hardware component—reaping the benefits of speed offered by the hardware. Yet another example is that a library of digital effects for both audio and video might be maintained on some community site. These effects would be implementations of the `Effect` `PlugIn`. Users wanting to employ an effect could simply download it from the repository and add it to their JMF installation on their machine. Those wanting to add a new effect (for example, motion blur) could implement a suitable `Effect` and place it on the site for all to use.

Conceptually, the task of extending the JMF is relatively simple, although the programming task might not be trivial (for example, adding support for a new video codec). The process consists of three steps:

1. Implement the appropriate interface (for example, `DataSink` interface if writing a new `DataSink`).
2. Register the new class with the JMF.

3. Employ the new feature or support in the same manner as that for the prepackaged features (for example, create an instance of the new `DataSink` through the central `Manager` class).

By registering the new classes with the JMF, they effectively become added to the pool of resources that the manager classes (chiefly `Manager`) oversee. The manager is then aware of the new class (and the features it provides) and can create an instance of that class as needed. Figure 9.9 shows the three-step process. A correctly registered class is subsequently available through the `Manager` class for any application.

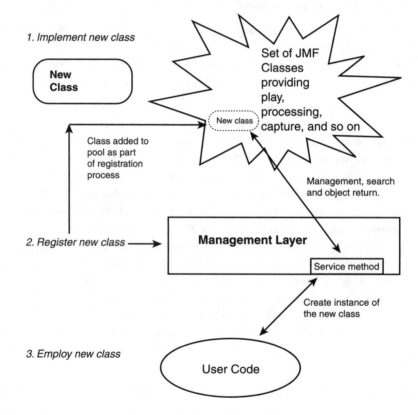

FIGURE 9.9

Registration of a new class that extends the JMF.

Before specifics are discussed, it is worth mentioning that extending the JMF isn't a trivial undertaking. The complexity does vary depending on the task at hand. However, a good understanding of the lower-level structures of the JMF (for example, `Buffer`, `Track`, `Format` and so on) is a virtual prerequisite for any such task. Those without such an understanding will no doubt acquire it if their extensions are successful.

Role of `Interfaces`

With the exception of `DataSource`, all the key infrastructure functional classes of the JMF employed repeatedly in user programs—`Player`, `Processor`, `DataSink`, and all the `PlugIns` (`Multiplexer`, `Demultiplexer`, `Codec`, `Effect`, and `Renderer`)—are all interfaces. Extending the JMF by adding another type of `Player` (for instance) is then a case of writing a class that implements the `Player` interface.

Implementing an interface is a case of writing a class that possesses all the methods that the interface lists. All methods must be present and must possess exactly the same signature as that in the interface. The *signature* of a method is its name, return type, visibility, argument numbers, type, and ordering.

No inheritance is involved in implementing an interface, so all code must be written by the user—there are no default versions for each method. On the other hand, the user class is free to extend another class (class, not interface) and thus inherit any methods and attributes it provides.

For instance an implementation of the `Codec` interface would have to possess 11 methods—five directly from the `Codec` interface along with four from the `PlugIn` interface that `Codec` extends, and two from the `Controls` interface that `Codec` also extends. Listing 9.6 shows an empty class that implements the `Codec` interface. It possesses all the necessary methods, but they are all *stubs* (empty methods that perform no useful task). As such, it is the bare skeleton of a real `Codec` implementation—it currently does nothing.

LISTING 9.6   An Empty Class that Implements the `Codec` Interface

```
import javax.media.*;

/***********************************************************
 * A stub or empty class with no functionality but which
 * shows the bare minimum methods a class must possess in
 * order to extend the Codec interface (to be a Codec).
 *
 * @author Spike Barlow
 ***********************************************************/
public class EmptyCodec implements Codec {

////////////////////////////////
// 5 methods of Codec itself
```

LISTING 9.6 Continued

```
//////////////////////////////
public Format[] getSupportedInputFormats() { return null; }

public Format[] getSupportedOutputFormats(Format in) { return null; }

public int process(Buffer in, Buffer out) {
  return PlugIn.INPUT_BUFFER_NOT_CONSUMED;
}

public Format setInputFormat(Format in) { return null; }

public Format setOutputFormat(Format out) { return null; }

////////////////////////////////////////////////
// The Controls interface that Codec extends
////////////////////////////////////////////////
public Object[] getControls() { return null; }

public Object getControl(String name) { return null; }

//////////////////////////////////////////////
// The PlugIn interface that Codec extends
//////////////////////////////////////////////

public void close() { }

public String getName() { return "EmptyCodec"; }

public void open() { }

public void reset() { }
}
```

Two minor catches exist for the unwary in implementing an interface. The first is that many interfaces are tiered, extending one or more other interfaces. If such an interface is being implemented, not only must its own methods be provided (written), but also all methods of interfaces that the interface in question extends. For instance, the Codec interface extends both Controls and PlugIn interfaces. Thus any class that implements Codec must possess at least 11 methods: five of Codec itself, four of PlugIn, and two of Controls. Second, the visibility of methods within the current version of the JMF API documentation often appear as though they are a package (that is, the method has no visibility modifier), whereas they are in fact public methods. Fixing these cases are simple however because the compiler will raise an error indicating that the interface specifies public visibility.

Registering the New Classes

For a new class such as a new `Player` to be automatically available for subsequent use, it must be registered with the JMF. In effect this registration process can be thought of as adding the new class to the database of classes that the JMF maintains. After that addition is made, the JMF is aware of the class. From then on, JMF will create instances of the class as appropriate (in response to user requirements).

Several of the manager classes have a role in registration of new classes:

> `PlugInManager`—New `PlugIns` (`Codecs`, `Renderers`, and so on) are added (registered) via the `PlugInManager`. They can also be removed via this class.
>
> `PackageManager`—New `MediaHandlers`—`Players`, `Processors`, `DataSource`, and `DataSink` classes—are registered via this class.
>
> `CaptureDeviceManager`—Newly attached capture devices are registered with the JMF via this class.

Registering a new class is a somewhat finicky process involving precise naming rules for the class (if a `MediaHandler`). It is also an uncommon process. Rather than writing code to register a new class, which is possible by making calls to the appropriate manager class, a new class can be registered interactively with the `JMFRegistry` program.

`JMFRegistry` is a GUI application that comes as part of the standard JMF distribution. Using menus, buttons, and text fields, it allows the user to interactively add or delete `PlugIns`, `CaptureDevices`, and packages to or from the database that the local implementation of the JMF maintains. Using `JMFRegistry` is simple (provided the user comprehends the JMF rules for naming) and is strongly recommended as an easier means for registering a new class. Sun maintains a short help document for `JMFRegistry`. It can be found at `http://java.sun.com/products/java-media/jmf/2.1.1/jmfregistry/jmfregistry.html`. Running `JMFRegistry` is as simple as `java JMFRegistry`.

The JMF employs naming rules as its means of keeping track of `MediaHandler` (`Player`, `Processor`, and `DataSink`) and `DataSource` classes, as well as knowing what they do. Classes are organized into packages, and the package name together with the classname indicates what the class does. The JMF employs these rules for all `MediaHandler` and `DataSink` classes that come as part of the JMF. If the same naming rules aren't followed for new `MediaHandler` classes, the `Manager` class will be unable to find the new class. Hence it will remain unavailable to the user.

These naming rules don't apply for `PlugIns`. Each `PlugIn` is added separately as a fully qualified classname.

However, for all `DataHandler` and `DataSource` classes, strict naming rules apply. All `DataHandler` classes (whether `Player`, `Processor`, or `DataSink`) must be called (has a class-name of) `Handler`, whereas all `DataSources` must be called (have a classname of) `DataSource`. This apparent confusion stemming from a profusion of `Handler` and `DataSource` classes is resolved by each of them existing in their own package. Hence the fully qualified name of the class uniquely differentiates it from all other classes.

Package names are split into several portions—an initial user assigned name followed by a fixed portion that reflects the type of class it is (`Processor`, `Player`, `DataSink`, and so on), followed by a name that reflects the protocol or content-type that the class supports. That is followed by the classname.

In particular,

- `Players` are named as `<content package-prefix>.media.content.<content-type>.Handler`

- `Processors` are named as `<content package-prefix>.media.processor.<content-type>.Handler`

- `DataSinks` are named as `<content package-prefix>.media.datasink.<protocol>.Handler`

- `DataSources` are named as `<protocol package-prefix>.media.protocol.<protocol>.DataSource`

The names *content package prefix* and *protocol package prefix* are Sun's terms for the user assigned prefix. The JMF provides for two categories of prefixes: one for `MediaHandlers` (content package prefix) and one for `DataSources` (protocol package prefix). For instance the prefixes that are part of the JMF 2.1.1 (Windows Performance) distribution are `javax`, `com.sun`, and `com.ibm`.

So, for instance, `com.sun.media.protocol.rtp.DataSource` is the name of the DataSource class provided by Sun, as part of the JMF, for RTP DataSources. A user writing her own processor for handling a new content type known as, for example, `cs9` and having selected a package prefix of `au.edu.adfa`, for instance, would name the class `au.edu.adfa.media.processor.cs9.Handler.java`.

Implementing `PlugIns`

Implementing a `PlugIn` is generally easier than writing a `DataSource` or `DataHandler`. Not only is the task generally smaller (which isn't always so), it doesn't require the strict class and package naming needed for `DataSources` and `DataHandlers`.

The discussion under the previous section concerning interfaces and Listing 9.6 provides an example of how implementing a Codec might be started. Similar approaches apply for Demultiplexers, Effects, Multiplexers, and Renderers.

Registering a new PlugIn with the JMF (either using JMFRegistry or PlugInManager directly) means that the PlugIn will henceforth be available to default Processors or those created with a ProcessorModel object.

It is possible to use a nonregistered PlugIn by creating an instance of the class directly and using the Processor object's TrackControl objects (one per track composing the media) to specify that the PlugIn be employed. This might, for instance, be used as a means of testing a PlugIn under development. However, in general, registering a PlugIn is far preferable.

Implementing DataHandlers

Implementing a new DataHandler—a Player, Processor, or DataSink—requires writing a class named Handler that is part of a larger package and which implements the particular interface (Player, Processor, or DataSink).

As for PlugIn implementation, implementing a DataHandler requires writing a class that possesses all the methods listed for that interface, as well as for all the interfaces it extends. This is a nontrivial task—a DataSink must possess at least 12 methods, a Player must have 32 methods, and a Processor must have 38. The complexity of Player stems from the fact that it extends Controller, which extends Clock. Processor extends Player and hence has an additional six methods.

As discussed in the previous section on registering new classes, a new MediaHandler class must be called Handler and exist in a package with a particular name structure. The exact naming rules are found previously, whereas the following code fragment shows the start of a Player class that handles a hypothetical content-type known as 4XXXX.

```
package com.samspublishing.mediaaips.media.content.4XXXX
import javax.media.*;
public class Handler implements Player {
:         :         :
}
```

Note that the package to which the class belongs begins with the top-level name. In this case, the hypothetical com.samspublishing.mediaapis, has the mandatory media.content as the mid-portion of the name, indicating it is a player, and 4XXXX as the suffix, indicating the particular content-type that it handles.

It is worth noting that individual Handlers aren't registered with the JMF, but simply the top-level, user package name. After that is registered, all subsequently implemented

MediaHandlers in the same top-level package will be automatically found by the Manager class when it is asked to create a new object.

Extending DataSource

The DataSource class is an exception in terms of extending the JMF. Whereas PlugIns and DataHandlers are interfaces and require one pattern for implementation, DataSource is a class and requires a different approach.

Writing a new DataSource means extending the existing DataSource class or one of its subclasses. When contrasted with implementing an interface, this can be an advantage because the default inherited behavior for some methods might not need to be altered. The following code fragment shows the start of a DataSource class that deals with a new protocol known as sdtb, which is a type of pull data source.

```
package com.samspublishing.mediaapis.media.protocol.sdtb
import javax.media.*;
import javax.media.protocol.*;
public class DataSource extends PullBufferDataSource {
    :        :        :
}
```

As for MediaHandlers, the top-level, user-supplied, package name must be registered with the JMF for the new DataSource to be accessible to the Manager class. This is most easily done through the JMFRegistry application. The JMF differentiates user-package names into those for DataHandlers, which it names content package prefix, and those for DataSources, which it calls protocol package prefix. Registration of each package prefix is separate even, as is the usual case, if the names are the same.

Sun's Examples

As mentioned previously, extending the JMF is a non-trivial task and often involves writing a relatively large class. This section doesn't possess a complete example because of space and complexity restrictions.

However, Sun has provided a number of excellent examples of writing PlugIns, MediaHandlers, and DataSources in both its JMF guide http://java.sun.com/products/java-media/jmf/2.1.1/guide/JMFTOC.html and on its solutions Web page http://java.sun.com/products/java-media/jmf/2.1.1/solutions/index.html. These are very good starting points for those wanting to extend the JMF and go beyond the information provided here. They also provide a good gauge for the complexity of the task.

In particular, the current version of the JMF guide contains a `Demultiplexer` `PlugIn` implementation for GSM, a gain control, a `Renderer` for RGB (employing `AWT's Image` class), an ftp `DataSource`, and a `Controller` for a hypothetical type of data known as TimeLine.

The solutions page contains a particularly clever implementation of a `DataSource` that provides screen capture facilities. By defining a new protocol called `screen`, the `DataSource` can be used to capture a particular region of the computer screen as a video. The implementation is highly recommended not only as an example of what can be done with the JMF, but also is a particularly useful utility—one that can be installed within the JMF in minutes.

JMFCustomizer

The JMF is a large, optional API that extends the functionality of the Java platform. For users to run JMF-based programs, they must download and install the JMF API on their own machines. That can be problematic for some users who don't feel confident to complete such tasks. This can limit both the distribution and appeal of JMF-based programs—many users are happy to run a prepackaged application (or applet), but will balk at the prospect of having to download and install some software first.

The `JMFCustomizer` application has been provided by Sun to help JMF developers address this issue. `JMFCustomizer` is a simple application that allows the user to select a subset of the classes that compose the JMF. Those classes are then encapsulated as a JAR file, which can be distributed with the application (or applet).

The intention of this approach is that the user doesn't need to have the JMF installed on his machine. The developer of the application selects the subset of the JMF that is required by the application and distributes that (as a JAR file) along with the application itself. The user then has all that he requires in a single distribution. Figure 9.10 shows such a usage of `JMFCustomizer`.

Running `JMFCustomizer` is as simple as `java JMFCustomizer`. After that GUI components such as check boxes and buttons lead the user through the selection of appropriate classes and the creation of the JAR file.

However, although the `JMFCustomizer` application is part of the standard JMF 2.1.1 distribution, it isn't (by default) in the classpath. As such the developer wanting to employ `JMFCustomizer` must modify the classpath to include the customizer.jar file (that is found in the same folder and directory as jmf.jar). The particulars of setting the classpath variable depend on the operating system in question. Sun's "Setting Up and Running JMF on a Java Client" at `http://java.sun.com/products/java-media/jmf/2.1.1/setup-java.html` describes the simple steps for all operating systems.

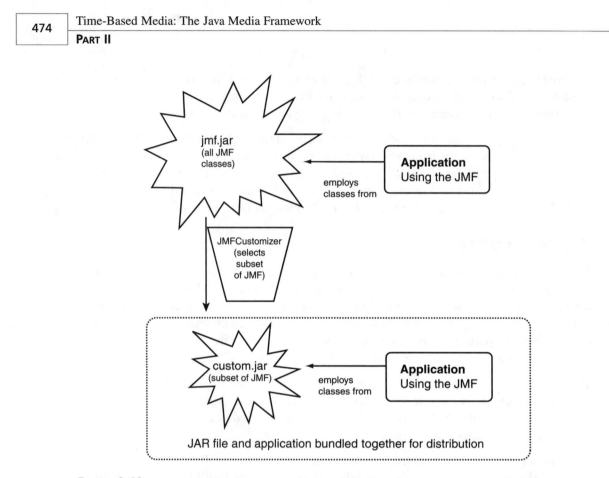

FIGURE 9.10

Use of JMFCustomizer *to create a JAR file containing the subset of the JMF necessary for a particular application.*

Synchronization

In some circumstances, it is necessary to have a number of individual Players (or perhaps Processors) as part of a single application. An example of such a situation might be an AV conference over RTP, particularly if there are multiple participants. Each participant is likely to send separate audio and video streams. Hence, recipients require a number of Players: one for each stream. Imagine such a three-way conference; each participant requires four Players, one audio player, and one video player for each of the two participants from which they are receiving. Figure 9.11 shows such a situation. Each player is controlled individually.

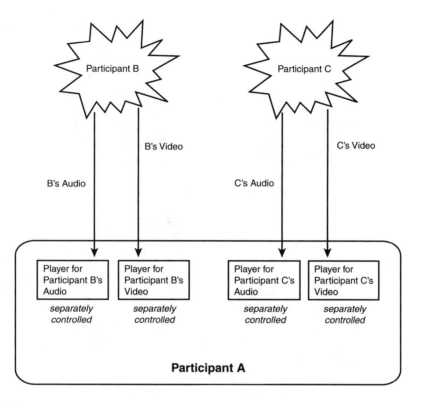

FIGURE 9.11

A three-way AV conference from the perspective of one of the participants showing the players needed in order to render the media being streamed to it.

Controlling all those players individually not only is tedious, but also often doesn't match the desired solution. Generally it is easier (both as a user and programmer) to centralize the control. Actions on the one centralized controller (Player) should then automatically propagate to all those it oversees. For instance, selecting Stop should stop all players. The JMF provides such a feature through the Player class.

A Player (Processors are also a type of Player) object is capable of controlling one or more additional Controllers (Players or Processors). Actions (methods) on the central Player are also propagated to all Controllers that the Player controls. For instance, invoking prefetch() on the central Player would cause prefetch() to be called on all Controllers that the Player controls. Figure 9.12 shows the previous scenario of a three-way AV conference from the perspective of one of the participants. However in this case, rather than controlling each Player separately, the Player for participant B's video is also the central control for all `Players`. Any actions carried out on that `Player` (such as stopping it) also affect the other players.

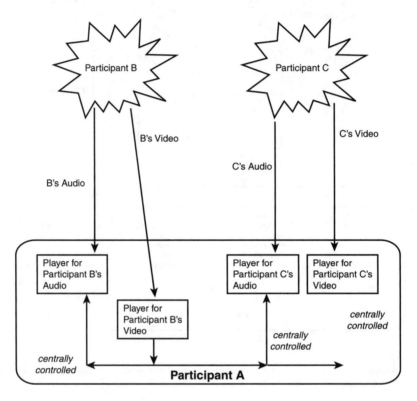

FIGURE 9.12

In this case, control of the players is centralized through one of their numbers.

A `Player` object is given control over another `Controller` with `Player`'s `addController()` method. Similarly you can remove a `Controller` object from a `Player` with the `removeController()` method. The following code fragment shows two `Players` being constructed, and `player1` is given control over `player2`. They are both brought to the realized state by invoking `realize()` on the central Player, which is `player1`.

```
Player player1 = Manager.createPlayer(...);
Player player2 = Manager.createPlayer(...);
player1.addController(player2);
player1.realize();
```

Several features of the synchronized control are worth noting:

- The added controller assumes the centralized `Player` object's `TimeBase`.

- The `Player` object's duration is the maximum of its own duration and that of all `Controller` objects under its direction.

- The start latency of the `Player` is the maximum of the `Player`'s own start latency and that of all `Controller` objects under its direction. This ensures that all `Controllers` will start simultaneously using the `syncStart()` method.

- The `Player` object only posts completion events (for example, `PrefetchCompleteEvent`) when all managed `Controllers` have also posted the event.

- All `Controller` methods invoked on the central `Player` object are propagated to all `Controllers` under its direction.

- Although `Controllers` are under the central direction of a `Player`, they shouldn't have their methods invoked individually. All method invocation should occur by way of the central `Player` object.

The JMF in Conjunction with Other APIs

The JMF is a powerful API, supporting a high-level and uniform approach to controlling, playing, and processing time-based media. An equally important JMF strength is that it is part of the larger Java platform. The implication of this is that the JMF approach to time-based media can be combined with other features of Java; either from the core platform, or one or more of the other specialist APIs that extend the functionality of Java. This leads to programs that can combine time-based media with other media (for example, 3D graphics) in either traditional multimedia paradigms, or in new and innovative approaches that are only possible because of the common platform-independent glue that is Java.

Consider an educational application dealing with Australian Aboriginal culture and civilization in the region of the Olgas (central Australian geographic formation) across the last 50,000 years. The application might combine a library of still images of the region, maps, hypertext about the languages and customs of the region, 3D interactive models of reconstructed camp sites, and audio and video interviews with tribal elders of today, perhaps telling some of the Dreamtime legends unique to the area. Such an application could be written entirely in Java, using features of the core platform, the JMF, and Java 3D (perhaps with other APIs also), and would run on any platform.

What about an application of tomorrow? A *virtual* or immersive audio-video conference with colleagues overseas who are speaking a different language unknown to the recipient. Such an application would use the JMF in conjunction with features of Java 3D, the JAI, and other

APIs such as Java Speech. Not only would the audio and video be streamed between participants and projected into a virtual environment (for example, a model of a new building that is being jointly designed), but the audio stream would be extracted, processed by a recognizer (for the speaker's language); then translated into the hearer's language and reintegrated with the video as subtitles or as a separate synthesized audio track. Again, Java provides the framework to enable such a future application.

Applications that involve the JMF in conjunction with other APIs fall into two broad categories. The simpler form, such as the preceding archaeological/cultural multimedia application, uses the JMF as a plug-in component of the entire application. The JMF portion (playing the interviews) is a logical, self-contained component of the entire application. Such applications, although often large, are relatively modular and don't hinge on low-level interfacing of different APIs. The more difficult applications, such as the virtual AV conference involving language translation, aren't so modular in their composition. They tend to rely on the fusing of APIs at a lower level of detail. In the multi-language AV conference application, the media streams must be demultiplexed and passed off to other APIs (the speech recognition and translation) that don't directly support the JMF data models. This requires a knowledge of the deeper data structures in the communicating APIs and the means of converting between them. For the JMF side, that might involve strong familiarity with the `Buffer`, `Format`, `Stream`, `Clock`, and related classes and interfaces.

Chapter 14, "Integrating Across the Java Media API," is explicitly concerned with combining the media APIs discussed in this book. As a prelude to that chapter, the following subsection discusses the key JMF classes that allow a video stream to be treated as a sequence of images by other APIs.

ImageToBuffer and BufferToImage

Two classes, `ImageToBuffer` and `BufferToImage`, play central roles as the lynchpins between the video component of the JMF and 2D or 3D graphics. For instance, with these classes, it is possible to grab individual images from a video, insert frames into a video, or even extract, modify, and reinsert them. Indeed, it is possible to write a video `Renderer` by using `BufferToImage`—simply pull out each frame and render that image (using Java's Graphics class). `BufferToImage` is one mechanism by which JMF originated video can be imported into other contexts. For instance, a JMF video could be applied as a texture in a Java 3D world by texturing the individual images that compose the video. Conversely, a video can be constructed as a sequence of (AWT) images.

`ImageToBuffer` and `BufferToImage` are the sole members of the `javax.media.util` package. As shown in Figure 9.13, the `BufferToImage` class provides the ability to convert from a JMF (video) `Buffer` to an AWT `Image` (`BufferedImage`), while `ImageToBuffer` provides the reverse functionality.

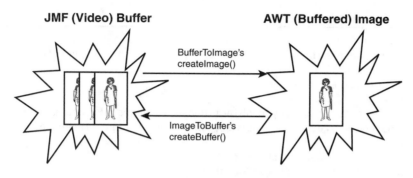

JMF (Video) Buffer

BufferToImage's
createImage()

ImageToBuffer's
createBuffer()

AWT (Buffered) Image

FIGURE 9.13

The roles of BufferToImage *and* ImageToBuffer *classes in moving between a JMF video frame and an AWT Image.*

The BufferToImage class possesses a single constructor, accepting a Format object. That Format object specifies the format of the video buffer that must be converted. Hence, BufferToImage objects are specific to a particular Format, but can convert any Buffer in that Format into its equivalent Image. The class has a single method createImage() that accepts a Buffer (of the Format specified in the constructor) and returns an AWT Image. Null is returned if the conversion cannot be done.

Obtaining an Image from a video sequence devolves into obtaining a Buffer object that corresponds to the video frame in question. BufferToImage's createImage() can then be applied to the Buffer to generate the Image. Obtaining a Buffer for a particular video frame can be achieved through use the FrameGrabbingControl interface. A FrameGrabbingControl can be exported by a Player or Renderer through the getControl() method. The interface possesses a single method grabFrame() that returns a Buffer object that corresponds to the current frame from the video stream. In addition to FrameGrabbingControl, there is also the useful FramePositioningControl that can be employed to precisely position a stream at a particular frame number. As shown in Listing 9.7, these can be used in conjunction so that a particular (known) frame number can be grabbed and turned into an image. In this case, the 500th frame is used.

9

RTP AND ADVANCED TIME-BASED MEDIA TOPICS

LISTING 9.7 A Particular Video Frame Is Grabbed and Transformed into an AWT Image

```
int     desiredFrame = 500;
Player      player = Manager.createRealizedPlayer(new MediaLocator(...));
FramePositioningControl positioner =
            player.getControl("javax.media.control.FramePositioningControl");
if (positioner==null) return;
FrameGrabbingControl grabber =
            Player.getControl("javax.media.control.FrameGrabbingControl");
if (grabber==null)  return;
```

LISTING 9.7   Continued

```
player.prefetch();
// Some sort of pause/polling/event listening to ensure its prefetched

positioner.seek(desiredFrame);

// Assumption here is that Player object doesn't "regress" into an earlier
// "less prepared" state. More generally should wait till Player returns to //
// prefetched.
Buffer inTheBuff = grabber.grabFrame();
Format videoFormat = inTheBuff.getFormat();
BufferToImage converter = new BufferToImage(videoFormat);
Image captured = converter.createImage(inTheBuff);

// Now do something useful with captured, the image that corresponds to the
// desired (500th) frame.
```

Going in the opposite direction—from an AWT Image to a JMF Buffer—employs the ImageToBuffer class. The class possesses a single static method that accepts an AWT Image and desired frame rate and returns a JMF Buffer with an RGB Format. Although that operation is simple, construction of a stream from the Buffers is somewhat more difficult. Sun's example Screen Grabber [DataSource] linked from their JMF solutions page, http://java.sun.com/products/java-media/jmf/2.1.1/solutions/index.html, is a good example of building a stream from individual images.

Java Sound

Java Sound (javax.sound) is a core API of the Java platform, meaning that it is part of all Java runtime environments that support Java 1.3 and later. The Java Sound API is low-level, concerning itself with the input and output plus processing of both sampled audio and *MIDI (Musical Instrument Digital Interface)* data.

The Java Sounds API provides the lowest-level of sound support on the Java platform, which incorporates explicit control over the resources concerned with sound input and output. Among the abilities provided by the API are direct access to system resources such as MIDI synthesizers, audio mixers, audio and MIDI devices, converters between sound formats, and file-based I/O.

The capabilities provided by Java Sound partially overlap with those of the JMF, although their target audiences are different. The JMF is larger, encompassing video and sound, and also high-level, providing a unified architecture for handling, processing, and transporting time-based media. On the other hand, Java Sound is both more specialized and lower level. It is concerned only with audio, but provides far finer control over the audio parameters of a system. In particular, Java Sound's MIDI functionality is considerably more sophisticated than that of the JMF (which has limited playback only as of 2.1.1), as well as providing the ability to control aspects such as buffering and mixing.

Java Sound is a large API. The programmer's guide from Sun can currently be found at `http://java.sun.com/products/java-media/sound/index.html`, and it runs more than 150 pages. If it has moved, do a search on the main Java Web page `http://java.sun.com`. This short section serves to inform you of the existence of the API. A number of audio-only applications are better suited to Java Sound than the JMF, and those developing a time-based application that is audio only should contrast the features of both APIs as to which is most suitable for the application.

Java Sound divides its MIDI and sampled audio support into two separate packages, with an additional two packages for service providers:

> `javax.sound.sampled`—Classes for playing, capturing, and processing (mixing) of digital (sampled) audio
>
> `javax.sound.midi`—Classes for MIDI synthesis, sequencing, and event transport
>
> `javax.sound.sampled.spi`—Service provider's package for sampled audio
>
> `javax.sound.midi.spi`—Service provider's package for MIDI sound

Implementations of the Java Sound API provide a basic set of audio services. The *Service Provider Interface (SPI)* packages are provided as a means for third-party software developers to develop new services. These new services then become another aspect of Java Sound.

The Java Sound API employs a similar approach to management of the services it provides to that of the JMF. Two central management classes act as registries or database managers for the audio components and audio resources on the system. Those management classes are `AudioSystem` for sampled audio and `MidiSystem` for MIDI resources. These classes act as *access points* for obtaining the services provided by Java Sound. For instance, the `AudioSystem` class provides a means of obtaining mixers, lines, format converters, and I/O functionality for sampled audio data.

The reader wanting to know more about Java Sound should consult Sun's "Java Sound API Programmer's Guide," as well as the API documentation. Both can be found at the Java Sound documentation page: `http://java.sun.com/j2se/1.3/docs/guide/sound/`.

Future Directions for the JMF

The JMF is a powerful and rapidly maturing API that provides a high-level and uniform structure for the handling of time-based media. All key structures and classes for capturing, playing, processing, receiving, and transmitting time-based media already exist in the API. Currently the API is undergoing a solidification phase—developers are exploring and adopting the API as suitable to a range of potential applications. Simultaneously, Sun is continuing its strong support for the API with the addition of further features (for example, new codecs and formats) and enhancements in the short term with specific goals for the longer term.

The next significant release of the JMF, 2.2, is expected shortly (perhaps around the time this book is released). JMF 2.2 is expected to incorporate a new RTP implementation, together with significant optimizations and fixes.

The JMF team at Sun has set supporting MPEG-2 and MPEG-4, the two most frequently requested codecs, as its highest priority. This support will hopefully be appearing in the next version of the JMF, but licensing and patent issues are likely to be the real decider of exactly when the support appears. In this regard, Sun has promised not only to continue to optimize and update the JMF, but also to add support for open-standard, industry-leading codecs.

The maturity, stability, and size of the JMF mean that it is unlikely to ever be incorporated into the core Java platform. However a closer integration with other optional packages (for example, Java 3D) is likely. In that sense, standards such as MPEG-4 might well act as drivers in that direction, stressing the coding of audio-visual objects and composite media that incorporates interactivity—for instance, combining 2D imagery and 3D synthetic objects with audio and video streams. Indeed Sun has stated that it believes MPEG-4 to be an important standard—one for which it will provide increased functionality in the future.

As an example of the directions that the JMF and related developments are headed, Sun is working closely with Nokia and other international telecommunication companies (including Motorola, Mitsubishi, Siemens, and NTT) on a multimedia API for J2ME (Java 2 Micro Edition). J2ME is the small footprint (less demanding of memory and processor power) version of the Java platform suitable for the newer generation of mobile devices including phones, pagers, digital set-top boxes, car navigation systems, and personal digital assistants.

The J2ME Multimedia API is being designed under the Java Community Process as *JSR (Java Specification Request)* 135. The publicly available documentation on the JSR can be found at `http://www.jcp.org/jsr/detail/135.prt`. The intention of the API, as described in the JSR documentation, is to provide a high-level interface to sound and multimedia capabilities on a device running J2ME, which would thus enable versatile and scalable multimedia applications on these devices. The package's proposed name is `javax.microedition.media`. Although its primary focus is sound, it also is intended to incorporate the control of other time-based multimedia formats. Both the JMF and Java Sound are listed as starting points for the new API. This development, and the future of platform-independent handling of media through the JMF and its derivatives, is put in context by the fact that Nokia (the filers of the JRS) plans to ship 50 million Java-enabled phones by the end of 2002 and 100 million by the end of 2003.

Summary

This chapter is the last of three covering the handling of time-based media with the JMF. It has covered more advanced topics in time-based media handling, including the streaming of media and extending the JMF. Chapter 8 served to cover the core functionality of the JMF, whereas Chapter 7 introduced time-based media and the JMF.

More than half of the chapter is dedicated to RTP—the Real-time Transport Protocol and its integration into the JMF to support the streaming of audio and video. The fundamentals of RTP and streaming data are introduced before the particular classes involved in managing an RTP session are discussed.

The other major topic of the chapter is extending the JMF. Details of writing a new `DataSource`, `Player`, `Processor`, or `DataSink` are covered as well as the means of registering the new class so that it is available for subsequent use in any JMF-based program.

The chapter concludes with a miscellany of topics including synchronization of multiple players, interfacing the JMF to other APIs, the Java Sound API, and finally a glimpse at some of the future paths for the JMF.

Visualization and Virtual Environments: The Java 3D API

IN THIS PART

3D Graphics, Virtual Reality, and Visualization

IN THIS CHAPTER

Immersive virtual environments and 3D data visualization are among the major goals of computer graphics. This chapter introduces the concepts behind the way that 3D works. The basic process is to create a model in a 3D mathematical space, define a viewing volume in that space, and project the objects within the viewing volume onto a 2D plane for rendering. Having a basic understanding of the fundamentals of 3D presented in this chapter will make the remaining chapters of this section on the Java 3D API more accessible.

What Is 3D?

Whether we can know and comprehend the kind of space we really live in is a philosophical question with no clear answer. Generally speaking, humans perceive space in three dimensions (height, width, and depth) and understand the fourth dimension as time.

Our goal in 3D graphics is to create a model of something with three dimensions and represent it to the user on some sort of 2D screen, such as a computer monitor or a head mount display. To do this, we first define a mathematical 3D space in which the locations and the shapes of objects can be described in terms of height, width, and depth within an arbitrary reference frame. This space can be thought of as *model space*.

When we want to see into this 3D space, we define a volume within the space (*the viewing volume, or frustum*), project the objects within that volume onto a flat plane, and obtain a rendering. The rendering can be considered to be in *screen space*. When we want to see an object move in the space over time or, alternatively, want to move around the space ourselves, we obtain a series of renderings and view them sequentially as an animation.

Interactive 3D

Interactive 3D graphics, such as is possible in Java 3D, requires the computer to calculate and render the view continuously in near real-time. This is by no means an easy task and requires many compromises. In general, the compromises are being mitigated by advances in technology, and there is little doubt that the next several generations of 3D graphics accelerators and faster computers will go a long way toward improving the situation. This is a particularly important point with regard to Java 3D because for some applications, Java 3D doesn't render sufficiently fast to be viable. It is probably safe to say that most current efficiency issues for interactive 3D graphics will become moot within one or two computer generations, but it is also safe to say that developers will want to throw bigger challenges at 3D systems: Therefore, the never ending cycle will continue.

Some consideration must be given to what we mean by the term interactive. There exists a kind of gray area on the spectrum of non-interactive to interactive 3D. Many games will prerender a large number of frames and then allow the user to choose which are displayed at various choice paths. Our usage of the term interactive doesn't include prerendered frames. Java 3D is a truly interactive 3D graphics package in that the user (if allowed to do so) can navigate to any place at any time and change the course of events to the maximum degree. We will see that this interactive capability is particularly useful in VR and visualization applications.

The Problem of Immersion

Generally speaking, developers of 3D graphics programs are hoping to create a sense of immersion—that is, a sense of the user somehow psychologically being inside the artificial computer space. The fundamental challenge in this enterprise is that the brain is highly evolved for extracting information in 3D; but as designers of virtual worlds, we have very limited ways of providing these 3D cues. Indeed, we don't have any access to the real 3D cues. We end up trying to trick the brain into thinking that a set of 2D cues is 3D.

Fortunately, throughout the long history of painting and the more recent history of visual psychophysics and computer graphics, a great deal of thought has been put into making an inherently 2D output (the painting canvas or the computer screen) appear as 3D. Although the whole topic of 3D perception is quite fascinating, the point we want to make here is that we are going to have a pretty tough time immersing our target audience using a 21-inch monitor.

Although it is certainly true that there are more output options than just a flat screen monitor (see Figures 10.1–10.4 for some examples from our own work), it is also true that the immersive impact of these other devices is still relatively small. Even considering a *head mounted display (HMD)*, multiprojector room system (generally known as a CAVE), a sound system, or a haptic glove or treadmill, our ability to remove the user from the real world and put him in the virtual world is limited. Some of our own research is concerned with how self-motion signals influence the brain mechanisms of navigation in real and virtual environments. The consensus is very strong that memory, spatial cognitive function, and wayfinding are highly influenced by the sum of the self-motion senses especially optic flow, vestibular (self-motion signals from the inner ear), and proprioception (feedback from the muscles indicating movement). These senses need to be in synch with each other to enable normal brain functioning in space.

FIGURE 10.1

Custom built wedge projection system using two projectors to increase the surround of the environment. (Photo courtesy of Dr. Michael Barlow, Australian National University Virtual Environment and Simulation Laboratory)

In Figure 10.2, wands track the position of the hand relative to the body using separate coordinate systems for each. The devices allow the user to make pointing movements within the coordinate system of the virtual world. This device is used to study how changes in the proprioception (the neural integration of limb movement) are kept in synch with the visual and vestibular system.

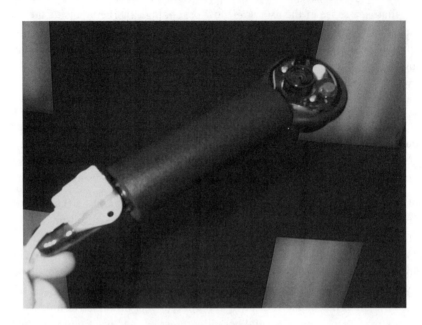

FIGURE 10.2
Haptic wand. (Photo courtesy of Jerry Roll, Michigan State University MIND Lab)

In Figure 10.3, the photo shows experimenters working with Immersadesk and haptic wand to study interaction in 3D. 3D glasses provide stereoscopic cues.

FIGURE 10.3
3D interaction task. (Photo courtesy of Dr. Frank Biocca, Michigan State University MIND Lab)

In Figure 10.4, this device allows subjects to "walk" through virtual space and has been used to demonstrate the importance of proprioception in wayfinding and spatial cognition in humans.

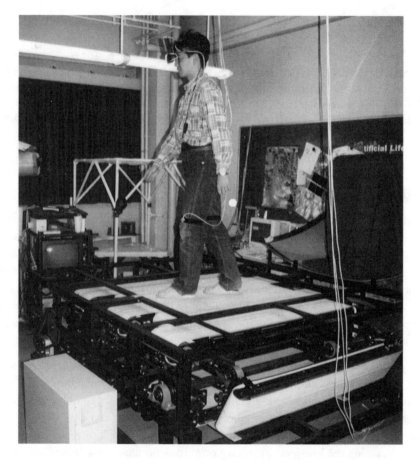

FIGURE 10.4

Torus Treadmill. (Photo courtesy of Dr. Hiroo Iwata, University of Tsukuba, Japan)

We also emphasize that the vast majority of users won't have access to advanced VR gear and will in fact be seeing the 3D application on a basic monitor. Occasionally, end users will have an HMD or goggles and almost all users will have a set of speakers. This fact will remain true at least several years into the future.

With this in mind, we attempt to do the best we can, and in many ways we computationally mimic the techniques of the painting masters. As we will see, the use of light and shadows, removal of hidden surfaces, and the convergence of lines all play a major part in our attempts to make a convincing virtual world. Much of our success will depend on how well we use these techniques in our 3D applications.

> **NOTE**
>
> One of Java 3D's real innovations is its capability to readily adapt to different input and output devices. This is achieved through a series of abstractions over specific implementations. As we will see later, this potential isn't yet fully realized; however, the abstractions are in place so that new devices can be incorporated into an application relatively easily. This topic will be the focus of Chapter 12, "Interaction with the Virtual World."

The Java 3D Scene Graph

The idea of using a graph as a way to organize the parts of a 3D scene has been around for a number of years and certainly isn't unique to Java 3D. The general purpose of the scene graph is to contain a complete description of the scene. Figure 10.5 contains a portion of a scene graph. This particular example shows scene elements (*LeafNodes*) grouped together under a *TransformGroup* that is the child of a *BranchGroup*. In most applications, the majority of the work is in making the *LeafNodes* and adding them to the appropriate *TransformGroup*. This particular partial scene graph example doesn't show the superstructure elements *Locale* and *Universe* that you will encounter later.

The scene graph also provides several levels of abstraction above the low-level APIs (OpenGL or DirectX). *Abstraction* is an important object-oriented programming concept that refers to the process of identifying and isolating generalized qualities in a set of objects. In terms of the scene graph, this means that the programmer is now free to think about the content and higher level conceptual aspects of creating the scene rather than the details of rendering or the complexities of managing the low-level geometry primitives because these things have been "abstracted away."

By virtue of being a scene graph based API, Java 3D provides free cross-platform optimization in terms of development effort. Each individual developer can thus get functionality and optimization in her 3D content without having to worry much about it. These low-level challenges would have previously been a major impediment to our beginning the project in the first place. Moreover, without the abstractions provided for in the scene graph model, we would end up with a platform-specific solution. The optimizations that were developed for one low-level implementation wouldn't necessarily benefit us on the other platform. In many ways, the scene graph is highly similar in nature to a high-level optimizing compiler in that it provides a platform independent API that is optimized for the particular hardware on which it is compiled.

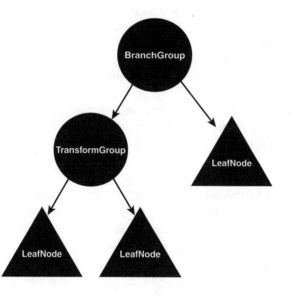

FIGURE 10.5
Portion of a scene graph.

> **NOTE**
>
> Java 3D performs the best optimizations on scene graphs that are properly organized spatially. It is critical that objects in close proximity moving in synchronization be grouped together.

The scene graph is the central structure of every application written in Java 3D, and it is highly recommended that programmers at least sketch a proposed scene graph prior to beginning programming. This point cannot be emphasized enough. A layout of the organization of the scene graph will both document the application and give the programmer insight into efficiencies that can be gained through better structuring of the model. A large amount of confusion will be avoided through understanding how scene graphs work.

> **NOTE**
>
> The name scene graph might be a little confusing to some people. We therefore describe the origin of this terminology here. A *graph*, in this case, refers to the definition used in discrete mathematics. In this sense, a graph attempts to describe a system schematically from the perspective of the states it can enter and the transitions between those states. Note that we worked from the standpoint of a rendering graph in some of our image processing examples from Chapter 6, "Java Advanced Imaging."
>
> A graph is made from two basic entities: *nodes* and *edges* that are arranged in a tree-like structure. Each edge is a pair of nodes. In a family tree, for example, the nodes are the individual people and the edges are the parent-child relationships.

The scene graph is built by instantiating both scene objects (for example, lights, textures, geometries) and special objects for defining the viewing parameters. These two fundamental scene graph branches are added in parallel structures to the scene graph and are known as the *content branch* and the *view branch*, respectively. The skill of scene graph design lies in recognizing meaningful groupings within the content subgraph. Generally, the view branch doesn't substantially change from application to application, although it certainly can. However, most of the real work is in describing the content subgraph.

In Java 3D, all nodes and components that can be added to the scene graph are subclasses of `SceneGraphObject`. All these are accessed and operated on by the `set()` and `get()` methods. Other important methods include `setUserData()` and `getUserData()`, which can be used to set and get user-defined states for the object, respectively. The `SceneGraphObject` is covered in more detail in Chapter 11, "Creating and Viewing the Virtual World."

In Java 3D, both the content and viewing subgraphs are contained in separate holders known as `BranchGroups`. Each `BranchGroup` is the root of a branch in the scene graph. `BranchGroups` are the only objects that can be added to a `Locale` (a collection of `BranchGroups` that occupies a high-resolution position within the "universe"). The `Locale` and `VirtualUniverse` objects are described next.

Once you understand how to organize content within a scene graph, most of the conceptual hurdles will have been overcome. Far more detail is given about scene graph organization in the next chapter. For now, you should remember that the basic purpose of the scene graph is to organize the view and content subgraphs in a logical and abstracted fashion.

Inside the Rendering Pipeline

As we have said, 3D graphics involves creating a 3D model, establishing a viewing volume, and then rendering that viewing volume as a 2D plane. A pretty standard series of steps is used in creating the pixels that are ultimately put on the screen. This series of steps is frequently referred to as the *rendering pipeline*. The vast majority of 3D APIs follow these steps (shown in Figure 10.6). The top row refers to the five basic steps in the pipeline with the arrow indicating the order of steps. The bottom row indicates roughly where Java 3D fits into this picture. Note, however, that major differences exist in what specifically happens at each step.

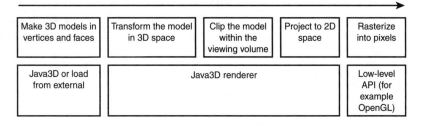

FIGURE 10.6

Schematic of the typical rendering pipeline.

You will gain some insight into the steps of the pipeline shortly, but for now we want to consider the role of Java 3D in this pipeline.

Because many of the steps in 3D graphics are so computationally expensive, they are often implemented in optimized native code. Most current 3D graphics cards have incorporated hardware acceleration to perform most of these low-level API calls. The two most prominent low-level 3D graphics APIs are OpenGL—which runs on Sun, SGI, Linux, and Windows—and DirectX, which runs on Windows machines. As yet, no hardware acceleration works directly with Java 3D (nor is there ever likely to be), and therefore Java 3D makes use of bindings to the low-level API (either DirectX or OpenGL) through separate versions of Java 3D for OpenGL and DirectX.

It is a mistake, however, to believe that Java 3D is simply a set of bindings to the low-level API. Because Java 3D is written in Java, it turns out that all low-level calls have to be made through the *Java Native Interface (JNI)*. Each call to the JNI is expensive, so the calls need to be used as sparingly as possible and scheduled appropriately. Therefore, Java 3D substantially reduces the computational problem within its own native rendering layer before calling the low-level API. This special rendering layer is the heart of the *Java 3D renderer*.

The low-level bindings that are the end product of the Java 3D renderer are largely invisible to the programmer, and for some applications this can be a problem. Future implementations promise to allow the programmer to make calls to the low-level API, but at present we must accept the fact that we cannot easily make low-level API calls. In general, this isn't a major problem, and unless a programmer is very good, there won't be much advantage to making these calls anyway. In the vast majority of the cases, Java 3D will be sufficient to the task without needing to get into low-level calls.

To reiterate, a developer might consider directly using either of the low-level APIs (OpenGL or DirectX) in order to get performance improvements. This brute force approach has been used successfully many times; however, for a huge majority of applications, this isn't a wise choice. Performance improvements are predicated by whether the programmer is good enough or experienced enough to beat Java 3D. Even if the programmer operating at a low level can do a better job of squeezing performance out of the application (again, by no means guaranteed), there will be a loss of the cross-platform capabilities (particularly with DirectX) and the development cycle will almost always be much longer.

The Framebuffer

Probably the most important innovation and concept to understand regarding raster graphics hardware is the idea of a framebuffer. The *framebuffer* is quite similar to the image buffer idea presented in Part I, "2D Graphics and Imaging on the Java Platform: The Java 2D, Java Advanced Imaging, and Java Image I/O APIs." Essentially, we are talking about a memory space to store pixel information.

The framebuffer in 3D graphics is more typically a set of buffers that store different types of information. The most commonly considered buffer (and the one used in the imaging section) is the color buffer. In the simplest case, the color buffer contains RGB plus alpha values for each pixel in the output image.

The second important component of the framebuffer that should be understood is the *depth buffer*. We will cover the depth buffer in more detail when we discuss hidden surface removal in the section "Reducing Unnecessary Rendering Through Culling." For now, understand that the depth buffer stores information about the distance of objects in the 3D view volume from the eye of the person doing the viewing. This information is later collapsed such that the closest object obscures the objects behind it.

Other buffers such as the accumulation buffer and the stencil buffer are less commonly used by application programmers and therefore aren't covered here. Both the color buffer and depth buffer will play a role in the discussions that follow.

Rasterization

We discussed the process of rasterization for 2D graphics in Chapter 2, "Imaging and Graphics on the Java Platform," under the section "What Is Rendering?" *Rasterization* is the conversion of the mathematical description of a primitive with its color information into screen coordinates. Extension of the 2D concept of rasterization to the case of 3D graphics is pretty straightforward with the exception of a few additional steps dealing with depth, which are covered next.

Java 3D Rendering Modes

Given an understanding of the general rendering process, we can now examine some aspects of the Java 3D rendering process.

Java 3D has four primary rendering modes that allow differing amounts of control over the low-level aspects of rendering. Generally, when the user has more control over rendering, Java 3D will be able to perform fewer optimizations. Java 3D's four rendering modes are listed in Table 10.1.

TABLE 10.1   Java Rendering Modes

Rendering Mode	Means of Entering	Properties
Retained	Default	Provides a large number of high-level optimizations.
Compiled-retained	Issuing `BranchGroup`'s `compile()` method	Allows for the greatest number of automatic optimizations
Pure immediate	`Canvas3D.stopRenderer()` to stop Java 3D's continuous rendering	Greatest flexibility for drawing to the screen. Automatic rendering is completely disabled until `Canvas3D.start Renderer()` is issued.
Mixed immediate	Through any one of 4 per-frame callbacks	Java 3D renderer continues to operate while the frame callbacks are issued.

The choice of rendering mode is usually quite easy: Stick with the retained or compiled-retained mode unless strongly compelled to do otherwise. Before discussing why we make this statement, a quick overview of the four rendering modes is presented.

Retained Mode

The retained mode is the default mode. In retained mode, the application remains in a continuous rendering state unless the `Canvas3D.stopRender()` method is invoked. Retained mode represents a happy medium between total capitulation to the Java 3D renderer with compiled-retained mode (covered next) and near total abandonment of the Java 3D renderer with the pure immediate mode (also covered next). The optimization that is automatically generated in the retained mode is substantial. In particular, the Java 3D renderer will attempt to build special structures for geometry handling and flatten transform operations. (Transforms are covered later in this chapter and the next.)

In many cases, picking objects in the 3D scene is most easily solved in retained mode because the geometry compression that occurs with compiling (discussed next) can interfere with some operations.

Capability Bits

Java 3D decides which optimizations to use depending on *capability bits*. Most of the default capability bits are set for optimal rendering speed, but not all. Setting capability bits can be among the most confusing aspects in Java 3D, and a great many programming errors are a result of improperly set bits. An example of setting a bit is as follows:

```
TransformGroup tg = new TransformGroup();
tg.setCapabilityBit(TransformGroup.ALLOW_TRANSFORM_WRITE);
```

Compiled-retained Mode

Compiled-retained mode gives Java 3D the freedom to perform the greatest number of optimizations. Important among these optimizations are scene graph compression and geometry compression and grouping.

To enter compiled-retained mode, the programmer calls the BranchGroup's compile() method. The compile() method optimizes the scene graph in two basic ways; first by sorting the attributes, and second by grouping shapes.

The disappointing truth is that you aren't likely to see much of an improvement in frame rate after compiling. This is for two primary reasons. The first reason is that most of the default capability bits aren't set up to allow for optimization of the scene graph. This is easily corrected by setting these bits at instantiation (covered in more detail in the following chapter; also see the previous sidebar). Manually setting the capability bits like this might be a lot of working for little gain.

The second reason that you might not see an increase in speed by compiling is that even if all the capability bits are set correctly, there might not be enough shapes to make much of a difference anyway. The main additional optimization that you get from compiling is geometry compression, and this is only useful with complex shapes. The other optimization that compiled-retained mode has over retained mode is geometry grouping, which is only an advantage when large numbers of shapes are part of the scene. In these cases, you might indeed be able to detect a difference by compiling.

Immediate Mode

The immediate mode, in contrast to the two modes previously described, provides a lot of run-time flexibility. This comes at the cost of severely limiting the kinds of optimizations that the Java 3D renderer can use.

Generally, a programmer who uses immediate mode is concerned with controlling rendering at the lowest possible level (that is, at the level of the frame buffer). Immediate-mode programmers often just want to take advantage of the geometry classes and to leave the other stuff behind. Their choice in using the immediate mode is often one of vanity rather than sanity because the optimizations that occur in retained or compiled-retained mode (for example, geometry compression, geometry grouping, scene graph flattening) are quite powerful. That said, Java 3D does provide a fairly robust immediate-mode rendering model and can accommodate most of the needs of immediate mode users. While in immediate mode, the Java 3D renderer is off and all rendering is done by direct calls. You should note that many of the rendering efficiencies built in an immediate-mode application on one platform won't necessarily result in the same efficiencies on a different platform.

To continue, the real rendering bottleneck is usually in scanning conversion and shading the triangles—not in the process of looping through frames. The Java 3D renderer helps us to avoid rendering unnecessary triangles, which, in most cases, is where the bulk of the optimizations are beneficial.

Mixed-mode Rendering

Finally, it should be noted that the immediate mode can be mixed with retained and compiled-retained modes. This option is often chosen in practice when low-level access to the frame buffer is needed. The mixed mode retains the property of continuous rendering from the retained and compile-retained modes. Four methods from the Canvas3D class (see the next chapter) can be overridden to allow the application to access the buffer at different stages of the pipeline. These methods are described in Table 10.2.

TABLE 10.2   Mixed-mode Rendering Methods

Mixed-mode Method	Pipeline Location
preRender()	Just prior to the Java 3D renderer's operation
postRender()	Just after the Java 3D renderer's operation
postSwap()	Just after the buffer swap
renderField()	During the Java 3D renderer's operation; particularly useful in stereoscopic imaging

Thread Scheduling

Java 3D requires a more robust thread scheduling system than the standard Java thread mechanism and therefore implements its own custom methods for thread execution. Under the Java 3D thread scheme, messages propagate through three separate mechanisms. One thread structure is spatially organized around geometric objects and is used for things such as picking, collision detection, and culling. The second thread mechanism is termed the *render bin* and represents the state of the scene graph associated with each view. This state impacts the rendering thread. Finally, object behaviors exist in yet another thread.

All three threads are run in an infinite loop. The thread scheduler runs all three threads once for each iteration of the loop and waits for all of them to terminate before entering the next iteration.

Geometric Modeling

Geometric modeling is at the heart of 3D graphics and is, quite frankly, among the most tedious and time-consuming parts of the entire enterprise. Although many people are born with a gift for creating models, the rest of us have to learn incrementally and through experimentation. Fortunately, there are programs to facilitate the process of building 3D shapes, and it also possible to purchase or download a large number of prebuilt shapes that can be imported into Java 3D. Finally, with 3D laser scanners becoming less expensive, the importation of 3D models will become more commonplace.

That said, it is strongly advised that you come to grips with the challenges of creating a 3D model. Geometric modeling can have a particularly steep learning curve but becomes considerably easier after the first couple of attempts.

In general, 3D models are best made incrementally. It is recommended that beginners start by specifying a single point or line and viewing that alone before adding new elements. It is also well worth the effort to make a list of parts and to begin thinking about these parts in terms of vertices and surfaces (see more next).

We present the basics here and develop these concepts as we work through several examples in the next chapter.

Wireframe and Solid Surface Models

A three-dimensional object can be described by the position of its points in an *Euclidean* three-dimensional space. The term Euclidean space is reserved for any n-dimensional space in which all points in the space are referenced to a single origin. The important idea here is that any point in an n-dimensional Euclidean space can be represented by n individual values (all implicitly referenced to the origin). For example, a Cartesian space is a special type of Euclidean space that is commonly used in 2D operations. In fact, we used numerous Cartesian spaces in the examples of Chapter 3, "Graphics Programming with the Java 2D API." A point in Cartesian space is represented by two values (x, y). For example, the point (10.0, 10.0) is meaningful because we assume the origin is (0.0, 0.0). A 2D shape can thus be described by a list of points, called *vertices*, in the 2D space. By drawing lines between the vertices and rasterizing them, a rendering of the shape is obtained.

Likewise, a 3D shape is also described by a list of vertices —this time using points with three values (x, y, z) . The simplest form of a 3D shape is the wireframe model in which vertices are connected by a series of straight lines (see Figure 10.7). Generally, wireframe models have been replaced in most applications by *solid surface models* but are still used in many computer aided design applications. A solid surface model is one in which the surface is approximated by a connected set of polygons (see Figure 10.8) .

FIGURE 10.7
A wireframe model created in Autodesk 3D Studio.

FIGURE 10.8
A solid surface version of the model from Figure 10.7.

A solid surface model can be built from a wireframe model and is essentially a wireframe with faces. We begin with the simplest example, building a cube in the center of a space. The first task is to specify eight three-dimensional points that define the corners of the cube. The points of the cube for this example are listed in Table 10.3.

TABLE 10.3 Points Defining a 10x10x10 Cube

Element	X	Y	Z
1	-10.0	-10.0	10.0
2	10.0	-10.0	10.0
3	-10.0	-10.0	-10.0
4	10.0	-10.0	-10.0
5	-10.0	10.0	10.0
6	10.0	10.0	10.0
7	-10.0	10.0	-10.0
8	10.0	10.0	-10.0

To make a wireframe version of this model, we would simply define a series of lines connecting the elements in series 1-2, 2-3,...7-8.

To make this wireframe model of a cube into a solid surface model, we need to add squares as shown in Table 10.4.

TABLE 10.4 One Possible Set of Faces for the Points in Table 10.3

Face #	Point #1	Point #2	Point #3	Point #4
1	1	3	4	2
2	5	6	8	7
3	1	2	6	5
4	2	4	8	6
5	4	3	7	8
7	3	1	5	7

Note that the particular polygons used in this example are defined with four points and are naturally called *quads*. The other commonly used polygon is the *triangle*. In fact, if we wanted to make a more efficient version of this particular surface mode, we would respecify each quad as two triangles. Returning to the problem of drawing quads, for the first face we would begin at point #1 (-10.0, -10.0, 10.0), move to point #3 (-10.0, -10.0, -10.0), to point #4 (10.0, -10.0, -10.0), to point #2 (10.0, -10.0, 10.0), and finally return to point #1. Indeed, this is directly analogous to the PathInterator and GeneralPath methods used in Java 2D (see Chapter 3). We would then proceed to draw the next face and so forth.

The object we just drew is from the general family of shapes known as *polyhedrons*. In a polyhedron, every edge is shared by exactly two faces. The basic process involved in creating a 3D geometric model is to first find a set of polygonal faces that describe the shape we intend to draw and then break this set of polygons into triangles (or quads), thus creating a triangle (or quad) mesh. Triangles are used because they are the optimal representation for hardware acceleration. At this stage, the effort of creating a sketch and parts list of the model really pays off. If the model is at all complicated—for example, a simple fighter jet or a room—there will be choices to be made.

Specifying geometry vertex by vertex is generally too time-consuming to be of much practical value. Thus, it is usually preferable to find an algorithm for programming these points or even to draw the object in a 3D drawing program first and then import it. Another very common way to get the model is to use a predefined *VRML (Virtual Reality Model Language)* model. It should be noted, however, that VRML still requires a significant effort and knowledge of scene creation. Regardless of which path or combination of paths a developer takes, there is often a need to operate at a pretty low level. Knowledge of these fundamental ideas is essential to understanding 3D graphics in general. You will have the opportunity to work through several examples in the next chapter.

Reducing Unnecessary Rendering Through Culling

Generally speaking, *culling* is a process through which a subset of a larger whole is selected and set aside for some purpose. This general definition applies to 3D graphics as well because many rendering algorithms attempt to extract only those polygons that are visible in a particular view. As an organism living in a 3D world, you are culling all the time. It is often helpful to consider what your brain and body do in real space to reduce the inordinate complexities of the world when considering what the computer can do as well. However, you must consider that the computer uses loops to accomplish what nature does by design.

View Frustum Culling

Because humans have eyes in the front of their heads, they don't see the majority of the visual field at all times. For many predatory animals, this is an evolutionary result of the need to focus high-resolution visual resources on objects in front of the organism. This constitutes a natural version of one of the most basic forms of 3D culling, *view frustum culling*. As an aside, we note that many animals have almost total surround vision and therefore perform very little of this *natural view frustum culling*.

The *frustum* (a pyramid with its top cut off) defines the shape of the viewing volume (that area of space within the user's view). The basic mantra of view frustum culling is *don't render anything that lies completely outside the user's field of view*. An example of basic view frustum culling is shown in Figure 10.9. In this example, objects A, B, C, and G are eliminated from further rendering of the view because they are outside the view frustum.

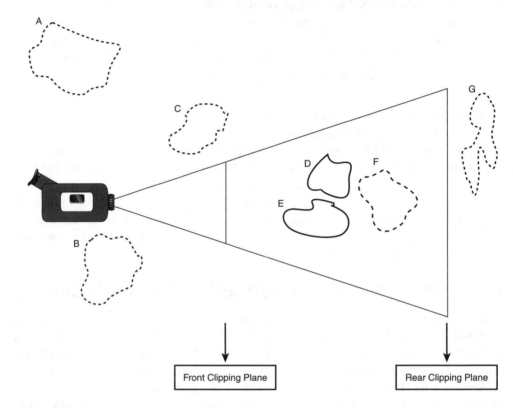

FIGURE 10.9
Some basic culling operations.

One efficient way to perform view frustum culling is to create a hierarchical map of the space that can be used to guide the frustum culling in an efficient manner. One popular form of the spatial hierarchy mapping is the *binary space partition tree (BSP)*. The general approach is as follows: 1) divide the space into arbitrary halves; 2) if the subdivided half of space has an object in it, continue dividing and testing for the presence of an object in the new space; otherwise stop processing this subspace and move onto another. (Figure 10.10 in the section "Particle Systems" shows a progression through a series of space partitions.)

Occlusion Culling

After the simple view frustum culling has been performed, we can still reduce the problem of what to render in a number of different ways. One additional form of culling operations that can be done is *occlusion culling*. Returning to Figure 10.9, you can see that object F is occluded by objects D and E. Therefore, in this particular view, it doesn't need to be rendered. Indeed, because we are creating and viewing a model in 3D space, there will always be parts of the model that are (or rather should be) obscured by other parts of the model. When multiple objects exist in the space, they too should obscure each other, depending on the viewing direction. Occlusion culling belongs to the general class of methods known as *hidden surface removal (HSR)* algorithms. Hidden surface removal is also commonly called *visible-surface determination*.

Two fundamental approaches to HSR, called image- and object-precision methods, derive their names from the inherent precision with which they can be calculated. The easiest and most commonly used of these two general classes of algorithm is image-precision, therefore we begin with it.

Image-Precision

The most obvious and generally preferable algorithm simply loops over the 2D rendering pixel by pixel and determines which object is closest to the viewer for every pixel. This type of algorithm is often referred to as *image-precision* because its precision is determined by the output image (rendering) that is to be produced. The time to calculate HSR on a single rendering of 10 objects and a resolution of 800x600 would require 10x800x600=4,800,000 comparisons. This is indeed a great number of comparisons, but each comparison can be handled pretty efficiently. It should also be noted that the image-precision algorithm can be tuned to process only pixels in a given subrectangle of the image and thus can be optimized for schemes that only process of subset of the pixels.

The most conceptually straightforward image-precision method to understand is the z-buffer algorithm. The z-buffer basically creates a series of frame buffers to hold depth layers of the scene. By laying down the layers in the proper order, an algorithm can eliminate the rendering and processing of any pixels that will be covered by a subsequent layer.

Object-Precision Methods

The second approach would be considered a more object-centered approach (sometimes called an *object-precision* algorithm). The idea behind this class of algorithms is to remain inside the 3D space and compare individual objects with themselves and other objects in the view volume. These comparisons can be more expensive than the image-precision methods and scale with the number of objects squared.

Inside- and Back-face Culling

The first step in both of the preceding algorithms is usually to remove the *inside faces* (faces that are on the inside of a solid surface model) and the *backfaces* (surfaces that are pointing away from the viewer). Generally speaking, these operations are best performed early in the rendering pipeline and usually make a substantial reduction in the dimensionality of the rendering problem.

Execution Culling

Another relevant form of culling is *execution culling*. In many applications, a great deal of the CPU overhead is in calculating events in the background. For example, in an environment with a lot of behaviors, it would be useful to create a scheduling tree that is activated only when the view is in certain spatially restricted areas. Consider a game in which a lot of computational resources are spent computing the trajectories of objects and appearances of objects, and so on. When these computations have no impact on the user and can be removed from the execution schedule, the CPU can be freed to compute what is relevant to the user's view. Of course, in multiplayer games, this becomes a far more complicated issue.

The general approach of an execution culler is to make a series of Boolean operations on a collection of bounding regions that are arranged into a *scheduling tree* (another hierarchical structure this time for organizing event contingencies). By keeping the scheduling regions a reasonable size, we are able to reduce the number of executions the renderer must make. You will see in Chapter 12 that Java 3D's `Behavior` objects usually have a wakeup criterion that must be met before the object performs its behavior. The scheduler won't activate the `Behavior` until something (e.g. the viewing volume) intersection with the object banding volume.

Spatially Organizing the SceneGraph

From the previous discussion on culling, you can see the benefit and necessity of creating a spatially organized scene graph. If the scene graph is organized intelligently, large branches of the tree can be collapsed and removed from the list of jobs to do in creating a rendering. This can *greatly increase* the efficiency of scene graph traversal.

Spatial Transformation

After a model is created, it exists in its original reference frame until it is somehow spatially transformed. Indeed, there isn't much point to go to all the trouble of geometric modeling unless the model can be moved or rotated. This is the domain of spatial transformation.

The definition of a *transformation* is a function that maps points from one space to another. There are two basic uses of transformation in 3D graphics.

The first use is to move, rotate, scale, and shear objects in three dimensions. The applications programmer will use transformations in this way time and time again.

The second use of transformation is less frequently encountered by the applications programmer but is present in every application. This is the use of transformation to project the 3D world onto a 2D screen or other output device. Much more detail about view projection will be given in Chapters 11 and 13.

We now introduce some of the basic mathematical background necessary for understanding transformations.

Model Transformations

Model Transformations are simply those spatial transformations that apply to the geometric model independently of the view of that model. Two general classes of model transformation are as follows:

- Rigid body transformations
- Deformation transformations

Rigid Body Transformations

A *rigid body transformation* is one in which the points are moved or rotated without changing the distances between them. Vectors, points, and scalars can undergo rigid body transformation. In three-dimensional space, there are six possible values that we can play with—three for translation (x, y, z) and three more for rotation (pitch, roll, and yaw). The six transformations are often referred to as having six degrees of freedom. Note that in the case of a Cartesian coordinate, we have three degrees of freedom (x, y, and rotation).

Sticking with the Cartesian coordinate system for a moment, we can see any point $P(x, y)$ specified in two dimensions can be moved to a new location in the same coordinate system $P(x+d_x, y+d_y)$ by simply adding d_x units to x and d_y units to y. This operation defines a translation in two dimensions and can be expressed in column vector form as

$$P' = P+T \text{ where}$$

$$P' = \begin{bmatrix} x' \\ y' \end{bmatrix}, \quad P = \begin{bmatrix} x \\ y \end{bmatrix}, \quad T = \begin{bmatrix} d_x \\ d_y \end{bmatrix},$$

As a further example, we consider scaling in 2D. Just as we added d_x and d_y to x and y, we can multiply x and y by scaling factors, s_x and s_y. Alternatively in matrix form, this is shown as

$$P' = S \cdot P \text{ where}$$

$$P' = \begin{bmatrix} x' \\ y' \end{bmatrix}, \quad S = \begin{bmatrix} s_x & 0 \\ 0 & s_y \end{bmatrix}, \quad P = \begin{bmatrix} x \\ y \end{bmatrix},$$

Finally, it is possible to rotate points about the origin. In this case, we have

$$P' = R \cdot P \text{ where}$$

$$P' = \begin{bmatrix} x' \\ y' \end{bmatrix}, \quad R = \begin{bmatrix} \cos\Theta & -\sin\Theta \\ \sin\Theta & -\cos\Theta \end{bmatrix}, \quad P = \begin{bmatrix} x \\ y \end{bmatrix},$$

You will notice that two of the three operations described previously are multiplications and that translation is the odd ball because it requires addition. It would be better if all three of these operations could be expressed in terms of multiplication and hence use a common set of methods for performing them. This is achieved through the use of a homogenous coordinate system.

Homogeneous coordinates are essential elements of projective geometry and permit the translation of points using matrix multiplication. By adding a *non-zero* third coordinate (the so-called W coordinate) to each of our 2D points, we can express each point in two dimensions as a line in three dimensions. Therefore, our point $P=(x, y)$ is now represented by $P = (x, y, W)$. Further, if we divide by W (often referred to as *homogenizing* the point), we get a point on a plane equal to $(x/W, y/W, 1)$. The addition of the W coordinate now mandates that a 3x3 matrix be used when translating our homogenous point a distance d_x and d_y. So, our translation operation, , in homogeneous coordinates is expressed as

$$\begin{bmatrix} x' \\ y' \\ 1 \end{bmatrix} = \begin{bmatrix} 1 & 0 & d_x \\ 0 & 1 & d_y \\ 0 & 0 & 1 \end{bmatrix} \cdot \begin{bmatrix} x \\ y \\ 1 \end{bmatrix}$$

So far, however, we have described no advantage to the use of homogeneous coordinates. The advantage comes from something that was alluded to previously. Homogeneous coordinates allow for the *composition* (also known as concatenation or compounding) of matrices. The advantage of composition is that a single transform can be used to make a series of spatial transformations, thereby often gaining a substantial improvement in efficiency.

The idea can be expanded to coordinate systems of any dimension. In our case, we are most interested in applying homogeneous coordinates in three dimensions. This time we will add W as the fourth coordinate of a point in 3D space, thereby representing a point as (x, y, z, W). Again, remember that W cannot equal 0 and is typically equal to 1 for convenience.

In short, by working with homogeneous coordinates, we can make efficient computations for any number of rotational, scaling, and translation operations through multiplication. The result of these operations will always be a matrix of the form:

$$M = \begin{bmatrix} r_{11} & r_{12} & r_{13} & t_x \\ r_{21} & r_{22} & r_{23} & t_y \\ r_{31} & r_{32} & r_{33} & t_z \\ 0 & 0 & 0 & 1 \end{bmatrix}$$

The preceding form is omnipresent in 3D graphs. Note that there are various submatrices that can be extracted. One of these is the upper-left 3x3 matrix denoted as R. R provides information on the aggregate scaling and translation. Likewise, the 1x3 column vector of ts provides the aggregate translation.

So far, we have only dealt with points in 3D, however, because lines and polygons are defined by their endpoints and vertices respectively, it is trivial to apply the transformations to these points as well.

> **NOTE**
>
> In Java 3D, it isn't really necessary to work directly with the 4x4 matrix because there are a number of methods for rotation, scaling, and translation. Nevertheless, the 4x4 matrix is such a staple of 3D graphics in general that you are encouraged to become familiar with the form. Java 3D's utility package includes a large number of methods for accessing matrices and performing mathematical operations on them (see Chapter 11) .

Deformation Transformations

The two primary forms of structure deformations are scaling and shearing. *Scaling* refers to proportionally reducing or increasing the distances between points. This can be thought of as contracting or expanding the space linearly.

The second deforming transformation is shearing. With a *shearing* transformation, the points are displaced on some axis by an amount proportional to that point's distance from the origin along another direction. For example, a shear in the Y direction will transform the values of X and Z according to the point's position in Y. Those with a larger Y projection will move the most in the X and Z directions.

Transforming in Local Coordinates

Another approach to the problem of transformation was also illustrated in Chapter 2 where we considered transformation in terms of a change in coordinate systems. This is often the approach used in practice and as you will see, a frequently used approach in Java 3D.

The basic idea is to think in terms of local coordinate systems within the global coordinate system. A good example of local coordinate systems is our solar system. One coordinate system can be defined for the Sun and yet another can be defined for each planet that orbits the Sun. The Earth is rotating in its coordinate system and is rotating around the Sun in the Sun's coordinate system. Of course, calculating the Earth's rotation about its axis within the Sun's coordinate system would be possible and far more challenging than computing the Earth's rotation about its own axis in its coordinate system and moving the entire coordinate system around the sun. More examples of the use of local coordinate systems are given in the next chapter.

Quarternions

There has been a lot of interest recently in using quarternions for computing rotations in space. *Quarternions* are a mathematical construct involving fourth dimensional vectors, complex numbers, and a special algebra. There is really nothing new about quarternions because they were discovered in the mid-1800s. The desirability of using Euler angles versus quarternions has been debated ever since.

The advantage of quarternions stems from the fact that for some rotations, executing the Euler angles in series can lead to the loss of one degree of freedom. The occurrence of this is termed *gimbal lock* and happens when two of the angles begin to describe the same rotation. Quarternions allow for rotations about an arbitrary axis and therefore aren't susceptible to the order of rotations problem encountered with some Euler angle sequences. Quarternions can be used to advantage in these cases. It should be noted that gimbal lock rarely poses any real problem for most applications but it does occasionally, and the developer should be aware of the opportunity to use quarternions.

A second reason why a programmer would want to specify rotation in quarternions is that the interpolation between two points on a curve can be smoother. This is where the real argument for using quarternions can be made. Rotational animations can be considerable smoother when quarternions are used to compute the transformations.

In practice, however, we haven't found the use of quarternions to yield a significant improvement in our visualizations. Our recommendation is for developers to attempt their visualizations first with the more traditional Euler rotations to see if the Euler angles are sufficient to the task before considering the more challenging quarternion approach. Of course, modelers with a solid understanding of quarternions should use whichever approach they feel the problem calls for. Java 3D's vecmath package fully supports quarternions.

Projection Transformations

As we have stated frequently in this chapter, the great irony of 3D modeling is that after we go to all the trouble to specify an object in terms of a 3D coordinate system, we are forced to render it to a 2D screen. This unfortunate fact of life adds another level of complexity to the transformations that we must use in order to render a 3D scene. The name for this process is *view projection*.

Two fundamental forms of projection exist: *perspective* and *parallel*. These are described next. Refer to Chapter 13 and Listing 13.1 for a detailed examination of these and other viewing concepts. We give a brief description here.

Perspective Projection

A *perspective projection* is the type that is most common in drawing and that matches how we view the environment in real life. The technique makes objects that are farther away smaller and makes lines that go into the distance converge (that is, a road running into the horizon). Perspective is the default for realism and is the choice to make in the vast majority of applications.

Perspective projections are created by placing the user's eye at the point of convergence of rays reflected from the objects in the virtual world. As each ray travels to the eye, it passes through the view plane. The set of these points are stored for later rendering.

The distance from the eye to the projection plane can be varied to produce different focal distances.

Parallel Projection

The idea behind *parallel projection* is that the depth dimension of the 3D space is collapsed such that all lines that are parallel in the 3D space map onto a single point on the projection plane. Parallel projection is often used when the visualization requires that the objects maintain their size dimensions on the output rendering; for example, when an architect draws construction plans. Another commonly used term for parallel projection is *orthographic projection*; however, this term refers only to projections at right angles (90 degree) to the projection plane. A parallel projection taken at any other angle is termed *oblique*.

See Figure 13.2 and 13.3 for examples of perspective and parallel projections.

The Java 3D View Model

Java 3D has a particularly sophisticated model for creating views into the virtual world. These views include both perspective and parallel projections as previously discussed as well as *stereoscopic* views that will be discussed in Chapter 13.

Java 3D's view model is controlled primarily through the View object. The View object contains all the information necessary to render a 3D scene from a single viewpoint and is attached to a virtual platform, called the ViewPlatform, which in many ways resembles a moveable camera. You should note, however, that the `ViewPlatform` object extends this traditional concept of a camera platform in several important ways. These additional capabilities have relevance to some advanced applications such as head tracking and the use of specialized input devices and will be expanded on in Chapter 13.

For the most part, you *should* think of the `ViewPlatform` as a camera while keeping in mind that advanced features come with it.

The View Model: A Chain of Coordinate Systems

After all is said and done, we are left with a fairly large number of coordinate systems and transformations. To begin with, we have the series of transforms that exist within the virtual world (for example, the position of our `ViewPlatform`, the scaling of our scene objects, the objects' positions, and so on), and we have a lot of coordinates in the real world (for example, the location of our display relative to our head position, that we have yet to even mention).

A fundamental dichotomy exists between coordinates in our 3D world and coordinates in our physical world. We refer to this dichotomy as the virtual/physical dichotomy. The coordinate systems that pertain to virtual and physical worlds are shown in Table 10.5 and 10.6, respectively.

TABLE 10.5   Relevant Coordinate Systems in the Virtual World

Coordinate System	Influence
Virtual	All the objects and coordinate systems that exist in the virtual world created by the programmer or user
ViewPlatform	The location of the platform in the virtual world

TABLE 10.6   Relevant Coordinate Systems in the Real World

Coordinate System	Influence
Image Plate	Represents the 2D coordinate system of the output display; can be further transformed into left and right eye images for HMDs and other stereoscopic displays.
Head	Specifies the basic location of the users head, including information about the locations of the eyes and ears.
Head Tracker	Represents the location of the user's head.
Tracker Base	Can be specified in absolute or relative coordinates depending on type of head tracker.

Let's not forget that we are typically writing an application that we hope will run on a variety of platforms and display options. How does Java 3D coordinate these coordinates? You will remember from our discussion of transformation mathematics that a set of homogeneous matrices can be composed into a single matrix. The use of matrix composition in conjunction with the Java 3D view model makes solving the series of transformations much more tenable and frees us to work on content instead of the details of each and every transformation in this long list.

Mapping the Virtual World to the Physical World and Vice Versa: The Coexistence Coordinate System

Our primary goal in creating virtual environments is to create a feeling of immersion in the virtual space. To this end, whatever can be done to link physical actions such as head movement or hand manipulation to appropriate changes in the virtual space is beneficial. In order to accomplish this dual existence, we need to determine the location of real objects in virtual space. To understand how Java 3D accomplishes this feat is to understand a special coordinate system called the *coexistence coordinate* system. The coexistence coordinate system sits in between the virtual world and the real world.

In Chapter 13, we develop a full 3D model of the Java 3D view model including the calibration and placement of trackers, the view plane projection, and view frustrum.

Particle Systems

Particle systems are an extremely hot topic in game design and simulation at present (see Figure 10.10 for an example). A particle system is basically a collection of small objects (particles) that obey some model of physics. Particle systems are real attention getters and are commonly used for effects such as explosions, fire, and gas trails. Moreover, in visualization, particle systems are often exactly what we are trying to model in the first place. In Figure 10.10, the particle system models the gaseous explosions and is based on a complex mathematical model developed by astrophysicists.

One aspect of a dynamical system is a certain amount of evolving randomness and possibly a fate for each particle. For example, part of what makes a realistic looking fire model is that the flames flicker in a fashion that isn't totally predictable. An explosion also contains a certain level of randomness and, further, the sparks and hot cinders tend to change state over the time course of the model. These examples clearly fall into the realm of particle systems.

A major challenge to building a particle system is abandoning the approach of having a unique transform and appearance for every particle. Any particle will contain a whole family of properties that describe things such as its position, velocity, color, life span, gravity, and wind force. All these properties will be dynamic (that is, the color of a burning ember will glow and

10

slowly turn to black). For a system with thousands of particles, keeping track of and computing these properties will be a large job. Transparency is another property widely used in this type of modeling.

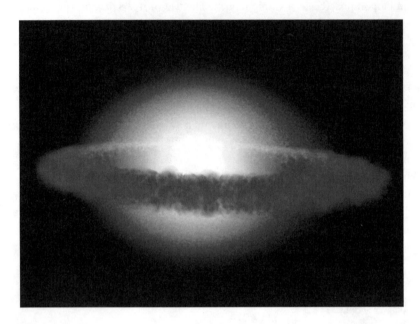

FIGURE 10.10

Particle system visualization of a super nova. (Photo courtesy Joe Berger, Michigan State University MIND Lab)

Often the approach is to have two interacting systems. The first represents the particle itself and the second is a particle manager.

Texture Mapping

One of the keys to making realistic looking environments is the proper use of texture maps. Texture maps are special images that are applied to 3D geometry and are most often used to simulate detail in the scene that would be impractical to create with geometric primitives (for example, grass). Texture maps are also used extensively to show mountainous scenes or cities in the far distance. When used properly, texturing can add a great deal of realism to virtual environments. When used improperly, texture mapping can destroy rendering performance. An understanding of basic texture mapping is invaluable to the applications developer. We provide a short introduction here and follow up with more detail in Chapter 11.

You saw in Chapter 2 how textures could easily be applied to 2D objects. The extension to 3D is slightly more complex. The process is a series of steps for mapping pixels from a 2D image onto coordinates on an arbitrary polygon. The standard notation for the coordinates of the texture is (u, v). By convention, (u, v) are each in the range of 0.0–1.0. The 3D shape is flattened so that it too occupies a 2D coordinate space, which is denoted by (s, t). The texture mapping algorithm's job is to fit the (u, v) coordinate system onto the (s, t) prior to rendering into screen coordinates.

The texture map, then, refers to a 2D array in which the first column is filled with the points of the polygon that are to receive the texture (u, v) and the second column is filled with the corresponding image values for each pair. Each element of this array is called a *texel*. The process of texture mapping is to determine the array of texels given the texture (a rectangular array of pixels) and the polygon (a list of triangles). Once the texels are determined, it becomes trivial to render them.

Determining the Texels

The easiest form of texture mapping is linear mapping. In this case, a reduced set of texture coordinates (u, v) is determined for each vertex of the polygon, basically anchoring the edges of the image to the edges of the polygon. It is then a simple matter to interpolate along vertical and then horizontal lines of the polygon, thus generating the remaining texels from the reduced set of texels at the anchor points.

Although linear mapping is the easiest to conceptualize and compute, it suffers from undesirable distortions when perspective projection is used to compute the polygon's image on the screen. This is because the transformation to the perspective projection is a non-linear transformation. In many cases, this linear mapping distortion might not be a problem. However, it is a serious problem when putting textures on walls and floors in virtual environments because the perspective transformations can be large in these cases.

MIPMAPing

MIPMAPing is an intimidating word for a fairly straightforward concept. The term MIPMAP was first introduced by Lance Williams in a 1983 SIGGRAPH paper. The MIP part of the acronym is derived from the Latin phrase *multum in parvo* (many in small) and refers to the central idea of a MIPMAP, which is to store many images in a memory buffer. The technique can be used to reduce a form of flicker that occurs when textures are reinterpolated as a result of a change in the size of the rendered texture polygon. Additionally, MIPMAPing can be used to perform *Level of Detail (LOD)* rendering (see the following discussion), which can be useful to reduce the rendering time for a scene.

Recall from the previous discussion on texture mapping that the texture is a fixed entity based on the number of pixels. If a large texture is mapped to a small polygon, there will be minification. Conversely, a small image mapped onto a large polygon will undergo magnification.

Occasionally both processes occur at the same time when, for example, a texture needs to be magnified in one dimension and minified in the other.

The need for MIPMAPing arises from the fact that the process of magnification and minification often exhibit discrete jumps as the size of the rendered polygon changes. These jumps can look like a brief flash or shimmering. Additionally, the magnification and minification processes can be computationally expensive (particularly in the case of minification). It is more efficient to have a stack of images available in memory.

Modeling Light and Shadows

In the real world, any object is visible because it reflects light. Various materials reflect light in different ways, and these differences add to our perception of individual objects. Computer renderings can only simulate the effects of real light using colors. This process, called *shading*, is an artistic technique used by painters to increase the realism of scenes. Shading is also a computational technique in 3D graphics that can be used to increase the immersive impact of any 3D scene.

There are three main types of computer generated lighting that we will consider here. The first, termed *radiosity*, gives the best approximation to real world lighting but is too computationally expensive to consider for interactive graphics. Radiosity works by computing the reflection of the simulated light from every point of every surface in the scene. The second type of lighting model used in 3D is *ray-tracing*, where the reflected light is computed for every pixel of every object. Indeed, ray-tracing is more efficient that radiosity, but it still isn't practical for interactive applications.

The third model, and the one used by Java 3D and OpenGL, is to compute reflection for each vertex of each polygon and then interpolates the points in between.

Five different types of light interactions are possible using Java 3D's lighting model and are listed in Table 10.7 with comments.

TABLE 10.7   Lighting Models and Their Interactions

Interaction	Comments
Ambient Scattering	Light is scattered uniformly; independent of viewer position or light location.
Diffuse Reflection	Light is scattered from a surface depending on the orientation of the light source and the surface.
Specular Reflection	Reflected light depends on direction of light, orientation of surface, and direction of view.

TABLE 10.7   Continued

Interaction	Comments
Transparent Transmission	Light penetrates and is scattered through a semitransparent object. Refraction isn't calculated.
Emitted Light	An object that glows (that is, a neon light).

A little lighting goes a long way. Good use of Java 3D's lighting will add substantial realism to the scene. The primary limitation is the inability to compute interactions among multiple objects. Java 3D won't model the light reflected from one object onto another.

Surface Normals: The Direction of Reflected Light

Of particular importance in performing many of the previous lighting computations is the surface normal. A *surface normal* is a unit line perpendicular to the surface of a face and is used in calculating how much light is reflected when a light source comes into contact with a surface.

User Interaction in 3D Space

One vision of virtual reality has us doing our shopping, filing our documents, and having many of our human interactions in interactive 3D spaces. To this end, a large number of devices exist on the market today such as gloves, wands, and body trackers, as well as other special devices such as head and eye trackers. We leave aside the idea of haptic or force feedback devices to focus on sensors or objects that are passive in nature. Some consideration of the problem of extending haptics and motion platforms capabilities to Java 3D through extension are covered in Chapter 13.

Picking

Picking, in particular, object picking, refers to the user selection of an object in the 3D scene. Such techniques allow the user to perform actions such as selecting 3D user interface elements that are in the environment or drag and drop objects in different locations (that is, arrange the environment). The trick in picking is to translate a mouse click on the 2D screen (or some other 2D device) into a position in the 3D world. This is accomplished by casting a ray from the user's eye position over the mouse click position and determining what objects that ray intersects the 3D world. We will cover picking in greater detail in Chapter 12.

Navigation

Obviously for any virtual environment application, navigation is going to be key. The psychologist Edward Tolman and his students at Berkley did much of the fundamental work in how rats build up cognitive maps of the environment through exploration. They showed convincingly that rats could use information about the environment to compute novel and optimal trajectories.

A fundamental question is whether we build robust cognitive maps of virtual environments, and the answer is pretty clear that in most cases we do not. Getting lost in virtual reality is commonplace, and this fact has serious implications for the use of virtual environments for things such as training and 3D experiential e-commerce.

In virtual spaces, navigation usually involves moving the viewing platform through the environment in a first-person fashion. We will explore different mechanisms for adding realism to VR-based navigation in Chapter 12.

Java 3D Sensors for External Devices

Java 3D provides an interface, the Sensor interface, that, along with the InputDevice interface, can be used to provide interaction with a variety of external devices. The major problem is that only a paucity of vendors have written implementations of these interfaces. If the Sensor to be used isn't one of the few that is supported, it is up to the programmer to develop a custom design.

Briefly, Java 3D communicates with a device driver through the InputDevice interface. If the input device is to be used by Java 3D, it must implement the InputDevice interface and make the object known to the PhysicalEnvironment object.

The Sensor interface contains the information about a real-time device such as a mouse, a headtracker, or a joystick.

Unjarring the Java 3D Utilities

You might want to copy the j3dutils.jar file into a new directory and run the jar extraction utility on it. This will unjar an enormous number of classes that are provided in the form of the utilities package. This is a great way for the developer to understand some ways to create classes and utilize packages in future development projects. One of the frequently used classes in the Java 3D.utils package is the SimpleUniverse class, which contains utilities for creating a ViewPlatform and moving it back for viewing. For reasons that will be explained later, we tend to avoid using the SimpleUniverse class.

Summary

Three dimensional graphics is a difficult topic that is made considerably easier by knowing some fundamental ideas about rendering, geometric modeling, and matrix transformations. Geometric objects, textures, lights, and other elements in the environment or visualization are organized together into a scene graph. A view volume is used to restrict rendering akin to what you would see by viewing the scene through a window. The elements of the scene that remain after clipping the viewing volume are rendered by the Java 3D renderer, which performs optimizations on the scene graph and its elements and then makes a reduced set of calls to a low-level API. Given an understanding of this basic information, the developer can proceed to understand the powerful high-level abstractions of Java 3D that are described in the next chapters.

Creating the Virtual World

IN THIS CHAPTER

Programming an application in Java 3D requires setting up a scene graph. All scene graphs contain two essential elements; the content subgraph and the view subgraph. This chapter guides you through the process of creating these two fundamental scene graph elements and culminates with the beginning installments of two comprehensive examples.

Revisiting the Java 3D Scene Graph

As discussed in the introduction to the 3D Visualization section in Chapter 10, the scene graph is the organizational structure for all Java 3D programs. It is worth the effort for you to develop a well thought out scene graph before beginning to code an application. At the very least, the scene graph will serve as documentation for the design. But just as importantly, the scene graph can guide the programmer's conceptual approach to the application. As a designer gains competence, the scene graph also serves as a way to see the optimization and grouping strategies that are always important considerations in any 3D application.

A Java 3D program, like a program developed in any other scene graph based API, is a collection of nodes and their relationships. (Recall the terminology of discrete mathematics, *nodes* and *edges* from Chapter 10, "3D Graphics, Virtual Reality, and Visualization.") For now, we will say these elements are organized in the form of a tree (they are actually directed acyclic graphs, which will be described later in the chapter). Implicit in the tree design are parent-child relationships; the children are attached to the parents and live below them within the tree structure (see Figure 11.1). The practical implication of this is that the parents' states are carried through to their children.

Because the tree is such a good analogy, we will continue with it. Java 3D includes nodes, called Group nodes, which serve as the major branches of the tree. Like a branch, a Group will typically contain more branches that eventually lead to a termination point (called a Leaf node). The scene graph acts as the organizing structure for a Java 3D application and is also useful as documentation. In Figure 11.1, groups are indicated by circles and leaves by triangles.

Like trees you would see in your own backyard, scene graph trees have a wide variety of branching patterns, some intricate and others pretty simple. There are some (but not many) restrictions on what types of branches can be added where. The complexity of the tree naturally builds from the base, but the majority of the work in developing Java 3D applications is in developing a particular branch, the *content branch*. Java 3D's ease of content creation is an important advance because it brings an entire class of scientists, engineers, and artists into the world of 3D and Web3D.

Returning to our analogy of the tree, we move up (increasing in detail) from the base. The first major functional division of the tree is into the two branches: the *content subgraph* and the *view subgraph*. Both the content and view subgraphs are represented by a special Group object known as a BranchGroup. Later, you will see that the BranchGroup has some special properties. The details of developing the content and view subgraphs are discussed later in this chapter. For now, we will consider the different types of branches that we can use to organize the scene graph.

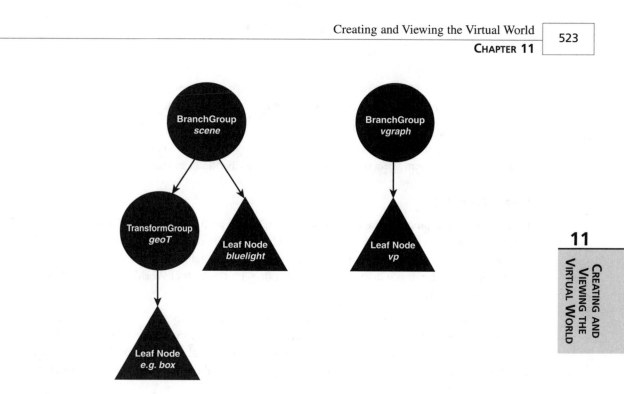

FIGURE 11.1

Simple scene graph for BasicRecipeJ3D.java.

Java 3D Group Nodes: The Branches

Six fundamental ways to group scene graph elements in Java 3D are listed in Table 11.1. The listed classes are used to organize the elements in Java 3D scene graphs. All these grouping classes extend the abstract class Group.

TABLE 11.1 Important Subclasses of Group

Subclass	Function
BranchGroup	The root of a subgraph; can be compiled or set as the child of another BranchGroup.
TransformGroup	Spatial transformations applied to a TransformGroup are applied to all children.
Switch	Allows switching among subgraphs.
SharedGroup	A subgraph that can be shared by multiple nodes (see Link leaf).
OrderedGroup	Puts nodes in a specific rendering order.
DecalGroup	Extends OrderedGroup; renders children in first to last order; useful for putting markings on top of objects (for example, packing labels on boxes, markings on a roadway, and so on).

The classes in Table 11.1 inherit two important qualities from Group: 1) each can have one (and only one) parent, and 2) each can have any number of children.

Three of these classes (BranchGroup, Switch, and TransformGroup) are used extensively in most applications, whereas the remaining three (OrderedGroup, SharedGroup, and DecalGroup) have more specialized uses that are described later in this chapter.

Leaf Nodes

In addition to Group nodes (the branches), Java 3D contains a second type of node called a Leaf node (the leaves). The difference is that while Group nodes act to organize the scene, the Leaf nodes represent specific elements in the scene such as lights, sounds, and shapes and behaviors (a major part of Chapter 12, "Interaction with the Virtual World," and partially covered in this chapter).

Leaf nodes are the lowest level constructs in the scene graph. They have no children and exactly one parent. The Leaf node class itself is abstract; therefore, the programmer would never instantiate a Leaf node object directly. From a conceptual scene graph design standpoint, it is important to recognize which objects are subclasses of the Leaf node class and which are subclasses of Group node.

Directed Acyclic Graph

Although we have been using the analogy of a tree to describe the organization of a scene graph, we should make it clear that Java 3D, as well as other scene graph APIs, are really a special kind of graph structure called a *directed acyclic graph (DAG)*. Two major distinctions exist between a DAG and other types of graphs. These differences are reflected in the terms *directed* and *acyclic*.

The *directed graph*, or *digraph*, has a fairly long history of use in logic, perhaps even dating back to Aristotle himself. A digraph can be thought of in terms of a series of one-way streets. The key concept to keep in mind is that although a graph is like a map of a neighborhood, a directed graph represents a particular route through that neighborhood. This distinction will become clearer as you progress through this chapter. In terms of the scene graph, it means that a unique path can be drawn from the trunk of the tree to each of the Leaf nodes that eventually terminates the branching patterns. This path is often referred to as a *scene graph path*.

The term *acyclic* refers to the complete absence of loops within the scene graph structure. In simple terms, you cannot take a path that starts and ends at the same node. This restriction usually isn't an issue in most applications; however in certain circumstances, it does come into play. In the interest of simplicity, we will not concern ourselves with these situations here except to note that they are forbidden.

Following a Scene Graph Path

As mentioned previously, it is important to realize that because we are dealing with a DAG, a unique path can be drawn from the root of the scene graph to any Leaf node in the scene graph. The presence of a unique scene graph path enables a number of important advantages in rendering optimization and is particularly useful in the area of object picking, a major topic of Chapter 10, in the section on "User Interaction in 3D Space." The important concept to understand now is that each unique scene graph path specifies the state attributes of the Leaf node at the termination of the path. As you will see throughout this chapter, a Leaf node can have numerous state attributes including location, orientation, color, and so on. Each Leaf Node's attributes represent the accumulation of acquired attributes as the scene graph path is traversed.

One of the important jobs of the *Java 3D renderer* is to determine the most efficient order in which to render the set of Leaf objects. This type of rendering optimization is precisely the advantage of a scene graph based API. Note that it is possible to specify a programmer defined rendering order using an OrderedGroup, discussed in the section "OrderedGroups" later in this chapter; however, this is only useful in certain rare circumstances and is generally ill-advised unless the application absolutely requires the use of OrderedGroup.

Recipe for Writing a Java 3D Application

We are now going to describe the basic paradigm for writing a Java 3D application. To repeat, most of the programming effort goes into creating one or more BranchGroups for holding content. BranchGroups are the fundamental organizational structure to use when building the scene graph and are a mandatory element of all Java 3D programs.

Required Ingredients

All Java 3D programs have a basic set of ingredients that must be present in order to do anything. The classes for these objects are listed in Table 11.2.

TABLE 11.2   Objects that Must Be Present in Any Java 3D Program

Major Class	Function
BranchGroup	The root of a subgraph; most commonly takes the form of a scene subgraph, but also represents the view graph
Locale	Stores the origin of attached BranchGroups in high resolution coordinates
ViewPlatform	Defines a coordinate frame with an attached view
VirtualUniverse	The top-level container for any scene graph

11

**CREATING AND
VIEWING THE
VIRTUAL WORLD**

Canvas3D—a Place to Draw 3D Scenes

Even though it isn't absolutely mandatory that a Java 3D application has a rendering area on the screen, the cases in which an application doesn't are extremely rare.

The Canvas3D class provides a Component on which the 3D scene is rendered. Because Canvas3D is an extension of Canvas, it can be added to containers just like the Graphics2D object we used in Chapter 3, "Graphics Programming with the Java 2D API." It is therefore present in practically all Java 3D applications.

> **CAUTION**
>
> The Canvas3D object is a *heavyweight* object (that is, has a native peer), whereas Swing components are lightweight. This can cause some problems when adding a Canvas3D object to a Swing component. Workarounds to these problems are provided in the examples that follow.

A Canvas3D object can be used for both onscreen and offscreen rendering. Onscreen and offscreen Canvas3Ds behave somewhat differently from each other. Onscreen Canvas3Ds are rendered automatically and continuously if they are attached to an active View object. This isn't true of offscreen Canvas3Ds, which are only rendered after a call to the renderOffScreenBuffer() method. A second difference is that onscreen Canvas3Ds can be either single- or double-buffered, whereas offscreen Canvas3Ds are only single-buffered. Finally, offscreen Canvas3Ds are only available as monoscopic entities. (Monoscopic and stereoscopic viewing are covered in Chapter 13, "The Java 3D View Model.")

First Programming Example

Listing 11.1, BasicRecipeJ3D.java, demonstrates the structure of a program that contains the elements listed in Table 11.2 as well as an instantiation of the Canvas3D object.

The first three of the components in Table 11.2 will be covered in more detail later. For now, we will focus on the critical fourth element in Table 11.2, the BranchGroup.

Two fundamental parts of the scene graph are contained in BranchGroups: the *content sub-graph* and the *view subgraph*. These two objects are instantiated and added to the Locale object in the last four lines of Listing 11.1.

LISTING 11.1   BasicRecipeJ3D.java Part 1 of 4

```java
public BasicRecipeJ3D() {
   setLayout(new BorderLayout());

   GraphicsConfigTemplate3D g3d = new GraphicsConfigTemplate3D();
   GraphicsConfiguration gc =
      GraphicsEnvironment.getLocalGraphicsEnvironment().
getDefaultScreenDevice().getBestConfiguration(g3d);

   Canvas3D c = new Canvas3D(gc);
   add("Center", c);
   universe = new VirtualUniverse();
   locale = new Locale(universe);

   BranchGroup scene = createSceneGraph();
   BranchGroup view = createViewGraph();

   locale.add(scene);
   locale.add(view);
}
public static void main(String[] args) {
    new MainFrame(new VoxelModeler(), 256, 256);
 }
}
```

In addition to the creating of the view and content subgraphs, there are several important aspects of the previous code to examine. First is the creation of the Canvas3D object, c. Notice that the Canvas3D constructor requires a GraphicsConfiguration object. The GraphicsConfiguration is an object of general use in Java and encapsulates information about the graphics and printer devices on a particular platform. More information about the GraphicsEnvironment, GraphicsDevice, and GraphicsConfiguration objects is provided in Chapter 2, "Imaging and Graphics on the Java Platform." To get a GraphicsConfiguration object for 3D operations, we must also use the GraphicsTemplate3D class to create an additional object that is used for setting 3D graphics defaults.

Also, note the somewhat unusual call to the MainFrame class. MainFrame is a utility class that extends the Applet class and is provided in

com.sunj3d.utils.applet.MainFrame;

The purpose of the MainFrame class is to allow the class (in the preceding case, our BasicRecipeJ3D class) to be run as either a standalone application or as an applet.

Finally, we add the scene and view subgraphs to the scene graph superstructure object Locale.

Organizing the Scene Graph Through BranchGroups

To repeat, in Listing 11.1 we instantiate two separate BranchGroup objects and add them to the Locale object; one to represent the content subgraph and the other to represent the view subgraph. You are urged to get used to this structure because it is always present.

In the vast majority of cases, there is only one Locale. (Occasionally, there are more than one.) In all cases, there is one and only one VirtualUniverse. Thus, "the trunk of the tree" of a Java 3D scene graph is fundamentally the same for every program.

From this discussion, you can see that the top operating level for the developer is at the BranchGroup level. You will be well served in understanding and thinking of the Java 3D program in this way. To gain insight into any Java 3D example, the programmer should find and chart the BranchGroups. This approach will permit the programmer to "see the forest from the trees" in any application.

> **CAUTION**
>
> Indeed, although six basic Group objects can be used to Group scene graph elements, the BranchGroup is the only object that can be added directly to a Locale object.

The BranchGroup has additional properties that separate it from the other subclasses of Group. First, BranchGroups are the only objects that can be detached from a live scene. Also, a BranchGroup is the only object that can be compiled.

When writing Java 3D programs, we will always want to create at least one scene graph and one view graph. Keep this in mind as we continue our discussion.

We will now discuss in detail the substructures of these two important branches:

    Content graph
    View graph

The Content Graph

The majority of the work in developing a Java 3D application typically occurs in creating the content graph. To create the content graph, the programmer will write a method that returns a BranchGroup. The BranchGroup returned from this method is then added to a Locale object.

After the BranchGroup is added to the Locale object, it is considered "live" and will go into a kind of continuous render mode. This is called "retained mode" versus the alternative "immediate mode."

The purpose of the content or scene BranchGroup is to glue together the scene elements and those operations performed on them.

The building of a content graph is illustrated with the following simple example.

Imagine that we want to develop a 3D scene with a single object in the center. In this case, our method to return a BranchGroup will be trivial. Because the content is so simple, most of the work will actually be in setting up the program outside of creating the content subgraph. You should note that this is the opposite of the usual case. In BasicReceipeJ3D, in Listing 11.2, we add a simple box to the content subgraph as seen in Figure 11.2.

FIGURE 11.2
Screenshot from BasicRecipeJ3D *with a box added to the scene graph.*

Regardless, the structure of the program isn't too difficult. In the application's constructor, we create an instance of VirtualUniverse and Locale. After this is done, we are free to call our custom method for creating the content BranchGroup and add that BranchGroup to the Locale. Part 2 of the code from our BasicRecipeJ3D.java example is shown in Listing 11.2.

LISTING 11.2   `BasicRecipeJ3D.java` Part 2 of 4

```java
public void BasicRecipeJ3D()

. . .


BranchGroup scene = createScene();
locale.addBranchGraph(scene);


. . .

}
```

The method to create our content subgraph is

```java
public BranchGroup createScene() {

  // Create the root of the branch graph; this will be returned
  BranchGroup objRoot = new BranchGroup();

  //Create an appearance object to apply to the geometry

  Appearance app = new Appearance();
  Color3f red = new Color3f(1.f, 0.f, 0.f);
  Color3f black = new Color3f(0.f, 0.f, 0.f);
  Color3f white = new Color3f(1.f, 1.f, 1.f);

  app.setMaterial(new Material(red, black, red, white, 100.0f));

  //Create some geometry
  Box box = new Box(1.f,1.f,1.f, app);

  // Create a simple shape leaf node, add it to the scene graph.
 objRoot.addChild(box)
  return objRoot;
}
```

Building the content graph is the focus of this chapter, and we will explore the range of options throughout. For now, it is enough to realize that there are a large number of ways in which we can enhance our content subgraph. One thing that we can do in our `createScene()` method is import prebuilt objects (detailed later in this chapter and in Chapter 12) from other software packages, such as 3D Studio or VRML 2.0 and most recently X3D (so called VRML on steroids). We can also use this method to add lights, specify animation behaviors, and place textures on objects in the scene.

If the objects within the environment are complex at all, we will want to create external classes to load them. For example, we develop a variety of geometric primitives in the section "Making Simple Geometry with the Java 3D Utilities." Objects from these classes are instantiated and added to the scene graph in the `createScene()` method.

BasicRecipeJ3D is used throughout the rest of this chapter as a way to quickly view content. You will be asked to comment and uncomment sections of the createScene() method. As we develop classes and then build applications around those classes, we will largely abandon BasicRecipeJ3D. However, it is recommended that the programmer keep the class handy for future applications because it is a quick way to view classes and test code. I recommend that the reader and developer write a demo frame class as an exercise in order to become familiar with the interaction of Java 3D and Java.

The key information to take away from this discussion is that if we plan to create a 3D world, we will need a content subgraph to add to the Locale object. You can do this by writing a method similar to the previous createScene() method and use it to return a BranchGroup that is added to the scene graph. Later, you will see that BranchGroups can contain other Group objects that further allow the programmer to organize the scene graph in an intelligent manner.

With this elementary concept in hand, we move on to the second major branch of the scene graph, the view graph.

The View Graph

Now that we have a way to bring content into our scene graph, we need a way to control how the content is viewed. For now, we will leave aside the technical details of the Java 3D viewing model in order to continue with our basic recipe for creating a Java 3D program; however, moving beyond a rudimentary understanding of Java 3D will require an in-depth knowledge of the view model (provided in Chapter 13).

The view graph, like the content graph, is contained in a BranchGroup object. Therefore, we will need to add the elements of our view graph to a BranchGroup and add the BranchGroup to the same (usually) Locale to which we added our content subgraph.

Remember that the BranchGroup represents major branches in our scene graph tree. In most cases, the view graph is considerably simpler than the content graph; however, this need not always be the case. It is possible to add geometry and other objects to the view graph just as in the scene graph. For now, we will focus on the common elements that form the view graph.

The key element that we will add to the view BranchGroup is a ViewPlatform object. For the sake of the immediate discussion, you can consider the ViewPlatform as a type of camera mounted on a platform but, as will be discussed in Chapter 12, this is a gross oversimplification of the ViewPlatform's role. Indeed, the sophistication of the ViewPlatform is one of the major aspects of Java 3D that separates it from other 3D APIs. Advanced use of the Java 3D view model is discussed in Chapter 13.

Listing 11.3 illustrates the creation of our view graph.

LISTING 11.3 BasicRecipeJ3D.java Part 3 of 4

```
. . .
BranchGroup viewgraph = createView();
locale.addBranchGraph(viewgraph);. . .

public BranchGroup createView() {
  //Create the root of the view graph to return
  BranchGroup viewRoot = new BranchGroup();

  //Create the ViewPlatform object
  ViewPlatform vp = new ViewPlatform();

  //Add the ViewPlatform object to the BranchGroup and return
  viewRoot.add(vp);
  return viewRoot;
}
```

In Listing 11.3, several objects that are part of the view model are instantiated. Specifically, these objects are `PhysicalBody` and `PhysicalEnvironment`. We defer coverage of these objects until Chapter 13 and encourage you to continue without worrying about the details. The important point here is that there is a separate `BranchGroup` for the view graph and that the view graph contains a `ViewPlatform` object that can be manipulated by the application.

At this point, you shouldn't be discouraged by the rather unsophisticated results of this program. Much more attractive geometry and materials will be used later. The purpose of this first program is to show the programming paradigm in the simplest possible fashion.

Grouping Scene Graph Elements

So far, we have only worked with `BranchGroup` objects, but—as mentioned previously—six subclasses of the `Group` node can be used to achieve different organization/functional groupings. We examine these other subclasses of `Group` here.

TransformGroup

Although the `TransformGroup` is not listed among the mandatory objects in any Java 3D program, it is effectively mandatory in the sense that spatial transformation is at the heart of 3D graphics, and `TransformGroups` are the mechanism by which spatial transformations are made in Java 3D.

If we wanted to add a second box to our simple scene in Listing 11.1, we could add the following lines to the `createScene()` method:

```
Public BranchGroup createScene() {
  . . .
```

```
   // Make a second object, a bigger box; use same material
   Box bigbox = new Box(6.f, 6.f, 6,f, app);
   ObjRoot.add(bigbox);
}
```

Obviously, this step isn't very useful because we cannot see the small box inside the big box we just created. At any rate, we are going to eventually want to distribute our objects around the scene and move different groups of them based on user actions.

Moving, rotating, and otherwise spatially transforming scene objects is accomplished through the use of the `Transform3D` class in conjunction with one or more `TransformGroups`. To see how these objects work together, add the following lines to the `createScene()` method:

```
//instantiate the TransformGroup and set its Capability bits
TransformGroup bigboxTG = new TransformGroup();

//add bigbox to the TransformGroup
bigboxTG.addChild(bigbox);

//set up a Transform3D object and translate the object in x
Transform3D bbtran =  new Transform3D()
bbtran.setTranslation(new Vector3f(7.f, 0.f, 0.f));1
//set the transform of the TransformGroup to bbtran
bigboxTG.setTransform(bbtran);
```

In order to invoke the preceding spatial transformation, we need to change the parent-child relationships of the over-simplified scene graph by adding `bigbox` to the newly created `TransformGroup` instead of directly to the `BranchGroup` as we did in the first example. In turn, we add the new `TransformGroup` to the `BranchGroup`. Indeed, it is less common to add scene elements (`Leaf` nodes) directly to the `BranchGroup`. The more usual case is to add the scene element to a `TransformGroup` and add the `TransformGroup` to the `BranchGroup`.

Now our scene graph looks as shown in Figure 11.3 and our scene looks like Figure 11.4.

In this context, the `TransformGroup` seems like an unnecessary branch to the scene graph. Why not just translate the geometry directly?

When we really start designing a simulation or a virtual environment, we will see that the `TransformGroup` is quite useful. If we wanted to make a wall with a window and some paintings on it, it would be much easier to attach the window and paintings to the wall and then move the entire group of objects with a single transform. A natural grouping will shake out of our design. Without having a formal structure for grouping transformations, things will get messy in a hurry. Moreover, without grouping, when the programmer wants to move the wall and its contents in the future, a new transform will have to be computed for each object. If the objects are moveable by the user, the programming is even more complicated and rapidly becomes inefficient. The answer to this problem is to group the elements together in a `TransformGroup`. Finally, we note that `TransformGroups` are the basis of many of the optimizations that can be achieved.

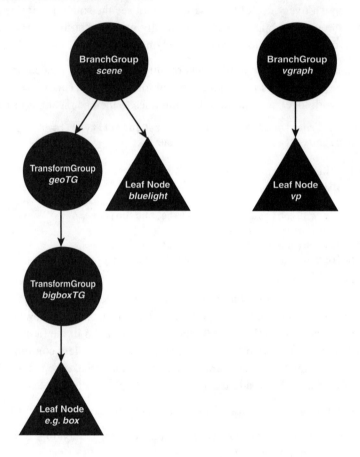

FIGURE 11.3

Reorganized scene graph from `BasicRecipeJ3D.java` *showing additional* `TransformGroup` *and alteration in the parent-child relationships.*

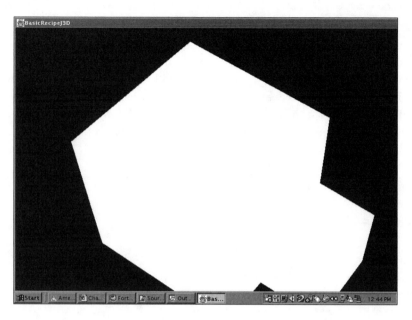

FIGURE 11.4

Screenshot from the application after adding and translating a second box using a TransformGroup.

Chains of TransformGroups

TransformGroups can be added to other TransformGroups to set up a hierarchy of transforms. A nice example of this would be making a visualization of a skeletal arm. Each individual joint of the arm can naturally be thought of in terms of a TransformGroup. The wrist, for example, would rather naturally form a TransformGroup that has as its children the bones of the hand (the carpal, metacarpal) and the bones of the fingers (phalanges). By changing the transform of the wrist (that is, by rotating or otherwise displacing it), the hand and fingers will move with it. The wrist with the forearm (radius and ulna) would, in turn, be added as a child to the TransformGroup of the elbow. Performing a rotation of the elbow would thus cause the wrist with all of its children and grandchildren to follow. Likewise, a TransformGroup of the shoulder (humerus) should be the parent of the TransformGroup of the elbow and its children such that when the shoulder rotates, the elbow will follow, as will the wrist. This hierarchical arrangement can be described further, of course, but the analogy has already served its purpose.

Adding the `ViewPlatform` to a `TransformGroup`

Note that the `ViewPlatform` can also be added to a `TransformGroup` and manipulated as well as in Listing 11.4. As we did in Listing 11.1, we will instantiate a `BranchGroup` object in the `createViewGraph()` method. However, this time we will also create a `TransformGroup` called `vpTrans`, and add the `ViewPlatform` to it. We can then translate the `ViewPlatform` back a bit getting and setting the `TransformGroup`'s `Transform3D`. Finally, we add the `TransformGroup` to the `BranchGroup` thereby producing the subgraph shown in Figure 11.5.

LISTING 11.4   `BasicRecipeJ3D.java` Part 4 of 4

```
public BranchGroup createViewGraph() {

    BranchGroup objRoot = new BranchGroup();

    Transform3D t = new Transform3D();

    t.setTranslation(new Vector3f(0.0f, 0.0f, 10.0f));
    ViewPlatform vp = new ViewPlatform();
    TransformGroup vpTrans = new TransformGroup();
    vpTrans.setCapability(TransformGroup.ALLOW_TRANSFORM_WRITE);
    vpTrans.setCapability(TransformGroup.ALLOW_TRANSFORM_READ);
    vpTrans.setTransform(t);
    vpTrans.addChild(vp);
    view.attachViewPlatform(vp);

    NavigationBehavior nav = new NavigationBehavior(vpTrans);
    vpTrans.addChild(nav);
    nav.setSchedulingBounds(bounds);

    objRoot.addChild(vpTrans);
    return objRoot;

}
```

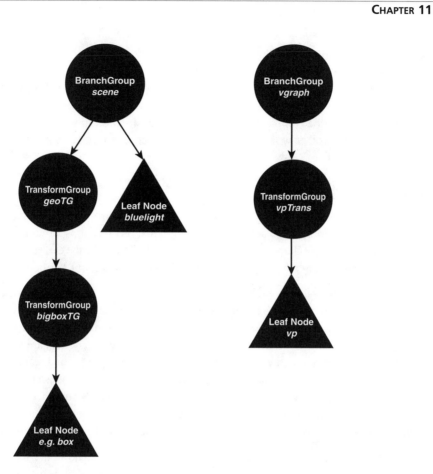

FIGURE 11.5
Scene graph after adding the ViewPlatform *to a* TransformGroup.

Thinking in Terms of Local Coordinates

From the previous discussion about the skeletal arm, it is pretty clear that TransformGroups can best be understood in terms of local coordinate systems. In other words, by placing ourselves in the local coordinate system of the wrist, we can easily understand the rotations there. It is far easier to enter the local coordinate system than to think of all transformations relative to some unifying coordinate system. One quickly develops the ability to shift coordinate systems. This concept is an integral part of many visualization problems and is basic to the KspaceModeller example, "Comprehensive Example #1: MR Physics Visualization," that begins near the end of this chapter. A clear hierarchy of TransformGroups is set up in order to have a rotatable and scalable net vector.

Rotating an Object Around the Origin

Rotations occur about the origin of the transform, so if the transform has any non-zero translation components, the object will move about the origin (that is, orbit). The whole issue of the order of operations becomes important in this situation. If the object is rotated and then translated, the result will be completely different from the situation in which the object is translated and then rotated. In other words, T(R(x,y,z)) is not equal to R(T(x,y,z) i), where T is translation and R is rotation.

Switch Nodes

Switch nodes are useful for choosing which among a number of children to render. Note that any number of children can be selected including none, one (the most common), or multiple. Choosing the child or children to render is accomplished through the Switch's setWhichChild() method or by specifying a bit mask and calling the setChildMask() method.

One of the primary uses of a Switch node is level of detail rendering in which different amounts of detail are rendered, depending on how near or far the viewer is from the part of the scene to be rendered. Using a model of New York City as an example, if the user is sitting on top of the Empire State Building, a lot of the Statue of Liberty's details are wasted because the viewer can't see the fine detail from such a great distance. It might be useful to set up a series of BranchGroups—the first containing the most detailed model of the Statue of Liberty and the last containing only a large rectangle with a texture map of the Statue of Liberty. As the user navigates closer to the Statue of Liberty, the more detailed geometric model would be switched on based on a proximity switch sensor, whereas the less detailed model would be switched off.

Another application is in hiding and unveiling an object(or objects) in the scene. Listing 11.5 shows an example of switching between two simple scenes based on pressing any key on the keyboard.

LISTING 11.5   SwitchExampleJ3D.java

```java
import java.applet.Applet;
import java.awt.BorderLayout;
import java.awt.event.*;
import java.awt.GraphicsConfiguration;
import com.sun.j3d.utils.applet.MainFrame;
import com.sun.j3d.utils.geometry.Box;
import com.sun.j3d.utils.geometry.Sphere;
import java.util.BitSet;

import com.sun.j3d.utils.geometry.Primitive;
import com.sun.j3d.utils.universe.*;
import javax.media.j3d.*;
```

LISTING 11.5   Continued

```java
import javax.vecmath.*;
import com.sun.j3d.utils.behaviors.mouse.MouseRotate;

public class SwitchExampleJ3D extends Applet {
  VirtualUniverse universe;
  Locale locale;
  TransformGroup vpTrans;
  View view;
  Bounds bounds;
  Switch sw;
  BitSet bitset;
    public BranchGroup createSceneGraph() {
// Create the root of the branch graph; this will be returned

        BranchGroup objRoot = new BranchGroup();
        sw = new Switch();
        sw.setCapability(Switch.ALLOW_SWITCH_READ);
        sw.setCapability(Switch.ALLOW_SWITCH_WRITE);

        sw.addChild(createScene1());
        sw.addChild(createScene2());
      //set up a bitset with 3 bits x x x
        bitset = new BitSet(3);
        bitset.set(0);
        bitset.set(1);
        objRoot.addChild(sw);

        objRoot.compile();
      return objRoot;
      }

    public BranchGroup createScene1() {

        BranchGroup scene1 = new BranchGroup();

        Color3f blue = new Color3f(0.f, 0.f, 0.9f);

        Appearance app = new Appearance();
        Material mat =  new Material();
        mat.setSpecularColor(blue);
        app.setMaterial(mat);

        TransformGroup geoTG = new TransformGroup();
        geoTG.setCapability(TransformGroup.ALLOW_TRANSFORM_WRITE);
      geoTG.setCapability(TransformGroup.ALLOW_TRANSFORM_READ);
```

LISTING 11.5   Continued

```java
        BoundingSphere bounds =
            new BoundingSphere(new Point3d(0.0,0.0,0.0), 100.0);

        MouseRotate mouseBeh = new MouseRotate(geoTG);
    geoTG.addChild(mouseBeh);
    mouseBeh.setSchedulingBounds(bounds);

        Sphere sphere = new Sphere(1.0f, Sphere.GENERATE_NORMALS |
                Sphere.GENERATE_TEXTURE_COORDS, 45);

        Sphere orbitsphere = new Sphere(.3f, Sphere.GENERATE_NORMALS |
                Sphere.GENERATE_TEXTURE_COORDS, 45);

        TransformGroup otranTG = new TransformGroup();
        Transform3D torbit = new Transform3D();
        torbit.setTranslation(new Vector3f(.5f, .5f, 1.5f));
        otranTG.setTransform(torbit);
        otranTG.addChild(orbitsphere);

        geoTG.addChild(otranTG);

        geoTG.addChild(sphere);

        // AmbientLight al = new AmbientLight(true, new Color3f(.1f,.9f, .1f));
        // AmbientLight al = new AmbientLight();

        Vector3f bluedir  = new Vector3f(0.0f, -8.0f, -8.0f);
        DirectionalLight bluelight = new DirectionalLight(blue, bluedir);


        bluelight.setInfluencingBounds(bounds);

        scene1.addChild(geoTG);

        scene1.addChild(bluelight);
        return scene1;

    }

    public BranchGroup createScene2() {

.   .//more or less the same as createScene1();

}
```

Creating and Viewing the Virtual World

CHAPTER 11

541

11

CREATING AND
VIEWING THE
VIRTUAL WORLD

LISTING 11.5 Continued

```
public SwitchExampleJ3D() {
   setLayout(new BorderLayout());
    //GraphicsConfiguration config =
        //  VirtualUniverse.getPreferredConfiguration();

   Canvas3D c = new Canvas3D(null);
   add("Center", c);
       universe = new VirtualUniverse();
   locale = new Locale(universe);
   PhysicalBody body = new PhysicalBody();
   PhysicalEnvironment environment = new PhysicalEnvironment();
   view = new View();
   view.addCanvas3D(c);
   view.setPhysicalBody(body);
       view.setPhysicalEnvironment(environment);
   // Create a simple scene and attach it to the virtual universe

       bounds = new BoundingSphere(new Point3d(0.0,0.0,0.0), 100.0);
       BranchGroup scene = createSceneGraph();
       BranchGroup vgraph = createViewGraph();


       KeyHandler kh = new KeyHandler(this);
       c.addKeyListener(kh);

      locale.addBranchGraph(vgraph);
   locale.addBranchGraph(scene);
   }

   public void changeScenes() {

       if (sw.getWhichChild()==0) {
          sw.setWhichChild(1);
       }
       else if (sw.getWhichChild()==1) {
         sw.setWhichChild(Switch.CHILD_MASK);
         sw.setChildMask(bitset);
       }
       else {
          sw.setWhichChild(0);
       }
   }

//make a custom keyhandler
class KeyHandler implements KeyListener {
```

LISTING 11.5 Continued

```
SwitchTextJ3D st;

public KeyHandler(SwitchTextJ3D st) {
    this.st = st;
}

public void keyReleased(java.awt.event.KeyEvent p1) {
}

public void keyPressed(java.awt.event.KeyEvent p1) {
    st.changeScenes();
}

public void keyTyped(java.awt.event.KeyEvent p1) {
}

}
```

Notice in the preceding code that we create a `BranchGroup` called `objRoot` and add it to the `Locale` object, just as we would in any Java 3D application. However, now we create two separate `BranchGroups` and add them to our Switch. The `Switch` is added to the top-level `BranchGroup`, `objRoot`.

The `changeScenes()` method simply switches rendering between the first `BranchGroup`, the second `BranchGroup`, and both `BranchGroups`, depending on the values set in the `BitSet` object.

Shared Groups

A `SharedGroup` can be used to hold shapes that are used repetitively in scenes and serves to reduce overhead (in some cases) and to simplify the program. In a road scene, for example, some elements will frequently be encountered (stop signs, yield signs, and so on). Instantiating these road elements each time would force us to have a high overhead and an unwieldy scene graph.

Importantly, `SharedGroups` aren't added to the scene graph directly, but instead are referenced through a `Link` leaf. The `Link` leaf is added to the scene graph.

> **TIP**
>
> A `SharedGroup` can be compiled prior to being referenced, and this often presents an important opportunity for optimization.

OrderedGroups

From our discussion of the z-buffer algorithm in Chapter 10, remember that conflicts some-times exist about which objects belong in front of each other in the scene and that this can add artifacts to the rendering. Gamers naturally refer to this problem as z-buffer fighting. In some cases—especially those in which many near coplanar surfaces are used—an `OrderedGroup` can be used to explicitly state the rendering order of all children. The rendering order is the order in which the children are added. The other `Group` subclasses allow the Java 3D renderer to create an optimized rendering order.

DecalGroups

The `DecalGroup` class is a subclass of `OrderedGroup` and is used for defining decal geometry that is placed over other geometry. As a subclass of `OrderedGroup`, `DecalGroup` provides an order for rendering its children. Further, `DecalGroup` specifies that its rendering should be coplanar with the object that is to receive the decal.

The object to receive a decal holds the 0 index position. All the polygons for each of the children must face in the same direction as this index 0 object.

Adding Prebuilt `Behaviors` to the Scene Graph

We digress from this chapter's main topic for a moment to introduce some standard `Behaviors` that we can add to our scene graph. For most projects, it is worthwhile to add these standard `Behaviors` to the application early in the development. The reason for this is some type of basic 3D user interaction (e.g. navigation, picking) is useful for debugging the scene when it is first created. Often, you might run a program only to discover that what appears to be an empty scene is actually not empty because the `ViewPlatform` is not properly oriented and positioned or the lighting too soft.

The following `Behaviors` are part of the Java 3D utilities package: `MouseRotate`, `MouseTranslate`, and `MouseZoom`. They are often attached to the highest level `TransformGroup` in the content or view subgraphs. Another useful `Behavior` included in the Java 3D utilities is the `OrbitBehavior`. Not included in the Java 3D utilities is a basic utility for navigating via the keyboard. Therefore, we develop the `NavigatorBehavior` class as part of Chapter 12.

`Behaviors` are typically added to the scene graph or view graph by attaching to the desired `TransformGroup` as follows:

```
TransformGroup tg = new TransformGroup();
Bounds bounds = new BoundingSphere(0.f,100.f);
MouseRotate mrotate = new MouseRotate();
mrotate.setTransformGroup(tg);
mrotate.setSchedulingBounds(bounds);
objRoot.addChild(mrotate);
```

The preceding section of code allows the user to rotate all elements that are added to the `TransformGroup` `tg` and is useful for examining a model.

Capability Bits

To provide the optimal rendering conditions in the default scene graph, Java 3D defaults to the most restrictive options. In other words, it is up to the programmer to turn on the appropriate capability bits for anything that is restricted. For the uninitiated, the errors generated because of "capability not set" can be mysterious and eat up a lot of time.

There are two basic ways to set the capability bits, and a preference for one over the other is a matter of personal style. We demonstrate the general approach using the most common application, allowing for reading and writing of the current transform for a `TransformGroup`.

The first is to set them at instantiation time using a construct such as

```
TransformGroup tg = new TransformGroup(TransformGroup.ALLOW_TRANSFORM_READ |
                    TransformGroup.ALLOW_TRANSFORM_WRITE);
```

The second is to use the `setCapability()` method as follows:

```
TransformGroup tg = new TransformGroup();
tg.setCapability(TransformGroup.ALLOW_TRANSFORM_READ);
tg.setCapability(TransformGroup.ALLOW_TRANSFORM_WRITE);
```

By setting these two particular capability bits, we are disabling some of the optimizations that can be used by the Java 3D renderer on this particular `TransformGroup`. You should avoid making the mistake of allowing all `TransformGroups` these capabilities because noticeable reductions in rendering speed can result.

Using 3D Geometry

Creating geometry is usually the most frustrating part of developing a 3D scene. Java 3D provides utilities for making basic geometric elements (for example, the `Box` used in our examples so far) and many scenes can be developed using these supplied elements. It is recommended that the beginning Java 3D programmer begin with these and not get too bogged down laying out vertices and faces (although doing so is enlightening). A brief summary of the geometry classes follows, but before that we should examine the basic elements of developing geometry in, or as will be seen shortly, for Java 3D.

The reason we emphasize creating geometry for Java 3D is that it is possible and sometimes highly desirable to use a third-party package to develop the geometry for a scene. Additionally, it is easy to find pre-existing geometric objects on the Internet. Finally, the developer might be restricted to using 3D models of a particular kind. For example, the 3D model of a human subject's cerebral cortex shown in Figure 11.6 was made more easily using a third-party package and then output as .OBJ. More information on the Loader interface is provided in the section "Using Loaders."

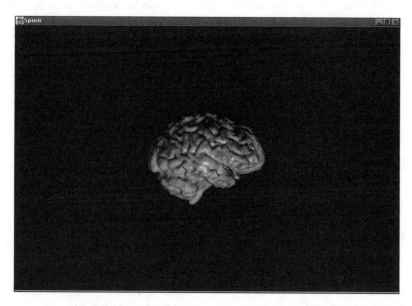

FIGURE 11.6

3D model of a human brain derived from MRI images.

Java 3D provides all the classes necessary to create geometry and in most cases offers a lot more flexibility than using loaders.

In developing an application that requires more than simple geometry, the programmer is always faced with a choice—to either program the geometry using the Java 3D classes or to build the geometry in another package and import it. Often a hybrid approach is optimal.

Following a description of using simple geometry, we will compare these two approaches and examine the tradeoffs therein.

Making Simple Geometry with the Java 3D Utilities

Java 3D provides several classes for the creation of some basic geometric primitives. These are often sufficient to get the programmer started with some simple examples and indeed can be used in more complex cases as well. You will see, throughout this chapter, that often the supplied geometric primitives aren't sufficient for many jobs. Therefore, geometry needs to be either custom programmed or alternatively imported from a third-party package in many cases.

The Java 3D geometry classes are found in com.sun.j3d.utils.geometry and, with the exception of the ColorCube class, all extend another supplied class called Primitive. Primitive extends Group. As mentioned in Chapter 10, it can be useful to examine these classes by unjarring the Java 3D-utils-src.jar file. Remember to copy this file to a new directory before unjarring it. After unjarring, it is possible to see how the Java 3D architects built various utilities such as the Box class described next.

Although the geometry classes are indeed very useful, you will see shortly that they certainly don't satisfy all of our geometric modeling needs. In those cases, it is necessary to either program the geometry or to use a loader. We begin with the simple geometry classes before addressing the more complicated topic of programming geometry and geometry loaders.

The Box Class

Four constructors are used to create a Box. The three most commonly used are

```
Public Box();
Public Box(float xdimension, float ydimension, float zdimension,
➥Appearance appearance);
Public Box(float xdimension, float ydimension, float zdimension,
➥Appearance appearance, int Capability);
```

There are five constructors for the Cone class; all of which require a radius for the base and length. Note that the number of divisions is specified in the radial direction.

```
Public Cone();
Public Cone(float radius, float length)
Public Cone(float radius, float length, Appearance appearance)
Public Cone(float radius, float length, int Capability, Appearance appearance);
Public Cone(float radius, float length, int Capability, Appearance appearance,
➥int ndivisions);
```

The Cylinder Class

Like all cylinders, the Cylinder class defines a tube with a radius and height. An object instantiated from this class is centered at the origin and aligned with the Y axis. The most common constructors are

```
Public Cylinder();
Public Cylinder(float radius, float height)
Public Cone(float radius, float height, Appearance appearance);
Public Cone(float radius, float height, int Capability, Appearance appearance);
Public Cone(float radius, float height, int Capability, Appearance appearance,
➥int ndivisions);
```

Creating and Viewing the Virtual World

CHAPTER 11

547

11

CREATING AND
VIEWING THE
VIRTUAL WORLD

The `Sphere` Class

As you would expect, the `Sphere` class produces a ball with a given radius.

```
Public Cylinder();
Public Cylinder(float radius)
Public Cylinder(float radius, Appearance appearance);
Public Cone(float radius, int Capability, Appearance appearance);
Public Cone(float radius,  int Capability, Appearance appearance,
➥int ndivisions);
```

Specifying the Appearance Bundle

Creating the geometry using the provided Java 3D utility classes is pretty easy because a number of important details were taken care of without our knowledge. One of the important things that occurs behind the scenes is the creation of a `Material` and an `Appearance` for the object. Note, however, that you can specify your own `Appearance` object in all the utility geometry constructors.

At this point, you should keep in mind that the `Shape3D` class contains both a `Geometry` object and an `Appearance` object (also known as an `Appearance` bundle).

Programming `Geometry` in Java 3D

The central class for creating geometry in Java 3D is `Shape3D`. In its most general form, a `Shape3D` object is a list of `Geometry` objects with an `Appearance` bundle. For now, we will focus on the geometry contained in the `Shape3D` node and defer a detailed discussion of the `Appearance` bundle until later. The geometry components are listed in Table 11.3 and are all subclasses of `Geometry`.

TABLE 11.3   Geometry Components

Compressed Geometry	*An efficient representation of geometry*
GeometryArray	Arrays of position coordinates, colors, normals, and texture coordinates for points, lines, and polygons
Raster	A special subclass for displaying a `Raster` in a 3D scene; defined as a point, therefore not able to use with picking or collision
Text3D	A 3D representation of a string; see the next section

To reiterate, a `Shape3D` is a collection of geometry components that reference a single `Appearance` object. We will now describe the geometry components listed in Table 11.3.

We begin with the `GeometryArray` class, which represents a collection of geometric primitives. Table 11.4 shows a list and description of the allowable primitives.

TABLE 11.4   Subclasses of `GeometryArray`

Class	Usage
`GeometryStripArray`	Specifies vertices in terms of variable length strips.
`IndexedGeometryArray`	A set of four arrays that specify per vertex color, texture coordinates, position, and normals.
`LineArray`	Lines specified by pair of points. Line attributes (for example, thickness) are specified through the `Appearance` bundle.
`PointArray`	Specifies a set of points in space. Point attributes are specified in the `Appearance` bundle.
`QuadArray`	Elements represent the corners of a quad.
`TriangleArray`	Elements represent the corner of a triangle.

The classes listed in Table 11.4 fall into three broad categories, strip-based geometry, indexed-based geometry, and basic vertex specification type geometry.

Strip-based Geometry

When one specifies geometry in strips, it is similar to building a model with long strips of cardboard or paper. The important thing to note about strip-based geometry is that there needs to be an index that specifies which elements belong to which strip. Table 11.5 shows the strip-based geometry classes. The classic example of strip-based geometry is a cocktail umbrella. Each of the umbrella's triangles meets in the center and shares two edges with its neighbors. This is exactly the way to format the data in a triangle fan array.

TABLE 11.5   Strip-based Geometry Classes

Class	Usage
`LineStripArray`	Defines a set of lines connecting pairs of vertices. Line attributes are set via the `Appearance` bundle.
`TriangleFanArray`	Represents a series of triangles in a fan formation. Functionally equivalent to a set of convex polygons.
`TriangleStripArray`	Specifies a series of triangles in strip formation.

Index-based Geometry

The `IndexedGeometryArray` is really an array of four vectors specifying the position coordinates, colors, normals, and texture coordinates for each primitive. Not all of these are necessarily specified. For example, in the class in Listing 11.6, only the position coordinates are specified. A series of bitmasks can be queried in order to find out which combinations of the four vectors have been specified. The `IndexedGeometryArray` classes are essentially index-based version of the classes specified in Table 11.4 with the prefix `Index` attached. We defer discussion until the examples later in this chapter.

Programming Example with Simple Vertex-based Geometry

We begin our examples of programming geometry by using the simplest `Geometry` class, the `PointArray`. The simplicity of this class makes it a good choice for gaining a basic understanding of the operations involved in programming geometry.

The `PointCloud` class (see Listing 11.6) generates *n* random 3D coordinates and puts them in a `PointArray`.

LISTING 11.6   `PointCloud.java`

```java
import javax.media.j3d.*;
import javax.vecmath.*;
import java.util.Random;

public class PointCloud {

    float verts[];
    Point3f[] rCoords;
    Random r;

    PointArray points = null;
    Shape3D shape;

    public PointCloud(int npoints, float x, float z, Appearance a) {

        r = new Random();
        genRandomCoordinates(npoints, spread);
        Appearance app = new Appearance();
        points = new PointArray(npoints, PointArray.COORDINATES);
        points.setCoordinates(0, rCoords);

        shape = new Shape3D(points, app);
    }
```

11

CREATING AND
VIEWING THE
VIRTUAL WORLD

LISTING 11.6   Continued

```
    public void genRandomCoordinates(int npoints, int spread) {

        for (int ii=1; ii <= npoints; ii++) {
            rCoords[ii] = new Point3f(r.nextFloat()*spread,
r.nextFloat()*spread,
➡r.nextFloat())*spread;

        }
    }

    public Shape3D getShape(){
        return shape;
    }
}
```

Let's take a deeper look at this class. The first thing to notice is that the class is a bit unusual because it doesn't extend any Java 3D classes. Other than the constructor, the PointCloud class has two methods. The first method, genRandomCoordinates(), generates random 3D points using the nextFloat() method of the Random class. Note that each Float value is multiplied by the float spread in order to spread the points out (nextFloat() generates numbers [0,1.0]. Each Point3f is stored in a one dimensional array rCoords. After rCoords is generated, it is used as an argument to the setCoordinates() method of our PointArray. The genRandomCoordinates() method isn't standard because it uses the random() method to generate the points. Usually, the coordinates represent a known object and must be specified.

The second method simply returns the shape that was just created in the constructor. This is the method that the calling class will use to get the Shape3D object into the scene. We therefore add the following from our standard createScene() method:

```
PointCloud pc = new PointCloud(10000);geoTG.addChild(pc.getShape());
```

The class in Listing 11.6 follows the standard recipe for creating a Shape3D. In this case, only the vertices are specified. If for example, we wanted to also generate colors for each vertex, we could add a method to generate arrays of length npoints such as follows:

```
GenRandomColors(nponts);
points.setColors(0, rColors);
```

The GenRandomColors method would be the following:

```
public void genRandomColor(int npoints) {
    for (int jj=0; jj <  npoints; jj++) {
            rColors[jj] = new Color3f(r.nextFloat(), r.nextFloat(),
➡r.nextFloat());
    }
}
```

Creating and Viewing the Virtual World

CHAPTER 11

551

11

CREATING AND
VIEWING THE
VIRTUAL WORLD

Finally, we need to modify the `creatScene()` method to incorporate our random colors:

```
points = new PointArray(npoints, PointArray.COORDINATES | PointArray.COLOR_3);
points.setCoordinates(0, rCoords);points.setColors(0, rColors);
```

A related example using the point array to plot real data in 3D is given in Listing 11.21 under `SpikeCloud.java` in the section "Comprehensive Example #2: Neuronal Spike Visualization."

A Hybrid Example of Geometry Programming

The importance of the GeometryArray is such that we follow it up with another example. We will continue to expand this particular example in "Comprehensive Example #1: MR Physics Visualization." In this case, we want to create a scalable tube with a cone at the end. This object will represent the net magnetization of a group of "spins" in a sample of brain tissue or other substance of interest. The net magnetization is a vector quantity because it has both direction and magnitude. This is different from the concept of a vector from computer science. We will increase the complexity of this object considerably as we develop it into a comprehensive example including adding the ability to shrink and grow this vector.

The first important idea is that, with the exception of the `PointArray` and `LineArray` (and their index-based relatives), `Geometry` objects represent surfaces. Except for explicitly bidirectional surfaces, a surface has only one side and thus can be invisible depending on the viewing direction. This can make programming them particularly challenging and prone to trial and error. You will remember that we recommend attaching one or two navigational or rotational `Behaviors` to the scene graph in order to avoid the danger of becoming lost in space. Using the `Geometry` classes is definitely a case in which having a way to move the object of `ViewPlatform` is beneficial. Often the developer is looking at the wrong side of the surface or is unknowingly sitting in the middle of the object.

The second important lesson from this example is that programming geometry can be tedious work. There is a particularly steep learning curve with the `Geometry` classes. We remind you that this advanced topic can be skimmed over for its gist and returned to later as necessary.

Finally, we take a tack slightly different from our first example and create our geometry within a class that extends `TransformGroup`. The reason for this is mostly academic. However, we choose this approach here because it is 1) commonly seen in examples, and 2) we intend to add children to the object and perform a series of spatial transformations on them as a group.

In this example, we create a `Shape3D` called `vbody` and add it to our class extending `TransformGroup` (the `VecBody` class). We also create a `Cone` object and add it to another class extending `TransformGroup` called `VecHead`. These two `TransformGroup` objects are then added to a higher level `TransformGroup` called `Mnet`.

We begin by showing the `VecBody` class (see Listing 11.7) because it contains the programmed `Geometry`.

LISTING 11.7   VecBody.java

```java
import java.lang.Math.*;
import javax.media.j3d.*;
import javax.vecmath.*;

public class VecBody extends TransformGroup {

    float length, radius;
    int nsegs;
    Appearance app;

    float xDirection, yDirection;
    float xVecBody, yVecBody;
    float endcapPos;
    float basecapPos;

    int nFaces;        // #(vertices) per VecBody face
    int VecBodyFaceTotalVertexCount;   // total #(vertices) in all teeth
    int nStrips[] = new int[1]; // per VecBody vertex count

    int VecBodyVertexCount;        // #(vertices) for VecBody
    int VecBodyStripCount[] = new int[1]; // #(vertices) in strip/strip

    Point3f coord = new Point3f(0.0f, 0.0f, 0.0f);

        boolean center;


    Vector3f rearNormal = new Vector3f(0.0f, 0.0f, 1.0f);

    // Outward facing normal
    Vector3f outNormal = new Vector3f(1.0f, 0.0f, 0.0f);

    // The angle subtended by a single segment
    double segmentAngle = 2.0 * Math.PI/nsegs;
    double tempAngle;

    public VecBody(int nsegs, float length, float radius, Appearance app) {

        this.nsegs = nsegs;
        this.length = length;
        this.radius = radius;
        this.app = app;

        //allow capability to write and read at runtime
```

LISTING 11.7 Continued

```
this.setCapability(TransformGroup.ALLOW_TRANSFORM_WRITE);
    this.setCapability(TransformGroup.ALLOW_TRANSFORM_READ);

    //create an empty shape to add Geometry to

    Shape3D vbody =  new Shape3D();
    vbody.setAppearance(app);

    //add the parts to vbody

    vbody.addGeometry(this.makeBody(0.f, length));
    vbody.addGeometry(this.makeDisk(1.f, new Vector3f(0.0f, 0.0f, 1.0f),
 length));
    vbody.addGeometry(this.makeDisk(-1.f, new Vector3f(0.0f,
 0.0f, -1.0f), 0.f));

    this.addChild(vbody);

  }

  public Geometry makeDisk(float dirmult, Vector3f faceNormal,
 float facePosition) {

    nFaces = nsegs + 2;
  nStrips[0] = nFaces;

    TriangleFanArray endCap
    = new TriangleFanArray(nFaces,
                GeometryArray.COORDINATES
                | GeometryArray.NORMALS,
                nStrips);


  coord.set(0.0f, 0.0f, facePosition);

    endCap.setCoordinate(0, coord);
  endCap.setNormal(0, faceNormal);


  for (int ii = 1; ii < nsegs+2; ii++) {
    tempAngle = dirmult * segmentAngle * -(double)ii;

      coord.set(radius * (float)Math.cos(tempAngle),
           radius * (float)Math.sin(tempAngle),
           facePosition);
```

LISTING 11.7   Continued

```java
          endCap.setCoordinate(ii, coord);
          endCap.setNormal(ii, faceNormal);

        }

        return endCap;

      }

    public Geometry makeBody(float basePos, float endPos) {

    // Construct VecBody's outer skin (the cylinder body)
    VecBodyVertexCount = 2 * nsegs + 2;
    VecBodyStripCount[0] = VecBodyVertexCount;

    TriangleStripArray vecBody
        = new TriangleStripArray(VecBodyVertexCount,
                    GeometryArray.COORDINATES
                    | GeometryArray.NORMALS,
                    VecBodyStripCount);

    outNormal.set(1.0f, 0.0f, 0.0f);

    coord.set(radius, 0.0f, basePos);
    vecBody.setCoordinate(0, coord);
    vecBody.setNormal(0, outNormal);

    coord.set(radius, 0.0f, endPos);
    vecBody.setCoordinate(1, coord);
    vecBody.setNormal(1, outNormal);

    for(int count = 0; count < nsegs; count++) {
        int index = 2 + count * 2;

        tempAngle = segmentAngle * (double)(count + 1);
        xDirection = (float)Math.cos(tempAngle);
        yDirection = (float)Math.sin(tempAngle);
        xVecBody = radius * xDirection;
        yVecBody = radius * yDirection;
        outNormal.set(xDirection, yDirection, 0.0f);

        coord.set(xVecBody, yVecBody, basePos);
        vecBody.setCoordinate(index, coord);
        vecBody.setNormal(index, outNormal);
```

LISTING 11.7   Continued

```
        coord.set(xVecBody, yVecBody, endPos);
        vecBody.setCoordinate(index + 1, coord);
        vecBody.setNormal(index + 1, outNormal);
    }
        /*
    newShape = new Shape3D(VecBody, app);
    this.addChild(newShape);
        */

        return vecBody;
    } //end method
} //end class
```

Note from the listing that we needed to create three `GeometryArray` objects; one each for the two endcaps of the vector body and one for the body itself. The `Geometry` for the endcaps is created with two successive calls to the `genCaps()` method. In that method, we specify a `TriangleFanArray` object called `face` and loop over the segments of the fan, specifying the vertices using the equation for a circle.

Special care must be taken when filling a `GeometryArray` or `IndexedGeometryArray` with values. The programmer must be sure to understand the proper order to specify the vertices and get the correct number of vertices for the particular class chosen.

Geometry Compression Classes

Java 3D has a number of classes for working with compressed geometry. Specifically, the `CompressedGeometry` class and the `CompressedGeometryHeader` class are used for this purpose. Geometry compression can often dramatically reduce the memory overhead associated with geometric objects. This can be particularly useful in Internet applications in which you have to send large models over limited bandwidth connections.

Like image compression methods, there is a loss of information during geometry compression. For the majority of applications, this isn't a major issue because geometric precision isn't the primary objective. However, the developer must keep these issues in mind.

Similar to the other preceding `Geometry` classes, the `CompressedGeometry` class allows geometry-by-reference and geometry-by-copy.

Using Raster Geometry

The name raster geometry is a bit confusing because the only link to a geometric primitive is that a point is used to specify the location of a 2D raster. Refer to Chapters 2–4 for the details of

11

CREATING AND
VIEWING THE
VIRTUAL WORLD

a Java `Raster`, which is basically a rectangular array of pixels (a `DataBuffer` plus `SampleModel`). In Java 3D, `Raster` is represented by a special utility class called `ImageComponent2D`.

Raster geometry is useful for presenting 2D images in the 3D environment. This can have applications for things such as placing sprite animations or text labels in the environment. An example of presenting information to the user with the `Raster` class is given in the Virtual Shopping Mall example in Chapter 14, "Integrating the Java Media APIs."

Using Loaders

As already mentioned, there are a lot of good reasons to use loaders to bring in geometry from a third-party package or file format. Undoubtedly, almost everyone who writes a Java 3D application will need to use a `loader` sometime, and it is often desirable to mix scene elements brought in with a `loader` with elements programmed using the `Geometry` classes.

Java 3D has provided a fairly robust infrastructure for creating custom loaders, and a reasonably large number of loader's are in existence. Go to `http://www.j3d.org/utilities/loaders.html` for an up-to-date listing. We will focus on the general structure and use of the `Loader Interface`.

In general, writing or even using a loader can be a challenge for several reasons, not the least of which is that little documentation is available. Another serious challenge results from matching the version of the third-party format with the version expected by the `Loader Interface`.

Inside the `Loader Interface`

The interface to implement when writing a custom loader is defined in the following:

```
com.sun.j3d.loaders
```

A class that implements the `Loader Interface` is basically a file parser that reads in the file; for example, a VRML 2.0 .wrl file converts the parts of text into Java 3D objects such as lights or objects and arranges these objects into an appropriate scene graph representation.

Java 3D's New Native File Format

The separate J3DFly download allows for the serialization of scene graph objects and thus corresponds to a native file format (of sorts) for Java 3D.

To add serialization to any custom object, the programmer will need to implement the following method:

```
public void writeSceneGraphObject( java.io.DataOutput ) throws IOException;
```

The procedure for serializing is to serialize the objects using `ByteArrayOutputStream`, count the resulting number of bytes, and then write these bytes into the `DataOutput` object before calling `writeSceneGraphObject`.

The resulting file contains all the objects and data associated with the object being serialized. Because a serialized object contains all the associated classes, the programmer is occasionally surprised by the ultimate size of the serialized object. For example, an object load from VRML might be some three times larger after serialization. The size increase is because of the added normals, transparency values, and other components added to it.

In the utility classes, Java 3D provides an interface called `LoaderBase`. If you have unjarred the Java 3D utilities as recommended in Chapter 10, this would be a good time to examine the `LoaderBase` interface. Any loader class implements this interface. A second interface, the `Scene` interface, is also important.

As an example that we will revisit later, consider an .obj file that contains a list of triangles. Taking the first seven lines of the file wm.obj, we have the following:

```
#- - - - - - - - - - - - - - -  X1_X2_BV  - - - - - - - - - - - - - -
v  2.940000  4.266000  6.430000
v  2.948000  4.326000  6.449000
v  2.912000  4.268000  6.500000
v  2.974000  4.395000  6.473000
v  2.943000  4.337000  6.539000
v  2.958000  4.259000  6.587000
v  3.022000  4.539000  6.506000
.  .  .

f  1  2  3
f  4  5  2
f  6  3  5
f  2  5  3
f  7  8  9
f  10 11  8
f  4  9  11
.  .  .
eof
```

Or alternatively in the VRML 2.0 file that we will use shortly:

```
#VRML V2.0 utf8
#A floor
Shape {
    geometry Box {
            size 20 0.1 30
    }

}
```

It is fairly easy to see how a parser could be written to recognize the first character as either a v or an f (in the case of this particular .obj file) and to construct an appropriate GeometryArray from the extracted information. Likewise for the office.wrl file, we could easily search for the string Shape and build up our scene from there. Parsing is in large part what a Loader does.

One confusing aspect of working with Loaders is that they are designed to return an object implementing the Scene interface. Listing 11.8 illustrates this point.

LISTING 11.8 vrmlLoad.java

```java
import javax.media.j3d.*;
import java.io.*;
import com.sun.j3d.loaders.vrml97.VrmlLoader;
import com.sun.j3d.loaders.Scene;

public class vrmlLoad extends BranchGroup{

    public vrmlLoad(String filename) {
      BranchGroup obj = new BranchGroup( );

    VrmlLoader loader = new VrmlLoader();
      Scene s = null;

      try{
        s = loader.load(filename);
      }
      catch (Exception e){
         System.err.println(e);
         System.exit(1);
      }

      obj.addChild(s.getSceneGroup( ) );
      this.addChild(obj);
    }
}
```

From the preceding, we can see the that the load() method of the Loader interface returns an object s of type Scene. Looking at the Scene.java code that we unjarred earlier, we can see that there are 10 methods that can be overridden when implementing Scene. The getSceneGroup() method is called in this code example because this is the most common case. However, keep in mind that it is also possible to get the lights, views, background, fog, and so on. Any particular custom Loader might or might not implement all these methods.

The question of how to access individual elements of the Scene can be tough. The following method is useful for accessing individual elements of the loaded file:

```java
public Hashtable getNamedObjects()
```

The `getNamedObjects` returns a `Hashtable` of all named objects in the imported scene with their associated Java 3D scene graph object names. You can simply print or list the objects in order to find their names.

Optimizing Geometry with the `GeometryInfo` Class

The `GeometryInfo` class can be used to save a great deal of effort in modeling geometry and can also provide several methods to improve the efficient representation of a model. The basic idea is to place the geometry in a `GeometryInfo` object before calling Java 3D's utilities. The Java 3D utilities can help in generating normals or in *stripification* (the process of turning geometry into long strips for more efficient rendering).

The `GeometryInfo` class itself contains several other methods for improving the efficient representation of geometry. These include *indexifying* (that is, calculating indexes) and *compacting* (removing unnecessary indexes).

Getting data into `GeometryInfo` can be a little more challenging than loading up a `GeometryArray` object because there are fewer options. It often isn't necessary to work with `GeometryInfo` except in cases where efficiency can be improved by stripification.

3D Text

Three-dimensional text can add visual appeal to certain 3D applications. Pickable text can serve as a nice user interface method and text can be useful for annotation. In many ways, it is easier to use Java 3D's 3D text classes than making 2D text and displaying it using textures or raster geometry.

To use 3D text, specify a `Point3d` where the text will be placed and a reference to a `Font3D` object. The `Font3D` object contains a list of extruded 2d glyphs (see Chapters 2 and 3 for a description of glyphs).

Examples of using 3D text are found throughout the examples in this and the next several chapters.

Making Changes to Live Geometry

As you saw previously, the `GeometryArray` class contains lists of vertex components: coordinates, normals, colors, and texture coordinates. Each is stored in a one-dimensional array (*vector*). From these values, we are able to create our own geometric shapes, just as we did in our `PointCloud` example. Further, you have seen that we can easily perform a number of rigid body transformations (translations, rotations, and scalings) on this data. You will see later that we can even morph between two shapes.

Although these capabilities are enough to handle many problems, a game or visualization developer would want to accomplish a number of things that are difficult or even impossible to achieve using linear transformations. In these cases, the developer must make some decisions based on the application.

A couple of options exist, but they have some drawbacks. Probably, the conceptually simplest thing we could do is instantiate new geometry and add it to the scene graph, but this is a poor approach in general.

One way to make changes to the geometry is through Geometry-by-reference. Geometry-by-reference is part of the set of classes that utilizes so-called by-reference functionality that is part of Java 3D version 1.2. By-reference is a way of accessing buffered data. The buffer data can be changed as it sits in accessible memory area (much like a BufferedImage). The GeometryUpdater class can be used to update the geometry during runtime.

Texture Mapping

As discussed in the introduction to the Java 3D section, texture mapping is an important technique for efficiently generating realism in a virtual environment. Texture maps can be used to create realistic looking floors, walls, and ceilings and are further useful as a way to reduce complex geometry, especially along the edges of an environment.

As an example of this last use of texture mapping, consider a model of an open space in the center of a city such as Central Park in New York City. Building geometry to represent the buildings in the far distance would take a lot of time to develop and would slow down rendering significantly. It wouldn't detract much from (and could even serve to increase) the realism of the scene to map photographic textures of the skyline on a simpler set of geometry placed in the distance.

A couple of options should be kept in mind while using texture mapping in Java 3D. The first is to understand how the source image will be loaded (or generated) so that it can be put in a format that works with Java 3D's Texture class (either Texture2D or Texture3D). There are only a couple of ways to instantiate a Texture2D or Texture3D object. Once a Texture object has been instantiated, it is included with the Appearance bundle.

Java 3D requires textures to be in an ImageComponent object (either ImageComponent2D or ImageComponent3D, depending on whether the texture is 2D or 3D. 3D texture mapping is covered later). Probably the easiest way to generate an ImageComponent is to use the TextureLoader utility (see the next section).

The more flexible and sophisticated way to get image data into an ImageComponent is by creating a BufferedImage (see Chapters 2–6 for information on using the BufferedImage class). Recall from those chapters that a BufferedImage is an image created in an accessible memory buffer. Later in this section, we will explore ways in which 2D texture animations can be incorporated into the environment. In order to do this, we will use Java 3D texture by reference capability.

One important aspect of using textures in Java 3D is that the dimension of all images must be a power of 2 (for example, 64x64, 128x128, 256x256, and so on). Note that the x and y dimensions don't have to be the same, however. For example, a 64x256 image is acceptable although this too can cause problems. Although this restriction can be a nuisance, it does provide some important rendering speed improvements. If you are not using images with a dimension that is a power of 2, you *must* resize the image in a graphics or paint program.

Finally, we will note that many additional texture mapping features can be specified with the `TextureAttributes()` object. These attributes dictate how the image is applied to the shape and color, for example, blending the texture with the underlying material or placing the texture on top of the material as a decal. The `TextureAttributes()` object also contains a method to translate, scale, and rotate the texture on the underlying shape.

Using the `TextureLoader`

To get the textures into Java 3D, the programmer will most often use the `TextureLoader` utility class. This utility takes the URL for a .jpg, .gif, or .bmp file as input and returns an `ImageComponent`. The `ImageComponent` class will be important not only for these more simple applications, but also later when we integrate JAI and JMF into our 3D scenes. Listing 11.9, `SimpleTextureExJ3D.java`, illustrates the use of the texture loader to perform a simple texturing of a box. The approach outlined in Figure 11.7 is good for placing static images in the environment, but it heavily restricts the techniques available relative to the `BufferedImaging` approach.

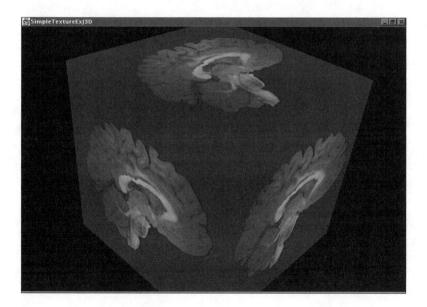

FIGURE 11.7
Screen shot from `SimpleTextureExJ3D.java`.

LISTING 11.9 SimpleTextureExJ3D.java

```java
import com.sun.j3d.utils.image.TextureLoader;
import com.sun.j3d.utils.behaviors.mouse.MouseRotate;
import java.applet.Applet;
import java.awt.*;
import java.awt.event.*;
import com.sun.j3d.utils.applet.MainFrame;
import com.sun.j3d.utils.geometry.Box;
import com.sun.j3d.utils.universe.*;
import javax.media.j3d.*;
import javax.vecmath.*;

public class SimpleTextureExJ3D extends Applet {

  public BranchGroup createSceneGraph() {
    // Create the root of the branch graph
    BranchGroup objRoot = new BranchGroup();

    // Create TransformGroup for scaling children
    TransformGroup objScale = new TransformGroup();
    Transform3D t3d = new Transform3D();
    t3d.setScale(0.5);
    objScale.setTransform(t3d);
    objRoot.addChild(objScale);

    // Create the TransformGroup for rotation;
    //   must enable WRITE and READ capability bits

    TransformGroup objTrans = new TransformGroup();
    objTrans.setCapability(TransformGroup.ALLOW_TRANSFORM_READ);
    objTrans.setCapability(TransformGroup.ALLOW_TRANSFORM_WRITE);

    objScale.addChild(objTrans);

    Appearance app = new Appearance();
    Box b = new Box(1.f,1.f,1.f, Box.GENERATE_TEXTURE_COORDS, app);
    objTrans.addChild(b);

    TextureLoader tex = new TextureLoader("c:/alexjava/texture.jpg",
➥ "RGB", this);  app.setTexture(tex.getTexture());

    BoundingSphere bounds =
      new BoundingSphere(new Point3d(0.0,0.0,0.0), 100.0);
```

LISTING 11.9   Continued

```
    // Create the rotate behavior node
    MouseRotate behavior = new MouseRotate(objTrans);
    objTrans.addChild(behavior);
    behavior.setSchedulingBounds(bounds);

    return objRoot;
}
```

The `createSceneGraph()` method creates the content subgraph for our texturing example. The vast majority of the method will look quite similar to what we have done in previous examples. We create a `BranchGroup` to eventually return and place two `TransformGroups` below it; one for scaling and the other for rotation with the `MouseRotate` behavior.

The texture mapping part of the scene graph begins after the `Box` node is added to the `objTrans TransformGroup`. We must first get our texture into the program using the `TextureLoader` utility. Note that a more complete program would verify that the texture is loaded by testing for null. For simplicity, we omit this important step. We next use the loaded texture as an argument to the `setTexture()` method of the `Appearance` object. This is the only step we need to take. The rest of the scene graph involves adding a `MouseRotate` behavior so that we can interact with our textured box.

NOTE

The `Box` was created with the `GENERATE_TEXTURE_COORDS` capability bit set. If this bit is not set, the texture will not be mapped and will appear white. No error or warning messages will appear.

Using a `BufferedImage` for Texturing

The `TextureLoader` is by far the most common way to load textures for texture mapping. The other approach is to use the `BufferedImage` class. Buffered imaging is described extensively in Chapters 2–6. Briefly, a `BufferedImage` is an area of memory containing pixel data.

Using a `BufferedImage` is the only way to produce dynamic textures and to incorporate image processing into the texture mapping. We will be utilizing this avenue in many of the examples in this section.

Listing 11.10 creates a `BufferedImage` and applies it to the same `Box` that we used in Listing 11.9.

LISTING 11.10   (Partial) `BufferedImageTextureJ3D.java`

```
import javax.media.j3d.ImageComponent2D;
import java.awt.image.*;
. . .
public class BufferedImageTextureJ3D extends Applet {

  int imgheight=256;
  int imgwidth=256;
. . .

  Appearance app = new Appearance();
  app.setCapability(Appearance.ALLOW_TEXTURE_WRITE);

  Box b = new Box(1.f,1.f,1.f, Box.GENERATE_TEXTURE_COORDS, app);
  objTrans.addChild(b);

  BufferedImage bi = new BufferedImage(imgwidth,
➥imgheight,BufferedImage.TYPE_INT_RGB);

  DataBuffer db = bi.getRaster().getDataBuffer();

//loop over the DataBuffer
  for (int ii=0;ii<imgwidth*imgheight;ii++ ) {
      db.setElem(ii,ii);
    }
```

Note the similarities with the `SimpleTextureExJ3D` example in Listing 11.9. The only difference is that we instantiated a `BufferedImage` and accessed the `DataBuffer`. The changes we made to the `DataBuffer` are pretty minor. In essence, we made a gradient paint texture. Of course, we really want to do much more sophisticated things with our texture. An animated texture, for example, would be nice. In Chapter 14, we will use JMF to generate a video texture and use the image processing capabilities of JAI to produce special effects.

In building up to that level of sophistication, we will first generate a simple animation by improving upon the `BufferedImageTextureJ3D` example in Listing 11.10.

Animating Textures Using Texture-by-reference

Texture-by-reference was introduced in Java 3D 2.1. We will need to use this feature when we bring in JAI and JMF objects into our 3D environment.

The basic idea of using texture-by-reference is that Java 3D may not need to make copies of images internally and can simply maintain a reference to the image. Similar to the Geometry-by-reference class described previously, image stored by-reference can be changed at runtime.

This can speed performance considerably and is needed for applications in which a dynamic texture is needed. Listing 11.11 illustrates the use of texture-by-reference. Each time a key is pressed, a number of random dots are added to the texture, as shown in Figure 11.8. Eventually, the texture becomes totally covered by spots.

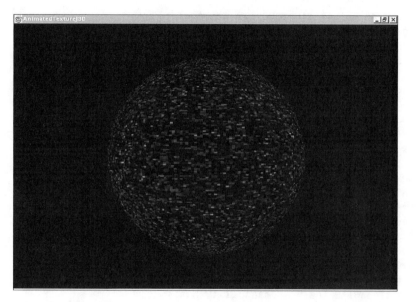

FIGURE 11.8

Screenshot from `AnimatedTextureJ3D.java`.

LISTING 11.11   `AnimatedTextureJ3D.java`

```
import java.applet.Applet;
import java.awt.*;
import java.awt.event.*;
import com.sun.j3d.utils.applet.MainFrame;
import com.sun.j3d.utils.geometry.Sphere;
import com.sun.j3d.utils.behaviors.mouse.MouseRotate;
import com.sun.j3d.utils.universe.*;
import javax.media.j3d.*;
import javax.vecmath.*;
import java.awt.image.*;
import java.awt.image.BufferedImage;
import javax.media.j3d.ImageComponent2D;
import java.awt.image.*;
```

LISTING 11.11   Continued

```java
import java.awt.geom.*;

import java.util.Random;

public class AnimatedTextureJ3D extends Applet{
  int imgwidth = 256;
  int imgheight = 256;
  Texture2D tex;
  Random r;
  BufferedImage bi;

  public BranchGroup createSceneGraph() {
    // Create the root of the branch graph
      BranchGroup objRoot = new BranchGroup();

    // Create TransformGroup for scaling children
    TransformGroup objScale = new TransformGroup();
    Transform3D t3d = new Transform3D();
    t3d.setScale(0.5);
    objScale.setTransform(t3d);
    objRoot.addChild(objScale);

    // Create the TransformGroup for rotation;
➥ must enable WRITE and READ capability bits

    TransformGroup objTrans = new TransformGroup();
    objTrans.setCapability(TransformGroup.ALLOW_TRANSFORM_READ);
    objTrans.setCapability(TransformGroup.ALLOW_TRANSFORM_WRITE);

    objScale.addChild(objTrans);

    Appearance app = new Appearance();
    app.setCapability(Appearance.ALLOW_TEXTURE_WRITE);

    bi = new BufferedImage(imgwidth,imgheight,BufferedImage.TYPE_INT_RGB);
    Sphere sphere = new Sphere(1.f, Sphere.GENERATE_NORMALS | Sphere.GENERATE_
➥TEXTURE_COORDS, 60, app);

    objTrans.addChild(sphere);
    tex = new Texture2D(Texture2D.BASE_LEVEL,Texture2D.RGB,imgwidth,imgheight);

    tex.setCapability(Texture2D.ALLOW_IMAGE_WRITE);
    tex.setCapability(Texture2D.ALLOW_IMAGE_READ);
```

Creating and Viewing the Virtual World

CHAPTER 11

567

11

CREATING AND
VIEWING THE
VIRTUAL WORLD

LISTING 11.11   Continued

```java
  this.genTexture();
  app.setTexture(tex);

  BoundingSphere bounds =
    new BoundingSphere(new Point3d(0.0,0.0,0.0), 100.0);

  // Create the rotate behavior node
  MouseRotate behavior = new MouseRotate(objTrans);
  objTrans.addChild(behavior);
  behavior.setSchedulingBounds(bounds);

  return objRoot;
}

public AnimatedTextureJ3D (){

  r = new Random();

  setLayout(new BorderLayout());
  GraphicsConfiguration config =
      SimpleUniverse.getPreferredConfiguration();

  Canvas3D c = new Canvas3D(config);
  add("Center", c);

  BranchGroup scene = createSceneGraph();

  KeyHandler kh = new KeyHandler(this);
  c.addKeyListener(kh);
  SimpleUniverse u = new SimpleUniverse(c);

  u.getViewingPlatform().setNominalViewingTransform();

  u.addBranchGraph(scene);
}

public void genTexture() {

  //instantiate a new ImageComponent; choose byRef and yUp
    ImageComponent2D ic = new ImageComponent2D(ImageComponent2D.FORMAT_RGB,
                                      256,256,true,true);
    //set bi as ImageComponenet object
    ic.set(bi);
```

LISTING 11.11   Continued

```
        // BufferedImage bi = ic.getImage();
        Graphics2D g2d = bi.createGraphics();

        RenderingHints antialiasHints =
➡ new RenderingHints(RenderingHints.KEY_ANTIALIASING,
➡                                 RenderingHints.VALUE_ANTIALIAS_ON);
        g2d.setRenderingHints(antialiasHints);

        for (int ii=0;ii<1000;ii++) {
          g2d.setPaint(Color.red);
            //generate a random dot size
          double dotsize = r.nextDouble();

          //paint blue and red dots
          g2d.setPaint(Color.red);
          g2d.fill(new Ellipse2D.Double(r.nextDouble()*256,r.nextDouble()*256,
                                    dotsize, dotsize));
          g2d.setPaint(Color.blue);
          g2d.fill(new Ellipse2D.Double(r.nextDouble()*256,r.nextDouble()*256,
                                    dotsize, dotsize));
        }

        ic.set(bi);
        tex.setImage(0,ic);
  }


  public static void main(String argv[]) {
     new MainFrame(new AnimatedTextureJ3D(), 750, 750);
  }
} //create an event handler to respond to key presses
class KeyHandler implements KeyListener {
     AnimatedTextureJ3D at;

     public KeyHandler(AnimatedTextureJ3D at) {
         this.at = at;
     }
     public void keyPressed(java.awt.event.KeyEvent p1) {
        at.genTexture();
     }
  . . .
}
```

Notice the genTexture() method in the previous example. The genTexture() method is a simple example of Java 2D graphics. Each time the KeyHandler object kh registers a key press, the genTexture() method is called, and the texture is progressively updated.

We will build on the use of texture by reference in our 3D shopping mall example.

Providing Texture Coordinate Information

Regardless of the initial size of the texture (say 128x128, for example), Java 3D maps textures onto the (s, t) coordinate system that goes from 0.f to 1.f.

Two basic modes are used when determining how to treat points outside of the boundary. The first mode is termed CLAMP and dictates that points outside the boundaries use a particular color (specified during creation of the boundaries). The other mode, WRAP, is used for creating repeating patterns such as wall and floor surfaces. In WRAP mode, the texture repeats continuously until the shape is covered.

Methods for specifying which mode to use are provided with the setBoundaryModeS() and setBoundaryModeT() methods. Note that the default is WRAP. You can thus specify WRAP in one direction and CLAMP in the other.

For example, to set the texture boundary mode to CLAMP along the horizontal dimension of a texture, you would use the following:

```
tex.setBoundaryModeS(Texture,CLAMP);
```

Note further that it is possible to use an affine transform to scale, translate, or rotate the (s, t) coordinates. This can have the effect of moving the texture across or down the shape in the case of translation, reorienting the image in the case of rotate, or enlarging or shrinking the texture in the case of scale.

The TextureAttributes object is used to specify the texture transformation and other information about the texture map to use. The getTextureTransform(Transform3D t) method will place the current texture transform in the Transform3D t. Similarly, the texture transform can be set with the setTextureTransform(Transform3D t) method.

One of the often used attributes in the TextureAttributes is related to the rendering quality versus speed tradeoff for texture rendering. The attributes are set with the following:

```
TextureAttributes.FASTEST
TextureAttributes.NICEST
```

11

CREATING AND VIEWING THE VIRTUAL WORLD

It is also possible, through the `TextureAttributes` object, to have some control over the blending of textures on a shape. This is done by specifying an alpha value for the textures. Finally, several important flags can be set in the `TextureAttributes` object. For example,

```
TextureAttributes.ALLOW_TRANSFORM_READ
TextureAttributes.ALLOW_TRANSFORM_WRITE
```

are important when using the `get` and `set` `TextureTransform` methods.

MIPMapping

The rationale behind using MIPMapping is presented in Chapter 10.

Java 3D allows two approaches to MIPMapping. The easiest avenue is to specify a single base image and allow Java 3D to automatically generate the rest of the MIPMap images. This is generally acceptable for most applications.

In situations in which this first approach is not usable or in situations in which the programmer wants to use MIPMapping for a different purpose, Java 3D allows the programmer to explicitly set the MIPMap array. Listing 11.12 demonstrates a simple example of explicitly setting the MIPMap array.

LISTING 11.12   MIPMapExample.java

```java
import com.sun.j3d.utils.behaviors.mouse.MouseRotate;

import java.applet.Applet;
import java.awt.*;
import java.awt.event.*;
import com.sun.j3d.utils.applet.MainFrame;
import com.sun.j3d.utils.geometry.Sphere;
import com.sun.j3d.utils.geometry.Box;
import java.awt.font.*;

import com.sun.j3d.utils.universe.*;
import javax.media.j3d.*;
import javax.vecmath.*;
import java.awt.image.*;

import java.awt.image.BufferedImage;
import javax.media.j3d.ImageComponent2D;
import java.awt.image.*;

import java.awt.geom.*;
```

LISTING 11.12 Continued

```java
import java.util.Random;
import java.awt.geom.*;

public class MIPMapExample extends Applet{
  int imgwidth = 256;
  int imgheight = 256;
  Texture2D tex;
  BufferedImage bi;

  VirtualUniverse universe;
  Locale locale;
  TransformGroup vpTrans;
  View view;
  Bounds bounds;
  public BranchGroup createSceneGraph() {
    // Create the root of the branch graph
      BranchGroup objRoot = new BranchGroup();

    // Create TransformGroup for scaling children
    TransformGroup objScale = new TransformGroup();
    Transform3D t3d = new Transform3D();
    t3d.setScale(0.5);
    objScale.setTransform(t3d);
    objRoot.addChild(objScale);

    // Create the TransformGroup for rotation;
➥ must enable WRITE and READ capability bits

    TransformGroup objTrans = new TransformGroup();
    objTrans.setCapability(TransformGroup.ALLOW_TRANSFORM_READ);
    objTrans.setCapability(TransformGroup.ALLOW_TRANSFORM_WRITE);

    objScale.addChild(objTrans);

    Appearance app = new Appearance();
    app.setCapability(Appearance.ALLOW_TEXTURE_WRITE);

   // Sphere sphere = new Sphere(1.f, Sphere.GENERATE_TEXTURE_COORDS, 32, app);
    Box box = new Box(5.f,5.f,5.f, Box.GENERATE_TEXTURE_COORDS, app);
    objTrans.addChild(box);
    tex = new Texture2D(Texture2D.MULTI_LEVEL_MIPMAP,Texture2D.RGB,
➥imgwidth,imgheight);
    //tex = new Texture2D(Texture2D.BASE_LEVEL,Texture2D.RGB,imgwidth,
➥imgheight);
```

LISTING 11.12   Continued

```
    //tex.setCapability(Texture2D.ALLOW_IMAGE_WRITE);
    //tex.setCapability(Texture2D.ALLOW_IMAGE_READ);

    tex.setMagFilter(Texture2D.BASE_LEVEL_POINT);
    tex.setMinFilter(Texture2D.MULTI_LEVEL_POINT);

    this.genMIPMap();

    app.setTexture(tex);
     MouseRotate behavior = new MouseRotate(objTrans);
    objTrans.addChild(behavior);
    behavior.setSchedulingBounds(bounds);

    return objRoot;
  }

. . .
  public void genMIPMap() {
      System.out.println("genMIPMap");
    //bi = new BufferedImage(imgwidth,imgheight,
➡BufferedImage.TYPE_INT_RGB);

    //Generate a series of n mipmaps
    int [] miplevels = {256, 128, 64, 32, 16, 8, 4, 2, 1};

    for (int ii=0; ii< miplevels.length; ii++) {
        System.out.println("miplevel: ii: " + miplevels[ii] + " " + ii );
        BufferedImage bi = new BufferedImage(miplevels[ii],miplevels[ii],
➡BufferedImage.TYPE_INT_RGB);

        ImageComponent2D ic = new ImageComponent2D
➡(ImageComponent2D.FORMAT_RGB,
                                        miplevels[ii],miplevels[ii]);

    // BufferedImage bi = ic.getImage();
        Graphics2D g2d = bi.createGraphics();

        RenderingHints antialiasHints =
➡ new RenderingHints(RenderingHints.KEY_ANTIALIASING,
➡             RenderingHints.VALUE_ANTIALIAS_ON);
        g2d.setRenderingHints(antialiasHints);
        g2d.setPaint(Color.blue);
        g2d.fill(new Rectangle2D.Double(0, 0,bi.getWidth(),bi.getHeight()));
        Ellipse2D r = new Ellipse2D.Double(50,50,100,100);
```

LISTING 11.12   Continued

```
                g2d.setPaint(Color.red);
                g2d.fill(r);
                g2d.setPaint(Color.white);
                Font f1 = new Font("Helvetica", Font.BOLD, 24/(ii+1));
                g2d.setFont(f1);
                String s = "SIZE: " + bi.getHeight() + " x " + bi.getHeight();
                g2d.drawString(s, 2,bi.getHeight()/2);

                ic.set(bi);
                tex.setImage(ii,ic);
        }
    }
```

Note the interesting and enlightening error that can occur in this example (shown in Figure 11.9). When the object is not "dead on" to the viewer, there exists transitionary zones that have a part of one level of the MIPMap and another part covered by the neighboring level of the MIPMap. When object views are at an angle, two different levels of the MIPMap will apply to individual surfaces at certain distances from the object. Although there are some ways to mitigate this artifact by changing the interpolation methods used, we are in essence exchanging one artifact for another.

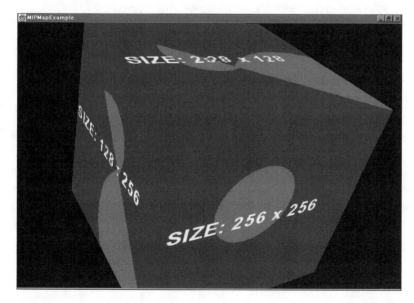

FIGURE 11.9

Screen shot from `MIPMapExample.java`.

Using Large Textures

Generally, small textures are used for texture mapping. In some cases, however, a large texture is desired. One technique that uses large textures is when a large digital photograph is pasted in the far distance of an environment.

Large textures can be problematic. Most of the problems are hardware related and not a specific limitation of Java 3D. Many graphics accelerators will only work with textures that are less than 256x256. In order to write the most generic program, textures should be kept at less than 256x256. Should a larger texture be needed, it might be necessary to split the texture and the object to be textured into smaller segments. Even if the graphics card will allow big textures, they will tend to eat up all the memory on the card anyway.

Java 3D 1.3 will most likely include methods for querying the maximum texture size supported by a device; therefore, textures that are too large can be scaled appropriately.

Backgrounds

Backgrounds are very useful in providing a sense of immersion in virtual environments and have other special uses in some areas of visualization. Java 3D provides three different types of backgrounds, and they are listed in Table 11.6.

TABLE 11.6   Different Types of Backgrounds and Their Usage

Background Type	Usage
Color	Specifies a basic color background.
Geometry	Tesselates geometry onto a sphere surrounding the entire scene.
Image	Uses an image as the background.

The Background Node contains a Bounds object that specifies the region in which the Background is active. Thus, whenever the ViewPlatform intersects the Bounds object, the Background is rendered. Note that it is possible to specify multiple Backgrounds that become active when the ViewPlatform is in different locations in the environment. In this case, the Background closest to the ViewPlatform is active even if the ViewPlatform intersects more than one. An example is provided next.

Using a Colored Background

A colored background is by far the easiest to implement. The following code can be added directly into the createScene() method of BasicRecipeJ3D.java:

```
//create a large sphere to contain applications bounds
BoundingSphere bounds =
     new BoundingSphere(new Point3d(0.0,0.0,0.0), 100.0);

//make a custom color
Color3f bgColor = new Color3f(0.2f, 0.05f, 0.28);
Background bg = new Background(bgColor);
bg.setApplicationBounds(bounds);

//add the background node to the scene graph
objRoot.addChild(bg);
```

Image Backgrounds

Image backgrounds add an additional degree of realism except for the fact that the background is the same for all views of the environment. For backgrounds like stars or clouds, the static nature of an image background isn't a large problem; however, in many virtual environment applications, the programmer might want to use background geometry (see the next section) in order to provide a different view for each orientation. The following code snippet demonstrates how to add a Background to the scene graph:

```
TransformGroup group = new TransformGroup();
. . .
TextureLoader l = new TextureLoader("clouds.jpg", this);
ImageComponent2D image = l.getImage();
. . .
Background back = new Background();
Back.setImage(image);
. . .
back.setApplicationBounds(bounds);
group.addChild(back);
```

Using Background Geometry

Using background geometry is slightly more complicated than using color or image backgrounds; however, the improvement in realism might be well worth it. The primary advantage is that the viewer sees different parts of the background from different view perspectives.

To create background geometry, it is necessary to add the elements to a `BranchGroup` and add `BranchGroup` to the scene graph.

For example, if the programmer wants a city scene in the background, we could use the following code segment:

```
TransformGroup tg = new TransformGroup();
BranchGroup branch = createBackground();
Background back = new Background();
back.setGeometry(branch);
back.setApplicationBounds(bounds);
group.addChild(back);
. . .
public BranchGroup createBackground() {
    BranchGroup objRoot = new BranchGroup();
return objRoot;
}
```

Note that the snippet doesn't show the creation of the `BranchGroup` containing the city scene, but only show the structure necessary to set up background geometry.

Multiple Backgrounds

It is possible to specify multiple backgrounds that are differentially activated when the `ViewPlatform` is within a certain range. Remember that when multiple backgrounds exist, Java 3D automatically chooses the one nearest the `ViewPlatform`.

Lighting

The proper lighting of a scene is one of the most important yet under-utilized techniques for adding a sense of immersion and realism in a 3D scene. A single directional light source exerts a powerful influence over wayfinding (navigation) in animals and should be incorporated into any virtual environment in which navigation is critical.

A great deal of current research in 3D graphics is centered around developing new lighting algorithms. The entire research enterprise is mathematically intense and relies on a knowledge of physics. However, proper use of lighting can be learned by getting a basic understanding of the basic forms of lighting and then doing experimentation to get the desired effect.

Java 3D Lighting Model

Only a reduced lighting model is currently practical for use with interactive graphics anyway. These limitations will be discussed shortly. For now, consider that Java 3D supports four fundamental lighting types (listed in Table 11.7).

TABLE 11.7 Basic Lighting Available in Java 3D

Light *Class*	*Usage*
AmbientLight	Light without a concentrated source; provides equal illumination throughout the environment.
DirectionalLight	A light with a specified direction; source is modeled as infinitely far away.
PointLight	An attenuated light source at a fixed point in space; radiates in all directions.
SpotLight	An attenuated light source at a fixed point in space; radiates in a specified direction.

All these classes are subclasses of the common parent Light. Light serves as a node to contain parameters that are common to all four of these subclasses (and others that can be created through extension). The common parameters shared by all light in Java 3D are color, enable/disable, region of influence, and scope.

Java 3D's lighting model is based on three key vector values pointing from a vertex on the object and pointing to 1) the viewer's eye, 2) back in the direction of the light, and 3) along the surface normal. These three vectors provide an important subset of the information necessary to render object shadings in Java 3D.

Three basic reflections are calculated in Java 3D: ambient, diffuse, and specular. Refer to Chapter 10 for a description of these from a more general computer graphics standpoint.

Implementing Java 3D's Lighting Model

Beginning to use lighting in Java 3D presents some potential pitfalls that you must be cautious to avoid. These pitfalls are related to not having the appropriate objects in the scene in order to see the effects of lighting.

First and foremost, you must remember that without objects in a scene, you cannot see a light. Lights are only visible when they interact with 3D surfaces.

The second prerequisite for implementing lighting effects is that all objects to be shaded must have surface normals and material properties.

AmbientLight

Because an ambient light source projects light uniformly throughout the environment, it is impossible to determine the origin of the source. For this reason, the `AmbientLight` node is the simplest light to use because you don't have to specify the direction of light. To create an instance of an `AmbientLight`, use on the following three constructors:

```
public AmbientLight()
public AmbientLight(Color3f color)
public AmbientLight(Boolean lighton, Color3f color)
```

It is possible to change the color of the light or turn it on or off using `setColor()` and `setEnable()`. Note that as with many other scene elements, it is necessary to set the proper capability bits in order to make post-instantiation changes to lights.

DirectionalLight

As mentioned previously, one of the strongest spatial cues that is used by animals for navigation is the perception of a directional light. Given that Virtual Reality is a perceptually degraded form of navigation, it is highly recommended that at least one directional light be placed in any environment.

Instantiating a `DirectionalLight` is similar to instantiating an `AmbientLight` with one additional step. When specifying a `DirectionalLight`, it is necessary to add a directional vector indicating the source and target locations of the light.

```
Vector3f light = new Vector3f(3.f, 3.f, 3.f);
```

PointLight

A `PointLight` is basically like a light bulb in the real world; it radiates in all directions and attenuates with distance from the source. In Java 3D, the programmer must specify the attenuation through three parameters that contribute to the calculation of the falloff from the `PointLight`. The attenuation parameters can be set dynamically (given that the programmer has set the proper capability bits) or specified at the time of instantiation using the following constructors:

```
public PointLight()
public PointLight(Boolean lightOn, Color3f color, Point3f position,
➥ Point3f attenuation)
public PointLight(Color3f color, Point3f position, Point3f attenuation)
```

To set the attenuation during runtime, use the `setAttenuation()` method.

Note that the attenuation is specified as a `Point3f` in which the three coordinates represent color, linear, and quadratic attenuation parameters, respectively.

SpotLight

A SpotLight is similar to a DirectionalLight except that it radiates from a point inside a cone. The diameter of the cone can be specified in order to control whether the light is wide or narrow. In addition, the programmer can set the focus from sharp to soft in a range of 128.f to 0.f. Instantiation is the same as for a PointLight with two additional parameters for controlling the spread and focus of the light. Use the following constructors to create a SpotLight:

```
SpotLight()
SpotLight(Boolean lightOn, Color3f color, Point3f position, Point3f
attenutation,
➥        Vector3f direction, float spreadAngle, float concentration)
SpotLight(Color3f color, Point3f position, Point3f attenutation,
➥        Vector3f direction, float spreadAngle, float concentration);
```

Specifying Scope and Influencing Bounds

It is possible to specify a scope (in terms of the scene graph) to use for lights. The scope, in this case, refers a list of Group nodes (called the *scope list*) that are influenced by a light. If the scope list is empty or not specified, the scope covers the entire universe. Otherwise, only those Leaf nodes that belong to the Groups in the scope list are influenced by the scoped light.

One sometimes confusing aspect of using influencing bounds is that there are two choices for specifying bounds that reflect subtle differences in how the lights are applied to the scene. The more commonly used bounds is for applying the light over the entire scene and works in light centered coordinates (that is, when the light moves, so do the bounds).

The BoundingLeaf doesn't move with the light. To move the influencing bounds, you must move the BoundingLeaf.

Listing 11.13 shows an example of two DirectionalLights with one of the lights attached to a TransformGroup and rotation Behavior. In Figure 11.10, by rotating the red light with the MouseRotate Behavior, the user can observe the different effects of mixing and influence with the static blue light.

LISTING 11.13   DirectionalLightEx.java

```
import com.sun.j3d.utils.behaviors.mouse.MouseRotate;

import java.applet.Applet;
import java.awt.*;
import java.awt.event.*;
import com.sun.j3d.utils.applet.MainFrame;
import com.sun.j3d.utils.geometry.Sphere;
import com.sun.j3d.utils.geometry.Cylinder;
```

LISTING 11.13 Continued

```java
import com.sun.j3d.utils.geometry.Box;
import com.sun.j3d.utils.universe.*;
import javax.media.j3d.*;
import javax.vecmath.*;

public class DirectionalLightEx extends Applet {

  public BranchGroup createSceneGraph(String[] args) {
    // Create the root of the branch graph
    BranchGroup objRoot = new BranchGroup();

    // Create a Transform group to scale all objects so they
    // appear in the scene.
    TransformGroup objScale = new TransformGroup();
    Transform3D t3d = new Transform3D();
    t3d.setScale(0.4);
    objScale.setTransform(t3d);
    objRoot.addChild(objScale);

    // Create the transform group node and initialize it to the
    // identity.  Enable the TRANSFORM_WRITE capability so that
    // our behavior code can modify it at runtime.
    TransformGroup objTrans = new TransformGroup();
    //read/write-enable for behaviors
    objTrans.setCapability(TransformGroup.ALLOW_TRANSFORM_READ);
    objTrans.setCapability(TransformGroup.ALLOW_TRANSFORM_WRITE);
    objScale.addChild(objTrans);

    //Create a Sphere
    Sphere sphere = new Sphere(1.0f, Sphere.GENERATE_NORMALS |
                Sphere.GENERATE_TEXTURE_COORDS, 45);

    Appearance ap = sphere.getAppearance();


    // add it to the scene graph.
    objTrans.addChild(sphere);

    BoundingSphere bounds =
      new BoundingSphere(new Point3d(0.0,0.0,0.0), 100.0);

    // Create the rotate behavior node
    MouseRotate behavior = new MouseRotate(objTrans);
```

LISTING 11.13   Continued

```
    objTrans.addChild(behavior);
    behavior.setSchedulingBounds(bounds);

    //Illuminate the object with two lights.
    Color3f red = new Color3f(1.f, 0.f, 0.f);
    Color3f blue = new Color3f(0.f, 0.f, 1.f);
    Vector3f reddir  = new Vector3f(0.f, 2.f, -2.f);
    Vector3f bluedir  = new Vector3f(0.0f, -2.0f, -2.0f);

    DirectionalLight redlight = new DirectionalLight(red, reddir);
    DirectionalLight bluelight = new DirectionalLight(blue, bluedir);

    redlight.setInfluencingBounds(bounds);
    bluelight.setInfluencingBounds(bounds);
  // objScale.addChild(lgt1);

    objTrans.addChild(redlight);
    objScale.addChild(bluelight);
    // Let Java 3D perform optimizations on this scene graph.
    objRoot.compile();

    return objRoot;
  }

  public DirectionalLightEx (String argv[]){
    setLayout(new BorderLayout());
    GraphicsConfiguration config =
        SimpleUniverse.getPreferredConfiguration();

    Canvas3D c = new Canvas3D(config);
    add("Center", c);

    BranchGroup scene = createSceneGraph(argv);
    SimpleUniverse u = new SimpleUniverse(c);

    // This will move the ViewPlatform back a bit so the
    // objects in the scene can be viewed.
    u.getViewingPlatform().setNominalViewingTransform();

    u.addBranchGraph(scene);
  }

. . .
```

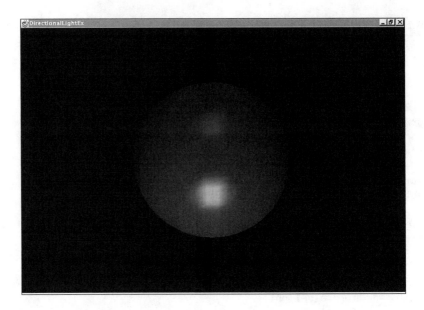

FIGURE 11.10

Screen shot from `DirectionLightEx.java`.

Fog

Fog is a powerful cue giving the impression of 3D. In addition, use of fog can result in the rather surprising benefit of improved rendering time for many scenes. Note that fog doesn't necessarily have to be thick or even strongly apparent to add to the 3D scene or to give improvement in rendering time. Fog can be used to soften edges much like one would use antialiasing.

The key to using fog in Java 3D is to first understand the difference among the three fundamental uses of fog. This first is the more obvious use for simulating weather patterns and providing additional parallax when moving through the environment.

The second use of fog is for depth cueing. As mentioned throughout this section, the sense of immersion (again, a central goal of 3D) is severely limited in VR. Most of the things that are done to improve the sense of immersion (for example, lighting, adding textures, or additional geometry, and so on) are computationally expensive. We return to this point here to emphasize the third use of fog, which is to reduce the number of rendered details in the scene.

Indeed, a good portion of any rendering contains computations that are simply not necessary, and even worse, detract from the sense of immersion. Fog provides one of the easiest ways to address this problem and amounts to a further form of culling (described in Chapter 10).

In Java 3D, the Fog class is the superclass for two subclasses that generate basic fog. The two subclasses differ in the mathematical model used to generate the fog. Both subclasses contain two fundamental pieces of information: the color of the fog (blue haze, black, and so on) and the spatial region and scope affected by the fog.

The ExponentialFog subclass is the class to use for creating strongly apparent fog that gives the look of foggy weather or a smoke filled environment. The thickness of an ExponentialFog increases exponentially with distance with the following equation:

EF = e(-density*distance)

where EF is the effect of the fog at any particular distance.

For a denser fog, one can simply increase the density value.

The constructors for an ExponentialFog are

```
public ExponentialFog()
public ExponentialFog(Color3f color)
public ExponentialFog(Color3f color, float density)
public ExponentialFog(float red, float green, float blue)
public ExponentialFog(float red, float green, float blue, float density)
```

To read out or to change the density of an ExponentialFog after it has been instantiated, the following capability bits must be set:

```
ALLOW_DENSITY_READ
ALLOW_DENSITY_WRITE
```

The LinearFog class is most appropriate for depth cueing because it allows for the setting of the front and back distance. As with the ExponentialFog, a LinearFog increases with distance, but this time in a linear fashion. Instead of specifying a density for the ExponentialFog, a front and back distance are used. To use a LinearFog for depth cueing, use a black fog and specify the front distance at the front of the object and the back distance for the back of the object. Depending on what type of object is being viewed, this can make a fairly dramatic difference in the perception of depth (see "Comprehensive Example #1: MR Physics Visualization").

The equation for the thickness of a LinearFog is

EF = (backDistance-distance)/(backDistance-frontDistance)

The constructors for a LinearFog are

```
public LinearFog()
public LinearFog(Color3f color)
public LinearFog(Color3f, double frontDistance, double backDistance)
public LinearFog(float red, float green, float blue)
public LinearFog(float red, float green, float blue, double frontDistance,
➡ double backDistance)
```

11

CREATING AND
VIEWING THE
VIRTUAL WORLD

The rendered color of any shape that is influenced by either an ExponentialFog or LinearFog can be determined from the calculated value EF:

color = EF * shapeColor + (1-EF)*fogColor

Adding 3D Sound

Three dimensional sound can add to the feeling of immersion in a virtual environment, but it generally isn't as important as lighting or 3D user interaction. As has been stated often in this book, spatial navigation in the real world is multisensory in nature. As with any spatial cue, lack of or improper use of aural cues will detract from the user's feeling of immersion.

Java 3D has a fairly sophisticated 3D Sound model that can be used to advantage in many situations. At present, the Java 3D Sound model is based on panning only. *Panning* is the gradual switching between speakers. When we develop our 3D shopping mall demonstration in Chapter 14, we will use the JMF Sound Player in conjunction with the Java 3D Sound classes.

In general, it is helpful to think of Sound nodes in terms of some of the ideas presented in the section on "Lighting." Like lighting, sounds can be directional and can fall off over distance. For many of the same reasons that lighting can be challenging, sound too can be difficult to use. It is often difficult to notice the subtleties of sound effects.

The Java 3D sound package supports three basic types of sounds: 1) Background sounds that are present throughout the environment (much like an ambient light), 2) Point sounds that emanate in all directions and have an attenuation (much as a PointLight simulates light energy), and 3) Cone sounds that act like a SpotLight to provide a directional source of sound.

Two additional classes are useful in creating sounds. The SoundScape node class specifies the area of space in which a sound is active, much like Bounds are used in lighting the scene.

The second class used to create sounds is the AuralAttributes object. This object is used to control how the amplitude of the sound attenuates with respect to distance from the object (like the Fog and Light nodes). Other properties are contained in the AuralAttributes object including looping and playback properties.

Because the sound objects are Leaf nodes, they can be added the same way as any Leaf node.

You must remember to set the SchedulingBounds for any sound that is to be heard. Again, this is directly analogous to the situation for lighting.

Listing 11.14 demonstrates the use of Directional and Point Sound Nodes.

LISTING 11.14   SoundExample.java

```java
import java.applet.Applet;
import java.awt.*;
import java.awt.event.*;
import com.sun.j3d.utils.applet.MainFrame;
import com.sun.j3d.utils.geometry.ColorCube;
import com.sun.j3d.utils.geometry.Sphere;
import com.sun.j3d.utils.geometry.Box;

import com.sun.j3d.utils.universe.*;
import java.io.File;
import javax.media.j3d.*;
import javax.vecmath.*;
import com.sun.j3d.audioengines.javasound.*;

public class SoundExample extends Applet {

  VirtualUniverse universe;
  Locale locale;
  TransformGroup vpTrans;
  View view;
  Bounds bounds;

. . .

  Point2f[] gainfield;

  public BranchGroup createSceneGraph() {
  // Create the root of the subgraph
    BranchGroup objRoot = new BranchGroup();

    TransformGroup objTrans = new TransformGroup();
      objTrans.setCapability(TransformGroup.ALLOW_TRANSFORM_WRITE);
    objTrans.setCapability(TransformGroup.ALLOW_TRANSFORM_READ);
    objRoot.addChild(objTrans);

  // Create a simple shape leaf node and add it into the scene graph.
    objTrans.addChild(new ColorCube(0.02));

    TransformGroup sphereTrans = new TransformGroup();
        sphereTrans.setCapability(TransformGroup.ALLOW_TRANSFORM_WRITE);
      sphereTrans.setCapability(TransformGroup.ALLOW_TRANSFORM_READ);

    Sphere sphere = new Sphere(.4f, Sphere.GENERATE_NORMALS |
                Sphere.GENERATE_TEXTURE_COORDS, 45);
        sphereTrans.addChild(sphere);
```

11

CREATING AND
VIEWING THE
VIRTUAL WORLD

Listing 11.14   Continued

```
      Transform3D tmptrans = new Transform3D();
      sphereTrans.getTransform(tmptrans);
      tmptrans.setTranslation(new Vector3f(0.f, 0.f, 7.f));
          sphereTrans.setTransform(tmptrans);
          objRoot.addChild(sphereTrans);

      objTrans.addChild(new OpenRoom());

       BoundingSphere bounds =
           new BoundingSphere(new Point3d(0.0,0.0,0.0), 100.0);

      Transform3D yAxis = new Transform3D();
      sphereTrans.getTransform(yAxis);

      Alpha rotationAlpha = new Alpha(-1, Alpha.INCREASING_ENABLE,
                          0, 0,
                          2500, 0, 0,
                          0, 0, 0);

      RotationInterpolator rotator =
              new RotationInterpolator(rotationAlpha, sphereTrans, yAxis,
                          0.0f, (float) Math.PI*2.0f);

      rotator.setSchedulingBounds(bounds);
  . . .
          Color3f red = new Color3f(1.f, 0.f, 0.f);
          Color3f blue = new Color3f(0.f, 0.f, 1.f);

          Point3f Point1 = new Point3f(2.f, 2.f, -2.f);
          Point3f atten = new Point3f(.1f,0.4f,0.01f);


      AmbientLight al = new AmbientLight();
         al.setInfluencingBounds(bounds);

         PointLight redlight = new PointLight(red, Point1, atten);

         redlight.setInfluencingBounds(bounds);


         objTrans.addChild(al);
          sphereTrans.addChild(rotator);

         objTrans.addChild(redlight);
```

LISTING 11.14 Continued

```java
        // Create an AuralAttribute with reverb params set

        Soundscape soundScape2 = new Soundscape();
        AuralAttributes attributes2 = new AuralAttributes();
        attributes2.setReverbOrder(2);
        attributes2.setReverbDelay(2.f);
        attributes2.setReflectionCoefficient(0.f);

        attributes2.setFrequencyScaleFactor(10.5f);
        attributes2.setVelocityScaleFactor(1000.f);

        soundScape2.setApplicationBounds(bounds);
        soundScape2.setAuralAttributes(attributes2);

        objRoot.addChild(soundScape2);

        //
        // Instantiatiate a PointSound and add it to the scene graph
        //
        PointSound sound = new PointSound();
        sound.setCapability(PointSound.ALLOW_ENABLE_WRITE);
        sound.setCapability(PointSound.ALLOW_INITIAL_GAIN_WRITE);
        sound.setCapability(PointSound.ALLOW_SOUND_DATA_WRITE);
        sound.setCapability(PointSound.ALLOW_DURATION_READ);
        sound.setCapability(PointSound.ALLOW_POSITION_WRITE);
        sound.setCapability(PointSound.ALLOW_LOOP_WRITE);
        sound.setCapability(Sound.INFINITE_LOOPS);
        sound.setSchedulingBounds(bounds);

         MediaContainer sample  = new MediaContainer();

        sample.setCacheEnable(true);
        sample.setURLString(filename[0]);
        System.out.println("urlstring: " + sample.getURLString());
        sound.setSoundData(sample);
        Point3f soundPos = new Point3f(0.0f, 0.0f, 0.0f);
        sound.setPosition(soundPos);

        Point2f[] gf = {
            new Point2f(0.f, 1.0f),
            new Point2f(5.f, 0.4f),
            new Point2f(10.f, 0.2f),
            new Point2f(15.f, 0.1f),
            new Point2f(20.f, 0.0025f),
```

LISTING 11.14   Continued

```
                new Point2f(25.f, 0.0f)

        };

        sound.setDistanceGain(gf);
        sound.setLoop(Sound.INFINITE_LOOPS);

        sound.setEnable(true);

//objTrans.addChild(sound);
    sphereTrans.addChild(sound);
return objRoot;
}

public void genGainField() {

    System.out.println("generating gain parameters");
    gainfield = new Point2f[4];
    float gain = .5f;
    float distance = 10.f;

    for (int ii=0; ii< 4; ii++) {
        distance = distance - 2.5f;
        gain = gain + .5f;

      //  System.out.println("distance: " + distance + " gain: " +  gain);
        gainfield[ii] = new Point2f(distance, gain);
    }

  }
. . .
```

Vector Math Library

The Vector Math Library is a required library for creating Java 3D objects. The Vector Math Library is packaged separately so that other Java APIs or non-3D applications might make use of it.

The main purpose of the Vector Math Library is to provide methods for matrix and vector mathematics as well as methods for dealing with color, positions, and volumes.

A brief review of the methods is provided here.

Tuples

Tuples store two, three, and four element values that are used to represent points, coordinates, and vectors. For example, a color can be stored in the tuple with three floating-point values (one each for red, green, and blue). The Java 3D class for a color specified in this way is `Color3f`. Note that there are tuples for representing bytes, double precision, and floating point values.

Matrix Objects

As we saw previously, matrix operations are a fundamental part of 3D graphics. Most applications won't need access to the matrices directly; however, there are many situations in which matrix manipulation is the only avenue available to achieve a particular transformation. The Vector Math Library contains a basic set of matrix objects that can be used to perform matrix operations (listed in Table 11.8).

TABLE 11.8 Matrix Classes

Matrix Object	Description
Matrix3f	Single-precision, floating-point 3x3 matrix
Matrix3d	Double-precision, floating-point 3x3 matrix
Matrix4f	Single-precision, floating-point 4x4 matrix
Matrix4d	Double-precision, floating-point 4x4 matrix
Gmatrix	Double-precision NxM matrix; can be dynamically resized

For many projects, it simply isn't necessary to directly use any of the objects in the Vector Math Library. Indeed, `TransformGroup` has several utility methods for rotation, translation, and scaling. (You have seen these in action already.) However, in many cases these aren't sufficient to achieve the desired effect, and moreover, many 3D programmers would prefer to perform their own matrix operations.

Regardless, the Vector Math Library is useful in many situations and worth understanding. Listing 11.15 shows a solution to the problem of scaling an object along a single dimension using matrix operations.

LISTING 11.15 `MatrixExampleJ3D.java`

```java
import java.applet.Applet;
import java.awt.BorderLayout;
import java.awt.event.*;
import java.awt.GraphicsConfiguration;
```

LISTING 11.15 Continued

```java
import com.sun.j3d.utils.applet.MainFrame;
import com.sun.j3d.utils.geometry.Box;

import com.sun.j3d.utils.geometry.Primitive;
import com.sun.j3d.utils.universe.*;
import javax.media.j3d.*;
import javax.vecmath.*;
//import javax.vecmath.Matrix3d;
import com.sun.j3d.utils.behaviors.mouse.MouseRotate;

public class MatrixExamplesJ3D extends Applet {
  VirtualUniverse universe;
  Locale locale;
  TransformGroup vpTrans;
  View view;
  Bounds bounds;
  TransformGroup geoTG;
  float sval=.1f;

    public BranchGroup createSceneGraph() {
        // Create the root of the branch graph; this will be returned
        Appearance app = new Appearance();
        BranchGroup objRoot = new BranchGroup();
        geoTG = new TransformGroup();
        geoTG.setCapability(TransformGroup.ALLOW_TRANSFORM_WRITE);
    geoTG.setCapability(TransformGroup.ALLOW_TRANSFORM_READ);

        Box box = new Box(1.f,1.f,1.f, app);

        objRoot.addChild(geoTG);
        MouseRotate behavior = new MouseRotate(geoTG);

        geoTG.addChild(behavior);
        behavior.setSchedulingBounds(bounds);
        geoTG.addChild(box);

    return objRoot;
      }


    . . .
    public void scaleBox() {
        sval=sval+0.08f;

        Transform3D currentTran = new Transform3D();
        geoTG.getTransform(currentTran);
```

Creating and Viewing the Virtual World
Chapter 11
591

11
CREATING AND
VIEWING THE
VIRTUAL WORLD

Listing 11.15 Continued

```
        Matrix3f xmat = new Matrix3f();
        currentTran.get(xmat);

        /* System.out.println("before " + xmat.m00 + " " +
➥ xmat.m01 + " " + xmat.m02 + " "
                            + xmat.m10 + " " + xmat.m11 + " " + xmat.m12 + " "
                            + xmat.m20 + " " + xmat.m21 + " " + xmat.m22);
        */
        Matrix3f newmat = new Matrix3f();
        newmat.setIdentity();

        newmat.setElement(1,1,sval);

        xmat.mul(newmat);

        /* System.out.println("after " + xmat.m00 + " " +
➥ xmat.m01 + " " + xmat.m02 + " "
                            + xmat.m10 + " " + xmat.m11 + " " + xmat.m12 + " "
                            + xmat.m20 + " " + xmat.m21 + " " + xmat.m22);
        */
        currentTran.set(xmat);

         geoTG.setTransform(currentTran);


    }
}
. . .


 class KeyHandler implements KeyListener {
    MatrixExamplesJ3D me;

    public KeyHandler(MatrixExamplesJ3D me) {
        this.me = me;
    }
    public void keyReleased(java.awt.event.KeyEvent p1) {
    }

    public void keyPressed(java.awt.event.KeyEvent p1) {
       me.scaleBox();

    }

    public void keyTyped(java.awt.event.KeyEvent p1) {
    }

}
```

Using the matrix notation m_{ij}, we can see one way in which we gain access to the different elements of the matrix. For example, one of the constructors for a `Matrix3f` object is

```
public Matrix3f(float m00, float m01, float m02,
                float m10, float m11, float m12
                float m20, float m21, float m22)
```

It is also possible to use the `setElement()` and `getElement()` methods to get and set individual elements directly.

Comprehensive Example #1: MR Physics Visualization

In Chapter 3, we developed a fairly simple Java 2D application to plot a trajectory through Kspace as part of the KspaceModeller application. We now begin to expand on this application using Java 3D models.

Our goal in this part of the ongoing example is to create a model voxel to examine the behavior of spins in magnetic resonance. Briefly, let's begin by sketching the scene graph for the part of the application we will do here (shown in Figure 11.11).

FIGURE 11.11

Scene graph diagram for MRVector.java.

We begin by creating a 3D axis in a separate class MRAxis.java (see Listing 11.16).

LISTING 11.16 MRAxis.java

```java
import java.lang.Math.*;
import javax.media.j3d.*;
import javax.vecmath.*;
import com.sun.j3d.utils.geometry.Cone;

public class MRAxis extends TransformGroup {

    public MRAxis() {

        Appearance axisapp = new Appearance();
        Material axismat = new Material();
        axismat.setShininess(60.f);
        axismat.setSpecularColor(.5f, 01.f, 01.f);
        axismat.setDiffuseColor(.5f, .1f, 0.1f);

        axismat.setLightingEnable(true);
        axisapp.setMaterial(axismat);

        this.setCapability(TransformGroup.ALLOW_TRANSFORM_WRITE);
        this.setCapability(TransformGroup.ALLOW_TRANSFORM_READ);

        Axis3D axis3d = new Axis3D(10, 8.f, .05f, axisapp);
        this.addChild(axis3d);

    }

} //end MRAxis
```

In its current state, the MRAxis class does little more than instantiate an Axis3D object. The Axis3D is substantially similar to the MRVector class; therefore, we don't include it in the text for brevity. As we continue to develop this example in the next few chapters, you will see that having the classes separated in this fashion will allow you to easily add several ornaments to the axis, including some labels that always face the viewer regardless of orientation and some other objects related to enhancing the visualization. These ornaments will be added in the next chapter when we take up OrientedShape3D and the Billboard Behavior.

We are now at an intermediate step and will examine our results. The 3D axis can be seen by instantiating the object in our BasicRecipeJ3D application. Uncomment the lines for MRAxis to see our axis triplet (see Figure 11.12).

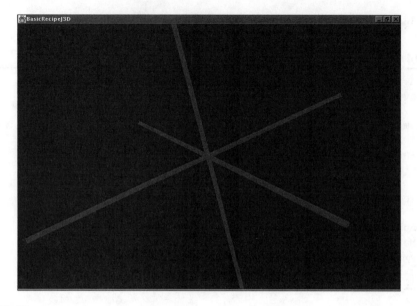

FIGURE 11.12

Screenshot from BasicRecipeJ3D with an object of MRAxis *class added to the scene.*

Now that we have an axis, we want to create a series of vectors (in the sense of a physical entity with a magnitude and direction). These vectors will be represented by an arrow. The first vector that we will add to the scene is called Mnet and represents the macroscopic sum of a large number of individual spins (as described previously). The code in Listing 11.17 is used to create each vector in a set.

LISTING 11.17 MRVector.java

```java
public class MRVector extends TransformGroup {

    Appearance app;
    private float length;
    private float sval = -0.1f;
    Transform3D currentTran;

    public MRVector(Appearance app, float length) {

        this.app = app;
        this.length = length;

        this.setCapability(TransformGroup.ALLOW_TRANSFORM_WRITE);
        this.setCapability(TransformGroup.ALLOW_TRANSFORM_READ);
```

LISTING 11.17   Continued

```
        this.setCapability(TransformGroup.ALLOW_CHILDREN_READ);
        this.setCapability(TransformGroup.ALLOW_CHILDREN_WRITE);

        VecBody vb = new VecBody(10, length, .1f, app);
        VecHead vh = new VecHead(50, length, app);

        this.addChild(vb);
        this.addChild(vh);

    }
```

Listing 11.17 is quite simple at present but a great deal of changes will occur when we add the ability to scale the Mnet vector. These changes will take place in the next chapter. For now, we will leave this class as a simple, non-scalable vector.

We are now ready to create the series of vectors that will represent the activity of a family of spins contained within a voxel. Listing 11.18 is the code for the MRVoxel class.

LISTING 11.18   MRVoxel.java

```java
import java.lang.Math.*;
import javax.media.j3d.*;
import javax.vecmath.*;
import com.sun.j3d.utils.geometry.Cone;

public class MRVoxel extends TransformGroup {

    int nspins = 8;

    public MRVoxel() {

        //part 1 - set the capabilities of this object to allow
        //reading and writing of
        //the Transform3D
    this.setCapability(TransformGroup.ALLOW_TRANSFORM_WRITE);
        this.setCapability(TransformGroup.ALLOW_TRANSFORM_READ);

        //set capabilities to allow reading and writing of the children
        this.setCapability(Group.ALLOW_CHILDREN_READ);
        this.setCapability(Group.ALLOW_CHILDREN_WRITE);
```

LISTING 11.18   Continued

```
        //part 2 - set up the appearance bundles
        Appearance mnetapp = new Appearance();
        Material mnetmat = new Material();

        mnetmat.setSpecularColor(1.f, 0.f, 0.f);
        mnetmat.setShininess(5.f);
         mnetapp.setMaterial(mnetmat);

        Appearance spinapp = new Appearance();
        Material spinmat = new Material();

        spinmat.setShininess(5.f);
        spinmat.setLightingEnable(true);
        spinapp.setMaterial(spinmat);

        Bounds bounds = new BoundingSphere(new Point3d(0.0,0.0,0.0), 100.0);
        MRVector mnet = new MRVector(mnetapp, nspins*1.f);

        float dephaseFac = -1.f*nspins/2;
        float dephaseFacGlobal = 20.f;

        //part 3 - instantiate the spins and
        //setUserData for diphase rate and type
        MRVector[] spins = new MRVector[nspins];

        for (int ii=0; ii<nspins; ii++) {
            spins[ii] = new MRVector(spinapp,2.f);   //unit vectors
            spins[ii].setUserData(new
➥ MRVectorProperties(dephaseFac/dephaseFacGlobal, "spin"));
            this.addChild(spins[ii]);

            dephaseFac += 1.f;
            if (dephaseFac == 0.f)
                dephaseFac += 1.f;
➥ //center frequency (dephaseFac=0) occupied by Mnet
        }

        this.addChild(mnet);

        mnet.setUserData(new MRVectorProperties(0.f, "mnet"));

        //add a T2Behavior for spinning
        T2Behavior t2 = new T2Behavior(this, 2.f);
        this.addChild(t2);
        t2.setSchedulingBounds(bounds);
```

LISTING 11.18   Continued

```
   }

} //end class
```

Listing 11.18 shows the results of adding MRVoxel and MRAxis to the scene and is displayed in Figure 11.13.

FIGURE 11.13

Screenshot from BasicRecipeJ3D.java *with objects from* MRVoxel *and* MRAxis *added to the scene.*

There are several aspects of the class in Listing 11.18 to notice. One of the main functions of the MRVoxel class is to instantiate the spin vectors and give them properties. This occurs in part two. Note that we use the setUserData() method to label each vector as either a "spin" or as an "mnet". The setUserData() method is one of the methods of the SceneGraphObject class and is a useful method for working around sometimes difficult problems. In this case, we need to identify which type of vector we are dealing with and to store information about the dephasing rate of the vector. In the next chapter, we will access this data in a custom Behavior.

Listing 11.19 shows the MRVectorProperties class that we will use to access and store vector properties.

LISTING 11.19   MRVectorProperties.java

```java
class MRVectorProperties {
   float dephaseRate;
   String vectype;

   public MRVectorProperties(float dephaseRate, String vectype) {
      this.dephaseRate = dephaseRate;
      this.vectype = vectype;
   }

   public float getDephaseRate() {
      return dephaseRate;
   }

   public String getVecType() {
      return vectype;
   }

   public void setDephaseRate(float dephaseRate) {
      this.dephaseRate = dephaseRate;
   }

}
```

Spins dephase over time because of the physical environment in which they exist. One of these dephasing mechanisms is termed T2* relaxation. As a preview, we will add one of the Behaviors that is developed in the next chapter. The purpose of the T2StarBehavior (see Listing 11.20) is to control the speed of the spin vectors so that they dephase over time.

LISTING 11.20   T2Behavior.java

```java
import java.awt.*;
import java.awt.event.*;
import java.util.*;
import javax.media.j3d.*;
import javax.vecmath.*;


public class T2Behavior
    extends Behavior
{
    private TransformGroup targetTG;
    private Transform3D rotation = new Transform3D();
    private double[] T2angle;
    private double T2Weight;
;
```

LISTING 11.20   Continued

```
    public T2Behavior( TransformGroup targetTG, double T2Weight )
    {
        super( );
        this.targetTG = targetTG;
        this.T2Weight = T2Weight;
            T2angle = new double[targetTG.numChildren()];
    }

    public void initialize()
    {
      this.wakeupOn(new WakeupOnAWTEvent(KeyEvent.KEY_PRESSED));
    }

    public void processStimulus(Enumeration criterion)
    {
        for (int ii=0; ii<targetTG.numChildren(); ii++) {

            MRVectorProperties vecprop =
➥ (MRVectorProperties)targetTG.getChild(ii).getUserData();

            if (vecprop != null) {

                T2angle[ii] += 0.045*(T2Weight+vecprop.getDephaseRate());
                MRVector tmpTG = (MRVector)targetTG.getChild(ii);
                if (vecprop.getVecType() == "mnet") {
                    System.out.println("Mnet encountered; scale");
                }

                Transform3D rot = new Transform3D();
                //System.out.println("T2Angle: " + T2angle[ii]);
                tmpTG.getTransform(rot);
            rot.rotY(T2angle[ii]);
                tmpTG.setTransform(rot);

            //targetTG.setChild(tmpTG,ii);
                //System.out.println("vectype: " + vecprop.getVecType()...
            }
        }

        this.wakeupOn(new WakeupOnAWTEvent(KeyEvent.KEY_PRESSED));
    }
}
```

Note that the T2StarBehavior retrieves the MRVectorProperties of each vector and uses that
to compute a rotational transform. In the next chapter, we will add scaling of Mnet as well as
more complex Behaviors for modeling the physic behavior of the voxel.

Comprehensive Example #2: Neuronal Spike Visualization

Neurons in the brain convey information by firing spikes (also known as action potentials). By placing a wire probe near a neuron, it is possible to record its electrical potential and thus determine when the neuron fired. These spiking events can be related to the behavior of an animal during a task. This is a fundamental technique in cognitive neuroscience.

A recent advancement in extracellular recording is the invention of the tetrode by Bruce McNaughton and colleagues at the University of Arizona. A *tetrode* is a twisted set of four wires that can be used to resolve the activities of up to 20 neurons simultaneously. The idea is that if a tetrode sits in a bed of neurons, different neurons will have a different signature on the four wires because the electrical potential seen at each wire will depend on its distance from the spiking neuron.

We can see that the amplitudes of the spikes tend to cluster in slightly fuzzy groups. Our goal here is to plot the peak amplitude of the data recorded on the wires in three dimensions and to develop this prototype into an interactive program for isolating these clusters. In the next chapter, we will add a picking behavior so that we can plot the spike waveform for different clusters of spikes. We will also add some Swing user interface components and multiple projections.

The important class in this example is `SpikeCloud.java`, shown in Listing 11.21, and Figure 11.14 displays the sample output.

LISTING 11.21 SpikeCloud.java

```java
import javax.media.j3d.*;
import javax.vecmath.*;
import java.util.Random;
import java.math.BigInteger;

public class SpikeCloud {

    float verts[];
    Point3f[] sCoords;
    Color3f[] sColors;
    int npoints;
    PointArray points = null;
    Shape3D shape;

    public SpikeCloud() {
        ReadSpikes s = new ReadSpikes(1,60000);
        this.npoints = s.nrecs;

        sCoords = new Point3f[this.npoints];
        sColors = new Color3f[this.npoints];
```

LISTING 11.21   Continued

```
        for (int ii=0; ii<this.npoints;ii++) {

            sCoords[ii] = new Point3f(s.sdata[ii][0].floatValue()/1000,
                                      s.sdata[ii][1].floatValue()/1000,
                                      s.sdata[ii][2].floatValue()/1000);
          sColors[ii] = new Color3f(1.f,0.f,1.f);

          }

      Appearance app = new Appearance();
      points = new PointArray(this.npoints, PointArray.COORDINATES |
                              PointArray.COLOR_3);
      points.setCoordinates(0, sCoords);
      points.setColors(0, sColors);
      shape = new Shape3D(points, app);
  }

  public Shape3D getShape(){
     return shape;
  }
}
```

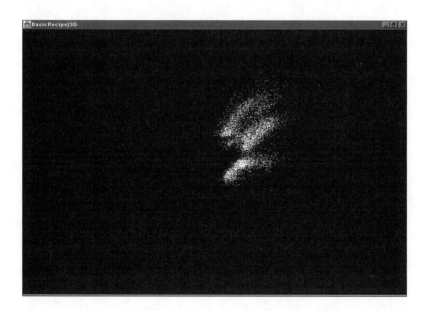

FIGURE 11.14

Screenshot from BasicRecipeJ3D.java *with an object of the* SpikeCloud *class added to the content subgraph.*

Note the instantiation of the ReadSpikes class. This class isn't shown because it doesn't specifically apply to Java 3D. However, the class illustrates how to load existing data into Java 3D. For the interested reader, we include ReadSpikes.java in the download from the Web site for the book.

Summary

In this chapter, we have examined some the basic classes necessary to create and put content into a Java 3D content subgraph. We have looked at the structure of a Java 3D program, which is, in fact, pretty straightforward. The challenge is to organize the scene graph into the appropriate Groups.

Along the way, we have hinted at the use of Behaviors to enable interaction in the 3D scene. The next chapter will help lay in the framework of user interaction with Java 3D.

Interaction with the Virtual World

IN THIS CHAPTER

All the Java 3D programs presented so far have been rather poor from an interaction standpoint. While trying to shield you from the details, we have used several Behaviors that allow us to do enough interaction to examine the scene graph, but our focus so far has been on getting the content into the scene. We now turn our attention to the important topic of human-computer interaction with 3D content.

Types of 3D User Interaction

There are two basic forms of interaction that we will consider in this chapter. The first is 2D based and is familiar to anyone who uses a computer. Examples of 2D interaction include the use of icons, buttons, and other widgets that exist on the user's desktop. In Java 3D, changes to the scene graph are made using the standard Swing and AWT components.

The second form of user interaction is 3D based and involves events detected within the *coexistence space* of the user and the 3D scene. In other words, user interaction in 3D requires that the user's actions in the real world be interpreted in coordinates in the virtual world and vice versa. This can be a challenging problem and is solved by finding a common space for a whole series of transforms. In order to address these challenges, Java 3D provides two important abstractions. We begin by describing the central class for interaction in Java 3D, the Behavior class.

The Behavior Class

The Behavior class is an abstract class in which code for manipulating the scene graph is typically placed. We say typically because you will see that a Behavior can perform important functions *not* related to the manipulation of the scene graph. Nevertheless, Behavior objects are the primary way in which user input can communicate with the virtual universe. Recall that an abstract class is never instantiated directly but rather is subclassed (extended) to accomplish some particular goal.

Similar to an event listener, the general idea of a Behavior object is to specify what to do and when to do it. As you will soon see, these two functions are handled in the processStimulus() and initialization() methods, respectively. A big part of the initialization() method is to specify one or more *wakeup conditions*. The wakeup conditions designate the specific condition that activates the processStimulus() method of the Behavior.

Basically all the work in writing a Behavior occurs in overriding these two methods: processStimulus() and initialization(). A constructor is also needed, but writing that is, of course, typically simple.

An important conceptual point should be understood at this time. A `Behavior` does not run synchronously with the Java 3D renderer. In other words, there is no guarantee that a `Behavior`'s action will impact the current frame. One exception to this rule is `wakeupOnElapsedFrames()`.

It should also be noted that many useful `Behaviors` already exist and are provided in the utilities package. It is obviously always a good idea to first see if an existing class exists or can be extended or modified. For example, the `MouseMover` and `MouseRotation` `Behaviors` are frequently and conveniently used. Nevertheless, it is important to understand how `Behaviors` work and in what situations they are used.

The `initialize()` Method

The first method that we must override is the `initialize()` method. The purpose of this method is to specify what events will awaken the quiescent `Behavior` and cause it to act. It is probably worthwhile to diverge for a moment and discuss terminology and class hierarchy of wakeup conditions and criteria.

The `WakeupCondition` class is the highest level of abstraction used to represent a condition that activates the `processStimulus()` method. It has several subclasses, the most elementary of which is the `WakeupCriterion` class. The `WakeupCriterion` class represents all unitary events that cause `WakeupCondition` to call `processStimulus()` and is itself extended into numerous subclasses. Combinations of `WakeupCirteria` can be specified with Boolean operations (see the section "Boolean `WakeupCriteria`").

There are several general categories of wakeup criteria, and these are listed in Table 12.1.

TABLE 12.1 General Classes of Wakeup Criterion

`WakeupCriterion`	*Usage*
`ViewPlatform` entry/exit	Collision avoidance; turning on lights upon entering an area
`Behavior` Post	Wake up or go to sleep when another `Behavior` posts a specific event
`TransformGroup` changes	Link to any `TransformGroup` and monitor changes to it
AWT Event	Making changes based on key strokes
Geometry collision/decollision	Wake up upon collision of a `Shape3D` node's `Geometry` with any other object
Elapsed time or frames	User gets specified time to make decision
`Sensor` activation	Entry or exit of a `Sensor`

The processStimulus() Method

The majority of the programming work necessary to develop a custom Behavior occurs in the processStimulus() method. The purpose of the processStimulus() method is to handle all the internal messages (stimuli) of the Behavior. These stimuli result from the activation of one of more wakeup criterions (as described previously). To repeat, the processStimulus() method implements the "what to do" function.

The first part of this process is to determine which stimulus prompted the particular incoming call to the processStimulus() method. This sorting out of stimuli is usually accomplished in a series of if else or case switch statements and is directly analogous to what happens in EventListeners in Java.

The next step is *typically* to make a change to the scene based on the stimulus. We emphasize the word *typically* to note that the processStimulus() method can execute any kind of Java code, not just methods related to the scene graph. You could just as easily invoke an RMI method, access a JNI executable, or launch another application. Generally, however, the developer will be making changes to the scene graph.

The scene element(s) to be acted on are often termed the *object(s) of change*, which simply means that the enumerated objects are candidates for the Behavior to act on. The objects of change must have the proper capability bits set for the manipulation to take place.

Writing a Behavior is about as easy as writing a Listener using AWT except that the methods have different names. Listings 12.1 and 12.2 demonstrate the simplest possible Behavior that can be written. In this case, the Behavior is set to wake up when any key is pressed on the keyboard. Instead of specifying an object of change, the Behavior just prints that the key has been pressed.

LISTING 12.1 SimpleBehaviorApp.java

```
import java.awt.event.*;
import javax.media.j3d.*;
import java.util.Enumeration;

  public class SimpleBehavior extends Behavior {

      WakeupCriterion criterion;

      public SimpleBehavior() {
          super();
      }

      public void initialize() {
          criterion = new WakeupOnAWTEvent( KeyEvent.KEY_PRESSED );
```

LISTING 12.1 Continued

```
        wakeupOn(criterion);
    }

    public void processStimulus( Enumeration criteria) {
            System.out.println("processStimulus of SimpleBehavior");

        wakeupOn(criterion);
    }
}
```

We now show how an application sets up the simple `Behavior`.

LISTING 12.2 SimpleBehavior.java

```java
import java.applet.Applet;
import java.awt.BorderLayout;
import com.sun.j3d.utils.applet.MainFrame;

import java.awt.event.*;
import java.awt.GraphicsConfiguration;
import com.sun.j3d.utils.universe.*;
import javax.media.j3d.*;
import javax.vecmath.*;

public class SimpleBehaviorEx extends Applet {

    SimpleBehavior  sb;

    public BranchGroup createSceneGraph() {
        // Create the root of the branch graph
        BranchGroup objRoot = new BranchGroup();

        // Create a SimpleBehavior ;

        sb = new SimpleBehavior();
        // set scheduling bounds
        BoundingSphere bounds =
➥ new BoundingSphere(new Point3d(0.0,0.0,0.0), 100.0);
        sb.setSchedulingBounds(bounds);
        // add the SimpleBehavior to the scene graph
        objRoot.addChild(sb);

        return objRoot;
    }
```

LISTING 12.2 Continued

```
public SimpleBehaviorEx() {
    GraphicsConfiguration config =
        SimpleUniverse.getPreferredConfiguration();

    Canvas3D canvas = new Canvas3D(config);
    canvas.setSize(800, 800);
    add("Center", canvas);
    // Create an empty scene and attach it to the virtual universe
    BranchGroup scene = createSceneGraph();
    SimpleUniverse u = new SimpleUniverse(canvas);

    u.getViewingPlatform().setNominalViewingTransform();

    u.addBranchGraph(scene);

}
```

. . .

Figure 12.1 shows a screenshot after running `SimpleBehavior.java`. A text string is printed to the output window each time the user presses a key. This program is the simplest possible `Behavior` and it does no more than a simple key listener.

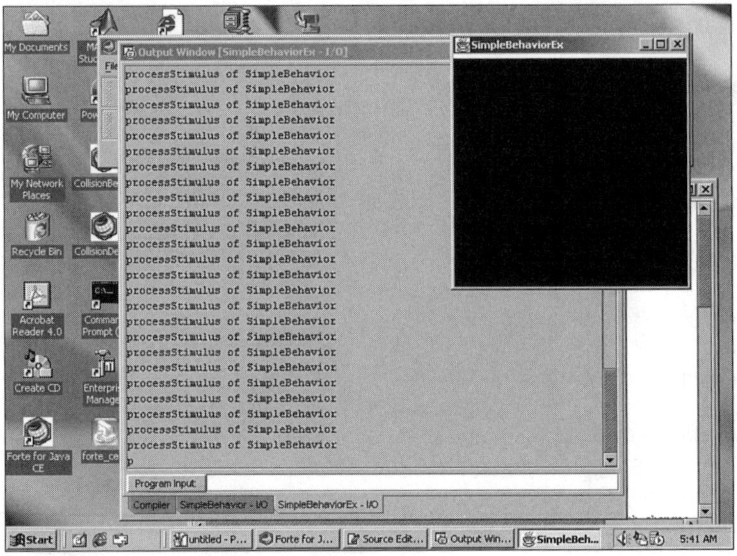

FIGURE 12.1
Running `SimpleBehavior.java`.

Note that in this case we have done little more than create a simple key listener using the Java 3D version of a listener. The one major difference is that the Java 3D `Behavior` runs in a single thread. Therefore, scene graph changes are grouped to avoid frame discontinuities. There is some talk of changing the single thread rule in a future release but as of the writing of this book, all `Behaviors` run in a single thread.

We now provide a second example (see Listings 12.3 and 12.4) that demonstrates using a `Behavior` in combination with Swing components to translate and rotate boxes depending on the state of `JRadioButtons`.

LISTING 12.3   MoveBoxBehavior.java

```
import java.awt.AWTEvent;
import java.awt.event.*;
import java.util.Enumeration;
import javax.media.j3d.*;
import javax.vecmath.*;

import com.sun.j3d.utils.universe.*;
import javax.swing.JRadioButton;

public class MoveBoxBehavior extends Behavior {


 // protected static final double FAST_SPEED = 2.0;
 // protected static final double NORMAL_SPEED = 1.0;
 // protected static final double SLOW_SPEED = 0.5;

  private TransformGroup tg;
  private Transform3D transform3D;
  private WakeupCondition keyCriterion;

  JRadioButton rb;

  public MoveBoxBehavior(JRadioButton rb, TransformGroup tg )
  {
    this.rb = rb;
    this.tg = tg;
    transform3D = new Transform3D();
  }

  public void initialize()
  {
    WakeupCriterion[] keyEvents = new WakeupCriterion[2];
```

LISTING 12.3   Continued

```java
    keyEvents[0] = new WakeupOnAWTEvent( KeyEvent.KEY_PRESSED );
    keyEvents[1] = new WakeupOnAWTEvent( KeyEvent.KEY_RELEASED );
    keyCriterion = new WakeupOr( keyEvents );
    wakeupOn( keyCriterion );
}


public void processStimulus( Enumeration criteria )
{

    WakeupCriterion wakeup;
    AWTEvent[] event;

    while( criteria.hasMoreElements() )
    {
     wakeup = (WakeupCriterion) criteria.nextElement();
     if( !(wakeup instanceof WakeupOnAWTEvent) )
      continue;

    event = ((WakeupOnAWTEvent)wakeup).getAWTEvent();
    for( int i = 0; i < event.length; i++ ) {
        if( event[i].getID() == KeyEvent.KEY_PRESSED )
        {
          if (rb.isSelected()==true)
              processKeyEvent((KeyEvent)event[i]);
        }
      }
    }
    wakeupOn( keyCriterion );
}
protected void processKeyEvent(KeyEvent event)  {
  int keycode = event.getKeyCode();
  tg.getTransform(transform3D);
  Transform3D t = new Transform3D();

  if(keycode == KeyEvent.VK_UP)
   t.setTranslation(new Vector3d(0.0, 0.0, 0.3));
  else if(keycode == KeyEvent.VK_DOWN)
   t.setTranslation(new Vector3d(0.0, 0.0, -0.3));
  else if(keycode == KeyEvent.VK_LEFT)
    t.rotY((2*Math.PI)/36);
  else if(keycode == KeyEvent.VK_RIGHT)
    t.rotY((-2*Math.PI)/36);
```

LISTING 12.3   Continued

```
    transform3D.mul(t);
    tg.setTransform(transform3D);

  }

}
```

The following application uses the preceding MoveBoxBehavior class.

LISTING 12.4   MoveBox.java

```java
import java.applet.Applet;
import java.awt.BorderLayout;
import java.awt.Panel;
import java.awt.event.*;
import java.awt.GraphicsConfiguration;
import com.sun.j3d.utils.applet.MainFrame;
import com.sun.j3d.utils.geometry.Box;

import com.sun.j3d.utils.geometry.Primitive;
import com.sun.j3d.utils.universe.*;
import com.sun.j3d.utils.behaviors.mouse.MouseRotate;
import javax.media.j3d.*;
import javax.vecmath.*;
import javax.swing.JRadioButton;

public class MoveBox extends Applet {
  VirtualUniverse universe;
  Locale locale;
  TransformGroup vpTrans;
  TransformGroup[] boxTGs;
  JRadioButton rb0, rb1, rb2, rb3, rb4;
  View view;
  Bounds bounds;

    public BranchGroup createSceneGraph() {
        // Create the root of the branch graph; this will be returned

        BranchGroup objRoot = new BranchGroup();

        TransformGroup geoTG = new TransformGroup();
        geoTG.setCapability(TransformGroup.ALLOW_TRANSFORM_WRITE);
    geoTG.setCapability(TransformGroup.ALLOW_TRANSFORM_READ);
```

LISTING 12.4   Continued

```
        BoundingSphere bounds =
            new BoundingSphere(new Point3d(0.0,0.0,0.0), 100.0);

    MouseRotate mouseBeh = new MouseRotate(geoTG);
geoTG.addChild(mouseBeh);
mouseBeh.setSchedulingBounds(bounds);

    boxTGs = new TransformGroup[4];

for (int ii=0; ii<4; ii++) {
        boxTGs[ii] = new TransformGroup();
    boxTGs[ii].setCapability(TransformGroup.ALLOW_TRANSFORM_WRITE);
            boxTGs[ii].setCapability(TransformGroup.ALLOW_TRANSFORM_READ);
}

    Transform3D t3d = new Transform3D();

    Material mat0 = new Material();
    mat0.setDiffuseColor(new Color3f(.8f, 0.f, 0.f));
    mat0.setSpecularColor(new Color3f(.9f, 0.f, 0.f));
    Appearance ap0 = new Appearance();
    ap0.setMaterial(mat0);

    t3d.set(new Vector3f(-1.f, 0.f, -1.f));
    boxTGs[0].setTransform(t3d);
    boxTGs[0].addChild(new Box(.3f,.3f,.3f,ap0));
    geoTG.addChild(boxTGs[0]);

    Material mat1 = new Material();
    mat1.setDiffuseColor(new Color3f(.0f, 0.f, 0.8f));
    mat1.setSpecularColor(new Color3f(.0f, 0.f, 0.9f));
    Appearance ap1 = new Appearance();
    ap1.setMaterial(mat1);

    t3d.set(new Vector3f(1.f, 0.f, -1.f));
    boxTGs[1].setTransform(t3d);
    boxTGs[1].addChild(new Box(.3f,.3f,.3f,ap1));
    geoTG.addChild(boxTGs[1]);

        . . .

        //add the Behaviors
    MoveBoxBehavior mbb0 = new MoveBoxBehavior(rb0,boxTGs[0]);
    mbb0.setSchedulingBounds(bounds);
    objRoot.addChild(mbb0);
```

LISTING 12.4   Continued

```
        MoveBoxBehavior mbb1 = new MoveBoxBehavior(rb1,boxTGs[1]);
        mbb1.setSchedulingBounds(bounds);
        objRoot.addChild(mbb1);

        MoveBoxBehavior mbb2 = new MoveBoxBehavior(rb2,boxTGs[2]);
        mbb2.setSchedulingBounds(bounds);
        objRoot.addChild(mbb2);

        MoveBoxBehavior mbb3 = new MoveBoxBehavior(rb3,boxTGs[3]);
        mbb3.setSchedulingBounds(bounds);
        objRoot.addChild(mbb3);

        Color3f lcolor = new Color3f(0.9f, 0.9f, 0.9f);
        Vector3f ldir  = new Vector3f(0.0f, -8.0f, -8.0f);

        DirectionalLight dirlight = new DirectionalLight(lcolor, ldir);

        dirlight.setInfluencingBounds(bounds);


    objRoot.addChild(dirlight);

    objRoot.compile();
  return objRoot;
  }

. . .

  public MoveBox() {
  setLayout(new BorderLayout());

. . .


      Panel uipanel = new Panel();

      rb0 = new JRadioButton("Box 1");
      rb1 = new JRadioButton("Box 2");
      rb2 = new JRadioButton("Box 3");
      rb3 = new JRadioButton("Box 4");
      rb4 = new JRadioButton("ViewPlatform");

      uipanel.add(rb0);
      uipanel.add(rb1);
      uipanel.add(rb2);
      uipanel.add(rb3);
```

LISTING 12.4   Continued

```
        uipanel.add(rb4);

        add("North", uipanel);
        bounds = new BoundingSphere(new Point3d(0.0,0.0,0.0), 100.0);
        BranchGroup scene = createSceneGraph();

    . . .

}
```

Figure 12.2 show the screen output from MoveBox.java. By selecting different radio buttons, the user can move and rotate any combination of boxes and the ViewPlatform.

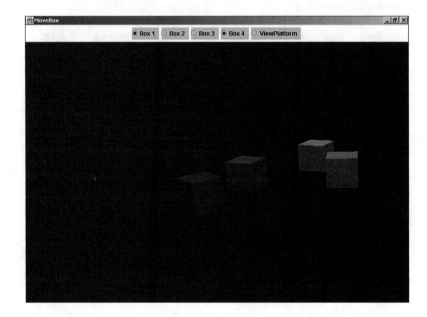

FIGURE 12.2

Screen output from MoveBox.java.

In order to reinforce the fundamental concepts for developing a custom Behavior, we include a third example. Listings 12.5 and 12.6 demonstrate the use of a Behavior for changing the emissive color of an object in the scene graph.

LISTING 12.5   EmissiveBall.java

```java
public class EmissiveBall extends Applet {

    private SimpleUniverse u = null;
public EmissiveBall() {
  super();
}


public void init() {
  setLayout(new BorderLayout());

  GraphicsConfiguration config =
          SimpleUniverse.getPreferredConfiguration();
  Canvas3D c = new Canvas3D(config);
  add("Center", c);


  u = new SimpleUniverse(c);
  BranchGroup scene = createSceneGraph(u);
        // This will move the ViewPlatform back a bit so the
        // objects in the scene can be viewed.
        u.getViewingPlatform().setNominalViewingTransform();
  u.addBranchGraph(scene);
    }

    public BranchGroup createSceneGraph(SimpleUniverse su) {
// Create the root of the branch graph
BranchGroup objRoot = new BranchGroup();
TransformGroup rotation = new TransformGroup();
rotation.setCapability(TransformGroup.ALLOW_TRANSFORM_WRITE);
rotation.setCapability(TransformGroup.ALLOW_TRANSFORM_READ);
objRoot.addChild(rotation);

    Transform3D sphereOffset = new Transform3D();
    sphereOffset.set(new Vector3d(1.1,0.7,0));
    TransformGroup sphereGroup = new TransformGroup(sphereOffset);
    rotation.addChild(sphereGroup);
    Appearance sphereAppearance = new Appearance();

    Material ballMaterial = new Material(
      new Color3f(Color.black), new Color3f(Color.black),
➥ new Color3f(Color.black),
      new Color3f(Color.white), 100f);
    sphereAppearance.setMaterial(ballMaterial);
    sphereGroup.addChild(new Sphere(0.6f,sphereAppearance));
```

LISTING 12.5   Continued

```java
    // Create the behaviour that will control the varying of the
    // emissive colour of the sphere. In this case it will vary
    // from red to green, be updated at 10 millisecond intervals,
    // and take 50 updates to go from one colour to the other. It
    // will also cycle (meaning it will go back and forwards between
    // the two colours rather than stopping after 1 complete change.

    EmissiveBehaviour ballLight = new EmissiveBehaviour(
      ballMaterial,new Color3f(Color.red), new Color3f(Color.green),
      10,50,true);
    ballLight.setSchedulingBounds(new BoundingSphere(new Point3d(),100.0));
    rotation.addChild(ballLight);

    Transform3D boxRotation = new Transform3D();
    boxRotation.setRotation(new AxisAngle4d(1.0,1.0,0.0,-Math.PI/1.3));
    TransformGroup boxGroup = new TransformGroup(boxRotation);
    rotation.addChild(boxGroup);
    Appearance cubeAppearance = new Appearance();
    cubeAppearance.setMaterial(new Material(
      new Color3f(Color.blue), new Color3f(Color.black),
➥ new Color3f(Color.blue),
      new Color3f(Color.white), 40f));
    Box ourBox = new Box(0.5f,0.5f,0.5f,cubeAppearance);
    boxGroup.addChild(ourBox);

    DirectionalLight light1 = new DirectionalLight(
      new Color3f(Color.white), new Vector3f(-1.0f,-1.0f,-1.0f));
    light1.setInfluencingBounds(new BoundingSphere(new Point3d(),100.0));
    rotation.addChild(light1);

    KeyNavigatorBehavior navigator = new KeyNavigatorBehavior(
        su.getViewingPlatform().getViewPlatformTransform());
    navigator.setSchedulingBounds(new BoundingSphere(
        new Point3d(), 1000.0));
    objRoot.addChild(navigator);

    MouseRotate rotator = new MouseRotate();
    rotator.setTransformGroup(rotation);
    rotator.setSchedulingBounds(new BoundingSphere(
        new Point3d(), 1000.0));
    objRoot.addChild(rotator);

    return objRoot;
}
```

Interaction with the Virtual World

CHAPTER 12

617

12

INTERACTION WITH
THE VIRTUAL
WORLD

LISTING 12.5   Continued

```java
/******************************************************************
* Free up all resources.
******************************************************************/
public void destroy() {
  u.removeAllLocales();
    }

public static void main(String[] args) {
    new MainFrame(new EmissiveBall(), 512, 512);
 }
}
```

LISTING 12.6   EmissiveBehavior.java

```java
import java.util.*;
import javax.media.j3d.*;
import javax.vecmath.*;
import java.awt.*;

public class EmissiveBehaviour extends Behavior {

  /** What makes the behaviour wake. */
  protected WakeupOnElapsedTime wakeCriteria;

  protected Material    material;
  protected Color3f     startColour;

  protected Color3f     stopColour;

  /** Time (in milliseconds) between updates of the colour. */
  protected int         timeBetweenUpdates;

  /** Number of updates for the colour to max one complete
  * cycle from the start to stop colour. ******************/
  protected int         totalUpdates;

  /** Whether the Behavior will continue to cycle. **/
  protected boolean     cycle;

  /** Current emissiveColor for the Material. */
  protected Color3f     currentColour;

  /** The amount of colour change each update. */
  protected Color3f     colourStep;
```

LISTING 12.6   Continued

```
/** Current count of number of updates performed. */
protected int          stepNumber;


/**************************************************************
 * Constructs an EmissiveBehaviour object that will vary the
 * emissiveColr of the passed material between the 2 colours
 * passed and according to the timing information provided.
 **************************************************************/
EmissiveBehaviour(Material mat,Color3f start, Color3f stop,
  int updateInterval, int numUpdates, boolean cyclic) {

  material = mat;
  mat.setCapability(Material.ALLOW_COMPONENT_WRITE);
  startColour = start;
  stopColour = stop;
  timeBetweenUpdates = updateInterval;
  wakeCriteria = new WakeupOnElapsedTime(timeBetweenUpdates);
  totalUpdates = numUpdates;
  cycle = cyclic;
  stepNumber = 0;

  currentColour = startColour;
  //////////////////////////////////
  // The colour change at each update
  //////////////////////////////////
  colourStep = new Color3f(
    (stopColour.x-startColour.x)/totalUpdates,
    (stopColour.y-startColour.y)/totalUpdates,
    (stopColour.z-startColour.z)/totalUpdates);
}


public void initialize() {

  wakeupOn(wakeCriteria);
  material.setEmissiveColor(currentColour);
}


public void processStimulus(Enumeration criteria) {

  currentColour.add(colourStep);
  stepNumber++;
  material.setEmissiveColor(currentColour);
```

LISTING 12.6   Continued

```
///////////////////////////////////////////
// If cyclic and reached the end then colour
// change needs to occur in other direction
// (negate RGB change values).
///////////////////////////////////////////
if (stepNumber==totalUpdates && cycle) {
  stepNumber = 0;
  colourStep.x = -colourStep.x;
  colourStep.y = -colourStep.y;
  colourStep.z = -colourStep.z;
}
///////////////////////////////////////////
// Set "alarm" for next update as long as it is
// appropriate
///////////////////////////////////////////
if (cycle || stepNumber!=totalUpdates)
  wakeupOn(wakeCriteria);
}
}
```

Figure 12.3 shows the screen output from the Emissive Ball application. `Behavior` cycles through different levels of emissiveness using a `Behavior` that wakes up on elapsed time.

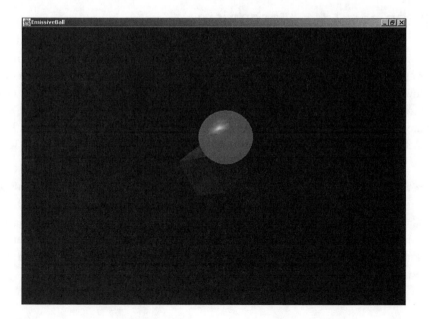

FIGURE 12.3
Screen output from Emissive Ball application.

Boolean `WakeupCriteria`

As we stated previously, a special class, `WakeupCriterion`, is used to encapsulate information about singleton wakeup conditions. The `WakeupCriterion` is an extension of the abstract class `WakeupCondition`. `WakeupCriterion` is itself extended to provide for Boolean operations on these conditions. For example, if the programmer wants the `Behavior` to wake up when both the `ViewPlatform` intersects the object `Bounds` and the key k is pressed, the user would use the `WakeupAnd` class and specify the two conditions that have to be met. The full list of these Boolean `WakeupCriteria` is given in Table 12.2 below. Note that a `WakeupCriteria` represents multiple `WakeupCriterion`.

TABLE 12.2   Boolean `WakeupConditions`

Boolean `WakeupCondition`	*Usage*
`WakeupAnd`	Like an AND gate, returns true when all inputs are simultaneously true.
`WakeupOr`	Like an OR gate, returns true when any inputs are true.
`WakeupAndOfOrs`	Triggers when a series of `WakeUpOrs` are all true.
`WakeupOrOfAnds`	Triggers when any of a series of `WakeUpAnds` are true.

Using the `postId()` Mechanism

In many of the examples used so far, we have used `Listeners` to monitor `Swing` and `AWT` events generated by the user interface. This is a perfectly fine solution when only single changes to the scene graph are required (for example, turn on/off a light or move an object, and so on). However, this approach can introduce problems when multiple and complex changes are made to the scene graph. One particular problem is that a time-consuming set of scene graph changes might not necessarily be ready in its entirety at the same frame/time. In these cases, the changes occur over several frames and can cause some undesirable transitions with part of one scene intermixing with parts of another.

When several changes are to be made to the scene, the recommended approach is to use a `Behavior` that is activated with the `postId()` method. The `postId()` method is used to cause another `Behavior` to be run and can thus be used to set up a sequential run of `Behaviors`. Using this method can at first seem a little unintuitive. Therefore, we present a rather simple example that has no 3D content. Listing 12.7 uses a `KeyListener` to call the `postId()` method of a `Behavior`.

LISTING 12.7   BehaviorPostEx.java

```java
import javax.swing.*;
import javax.swing.event.*;
import java.awt.BorderLayout;
import java.awt.event.*;
import com.sun.j3d.utils.applet.MainFrame;
import com.sun.j3d.utils.universe.*;
import javax.media.j3d.*;
import javax.vecmath.*;
import java.util.Enumeration;

public class BehaviorPostEx extends JFrame {

    PostBehavior  pb;

    public BranchGroup createSceneGraph() {

        BranchGroup objRoot = new BranchGroup();

        TransformGroup objTrans = new TransformGroup();
        objTrans.setCapability(TransformGroup.ALLOW_TRANSFORM_WRITE);
        objRoot.addChild(objTrans);

        // Create a PostBehavior to handle external scene graph changes
         pb = new PostBehavior(this);
        // set scheduling bounds
        BoundingSphere bounds = new BoundingSphere(new Point3d(0.0,0.0,0.0),
100.0);

        pb.setSchedulingBounds(bounds);

        objTrans.addChild(pb);

        return objRoot;
    }


    public void updateScene() {
       System.out.println("Update scene here");
    }


     public BehaviorPostEx() {
        super("BehaviorPostEx");
```

12

LISTING 12.7   Continued

```java
        JPanel contentPane = new JPanel();
        contentPane.setLayout(new BorderLayout());

        GraphicsConfiguration config =
            SimpleUniverse.getPreferredConfiguration();

        Canvas3D canvas = new Canvas3D(config);
        canvas.setSize(800, 800);

        KeypressHandler kh = new KeypressHandler(this);
        canvas.addKeyListener(kh);
        contentPane.add(canvas, BorderLayout.CENTER);
        setContentPane(contentPane);

        // Create a simple scene and attach it to the virtual universe
        BranchGroup scene = createSceneGraph();
        SimpleUniverse u = new SimpleUniverse(canvas);

        // This will move the ViewPlatform back a bit so the
        // objects in the scene can be viewed.
        u.getViewingPlatform().setNominalViewingTransform();

        u.addBranchGraph(scene);


        pack();
        show();
    }

public static void main(String[] args) {
        new BehaviorPostEx();
    }
}

//inner class for handling key events

class KeypressHandler implements KeyListener {

    BehaviorPostEx bpe;

    public KeypressHandler(BehaviorPostEx bpe) {
        this.bpe = bpe;
        System.out.println("constructor of KeypressHandler");
    }
    public void keyReleased(java.awt.event.KeyEvent p1) {
    }
```

LISTING 12.7   Continued

```
public void keyPressed(java.awt.event.KeyEvent p1) {
  System.out.println("keyPressed");
  bpe.pb.postId(1);

}

public void keyTyped(java.awt.event.KeyEvent p1) {
}

}
```

The PostBehavior class (as shown in Listing 12.8) is only intended to demonstrate the postId() method. The idea in this case is not to make any changes to the scene graph, but rather to show how the mechanism works by printing messages to the screen. In practice, it is only necessary to use the posted() method when the scene changes are complex.

Indeed, in most of the cases we examined in Chapter 11, "Creating and Viewing the Virtual World," the changes to the scene graph were such that they easily play out within one frame (sometimes two). In many other cases, the changes to the scene graph occur over a longer period of time, and these are the cases when postId() is needed. The postId() method allows you to specify changes to the scene graph in a Behavior and this guarantees that all changes show up in the same frame. One example that illustrates the need for this mechanism is a particle system where it is likely that a great number of objects would be changing in the scene graph. The calculations that occur over these objects is likely complex. Data coming back from these operations might arrive at different times and on different frames, thus producing the artifact. By virtue of taking part in the general Java 3D behavior loop, the postId() method guarantees that all changes will be gathered together and executed at the same time.

Note that this does not mean that the rendering loop and the behavior loop are synchronized to each other. They are indeed independent. The example in Listing 12.8 demonstrates using the postId() method.

LISTING 12.8   PostBehavior.java

```
import javax.swing.*;
import javax.swing.event.*;
import java.awt.BorderLayout;
import java.awt.Dimension;
import java.awt.event.*;
import java.awt.GraphicsConfiguration;
import com.sun.j3d.utils.applet.MainFrame;
import com.sun.j3d.utils.geometry.Sphere;
import com.sun.j3d.utils.universe.*;
import javax.media.j3d.*;
```

Listing 12.8   Continued

```java
import javax.vecmath.*;
import java.util.Enumeration;

    public class PostBehavior extends Behavior {
        BehaviorPostEx     master; // whom to notify

        // Define a number of postids.
        public static final int POST1_CHANGE = 1;
        public static final int POST2_CHANGE = 1;

        // Add a criteria for each post id
        WakeupCriterion criterion[] = {
                new WakeupOnBehaviorPost(null, POST1_CHANGE)
                };
        WakeupCondition conditions = new WakeupOr( criterion );

        public PostBehavior(BehaviorPostEx owner) {
            super();
            this.owner = owner;
        }

        public void initialize() {
            wakeupOn(conditions);
        }

        public void processStimulus( Enumeration criteria) {
            while (criteria.hasMoreElements()) {
                System.out.println("processStimulus of PostBehavior");
                WakeupOnBehaviorPost post =
                            (WakeupOnBehaviorPost)criteria.nextElement();
                switch (post.getPostId()) {
                  case POST1_CHANGE:
                    master.updateScene();
                    break;
                  default:
                    System.out.println("Unknown post id: " +
                                            post.getPostId());
                    break;
                }
            }

            wakeupOn(conditions);
        }
    }
```

Behavior Culling

Another advantage to using a `Behavior` is the potential optimizations that can be gained through the use of scheduling bounds. Remember that when Java 3D is creating optimizations during rendering, a big savings can be achieved by disregarding objects that are not within the spatial sphere of the `View Platform`. This can be a useful assumption. In many cases, however we do indeed want computations to occur in the background. For example in simulation, we do not necessarily want the world to stop just because our `View Platform` is not nearby. This situation can be rectified by having the bounds set to infinity for objects that should always be active thereby ensuring that activation is always met.

Other Uses of `Behaviors`

The main purpose of a `Behavior` is to control scene graph elements. However, we note again that `Behaviors` can be used in a variety of contexts. In our research on navigation, for example, we often need to move the `ViewPlatform` in response to a joystick or keyboard user event. At the same time, we need to have file output relating to the current location of the platform as well as precise timing and user event data. This is all accomplished in a series of custom `Behaviors`. We also use `Behaviors` to start movies inside the 3D environment, which is a topic we will cover in Chapter 14, "Integrating the Java Media APIs."

Most, if not all, user interface procedures are achieved through `Behaviors`. Now that you have the fundamentals of `Behaviors`, it is possible for you to understand more advanced topics such as picking and navigation. We begin with the important topic of picking.

Picking

Picking is a bread and butter user interface technique for 3D. There are many forms of picking which we will discuss shortly, but the general idea is that picking is the process of selecting an object or polygon with an input device.

A general algorithm for picking is depicted in Figure 12.4, and the steps are as follows:

1. Convert the mouse click or other input event into the display device coordinates (that is, screen).
2. Cast a ray from the user's eye position through the display device coordinates.
3. Convert the ray into the virtual space.
4. Test for the intersection of any eligible model parts with the ray and report these as picked.

Restricting our discussion to mouse picking only, we consider the challenge involved with selecting between two shapes.

12

INTERACTION WITH
THE VIRTUAL
WORLD

Recall our discussion from Chapter 10, "3D Graphics, Virtual Reality, and Visualization," of the virtual and physical coordinate systems and how they relate to the coexistence coordinate system. The coexistence coordinate system is also covered in Chapter 13, "The Java 3D View Model." In those discussions, you saw that the physical coordinate system reflects the real world in which the user exists. In order to interpret the user's action with the mouse, we must compute where the mouse arrow is relative to the eye of the user and "shoot an arrow" from the user's eye through the point on the screen and into our 3D scene (see Figure 12.4).

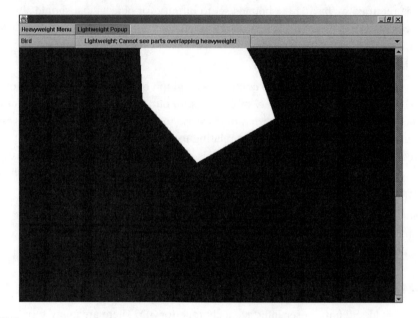

Figure 12.4
Ray casting. The user shoots an arrow from the eye through the screen and tests for intersection.

Once the arrow is shot, we have achieved steps 1, 2, and 3. These steps fall under the general heading of ray casting. That's the easy part. The challenge arises in step 4. A model of any complexity will have a large number of objects and faces that are eligible to be picked. Furthermore, the issue of spatial precision becomes critical. We do not want to pick at too high or too low of a precision, or the whole thing will fall apart. If the spatial resolution is too low, the algorithm will not be able to distinguish nearby objects from each other. Conversely, if the spatial resolution is too high, we will experience a performance hit because too many small objects will be selectable.

Java 3D achieves step 4 of the picking algorithm by offering two levels of spatial precision that are evaluated in two passes. The first, *bounds testing*, tests the intersection of the ray and the bounds of all eligible objects. Remember that bounds are similar to an invisible field surrounding an object. Because bounds are almost always larger than their objects and because there are

Interaction with the Virtual World

CHAPTER 12

627

12

INTERACTION WITH
THE VIRTUAL
WORLD

oftentimes few objects with bounds specified, bounds picking is the algorithm with the lowest level of spatial precision.

After bounds testing is completed, it is possible to refine the search based on the actual geometry of the object. This is the second level of spatial precision for picking and is termed *geometry-based*. Geometry-based picking provides far better quality in terms of accuracy but, again, the price paid is performance.

In general, bounds testing is a good place to begin. When the scene is complex and the objects aren't well separated, geometry-based picking might be necessary.

Essential Objects for Picking

In Chapter 10, we introduced the concept of a scene graph path that is unique for every leaf in the scene graph. This concept is central to the idea of a directed acyclic graph or DAG. Java 3D has a corresponding object (the SceneGraphPath object) for representing each unique path from a BranchGroup (or Locale) to an eligible Leaf node.

An eligible Leaf node refers to any Leaf object that has the ENABLE_PICK_REPORTING flag set somewhere along the parent-child hierarchy. The fact that if any part of the path is set to ENABLE_PICK_REPORTING then all children are likewise set is an important consideration when optimizing the code. In general, the programmer should not set this flag at too high of a level in the scene graph path because a potential large number of children will be ineligible for some important optimizations.

To instantiate a SceneGraphPath object, the programmer can choose from one of the following three constructors:

```
Public SceneGraphPath()
Public SceneGraphPath(Locale root, Node object)
Public SceneGraphPath(Locale root, Node nodes[], Node object)
```

In general, however, one does not construct a SceneGraphPath *de novo*, but rather returns the SceneGraphPath using an accessor method.

Making an Object Eligible for Picking

Throughout this section on picking, we have frequently referred to *eligible* objects. We now discuss more precisely what eligible means.

First and foremost, *only Leaf nodes are directly pickable*. The most common Leaf node for picking is an object of the Shape3D class. Group Nodes are not directly pickable but can be selected as a function of their Leaf node children by passing the information up the scene graph path.

Further, a Leaf node object must satisfy two conditions in order to be eligible for picking. The first is that the object must be set as pickable using the setPickable() method.

The second requirement is that pick reporting must be enabled. This requirement is independent of the requirement of having `setPickable` set.

As a general aside, picking can often be a challenge to program. It is often difficult to know which objects have been picked. As with any complex task, it is best to begin with simple examples that verify the strategy and show its feasibility before attacking the entire problem. In that spirit, we begin with a very simple example that demonstrates how to figure out which object has been chosen among many. We then proceed to more complex examples.

Picking Examples

We begin with the simple example of selecting among four boxes. The basic picking program uses two classes. Listing 12.9 shows the creation of the scene graph and the addition of the `Behavior`, and Listing 12.10, called `BasicPickBehavior`, shows the pick `Behavior`.

LISTING 12.9   BasicPicking.java

```
import java.applet.Applet;
import java.awt.BorderLayout;
import java.awt.Panel;
import java.awt.event.*;
import java.awt.GraphicsEnvironment;
import java.awt.GraphicsConfiguration;
import com.sun.j3d.utils.applet.MainFrame;
import com.sun.j3d.utils.geometry.Box;

import com.sun.j3d.utils.geometry.Primitive;
import com.sun.j3d.utils.universe.*;
import com.sun.j3d.utils.behaviors.mouse.MouseRotate;
import javax.media.j3d.*;
import javax.vecmath.*;
import javax.swing.JRadioButton;

public class BasicPicking extends Applet {
  VirtualUniverse universe;
  Locale locale;
  TransformGroup vpTrans;
  TransformGroup[] boxTGs;
  Canvas3D c;

  View view;
  Bounds bounds;

    public BranchGroup createSceneGraph() {
        // Create the root of the branch graph; this will be returned
```

LISTING 12.9   Continued

```
BranchGroup objRoot = new BranchGroup();
objRoot.setCapability(BranchGroup.ENABLE_PICK_REPORTING);


TransformGroup geoTG = new TransformGroup();
geoTG.setCapability(TransformGroup.ALLOW_TRANSFORM_WRITE);
geoTG.setCapability(TransformGroup.ALLOW_TRANSFORM_READ);
geoTG.setCapability(TransformGroup.ENABLE_PICK_REPORTING);

BoundingSphere bounds =
    new BoundingSphere(new Point3d(0.0,0.0,0.0), 100.0);

boxTGs = new TransformGroup[4];

Transform3D t3d = new Transform3D();
t3d.rotX(Math.PI/12);
geoTG.setTransform(t3d);


Material mat0 = new Material();
mat0.setDiffuseColor(new Color3f(.8f, 0.f, 0.f));
mat0.setSpecularColor(new Color3f(.9f, 0.f, 0.f));
Appearance ap0 = new Appearance();
ap0.setMaterial(mat0);

t3d.set(new Vector3f(-1.f, 0.f, -1.f));
boxTGs[0] = new TransformGroup();
boxTGs[0].setCapability(TransformGroup.ALLOW_TRANSFORM_WRITE);
boxTGs[0].setCapability(TransformGroup.ALLOW_TRANSFORM_READ);
boxTGs[0].setCapability(TransformGroup.ENABLE_PICK_REPORTING);
boxTGs[0].setTransform(t3d);
Box redbox = new  Box(.3f,.3f,.3f,
                        Box.ENABLE_GEOMETRY_PICKING |
Box.GENERATE_NORMALS,ap0);

redbox.setAppearance(ap0);
//Box redbox = new  Box(0.3f,0.3f,0.3f,ap0);
boxTGs[0].addChild(redbox);
geoTG.addChild(boxTGs[0]);

PickName pn = new PickName("red box");
Shape3D shape = redbox.getShape(1);
shape.setUserData(pn);


. . .
```

LISTING 12.10   BasicPickBehavior.java

```java
import javax.media.j3d.*;
import com.sun.j3d.utils.picking.PickTool;
import com.sun.j3d.utils.picking.PickResult;
import com.sun.j3d.utils.picking.behaviors.PickMouseBehavior;
import java.util.*;
import java.awt.*;
import java.awt.Event;
import java.awt.AWTEvent;
import java.awt.event.MouseEvent;
import javax.vecmath.*;
import java.awt.event.MouseListener;

public class BasicPickBehavior extends PickMouseBehavior {
    boolean ispicked = false;

        PickResult[] pickResult;

  public BasicPickBehavior(Canvas3D canvas, BranchGroup root,
                    Bounds bounds) {
      super(canvas, root, bounds);

      this.setSchedulingBounds(bounds);
      root.addChild(this);
      pickCanvas.setMode(PickTool.GEOMETRY);
     // pickCanvas.setTolerance(0.01f);
      System.out.println(pickCanvas.getTolerance());
  }

    public void updateScene(int x, int y) {
    Shape3D shape = null;

    pickCanvas.setShapeLocation(x, y);
        System.out.println("x: " + x + " y" +  y);
        //PickResult pickResult = null;
    //pickResult = pickCanvas.pickClosest();
        pickResult = pickCanvas.pickAllSorted();
        System.out.println("updateScene");

    if (pickResult != null) {

            System.out.println("length of pickResult " + pickResult.length);

            for (int i=0; i<pickResult.length; i++) {

                shape = (Shape3D) pickResult[i].getNode(PickResult.SHAPE3D);
                System.out.println(shape);
```

LISTING 12.10 Continued

```
                try {
                  PickName pn =  (PickName) shape.getUserData();
                  if (pn != null) {
                    System.out.println("pn.get(): " +
pn.get().toCharArray());
                  }
                }
                catch (CapabilityNotSetException e) {
                  System.out.println("CapabilityNotSetException");
                }
            }
        }


    }

}
```

Figure 12.5 shows the Canvas3D and output window while running the BasicPicking example.
Note that we have used Geometry picking (as opposed to Bounds picking). By clicking on a
box, the scene graph path and objects in the path are displayed in the output window.

FIGURE 12.5

Screen output showing Canvas3D and output window.

Navigation

Navigation is an area of psychological study influenced heavily by the pioneering work of the psychologist Edward Tollman and his students at Berkley in the '40s. Tollman showed that rats used mental maps of the environment to perform rather amazing navigational feats such as shortcut taking and escape route planning. A key argument was based on the fact that rats showed so-called *incidental learning*. It was shown that rats took in information about many aspects of the environment that were not necessary to the performance of the task they were trained on.

A paucity of data addresses how humans navigate in virtual environments, but it is clear that navigation behaviors can make a big difference in the feeling of presence. There is a general consensus among VR researchers that most users end up lost in space. If the goal is to get the user immersed in the environment, it is worth the effort to either find or develop the best navigational behavior possible. A marginally realistic navigational behavior will likely include free ranging ability, a walking semantic (for example, a slight bounce as would be experienced in real walking), gravity, and collision avoidance.

The degree of attention that the developer needs to give the issue of navigation is strongly dependent on the application. Many applications only need to have a 3D representation of the product or visualization and don't require navigation. Other applications are all about navigation. Examples include a 3D shopping mall, 3D chat rooms, and first person shooter games. What makes or breaks a virtual experience in a navigational application is the quality of the spatial experience.

Free Ranging Navigation

Except when restricted by walls and other barriers, humans and other animals have a degree of free range in their natural settings. Although animals do indeed tend to travel in paths, they also tend to stop and look around. Interestingly, rats have a visual field of nearly 300° and therefore take in data about the environment all around them. Humans and other primates appear to be more dependent on the view directly in front of them.

Humans often move their heads 60-100° in plane while walking forward and then make larger movements during stops. There is also a slight out of plane movement due to steps. Turning around 360° is always a possibility but is not usually part of goal directed movements.

It is often the case that the environment also tends to guide the user during navigation. A good navigational utility would force the user back toward the middle of a hallway should the user get too close to an impermeable wall, for example.

Collision Detection and Avoidance

One of the most basic behaviors in 3D graphics is *collision detection*, defined here as the ability to detect the presence of one object relative to another. Collision detection is most often used to prevent the user from crashing through walls or tables and in this case is more precisely termed *collision avoidance*. We will generally refer to both detection and avoidance as *collision processing* unless the distinction is important to the discussion at hand.

In the design of virtual environments for free ranging navigation, collision avoidance is almost a requirement. Crashing through walls causes a great deal of spatial disorientation and tends to make users want to quit.

In Java 3D, collision processing (similar to pretty much all user behavior processing) is implemented through the `Behavior` mechanism described previously. The programmer must therefore go back to the idea of what to do and when to do it. For simple collision detection, there already exist some very basic but useful classes. The `wakeupOnCollisionEntry` and `wakeupOnCollisionExit` classes do an adequate job of detecting the collision of two objects. Likewise, the `wakeupOnViewPlatformEntry` and the `wakeupOnViewPlatformExit` classes can be used to detect when the `ViewPlatform` is in contact with a single object. We demonstrate the use of these classes with a simple example (see Listing 12.11).

Collision Detection Example

To reiterate, simple collision detection is pretty straightforward. To demonstrate, we give the following example. The `TransformGroup` of the `ViewPlatform` is allowed to go forward and backward depending on whether the user pushes the up arrow key (VK_UP) or the down arrow key (VK_DOWN). Each movement is proposed, a pick cone is created, and a test is made to see whether the movement will collide.

Listing 12.11 is the simplest possible example and is elaborated on in the Collision Avoidance example (Listing 12.13 and 12.14) in the next section, "Collision Avoidance Example."

LISTING 12.11   CollisionDetection.java

```
. . .

public class CollisionDetection extends Applet {

  VirtualUniverse universe;
  Locale locale;
  TransformGroup vpTrans;
  TransformGroup[] boxTGs;
  View view;
  Bounds bounds;
```

LISTING 12.11 Continued

```java
    Random r;


    public BranchGroup createSceneGraph() {
        // Create the root of the branch graph; this will be returned

        BranchGroup objRoot = new BranchGroup();
. . .

            //generate random boxes here//
        for (int ii=0; ii<20; ii++) {
          System.out.println("making and adding a box");
          geoTG.addChild(makeBox(ii));
        }

        TransformGroup geoTG = new TransformGroup();
        geoTG.setCapability(TransformGroup.ALLOW_TRANSFORM_WRITE);
        objRoot.compile();
        return objRoot;
    }

    public TransformGroup makeBox(int boxnum) {

        Transform3D t3d = new Transform3D();

        Material mat = new Material();
        mat.setDiffuseColor(new Color3f(r.nextFloat(),r.nextFloat(),
➡ r.nextFloat())));
        Appearance app = new Appearance();
        app.setMaterial(mat);

        t3d.set(new Vector3f(0.f,0.f, boxnum*6));
        TransformGroup boxTG = new TransformGroup();
        boxTG.setCapability(TransformGroup.ALLOW_TRANSFORM_WRITE);
        boxTG.setCapability(TransformGroup.ALLOW_TRANSFORM_READ);
        boxTG.setTransform(t3d);
        Box box = new Box(2*r.nextFloat(),2*r.nextFloat(),2*r.nextFloat(),
                          Box.ENABLE_GEOMETRY_PICKING | Box.GENERATE_NORMALS,
                          app);
        box.setAlternateCollisionTarget(true);
        boxTG.addChild(box);
        return boxTG;

    }

    public CollisionDetection() {
. . .
}
```

LISTING 12.12   CollisionBehavior.java

```java
import java.awt.AWTEvent;
import java.awt.event.*;
import java.util.Enumeration;
import javax.media.j3d.*;
import javax.vecmath.*;

import com.sun.j3d.utils.universe.*;
import javax.swing.JRadioButton;

import com.sun.j3d.utils.picking.PickTool;
import com.sun.j3d.utils.picking.PickResult;
// import com.sun.j3d.demos.utils.scenegraph.traverser.TreeScan;
//import com.sun.j3d.demos.utils.scenegraph.traverser.NodeChangeProcessor;

public class CollisionBehavior extends Behavior {

  private TransformGroup tg;
  private Transform3D transform3D;
  private WakeupCondition keyCriterion;

  private final static double TWO_PI = (2.0 * Math.PI);

  private double moveRate = 0.3;
  int keycode;

  Locale locale;
  PickTool pickTool;
  double rotateXAmount = Math.PI / 16.0;
  double rotateYAmount = Math.PI / 16.0;
  double rotateZAmount = Math.PI / 16.0;

  double speed;

  public CollisionBehavior(TransformGroup tg, Locale locale ) {

    this.tg = tg;
    this.locale = locale;
    transform3D = new Transform3D();

    pickTool = new PickTool( locale );
    pickTool.setMode( PickTool.GEOMETRY_INTERSECT_INFO );

  }
  public void setSpeed(double speed) {
      this.speed = speed;
  }

  public void initialize()
  {
```

12

INTERACTION WITH
THE VIRTUAL
WORLD

LISTING 12.12 Continued

```java
    WakeupCriterion[] keyEvents = new WakeupCriterion[2];

    keyEvents[0] = new WakeupOnAWTEvent( KeyEvent.KEY_PRESSED);
    keyEvents[1] = new WakeupOnAWTEvent( KeyEvent.KEY_RELEASED );
    keyCriterion = new WakeupOr( keyEvents );
    wakeupOn( keyCriterion );
}

    public void processStimulus( Enumeration criteria )
{
    WakeupCriterion wakeup;
    AWTEvent[] event;

    while( criteria.hasMoreElements() )
    {
      wakeup = (WakeupCriterion) criteria.nextElement();
      if( !(wakeup instanceof WakeupOnAWTEvent) )
        continue;

      event = ((WakeupOnAWTEvent)wakeup).getAWTEvent();
      for( int i = 0; i < event.length; i++ )
      {
        if( event[i].getID() == KeyEvent.KEY_PRESSED )
        {
          processKeyEvent((KeyEvent)event[i]);
        }
      }
    }
    wakeupOn( keyCriterion );
}

protected void processKeyEvent(KeyEvent event)
{
  keycode = event.getKeyCode();
  if(keycode == KeyEvent.VK_UP)
    prepareMove(new Vector3d(0.f, 0.f, -1.f));
  else if(keycode == KeyEvent.VK_DOWN)
    prepareMove(new Vector3d(0.f, 0.f, 1.f));
  else if(keycode == KeyEvent.VK_LEFT)
    System.out.println("rot left");
  else if(keycode == KeyEvent.VK_RIGHT)
    System.out.println("rot right");

  executeMove();
}

protected void checkDistance(Vector3d preMove, Vector3d postMove) {
    System.out.println("checking distances to collidable objects");
    int lookahead = -5;
```

LISTING 12.12   Continued

```
      pickTool.setShapeSegment(new Point3d(preMove.x,
                                            preMove.y,
                                            preMove.z),
                               new Point3d(preMove.x,
                                            preMove.y,
                                            preMove.z + lookahead));

      System.out.println("preMove.x: " + preMove.x +
                         "preMove.y: " + preMove.y +
                         "preMove.z: " + preMove.z +
                         "postMove.x: " + postMove.x +
                         "postMove.y: " + postMove.y +
                         "postMove.z: " + preMove.z);

      PickResult pickRes = pickTool.pickClosest();
      if (pickRes!=null) {

        System.out.println(pickRes.toString());
      }
  }
```

Figure 12.6 shows the screen output from `CollisionDetection.java`. A small pick shape, in this case a Pick Segment, is used to test each successive move for a collision. Regardless of the collision, the platform advances. The program is the simplest form of detection algorithm and is used only to reinforce the concepts.

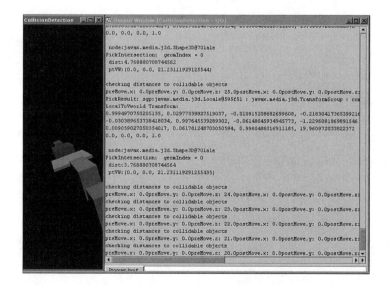

FIGURE 12.6

Screen output from `CollisionDetection.java`.

Collision Avoidance Example

Collision avoidance is tougher to implement because it requires a type of look ahead function that makes intelligent guesses about where the ViewPlatform will be sometime in the future. The need for the look ahead function is that by the time a collision is detected, it is probably too late to do anything about it. Looking ahead is a common problem in tracking.

Returning to the issue of navigation, we note that if the user is moving faster or slower, the computations of the future location (in a frame or two) are greatly affected. Therefore, it is necessary to have an idea of the user's speed and acceleration in order to do a reasonable job of predicting.

Deciding whether the user will collide with an object in the next frame or two can be solved a number of ways, however: The most straightforward mechanism is an extension of the ray casting picking algorithm described in the previous section. Recall that in mouse-based picking, we shoot a ray from our best guess of the user's eye position through the point of the screen where the user clicked and into the virtual world. Any pickable objects that intersected this ray are put in a cue for future processing.

In the standard Java 3D collision avoidance scheme, a ray (often multiple rays in different directions) is cast from the object of interest (most often the camera position of the ViewPlatform) through the scene. Just as in picking, an array of objects (this time, *collidable* objects) is returned for future processing. This is the step in which you can estimate the objects that the user is likely to contact in the next frame.

We now present our virtualMSU navigation (see Listing 12.13) that closely approaches a full fledged navigation behavior.

LISTING 12.13   virtualMSU.java

```java
import java.awt.event.*;
import java.awt.AWTEvent;
import java.util.Enumeration;
import javax.media.j3d.*;
import javax.vecmath.*;
import com.sun.j3d.utils.picking.PickIntersection;
import com.sun.j3d.utils.picking.PickResult;
import com.sun.j3d.utils.picking.PickTool;
import com.sun.j3d.utils.universe.*;
import Joystick;

public class VMSUBehavior extends Behavior {

    // the CollisionBehavior Class's member variables
    private Canvas3D canvas;
    private TransformGroup Target;
```

Interaction with the Virtual World

CHAPTER 12

639

12

INTERACTION WITH
THE VIRTUAL
WORLD

LISTING 12.13 Continued

```java
    private TransformGroup BackTrans;
    private Transform3D Translation = new Transform3D();
    private Transform3D XRotation = new Transform3D();
    private Transform3D YRotation = new Transform3D();
    private PickTool pickTool;
    private Vector3d UserThrust = new Vector3d(0.0,0.0,0.0);
    private Vector3d Direction = new Vector3d(0.0,0.0,-1.0);
    private Vector3d Velocity = new Vector3d(0.0,0.0,0.0);
    private Point3d CurrentLocation = new Point3d(0.0,5.0,0.0);
    private WakeupCondition WakeCriterion;

    private boolean ForwardKey = false, BackKey = false, RightKey = false,
                    LeftKey = false, UpKey = false, DownKey = false,
➥ JumpKey=false;

    private double XAngle = 0.0;
    private double YAngle = 0.0;
    private int old_mouse_x=-1, old_mouse_y=-1, mouse_x=-1, mouse_y=-1;

    private Vector3d Gravity = new Vector3d(0.0,-0.06,0.0);
    private double CollisionRadius = 0.8;
    private double Friction = 0.0;
    private double speed = 0.08;
    private int InputDevice = 0;                    // 0 - mouse + keyboard
                                                    // 1 - Joystick
    private Joystick joy = new Joystick(0);
    private double InputSensitivity = 0.01;

    //
    // Constructor with the simple universe to use
    //
    public VMSUBehavior(SimpleUniverse u) {
        this.Target=u.getViewingPlatform().getViewPlatformTransform();
        this.canvas = u.getCanvas();
        pickTool = new PickTool(u.getLocale());
    }

    //
    // this method gets called automatically.  I use it to set the
    // conditions for what triggers the behavior
    //
    public void initialize() {
        pickTool.setMode(PickTool.GEOMETRY_INTERSECT_INFO);
        WakeupCriterion[] MouseWakeEvents = new WakeupCriterion[5];
```

LISTING 12.13   Continued

```
            MouseWakeEvents[0] = new WakeupOnAWTEvent( MouseEvent.MOUSE_MOVED);
            MouseWakeEvents[1] = new WakeupOnAWTEvent( MouseEvent.MOUSE_DRAGGED );
            MouseWakeEvents[2] = new WakeupOnAWTEvent( KeyEvent.KEY_PRESSED );
            MouseWakeEvents[3] = new WakeupOnAWTEvent( KeyEvent.KEY_RELEASED );
            MouseWakeEvents[4] = new WakeupOnElapsedFrames(0);

            WakeCriterion = new WakeupOr( MouseWakeEvents );
            wakeupOn( WakeCriterion );
    }


    //
    // called whenever the wakeup conditions are met,
    // does Physics() every frame and MouseControl whenever the mouse
    // is moved
    //
    public void processStimulus(java.util.Enumeration enumeration) {
        // stop the renderer so it doesn't show stuff while we are in
 ➥ the middle of calculating
        canvas.stopRenderer();

        WakeupCriterion wakeup;
        // determine what event awoke it
        while (enumeration.hasMoreElements() ){
            wakeup = (WakeupCriterion) enumeration.nextElement();
            if ( wakeup instanceof WakeupOnElapsedFrames)
                Physics();
            if ( InputDevice == 0 ){
                if ( wakeup instanceof WakeupOnAWTEvent ) {
                    // determine if it is a mouse event
                    AWTEvent[] events = ((WakeupOnAWTEvent)wakeup)
 ➥.getAWTEvent();
                    for (int i = 0; i<events.length; i++) {
                        if (events[i] instanceof MouseEvent){
                            MouseControl( (MouseEvent)events[i] );
                        } else if (events[i] instanceof KeyEvent){
                            KeyControl( (KeyEvent)events[i] );
                        }
                    }
                }
            } else {
                JoystickControl();
            }
        }
        wakeupOn( WakeCriterion );
```

LISTING 12.13   Continued

```java
            // ok we're done
            canvas.startRenderer();
    }

    //
    // allows you to change the internal variables
    //
    public void setCurrentLocation(double x, double y, double z) {
        CurrentLocation.set(x,y,z);
    }
    public void setGravity(double x, double y, double z) {
        Gravity.set(x,y,z);
    }
    public void setFriction(double friction) {
        Friction = friction;
    }
    public void setCollisionRadius(double radius) {
        CollisionRadius = radius;
    }
    public void setSpeed(double NewSpeed) {
        speed = NewSpeed;
    }

    //
    // lets the you attach a background object to the Behavior
    //
    public void addBack( TransformGroup trans){
        BackTrans = trans;
    }

    //
    // KeyEvent code below
    //
    public void keyPressed(java.awt.event.KeyEvent keyEvent) {
        if (InputDevice==0) {
            switch (keyEvent.getKeyCode()){
                // Forward
                case KeyEvent.VK_W:
                    ForwardKey = true;
                    break;
                // Backward
                case KeyEvent.VK_S:
                    BackKey = true;
                    break;
                // Right
```

12

LISTING 12.13   Continued

```
                case KeyEvent.VK_D:
                    RightKey = true;
                    break;
                // Left
                case KeyEvent.VK_A:
                    LeftKey = true;
                    break;
                // go up
                case KeyEvent.VK_SPACE:
                    JumpKey = true;
                    break;
                // garbage collect
                case KeyEvent.VK_ESCAPE:
                    System.gc();
            }
        }
    }
    public void keyReleased(java.awt.event.KeyEvent keyEvent) {
        if (InputDevice==0) {
            switch (keyEvent.getKeyCode()){
                // Forward
                case KeyEvent.VK_W:
                    ForwardKey = false;
                    break;
                // Backward
                case KeyEvent.VK_S:
                    BackKey = false;
                    break;
                // Right
                case KeyEvent.VK_D:
                    RightKey = false;
                    break;
                // Left
                case KeyEvent.VK_A:
                    LeftKey = false;
                    break;
                // go up
                case KeyEvent.VK_SPACE:
                    JumpKey = false;
                    break;
            }
        }
    }

    //
    // Turns the transform when the mouse is moved
    //
```

Listing 12.13   Continued

```
private void MouseControl( MouseEvent mevt){
    int dx, dy;
    mouse_x = mevt.getX();
    mouse_y = mevt.getY();
    dx = (mouse_x - old_mouse_x);
    dy = (mouse_y - old_mouse_y);
    old_mouse_x = mouse_x;
    old_mouse_y = mouse_y;
    if (old_mouse_x!=-1){
        YAngle += dx * -1 * InputSensitivity;
        XAngle += dy * -1 * InputSensitivity;
        if (XAngle > Math.PI/2.0)
            XAngle = Math.PI/2.0;
        if (XAngle < 0.0-Math.PI/2.0)
            XAngle = 0.0 - Math.PI/2.0;
    }
}

//
// Joystick Control
//
private void JoystickControl(){
    XAngle += joy.getYPos()*InputSensitivity;
    YAngle -= joy.getXPos()*InputSensitivity;
    if (XAngle > Math.PI/2.0)
        XAngle = Math.PI/2.0;
    if (XAngle < 0.0-Math.PI/2.0)
        XAngle = 0.0 - Math.PI/2.0;
}

//
// Sets the acceleration in response to key presses
//
private void KeyControl( KeyEvent kevt){
    switch (kevt.getID()){
        case KeyEvent.KEY_PRESSED:
            keyPressed(kevt);
            break;
        case KeyEvent.KEY_RELEASED:
            keyReleased(kevt);
            break;
    }

}

//
// handles collisions -  I'm sure this could be written
```

LISTING 12.13 Continued

```java
// more efficiently but I finally got it working and I'm
// afraid of changing it
//
private void Collisions() {
    // might not have to do anything
     if (Velocity.lengthSquared() < 0.0001)
        return;

    // Prepare to pick
    pickTool.setShapeRay( CurrentLocation, Velocity);
    // a few variables to be used in this function
    Vector3d Normal = new Vector3d();
    Point3d pickHit = new Point3d();
    Vector3d a = new Vector3d();
    double d1=0.0;

    // do the pick
    PickResult pr = pickTool.pickClosest();
    if (pr!=null){
        PickIntersection pi = pr.getClosestIntersection( CurrentLocation );
            if ((pi!=null)&&(pi.getPointNormal()!=null)){
                Normal.set(pi.getPointNormal());
                Normal.normalize();
                pickHit = pi.getPointCoordinatesVW();
                // a is the vector from the collision point to
// the future location
                a.set(CurrentLocation);
                a.add(Velocity);
                a.sub(pickHit);
                // use a dot product to see how far he is from the
// collision plane
                d1 = a.dot(Normal);
                if (d1 < CollisionRadius){
                    //CurrentLocation.scaleAdd((CollisionRadius-d1), Normal,
// CurrentLocation);
                    Velocity.scaleAdd( (CollisionRadius-d1), Normal, Velocity);
                    Velocity.scaleAdd( -1.0*(Velocity.dot(Normal)), Normal,
// Velocity);
                }
            }
    }
    // re-pick, this time checking the downward direction
    pickTool.setShapeRay( CurrentLocation, Gravity);
    pr = pickTool.pickClosest();
    if (pr!=null){
        PickIntersection pi = pr.getClosestIntersection( CurrentLocation );
```

LISTING 12.13 Continued

```
            if ((pi!=null)&&(pi.getPointNormal()!=null)){
                Normal.set(pi.getPointNormal());
                Normal.normalize();
                pickHit = pi.getPointCoordinatesVW();
                // a is the vector from the collision point to the
➥ future location
                a.set(CurrentLocation);
                a.add(Velocity);
                a.sub(pickHit);
                // use a dot product to see how far he is from
➥ the collision plane
                d1 = a.dot(Normal);
                if (d1 < CollisionRadius){
                    //CurrentLocation.scaleAdd((CollisionRadius-d1), Normal,
➥ CurrentLocation);
                    Velocity.scaleAdd( (CollisionRadius-d1), Normal, Velocity);
                    //Velocity.scaleAdd( -1.0*(Velocity.dot(Normal)),
➥ Normal, Velocity);
                }
            }
        }
    }


    //
    // Calls the functions associated with the physics simulation
    //
    private void Physics() {
        //
        UserAcceleration();
        Collisions();
        Movement();

        UpdateTransform();
    }


    //
    // Updates the position of the transform
    //
    private void Movement() {
        // I don't really like this, but it is necessary to
        // prevent there from being too much sliding
        if (Velocity.lengthSquared() < 0.0001)
            Velocity.set(0.0,0.0,0.0);
        else
            CurrentLocation.add(Velocity);
    }
```

LISTING 12.13 Continued

```
    //
    // Lets the user accelerate
    //
    private void UserAcceleration() {
        CalcUserThrust();
        Velocity.set(UserThrust);
        Velocity.add(Gravity);
    }

    //
    // Forces the player to head down
    //
    private void GravityAcceleration() {
        Velocity.set(Gravity);
    }

    //
    // applies the changes to the transform
    //
    private void UpdateTransform() {
        YRotation.rotY(YAngle);
        XRotation.rotX(XAngle);
        YRotation.mul(XRotation);
        YRotation.setTranslation( new Vector3d(CurrentLocation) );
        Target.setTransform(YRotation);

        if (BackTrans!=null){
            Translation.setTranslation( new Vector3d(CurrentLocation) );
            BackTrans.setTransform(Translation);
        }
    }

    //
    // find new thrust vector based on user input
    //
    private void CalcUserThrust() {
        UserThrust.set(0.0,0.0,0.0);
        // handle the acceleration vector control
        if (InputDevice==0) {
            if (ForwardKey){
                Direction.set(-1.0*(float)Math.cos(Math.PI/2.0-YAngle),
➥0.0, -1.0*(float)Math.sin(Math.PI/2.0-YAngle));
                UserThrust.add(Direction);
            } if (BackKey) {
                Direction.set((float)Math.cos(Math.PI/2.0-YAngle), 0.0,
➥ (float)Math.sin(Math.PI/2.0-YAngle));
```

LISTING 12.13   Continued

```
                    UserThrust.add(Direction);
            } if (RightKey) {
                Direction.set(-1.0*(float)Math.cos(Math.PI-YAngle), 0.0,
➡ -1.0*(float)Math.sin(Math.PI-YAngle) );
                UserThrust.add(Direction);
            } if (LeftKey) {
                Direction.set((float)Math.cos(Math.PI-YAngle), 0.0,
➡ (float)Math.sin(Math.PI-YAngle) );
                UserThrust.add(Direction);
            } if (UpKey) {
                Direction.set(0.0, 1.0, 0.0);
                UserThrust.add(Direction);
            } if (DownKey) {
                Direction.set(0.0, -1.0, 0.0);
                UserThrust.add(Direction);
            } if (JumpKey) {
                Direction.set(0.0, 1.0, 0.0);
                UserThrust.add(Direction);
            }
            // set it to the correct magnitude
            if (UserThrust.length()>0.0) {
                UserThrust.normalize();
                UserThrust.scale(speed);
            }
        } else if (InputDevice==1) {
            if (joy.getButtons()==1){
                Direction.set(-1.0*(float)Math.cos(Math.PI/2.0-YAngle),
                            0.0, -1.0*(float)Math.sin(Math.PI/2.0-YAngle));
                UserThrust.add(Direction);
            }
            // set it to the correct magnitude
            if (UserThrust.length()>0.0) {
                UserThrust.normalize();
                UserThrust.scale(speed);
            }
        }
    }

    //
    // changes the control system
    //
    public void useJoystick(double sensitivity){
        InputDevice = 1;
        InputSensitivity = sensitivity;
    }
```

LISTING 12.13 Continued

```
//
// changes the control system
//
private void useMouseAndKeyboard(){
    InputDevice = 0;
}
}
```

Figure 12.7 shows screen output from the VirtualMSU.java. The user is able to navigate and look around a virtual reality model of various parts of the VirtualMSU Campus using the virtualMSUBehavior navigator.

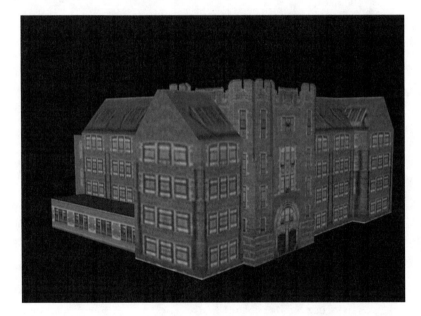

FIGURE 12.7
Screen output from the VirtualMSU.java.

Level of Detail

As mentioned in Chapter 10, *level of detail (LOD)* is an important optimization technique because it reduces the number of vertices that need to be rendered. It is often stated that the most efficient vertex to render is one that isn't rendered at all.

Remember from that discussion that a texture map pasted on a box will represent the Statue of Liberty just fine when shown from Battery Park but as you get closer, the flat nature of the 2D texture becomes more obvious. What we would really like is multiple levels of detail that switch into the scene systematically as we approach and move away from the model.

LODs fall naturally under the Behavior class abstraction. When looking at the Java 3D documentation for the LOD class, you will note that LOD itself is abstract and that the only subclass is DistanceLOD. There are three constructors for DistanceLOD.

```
DistanceLOD()
DistanceLOD(float[] distances)
DistanceLOD(float[] distances, Point3f() position)
```

Note that the first constructor used the default value of 1 and is therefore not necessarily useful unless the values are subsequently set. In the second constructor, an array of floats is used to specify the discrete distances over which the LOD will operate. Note that in the second constructor, the origin of the object is not specified and is assumed to be (0.f, 0.f, 0.f) by default. This can cause some confusion when using this class because the programmer most often wants the origin of the LOD to be the same location as the object and not at the center of the universe typically. The third constructor allows the position of the LOD object (or some other position) to be specified explicitly.

One critical aspect to using the DistanceLOD class is to understand the SwitchNode class presented in Chapter 11. The relationship between the distance and SwitchNode value is determined by breaking up the distance into *n* discrete bins and then assigning the Switch values to each bin.

Using Swing with Java 3D

The Java Swing API is a nearly exhaustive collection of user interface widgets that can be used to build a user interface around a Java 3D application. There are some real challenges to mixing Swing and Java 3D components. This is largely because Swing components are *lightweight* whereas the Java 3D Canvas3D component is *heavyweight*.

Lightweight Versus Heavyweight

The difference between lightweight and heavyweight components is a bit obscure. Simply stated, heavyweight components reference their own native screen resource called a *peer*. A lightweight component has no *native* peer and therefore temporarily uses the resources of a nearby native peer.

In general, lightweight UI components have many advantages including having a smaller resource footprint and also the ability to maintain a consistent look and feel across platforms. The downside is that some components do not have lightweight versions; therefore, it becomes necessary to mix lightweight and heavyweight. This is the exact situation that happens when we want to use the heavyweight Canvas3D object (which, as you know, is necessary to view our 3D scene) in conjunction with Swing components. There is no lightweight version of the Canvas3D object.

We should note that several of the Swing components are indeed heavyweight by design. In particular, the top-level components JWindow, JFrame, JApplet, and JDialog are all heavyweight. These components can be mixed with a Canvas3D object without concern. All AWT components are heavyweight as well.

Mixing Problems

Three main problems occur when mixing heavyweight and lightweight components:

- Mouse events for lightweight components filter up to the heavyweight parent, whereas mouse events for heavyweight components do not.
- Heavyweight components always appear on top of lightweight components regardless of the z order in which they are rendered.
- Lightweight components can have transparent pixels, whereas heavyweight components do not.

This section focuses on the second and third problems, which are of the most concern in Java 3D. The first problem does not interfere with the working of Java 3D in general, and thus won't be discussed further.

Returning to the second and third problems, we can see issues with the display of the Canvas3D. A partial solution to these display problems can be solved by avoiding certain situations or, alternatively, setting a flag to override lightweight functioning of the component.

First and foremost, avoid mixing lightweight and heavyweight components. This can be accomplished by keeping the heavyweight components in an area of the screen where lightweight components are not expected to overlap.

Also in terms of mixing components, certain lightweight components should never have a heavyweight component added to them. The two most common examples of this are adding a Canvas3D to a JInternalFrame or JScrollPane.

The same problems can occur when using pop-up components such as JComboBox or JPopupMenu. In this case, Java determines what the ideal weight of these objects should be in the context of the application. This decision is dependent on whether a property called LightWeightPopupEnabled is set to true or false. For example, if a JPopupMenu is activated, it can be heavyweight if the component does not fit entirely in its container, mediumweight if the pop-up fits within the top-level component but the lightweightPopupEnabled property is set to false, or truly lightweight if the pop-up fits within the top-level component but lightweightPopupEnabled is set to true (the default).

Therefore, you can set the LightWeightPopupEnabled property to false to ensure that the component is heavyweight. There are two methods for setting this property—one global (applies to all pop-ups) and the other more restricted (on a pop-up by pop-up basis).

The global method is

```
public static void setDefaultLightweightPopupEnabled(boolean)
```

To change the property for an individual pop-up component, use the following:

```
public void setLightweightPopupEnabled(Boolean)
```

The `BadMix.java` example in Listing 12.14 illustrates the preceding two approaches to mixing heavy- and lightweight components.

LISTING 12.14   BadMix.java

```
. . .
public class BadMix extends JFrame {
  VirtualUniverse universe;
  Locale locale;
  TransformGroup vpTrans;
  View view;
  Bounds bounds;

    public BranchGroup createSceneGraph() {
        // Create the root of the branch graph; this will be returned
        Appearance app = new Appearance();
        BranchGroup objRoot = new BranchGroup();

        TransformGroup geoTG = new TransformGroup();
        geoTG.setCapability(TransformGroup.ALLOW_TRANSFORM_WRITE);
      geoTG.setCapability(TransformGroup.ALLOW_TRANSFORM_READ);

        BoundingSphere bounds =
            new BoundingSphere(new Point3d(0.0,0.0,0.0), 100.0);

        MouseRotate mouseBeh = new MouseRotate(geoTG);
      geoTG.addChild(mouseBeh);
      mouseBeh.setSchedulingBounds(bounds);


        geoTG.addChild(new Box(.5f,.5f,.5f,app));
        objRoot.addChild(geoTG);

        //objRoot.addChild(pc.getShape());
        // objRoot.addChild(tc.getShape());


        Color3f blue = new Color3f(0.f, 0.9f, 0.f);
        Vector3f bluedir  = new Vector3f(0.0f, -8.0f, -8.0f);
```

LISTING 12.14   Continued

```java
//  AmbientLight al = new AmbientLight(true, new Color3f(.1f,.9f, .1f));
    AmbientLight al = new AmbientLight();

    DirectionalLight bluelight = new DirectionalLight(blue, bluedir);

    al.setInfluencingBounds(bounds);
    bluelight.setInfluencingBounds(bounds);

    objRoot.addChild(al);

  objRoot.addChild(bluelight);

    objRoot.compile();
return objRoot;
 }

. . .

public BadMix(int xsize, int ysize) {

. . .

    c.setSize(90,900);
    JScrollPane jscroll = new JScrollPane(c);
    jscroll.setPreferredSize(new Dimension(2, 1));


JScrollBar scrollv = new JScrollBar(JScrollBar.VERTICAL);
scrollv.setBounds(129,4,13,97);
scrollv.setForeground(new Color(-987431));

    JScrollBar scrollh = new JScrollBar(JScrollBar.HORIZONTAL);
scrollh.setBounds(129,4,13,97);
scrollh.setForeground(new Color(-987431));

  JMenuBar menubar= new JMenuBar();
  setJMenuBar(menubar);

  JMenu menu1 = new JMenu("Heavyweight Menu");
  menubar.add(menu1);
  JMenu menu2 = new JMenu("Lightweight Popup");
  menubar.add(menu2);


    String[] jazzPlayers = { "Bird", "Monk", "Coltrane", "Dizzy", "Miles" };
    JComboBox jcombo = new JComboBox(jazzPlayers);
```

LISTING 12.14   Continued

```
        this.getContentPane().add(jcombo, BorderLayout.NORTH);

        jcombo.setLightWeightPopupEnabled(false);


        menu1.add(new JMenuItem("Heavyweight; Should see this! "));
         menu1.add(new JMenuItem("Heavyweight; Should see this!! "));
         menu1.add(new JMenuItem("Heavyweight; Should see this!! "));


        JPopupMenu popup = menu1.getPopupMenu();
        popup.setLightWeightPopupEnabled(false);

        menu2.add(new JMenuItem("Lightweight;
➥ Cannot see parts overlapping heavyweight! "));
        menu2.add(new JMenuItem("Lightweight;
➥ Cannot see parts overlapping heavyweight!! "));
        menu2.add(new JMenuItem("Lightweight;
➥ Cannot see parts overlapping heavyweight!!! "));

        int num_menus = menubar.getMenuCount();
        System.out.println(num_menus);

. . .

        jscroll.add(scrollv);
        jscroll.add(scrollh);
        locale.addBranchGraph(vgraph);
    locale.addBranchGraph(scene);
    }

    //
    // The following allows HelloUniverse to be run as an application
    // as well as an applet
    //
}
```

The `BillboardBehavior`

It is often the case that the programmer wants some scene graph elements to always face a particular way. This situation arises in 3D text labeling of axis and other objects where it would look strange to see the side of the text object.

Java 3D provides an extension to the `Behavior` class called `Billboard` that forces the +z direction of an object to always face the viewer. The `Billboard` class can be quite useful in this regard as we demonstrate in Listing 12.15.

Recall from our MRPhysics visualization that our axes were missing labels. This is a severe limitation in our ability to see where all the movement is oriented. In other words, we cannot tell which way is up as we rotate the axis. We now modify `AxisBody` by adding a billboard behavior for keeping the axis labels facing the user.

LISTING 12.15 `AxisBody.java`

```java
import java.lang.Math.*;
import javax.media.j3d.*;
import javax.vecmath.*;
import javax.media.j3d.Text3D;
import java.awt.Font;

public class AxisBody extends TransformGroup {

    float length, radius;
    int nsegs;
    Appearance app;

     float xDirection, yDirection;
     float xVecBody, yVecBody;
     float endcapPos;
     float basecapPos;

     private String fontName = "TestFont";
     int nFaces;        // #(vertices) per VecBody face
     int VecBodyFaceTotalVertexCount;        // total #(vertices) in all teeth
     int nStrips[] = new int[1]; // per VecBody vertex count

     int VecBodyVertexCount;        // #(vertices) for VecBody
     int VecBodyStripCount[] = new int[1]; // #(vertices) in strip/strip

     Point3f coord = new Point3f(0.0f, 0.0f, 0.0f);


     // The angle subtended by a single segment
     double segmentAngle = 2.0 * Math.PI/nsegs;
     double tempAngle;
```

LISTING 12.15   Continued

```
public AxisBody(int nsegs, float length, float radius, Appearance app) {

    this.nsegs = nsegs;
    this.length = length;
    this.radius = radius;
    this.app = app;

    //allow capability to write and read at runtime

this.setCapability(TransformGroup.ALLOW_TRANSFORM_WRITE);
    this.setCapability(TransformGroup.ALLOW_TRANSFORM_READ);

    Transform3D tempTrans = new Transform3D();

    //create an empty shape to add Geometry

    Shape3D zaxis =  new Shape3D();
    zaxis.setAppearance(app);
    zaxis.addGeometry(this.makeBody(-length/2, length/2));

    this.addChild(zaxis);
    Point3f zlabelpt = new Point3f( 0.f, 0.f, length/2);
    this.addChild(MakeLabels("X",zlabelpt));


    Shape3D ztxt = new Shape3D();

    TransformGroup xTG = new TransformGroup();

    tempTrans.rotX(Math.PI/2);
    xTG.setTransform(tempTrans);

    Shape3D xaxis =  new Shape3D();
    xaxis.setAppearance(app);
    xaxis.addGeometry(this.makeBody(-length/2, length/2));

    xTG.addChild(xaxis);
    this.addChild(xTG);
    Point3f xlabelpt = new Point3f(length/2, 0.f, 0.f);
    this.addChild(MakeLabels("Y",xlabelpt));


    tempTrans.setIdentity();
    TransformGroup yTG = new TransformGroup();
    tempTrans.rotY(Math.PI/2);
```

LISTING 12.15   Continued

```
            yTG.setTransform(tempTrans);
            Shape3D yaxis =  new Shape3D();
            yaxis.setAppearance(app);
            yaxis.addGeometry(this.makeBody(-length/2, length/2));
            yTG.addChild(yaxis);
            this.addChild(yTG);
            Point3f ylabelpt = new Point3f(0.f, length/2, 0.f);
            this.addChild(MakeLabels("Z",ylabelpt));

    }
    public TransformGroup MakeLabels(String s, Point3f p) {

        Font3D f3d = new Font3D(new Font(fontName, Font.PLAIN, 1),
                                new FontExtrusion());

        int sl = s.length();

        Appearance apText = new Appearance();
. . .

        Text3D txt = new Text3D(f3d, s, p);
        Shape3D textShape = new Shape3D();
        textShape.setGeometry(txt);
        textShape.setAppearance(apText);

    // Using billboard behavior on text3d

        TransformGroup bbTransPt = new TransformGroup();
        bbTransPt.setCapability(TransformGroup.ALLOW_TRANSFORM_WRITE);
        bbTransPt.setCapability(TransformGroup.ALLOW_TRANSFORM_READ);
        Billboard bboardPt = new Billboard( bbTransPt );
        this.addChild( bboardPt );
        BoundingSphere bounds =
        new BoundingSphere(new Point3d(0.0,0.0,0.0), 100.0);

        bboardPt.setSchedulingBounds( bounds );
    bboardPt.setAlignmentMode(Billboard.ROTATE_ABOUT_POINT);

    // text is centered around 0, 3, 0.  Make it rotate around 0,5,0
    Point3f rotationPt = new Point3f(0.0f, 5.0f, 0.0f);
    bboardPt.setRotationPoint(p);
        bbTransPt.addChild( textShape );

        return bbTransPt;
    }
```

Figure 12.8 shows the output of the BasicRecipeJ3D using the AxisBody class added to the scene graph. Note how the axis labels always face the viewer.

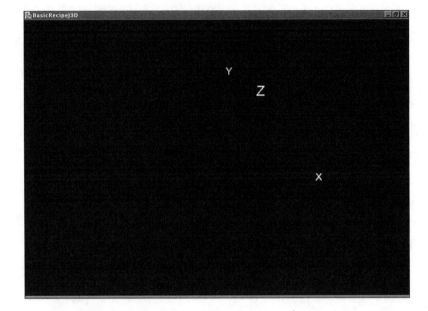

FIGURE 12.8

Screenshot from BasicRecipeJ3D *using the new* AxisBody *class.*

Note that we could have achieved the same effect using the OrientedShape3D class. The difference is that usage between the Billboard class and the OrientedShape3D class can be subtle. Another difference is that the OrientedShape3D can function well when multiple View objects are specified. A Billboard object will stay aligned with the primary View only (that is, the first View added to the Canvas3D). Also, remember that the OrientedShape3D extends Shape3D, and the Billboard class extends Behavior. This means that the OrientedShape3D can be used in a SharedGroup, whereas a Billboard cannot.

Animation Through Interpolators and Alpha Objects

The Interpolator class extends Behavior that is used in conjunction with an Alpha object to provide animation to the scene graph. We use the term *animation* to refer to basically non-interactive changes to the scene graph.

The name Interpolator reflects the use of these classes in interpolating between sets of values. We all remember having to interpolate tables and such in math class. This idea is the same. Often, the programmer will specify two values, and the Interpolator will provide a smooth set of values between the pair. Other Interpolators can have a variable number of points called *knots* to interpolate between.

Note that `Interpolators` are almost always considered with respect to an `Alpha` value. In rare cases, an `Alpha` object is used alone; however, the two are intended to be used together.

The role of the `Alpha` object is to map time to the referencing `Interpolator`. In other words, the purpose of the `Alpha` object is to scale (normalize) time into a series of values between 0 and 1 and to map those values to other objects (especially `Interpolators`) as input. The scaled time values are called the `Alpha` values.

`Interpolator/Alpha` pairings are generally used for ballistic events; that is, events that are triggered and run to completion without further changes. The typical example of a ballistic event is the firing of a missile. Once the missile is launched, little can be done to change the course of events (modern guided missiles notwithstanding). Regardless, the general idea is to turn on the `Interpolator` and let it go. We note, however, that in Java 3D version 1.3, `Interpolators` do allow for starting and stopping of their action through the `pause()` and `resume()` methods.

Existing `Interpolators`

Java 3D provides a number of prewritten `Interpolators` as part of the base API in `javax.media.j3d.Behavior.Interpolator` as well as extensions of these as part of the utilities in `com.sun.j3d.utils.behaviors.interpolators`. Note that as of Java 3D v 1.3, there are new methods to pause and restart `Interpolators`. `Interpolators` used for rotating or translating objects in the scene graph extend the abstract class `TransformInterpolator`. The `ColorInterpolator` and `SwitchInterpolator` classes still extend `Interpolator`.

Specifying `Alpha` Objects

To examine `Alpha` objects in more detail, consider some arbitrary function of time f(t) = 10*t. Table 12.3 shows this very simple relationship that would have two columns, one containing the value of f(t) and the other containing discrete values of t.

TABLE 12.3   Sample Table for f(t) and Alpha Evaluated at Different Values of t

f(t) (seconds)	t (seconds)	Alpha
0	0	0.0
10	1	0.01
20	2	0.02
...	...	...
990		0.99
1000	100	1.0

In this particular example, computation of the `Alpha` object is simple because the time points are equidistant and therefore could be easily specified in a `Behavior` with a `wakeupOnElapsedTime()` wakeup condition. Indeed, all the `Interpolators` can be specified in this way.

To understand the `Alpha` object, it is important to understand two *mappings* (input-output pairings) that are computed for each `Alpha` object. The first is termed the *time-to-Alpha* mapping and describes how the `Alpha` value, restricted to the range of 0-1 floating point, relates to time (which is, of course, continuous). The second mapping, *Alpha-to-value*, specifies how the `Alpha` values relate to changes in the Java 3D object (for example, `TransformGroup`, `Color`, or `Switch`).

Indeed, the `Alpha` class can be used to produce almost any time sequence. For example, the `setPhaseDelayDuration()` method is used to specify a period of time before the interpolation begins. A fixed (or infinite) number of loops can be specified using the `setLoopCount()` method. (Note that setting the `LoopCount` to `-1` specifies infinite looping.)

Specifying Knots

Knots are much like key frames. In a complex sequence of movements, knots specify where the object is to be at different times in the sequence. In Listing 12.16, knots are used in conjunction with the `Interpolator` to specify some interesting movements of a cube through space.

The important thing to remember when using knots is that the first and last knots in the sequence are 0.f and 1.f, respectively. Furthermore, a sequence of knots always progresses upward (for example, knot 2 is higher than knot 1, knot 3 is higher than knot 2, and so on).

The `InterpolationPlotter` Example

Partly because there are so many options that can be specified in an `Alpha` object and further because we want to demonstrate the interaction between an `Alpha` object and its `Interpolator`, we provide an example program for experimentation. In Listing 12.16, the `InterpolationPlotter` application allows the user to create `Alphas` and then instantiate one of several `Interpolators` to see the results.

LISTING 12.16   `InterpolationPlotter.java`

```
import java.applet.Applet;
import java.awt.BorderLayout;
import java.awt.event.*;
import java.awt.GraphicsConfiguration;
import com.sun.j3d.utils.applet.MainFrame;
import com.sun.j3d.utils.geometry.Box;
import com.sun.j3d.utils.geometry.ColorCube;
import com.sun.j3d.utils.geometry.Primitive;
import com.sun.j3d.utils.universe.*;
```

LISTING 12.16 Continued

```java
import com.sun.j3d.utils.behaviors.mouse.MouseRotate;
import javax.media.j3d.*;
import javax.vecmath.*;
import javax.swing.*;
//import javax.swing.JScrollPane.ScrollBar;
import java.util.Random;
import javax.media.j3d.Text3D;

import java.awt.*;
import javax.swing.border.*;

public class InterpolationPlotter extends JFrame {
  VirtualUniverse universe;
  Locale locale;
  TransformGroup vpTrans, geoTG;
  View view;
  Bounds bounds;
  InterpPlot2D ip2d;
  JButton newAlpha, newRandomInterp;
  Alpha a;
  Random r = new Random();

  int n_knots;
  Quat4f[] quats;

  float[] knots;

  Point3f[] points;

  JRadioButton inc_alpha_enabledButton, dec_alpha_enabledButton,
➥ inc_dec_alpha_enabledButton;
    private String fontName = "TestFont";
  BranchGroup scene;

  WholeNumberField phaseDelayDuration,triggerTime,
                   increasingAlphaDuration, decreasingAlphaDuration,
                   increasingAlphaRampDuration, decreasingAlphaRampDuration,
                   alphaAtOneDuration, alphaAtZeroDuration,
                   n_points, n_loops;
```

LISTING 12.16   Continued

```java
public BranchGroup createSceneGraph(boolean newPath) {

    // Create the root of the branch graph; this will be returned
    Appearance app = new Appearance();
    BranchGroup objRoot = new BranchGroup();
    objRoot.setCapability(BranchGroup.ALLOW_DETACH);


    geoTG = new TransformGroup();
    geoTG.setCapability(TransformGroup.ALLOW_TRANSFORM_WRITE);
    geoTG.setCapability(TransformGroup.ALLOW_TRANSFORM_READ);

    TransformGroup boxTG = new TransformGroup();
    boxTG.setCapability(TransformGroup.ALLOW_TRANSFORM_WRITE);
    boxTG.setCapability(TransformGroup.ALLOW_TRANSFORM_READ);

    geoTG.addChild(boxTG);

    BoundingSphere bounds =
        new BoundingSphere(new Point3d(0.0,0.0,0.0), 1000.0);

    MouseRotate mouseBeh = new MouseRotate(geoTG);
    geoTG.addChild(mouseBeh);
    mouseBeh.setSchedulingBounds(bounds);

    PlotBehavior pb = new PlotBehavior(this);
    pb.setSchedulingBounds(bounds);
    objRoot.addChild(pb);

    Transform3D yAxis = new Transform3D();

    knots[n_points.getValue()-1]=1.f;
    for (int ii=1; ii<n_points.getValue()-1; ii++) {
      knots[ii] = (float)ii/(float)(n_points.getValue()-1);
      System.out.println("ii: " + ii + " knots[ii]: " + knots[ii]);
    }

    if (newPath==true) {

        for (int ii=0; ii<n_points.getValue(); ii++) {
            quats[ii] = genRandomQuat();
            points[ii] = genRandomPoint();
        }
    }
     for (int ii=0; ii<n_points.getValue(); ii++) {
         String label = " " + ii;
```

LISTING 12.16   Continued

```
            geoTG.addChild(MakeLabels(label,points[ii]));
        }

  . . .


        PointArray pathLine = new PointArray(n_points.getValue(),
➥ GeometryArray.COORDINATES);
        pathLine.setCoordinates(0, points);
        Shape3D path = new Shape3D(pathLine, app);
        geoTG.addChild(path);

        for (int ii=0; ii<n_knots; ii++) {
          String label = " " + ii;
          geoTG.addChild(MakeLabels(label,points[ii]));
        }

        RotPosPathInterpolator interp =
                new RotPosPathInterpolator( a,
                    boxTG,
                yAxis,
                knots,
                quats,
                points);


    PositionPathInterpolator interp =
        new PositionPathInterpolator(a, geoTG, yAxis, knots,points);

    */


        interp.setSchedulingBounds(bounds);

        objRoot.addChild(interp);

        boxTG.addChild(new ColorCube(.8f));
        objRoot.addChild(geoTG);

        Color3f blue = new Color3f(0.f, 0.9f, 0.f);
        Vector3f bluedir  = new Vector3f(0.0f, -8.0f, -8.0f);

    // AmbientLight al = new AmbientLight(true, new Color3f(.1f,.9f, .1f));
        AmbientLight al = new AmbientLight();

        DirectionalLight bluelight = new DirectionalLight(blue, bluedir);

        objRoot.addChild(al);
```

LISTING 12.16   Continued

```
    objRoot.addChild(bluelight);

return objRoot;
 }

 public BranchGroup createViewGraph() {

     BranchGroup objRoot = new BranchGroup();

Transform3D t = new Transform3D();
t.setTranslation(new Vector3f(0.0f, 0.2f,30.0f));
ViewPlatform vp = new ViewPlatform();
TransformGroup vpTrans = new TransformGroup();
    vpTrans.setCapability(TransformGroup.ALLOW_TRANSFORM_WRITE);
vpTrans.setCapability(TransformGroup.ALLOW_TRANSFORM_READ);
vpTrans.setTransform(t);
vpTrans.addChild(vp);
view.attachViewPlatform(vp);

     NavigationBehavior nav = new NavigationBehavior(vpTrans);
     vpTrans.addChild(nav);
     nav.setSchedulingBounds(bounds);

     objRoot.addChild(vpTrans);
     return objRoot;

}

public TransformGroup MakeLabels(String s, Point3f p) {

     Font3D f3d = new Font3D(new Font(fontName, Font.PLAIN, 1),
                           new FontExtrusion());

     int sl = s.length();

     Appearance apText = new Appearance();


     Text3D txt = new Text3D(f3d, s, p);
     Shape3D textShape = new Shape3D();
     textShape.setGeometry(txt);
     textShape.setAppearance(apText);

// Using billboard behavior on text3d
```

LISTING 12.16 Continued

```java
        TransformGroup bbTransPt = new TransformGroup();
        bbTransPt.setCapability(TransformGroup.ALLOW_TRANSFORM_WRITE);
        bbTransPt.setCapability(TransformGroup.ALLOW_TRANSFORM_READ);
        Billboard bboardPt = new Billboard( bbTransPt );
        geoTG.addChild( bboardPt );
        BoundingSphere bounds =
        new BoundingSphere(new Point3d(0.0,0.0,0.0), 100.0);

        bboardPt.setSchedulingBounds( bounds );
    bboardPt.setAlignmentMode(Billboard.ROTATE_ABOUT_POINT);

    Point3f rotationPt = new Point3f(0.0f, 5.0f, 0.0f);
    bboardPt.setRotationPoint(p);
        bbTransPt.addChild( textShape );

        return bbTransPt;
    }

    public Point3f genRandomPoint() {
        float x = r.nextFloat()*15;
        float y = r.nextFloat()*15;
        float z = r.nextFloat()*15;
        Point3f p = new Point3f(x,y,z);
        // System.out.println("Point3f is made of x:
➥ " + x + " y: " + y + " z: " + z);
        return p;
    }

    public Quat4f genRandomQuat() {

        float x = r.nextFloat()*200;
        float y = r.nextFloat()*200;
        float z = r.nextFloat()*200;
        float w = r.nextFloat()*1;
        Quat4f q = new Quat4f(x,y,z,w);
        // System.out.println("Quat4f is made of x:
➥ " + x + " y: " + y + " z: " + z + "w: " + w);
        return q;
    }

    public InterpolationPlotter() {
     super("Interpolation Plotter");

    . . .

        universe = new VirtualUniverse();
     locale = new Locale(universe);
```

LISTING 12.16 Continued

```
        GraphicsConfigTemplate3D g3d = new GraphicsConfigTemplate3D();
        GraphicsConfiguration gc=
        GraphicsEnvironment.getLocalGraphicsEnvironment().
                    getDefaultScreenDevice().getBestConfiguration(g3d);

    Canvas3D c = new Canvas3D(gc);

. . .

        plotpanel.add(c);
        PhysicalBody body = new PhysicalBody();
    PhysicalEnvironment environment = new PhysicalEnvironment();
    view = new View();

    view.addCanvas3D(c);
    view.setPhysicalBody(body);
        view.setPhysicalEnvironment(environment);
    // Create a simple scene and attach it to the virtual universe

        bounds = new BoundingSphere(new Point3d(0.0,0.0,0.0), 100.0);
        scene = createSceneGraph(true);
        BranchGroup vgraph = createViewGraph();

        locale.addBranchGraph(vgraph);
    locale.addBranchGraph(scene);

}

public void newAlpha() {
    System.out.println("new Alpha");

    a = new Alpha(-1,
                    Alpha.INCREASING_ENABLE | Alpha.DECREASING_ENABLE,
                    //Alpha.DECREASING_ENABLE,
                    triggerTime.getValue(),
                    phaseDelayDuration.getValue(),
                    increasingAlphaDuration.getValue(),
                    increasingAlphaRampDuration.getValue(),
                    alphaAtOneDuration.getValue(),
                    decreasingAlphaDuration.getValue(),
                    decreasingAlphaRampDuration.getValue(),
                    alphaAtZeroDuration.getValue());
}

public void resetScene() {
  scene.detach();
  ip2d.setNewAlpha(a);
```

12

INTERACTION WITH
THE VIRTUAL
WORLD

LISTING 12.16   Continued

```
    ip2d.refreshPlot();
    scene = createSceneGraph(false);
    locale.addBranchGraph(scene);
}

public void newScene() {
    scene.detach();
    quats = new Quat4f[n_points.getValue()];
    knots = new float[n_points.getValue()];
    points= new Point3f[n_points.getValue()];
    scene = createSceneGraph(true);
    locale.addBranchGraph(scene);


}

. . .
```

Figure 12.9 shows the screen output for InterpolationPlotter. The InterpolationPlotter program allows for the adjustment of several parameters of the Alpha object to be manipulated. The program also allows for placement of the knots.

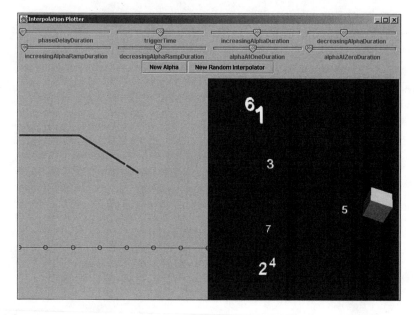

FIGURE 12.9

Screen output for InterpolationPlotter.

Introduction to Sensors

The use of sensors is a fairly advanced topic in 3D graphics and generally refers to detecting or sensing some signal in the environment. In 3D graphics, it is usually some movement of the user that we want to sense. Common forms of motion sensing are those involving joysticks, head tracking, motion suits, and hand/arm movements.

Developing a sensor requires some knowledge of how device drivers work. A *device driver* is software that helps a computer communicate with a hardware device. To fully explore this topic, you should have access to an input device such as a head tracker or special mouse (for example, the Magellan Space Mouse). However, we are able to approximate the workings of special devices using a simulated device. Included is the `SimulatedDevice` class that will act as a prototypical input device for these purposes.

Two classes and one interface are used together to implement a sensor in Java 3D: the `InputDevice` interface and the `Sensor` and `SensorRead` classes.

The `InputDevice` Interface

The `InputDevice` interface is used to communicate with a device driver. In order to be recognized by a Java 3D application, an object instantiated from a class implementing `InputDevice` must first be initialized and then registered through the `PhysicalEnvironment.addInputDevice()` method.

The most important aspect of device drivers to understand is the different types of drivers. There are three primary types, *blocking, non-blocking,* and *demand driven.* Blocking and non-blocking drivers are accessed by a scheduling thread that looks for inputs at regular time intervals. The difference between blocking and non-blocking is that a blocking driver causes the calling thread to block (wait) until the input data is completely read before returning, whereas non-blocking does not necessarily wait until the input data is completely read.

A demand driven sensor is not queried at specific intervals, but is only retrieved when the application program asks for it. The buttons can be turned on or off multiple times without the sensor doing anything. The only changes that will be recognized are those that are in place when the application asks for the status.

As already mentioned, `InputDevice` is an interface. As such, several methods must be developed in order to implement the interface. One of these is called `pollAndProcessInput()`. The purpose of this method is to update the values in the `Sensor` class (discussed next) with the values provided by the device driver.

The Sensor Class

There is a tight coupling of the InputDevice with the Sensor class. Indeed, the main purpose of any class implementing InputDevice is to update the Sensor class.

The Sensor class is an abstraction of all input devices such as six degrees of freedom trackers, joysticks, and haptic gloves. Another possibility is for a file to act as an InputDevice and provide input to the Sensor. This is a way to play back a user's experience for example.

At its most basic level, a Sensor represents a series of timestamps with the corresponding input values (stored in a transform) and the states of buttons and switches at the time of the read.

By way of example, let's consider a simple joystick that can only go forward and backward and has one button that can be pushed. When the pollAndProcessInput() method of the InputDevice is called, it will return a timestamp of when the method was called along with the digitized value of the front-back position of the joystick and whether the button was depressed. Note that Java 3D will normalize the input value of the front-back position to [-1,+1].

Prediction

It has been noted that the Sensor class encapsulates a series of timestamps. You might have been wondering why this series is kept when a single read is probably sufficient for the task. The answer is that the series of values enables prediction. It turns out that in tracking, prediction is almost always required in order to do a reasonable job of updating the scene. Much as we did in our collision avoidance examples, we have to look into the future and guess where the sensor will be. Otherwise, it might be too late to do anything.

This is where the series of timestamps become important. If the series of timestamps and values indicates acceleration in a particular direction, then the predicted value can reflect this information. Likewise, deceleration can also be used to better predict the sensors future value. There are two fields that are set to enable or disable prediction, PREDICT_NONE and PREDICT_NEXT_FRAME_TIME.

Finally, the prediction algorithm can be adjusted for the prediction of head and hand position and orientation. The reason for this is that the two fundamental types of prediction can be made much better by using certain constraints. For example, head movements are quite characteristic because heads do not typically move upward by more than a couple of inches, whereas hands can often move several feet.

The SensorRead Class

The SensorRead class encapsulates the data from a single read of a sensor. This includes a single timestamp, the transform value of the sensor, and the status of the buttons and switches.

This class is used in conjunction with the `Sensor` class through the `setNextSensorRead` class. A full example of the use of the `SensorRead` is shown in Chapter 13.

Developing a Sensor

Given the `InputDevice` interface and the `Sensor` and `SensorRead` classes previously described, it is still difficult to understand the entire process of writing and implementing a sensor in an application. Once the `Sensor` is developed and is reading the data properly, an important choice has to be made regarding linking the `Sensor` to the scene. Does the developer want to use a `Behavior` class to implement the changes, or should the developer use one of Java 3D's existing mechanisms for this purpose? The most common example of the built-in mechanisms is the `setUserHead()` method demonstrated in Chapter 13.

In general, if you want to drive the `View` from either the user head position (head tracked) or the dominant or non-dominant hand (hand tracked), the built-in mechanisms are preferable. Other than using a joystick, head tracking is the most common application of `Sensors`. Examples of how to link the tracker to the `View` are given in the next chapter. You might consider cheating and telling Java 3D that some `Sensor` that doesn't really represent the user's head is, in fact, the user's head. In this case, prediction algorithms specific to head tracking might cause some problems. In the next chapter, we will show how prediction can be turned off.

Otherwise, you might consider working through a `Behavior`. Many non-tracking based sensor applications (that is, button events) will work well through the `Behavior` mechanism. Some tracking applications can also work well enough without using the built-in mechanisms.

Summary

Java 3D provides a well-conceived behavioral abstraction that can be used effectively for user interaction tasks. Using the `Behavior` class is preferable in many ways to writing a standard AWT or Swing listener because the `Behavior` class runs in a single thread and gathers all changes together so that they occur in the same frame. Otherwise, a `Behavior` is quite similar to a listener.

Important forms of user interaction in 3D environments include 2D and 3D mechanisms. Examples of 2D interaction include clicking on a button or icon, whereas 3D mechanisms include picking, collisions, and navigation.

Finally, the `Sensor` class is introduced as a way to feed data from the environment to the Java 3D renderer. This information is used to make changes to the rendered scene. The use of `Sensors` to affect the scene graph rendering is discussed in the next chapter.

The Java 3D View Model

IN THIS CHAPTER

The view model is one of the high-level features that sets Java 3D apart from all other 3D APIs. In many ways, learning the Java 3D view model is more complicated than learning other models, and hence this poses a significant challenge to the uninitiated.

Use of the Java 3D view model can be simplified for basic applications using the ConfiguredUniverse class (available in Java 3D 1.3). Regardless, a basic understanding of the model is useful and often necessary. We suggest that a more complete understanding of the Java 3D viewing model has great heuristic value for learning 3D in general.

It should be further noted that most applications do not need the vast majority of the options specified as part of the view model. Developers who do not want to get into the vast details of head tracking and display technologies will benefit from the overview and the sections on using the view model in camera mode (see the section, "Using Java 3D's View Model as a Camera Model").

The Big Chain of Transforms

On the way through the graphics pipeline, the 3D content undergoes numerous transformations to become a rendered output. This part of the pipeline is what we have covered throughout this section of the book so far as we have examined content creation. The pipeline transformations occur over all the many reference frames in the scene (represented by TransformGroups and Transform3Ds). The basic set of transformations in any 3D graphics pipeline was established early on by Sutherland, who recognized the utility of projective geometry in chaining them together for computational ease. In fact, when we refer to "the 3D graphics pipeline," for all intents and purposes, we are describing what is frequently called *the Sutherland pipeline*.

It turns out that the physical environment in which the user exists also corresponds to a kind of Sutherland pipeline going the other way. Because both pipelines converge at a common point, the screen, a common space can be created in which a point in one space maps on to a point in the other space. This space can be considered a *coexistence space*.

None of this is very important when you simply want to display a 3D model on a single flat screen as we have done throughout the last two chapters. Java 3D makes some basic assumptions about where your head and eyes are and renders the correct view.

However, when you want to use more advanced 3D graphics displays such as stereo viewing or controlling the view with head tracking, you will quickly run into a complex series of transformations that must be used to get the correct view. Encountering these transforms will most likely make you a little nauseated because knowing them all is quite challenging. Nonetheless, a number of simplifying assumptions can be used to make the problem more tractable. In general, there are two basic series of transformations corresponding to two general classes of viewing situations. We describe these next.

Two Fundamental Series of Transforms

Most viewing situations fall into one of two classes depending on whether the display (by this, we mean the physical screen) is *head mounted* and *room mounted*. The vast majority of output situations are single screens without head tracking. Such systems are the simplest form of room mounted display. In the case of the head mounted situation, the screens are attached to the head (that is, when the head moves, the screens follow).

Whether the screen is head mounted or room mounted only really makes a difference when head tracking is incorporated. We want to use head tracking for two different purposes, depending on which of the two viewing situations are in play. The following descriptions apply to head tracking setups only. Remember that a typical head tracking setup has two relevant hardware components—the *tracker base*, a base station that emits and receives data, and the *tracker sensor*, a measurement device for detecting x, y, z, pitch, roll, and yaw. An excellent review of head tracking hardware and theory was presented at SIGGRAPH 2001 by Danette Allen, Gary Bishop, andAllen, Gary Bishop and Gregory Gregory Walsh from UNC. The course notes are available from

```
http://cave.cs.nps.navy.mil/Courses/cd1/courses/11/11cdrom.pdf
```

In the head-mount situation, we want the camera to be slaved to the user's head such that when the user's head moves and rotates, the 3D view of the scene moves with it. Importantly, the relationship between our eyes and the screen does not change in the head-mount situation. Therefore, the projection matrix remains constant. In the head-mount situation, the sensor is rigidly attached to thehead tracking display device.

In the room-mount situation, movement of our head changes the projection matrix but has no effect on the camera. This is only an issue when viewing stereo. With a room mounted display, there is no reason to use head tracking unless you are viewing in stereo. In this case, the *tracker base* (and **not** the sensor) is attached to the display (or some central point among multiple displays).

To summarize, when the screen(s) are fixed in the room, Java 3D operates under the assumption that the tracker base is fixed to the display. Thus the room, the screen, and the tracker base all exist in the same reference frame. Alternatively, when the screen(s) are fixed to the user's head, Java 3D computes the transforms assuming that the tracker sensor is attached to the display. In this case the head, display screen, and tracker sensor exist in the same reference.

Java 3D determines which of these two situations to use in rendering by seeing whether the View policy is View.HMD_VIEW or View.SCREEN_VIEW.

Understanding Viewing Through a Remote Telepresence Robot

One way to understand the different viewing situations is to consider a remote controlled video equipped robot. Such a robot was used in psychological and brain imaging investigations during my time at Michigan State University (see Figure 13.1). The robot work described here was developed in collaboration with the Robotics and Automation Lab in the College of Engineering at MSU.

FIGURE 13.1
Telerobot with control system.

The robot can be configured in a number of ways and makes a nice heuristic model for understanding the Java 3D view model.

The robot is drivable by a remote user from a distant location using a joystick. In the most basic configuration, the robot has a single camera attached to it that continuously streams video to the remote user.

The robot platform corresponds well to the ViewPlatform in Java 3D. Moving the joystick moves the robot (including the camera) around in the remote location, much as we experience when we use a navigation behavior (see Chapter 12, "Interaction with the Virtual World"). The remote user can see the world from the perspective of the robot. The user's *eyes* are in the world of the robot, and hence everything the user sees is from the robot's cyclopean view.

One important point to note is that what the remote user sees on the screen is determined partially by the properties of the camera lens and partially by the properties of the display device. For example, the cameras could have a wide-angle lens, and the user could have a simple monitor on which to view the video. We want the user to suspend reality and imagine being embodied by the robot. One way to help suspend the user's reality is to project the video so that the objects in the remote world are their proper size in the user's world. In other words, if we know the amount of space that the robot's video camera covers, we can create a nice immersive effect by projecting the image to the user at the same *apparent* size as he would encounter if he actually were the robot. For example, we could have some very large screens several feet from the user and project large images, or we could have small screens right in front of the user's eyes and project little images thereby achieving roughly the same effect. That, in essence, is the important idea of apparent size.

A number of interesting configurations are possible given sufficient bandwidth, including another simple configuration in which three cameras are mounted on the robot—the original camera pointing straight ahead with two additional cameras rotated 45° to either side within the view plane. The remote user could then sit in a room with three screens and three projectors in back projection mode. Again, in order for the subject to feel more embodied within the robot, we need to maintain the apparent size of the robot's scene.

Adding Immersive Head Tracking to the Robot

Now consider what would happen if we configured the system so that a head tracker is attached to the head of the remote user. Moreover, say that we mount cameras to a 3° of freedom motorized tripod that is slaved to the head tracker of the remote user. Thus, when the remote user moves his head, the camera will rotate around the x, y, and z axis accordingly. (For now, we will leave out the translations.)

Two very different view scenarios occur with this setup. We could have the screen(s) attached to the user's head or attached to the room. If we have a little single screen (say .3mx.2m attached to the user's head, immediately in front of the eyes), we could have a pretty realistic robot's perspective. Even if we don't scale the image to the size of the screen, we will feel "pretty robotic." A scaling problem will only make us feel big or small.

The virtual analogy of this can easily be seen in the virtual world. In the virtual world, the camera (defined by the view frustum) is slaved to the head tracker. Again, the ViewPlatform always corresponds to the robot itself. Because the tripod and camera are attached to the robot, they form a parent-child relationship, just as the view platform and camera do in the virtual world.

Note that a human would generally return his head to the forward position when walking, although not always. This can be accomplished by incorporating some *body* reference such as a fake set of shoulders mounted on the robot or by reference to the robot's arm. The body reference is analogous to geometry attached to the ViewPlatform.

Robot View as a Window

The last part of the robot analogy is a little harder to imagine. This is the case in which the screen is not attached to the remote operator's head. We begin by returning to the original one camera cyclopean case with no head tracking. In this case, we are looking at the robot's remote world as if we were sitting on the robot with our faces in front of a large window. This window is defined by the field of view of our camera lens. The viewing volume is analogous to viewing a large fish tank through a small window, much like those underground exhibits at the zoo in which you get a little view of the underground or underwater life of beavers and other such creatures. Note that with a single camera, we get little depth information. Furthermore, if we move our heads relative to the window, it does not matter much for our viewing.

But now imagine what would happen if we had a pair of video cameras streaming video to the remote user. In this case, when we move back and forth, our stereo vision is going to be seriously affected. Each eye is going to have a slightly different and separate view frustum. When the head moves, the view frustum for each eye is going to change differently. Thus if we use the same projection matrix we were using at the start, our stereo cues are going to be invalid. In the case of the robot's video cameras, we are going to translate and rotate the cameras independently to get a proper 3D capture. Indeed, the brain does some remarkable occulomotor control to do just that in the real world. Similar to the brain, our robot will need to use head tracking in order to appropriately change the view frustum.

Attaching the Reference Frames to the Renderer

All that remains is to attach one of the two reference frames described previously to the scene. This is achieved through setting the matrix representing the physical world to a place in the virtual world, and it can be done because we know the transformation between the physical world and coexistence and the transformation from coexistence to the virtual world.

We will give examples of these two situations and how to attach coexistence later. For the moment, we want to discuss why the Java 3D view model is powerful for addressing the many variations of these two basic setups.

Advantages of the Java 3D View Model

As we said previously, for specific applications, you can make some simplifying assumptions and just recompute the projection matrix for the given situation. Unfortunately, when the viewing situation changes, the projection matrix has to be reanalyzed and recomputed. This means that even small variations in display size and other parameters can force the developer to maintain a different version of the source code. The ideal of Java is "Write once, run anywhere," and most of us who program in Java believe strongly in this ideal even when it sometimes isn't fully true. The Java 3D view model takes this further by attempting to achieve "write once, view anywhere." Even in the research environment in which code is not generally distributed to the general public, it is extremely handy to be able to change the display environment and computer platform and not have to worry about reprogramming the projection matrix.

The power of the Java 3D view model is that it allows you to specify one or more screens, where they are in relationship to each other, and where the eyes and head are relative to the screen. This physical configuration is then placed in the virtual world by establishing a coexistence point. The renderer can now blindly compute each frame based on one of the two big transform chains described previously.

Exactly how many transforms are there? The answer is a lot. Indeed, up to eight coordinate systems are at play in the Java 3D view model depending on which of the two chains of transforms is selected. By understanding these basic reference frames, the student will naturally begin to understand the transformations in and out of those coordinate systems in turn. Always try to remember that the purpose of a transformation is to convert data from one coordinate system to another.

Table 13.1 lists all the coordinate systems that are part of the Java 3D view model.

TABLE 13.1 Java 3D View Model Coordinate Systems

Coordinate System	Relevant Classes and Methods
HeadTracker	PhysicalBody.setHeadToHeadTracker
	Screen3D.setHeadTrackerToLeftImagePlate()
	Screen3D.setHeadTrackerToRightImagePlate()
TrackerBase	PhysicalEnvironment.setCoexistenceToTrackerBase()
	Screen3D.setTrackerBaseToImagePlate()
Head	PhysicalBody
Image Plate (Screen) RightImagePlate (HMD) LeftImagePlate (HMD)	Screen3D
Coexistence	PhysicalEnvironment.setCoexsistence ToTrackerBase ViewPlatform.setViewAttachPolicy()
View Platform	ViewPlatform View.attachViewPlatform()
Virtual World	Locale

Policy Matters

As we said earlier, the Java 3D renderer needs to know where the eyes are relative to the screen. This information uniquely defines the view frustum and constitutes the first part of the viewing computation. Given the eye to screen transforms, there are a number of options for using that information to render a frame. Java 3D sets most of these options through *policies*. The name policy might sound a bit foreboding, but it's really nothing more than a set of rules and operating principles. The idea here is that policies establish the general set of rules for rendering views and really serve to group the options in a logical fashion.

Commonly Used Policies

Several primary policies exist that pertain to most situations. They are as follows:

- View policy
- Monoscopic View policy
- Screen Scale policy
- Projection policy
- View Attach policy

View Policy

One of the primary policies that comes into play is the view policy. The view policy determines which of two basic sets of transforms are to be used in rendering views. Thus, there are two view policy options, referring to the two distinct series of transforms. The first, SCREEN_VIEW is the default and is suitable for displays such as multiple projection CAVE systems, FishTank VR, and VR desks such as the ImmersaDesk. SCREEN_VIEW requires that the tracker base is rigidly attached to the display screen.

The second policy option is the HMD_VIEW policy, which is used when the screen is attached to the user's head (that is, an HMD). Remember, when the screen is attached the user's head, the *camera* (not the ViewPlatform) must be translated and rotated rapidly whenever the head moves and rotates. The difference between moving the camera and moving the ViewPlatform is a common source of confusion when learning the view model. The only way to affect the position of the ViewPlatform is to access the TransformGroup that contains the ViewPlatform (as we have done in the previous two chapters). Note that it is possible to set up a chain of transforms so that the ViewPlatform would be chained to the head tracker, but this is not the optimal approach.

To reiterate, the ViewPlatform is only one frame of reference in the chain of transforms that determines the final viewing and projection matrices for each eye and each screen. In the default case, appropriate for the typical desktop display, the ViewPlatform orientation and position is equivalent to the view matrix because we have fixed screen and eye positions centered about the origin of the view platform. On the other hand with head tracking, the screens (eyes) are moving about relative to the view platform. Their positions and orientations relative to the view platform have to be concatenated with the ViewPlatform position and orientation to get the final view transform.

With an HMD_VIEW policy, the left and right screens are the only things slaved to head movement with the HMD_VIEW policy. This relationship is established with the Screen3D setHeadTrackerToLeftImagePlate() and setHeadTrackerToRightImagePlate() methods. From the sensor read and the CoexistenceToTrackerBase transform, we get the position and orientation of the screens and eyes in coexistence coordinates. The view attach policy and screen scale defines the transform from coexistence coordinates to ViewPlatform coordinates. From there we get to the virtual world coordinates and final viewing transform. Recall that the projection transform is determined by the position of the eyes relative to the image plates.

Monoscopic View Policy

The monoscopic view policy is used when Java 3D is creating a monoscopic image (that is, a rendering from the perspective of a single eye). Somewhat counterintuitive is the fact that in most cases when using an HMD, even though you are generating stereo pairs, you are really in a monoscopic view mode because the application is generating two monoscopic views to produce the stereo perception. Of course, fixed screens, when not in stereo mode, also have a monoscopic view policy. However, they can generally accept the default, and therefore we have not had to change this parameter. There are three options for monoscopic view policy—LEFT_EYE_VIEW, RIGHT_EYE_VIEW, and CYCLOPEAN_EYE_VIEW (the default). We also note that not all HMDs have a separate screen for each eye. Some HMDs display interleaved stereo and therefore would have a monoscopic view policy of CYCLOPEAN_EYE_VIEW. Java 3D can accommodate both types of HMD easily.

In the HMD example, LEFT_EYE_VIEW and RIGHT_EYE_VIEW are used in the two Canvas3Ds that we use to display the image to each eye. In the single and multiple monitor situations, we need the CYCLOPEAN_EYE_VIEW. CYCLOPEAN_EYE_VIEW is the default and represents the view from a point halfway between the two eyes (hence the name cyclopean). CYCLOPEAN_EYE_VIEW is also the correct policy to have for those stereo situations in which alternate images are shown to each eye.

Screen Scale Policy

It is occasionally necessary to change the screen scale policy particularly for ease of calibration. In this case, the screen scale policy should be changed from its default value of View.SCALE_SCREEN_SIZE to View.SCALE_EXPLICIT. The screen scale would then be set to 1.0 with the View object's setScreenScale() method. Values other than 1.0 are also useful in certain situations, however, by and large, 1.0 is most common.

Projection Policy

The projection policy determines whether the projection matrix is computed for parallel or perspective. The two possible values are View.PARALLEL_PROJECT and View.PERSPECTIVE_PROJECTION. Recall from Chapter 1, "Media, Imaging, and Visualization Programming on the Java Platform," that most applications use perspective viewing, but some CAD/CAM and other applications require parallel projection.

View Attach Policy

Understanding the view attach policy is critical to understanding how the physical world of screens, trackers, and the body are mapped in the virtual world through coexistence. In other words, the view attach policy defines the mapping of coexistence coordinates and view platform coordinates.

There are three options for attaching the view: View.NOMINAL_HEAD (the default), View. NOMINAL_FEET, and View.NOMINAL_SCREEN. Generally, you do not have to change this policy from its default.

For a ViewAttachPolicy of NOMINAL_HEAD, the ViewPlatform origin is at the origin of the nominal head—the center eye halfway between the left and right eyes. If the WindowEyepointPolicy is the default RELATIVE_TO_FIELD_OF_VIEW, the nominal head origin is centered about the +Z axis of coexistence coordinates at the offset required to produce the desired field of view relative to the width of the canvas at the coexistence origin. Otherwise, the Z offset is defined by the NominalEyeOffsetFromNominalScreen attribute of PhysicalBody.

The View.NOMINAL_FEET is used to anchor the user's virtual feet to the virtual ground. Rendering is done to ensure that the Y component is zero in the ViewPlatform's coordinate system.

For a ViewAttachPolicy of NOMINAL_SCREEN, the ViewPlatform origin is set directly to the origin of coexistence so that ViewPlatform coordinates and coexistence coordinates are identical except for scale (reflected in the screen scale). Because of this easy mapping, the NOMINAL_SCREEN ViewAttachPolicy is preferable with head tracking and multiple screens.

In truth, this is only correct if CoexistenceCenterInPworldPolicy is NOMINAL_SCREEN. NOMINAL_SCREEN is the default value, and there really isn't any need to set it to anything else because the proper effects can always be achieved with it set to that default. Most developers can and should ignore the CoexistenceCeenterInPworldPolicy because it adds yet another level of complexity to the view model with little benefit. It is important, however, not to confuse the CoexistenceCenterInPworldPolicy with the ViewAttachPolicy.

Finally, we note again that in HMD_VIEW mode, the ViewAttachPolicy setting is ignored and NOMINAL_SCREEN is always used instead.

The Most Basic Example

Again, the most fundamental relationship we want to know is where the user's eyes are with respect to the screen. This allows Java 3D to compute the projection matrix. For the case in which the screen is not attached to the user's head, the renderer already has enough information to generate a frame. When there is one display and no tracking is being used, the problem is relatively trivial. We only need to assume a fixed distance from the eyes to the display. Regardless of the true position of the head, Java 3D is rendering a frame appropriate for an assumed head, sitting in front of the screen.

In this most simple case, we can set several of the transforms to unity. Setting the transform to unity has the effect of canceling the transform and simplifying the series.

Let's test the water by showing the most common configuration. Listing 13.1 gives code for checking the graphics and default parameters for any system.

LISTING 13.1   ShowJ3DGraphics.java

```java
import java.awt.Frame;
import java.awt.BorderLayout;
import java.awt.GraphicsEnvironment;
import java.awt.GraphicsDevice;
import java.awt.GraphicsConfiguration;
import java.awt.event.*;
import com.sun.j3d.utils.universe.*;
import javax.media.j3d.*;

public class ShowJ3DGraphics {
    PhysicalBody body;
    PhysicalEnvironment environment;
    View view;
    Locale locale;

    public ShowJ3DGraphics(Canvas3D[] canvases) {
        // Create an empty scene and attach it to the universe
        BranchGroup scene = new BranchGroup();
        BranchGroup vgraph = new BranchGroup();
        VirtualUniverse universe = new VirtualUniverse();
        Locale locale = new Locale(universe);
        body = new PhysicalBody();
        System.out.println("PhysicalBody ear and eye positions (Left,Right):
 \n" + body.toString());
        System.out.println("***PhysicalBody Transforms***");
        Transform3D t = new Transform3D();
        body.getHeadToHeadTracker(t);
        System.out.println("HeadToHeadTracker: \n" + t.toString());

        environment = new PhysicalEnvironment();
        environment.getCoexistenceToTrackerBase(t);

        System.out.println("***PhysicalEnvironment Transforms***");
        System.out.println("CoexistenceToTrackerBase: \n" + t.toString()); ok?
        view = new View();
        view.setPhysicalBody(body);
        view.setPhysicalEnvironment(environment);

        System.out.println("canvases.length: " + canvases.length);
        for (int i = 0; i < canvases.length; i++) {
```

LISTING 13.1 Continued

```java
            // Attach the new canvas to the view
            view.addCanvas3D(canvases[i]);
        }

    ViewPlatform vp = new ViewPlatform();
    TransformGroup vpTrans = new TransformGroup();
        vpTrans.setCapability(TransformGroup.ALLOW_TRANSFORM_WRITE);
    vpTrans.setCapability(TransformGroup.ALLOW_TRANSFORM_READ);
    vpTrans.addChild(vp);
        vgraph.addChild(vpTrans);
        locale.addBranchGraph(vgraph);
        locale.addBranchGraph(scene);
        //u.addBranchGraph(scene);
    }

    public static void main(String[] args) {

        GraphicsDevice[] allScreenDevices = GraphicsEnvironment.
                getLocalGraphicsEnvironment().getScreenDevices();
        System.out.println("Found " + allScreenDevices.length +
                            " screen devices");
        for (int i = 0; i < allScreenDevices.length; i++)
            System.out.println(allScreenDevices[i]);
        System.out.println();
        GraphicsDevice[] graphicsDevices =
                        new GraphicsDevice[allScreenDevices.length];
        for (int i = 0; i < allScreenDevices.length; i++) {
            graphicsDevices[i] = allScreenDevices[i];
        }

        GraphicsConfigTemplate3D template;
        GraphicsConfiguration gConfig;
        Canvas3D[] canvases = new Canvas3D[allScreenDevices.length];
        for (int i = 0; i < allScreenDevices.length; i++) {
            template = new GraphicsConfigTemplate3D();
            gConfig = graphicsDevices[i].getBestConfiguration(template);
            canvases[i] = new Canvas3D(gConfig);
            Screen3D screen = canvases[i].getScreen3D();
            System.out.println("***Screen parameters for screen# "
                                + i + "*** \n");
            System.out.println(screen.toString());
            System.out.println("Screen3D transformations");
            Transform3D t = new Transform3D();
            screen.getTrackerBaseToImagePlate(t);
            System.out.println("TrackerBaseToImagePlate: \n" + t.toString());
            screen.getHeadTrackerToLeftImagePlate(t);
```

LISTING 13.1 Continued

```
          System.out.println("HeadTrackerToLeftImagePlate: \n"
                             + t.toString());
          screen.getHeadTrackerToRightImagePlate(t);
          System.out.println("HeadTrackerToRightImagePlate: \n"
                             + t.toString());
          System.out.println("Screen3D[" + i + "] = " + screen);
      }

      new ShowJ3DGraphics(canvases);

   }
}
```

The output of this program (when run on my computer) is:

```
Found 1 Screen Device
Win32GraphicsDevice[screen=0]
***Screen parameters for screen # 0 ***
Screen3D: size = (1024 x 768),
physical size = (0.288995555555555556m x .2167466666667m)
***Screen3D transformations***
TrackerBaseToImagePlate:
1.0, 0.0, 0.0, 0.0
0.0, 1.0, 0.0, 0.0
0.0, 0.0, 1.0, 0.0
0.0, 0.0, 0.0, 1.0

HeadTrackerToLeftImagePlate:
1.0, 0.0, 0.0, 0.0
0.0, 1.0, 0.0, 0.0
0.0, 0.0, 1.0, 0.0
0.0, 0.0, 0.0, 1.0

HeadTrackerToRightImagePlate:
1.0, 0.0, 0.0, 0.0
0.0, 1.0, 0.0, 0.0
0.0, 0.0, 1.0, 0.0
0.0, 0.0, 0.0, 1.0

PhysicalBody ear and eye positions (Left,Right):
eyePosition = ((-.033, 0.0, 0.0), 0.033, 0.0, 0.0))
earPosition = ((-0.08, -0.03, 0.095), (0.08, -0.03, 0.095))
***PhysicalBody Transforms***
```

```
HeadToHeadTracker:
1.0, 0.0, 0.0, 0.0
0.0, 1.0, 0.0, 0.02
0.0, 0.0, 1.0, 0.035
0.0, 0.0, 0.0, 1.0

***PhysicalEnvironment Transforms***
CoexistenceToTrackerBase
1.0, 0.0, 0.0, 0.0
0.0, 1.0, 0.0, 0.0
0.0, 0.0, 1.0, 0.0
0.0, 0.0, 0.0, 1.0
```

The particular computer used to run this example has one graphics card and is typical of the general computer available on the market. We will examine a case with multiple graphics pipelines shortly. For now, notice that one screen was found and that it occupies the 0 place in the array of Screen3Ds.

Quite a bit of information is contained in this simple example. First, let's talk about the reference frames. Recall that we have the eye reference, the head reference, the environment reference, the tracker reference, the tracker base reference, and the screen reference. We also have the coexistence reference, which will be explained in more detail later.

In this case, our goal is to find the location of the eyes relative to the screen because this information can be used to uniquely define the viewing frustum. In this very simple case, tracking is not being used, so we can simplify many of the transformations. Indeed, notice that all the transforms out of the tracker and tracker base reference frames are set to identity (that is, the transforms, TrackerBaseToImagePlate, HeadTrackerToLeftImagePlate, and HeadTrackerToRightImagePlate). In this case, we are only concerned with the TrackerBaseToImagePlate transform because we do not have separate left and right image plates. What this means is that tracker, tracker base, and image plate coordinate systems are all in the same reference frame. Specifying a point in one reference frame is the same as specifying the point in the other.

Next, observe the off-diagonal values in the HeadToHeadTracker transform. There is indeed a small translation specified for the HeadToHeadTracker transformation. This transformation specifies the Y and Z distances of the head to the sensor mounted on the head. As an exercise, you are encouraged to take any of the examples from Chapters 11 or 12 and add the following lines after the PhysicalBody object is created:

```
//create a transform to modify
Transform3D htoht = new Transform3D();
htoht.rotX(Math.PI/16);
htoht.setTranslations(new Vector3d(0.0, .5, 0.0));
body.setHeadToHeadTracker(htoht);
```

A second part of the output from Listing 13.1 to pay attention to is the size of the screens. Screens have both resolution and a physical size. Note that the physical size of the screen can be set to most dimensions.

What would the output look like in a different graphics pipeline? Rerunning this same code on our PC with the dual-head Wildcat card gives

```
Found 2 Screen Device
Win32GraphicsDevice[screen=0]
Win32GraphicsDevice[screen=1]
TrackerBaseToImagePlate:
1.0, 0.0, 0.0, 0.0
0.0, 1.0, 0.0, 0.0
0.0, 0.0, 1.0, 0.0
0.0, 0.0, 0.0, 1.0

HeadTrackerToLeftImagePlate:
1.0, 0.0, 0.0, 0.0
0.0, 1.0, 0.0, 0.0
0.0, 0.0, 1.0, 0.0
0.0, 0.0, 0.0, 1.0

HeadTrackerToRightImagePlate:
1.0, 0.0, 0.0, 0.0
0.0, 1.0, 0.0, 0.0
0.0, 0.0, 1.0, 0.0
0.0, 0.0, 0.0, 1.0

Screen3D[0] = Screen3D: size = (640 x 480),
physical size = (0.180622222222224mm x .135466666666668m)
hashCode = 914691
Screen3D[1] = Screen3D: size = (640 x 480),
physical size = (0.180622222222224mm x .135466666666668m)
hashCode = 11914793

canvases.length: 2
```

In the preceding output listing, you can see that two Canvas3Ds are created and their corresponding Screen3D objects are shown. In this case, the two screens are set at 640x480.

The multiple-screen situation is somewhat more complex, naturally, than the single screen situation. We might have a CAVE or Wedge setup, (as described in Chapter 10, "3D Graphics, Virtual Reality, and Visualization," and the later section, "Building a CAVE or Wedge with Java 3D") or we might have an HMD with a separate screen for each eye. In all these cases, we are faced with different screen sizes and positions relative to the eyes and virtual world. If we want to display a stereoscopic view on the two screens of the HMD, for example, we will need to compute different views corresponding to each eye. In addition, we might want to adjust for different eye separations.

So far, we have kept the head tracker rigidly attached to some point in the physical environment just to keep things simple. The situation becomes *almost* hopelessly complicated when we add head tracking. In the HMD cases, we will want the camera slaved to the tracker so that when we look up we see the environment's ceiling and when we look down we see the environment's floor. To avoid making our subjects sick and to create the most immersive experience, we need the changes to occur with minimal lag. Moreover, calibration becomes important when we leave the non-head tracker environment.

Java 3D view model saves us from having to write a custom viewing engine for every viewing situation. The chain of transforms is quite diverse in all these different cases. That it not to say that an application merely has to set one switch and the head tracker is working. It is still considerably challenging to set up the whole sequence properly. This includes doing some basic calibration and making sure that several transforms and coordinate systems are set. We now describe different transformation series incorporated in to the view model.

Stereo Viewing

As mentioned already, there are a couple of different options for stereo viewing. The first uses so-called shutter glasses that alternate between eyes in sync with the computer monitor. Recall that stereoscopic perceptions require that each eye receives a separate view of the scene. The view must be from a slightly different angle and roughly matched to the separation of the eyes. The distance between an individual's pupils is called the *interocular distance*.

The second way to generate stereoscopic objects and scenes is by having two separate monitors, one for each eye. In this case, no flickering is required. This is exactly how an HMD is set up to work. In essence, each eye has its own little monitor. Again, a slightly different view is needed for each eye, but there is no switching between eyes; both monitors are constantly on.

Listing 13.2 demonstrates how to generate stereo images with Java 3D. There are several issues to keep in mind when setting up the displays for stereo. The first and most frequently encountered problem is that the user has a stereo card that is not supported by Java 3D. One source of confusion arises when the target system has a card that is indeed stereo capable but that is not supported in stereo by Java 3D. Many cards are supported by Java 3D, but some are not. Regardless, this is an important factor to consider, and it is worth investigating a particular card before spending too much time with it.

Otherwise, most of the other challenges are the result of not setting the options correctly. The first procedural rule is to run a stereo program using the command line option

```
-Dj3d.stereo=REQUIRED
```

The second necessary change for setting up stereo is to set the GraphicsConfiguration options in the code itself. In Listing 13.2, take special notice of the following lines:

```
GraphicsConfigTemplate3D g3d = new GraphicsConfigTemplate3D();
g3d.setStereo(GraphicsConfigTemplate3D.REQUIRED);
GraphicsConfiguration gc =
GraphicsEnvironment.getLocalGraphicsEnvironment().
➥        getDefaultScreenDevice().getBestConfiguration(g3d);
```

Finally, the program must set a flag on the Canvas3D object with

```
Canvas3D.setStereoEnable(true)
```

After these steps are taken care of, the application is ready for stereo. The full listing is given in Listing 13.2.

LISTING 13.2   StereoRecipdeJ3D.java

```
import com.sun.j3d.loaders.objectfile.ObjectFile;
import com.sun.j3d.loaders.ParsingErrorException;
import com.sun.j3d.loaders.IncorrectFormatException;
import com.sun.j3d.loaders.Scene;
import java.applet.Applet;
import java.awt.*;
import java.awt.event.*;
import com.sun.j3d.utils.applet.MainFrame;
import com.sun.j3d.utils.universe.*;
import javax.media.j3d.*;
import javax.vecmath.*;
import java.io.*;
import com.sun.j3d.utils.image.TextureLoader;
import com.sun.j3d.utils.behaviors.vp.*;
import com.sun.j3d.utils.geometry.ColorCube;

import java.applet.Applet;
import java.awt.BorderLayout;
import java.awt.event.*;
import java.awt.GraphicsEnvironment;

import java.awt.GraphicsConfiguration;
import com.sun.j3d.utils.applet.MainFrame;
import com.sun.j3d.utils.geometry.Box;
import com.sun.j3d.utils.geometry.Cone;
 import com.sun.j3d.loaders.ParsingErrorException;
import com.sun.j3d.loaders.IncorrectFormatException;
```

LISTING 13.2   Continued

```java
import com.sun.j3d.utils.geometry.Primitive;
import com.sun.j3d.utils.universe.*;
import javax.media.j3d.*;
import javax.vecmath.*;
import com.sun.j3d.utils.behaviors.mouse.MouseRotate;

public class StereoRecipeJ3D extends Applet {
  VirtualUniverse universe;
  Locale locale;
  TransformGroup vpTrans;
  View view;
  Bounds bounds;
  PhysicalBody body;
    public BranchGroup createSceneGraph() {
        // Create the root of the branch graph; this will be returned
        Appearance app = new Appearance();
        BranchGroup objRoot = new BranchGroup();
        TransformGroup geoTG = new TransformGroup();
        geoTG.setCapability(TransformGroup.ALLOW_TRANSFORM_WRITE);
        geoTG.setCapability(TransformGroup.ALLOW_TRANSFORM_READ);

        BoundingSphere bounds =
              new BoundingSphere(new Point3d(0.0,0.0,0.0), 1000.0);
        MouseRotate mouseBeh = new MouseRotate(geoTG);
        geoTG.addChild(mouseBeh);
        mouseBeh.setSchedulingBounds(bounds);

        geoTG.addChild(new ColorCube(2));
        objRoot.addChild(geoTG);

        Color3f blue = new Color3f(0.f, 0.9f, 0.f);
        Vector3f bluedir  = new Vector3f(0.0f, -8.0f, -8.0f);
      Color3f bgColor = new Color3f(0.9f, 0.9f, 0.0f);
        AmbientLight al = new AmbientLight(true, new Color3f(.5f,.5f, .5f));
        DirectionalLight bluelight = new DirectionalLight(blue, bluedir);
        al.setInfluencingBounds(bounds);
        bluelight.setInfluencingBounds(bounds);

        objRoot.addChild(al);
        objRoot.addChild(bluelight);

        return objRoot;
    }

  public BranchGroup createViewGraph() {
        BranchGroup objRoot = new BranchGroup();
```

LISTING 13.2   Continued

```java
        Transform3D t = new Transform3D();
        t.setTranslation(new Vector3f(0.0f, 0.0f,10.0f));
        ViewPlatform vp = new ViewPlatform();
        vpTrans = new TransformGroup();
        vpTrans.setCapability(TransformGroup.ALLOW_TRANSFORM_WRITE);
        vpTrans.setCapability(TransformGroup.ALLOW_TRANSFORM_READ);
        vpTrans.setTransform(t);
        DisparityBehavior db = new DisparityBehavior(body);
        NavigationBehavior nav = new NavigationBehavior(vpTrans);
        vpTrans.addChild(nav);
        nav.setSchedulingBounds(bounds);

        db.setSchedulingBounds(bounds);
        vpTrans.addChild(db);

        vpTrans.addChild(vp);
        view.attachViewPlatform(vp);
        objRoot.addChild(vpTrans);
        return objRoot;

    public StereoRecipeJ3D() {
        setLayout(new BorderLayout());
        GraphicsConfigTemplate3D g3d = new GraphicsConfigTemplate3D();
        g3d.setStereo(GraphicsConfigTemplate3D.REQUIRED);
        GraphicsConfiguration gc =
                GraphicsEnvironment.getLocalGraphicsEnvironment().
                getDefaultScreenDevice().getBestConfiguration(g3d);
        Canvas3D c = new Canvas3D(gc);
        add("Center", c);
        universe = new VirtualUniverse();

        locale = new Locale(universe);
        body = new PhysicalBody();
        PhysicalEnvironment environment = new PhysicalEnvironment();
        view = new View();
        view.setTrackingEnable(true);
        c.setStereoEnable(true);
        System.out.println("stereo enable: " + c.getStereoEnable());
        System.out.println("stereo available: " + c.getStereoAvailable());
        view.addCanvas3D(c);
        view.setPhysicalBody(body);
        view.setPhysicalEnvironment(environment);
        // Create a simple scene and attach it to the virtual universe

        bounds = new BoundingSphere(new Point3d(0.0,0.0,0.0), 100.0);
        BranchGroup scene = createSceneGraph();
```

LISTING 13.2   Continued

```
        BranchGroup vgraph = createViewGraph();
        locale.addBranchGraph(vgraph);
        locale.addBranchGraph(scene);
    }
    //
    //
    public static void main(String[] args) {
        new MainFrame(new StereoRecipeJ3D(), 256, 256);
    }
}
```

Head Tracking and the Sensor Class

At the end of Chapter 12, we introduced the Sensor class as an abstract sensor for all kinds of inputs including buttons, joysticks, and 6DOF devices. We will now focus specifically on 6DOF devices for head tracking.

Recall that a Sensor is a variable length circular buffer of time stamps each with a Transform3D and the state of various buttons. In the head tracking scenario, it is the values of this Transform3D that we want to use to control our view. The reason for maintaining the information in a circular buffer is that this enables some flexibility in choosing which timestamp and data elements to use in assigning the *best approximate* position of whatever device is being monitored. The buffer of SensorReads can also be used in prediction, which is an invaluable technique in tracking systems in general.

The PhysicalBody class contains a specific method for slaving a 6DOF Sensor to the output, rendering the setUserHead() method.

Exploring Head Tracking through the **Virtual6DOF** Class

In order to explore tracking in more detail as well as to make this section accessible to readers without access to a head tracker, we develop a virtual 6 degree of freedom device, Virtual6DOFSensor (see Listing 13.3) and use it to illustrate some basic aspects of using head tracking in Java 3D.

LISTING 13.3   Virtual6DOF.java

```
import javax.media.j3d.*;
import javax.vecmath.*;
import java.awt.*;
import java.awt.event.*;
```

LISTING 13.3   Continued

```java
public class Virtual6DOF implements InputDevice {
    private Vector3f position = new Vector3f();
    private Transform3D newTransform = new Transform3D();

    Sensor sensors[] = new Sensor[1];
    private int processingMode;
    private SensorRead sensorRead = new SensorRead();

    public Virtual6DOF() {
        processingMode = InputDevice.BLOCKING;
    sensors[0] = new Sensor(this);
        TransformGroup tg = new TransformGroup();
        this.outsideTG = tg;
    }
    public void close() {
    }

    public int getProcessingMode() {
        return processingMode;
    }

    public int getSensorCount() {
    return sensors.length;
    }

    public Sensor getSensor( int sensorIndex ) {
    return sensors[sensorIndex];
    }

    public boolean initialize() {
    return true;
    }

    public void pollAndProcessInput() {
      sensorRead.setTime( System.currentTimeMillis() );
      sensorRead.set(newTransform);
      sensors[0].setNextSensorRead(sensorRead);
    }

    public void processStreamInput() {
    }

    public void setNominalPositionAndOrientation() {
        sensorRead.setTime( System.currentTimeMillis() );
```

LISTING 13.3 Continued

```
        //setting noimalPosition and Orientation to identity
        sensorRead.set( new Transform3D());
        sensors[0].setNextSensorRead( sensorRead );
    }

public void setRotationX() {
        sensorRead.get(newTransform);
        Transform3D t = new Transform3D();
        t.rotX(Math.PI/36);
        newTransform.mul(t);
    }

    public void setRotationY() {
        sensorRead.get(newTransform);
        Transform3D t = new Transform3D();
        t.rotY(Math.PI/36);
        newTransform.mul(t);
    }

    public void setRotationZ() {
        sensorRead.get(newTransform);
        Transform3D t = new Transform3D();
        t.rotZ(Math.PI/36);
        newTransform.mul(t);
    }

public void setTranslationX() {
        sensorRead.get(newTransform);
        Transform3D t = new Transform3D();
        t.setTranslation(new Vector3d(0.1, 0.0,0.0));
        newTransform.mul(t);
    }

    public void setTranslationY() {
        sensorRead.get(newTransform);
        Transform3D t = new Transform3D();
        t.setTranslation(new Vector3d(0.0, 0.1,0.0));
        t.rotY(Math.PI/36);
        newTransform.mul(t);
    }

    public void setTranslationZ() {
        sensorRead.get(newTransform);
        Transform3D t = new Transform3D();
        t.setTranslation(new Vector3d(0.0, 0.0,0.1));
```

LISTING 13.3 Continued

```
        newTransform.mul(t);
    }

public void setProcessingMode( int mode ) {
        switch(mode) {
            case InputDevice.DEMAND_DRIVEN:
            case InputDevice.NON_BLOCKING:
            case InputDevice.BLOCKING:
                processingMode = mode;
            break;
            default:
                throw new IllegalArgumentException("Processing mode must " +
                        "be one of DEMAND_DRIVEN, NON_BLOCKING, or BLOCKING");
        }
    }

}
```

Note that once this device is registered with the PhyscialEnvironment object, as in the excerpt from the SimulatedHeadTracking.java application shown in Listing 13.4, it is polled continuously by the Java 3D rendering thread. Each time the renderer loops, it calls the pollAndProcessInput() method of the Sensor object. Within the pollAndProcessInput() method, we have put the appropriate code for setting the transform and updating the timestamp.

LISTING 13.4 SimulatedHeadTracking.java

```
import java.awt.Frame;
import java.awt.Panel;
import java.awt.BorderLayout;
import java.awt.GraphicsEnvironment;
import java.awt.GraphicsDevice;
import java.awt.GraphicsConfiguration;
import java.awt.event.*;
import com.sun.j3d.utils.universe.*;
import com.sun.j3d.utils.geometry.ColorCube;
import javax.media.j3d.*;
import javax.vecmath.*;
import com.sun.j3d.utils.behaviors.mouse.MouseRotate;
import com.mnstarfire.loaders3d.Loader3DS;
//import com.mnstarfire.loaders3d.Loader3DS;

import java.applet.*;
//import com.sun.j3d.*;
```

LISTING 13.4 Continued

```java
import com.sun.j3d.utils.applet.*;
import java.awt.*;

import java.io.*;
public class SimulatedHeadTracking extends Applet {
    PhysicalBody body;
    PhysicalEnvironment environment;
    View view;
    Locale locale;
    public BranchGroup createSceneGraph() {
        // Create the root of the subgraph
        BranchGroup objRoot = new BranchGroup();
        // Create the transform group node and initialize it to the identity.
        // Enable the TRANSFORM_WRITE capability so that our behavior code
        // can modify it at runtime.  Add it to the root of the subgraph.
        TransformGroup objTrans = new TransformGroup();
        objTrans.setCapability(TransformGroup.ALLOW_TRANSFORM_WRITE);
        objTrans.setCapability(TransformGroup.ALLOW_TRANSFORM_READ);
        objRoot.addChild(objTrans);
        Bounds bounds =
            new BoundingSphere(new Point3d(0.0,0.0,0.0), 1000.0);

        //Create a 20cm wide cube spaning -10cm .. +10cm about the virtual
        // world origin.
        objTrans.addChild(new ColorCube(0.10));
        // Create a new Behavior object that will perform the desired
        objRoot.compile();
        return objRoot;
    }
    public BranchGroup createViewGraph() {
        BranchGroup objRoot = new BranchGroup();
        Transform3D t = new Transform3D();
        t.setTranslation(new Vector3f(0.0f, 0.0f,0.0f));
        ViewPlatform vp = new ViewPlatform();
        TransformGroup vpTrans = new TransformGroup();
        vpTrans.setCapability(TransformGroup.ALLOW_TRANSFORM_WRITE);
        vpTrans.setCapability(TransformGroup.ALLOW_TRANSFORM_READ);
        vpTrans.setTransform(t);
        vpTrans.addChild(vp);
        view.attachViewPlatform(vp);
        Bounds bounds = new BoundingSphere(new Point3d(0.0,0.0,0.0), 1000.0);
        NavigationBehavior nav = new NavigationBehavior(vpTrans);
        vpTrans.addChild(nav);
        nav.setSchedulingBounds(bounds);
```

LISTING 13.4   Continued

```java
            objRoot.addChild(vpTrans);
            return objRoot;


    }

    public SimulatedHeadTracking() {
        // Create a simple scene and attach it to the virtual universe
        BranchGroup scene = createSceneGraph();
        // SimpleUniverse u = new SimpleUniverse(canvases[0]);
    setLayout(new BorderLayout());
        GraphicsConfigTemplate3D g3d = new GraphicsConfigTemplate3D();
        GraphicsConfiguration gc =
                    GraphicsEnvironment.getLocalGraphicsEnvironment().
                    getDefaultScreenDevice().getBestConfiguration(g3d);
    Canvas3D c = new Canvas3D(gc);
    add("Center", c);
        // This will move the ViewPlatform back a bit so the
        // objects in the scene can be viewed.
        //View view = u.getViewer().getView();
        VirtualUniverse universe = new VirtualUniverse();
        Bounds bounds = new BoundingSphere(new Point3d(0.0,0.0,0.0), 1000.0);
        Locale locale = new Locale(universe);
        body = new PhysicalBody();
        environment = new PhysicalEnvironment();

        Virtual6DOF tracker = new Virtual6DOF();
        tracker.initialize();
        environment.addInputDevice(tracker);

        Transform3D ctotb = new Transform3D();
        environment.getCoexistenceToTrackerBase(ctotb);
        //the following command makes environment call pollAndProcessInput()
        environment.setSensor(0,tracker.getSensor(0));
        environment.setHeadIndex(0);

        //   environment.setSensor(0,v6dof.getSensor(0));
    //   environment.setHeadIndex(0);
        view = new View();
        view.setPhysicalBody(body);
        view.setPhysicalEnvironment(environment);

        view.setViewPolicy(View.HMD_VIEW);
        view.setTrackingEnable(true);
            // Attach the new canvas to the view
➥c.setMonoscopicViewPolicy(View.LEFT_EYE_VIEW); view.addCanvas3D(c);
```

LISTING 13.4   Continued

```
        // With HMD_VIEW, coexistence coordinates in the physical world are
        // mapped exactly to view platform coordinates in the virtual world
        // except for scale.  To verify the image plate calibration, let's
        // set the scale to 1.0 so that objects in the virtual world are the
        // same size as objects in the physical world.
        view.setScreenScalePolicy(View.SCALE_EXPLICIT);
        view.setScreenScale(1.0);

        // Neither HeadToHeadTracker, CoexistenceToTrackerBase, nor the
        // initial head sensor read (from head tracker to tracker base) have
        // been set from their identity defaults.  We've set a unity screen
        // scale so that coexistence coordinates to view platform coordinates
        // is identity as well.
        //
        // This means that the initial view has view platform coordinates
        // equal to head coordinates.  Move the view platform in the virtual
        // world back by the focal plane distance of the HMD + 10cm so that
        // the front face of a 20cm wide cube centered about the virtual
        // world origin lies on the focal plane of the HMD screen image.  If
        // the HMD image plate calibration is correct then the cube image
        // will appear to be 20cm wide.
        BranchGroup vgraph = createViewGraph();
        Transform3D t = new Transform3D();
        t.setTranslation(new Vector3f(0.0f, 0.0f, 0.9144f + 0.10f));

      Set6DOFBehavior set6dof = new Set6DOFBehavior(tracker);
       vgraph.addChild(set6dof);
       set6dof.setSchedulingBounds(bounds);

       view.setBackClipDistance(80.0);
       locale.addBranchGraph(vgraph);
      locale.addBranchGraph(scene);
      //u.addBranchGraph(scene);
    }
   public static void main(String[] args) {
     new MainFrame(new SimulatedHeadTracking(), 256, 256);

   }
}
```

Finally, in order to invoke changes in our simulated 6DOF device, we include a Behavior,
Set6DOFBehavior.java (see Listing 13.5), that listens for key events (pressing X, Y, Z) and
changes the SensorRead Transform3D accordingly. This Behavior takes the place of a driver
that would be used in a real tracking environment. The use of such a driver is demonstrated in
the next section, "Real Head Tracking Example."

LISTING 13.5   Set6DOFBehavior.java

```java
import java.awt.AWTEvent;
import java.awt.event.*;
import javax.media.j3d.*;
import java.util.*;
import javax.vecmath.*;

public class Set6DOFBehavior extends Behavior {
   Virtual6DOF v6dof;
   private WakeupCondition keyCriterion;
   public Set6DOFBehavior(Virtual6DOF v6dof) {
     this.v6dof = v6dof;
    }

   public void initialize() {
   //wakeupOn( conditions );
      System.out.println("Set6DOFBehavior initialize");
      WakeupCriterion[] keyEvents = new WakeupCriterion[2];
      keyEvents[0] = new WakeupOnAWTEvent( KeyEvent.KEY_PRESSED );
      keyEvents[1] = new WakeupOnAWTEvent( KeyEvent.KEY_RELEASED );
      keyCriterion = new WakeupOr( keyEvents );
      wakeupOn( keyCriterion );
}

   public void processStimulus( Enumeration criteria ) {
      // System.out.println("processStimulus");
      WakeupCriterion wakeup;
      AWTEvent[] event;
      while( criteria.hasMoreElements() ) {
      wakeup = (WakeupCriterion) criteria.nextElement();
      if( !(wakeup instanceof WakeupOnAWTEvent) )
       continue;

      event = ((WakeupOnAWTEvent)wakeup).getAWTEvent();
      for( int i = 0; i < event.length; i++ ) {
         processKeyEvent((KeyEvent)event[i]);
      }

   }
   wakeupOn( keyCriterion );

 }

protected void processKeyEvent(KeyEvent event) {
    int keycode = event.getKeyCode();
 // System.out.println("what: " + (.getID());
        if (keycode == KeyEvent.VK_X) {
```

LISTING 13.5   Continued

```
        v6dof.setRotationX();
    }
    else if (keycode == KeyEvent.VK_Y) {
      v6dof.setRotationY();
    }
    else if (keycode == KeyEvent.VK_Z) {
      v6dof.setRotationZ();
    }
  }
}
```

Figure 13.2 shows a screen shot from the `SimulatedHeadTracking.java` example. The program sets up a situation analogous to having the cyborg's head attached to a single camera. Moving the remoted user's head (in this case using keystrokes) is akin to having the robot's camera mounted to a motorized tripod bevel.

FIGURE 13.2

Screen shot from `SimulatedHeadTracking` *example.*

Real Head Tracking Example

The first challenge to overcome in developing a Sensor for head tracking is in reading the data values correctly. Remember that we want our Sensor to contain two things; time stamps and a Transform3D. Our tracker, in the case of this example, is a Polhemus Fastrack that provides six values each time it is polled. The data values for each read correspond to x, y, z, pitch, roll, and yaw. We need to store these values in a Transform3D within the Sensor. Putting the data in the Transform3D is done by instantiating a new Transform3D object. The new Transform3D is an identity matrix. We can therefore rotate, multiply, and translate the matrix directly without inverting it. We will return to the development of the Sensor class after digressing a little to discuss the general challenge of setting up head tracking.

Preparing for Head Tracking

Before getting too frustrated trying to set up tracking, it is wise to remember that tracking is difficult work. It is difficult to know which way is up (or left or in front, for that matter).

Some general recommendations regarding tracking are now provided followed by a specific example of reading data on the serial port.

- Test your tracker *completely outside of Java*. This simple rule is so often over looked, yet it can save days or even weeks of work in debugging.
- Understand which of the two choices of transform chain you are working with.
- Do be frustrated if you cannot see anything on the screen or the objects look strange when you first run your application. Make sure that you have a way to move around the scene to try to find your objects.

Reading the Values

The example in Listing 13.6 uses the Java Comm API to read the serial port. It is worth the effort to guarantee to yourself (and your boss) that you are getting reasonable values from the serial port read before moving on to slaving the view to the tracker values. Indeed, it is impossible to do tracking any other way. We cannot overemphasize this point enough because starting at the very beginning and testing at every point along the way is what everyone does eventually.

Listing 13.6 shows the extension of the InputDevice interface for reading the Polhemus Fastrak.

13

LISTING 13.6   FastTracInputDevice.java

```java
import javax.media.j3d.*;
import javax.vecmath.*;

public class FastrakInputDevice implements InputDevice {
    private FastrakDriver polhemus;
    private Sensor [] polhemusSensor;
    private SensorRead [] polhemusSensorRead;

    private Transform3D [] initPosTransform;
    private Transform3D [] initOriTransform;

    private int polhemusActiveReceivers;
    private Transform3D polhemusTransform = new Transform3D();
    private float [] polhemusPos = new float[3];
    private float [] polhemusOri = new float[3];

    private Transform3D posTransform = new Transform3D();
    private Transform3D oriTransform = new Transform3D();
    private Vector3f posVector = new Vector3f();
    private Transform3D trans = new Transform3D();

    private float sensitivity = 1.0f;
    private float angularRate = 1.0f;
    private float x, y, z;

    int ii=0;
        public FastrakInputDevice(FastrakDriver polhemus)
    {
        //System.out.println("FastrakInputDevice constructor");
                this.polhemus = polhemus;
        polhemusActiveReceivers = polhemus.getActiveReceivers();
        polhemusSensor     = new Sensor[polhemusActiveReceivers];
        polhemusSensorRead = new SensorRead[polhemusActiveReceivers];
        initPosTransform = new Transform3D[polhemusActiveReceivers];
        initOriTransform = new Transform3D[polhemusActiveReceivers];
                for (int n=0; n<polhemusActiveReceivers; n++)
        {
            polhemusSensor[n] = new Sensor(this);
            polhemusSensorRead[n] = new SensorRead();
            initPosTransform[n] = new Transform3D();
            initOriTransform[n] = new Transform3D();
            try {
               polhemus.readData();
               // System.out.println("readData on polhemus from InputDevice");
            } catch( Exception e ) {
```

LISTING 13.6   Continued

```java
                System.err.println( "PID: " + e.toString() );
        }
         getPositionTransform( n+1, initPosTransform[n] );
         getOrientationTransform( n+1, initOriTransform[n] );
    }
    setSensitivity(0.1f);
    setAngularRate(0.01f);
}

public boolean initialize()
{
    for (int i=0; i<3; i++)
    {
        polhemusPos[i] = 0.0f;
        polhemusOri[i] = 0.0f;
    }
    return true;
}

public void close()
{
}

public int getProcessingMode()
{
    return DEMAND_DRIVEN;
}

public int getSensorCount()
{
    return polhemusActiveReceivers;
}

public Sensor getSensor( int id )
{
    return polhemusSensor[id];
}

public void setProcessingMode(int mode)
{
}

public void getPositionTransform(int n, Transform3D posTrans)
{
        //  System.out.println("getPositionTransform()");
          polhemusPos = polhemus.getLocation(n);
```

LISTING 13.6 Continued

```java
            posVector.x = polhemusPos[0];
            posVector.y = polhemusPos[1];
            posVector.z = polhemusPos[2];
             posTrans.setIdentity();
             posTrans.setTranslation(posVector);
    }

    public void getOrientationTransform(int n, Transform3D oriTrans)
    {
        //System.out.println("getOrientationTransform()");
                polhemusOri = polhemus.getRotation(n);
         oriTrans.setIdentity();
         // Fastrak gives azimuth, elevation and roll, which
             // do not translate to Java3D X, Y and Z directly, so
        // some assembly is required. Glue included.
         trans.setIdentity();
        trans.rotY(-Math.toRadians((double)polhemusOri[0]));
         //  System.out.println("polhemusOri[0]: "
             + (double)polhemusOri[0]);
        oriTrans.mul(trans);
                trans.setIdentity();
        trans.rotX(Math.toRadians((double)polhemusOri[1]));
        oriTrans.mul(trans);
                trans.setIdentity();
        trans.rotZ(-Math.toRadians((double)polhemusOri[2]));
         //    System.out.println("polhemusOri[2]: " +
                (double)polhemusOri[2]);
            oriTrans.mul(trans);
    }

    public void pollAndProcessInput() {
                ii++;
          // System.out.println("pollAndProcessInput; interation: " + ii);
                try
        {
            polhemus.readData();
        }
        catch( Exception e )
        {
            System.err.println( "PID: " + e.toString() );
        }
        for (int n=0; n<polhemusActiveReceivers; n++) {
                //System.out.println("setting polhemus xform");
                polhemusSensorRead[n].setTime(System.currentTimeMillis());
            getPositionTransform(n, posTransform);
            getOrientationTransform(n, oriTransform);
```

LISTING 13.6   Continued

```java
                polhemusTransform.setIdentity();
                polhemusTransform.mulInverse(initOriTransform[n]);
                polhemusTransform.mul(oriTransform);
                Vector3d translation = new Vector3d();
                posTransform.get( translation );
                translation.scale( (double)sensitivity );
                polhemusTransform.setTranslation( translation );

                polhemusSensorRead[n].set(polhemusTransform);
                polhemusSensor[n].setNextSensorRead(polhemusSensorRead[n]);
        }
    }

    public void processStreamInput()
    {
    }

    public void setNominalPositionAndOrientation() {
        initialize();
        for (int n=0; n<polhemusActiveReceivers; n++) {
            polhemusSensorRead[n].setTime(System.currentTimeMillis());
            polhemusTransform.setIdentity();
            polhemusSensorRead[n].set(polhemusTransform);
            polhemusSensor[n].setNextSensorRead(polhemusSensorRead[n]);
        }
    }

    public void setSensitivity(float value)
    {
        sensitivity = value;
    }

    public float getSensitivity() {
        return sensitivity;
    }

    public void setAngularRate(float value) {
        angularRate = value;
    }

    public float getAngularRate() {
        return angularRate;
    }
}
```

The `Sensor` objects that are written for this class must generate values that transform the local tracker coordinates to the tracker base coordinates. Remember that the tracker base corresponds to a point in the physical world. The tracker base is a receiver/transmitter attached somewhere in the room.

Head Tracking Scenarios

Now that you can read the values and set the tracker to the tracker base transform, it is time to tell the renderer how to deal with this situation. There are two basic setups in which head tracking is used. The first setup is *attached*, in which the screens are attached to the user's head and therefore the reference frame of the screens is that of the tracker itself. The attached configuration is the correct one to use with an HMD. The second setup is called *non-attached* and pertains to the situation in which the screen(s) are attached rigidly to the reference frame of the physical environment.

These two situations are handled differently by the Java 3D renderer.

One tip for setting up both head tracking situations is to use a `ViewAttachPolicy` of `NOMINAL_SCREEN`. This is because with `NOMINAL_SCREEN`, the tracker is mapped directly onto the virtual world (again, except for scaling). When in `HMD_VIEW` mode, the `ViewAttachPolicy` is automatically `NOMINAL_SCREEN`. Note that it is also possible to set the `ViewAttachPolicy` as `NOMINAL_SCREEN` when in `SCREEN_VIEW` mode as well, thus also gaining the same simplifying benefits of having tracker coordinates being the same as virtual coordinates. That might seem a little counterintuitive to those of you who have used a different view model. Having the tracker mapped to the virtual world makes the coexistence coordinates pretty straightforward. Simply set the coexistence relative to the tracker base such that the origin of coexistence is directly in front of the user's nominal front facing direction (looking straight toward -Z with +Y pointing up toward the ceiling).

Note that when head tracking is enabled AND we are NOT in `HMD_VIEW` mode, the `setCoexistenceCenteringEnable` flag should be set to `false` because by definition coexistence centering is only appropriate when the `trackerBaseToImagePlate` transform is set to the identity matrix.

Beginning with the case of the HMD and moving on to the FishTank VR, we now show in more detail the head tracking necessary steps for using tracking with the Java 3D view model.

Transforms and Settings for an HMD

As we said previously, the HMD is an attached device. Because it is attached, we really just need to slave the camera object to the tracker. This is just as we imagined in one of our robot examples. In this case, the coexistence coordinates in the physical world correspond exactly to view platform coordinates in the virtual world (with the exception of scale). In other words, if you rotate the head tracker—90° in the x direction for example—you get the same rotation of the view platform.

The remaining challenge is to scale the screens appropriately. This requires getting out the manual for your HMD and looking up some numbers. The HMD used in our lab is a Virtual Research V8. The relevant numbers for this particular HMD specify 60° diagonal field of view, focal plane of 3ft, 100% overlap between right/left images, and a 4:3 aspect ratio. In addition, the *apparent* screen width is 0.8447 and the height is .6335. Again, these are apparent values because they are derived from the optics and are only meaningful when considered relative to the head. This can be confusing because the Screen3D asks for the physical width, height, and position. But really the only parameters that make any sense to apply to a Screen3D are the virtual size and position of the screen images as projected by the HMD optics onto the physical screen.

The approximate transformation from head to image plate is .4223 x, .3168 y, and .9144 z. These values are set in main().

Also, note that because there is 100% overlap in the screen images in the case of the V8, the same head tracker to image plate transformation can be used for both the left and right eyes. However, in many cases this is not true. Be prepared to set these values separately in some situations.

Note that the program in Listing 13.7 will not run properly on your machine unless you have at least two graphics pipelines. On a PC, this can be achieved through a dual head graphics card or a single head AGP with a single head PCI. Multiple PCI cards can work as well, but the bus becomes overcrowded with multiple pipes. Sun and SGI machines typically have multiple pipes. The situation for PCs is likely to change in the near future as more multiple pipe options enter the market.

We have shown the HMD program using our Virtual6DOF as the tracker. However, if you do have access to the 6 DOF tracker, you can add it as we have done shown in commented form. Just remove the comments and run it with your tracker.

LISTING 13.7   BasicHMDSetup.java

```java
import java.awt.Frame;
import java.awt.Panel;
import java.awt.BorderLayout;
import java.awt.GraphicsEnvironment;
import java.awt.GraphicsDevice;
import java.awt.GraphicsConfiguration;
import java.awt.event.*;
import com.sun.j3d.utils.universe.*;
import com.sun.j3d.utils.geometry.ColorCube;
import javax.media.j3d.*;
import javax.vecmath.*;
import com.sun.j3d.utils.behaviors.mouse.MouseRotate;
```

LISTING 13.7   Continued

```
public class BasicHMDSetup {
    PhysicalBody body;
    PhysicalEnvironment environment;
    View view;
    Locale locale;
    public BranchGroup createSceneGraph() {
        // Create the root of the subgraph
        BranchGroup objRoot = new BranchGroup();
        TransformGroup objTrans = new TransformGroup();
        objTrans.setCapability(TransformGroup.ALLOW_TRANSFORM_WRITE);
        objTrans.setCapability(TransformGroup.ALLOW_TRANSFORM_READ);
        objRoot.addChild(objTrans);
        Create a 20cm wide cube spanning -10cm ..
           +10cm about the virtual  world origin.
         objTrans.addChild(new ColorCube(0.10));
         Bounds bounds =
             new BoundingSphere(new Point3d(0.0,0.0,0.0), 1000.0);
         MouseRotate mouseBeh = new MouseRotate(objTrans);
        objTrans.addChild(mouseBeh);
         mouseBeh.setSchedulingBounds(bounds);
        objRoot.compile();

        return objRoot;
    }

    public BasicHMDSetup(Canvas3D[] canvases) {
        BranchGroup scene = createSceneGraph();
        BranchGroup vgraph = new BranchGroup();
         VirtualUniverse universe = new VirtualUniverse();
         Bounds bounds =
             new BoundingSphere(new Point3d(0.0,0.0,0.0), 1000.0);
         Locale locale = new Locale(universe);
         body = new PhysicalBody();
         environment = new PhysicalEnvironment();
     /* Uncomment this section to use the actual Fastrak Driver
        FastrakDriver polhemus = new FastrakDriver();
         System.out.println( "Fastrak opened--" );
      try {
        polhemus.initialize();
          }
     catch( Exception e )
     {
         System.err.println( e.toString() +
                             "\nError initializing Fastrak, exiting... " );
         System.exit(0);
     }
```

LISTING 13.7   Continued

```
    tracker = new FastrakInputDevice( polhemus );
    tracker.initialize();

        tracker.setSensitivity(1.175f );
*/

        Virtual6DOF tracker = new Virtual6DOF();
        tracker.initialize();
        environment.addInputDevice(tracker);
        environment.setSensor(0,v6dof.getSensor(0));
        environment.setHeadIndex(0);

        view = new View();
        view.setPhysicalBody(body);
        view.setPhysicalEnvironment(environment);
        view.setViewPolicy(View.HMD_VIEW);
        view.setTrackingEnable(true);

        System.out.println("canvases.length: " + canvases.length);
        for (int i = 0; i < canvases.length; i++) {
            // Attach the new canvas to the view
            view.addCanvas3D(canvases[i]);
        }

    // With HMD_VIEW, coexistence coordinates in the physical world are
    // mapped exactly to view platform coordinates in the virtual world
    // except for scale.  To verify the image plate calibration, let's
    // set the scale to 1.0 so that objects in the virtual world are the
    // same size as objects in the physical world.
    view.setScreenScalePolicy(View.SCALE_EXPLICIT);
    view.setScreenScale(1.0);

    // Neither HeadToHeadTracker, CoexistenceToTrackerBase, nor the
    // initial head sensor read (from head tracker to tracker base) have
    // been set from their identity defaults.  We've set a unity screen
    // scale so that coexistence coordinates to view platform coordinates
    // is identity as well.
    //
    // This means that the initial view has view platform coordinates
    // equal to head coordinates.  Move the view platform in the virtual
    // world back by the focal plane distance of the HMD + 10cm so that
    // the front face of a 20cm wide cube centered about the virtual
    // world origin lies on the focal plane of the HMD screen image.  If
    // the HMD image plate calibration is correct then the cube image
    // will appear to be 20cm wide.
    Transform3D t = new Transform3D();
```

LISTING 13.7 Continued

```java
        t.setTranslation(new Vector3f(0.0f, 0.0f, 0.9144f + 0.10f));
        ViewPlatform vp = new ViewPlatform();
        TransformGroup vpTrans = new TransformGroup();
        vpTrans.setCapability(TransformGroup.ALLOW_TRANSFORM_WRITE);
        vpTrans.setCapability(TransformGroup.ALLOW_TRANSFORM_READ);
        vpTrans.setTransform(t);
        vpTrans.addChild(vp);
        Set6DOFBehavior set6dof = new Set6DOFBehavior(v6dof);
        vpTrans.addChild(set6dof);
        set6dof.setSchedulingBounds(bounds);

        NavigationBehavior nav = new NavigationBehavior(vpTrans);
        nav.setSchedulingBounds(bounds);
        vpTrans.addChild(nav);
        view.attachViewPlatform(vp);

        vgraph.addChild(vpTrans);
        locale.addBranchGraph(vgraph);
        locale.addBranchGraph(scene);
        //u.addBranchGraph(scene);
    }


    public static void main(String[] args) {
        int nScreens = 2;
        if (args.length > 0) {
            try {
                nScreens = Integer.parseInt(args[0]);
            }
            catch (NumberFormatException e) {
                System.out.println("Usage: java MultiScreens [#screens]");
                System.exit(1);
            }
        }

        int i;
        GraphicsDevice[] graphicsDevices = GraphicsEnvironment.
            getLocalGraphicsEnvironment().getScreenDevices();
        System.out.println("Found " + graphicsDevices.length +
                        " screen devices");
        for (i = 0; i < graphicsDevices.length; i++)
            System.out.println(graphicsDevices[i]);
        System.out.println();
        GraphicsConfigTemplate3D template;
        GraphicsConfiguration gConfig;
        Screen3D[] screens = new Screen3D[nScreens];
```

LISTING 13.7   Continued

```java
Canvas3D[] canvases = new Canvas3D[nScreens];
Frame[] frames = new Frame[nScreens];
Panel[] panels = new Panel[nScreens];
java.awt.Rectangle bounds;
template = new GraphicsConfigTemplate3D();

for (i = 0; i < nScreens; i++) {
    gConfig = graphicsDevices[i].getBestConfiguration(template);
    bounds = gConfig.getBounds();
    canvases[i] = new Canvas3D(gConfig);
    // Gotta do this for the new focus model in JDK 1.4, otherwise
    // full screen windows won't get keyboard focus.
    canvases[i].setFocusable(true);
    screens[i] = canvases[i].getScreen3D();
    System.out.println("Screen3D[" + i + "] = " + screens[i]);
    System.out.println("    hashCode = " + screens[i].hashCode());
    panels[i] = new Panel();
    panels[i].setLayout(new BorderLayout());
    panels[i].add("Center", canvases[i]);

    frames[i] = new Frame(gConfig);
    frames[i].setLocation(bounds.x, bounds.y);

    // Set to the full screen size with no borders.
    frames[i].setSize(bounds.width, bounds.height);
    frames[i].setUndecorated(true);
    frames[i].setLayout(new BorderLayout());
    frames[i].setTitle("Canvas " + (i+1));
    frames[i].add("Center", panels[i]);
    frames[i].addWindowListener(new WindowAdapter() {
        public void windowClosing(WindowEvent winEvent) {
            System.exit(0);
        }
    });
}

//
// HMD image plate calibration.  Assume 2-channel input, 60 degree
// diagonal field of view, focal plane at 3ft, 100% overlap between
// right/left images, 4:3 aspect ratio.
//
canvases[0].setMonoscopicViewPolicy(View.RIGHT_EYE_VIEW);
// Apparent screen width and height in meters at focal plane.
screens[0].setPhysicalScreenWidth(0.8447);
screens[0].setPhysicalScreenHeight(0.6335);
```

LISTING 13.7   Continued

```
        // Transform from head coordinates to apparent image plate location.
        Transform3D headToImagePlate = new Transform3D();
        headToImagePlate.set(new Vector3d(0.4223, 0.3168, 0.9144));
        // Use headToImagePlate for now, assuming HeadToHeadTracker is I.
        screens[0].setHeadTrackerToRightImagePlate(headToImagePlate);
        // Same for left eye view.  The apparent screen size is the same and
        // there is 100% overlap with the right eye view, so the same
        // head tracker to image plate transform can be used.
        canvases[1].setMonoscopicViewPolicy(View.LEFT_EYE_VIEW);
        screens[1].setPhysicalScreenWidth(0.8447);
        screens[1].setPhysicalScreenHeight(0.6335);
        screens[1].setHeadTrackerToLeftImagePlate(headToImagePlate);

        new MultiScreens(canvases);
        for (i = 0; i < nScreens; i++) {
            frames[i].setVisible(true);
        }
    }
}
```

FishTank VR Example

As we said, FishTank VR is a term for a head tracked VR system that uses stereo but that, unlike the HMD setup, has the screen fixed in the room and not in to the user's head.

The next step is to set the position and orientation of each screen to the tracker base. In the nonattached mode, this is accomplished through the setTrackerBaseToImagePlate method of Screen3D (accessed from Canvas3D). The orientation position of each screen is thus *indirectly* mapped to coexistence through the CoexistenceToTrackerBase transform.

Finally, the user must set the location and orientation of the center of coexistence relative to the tracker base using the setCoexistenceToTrackerBase() method of the PhysicalEnvironment method. The center of coexistence locates the center of the nominal screen. For one, three, or five screens, set this to the center of the middle screen. For two screens this center point would be the middle edge.

Yet another setting that must be considered is the CoexistenceCenteringEnable() method of the View object. This flag is set to true by default, but this is not appropriate for head tracking. When this flag is set, the center of coexistence is set to the middle of the screen and assumes that trackerBaseToImagePlate and coexistenceToTrackerBase are both identity, which is also not correct for head tracking. Therefore, in the head tracking situation, the setCoexistenceCenteringEnable() method must be called with the argument set to false.

Listing 13.8 is code for use in a Fishtank VR setup.

LISTING 13.8   FishTankVR.java

```java
import java.awt.Frame;
import java.awt.Panel;
import java.awt.BorderLayout;
import java.awt.GraphicsEnvironment;
import java.awt.GraphicsDevice;
import java.awt.GraphicsConfiguration;
import java.awt.event.*;
import com.sun.j3d.utils.universe.*;
import com.sun.j3d.utils.geometry.ColorCube;
import javax.media.j3d.*;
import javax.vecmath.*;
import java.awt.BorderLayout;
import java.applet.Applet;
import com.sun.j3d.utils.behaviors.mouse.MouseRotate;
//import com.mnstarfire.loaders3d.Loader3DS;

import java.applet.*;
//import com.sun.j3d.*;
import com.sun.j3d.utils.applet.*;
import java.awt.*;

import java.io.*;
public class FishTank extends Applet {
    PhysicalBody body;
    PhysicalEnvironment environment;
    View view;
    Locale locale;
  FastrakInputDevice tracker;
  // static final String filename = "C:\\Cyclotron\\cyclotron.3ds";
  public BranchGroup createSceneGraph() {
      // Create the root of the subgraph
      BranchGroup objRoot = new BranchGroup();
      // Create the transform group node and initialize it to the identity.
      // Enable the TRANSFORM_WRITE capability so that our behavior code
      // can modify it at runtime.  Add it to the root of the subgraph.
      TransformGroup objTrans = new TransformGroup();
      objTrans.setCapability(TransformGroup.ALLOW_TRANSFORM_WRITE);
      objTrans.setCapability(TransformGroup.ALLOW_TRANSFORM_READ);
      objRoot.addChild(objTrans);

      // Create a 20cm wide cube spanning -10cm .. +10cm about the virtual
      // world origin.
      objTrans.addChild(new ColorCube(0.10));
      // Create a new Behavior object that will perform the desired
      // operation on the specified transform object and add it into the
      // scene graph.
```

LISTING 13.8   Continued

```java
            Bounds bounds =
                new BoundingSphere(new Point3d(0.0,0.0,0.0), 1000.0);
            MouseRotate mouseBeh = new MouseRotate(objTrans);
        objTrans.addChild(mouseBeh);
        mouseBeh.setSchedulingBounds(bounds);
        // Have Java 3D perform optimizations on this scene graph.
        objRoot.compile();

        return objRoot;
    }


    public FishTank() {
        // Create a simple scene and attach it to the virtual universe
        System.out.println("FISH TANK");
        BranchGroup scene = createSceneGraph();
       // SimpleUniverse u = new SimpleUniverse(canvases[0]);
        // This will move the ViewPlatform back a bit so the
        // objects in the scene can be viewed.
        //u.getViewingPlatform().setNominalViewingTransform();
        //View view = u.getViewer().getView();
        setLayout(new BorderLayout());
        GraphicsConfigTemplate3D g3d = new GraphicsConfigTemplate3D();
        g3d.setStereo(GraphicsConfigTemplate3D.REQUIRED);
        GraphicsConfiguration gc =
                GraphicsEnvironment.getLocalGraphicsEnvironment().
                    getDefaultScreenDevice().getBestConfiguration(g3d);
        Canvas3D c = new Canvas3D(gc);
        Screen3D screen = c.getScreen3D();
        screen.setPhysicalScreenWidth(.350);
        screen.setPhysicalScreenHeight(.245);

        Transform3D t = new Transform3D();
        t.setTranslation(new Vector3d(.175, .0845, .020));
        screen.setTrackerBaseToImagePlate(t);
        c.setStereoEnable(true);
    add("Center", c);

      //   c.setStereoEnable(true);
        BranchGroup vgraph = new BranchGroup();
        VirtualUniverse universe = new VirtualUniverse();
        Bounds bounds =
                new BoundingSphere(new Point3d(0.0,0.0,0.0), 1000.0);
        Locale locale = new Locale(universe);
        body = new PhysicalBody();
        t.setIdentity();
```

LISTING 13.8   Continued

```
        // t.setTranslation(new Vector3d(0.0, 0.02, 0.18));
        // body.setHeadToHeadTracker(t);

         environment = new PhysicalEnvironment();
        // t.setIdentity();
        // t.setTranslation(new Vector3d(0.0, -0.22, -0.02));
        // environment.setCoexistenceToTrackerBase(t);

        FastrakDriver polhemus = new FastrakDriver();
        System.out.println( "Fastrak opened--" );
try {
   polhemus.initialize();
     }
catch( Exception e )
{
    System.err.println( e.toString() +
            "\nError initializing Fastrak, exiting... " );
    System.exit(0);
}

tracker = new FastrakInputDevice( polhemus );
tracker.initialize();

 //    tracker.setSensitivity(1.175f );


/*   Virtual6DOF tracker = new Virtual6DOF();
    tracker.initialize();
*/
    environment.addInputDevice(tracker);
    //the following command makes environment call pollAndProcessInput()
    environment.setSensor(0,tracker.getSensor(0));
    environment.setHeadIndex(0);
    view = new View();


    view.setPhysicalBody(body);
    view.setPhysicalEnvironment(environment);
     //uncommenting the following makes box disappear
    // view.setCoexistenceCenteringEnable(false);
    view.setCoexistenceCenteringEnable(false);
    view.setTrackingEnable(true);
    view.addCanvas3D(c);
```

LISTING 13.8 Continued

```
    // view.setScreenScalePolicy(View.SCALE_EXPLICIT);
    // view.setScreenScale(1.0);

      t = new Transform3D();

      t.setTranslation(new Vector3f(0.0f, 0.0f, 0.9144f + 0.10f));
      ViewPlatform vp = new ViewPlatform();
      vp.setViewAttachPolicy(View.NOMINAL_SCREEN);
      TransformGroup vpTrans = new TransformGroup();
      vpTrans.setCapability(TransformGroup.ALLOW_TRANSFORM_WRITE);
      vpTrans.setCapability(TransformGroup.ALLOW_TRANSFORM_READ);
      vpTrans.setTransform(t);
      vpTrans.addChild(vp);
    //    Set6DOFBehavior set6dof = new Set6DOFBehavior(tracker);
    //    vpTrans.addChild(set6dof);
    //    set6dof.setSchedulingBounds(bounds);

      NavigationBehavior nav = new NavigationBehavior(vpTrans);
      nav.setSchedulingBounds(bounds);
      vpTrans.addChild(nav);
      view.attachViewPlatform(vp);

      vgraph.addChild(vpTrans);
      locale.addBranchGraph(vgraph);
      locale.addBranchGraph(scene);
      //u.addBranchGraph(scene);
    }

    public static void main(String[] args) {
        new MainFrame(new FishTank(), 512, 512);
    }
}
```

Coexistence Revisited

Recall that there exists a common space, the coexistence space, where the physical and the virtual world can both be represented. It is therefore possible to compute a transform of any point in coexistence space to a point in virtual space. Likewise, another transform exists for mapping coexistence space to the physical world. Given these transforms, it is possible to rotate, translate, or scale the virtual world relative to the physical world. This is the primary means through which Java 3D supports so many devices.

In non-head tracked setups, the center of coexistence is the same as the center of the tracker base. In head-tracked setups, there is a transformation between coexistence and the tracker base. This transformation is represented by the CoexistenceToTrackerBase transform.

Using Java 3D's View Model as a Camera Model

So far, we have avoided trying to think of the view model as a camera. However, the camera model is a stalwart approach to thinking about 3D and is the basis of most other packages and language. To use the view model as a camera model, you must set the compatibility mode to true using the View object's `setCompatibilityModeEnable()` method.

```
SetCompatibilityModeEnable(true)
```

Once the application is in compatibility mode, it becomes possible to use the tried and true camera model. The reason to incorporate compatibility mode is to provide a link to applications that incorporate the camera model. Remember, these applications do considerable work to control the view transformation. Developers who had gone to such trouble might want to import their custom view computations directly into Java 3D without worrying about making the application take advantage of the Java 3D view system. A new application would not choose to go this route.

Several functions are useful in compatibility mode. `Transform3D`'s `lookAt()` function creates the viewing matrix. The constructor is as follows:

```
lookAt(Point3d eye, Point3d center, Vector3d up)
```

After invoking this method on the `Transform3D`, remember to invert the `Transform3D` and then set the view platform's `TransformGroup` to the inverted `Transform3D`.

The following code snippet demonstrates this use:

```
. . .
Transform 3D tview = new Transform3D();
tview.lookAt(new Point3d(0., 0., Math.cos(angle),
             new Point3d(0., 0., 0.).
             new Vector3d(0., 1.0, 0.));
tview.invert();
vpTrans.setTransform(tview);
```

Alternatively, you can set the View's `setVpcToEc()` method directly with the result of `lookAt()`. That would work best if the view platform `TransformGroup` is identity.

Two other methods available in compatibility mode (not covered in this text) are `frustum()` and `perspective()`, which work just like the OpenGL equivalents and can be passed to View through the `setLeftProjection()` and `setRightProjection()` methods. Additionally compatibility methods allow the developer to set clipping planes and the field of view.

Building a CAVE or Wedge with Java 3D

As further testament to the flexibility of the Java 3D view model, we illustrate the building of a *Cave Automatic Virtual Environment (CAVE)* system. Before diving into the nuts and bolts, we need to acknowledge that some VR researchers might take exception to our use of the term

CAVE. Our definition of CAVE is really any multiprojector setup. A CAVE in the more precise sense is a multiprojector system setup in a very particular way. The CAVE was originally developed nearly 10 years ago at the University of Illinois at Chicago by Cruz-Neira, Sandin, and Defanti. In its traditional form, the CAVE is in place at several research institutions and includes stereo display and head tracking.

Recently, a spectacular high performance CAVE was built at the University of Calgary (see Figure 13.3). This particular CAVE was developed on a SUN platform and is, so far, difficult to implement on a PC-based system. Note that a two projector CAVE can be run on a PC with two graphics ports.

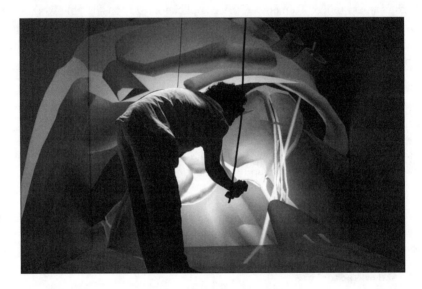

Figure 13.3

Paul Gordon of the University of Calgary interacting with a human heart model in a CAVE.

CAVEs (and multiprojector systems in general) can be highly immersive, can be viewed by multiple users at the same time, and overcome many of the drawbacks of HMDs, including the discomfort of having a monitor mounted to your head and the strange sensation of being out of register with the real space around you.

Setting up a multiprojector system poses special challenges such as having dual-head or multiple graphics cards. There are a lot of options. The simplest multiprojector system has two graphics pipelines that each drive a projector. On a PC, the two graphics pipelines can be built by installing a single AGP dual-head card such as the Wildcat II, 9100. Note that to use this configuration, Java 1.4 must be installed. Older versions did not recognize the dual-head card as having two pipelines. An alternative method is to have multiple PCI cards (two in the case of the Wedge) or an AGP and a PCI card. At the time of this writing, we have not seen PCs with multiple AGP pipelines.

Once the cards are installed into the PC, it is necessary to set up your system for multiple monitors.

On SGI Onyx systems, it is considerably easier to drive multiple pipelines from a hardware standpoint. The same is true for Sun Solaris systems.

Note that in the case of multiple projectors and no head tracking, we will have a separate Canvas3D for each device and a single View object to which all the Canvas3Ds are attached. Also, only one ViewPlatform is used with a CAVE. Listing 13.9 shows the code for setting up a two projector system.

LISTING 13.9   Wedge.java

```java
import java.awt.Frame;
import java.awt.Panel;
import java.awt.BorderLayout;
import java.awt.GraphicsEnvironment;
import java.awt.GraphicsDevice;
import java.awt.GraphicsConfiguration;
import java.awt.event.*;
import com.sun.j3d.utils.universe.*;
import com.sun.j3d.utils.geometry.ColorCube;
import javax.media.j3d.*;
import javax.vecmath.*;
import com.sun.j3d.utils.behaviors.mouse.MouseRotate;
public class Wedge {

    PhysicalBody body;
    PhysicalEnvironment environment;
    View view;
    Locale locale;
    public BranchGroup createSceneGraph() {
        // Create the root of the subgraph
        BranchGroup objRoot = new BranchGroup();
        // Create the transform group node and initialize it to the identity.
        // Enable the TRANSFORM_WRITE capability so that our behavior code
        // can modify it at runtime.  Add it to the root of the subgraph.
        TransformGroup objTrans = new TransformGroup();
        objTrans.setCapability(TransformGroup.ALLOW_TRANSFORM_WRITE);
objTrans.setCapability(TransformGroup.ALLOW_TRANSFORM_READ);
        objRoot.addChild(objTrans);
        // Create a simple shape leaf node and add it into the scene graph.
        objTrans.addChild(new ColorCube(0.4));
        // Create a new Behavior object that will perform the desired
        // operation on the specified transform object and add it into the
        // scene graph.
        Bounds bounds =
```

LISTING 13.9   Continued

```
                new BoundingSphere(new Point3d(0.0,0.0,0.0), 1000.0);
         MouseRotate mouseBeh = new MouseRotate(objTrans);
      objTrans.addChild(mouseBeh);
 mouseBeh.setSchedulingBounds(bounds);
    // Have Java 3D perform optimizations on this scene graph.
    objRoot.compile();
    return objRoot;
}

public Wedge(Canvas3D[] canvases) {
    // Create a simple scene and attach it to the virtual universe
    BranchGroup scene = createSceneGraph();
  // SimpleUniverse u = new SimpleUniverse(canvases[0]);
    // This will move the ViewPlatform back a bit so the
    // objects in the scene can be viewed.
    //u.getViewingPlatform().setNominalViewingTransform();
    //View view = u.getViewer().getView();
     BranchGroup vgraph = new BranchGroup();
     VirtualUniverse universe = new VirtualUniverse();
     Bounds bounds = new BoundingSphere(new Point3d(0.0,0.0,0.0), 1000.0);
     Locale locale = new Locale(universe);
     body = new PhysicalBody();
     environment = new PhysicalEnvironment();
     view = new View();
     view.setPhysicalBody(body);
     view.setPhysicalEnvironment(environment);
     view.setCoexistenceCenteringEnable(false);
     // view.setCoexistenceCenteringEnable(true);
     view.setWindowEyepointPolicy(View.RELATIVE_TO_SCREEN);
     //view.setWindowEyepointPolicy(View.RELATIVE_TO_COEXISTENCE);

     System.out.println("canvases.length: " + canvases.length);
     for (int i = 0; i < canvases.length; i++) {
        // Attach the new canvas to the view
        view.addCanvas3D(canvases[i]);
     }

     Transform3D t = new Transform3D();
  t.setTranslation(new Vector3f(0.0f, 0.0f,30.0f));
  ViewPlatform vp = new ViewPlatform();
  TransformGroup vpTrans = new TransformGroup();
     vpTrans.setCapability(TransformGroup.ALLOW_TRANSFORM_WRITE);
  vpTrans.setCapability(TransformGroup.ALLOW_TRANSFORM_READ);
  vpTrans.setTransform(t);
  vpTrans.addChild(vp);
```

LISTING **13.9**   Continued

```
            NavigationBehavior nav = new NavigationBehavior(vpTrans);
            nav.setSchedulingBounds(bounds);
            vpTrans.addChild(nav);
        view.attachViewPlatform(vp);
            vgraph.addChild(vpTrans);
            locale.addBranchGraph(vgraph);
            locale.addBranchGraph(scene);

    }


    public static void main(String[] args) {
        int nViews = 2;
        if (args.length > 0) {
            try {
                nViews = Integer.parseInt(args[0]);
            }
            catch (NumberFormatException e) {
                System.out.println("Usage: java Wedge [#views]");
                System.exit(1);
            }
        }

        int i;
        Panel[] panels = new Panel[nViews];
        for (i = 0; i < nViews; i++) {
            panels[i] = new Panel();
        }

        GraphicsDevice[] allScreenDevices = GraphicsEnvironment.
            getLocalGraphicsEnvironment().getScreenDevices();
        System.out.println("Found " + allScreenDevices.length +
                            " screen devices");
        for (i = 0; i < allScreenDevices.length; i++)
            System.out.println(allScreenDevices[i]);
        System.out.println();
        GraphicsDevice[] graphicsDevices = new GraphicsDevice[nViews];
        for (i = 0; i < nViews; i++) {
            graphicsDevices[i] = allScreenDevices[i % allScreenDevices.length];
        }

        GraphicsConfigTemplate3D template;
        GraphicsConfiguration gConfig;
        Canvas3D[] canvases = new Canvas3D[nViews];
        for (i = 0; i < nViews; i++) {
            template = new GraphicsConfigTemplate3D();
```

13

THE JAVA 3D
VIEW MODEL

LISTING 13.9   Continued

```
        gConfig = graphicsDevices[i].getBestConfiguration(template);
        canvases[i] = new Canvas3D(gConfig);
        panels[i].setLayout(new BorderLayout());
        panels[i].add("Center", canvases[i]);

    }

    Screen3D screenL = canvases[0].getScreen3D();
//screen.setPhysicalScreenWidth(2.05);
//screen.setPhysicalScreenHeight(1.05);
    System.out.println("Screen3D[" + i + "] = " + screenL);

    Screen3D screenR = canvases[1].getScreen3D();
    Transform3D tR = new Transform3D();
    tR.rotY(-.25*Math.PI);
    screenL.setTrackerBaseToImagePlate(tR);
    System.out.println("Screen3D[" + i + "] = " + screenR);
    Transform3D tL = new Transform3D();
    tL.rotY(.25*Math.PI);
    screenL.setTrackerBaseToImagePlate(tL);
    canvases[0].setSize(640,480);

    canvases[1].setSize(640,480);
    new Wedge(canvases);
    Frame[] frames = new Frame[nViews];
    for (i = 0; i < nViews; i++) {
        gConfig = graphicsDevices[i].getDefaultConfiguration();
        frames[i] = new Frame(gConfig);
        frames[i].setLayout(new BorderLayout());
        frames[i].setTitle("Canvas " + i);

        frames[i].addWindowListener(new WindowAdapter() {
            public void windowClosing(WindowEvent winEvent) {
                System.exit(0);
            }
        });

        frames[i].add("Center", panels[i]);
        frames[i].setLocation(300*(i % 3), 300*(i / 3));
        frames[i].setSize(640, 480);
        frames[i].setVisible(true);
    }

    try {
        Thread.sleep(5000);
    }
```

LISTING 13.9 Continued

```
        catch (InterruptedException e) {
        }

/*      for (i = 0; i < nViews; i++) {
            Screen3D screen = canvases[i].getScreen3D();
            System.out.println("Screen3D[" + i + "] = " + screen);
            System.out.println("    hashCode = " + screen.hashCode());
        }
*/
    }
}
```

At first the idea of having only one `ViewPlatform` might seem strange. The natural tendency of developers who are accustomed to the camera based model is that you would have multiple cameras mounted on the center of the platform—each pointing in a different non-overlapping direction. This particular scenario illustrates how the Java 3D view model is different. In the Java 3D case, you have multiple screens associated with a single view.

How does the view model handle this situation? Note the use of `Screen3D`'s `setTrackerBaseToImagePlate()` method. By supplying the correct transform to map each screen to the center of coexistence, the screens will all contain the correct information.

This is in stark contrast to the camera model in which we would have to recompute the camera view for each screen. In the case of the non-head tracked CAVE or any other non-head tracked scenario, the tracker base coordinates are the same as coexistence. Thus, the `TrackerBaseToImagePlate` transform simply maps the tracker base to the lower-left corner of each screen. By changing this transform, we tell the renderer where the screens are relative to the coexistence. Therefore, a nice mapping results. Again, the idea here is that the coexistence transform is mapping observer and display between the virtual world and the real world.

Continuing on with our CAVE example. Let's consider a driving simulator with six projectors arranged to project a dynamic scene onto each window of a car. This is a case in which putting a separate camera for each projector would be a real pain. This is not such a big deal in Java 3D. We would simply arrange our projectors around the car model, set their screen sizes to the sizes of each projection window, set the center of coexistence to the center of the car, and proceed to render with physically reasonable coordinates. Because the center of coexistence is set and head tracking is not in play, our viewer should be able to look out of each window and see the expected virtual items. Moreover, a passenger could sit in the car and have the same effect. Of course, the passenger situation would not work if head tracking were in play because the view would be slaved to the tracker.

Summary

The Java 3D view model is powerful because of the ideal of "write once, display anywhere." After the developer has mastered the concept of the view model, it becomes fairly easy to display on almost any device with minor modifications.

The key concept is that Java 3D needs to know where the eyes are relative to the screen(s). This information can be used to solve almost any viewing problem, including head tracking when the screens are attached to the head (HMD) and when the screens are not attached to the head but rather to the room (CAVE and FishTank VR).

Bringing It All Together: Integrated Java Media Applications

IN THIS PART

Integrating the Java Media APIs

IN THIS CHAPTER

A benefit of developing software in any one of the Java Media APIs lies in having the other Media APIs available for use. Indeed, the entire Java platform is available for writing an application. Many of the examples we have developed so far have made use of other Java components for user interactions (slider bars, buttons, and the like) as well as file I/O, communications, and networking. None, however, have specifically integrated multiple Media APIs.

This chapter concludes our exploration of the Java Media APIs by giving examples of Media API—Media API interactions.

Integrated Applications

Integrated media components are finding their way in to more and more applications all the time. That is no surprise given the visual appeal of these applications and the strong interest in multimedia in general.

Some interesting examples of this all-Java approach are already evident in examples, and you can even see some in the commercial marketplace.

Although the capabilities are there, the challenge is that there are not enough programmers with a background in even one of the Java Media APIs, let alone multiples of the APIs. Nor are there many books that emphasize more than one of the APIs. Image processing, 3D graphics, and streaming media are substantial challenges in and of themselves. Therefore, it is a rare person indeed who has these multiple skills.

Granted, we have only covered a portion of the Java Media APIs in this book. The possibility of integration with some of the other APIs not covered in this book is, of course, much larger.

In practice, many non-Java media, imaging, and visualization applications use other parts of the Java language to handle events, load applets, and perform networking operations. Consider the Java OpenGL bindings, for example. In this chapter, we present a few examples that show the value of integration.

JMF-J3D Interactions: Prototype for a Streaming 3D Chat Room

Video texturing is an important technique that allows the developer to put live or prerecorded digital video on surfaces in the 3D environment. Typical applications that would make use of video texturing would be a 3D chat room, a 3D shopping mall application, or a video game with dynamic and naturalistic texturing.

From a JMF standpoint, we need to write a class that implements the `VideoRenderer` interface. The question is where. Recall that a `VideoRenderer` is a subinterface of `Renderer`, which is in turn a subinterface of `Plug-In`. A `Plug-In` accepts data in a particular format and performs some process including output. In the case of our `Plug-In`, we want to output data on to the screen.

The avenue for the creation of a dynamic texture in Java 3D was explored in AnimatedTextureJ3D.java (from Listing 11.8 of Chapter 11, "Creating and Viewing the Virtual World"). Recall that we created a simple Graphics2D object, placed it in a BufferedImage, and added that image to a Texture2D. Although it was not necessary for performance reasons on that particular example, we also specified the image as byReference. With the video stream that we are about use, the byReference option is pretty much mandatory because the performance needs are great with the dynamic digital video.

In short, we need put the data stored in the Buffer of the VideoRenderer to the BufferedImage of an ImageComponent2D for every frame of video. Recall from our studies of JMF that the process() method of Renderer is called continually when a TrackControl object is started. This is the natural place to try to exchange the video data with the texture data.

The conceptual challenge is in realizing that the VideoRenderer is not putting the video directly on the screen, but instead is passing the data to a BufferedImage. After the video data is fed to a Texture2D object, the Java 3D renderer can make the necessary transformations to put it in the 3D environment. The result is a video playing in the environment that can be seen from different angles and distances (see Figure 14.1).

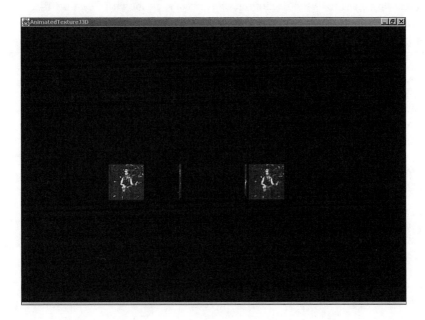

FIGURE 14.1
Screen shot from the VideoCubes application.

Extending `Texture2D` by Implementing `VideoRenderer`

In order to keep the code as simple as possible, we will hold off on swapping the video data into the `BufferedImage` data until later. We first want to concentrate on the control of the texturing using the `TrackControl` object and the `ByReference` option of `ImageComponent2D`.

Recall from Chapter 11 that the `ImageComponent2D` class encapsulates a texture to be used with a `Shape3D` Node. The `ImageComponent` class works together with the `Texture` class and the `Appearance` class to enable mapping of textures on objects. Any `ImageComponent` object comes in one of two flavors—ByReference and ByCopy. The fundamental difference is that `ByReference` establishes a reference to a `RenderedImage` (of which `BufferedImage` is the primary example).

Under certain conditions (see Table 14.1), `ByReference` can be used. In `By-Reference` image data can be swapped into the `ImageComponent` without making a new copy of the image. We can see the necessity of this when we consider a video texture that has 15 frames per second. Without `ByReference`, we would be subject to real memory problems because of the number of images that would have been created and destroyed.

The implementing class for VideoRenderer, `JMFTexture`, is shown in Listing 14.1.

LISTING 14.1   JMFTexture.java

```
import javax.media.*;
import javax.media.renderer.VideoRenderer;
import javax.media.control.*;
import javax.media.Format;
import javax.media.format.VideoFormat;
import javax.media.format.RGBFormat;
import java.awt.*;
import java.awt.image.*;
import java.awt.event.*;
import java.util.Vector;
import java.util.Random;
import java.awt.geom.*;
// Java 3D packages
import com.sun.j3d.utils.universe.*;
import com.sun.j3d.utils.geometry.Box;
import com.sun.j3d.utils.geometry.Sphere;
import com.sun.j3d.utils.geometry.Cylinder;

import javax.media.j3d.*;
import javax.vecmath.*;
import com.sun.j3d.utils.behaviors.mouse.*;
import javax.media.protocol.DataSource;
```

LISTING 14.1   Continued

```java
class JMFTexture2D extends Texture2D implements VideoRenderer {
    Processor p;
    protected RGBFormat inputFormat;
    protected RGBFormat supportedRGB;
    protected Format [] supportedFormats;

    boolean stateTransOK = true;
    private int textureHeight, textureWidth;
    private int videoHeight, videoWidth;

    boolean YUPFlag = true;

    int platformSpecificImageType;
    int[] waitSync = new int[0];
    BufferedImage bi;
    ImageComponent2D ic;

    byte[] textureData, jmfData;

    protected int scaledSize;

    protected Component component = null;
    protected Rectangle reqBounds = null;
    protected Rectangle bounds = new Rectangle();
    protected boolean started = false;
    protected Object lastData = null;
    Canvas3D c;

    boolean firstFrame = true;
    DataSource ds;

    public JMFTexture2D(Canvas3D c,
                        int textureHeight,
                        int textureWidth,
                        int videoHeight,
                        int videoWidth,
                        int platformSpecificImageType,
                        boolean YUPFlag) {


            super(Texture2D.BASE_LEVEL,
                  Texture2D.RGB,
                  textureHeight,
                  textureWidth);
```

LISTING 14.1   Continued

```java
        this.c = c;

        this.textureHeight = textureHeight;
        this.textureWidth = textureWidth;

        this.videoHeight = videoHeight;
        this.videoWidth = videoWidth;

        this.platformSpecificImageType = platformSpecificImageType;
        this.YUPFlag = YUPFlag;

        //must be able to read and write texture for image processing
        //and data swapping.
        this.setCapability(Texture2D.ALLOW_IMAGE_WRITE);
        this.setCapability(Texture2D.ALLOW_IMAGE_READ);

        supportedRGB =  new RGBFormat(null,
                                     Format.NOT_SPECIFIED,
                      Format.byteArray,
                      Format.NOT_SPECIFIED,
                      24,
                      3, 2, 1,
                      3, Format.NOT_SPECIFIED,
                      Format.TRUE,
                      Format.NOT_SPECIFIED);

     supportedFormats = new VideoFormat[] {supportedRGB };

        //create a BufferedImage to hold texture data;
        //return the data to bufferData

        bi = new BufferedImage(textureHeight,
                               textureWidth,
                               BufferedImage.TYPE_3BYTE_BGR);

  textureData=((DataBufferByte)bi.getRaster().getDataBuffer()).getData();

        //instantiate a new ImageComponent; choose byRef and yUp
        if (platformSpecificImageType == BufferedImage.TYPE_3BYTE_BGR) {

        ic = new ImageComponent2D(ImageComponent2D.FORMAT_RGB,
                                  textureHeight,
                                  textureWidth,
                                  true,
                                  YUPFlag);
```

LISTING 14.1 Continued

```
            } else {
              ic = new ImageComponent2D(ImageComponent2D.FORMAT_RGBA,
                                        textureHeight,
                                        textureWidth,
                                        true,
                                        YUPFlag);
            }

          //set bi as ImageComponenet object
            ic.set(bi);

      this.setImage(0, ic);

            this.start();
            System.out.println("JMFTexture2D constructor");
            // Prepare supported input formats and preferred format

    }

  public void setMedia(DataSource ds) {
        this.ds= ds;
  }

  public boolean openMedia() {

    try {
            System.out.println("Opening media ...");
          p = Manager.createProcessor(ds);
    } catch (Exception ex) {
          System.out.println("failed to create a processor for videostream "
➥+ ds);

      return false;
    }

    System.out.println("done opening; try to configure");
    p.configure();
    System.out.println("done configuring");

      if ( !waitForState(p.Configured)) {
      System.out.println("Failed to configure the processor");
      return false;
    } else {
            System.out.println("waiting for state");
      }
```

LISTING 14.1   Continued

```java
System.out.println("setting content descriptor");
// use processor as a player
p.setContentDescriptor(null);
System.out.println("done setting content descriptor");

// obtain the track control

    TrackControl[] tc = p.getTrackControls();

if ( tc == null ) {
    System.out.println("Failed to get the track control from processor");
    return false;
}

TrackControl vtc = null;

for ( int i =0; i < tc.length; i++ ) {
    if (tc[i].getFormat() instanceof VideoFormat ) {
    vtc = tc[i];
    break;
    }

}

if ( vtc == null ) {
     System.out.println("can't find video track");
    return false;
}

try {
    vtc.setRenderer(this);
} catch ( Exception ex) {
    ex.printStackTrace();
    System.out.println("the processor does not support effect");
    return false;
}
p.setContentDescriptor(null);

// prefetch
p.prefetch();

return true;
}
```

LISTING 14.1   Continued

```java
public void init() {

    p.start();

  System.out.println("start transmission");

}

public void movieOff() {
    p.stop();
  System.out.println("stop transmission");
}

  public void movieOn() {
    p.start();
  System.out.println("start transmission");
}

public void swapAndScaleRGB() {

    int op, ip, x, y;

op = 0;
int lineStride = 3 * videoWidth;
for ( int i = 0; i < textureHeight; i++ ) {
    for ( int j = 0; j < textureWidth; j++) {
        x = (videoWidth*j) >> 7;
        y = (videoHeight*i) >> 7;

        if ( x >= videoWidth || y >= videoHeight ) {
        textureData[op++]  = 0;
        textureData[op++]  = 0;
        textureData[op++]  = 0;
        } else {
        ip = y*lineStride + x*3;
        textureData[op++] = jmfData[ip++];
        textureData[op++] = jmfData[ip++];
        textureData[op++] = jmfData[ip++];
        }
    }
  }
}


  public void swapAndScaleARGB() {
```

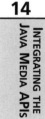

14

INTEGRATING THE
JAVA MEDIA APIS

LISTING 14.1   Continued

```
      int op, ip, x, y;

  op = 0;
  int lineStride = 3 * videoWidth;
      for ( int i = 0; i < textureWidth; i++ )
      for ( int j = 0; j < textureHeight; j++) {
          x = (videoWidth*j) >> 7;
          y = (videoHeight*i) >> 7;

          if ( x >= videoWidth || y >= videoHeight ) {
          textureData[op++] = (byte)0xff;
          textureData[op++]  = 0;
          textureData[op++]  = 0;
          textureData[op++]  = 0;
          } else {
          ip = y*lineStride + x*3;
          textureData[op++] = (byte)0xff;
          textureData[op++] = jmfData[ip++];
          textureData[op++] = jmfData[ip++];
          textureData[op++] = jmfData[ip++];
          }
      }
  }

  public int process(Buffer buffer) {


  //get the video data
      jmfData =(byte[])(buffer.getData());

      if (platformSpecificImageType == BufferedImage.TYPE_3BYTE_BGR) {
         swapAndScaleRGB();
      } else {
         swapAndScaleARGB();
      }

      ic = new ImageComponent2D (ImageComponent.FORMAT_RGB,
                                                bi,
                                                true,
                                                true);

  this.setImage(0, ic);
  return BUFFER_PROCESSED_OK;
```

LISTING 14.1   Continued

```java
    }

//the following methods must be implemented

    public java.lang.Object[] getControls() {
      // No controls
      return (Object[]) new Control[0];
    }

    /**
      * Return the control based on a control type for the PlugIn.
      */
    public Object getControl(String controlType) {
       try {
          Class  cls = Class.forName(controlType);
          Object cs[] = getControls();
          for (int i = 0; i < cs.length; i++) {
             if (cls.isInstance(cs[i]))
                 return cs[i];
          }
          return null;
       } catch (Exception e) {    // no such controlType or such control
          return null;
       }
    }

    /************************************************************************
      * PlugIn implementation
      ************************************************************************/

    public java.lang.String getName() {
       return "JMFTexture";
    }

    public java.awt.Rectangle getBounds() {
       return reqBounds;
    }

    public javax.media.Format[] getSupportedInputFormats() {
       return supportedFormats;
    }

    public boolean waitForState(int state) {
    synchronized (waitSync) {
```

LISTING 14.1   Continued

```
        try {
        while ( p.getState() != state && stateTransOK ) {

        }
        } catch (Exception ex) {}

        return stateTransOK;
    }
    }

  public boolean setComponent(java.awt.Component comp) {
        component = comp;
        return true;
    }

public void open() throws javax.media.ResourceUnavailableException {

}

public Format setInputFormat(Format format) {
        if ( format != null && format instanceof RGBFormat &&
            format.matches(supportedRGB)) {

            inputFormat = (RGBFormat) format;
            Dimension size = inputFormat.getSize();
          // inWidth = size.width;
         //   inHeight = size.height;
            return format;
        } else
            return null;
    }

  public void setBounds(java.awt.Rectangle rectangle) {
  }
  public synchronized void close() {
  }

public java.awt.Component getComponent() {
    return c;
    }
public void reset() {
        // Nothing to do
    }
  public void start() {
```

LISTING 14.1   Continued

```
    System.out.println("start called");
}

public void stop() {
    System.out.println("stop called");
}


}
```

Note the considerable amount of code that goes into setting up the imaging type and data format parameters for the different operating systems. This would seem to be distinctly non–cross-platform and, in fact, it is. The reason is that Java 3D does not treat all image formats the same when doing texture by reference. Indeed, various formats are handled differently depending on platform (Windows, Solaris, and so on). The reason for this is that there is a very large number of BufferedImage formats (including custom) but the low-level 3D APIs (for example, OpenGL and Direct3D) do not support all of these. Therefore, Java 3D creates an intermediate format that is compatible with OpenGL. The image in the intermediate format is therefore kept in case the texture does not change.

For performance reasons, we do not want a situation in which Java 3D is making multiple copies of an image; therefore we need to determine which platform the code is being run on and set up the images so that no copy is made.

Table 14.1 summarizes the combinations of the BufferedImage format and ImageComponent2D in which a second copy is *not* made. Therefore, these are the conditions that must be met in order to effectively use a dynamic texture.

TABLE 14.1   Image Types That Support By-Reference Under Different Platforms and Low-Level APIs

Platform/Low-Level API version	Format
OpenGL extension GL_EXT_abgr/ D3D version	BufferedImage.TYPE_4BYTE_ABGR + ImageComponent.FORMAT_RGBA8
OpenGL version 1.2 and above/ D3D version	BufferedImage.TYPE_3BYTE_BGR + ImageComponent.FORMAT_RGB
All others	BufferedImage.TYPE_BYTE_GRAY + ImageComponent.FORMAT_CHANNEL8

14

INTEGRATING THE
JAVA MEDIA APIs

The second condition that must be met in order to avoid making image copies is to specify Y-UP as true. It is necessary to include this parameter regardless of the target platform.

To create a JMFTexture and apply it to an object, you have to enable texture mapping and set up some RTP streaming or simple playback code. Listing 14.2 illustrates the use of the RTP Streaming mechanism.

Listing 14.2   VideoCubes.java

```java
import javax.media.control.*;
import com.sun.j3d.utils.behaviors.mouse.MouseRotate;
import javax.media.*;
import java.applet.Applet;
import java.awt.*;
import java.awt.event.*;
import com.sun.j3d.utils.applet.MainFrame;

import java.net.URL;
import com.sun.j3d.utils.universe.*;
import javax.media.j3d.*;
import javax.vecmath.*;
import java.awt.image.*;
import com.sun.j3d.utils.geometry.Box;
import java.awt.image.BufferedImage;
import javax.media.j3d.ImageComponent2D;
import java.awt.image.*;
import java.awt.geom.*;

import javax.media.format.*;
import java.io.File;

import com.sun.j3d.utils.picking.behaviors.*;
import com.sun.j3d.utils.picking.*;
import com.sun.j3d.utils.picking.behaviors.*;
import java.awt.BorderLayout;
import java.awt.Component;
import java.awt.Point;
import javax.swing.*;
import javax.swing.border.BevelBorder;

import java.net.*;
import java.io.*;
import java.net.*;
import java.util.Vector;
import javax.media.rtp.*;
import javax.media.rtp.event.*;
```

LISTING 14.2   Continued

```java
import javax.media.rtp.rtcp.*;
import javax.media.protocol.*;
import javax.media.protocol.DataSource;
import javax.media.format.AudioFormat;
import javax.media.format.VideoFormat;
import javax.media.Format;
import javax.media.format.FormatChangeEvent;
import javax.media.control.BufferControl;


/**
 * VideoCubes to receive RTP transmission using the new RTP API.
 */
public class VideoCubes extends Applet
        implements ReceiveStreamListener, SessionListener, ControllerListener {
    String sessions[] = null;
    RTPManager mgrs[] = null;

    boolean stateTransOK = true;
    boolean dataReceived = false;

    Object dataSync = new Object();

    private View view = null;
    private PickRotateBehavior behavior1;
    private PickZoomBehavior    behavior2;
    private PickTranslateBehavior behavior3;

    Canvas3D c;

    TransformGroup objScale;
    BranchGroup scene;
    BoundingSphere bounds;
    private VirtualUniverse universe;
    Locale locale;

    int platformSpecificImageType;

    int iter;
    int[] waitSync = new int[0];

    public VideoCubes(String sessions[]) {
this.sessions = sessions;
```

LISTING 14.2   Continued

```java
        String os = System.getProperty("os.name");
        System.out.println("running on " + os);



        if ( os.startsWith("W") || os.startsWith("w")) {
            platformSpecificImageType = BufferedImage.TYPE_3BYTE_BGR;
    } else if (os.startsWith("S") || os.startsWith("s")){
        platformSpecificImageType = BufferedImage.TYPE_4BYTE_ABGR;
    } else {
        platformSpecificImageType = BufferedImage.TYPE_3BYTE_BGR;
        }

    init3d();
}

public BranchGroup createViewGraph() {

    BranchGroup objRoot = new BranchGroup();

Transform3D t = new Transform3D();
t.setTranslation(new Vector3f(0.0f, 0.f,0.0f));
ViewPlatform vp = new ViewPlatform();
TransformGroup vpTrans = new TransformGroup();
    vpTrans.setCapability(TransformGroup.ALLOW_TRANSFORM_WRITE);
vpTrans.setCapability(TransformGroup.ALLOW_TRANSFORM_READ);
vpTrans.setTransform(t);
vpTrans.addChild(vp);
view.attachViewPlatform(vp);
    view.setBackClipDistance(200.f);
    NavigationBehavior nav = new NavigationBehavior(vpTrans);
    vpTrans.addChild(nav);

    nav.setSchedulingBounds(bounds);

    objRoot.addChild(vpTrans);
    return objRoot;

}



public void init3d() {
    setLayout(new BorderLayout());
```

LISTING 14.2   Continued

```
    bounds =
        new BoundingSphere(new Point3d(0.0,0.0,0.0), 100.0);

    universe = new VirtualUniverse();
  locale = new Locale(universe);

    GraphicsConfigTemplate3D g3d = new GraphicsConfigTemplate3D();
    GraphicsConfiguration gc = GraphicsEnvironment.
➥getLocalGraphicsEnvironment().
                                    getDefaultScreenDevice().
                                    ➥getBestConfiguration(g3d);

  Canvas3D c = new Canvas3D(gc);
    add("Center", c);

    PhysicalBody body = new PhysicalBody();
  PhysicalEnvironment environment = new PhysicalEnvironment();
  view = new View();

  view.addCanvas3D(c);
  view.setPhysicalBody(body);
    view.setPhysicalEnvironment(environment);
  // Create a simple scene and attach it to the virtual universe

    bounds = new BoundingSphere(new Point3d(0.0,0.0,0.0), 100.0);
    scene = createSceneGraph(c);

    scene.setCapability(Group.ALLOW_CHILDREN_EXTEND);
    BranchGroup vgraph = createViewGraph();

    locale.addBranchGraph(vgraph);
  locale.addBranchGraph(scene);


  // Create a scene and attach it to the virtual universe


  }

  protected boolean initialize() {
    try {
    InetAddress ipAddr;
    SessionAddress localAddr = new SessionAddress();
    SessionAddress destAddr;
```

LISTING 14.2   Continued

```java
mgrs = new RTPManager[sessions.length];

SessionLabel session;


    // Open the RTP sessions.
for (int i = 0; i < sessions.length; i++) {

 // Parse the session addresses.
try {
    session = new SessionLabel(sessions[i]);
} catch (IllegalArgumentException e) {
    System.err.println("Failed to parse the session address given: "
    ➥ + sessions[i]);
    return false;
}

System.err.println("  - Open RTP session for: addr: "
                    + session.addr + " port: "
                    + session.port + " ttl: " + session.ttl);

mgrs[i] = (RTPManager) RTPManager.newInstance();
mgrs[i].addSessionListener(this);
mgrs[i].addReceiveStreamListener(this);

ipAddr = InetAddress.getByName(session.addr);

if( ipAddr.isMulticastAddress()) {
    // local and remote address pairs are identical:
    localAddr= new SessionAddress( ipAddr,
                    session.port,
                    session.ttl);
    destAddr = new SessionAddress( ipAddr,
                    session.port,
                    session.ttl);
} else {
    localAddr= new SessionAddress( InetAddress.getLocalHost(),
                        session.port);
            destAddr = new SessionAddress( ipAddr, session.port);
}

mgrs[i].initialize( localAddr);

// You can try out some other buffer size to see
```

LISTING 14.2   Continued

```java
        // if you can get better smoothness.
        BufferControl bc = (BufferControl)mgrs[i].
        ➥getControl("javax.media.control.BufferControl");
        if (bc != null)
            bc.setBufferLength(350);

            mgrs[i].addTarget(destAddr);
        }

    } catch (Exception e){
        System.err.println("Cannot create the RTP Session: "
                            ➥+ e.getMessage());
        return false;
    }

// Wait for data to arrive before moving on.

long then = System.currentTimeMillis();
long waitingPeriod = 30000;

try{
    synchronized (dataSync) {
    while (!dataReceived &&
        System.currentTimeMillis() - then < waitingPeriod) {
        if (!dataReceived)
        System.err.println("  - Waiting for RTP data to arrive...");
        dataSync.wait(1000);
    }
    }
} catch (Exception e) {}

if (!dataReceived) {
    System.err.println("No RTP data was received.");
    //close();
    return false;
}

    return true;
}


public synchronized void update(SessionEvent evt) {
if (evt instanceof NewParticipantEvent) {
    Participant p = ((NewParticipantEvent)evt).getParticipant();
    System.err.println("  - A new participant had just joined: "
```

LISTING 14.2   Continued

```
                                          + p.getCNAME());
    }
    }



        private BranchGroup createVCube(DataSource ds,
                                        double scale,
                                        double xpos,
                                        double ypos,
                                        double zpos){

      BranchGroup newG = new BranchGroup();

    Transform3D t = new Transform3D();
    t.set(scale, new Vector3d(xpos, ypos, zpos));

    TransformGroup objTrans = new TransformGroup(t);
    objTrans.setCapability(TransformGroup.ALLOW_TRANSFORM_WRITE);
    objTrans.setCapability(TransformGroup.ALLOW_TRANSFORM_READ);
    objTrans.setCapability(TransformGroup.ENABLE_PICK_REPORTING);

    // Create a second transform group node and initialize it to the
    // identity.  Enable the TRANSFORM_WRITE capability so that
    // our behavior code can modify it at runtime.
    TransformGroup spinTg = new TransformGroup();
    spinTg.setCapability(TransformGroup.ALLOW_TRANSFORM_WRITE);
    spinTg.setCapability(TransformGroup.ALLOW_TRANSFORM_READ);
    spinTg.setCapability(TransformGroup.ENABLE_PICK_REPORTING);


    Appearance app = new Appearance();
    app.setCapability(Appearance.ALLOW_TEXTURE_WRITE);

    //determine which  platform code is running on


    JMFTexture2D jtex = new JMFTexture2D(c,
                                         128,
                                         128,
                                         144,
                                         176,
                                         platformSpecificImageType,
                                         platformSpecificYUP);
```

LISTING 14.2   Continued

```
jtex.setMedia(ds);

jtex.openMedia();
jtex.init();


app.setTexture(jtex);

BoundingSphere b = new BoundingSphere(new Point3d(xpos,ypos,zpos), 1.0);

Box stream = new Box(1.f,1.f,1.f,
                        Box.GENERATE_TEXTURE_COORDS |
                        Box.ENABLE_GEOMETRY_PICKING, app);


spinTg.addChild(stream);

    // add it to the scene graph.
objTrans.addChild(spinTg);
newG.addChild(objTrans);
return newG;
}


///end of createObject
public synchronized void update( ReceiveStreamEvent evt) {

RTPManager mgr = (RTPManager)evt.getSource();
Participant participant = evt.getParticipant();    // could be null.
ReceiveStream stream = evt.getReceiveStream();  // could be null.

if (evt instanceof RemotePayloadChangeEvent) {

    System.err.println("  - Received an RTP PayloadChangeEvent.");
    System.err.println("Sorry, cannot handle payload change.");
    System.exit(0);

}

else if (evt instanceof NewReceiveStreamEvent) {

    try {
    stream = ((NewReceiveStreamEvent)evt).getReceiveStream();
    DataSource ds = stream.getDataSource();
```

LISTING 14.2   Continued

```
                iter=iter+10;

        // Find out the formats.
        RTPControl ctl = (RTPControl)ds.
                        getControl("javax.media.rtp.RTPControl");
        if (ctl != null){
            System.err.println("  - Received new RTP stream: "
                                + ctl.getFormat());
        } else
            System.err.println("  - Received new RTP stream");

        if (participant == null)
            System.err.println(" The sender of this stream had yet to be
➥identified.");
        else {
            System.err.println(" The stream comes from: " +
                                participant.getCNAME());
        }


                scene.addChild(createVCube(ds, 0.5, 0.0, 0.0,iter));
                System.out.println("creating cube " );

        synchronized (dataSync) {
            dataReceived = true;
            dataSync.notifyAll();
        }

        } catch (Exception e) {
        System.err.println("NewReceiveStreamEvent exception " +
e.getMessage());
        return;
        }

    }

    else if (evt instanceof StreamMappedEvent) {

        if (stream != null && stream.getDataSource() != null) {
        DataSource ds = stream.getDataSource();
        // Find out the formats.
        RTPControl ctl = (RTPControl)ds.
                        getControl("javax.media.rtp.RTPControl");
        System.err.println("  - The previously unidentified stream ");
        if (ctl != null)
```

LISTING 14.2 Continued

```java
            System.err.println("        " + ctl.getFormat());
        System.err.println("  has now been identified as sent by: "
                             + participant.getCNAME());
        }
    }

    else if (evt instanceof ByeEvent) {

        System.err.println("   - Got \"bye\" from: " + participant.getCNAME());

    }

    }

    private Group createStructuralElement(double scale,
                                          Vector3d pos, Color3f color,
                                          float xdim, float ydim, float zdim,
                                          int tnumber) {
    // Create a transform group node to scale and position the object.
    Transform3D t = new Transform3D();
    t.set(scale, pos);
    TransformGroup objTrans = new TransformGroup(t);

    Appearance app = new Appearance();
        ColoringAttributes ca =
                    new ColoringAttributes(color,ColoringAttributes.
                    SHADE_GOURAUD);
        app.setColoringAttributes(ca);

        Box structelem = new Box(xdim, ydim, zdim, app);

        objTrans.addChild(structelem);
    return objTrans;
    }


    public BranchGroup createSceneGraph(Canvas3D canvas) {

    // Create the root of the branch graph
    BranchGroup objRoot = new BranchGroup();

    //add walls, floors etc.

    Group rightwall =
```

14

INTEGRATING THE
JAVA MEDIA APIs

LISTING 14.2   Continued

```
            createStructuralElement(1.f,
                                     new Vector3d( 50.0, 0.0, 0.0),
                                     new Color3f(1.f,0.f,0.f),
                                     2.0f, 14.0f, 100.0f, 1);
    objRoot.addChild(rightwall);

. . .



    behavior1 = new PickRotateBehavior(objRoot, canvas, bounds);
    objRoot.addChild(behavior1);

    behavior2 = new PickZoomBehavior(objRoot, canvas, bounds);
    objRoot.addChild(behavior2);

    behavior3 = new PickTranslateBehavior(objRoot, canvas, bounds);
    objRoot.addChild(behavior3);

    // Let Java 3D perform optimizations on this scene graph.
    objRoot.compile();

    return objRoot;
  }

public synchronized void controllerUpdate(ControllerEvent evt) {
    if ( evt instanceof ConfigureCompleteEvent ||
         evt instanceof RealizeCompleteEvent ||
         evt instanceof PrefetchCompleteEvent ) {
        synchronized (waitSync) {
        stateTransOK = true;
        waitSync.notifyAll();
        }
    } else if ( evt instanceof ResourceUnavailableEvent) {
        synchronized (waitSync) {
        stateTransOK = false;
        waitSync.notifyAll();
        }
    }
    }

    /*
      A utility class to parse the session addresses.
     */
    class SessionLabel {
```

LISTING 14.2 Continued

```java
public String addr = null;
public int port;
public int ttl = 1;

SessionLabel(String session) throws IllegalArgumentException {

    int off;
    String portStr = null, ttlStr = null;

    if (session != null && session.length() > 0) {
    while (session.length() > 1 && session.charAt(0) == '/')
        session = session.substring(1);

    // Now see if there's a addr specified.
    off = session.indexOf('/');
    if (off == -1) {
        if (!session.equals(""))
        addr = session;
    } else {
        addr = session.substring(0, off);
        session = session.substring(off + 1);
        // Now see if there's a port specified
        off = session.indexOf('/');
        if (off == -1) {
        if (!session.equals(""))
            portStr = session;
        } else {
        portStr = session.substring(0, off);
        session = session.substring(off + 1);
        // Now see if there's a ttl specified
        off = session.indexOf('/');
        if (off == -1) {
            if (!session.equals(""))
            ttlStr = session;
        } else {
            ttlStr = session.substring(0, off);
        }
        }
    }
    }

    if (addr == null)
    throw new IllegalArgumentException();
```

Listing 14.2 Continued

```
        if (portStr != null) {
        try {
            Integer integer = Integer.valueOf(portStr);
            if (integer != null)
            port = integer.intValue();
        } catch (Throwable t) {
            throw new IllegalArgumentException();
        }
        } else
        throw new IllegalArgumentException();

        if (ttlStr != null) {
        try {
            Integer integer = Integer.valueOf(ttlStr);
            if (integer != null)
            ttl = integer.intValue();
        } catch (Throwable t) {
            throw new IllegalArgumentException();
        }
        }
    }
    }

    public static void main(String argv[]) {
        if (argv.length == 0)
        prUsage();
        BranchGroup group;
    VideoCubes cubes = new VideoCubes(argv);
    new MainFrame(cubes,750,550);

        if (!cubes.initialize()) {
        System.err.println("Failed to initialize the sessions.");
        System.exit(-1);
    }

    }


    static void prUsage() {
    System.err.println("Usage: VideoCubes <session> <session> ...");
    System.err.println("     <session>: <address>/<port>/<ttl>");
    System.exit(0);
    }

}// end of VideoCubes
```

ROAM: Java-JAI-J3D Image Tiling Example

Terrain rendering is of major interest to game and simulation developers. Most developers who attempt to program a terrain algorithm soon discover that dynamic caching of the terrain data becomes necessary in order to represent a data structure of any reasonably large size.

One algorithm that has gathered a lot of interest in recent years is the Real-time Optimally Adapted Mesh algorithm (Duchaineau, et al., 1997). In collaboration with Paul Byrne of Sun and Justin Couch and Alan Hudson of Yumetech, we have developed a prototype implementation of the ROAM algorithm in Java 3D with image tiling for texture mapping. Another contributor to this project is one of the authors of the original paper, Mark Duchaineau from Jet Propulsion Labs.

Overview of Terrain Rendering

Real-time terrain rendering is a particularly challenging problem in 3D graphics. If the landscape is large, it is impossible to render the entire area, so some system needs to be implemented to load the visible parts of the terrain.

Think about the memory required to render a simple 10 meter terrain. If we used a float for each height value and represented one point per millimeter, our 10 meter square patch of terrain would require 400MB of RAM just for the height information. We would still need to render the terrain, and we haven't even put any objects in the environment.

Although detail down to the millimeter is extreme, it serves to illustrate the fundamental problem of terrain rendering. You must find a way to reduce the memory load of the terrain information.

If we were to reduce the sampling density of the heights to one sample per meter (instead of one per millimeter), we dramatically reduce our memory requirements, but we end up with a poor looking rendering.

Of course, with a perfectly flat terrain, only one height is needed. Conversely, with a mountainous terrain, much more detail is needed. What is needed is a way to determine the variability of heights in the region of interest and use this information to guide our rendering. This is the key to ROAM. The algorithm is based on a variance map that can be computed for any section of terrain. Before getting into the details of the Java 3D ROAM algorithm, we introduce the two basic approaches to terrain rendering and discuss the data structure necessary for ROAM.

Two Basic Approaches

All terrain rendering techniques begin with the idea of breaking the world into smaller, more manageable chunks. These chunks are more formally called *patches* or *tiles*. The application then controls memory usage by determining which patches are visible (or, equivalently, which chunks are not visible). As the user moves around, the application must update the visibility information.

Looking deeper into the various algorithms, there appear to be two basic approaches. One, termed *geo-mipmapping*, is similar in concept to the texture MIPMapping that we saw in Chapter 11. The patches are refined and reduced progressively. For example, the lowest-level patch would contain four corner points covering the entire patch. At this level, the terrain is represented by two triangles. The next level of detail would contain nine points. As in image MIPMapping, the level of detail used is determined by how close the user is to the object.

In the second basic approach, termed *adaptive meshing*, the code manages the terrain data by creating new triangles only when needed. If the surface is flat, only a few triangles are needed. But if the surface changes frequently over space, a lot of triangles will be needed.

Each of these approaches has its proponents. Geo-mipmapping is generally more commonly found in game applications, whereas adaptive meshing is more frequently encountered in scientific visualization.

The ROAM Algorithm

The ROAM algorithm is an adaptive meshing technique that offers a number of desirable features for terrain rendering and consists of a single preprocessing step coupled with several runtime processes. One of ROAM's advantages is that the execution time is proportional to the number of triangle *changes* that occur in each frame. The triangle changes are typically a few percent of the size of the mesh, and, therefore, faster rendering can be accomplished.

The goal of ROAM is to make a dynamic mesh based on a triangle bintree. A *bintree* is highly similar to a quadtree and can be used to organize both quads and triangles. The basic idea of a quadtree comes from image analysis and compression in which a planar image is first covered with a square and then subdivided into four neighbors until the squares become essentially uniform (based on color or spatial autocorrelation). Figure 14.2 illustrates this process with triangles. The tree becomes a sort of lookup table for triangles (or quads) and becomes progressively more detailed as you move down to lower levels in the hierarchy.

A triangle cannot undergo a split operation if its base neighbor is at a coarser level; likewise, it cannot undergo a merge operation if its neighbor is at a more detailed level. Therefore, it we want to force a split for a triangle with a coarser neighbor, we will need to recursively split the base neighbors up the tree. A merge will require a recursive merge up through the tree.

All the triangles, beginning with the base triangle, have split/merge priorities attached to them so that we can smoothly adjust the mesh. The main rule for generating the split priority is that no child can have a higher priority than its parent. Likewise, no parent can have a higher merge priority than its child. Therefore, the base triangulation has the highest priority of all possible splits, and the lowest level child has the highest priority for all possible merges.

FIGURE 14.2
Triangle bintree showing split and merge operations.

Integrating Data Structures with the Java 3D Scenegraph

As we just stated, we need to add and remove triangles during runtime. The problem is that scene graph APIs, including Java 3D, run faster when there are fewer changes to the scene graph during runtime.

One trick is to have the coordinate system of the terrain in the coordinate system of the highest branch group of the scene graph. The reason to organize the data in this way is that we don't want to include transforms in our real-time calculations. We therefore end up with a very simple scene graph.

The `Landscape` BranchGroup

Under the `Landscape` BranchGroup exist a series of `Shape3D`s that can be thought of as tiles. This is a natural structure for the JAI Tile Interface as you will see shortly. The `Landscape` class is a useful organization for terrain data regardless of the algorithm chosen for mesh updating.

Recall that a `BranchGroup` is an organizing entity for separable parts of the scene graph. Because the `Landscape` class represents the entire terrain, most of the changing logic occurs there. If we were working with a non-dynamic 3D terrain, we wouldn't need to organize the data in this way. We could simply make a `Shape3D` with an associated `GeometryArray`. In the case of ROAM, we need a dynamic change and we have yet to deal with visibility culling, so we really need a structure that will allow us to move data in and out of memory quickly without needing to determine whether every triangle will be visible.

Also, importantly, Java 3D's visibility culling works at the level of the `Shape3D`. Each `Shape3D`'s `Bounds` constitute the first step in the elimination decision. (Remember, the most efficient triangle to render is the one that isn't rendered at all.) We want to make sure that our expensive computations face this test early. Java 3D's internal mechanisms can take care of some of the management for us (which is one of the reasons we have chosen to work in Java 3D instead of a lower-level API).

Each `Patch` in the `Landscape`, therefore, uses its own instance of `Shape3D`. Note also that because of this, we can use the `GeometryUpdate` interface.

The particular `Geometry` subclass chosen in this case is `TriangleArray`. A trade-off must be made; on one hand, there is the expense of pushing triangles over the graphics bus to a card that can already triangulate for us. On the other hand, though, there is the simplicity and reduced CPU dependency of matching the data structure of our geometry to the inherent use of triangle in the ROAM algorithm.

Listing 14.3 shows the `Landscape` package that is part of the J3D.org terrain rendering download. To get this download, go to `http://code.j3d.org`. It is then possible to unjar the code examples.

LISTING 14.3   Landscape class

```
package org.j3d.terrain;

// Standard imports
import javax.media.j3d.Transform3D;

import javax.vecmath.Matrix3f;
import javax.vecmath.Tuple3f;
import javax.vecmath.Vector3f;

// Application specific imports
import org.j3d.ui.navigation.FrameUpdateListener;
import org.j3d.ui.navigation.HeightMapGeometry;


public abstract class Landscape extends javax.media.j3d.BranchGroup
    implements FrameUpdateListener, HeightMapGeometry
{
    /** The current viewing frustum that is seeing the landscape */
    protected ViewFrustum landscapeView;

    /** Raw terrain information to be rendered */
    protected TerrainData terrainData;

    /**
     * Temporary variable to hold the position information extracted from
     * the full transform class.
```

LISTING 14.3 Continued

```java
 */
private Vector3f tmpPosition;

/**
 * Temporary variable to hold the orientation information extracted from
 * the matrix class.
 */
private Vector3f tmpOrientation;

/**
 * Temporary variable to hold the orientation matrix extracted from
 * the full transform class.
 */
private Matrix3f tmpMatrix;

/**
 * Create a new Landscape with the set view and data. If either are not
 * provided, an exception is thrown.
 *
 * @param view The viewing frustum to see the data with
 * @param data The raw data to view
 * @throws IllegalArgumentException either parameter is null
 */
public Landscape(ViewFrustum view, TerrainData data)
{
    if(view == null)
        throw new IllegalArgumentException("ViewFrustum not supplied");

    if(data == null)
        throw new IllegalArgumentException("Terrain data not supplied");

    terrainData = data;
    landscapeView = view;

    tmpPosition = new Vector3f();
    tmpOrientation = new Vector3f();
    tmpMatrix = new Matrix3f();
}

//----------------------------
// Methods required by FrameUpdateListener
//----------------------------

/**
 * The transition from one point to another is completed. Use this to
```

LISTING 14.3   Continued

```java
 * update the transformation.
 *
 * @param t3d The position of the final viewpoint
 */
public void transitionEnded(Transform3D t3d)
{
    landscapeView.viewingPlatformMoved();
    setView(t3d);
}

/**
 * The frame has just been updated with the latest view information.
 * Update the landscape rendered values now.
 *
 * @param t3d The position of the viewpoint now
 */
public void viewerPositionUpdated(Transform3D t3d)
{
    landscapeView.viewingPlatformMoved();
    setView(t3d);
}

//----------------------------------
// Methods required by FrameUpdateListener
//----------------------------------

/**
 * Get the height at the given X,Z coordinate in the local coordinate
 * system. This implementation delegates to the underlying terrain data
 * to do the real resolution.
 *
 * @param x The x coordinate for the height sampling
 * @param z The z coordinate for the height sampling
 * @return The height at the current point or NaN
 */
public float getHeight(float x, float z)
{
    return terrainData.getHeight(x, z);
}

//----------------------------------
// Local methods
//----------------------------------
```

LISTING 14.3   Continued

```
    /**
     * Set the current viewing direction for the user. The user is located
     * at the given point and looking in the given direction. All information
     * is assumed to be in world coordinates.
     *
     * @param position The position the user is in the virtual world
     * @param direction The orientation of the user's gaze
     */
    public abstract void setView(Tuple3f position, Vector3f direction);

    /**
     * Set the current view location information based on a transform matrix.
     * Only the position and orientation information are extracted from this
     * matrix. Any shear or scale is ignored. Effectively, this transform
     * should be the view transform (particularly if you are using navigation
     * code from this codebase in the {@link org.j3d.ui.navigation} package.
     *
     * @param t3d The transform to use as the view position
     */
    public void setView(Transform3D t3d)
    {
        t3d.get(tmpMatrix, tmpPosition);
        tmpOrientation.set(0, 0, -1);
        tmpMatrix.transform(tmpOrientation);

        setView(tmpPosition, tmpOrientation);
    }
}
```

The ROAM algorithm extends `Landscape` to make `SplitMergeLandscape`, as shown in Listing 14.4.

LISTING 14.4   SplitMergeLandscape

```
public class SplitMergeLandscape extends Landscape
{
    static final int PATCH_SIZE = 64;

    /** The collection of all patches in this landscape */
    private ArrayList patches = new ArrayList();

    /** Queue manager for the patches needing splits or merges each frame */
    private TreeQueueManager queueManager = new TreeQueueManager();
```

LISTING 14.4 Continued

```java
/** Number of visible triangles */
private int triCount = 0;

/**
 * Creates new Landscape based on the view information and the terrain
 * data.
 *
 * @param view The view frustum looking at this landscape
 * @param terrain The raw data for the terrain
 */
public SplitMergeLandscape(ViewFrustum view, TerrainData terrain)
{
    super(view, terrain);

    createPatches();
}

/**
 * Change the view of the landscape. The virtual camera is now located in
 * this position and orientation, so adjust the visible terrain to
 * accommodate the changes.
 *
 * @param position The position of the camera
 * @param direction The direction the camera is looking
 */
public void setView(Tuple3f position, Vector3f direction)
{
    queueManager.clear();
    landscapeView.viewingPlatformMoved();
    float accuracy = (float)Math.toRadians(0.1);
    TreeNode splitCandidate;
    TreeNode mergeCandidate;
    boolean done;
    int size = patches.size();

    for(int i = 0; i < size; i++)
    {
        Patch p = (Patch)patches.get(i);

        p.setView(position, landscapeView, queueManager);
    }

    done = false;
```

LISTING 14.4 Continued

```
while(!done)
{
    splitCandidate = queueManager.getSplitCandidate();
    mergeCandidate = queueManager.getMergeCandidate();

    if(mergeCandidate == null && splitCandidate != null)
    {
        if (splitCandidate.variance > accuracy)
        {
            triCount += splitCandidate.split(position,
                                             landscapeView,
                                             queueManager);
        }
        else
            done = true;
    }
    else if(mergeCandidate!=null && splitCandidate == null)
    {
        if(mergeCandidate.diamondVariance < accuracy)
        {
            triCount -= mergeCandidate.merge(queueManager);
            //System.out.println("No split merge "+mergeCandidate+"
"+mergeCandidate.diamondVariance);
        }
        else
            done = true;
    }
    else if(mergeCandidate != null && splitCandidate != null &&
            (splitCandidate.variance > accuracy ||
              splitCandidate.variance > mergeCandidate.diamondVariance))
    {
        if (splitCandidate.variance > accuracy)
        {
            triCount += splitCandidate.split(position,
                                             landscapeView,
                                             queueManager);
        }
        else if (mergeCandidate.diamondVariance < accuracy)
        {
            triCount -= mergeCandidate.merge(queueManager);
        }
    }
    else
    {
```

LISTING 14.4   Continued

```
                    done = true;
            }
        }


        for(int i = 0; i < size; i++)
        {
            Patch p = (Patch)patches.get(i);
            p.updateGeometry();
        }
    }

    /**
     * Create a new set of patches based on the given terrain data.
     */
    private void createPatches()
    {
        int depth = terrainData.getGridDepth() - PATCH_SIZE;
        int width = terrainData.getGridWidth() - PATCH_SIZE;

        Appearance app = new Appearance();

        app.setTexture(terrainData.getTexture());

        Material mat = new Material();
        mat.setLightingEnable(true);

        app.setMaterial(mat);

//          PolygonAttributes polyAttr = new PolygonAttributes();
//          polyAttr.setPolygonMode(PolygonAttributes.POLYGON_LINE);
//          polyAttr.setCullFace(PolygonAttributes.CULL_NONE);
//          app.setPolygonAttributes(polyAttr);

        Patch[] westPatchNeighbour = new Patch[width];
        Patch southPatchNeighbour = null;
        Patch p = null;

        for(int east = 0; east <= width; east += PATCH_SIZE)
        {
            for(int north = 0; north <= depth; north += PATCH_SIZE)
            {
                p = new Patch(terrainData,
                        PATCH_SIZE,
```

LISTING 14.4   Continued

```
                                east,
                                north,
                                app,
                                landscapeView,
                                westPatchNeighbour[north/PATCH_SIZE],
                                southPatchNeighbour);

                patches.add(p);
                triCount += 2;
                this.addChild(p.getShape3D());
                southPatchNeighbour = p;
                westPatchNeighbour[north/PATCH_SIZE] = p;
            }

            southPatchNeighbour = null;
        }
    }
}
```

The split and merge queues and their usage are shown in Listing 14.4 in the setView method.

Another key component of this process is the Patch class, as shown in Listing 14.5. Note that the Patch class extends GeometryUpdater and therefore is built for updating a Shape3D. Any class that implements GeometryUpdater must override the updateData() method.

LISTING 14.5   Patch.java

```
package org.j3d.terrain.roam;

// Standard imports
import java.util.LinkedList;

import javax.media.j3d.Appearance;
import javax.media.j3d.Geometry;
import javax.media.j3d.TriangleArray;
import javax.media.j3d.BoundingBox;
import javax.media.j3d.Shape3D;
import javax.media.j3d.GeometryUpdater;

import javax.vecmath.Point3d;
import javax.vecmath.Tuple3f;
```

LISTING 14.5   Continued

```java
// Application specific imports
import org.j3d.terrain.ViewFrustum;
import org.j3d.terrain.TerrainData;

/**
 * A patch represents a single piece of terrain geometry that can be
 * rendered as a standalone block.
 * <p>
 *
 * A patch represents a single block of geometry within the overall scheme
 * of the terrain data. Apart from a fixed size nothing else is fixed in this
 * patch. The patch consists of a single TriangleArray that uses a geometry
 * updater (geometry by reference is used) to update the geometry frame
 * as necessary. It will, when instructed, dynamically recalculate what
 * vertices need to be shown and set those into the geometry array.
 *
 * @author  Paul Byrne, Justin Couch
 * @version
 */
class Patch implements GeometryUpdater
{
    /** The final size in number of grid points for this patch */
    private final int PATCH_SIZE;

    /** The values of the nodes in the NW triangle of this patch */
    TreeNode NWTree;

    /** The values of the nodes in the NW triangle of this patch */
    TreeNode SETree;

    private VarianceTree NWVariance;
    private VarianceTree SEVariance;

    /** The J3D geometry for this patch */
    private Shape3D shape3D;

    private int xOrig;
    private int yOrig;

    private TerrainData terrainData;
    private Patch westPatchNeighbour;
    private Patch southPatchNeighbour;
    private VertexData vertexData;
```

LISTING 14.5 Continued

```java
private TriangleArray geom;

/** The maximum Y for this patch */
private float maxY;

/** The minimumY for this patch */
private float minY;

/**
 * Create a new patch based on the terrain and appearance information.
 *
 * @param terrainData The raw height map info to use for this terrain
 * @param patchSize The number of grid points to use in the patch on a side
 * @param xOrig The origin of the X grid coord for this patch in the
 *     global set of grid coordinates
 * @param yOrig The origin of the Y grid coord for this patch in the
 *     global set of grid coordinates
 * @param app The global appearance object to use for this patch
 * @param landscapeView The view frustum container used
 * @param westPatchNeighbour the Patch to the west of this patch
 * @param southPatchNeighbour the Patch to the south of this patch
 */
Patch(TerrainData terrainData,
      int patchSize,
      int xOrig,
      int yOrig,
      Appearance app,
      ViewFrustum landscapeView,
      Patch westPatchNeighbour,
      Patch southPatchNeighbour)
{
    int height = yOrig + patchSize;
    int width = xOrig + patchSize;

    this.xOrig = xOrig;
    this.yOrig = yOrig;
    this.PATCH_SIZE = patchSize;
    this.terrainData = terrainData;
    this.westPatchNeighbour = westPatchNeighbour;
    this.southPatchNeighbour = southPatchNeighbour;

    boolean has_texture = (app.getTexture() != null);

    vertexData = new VertexData(PATCH_SIZE, has_texture);
```

14

LISTING 14.5 Continued

```
int format = TriangleArray.COORDINATES |
              TriangleArray.BY_REFERENCE;

if(has_texture)
    format |= TriangleArray.TEXTURE_COORDINATE_2;
else
    format |= TriangleArray.COLOR_3;

geom = new TriangleArray(PATCH_SIZE * PATCH_SIZE * 2 * 3, format);

geom.setCapability(TriangleArray.ALLOW_REF_DATA_WRITE);
geom.setCapability(TriangleArray.ALLOW_COUNT_WRITE);
geom.setCoordRefFloat(vertexData.getCoords());

if(has_texture)
    geom.setTexCoordRefFloat(0, vertexData.getTextureCoords());
else
    geom.setColorRefByte(vertexData.getColors());

NWVariance = new VarianceTree(terrainData,
                             PATCH_SIZE,
                             xOrig, yOrig,
                             width, height,
                             xOrig, height);

NWTree = new TreeNode(xOrig, yOrig,         // Left X, Y
                      width, height,        // Right X, Y
                      xOrig, height,        // Apex X, Y
                      1,
                      terrainData,
                      landscapeView,
                      TreeNode.UNDEFINED,
                      1,
                      NWVariance);

SEVariance = new VarianceTree(terrainData,
                             PATCH_SIZE,
                             width, height,      // Left X, Y
                             xOrig, yOrig,       // Right X, Y
                             width, yOrig);      // Apex X, Y

SETree = new TreeNode(width, height,        // Left X, Y
                      xOrig, yOrig,         // Right X, Y
                      width, yOrig,         // Apex X, Y
```

LISTING 14.5 Continued

```
                    1,
                    terrainData,
                    landscapeView,
                    TreeNode.UNDEFINED,
                    1,
                    SEVariance);

maxY = Math.max(NWVariance.getMaxY(), SEVariance.getMaxY());
minY = Math.min(NWVariance.getMinY(), SEVariance.getMinY());

NWTree.baseNeighbour = SETree;
SETree.baseNeighbour = NWTree;

if(westPatchNeighbour!=null)
{
    NWTree.leftNeighbour = westPatchNeighbour.SETree;
    westPatchNeighbour.SETree.leftNeighbour = NWTree;
}

if(southPatchNeighbour!=null)
{
    SETree.rightNeighbour = southPatchNeighbour.NWTree;
    southPatchNeighbour.NWTree.rightNeighbour = SETree;
}

Point3d min_bounds =
    new Point3d(xOrig * terrainData.getGridXStep(),
                minY,
                -(yOrig + height) * terrainData.getGridYStep());

Point3d max_bounds =
    new Point3d((xOrig + width) * terrainData.getGridXStep(),
                maxY,
                -yOrig * terrainData.getGridYStep());

shape3D = new Shape3D(geom, app);
shape3D.setBoundsAutoCompute(false);
shape3D.setBounds(new BoundingBox(min_bounds, max_bounds));

// Just as a failsafe, always set the terrain data in the user
// data section of the node so that terrain code will find it
// again, even if the top user is stupid.
shape3D.setUserData(terrainData);
}
```

14

INTEGRATING THE
JAVA MEDIA APIS

LISTING 14.5   Continued

```java
// — — — — — — — — — — — — — — — — — — — — — — — — — — — — — —
// Methods required by GeometryUpdater
// — — — — — — — — — — — — — — — — — — — — — — — — — — — — — —

/**
 * Update the J3D geometry array for data now.
 *
 * @param geom The geometry object to update
 */
public void updateData(Geometry geom)
{
    createGeometry((TriangleArray)geom);
}


// — — — — — — — — — — — — — — — — — — — — — — — — — — — — — —
// local convenience methods
// — — — — — — — — — — — — — — — — — — — — — — — — — — — — — —

void reset(ViewFrustum landscapeView)
{
    NWTree.reset(landscapeView);
    SETree.reset(landscapeView);

    NWTree.baseNeighbour = SETree;
    SETree.baseNeighbour = NWTree;

    if(westPatchNeighbour != null)
    {
        NWTree.leftNeighbour = westPatchNeighbour.SETree;
        westPatchNeighbour.SETree.leftNeighbour = NWTree;
    }

    if(southPatchNeighbour != null)
    {
        SETree.rightNeighbour = southPatchNeighbour.NWTree;
        southPatchNeighbour.NWTree.rightNeighbour = SETree;
    }
}

/**
 * Change the view to the new position and orientation. In this
 * implementation the direction information is ignored because we have
 * the view frustum to use.
 *
 * @param position The location of the user in space
```

LISTING 14.5   Continued

```
 * @param landscapeView The viewing frustum information for clipping
 * @param queueManager Manager for ordering terrain chunks
 */
void setView(Tuple3f position,
             ViewFrustum landscapeView,
             QueueManager queueManager)
{
    NWTree.updateTree(position,
                      landscapeView,
                      NWVariance,
                      TreeNode.UNDEFINED,
                      queueManager);

    SETree.updateTree(position,
                      landscapeView,
                      SEVariance,
                      TreeNode.UNDEFINED,
                      queueManager);
}

/**
 * Request an update to the geometry. If the geometry is visible then
 * tell J3D that we would like to update the geometry. It does not directly
 * do the update because we are using GeomByRef and so need to wait for the
 * renderer to tell us when it is OK to do the updates.
 */
void updateGeometry()
{
    if(NWTree.visible != ViewFrustum.OUT ||
       SETree.visible != ViewFrustum.OUT ||
       vertexData.getVertexCount() != 0)
    {
        geom.updateData(this);
    }
}

/**
 * Fetch the number of triangles that are currently visible in this patch.
 *
 * @return The number of visible triangles
 */
int getTriangleCount()
{
    return vertexData.getVertexCount() / 3;
}
```

14

INTEGRATING THE
JAVA MEDIA APIS

LISTING 14.5 Continued

```java
/**
 * Get the shape node that is used to represent this patch.
 *
 * @return The shape node
 */
Shape3D getShape3D()
{
    return shape3D;
}

/**
 * Create the geometry needed for this patch. Just sets how many vertices
 * are to be used based on the triangles of the two halves of the tree.
 *
 * @param geom The geometry array to work with
 */
private void createGeometry(TriangleArray geom) {
    vertexData.reset();

    if(NWTree.visible!=ViewFrustum.OUT)
        NWTree.getTriangles(vertexData);

    if(SETree.visible != ViewFrustum.OUT)
        SETree.getTriangles(vertexData);

    geom.setValidVertexCount(vertexData.getVertexCount());
}
}
```

The updateData() method calls the createGeometry() method, which determines if neighboring TreeNodes need to be loaded. The TreeNode class is given in Listing 14.6.

LISTING 14.6 TreeNode.java

```java
package org.j3d.terrain.roam;

// Standard imports
import java.util.LinkedList;

import javax.vecmath.Tuple3f;

// Application specific imports
import org.j3d.terrain.ViewFrustum;
import org.j3d.terrain.TerrainData;
```

LISTING 14.6   Continued

```java
/**
 * Represents a single node of the triangle mesh of the patch.
 *
 * @author   Paul Byrne, Justin Couch
 * @version
 */
class TreeNode
{
    /** The visibility status of this node in the tree is not known. */
    public static final int UNDEFINED = -1;

    TreeNode leftChild;
    TreeNode rightChild;

    TreeNode baseNeighbour;
    TreeNode leftNeighbour;
    TreeNode rightNeighbour;

    TreeNode parent;

    private int leftX, leftY;          // Pointers into terrainData
    private int rightX, rightY;
    private int apexX, apexY;

    private int node;

    private int depth;          // For debugging

    int visible = UNDEFINED;

    // The three corners of the triangle
    private float p1X, p1Y, p1Z;
    private float p2X, p2Y, p2Z;
    private float p3X, p3Y, p3Z;

    // Texture coordinates or colour values
    private float p1tS, p1tT, p1tR;
    private float p2tS, p2tT, p2tR;
    private float p3tS, p3tT, p3tR;

    private TerrainData terrainData;
    private VarianceTree varianceTree;

    float variance = 0f;
    float diamondVariance = 0f;
```

LISTING 14.6   Continued

```java
boolean diamond = false;

private boolean textured;

/**
 * A cache of instances of ourselves to help avoid too much object
 * creation and deletion.
 */
private static LinkedList nodeCache = new LinkedList();


/**
 * Default constructor for use by TreeNodeCache.
 */
TreeNode()
{
}

/**
 * Creates new TreeNode customised with all the data set.
 */
TreeNode(int leftX,
         int leftY,
         int rightX,
         int rightY,
         int apexX,
         int apexY,
         int node,
         TerrainData terrainData,
         ViewFrustum landscapeView,
         int parentVisible,
         int depth,
         VarianceTree varianceTree)
{
    this.leftX = leftX;
    this.leftY = leftY;
    this.rightX = rightX;
    this.rightY = rightY;
    this.apexX = apexX;
    this.apexY = apexY;
    this.node = node;
    this.terrainData = terrainData;
    this.depth = depth;
    this.varianceTree = varianceTree;
```

LISTING 14.6 Continued

```java
        init(landscapeView, parentVisible);
}

/**
 * Used to populate a node retrieved from the TreeNodeCache
 * setting the same state as creating a new TreeNode would.
 */
void newNode(int leftX,
             int leftY,
             int rightX,
             int rightY,
             int apexX,
             int apexY,
             int node,
             TerrainData terrainData,
             ViewFrustum landscapeView,
             int parentVisible,
             int depth,
             VarianceTree varianceTree)
{
    this.leftX = leftX;
    this.leftY = leftY;
    this.rightX = rightX;
    this.rightY = rightY;
    this.apexX = apexX;
    this.apexY = apexY;
    this.node = node;
    this.terrainData = terrainData;
    this.depth = depth;
    this.varianceTree = varianceTree;


    init(landscapeView, parentVisible);
}

/**
 * Reset this node by removing all it's children, set visible depending
 * on visibiling in view.
 *
 * @param landscapeView The latest view of the tree
 */
void reset(ViewFrustum landscapeView)
{
    if(leftChild != null)
    {
```

LISTING 14.6   Continued

```java
            leftChild.freeNode();
            leftChild = null;
        }

        if(rightChild != null)
        {
            rightChild.freeNode();
            rightChild = null;
        }

        baseNeighbour =null;
        leftNeighbour =null;
        rightNeighbour = null;

        visible = landscapeView.isTriangleInFrustum(p1X, p1Y, p1Z,
                                                    p2X, p2Y, p2Z,
                                                    p3X, p3Y, p3Z);
    }

    /**
     * Check to see if this treenode is a leaf or a branch. A leaf does not
     * have a left-hand child node.
     *
     * @return true if this is a leaf
     */
    boolean isLeaf()
    {
        return (leftChild == null);
    }

    /**
     * Place this node and all its children in the TreeNodeCache
     */
    void freeNode()
    {
        if(leftChild != null)
        {
            leftChild.freeNode();
            leftChild = null;
        }

        if(rightChild != null)
        {
            rightChild.freeNode();
```

LISTING 14.6 Continued

```java
            rightChild = null;
        }

        baseNeighbour = null;
        leftNeighbour = null;
        rightNeighbour = null;
        parent = null;
        diamond = false;

        addTreeNode(this);
    }

    /**
     * Request the recomputation of the variance of this node and place the
     * node on the queue ready for processing.
     *
     * @param position The location to compute the value from
     * @param queueManager The queue to place the node on
     */
    void computeVariance(Tuple3f position, QueueManager queueManager)
    {
        computeVariance(position);

        queueManager.addTriangle(this);
    }

    /**
     * If this triangle was half of a diamond then remove the
     * diamond from the diamondQueue
     *
     * @param queueManager The queue to remove the node from
     */
    void removeDiamond(QueueManager queueManager)
    {
        if(diamond)
        {
            queueManager.removeDiamond(this);
            diamondVariance = 0f;
            diamond = false;
        }
        else if(baseNeighbour != null && baseNeighbour.diamond)
        {
            queueManager.removeDiamond(baseNeighbour);
            baseNeighbour.diamondVariance = 0f;
            baseNeighbour.diamond = false;
```

LISTING 14.6   Continued

```java
        }
    }

    /**
     * Split this tree node into two smaller triangle tree nodes.
     *
     * @param position The current view location
     * @param landscapeView The view information
     * @param queueManager The queue to place newly generated items on
     * @return The number of triangles generated as a result
     */
    int split(Tuple3f position,
              ViewFrustum landscapeView,
              QueueManager queueManager)
    {
        int triCount = 0;

        //System.out.println(" — — — — — -> Splitting "+node);

        //if(mergedThisFrame)
        //    System.out.println("SPLITTING Tri that has been merged");
        //splitThisFrame = true;

        if(leftChild != null || rightChild != null)
        {
            throw new RuntimeException(" Triangle is already split "+node);
        }

        if(baseNeighbour != null)
        {
            if(baseNeighbour.baseNeighbour != this)
                triCount += baseNeighbour.split(position,
                                                landscapeView,
                                                queueManager);

            split2(position, landscapeView, queueManager);
            triCount++;
            baseNeighbour.split2(position, landscapeView, queueManager);
            //if(baseNeighbour.visible!=ViewFrustum.OUT)
            triCount++;

            leftChild.rightNeighbour = baseNeighbour.rightChild;
            rightChild.leftNeighbour = baseNeighbour.leftChild;
            baseNeighbour.leftChild.rightNeighbour = rightChild;
            baseNeighbour.rightChild.leftNeighbour = leftChild;
```

LISTING 14.6   Continued

```
            diamondVariance = Math.max(variance, baseNeighbour.variance);
            diamond = true;
            queueManager.addDiamond(this);
        }
        else
        {
            split2(position, landscapeView, queueManager);
            triCount++;

            diamondVariance = variance;
            diamond = true;
            queueManager.addDiamond(this);
        }

        return triCount;
    }

    /**
     * Merge the children nodes of this node into a single triangle.
     *
     * @param queueManager The queue to put the merged node on
     * @return The number of triangles that were reduced as a result
     */
    int merge(QueueManager queueManager)
    {
        int trisRemoved = 0;

        //System.out.print("Merging ");
        //printNode(this);

        //if(splitThisFrame)
        //    System.out.println("Merging Tri that was split this frame");
        //mergedThisFrame = true;

        if(baseNeighbour != null && baseNeighbour.baseNeighbour != this)
        {
            System.out.println("***** Illegal merge ********");
            queueManager.removeDiamond(this);
            diamond = false;
            diamondVariance = 0f;
            return 0;
            //throw new RuntimeException("Illegal merge");
        }
```

14

LISTING 14.6   Continued

```
        merge(this, queueManager);
        trisRemoved++;
        checkForNewDiamond(this.parent, queueManager);
        if(baseNeighbour!=null)
        {
            merge(baseNeighbour, queueManager);
            trisRemoved++;
            checkForNewDiamond(baseNeighbour.parent, queueManager);
        }

        queueManager.removeDiamond(this);
        diamond = false;
        diamondVariance = 0f;

        return trisRemoved;
    }

    /**
     * Add the coordinates for this triangle to the list
     */
    void getTriangles(VertexData vertexData)
    {
        if(leftChild == null)
        {
            if((visible != ViewFrustum.OUT) && (visible != UNDEFINED))
            {
                if(vertexData.textured)
                {
                    vertexData.addVertex(p1X, p1Y, p1Z,
                                         p1tS, p1tT);
                    vertexData.addVertex(p2X, p2Y, p2Z,
                                         p2tS, p2tT);
                    vertexData.addVertex(p3X, p3Y, p3Z,
                                         p3tS, p3tT);
                }
                else
                {
                    vertexData.addVertex(p1X, p1Y, p1Z,
                                         p1tS, p1tT, p1tR);
                    vertexData.addVertex(p2X, p2Y, p2Z,
                                         p2tS, p2tT, p2tR);
                    vertexData.addVertex(p3X, p3Y, p3Z,
                                         p3tS, p3tT, p3tR);
                }
            }
```

LISTING 14.6   Continued

```java
        }
        else
        {
            leftChild.getTriangles(vertexData);
            rightChild.getTriangles(vertexData);
        }
    }

    /**
     * Update the tree depending on the view position and variance
     */
    void updateTree(Tuple3f position,
                    ViewFrustum landscapeView,
                    VarianceTree varianceTree,
                    int parentVisible,
                    QueueManager queueManager)
    {

        //splitThisFrame = false;
        //mergedThisFrame = false;

        if(parentVisible == UNDEFINED ||
           parentVisible == ViewFrustum.CLIPPED)
        {
            visible = landscapeView.isTriangleInFrustum(p1X, p1Y, p1Z,
                                                        p2X, p2Y, p2Z,
                                                        p3X, p3Y, p3Z);
        }
        else
            visible = parentVisible;

        if(leftChild == null &&
           rightChild == null &&
           depth < varianceTree.getMaxDepth() &&
           visible != ViewFrustum.OUT)
        {

            computeVariance(position);

            queueManager.addTriangle(this);
        }
        else
        {
            if(leftChild != null)
                leftChild.updateTree(position,
                                     landscapeView,
```

LISTING 14.6   Continued

```
                                        varianceTree,
                                        visible,
                                        queueManager);

            if(rightChild != null)
                rightChild.updateTree(position,
                                        landscapeView,
                                        varianceTree,
                                        visible,
                                        queueManager);

            //System.out.println(diamond+"  "+diamondVariance);
            if(diamond) {

// BUG Here, baseNeighbour may not have had its variance updated
// for the new position
                if(visible != ViewFrustum.OUT)
                {
                    computeVariance(position);

                    if(baseNeighbour != null)
                        diamondVariance = Math.max(variance,
                                                    baseNeighbour.variance);
                    else
                        diamondVariance = variance;
                }
                else
                {
                    diamondVariance = Float.MIN_VALUE;
                }

                queueManager.addDiamond(this);
            }
        }
    }

    public String toString() {
        return Integer.toString(node);
    }

    //—————————————————————————————————
    // local convenience methods
    //—————————————————————————————————
```

LISTING 14.6 Continued

```java
/**
 * Internal common initialization for the startup of the class.
 *
 * @param landscapeView view information at start time
 * @param parentVisible Flag about the visibility state of the parent
 *      tree node
 */
private void init(ViewFrustum landscapeView, int parentVisible)
{
    float[] tmp = new float[3];
    float[] texTmp = new float[3];

    boolean textured = terrainData.hasTexture();

    if(textured)
        terrainData.getCoordinateWithTexture(tmp, texTmp, leftX, leftY);
    else
        terrainData.getCoordinateWithColor(tmp, texTmp, leftX, leftY);

    p1X = tmp[0];
    p1Y = tmp[1];
    p1Z = tmp[2];

    p1tS = texTmp[0];
    p1tT = texTmp[1];
    p1tR = texTmp[2];

    if(textured)
        terrainData.getCoordinateWithTexture(tmp, texTmp, rightX, rightY);
    else
        terrainData.getCoordinateWithColor(tmp, texTmp, rightX, rightY);

    p2X = tmp[0];
    p2Y = tmp[1];
    p2Z = tmp[2];

    p2tS = texTmp[0];
    p2tT = texTmp[1];
    p2tR = texTmp[2];

    if(textured)
        terrainData.getCoordinateWithTexture(tmp, texTmp, apexX, apexY);
    else
        terrainData.getCoordinateWithColor(tmp, texTmp, apexX, apexY);
```

14

INTEGRATING THE
JAVA MEDIA APIS

LISTING 14.6   Continued

```java
        p3X = tmp[0];
        p3Y = tmp[1];
        p3Z = tmp[2];

        p3tS = texTmp[0];
        p3tT = texTmp[1];
        p3tR = texTmp[2];

        // Check the visibility of this triangle
        if(parentVisible == UNDEFINED ||
           parentVisible == ViewFrustum.CLIPPED)
        {
            visible = landscapeView.isTriangleInFrustum(p1X, p1Y, p1Z,
                                                        p2X, p2Y, p2Z,
                                                        p3X, p3Y, p3Z);
        }
        else
            visible = parentVisible;

        variance = 0;
    }

    /**
     * Compute the variance variable value.
     *
     * @param position The position for the computation
     */
    private void computeVariance(Tuple3f position)
    {
        float center_x = (p1X + p2X) * 0.5f;
        float center_z = -(p1Y + p2Y) * 0.5f;
        float pos_x = (position.x - center_x) * (position.x - center_x);
        float pos_z = (position.z - center_z) * (position.z - center_z);
        float distance = (float)Math.sqrt(pos_x + pos_z);

        float angle = varianceTree.getVariance(node) / distance;

        variance = (float)Math.abs(Math.atan(angle));
    }

    /**
     * Forceful split of this triangle and turns it into two triangles.
     */
    private void splitTriangle(Tuple3f position,
                               ViewFrustum landscapeView,
                               QueueManager queueManager)
```

LISTING 14.6   Continued

```java
{
    int splitX = (leftX+rightX)/2;
    int splitY = (leftY+rightY)/2;

    if(parent != null)
        parent.removeDiamond(queueManager);

    leftChild = getTreeNode();
    rightChild = getTreeNode();

    leftChild.newNode(apexX, apexY,
                           leftX, leftY,
                           splitX, splitY,
                           node << 1,
                           terrainData,
                           landscapeView,
                           visible,
                           depth + 1,
                           varianceTree);

    rightChild.newNode(rightX, rightY,
                           apexX, apexY,
                           splitX, splitY,
                           1 + (node << 1),
                           terrainData,
                           landscapeView,
                           visible,
                           depth + 1,
                           varianceTree);

    leftChild.parent = this;
    rightChild.parent = this;

    if(depth+1 < varianceTree.getMaxDepth() && visible!=ViewFrustum.OUT)
    {
        rightChild.computeVariance(position, queueManager);
        leftChild.computeVariance(position, queueManager);
    }
}

private void split2(Tuple3f position,
                    ViewFrustum landscapeView,
                    QueueManager queueManager)
{
    splitTriangle(position, landscapeView, queueManager);
```

LISTING 14.6   Continued

```
        queueManager.removeTriangle(this);

        leftChild.leftNeighbour = rightChild;
        rightChild.rightNeighbour = leftChild;
        leftChild.baseNeighbour = leftNeighbour;

        if(leftNeighbour != null)
        {
            if(leftNeighbour.baseNeighbour == this)
                leftNeighbour.baseNeighbour = leftChild;
            else
            {
                if(leftNeighbour.leftNeighbour == this)
                    leftNeighbour.leftNeighbour = leftChild;
                else
                    leftNeighbour.rightNeighbour = leftChild;
            }
        }

        rightChild.baseNeighbour = rightNeighbour;

        if(rightNeighbour != null)
        {
            if(rightNeighbour.baseNeighbour == this)
                rightNeighbour.baseNeighbour = rightChild;
            else
            {
                if(rightNeighbour.rightNeighbour == this)
                    rightNeighbour.rightNeighbour = rightChild;
                else
                    rightNeighbour.leftNeighbour = rightChild;
            }
        }
    }

    private void merge(TreeNode mergeNode, QueueManager queueManager)
    {
        if(mergeNode.leftChild == null ||
           mergeNode.rightChild == null ||
           !mergeNode.leftChild.isLeaf() ||
           !mergeNode.rightChild.isLeaf())
        {
            throw new RuntimeException("Illegal merge");
        }
```

LISTING 14.6   Continued

```
        if(mergeNode.leftNeighbour != null)
        {
            if(mergeNode.leftNeighbour.baseNeighbour == mergeNode.leftChild)
                mergeNode.leftNeighbour.baseNeighbour = mergeNode;
            else
            {
                if(mergeNode.leftNeighbour.leftNeighbour ==
mergeNode.leftChild)
                    mergeNode.leftNeighbour.leftNeighbour = mergeNode;
                else
                    mergeNode.leftNeighbour.rightNeighbour = mergeNode;
            }
        }

        if(mergeNode.rightNeighbour != null)
        {
            if(mergeNode.rightNeighbour.baseNeighbour == mergeNode.rightChild)
                mergeNode.rightNeighbour.baseNeighbour = mergeNode;
            else
            {
                if(mergeNode.rightNeighbour.rightNeighbour ==
mergeNode.rightChild)
                    mergeNode.rightNeighbour.rightNeighbour = mergeNode;
                else
                    mergeNode.rightNeighbour.leftNeighbour = mergeNode;
            }
        }

        if(mergeNode.leftChild.baseNeighbour != null &&
          mergeNode.leftChild.baseNeighbour.baseNeighbour
                                        == mergeNode.leftChild)
        {
            mergeNode.leftChild.baseNeighbour.baseNeighbour = mergeNode;
        }

        if(mergeNode.rightChild.baseNeighbour != null &&
         mergeNode.rightChild.baseNeighbour.baseNeighbour
                                        == mergeNode.rightChild)
        {
            mergeNode.rightChild.baseNeighbour.baseNeighbour = mergeNode;
        }

        mergeNode.leftNeighbour = mergeNode.leftChild.baseNeighbour;
        mergeNode.rightNeighbour = mergeNode.rightChild.baseNeighbour;
```

14

**INTEGRATING THE
JAVA MEDIA APIS**

LISTING 14.6   Continued

```java
        if(mergeNode.visible != ViewFrustum.OUT)
            queueManager.addTriangle(mergeNode);

        queueManager.removeTriangle(mergeNode.leftChild);
        queueManager.removeTriangle(mergeNode.rightChild);

        mergeNode.leftChild.freeNode();
        mergeNode.leftChild = null;
        mergeNode.rightChild.freeNode();
        mergeNode.rightChild = null;
    }

    /**
     * Check if tn forms a diamond
     */
    private void checkForNewDiamond(TreeNode tn, QueueManager queueManager)
    {
        if(tn == null)
            return;

        if(tn.leftChild.isLeaf() && tn.rightChild.isLeaf() &&
            (tn.baseNeighbour == null ||
            tn.baseNeighbour.leftChild == null ||
            (tn.baseNeighbour.leftChild.isLeaf() &&
             tn.baseNeighbour.rightChild.isLeaf())))
        {
            tn.diamond = true;

            if(tn.visible != ViewFrustum.OUT)
            {
                if(tn.baseNeighbour != null)
                    tn.diamondVariance = Math.max(tn.variance,
                                                  tn.baseNeighbour.variance);
                else
                    tn.diamondVariance = tn.variance;
            }
            else
                tn.diamondVariance = Float.MIN_VALUE;

            queueManager.addDiamond(tn);
        }
    }
```

LISTING 14.6   Continued

```java
    /**
     * Either return a node from the cache or if the cache is empty, return
     * a new tree node.
     */
    private static TreeNode getTreeNode()
    {
        TreeNode ret_val;

        if(nodeCache.size() > 0)
            ret_val = (TreeNode)nodeCache.removeFirst();
        else
            ret_val = new TreeNode();

        return ret_val;
    }

    /**
     * Add the node to the free cache.
     */
    private static void addTreeNode(TreeNode node)
    {
        nodeCache.add(node);
    }
}
```

Image Tiling in JAI

We have finally reached a place where we can assign JAI Image Tiles to `Patches`. Recall that tiles are rectangular segments of a `Raster` object. Instead of working with the entire image at once (essentially one huge tile), you can work with rectangular subsegments. This is particularly useful when dealing with large images that don't easily fit into memory all at once. This is precisely the case that exists with terrain data.

The output of the image tiling ROAM example is shown in Figure 14.3, and the `CachedTextureTileGenerator` class is shown in Listing 14.7.

LISTING 14.7   `CachedTextureTileGenerator`

```java
// Standard imports
import java.awt.*;
import java.awt.event.*;
import java.awt.image.*;
import java.awt.image.renderable.*;
import javax.media.j3d.*;
```

Listing 14.7   Continued

```java
import javax.media.jai.JAI;
import javax.media.jai.PlanarImage;
import javax.media.jai.ImageLayout;
import java.util.HashMap;

// Application Specific imports
import org.j3d.terrain.TextureTileGenerator;

/**
 * An example TextureTileGenerator.
 * Caches textures so we don't regenerate them, but never decreases memory
usage.
 *
 * @author Alan Hudson
 */
public class CachedTextureTileGenerator implements TextureTileGenerator {
    /** The source image */
    private PlanarImage source;

    /** A simple cache */
    private Texture tCache[][];

    /**
     * Construct a TileGenerator for the specified name.
     *
     * @param filename The texture to tile
     */
    public CachedTextureTileGenerator(String filename)
    {
        source = JAI.create("fileload", filename);

        ParameterBlock pb = new ParameterBlock();
        pb.addSource(source);
        pb.add(null).add(null).add(null).add(null).add(null);

        RenderableImage ren = JAI.createRenderable("renderable", pb);
        RenderedImage image = ren.createDefaultRendering();

        /* Create a texture cache of 8x8 tiles.  2K image / 256 bytes */
        tCache = new Texture[8][8];
    }

    /**
     * Get the size of each texture tile.
     *
```

LISTING 14.7   Continued

```
     * @return The dimensions of the tile
     */
    public Dimension getTextureSize()
    {
        return new Dimension(256,256);
    }

    /**
     * Get the texture tile for bounded region.
     *
     * @param bounds The region
     */
    public Texture getTextureTile(Rectangle bounds)
    {
        int x = bounds.x / 256;
        int y = bounds.y / 256;

        if (tCache[x][y] != null) {
            return (tCache[x][y]);
        }

        Rectangle rect = new Rectangle(bounds.x, bounds.y, bounds.width,
            bounds.height);

        BufferedImage bi = source.getAsBufferedImage(rect, null);

        int format = ImageComponent2D.FORMAT_RGB;

        ImageComponent2D img =
            new ImageComponent2D(format, bi, true, false);

        Texture texture = new Texture2D(Texture.BASE_LEVEL,
                                        Texture.RGB,
                                        img.getWidth(),
                                        img.getHeight());
        texture.setImage(0, img);

        tCache[x][y] = texture;

        return texture;
    }
}
```

Listing 14.8 is a shell program from running the ROAM code.

LISTING 14.8   TiledCullingDemo

```java
// Standard imports
import java.awt.*;
import java.awt.event.*;
import java.awt.image.*;
import java.awt.image.renderable.*;
import javax.swing.*;
import javax.media.j3d.*;
import javax.vecmath.*;
import javax.media.jai.JAI;
import javax.media.jai.PlanarImage;
import javax.media.jai.ImageLayout;
import java.io.File;
import java.io.FileInputStream;
import java.io.IOException;
import java.util.HashMap;
import java.util.Hashtable;

// Application Specific imports
import org.j3d.geom.Box;

import org.j3d.loaders.HeightMapTerrainData;
import org.j3d.loaders.SimpleTiledTerrainData;
import org.j3d.loaders.vterrain.BTHeader;
import org.j3d.loaders.vterrain.BTParser;

import org.j3d.terrain.AbstractStaticTerrainData;
import org.j3d.terrain.AbstractTiledTerrainData;
import org.j3d.terrain.AppearanceGenerator;
import org.j3d.terrain.Landscape;
import org.j3d.terrain.TerrainData;
import org.j3d.terrain.TextureTileGenerator;
import org.j3d.terrain.roam.SplitMergeLandscape;

import org.j3d.texture.TextureCache;
import org.j3d.texture.TextureCacheFactory;

import org.j3d.ui.navigation.MouseViewHandler;
import org.j3d.ui.navigation.NavigationStateManager;
import org.j3d.ui.navigation.NavigationState;

import org.j3d.util.interpolator.ColorInterpolator;
import org.j3d.util.frustum.ViewFrustum;
```

LISTING 14.8 Continued

```java
/**
 * Demonstration of the ROAM code using tiled textures.
 *
 *
 * @author Alan Hudson
 * @version $Revision: 1.1 $
 */
public class TiledCullingDemo extends DemoFrame
    implements ItemListener, AppearanceGenerator
{
    private static final double BACK_CLIP_DISTANCE = 3000.0;
    private static final double FRONT_CLIP_DISTANCE = 1;

    /** The main canvas that we are navigating on */
    private Canvas3D navCanvas;

    /** The canvas that provides a birds-eye view of the scene */
    private Canvas3D topDownCanvas;

    /** Global material instance to use */
    private Material material;

    /** Global polygon attributes to use */
    private PolygonAttributes polyAttr;

    private MouseViewHandler groundNav;
    private MouseViewHandler topDownNav;

    /** The view frustum for the ground canvas */
    private ViewFrustum viewFrustum;

    /** The landscape we are navigating around */
    private Landscape landscape;

    /** The branchgroup to add our terrain to */
    private BranchGroup terrainGroup;

    /** TG that holds the user view position. Used when new terrain set */
    private TransformGroup gndViewTransform;

    /** TG that holds the top-down user view position. Used when new terrain
 ↪set */
    private TransformGroup topViewTransform;
```

LISTING 14.8   Continued

```java
private HashMap terrainFilesMap;
private HashMap textureFilesMap;

/** Mapping of the button to the polygon mode value */
private HashMap polyModeMap;

/** The color interpolator for doing height interpolations with */
private ColorInterpolator heightRamp;

/**
 * Construct a new demo with no geometry currently showing, but the
 * default type is set to quads.
 */
public TiledCullingDemo()
{
    super("Tiled Culling Demo");

    topDownCanvas = createCanvas();
    navCanvas = createCanvas();

    Cursor curse = Cursor.getPredefinedCursor(Cursor.CROSSHAIR_CURSOR);
    navCanvas.setCursor(curse);

    terrainFilesMap = new HashMap();
    textureFilesMap = new HashMap();

    Panel p0 = new Panel(new GridLayout(1, 2));
    p0.add(navCanvas);
    p0.add(topDownCanvas);

    add(p0, BorderLayout.CENTER);

    JPanel p1 = new JPanel(new FlowLayout());

    ButtonGroup grp = new ButtonGroup();
    JRadioButton button = new JRadioButton("Crater Lake");
    button.addItemListener(this);
    grp.add(button);
    p1.add(button);

    terrainFilesMap.put(button, "crater_0513.bt");
    textureFilesMap.put(button, null);

    add(p1, BorderLayout.SOUTH);
```

LISTING 14.8   Continued

```java
// Panel for the polygon mode style
polyModeMap = new HashMap();

JPanel p2 = new JPanel(new GridLayout(4, 1));

p2.add(new JLabel("Render As..."));

grp = new ButtonGroup();
button = new JRadioButton("Polygons", true);
button.addItemListener(this);
grp.add(button);
p2.add(button);
polyModeMap.put(button, new Integer(PolygonAttributes.POLYGON_FILL));


button = new JRadioButton("Lines");
button.addItemListener(this);
grp.add(button);
p2.add(button);
polyModeMap.put(button, new Integer(PolygonAttributes.POLYGON_LINE));


button = new JRadioButton("Points");
button.addItemListener(this);
grp.add(button);
p2.add(button);
polyModeMap.put(button, new Integer(PolygonAttributes.POLYGON_POINT));


JPanel p3 = new JPanel(new BorderLayout());
p3.add(p2, BorderLayout.NORTH);

add(p3, BorderLayout.EAST);

groundNav = new MouseViewHandler();
groundNav.setCanvas(navCanvas);
groundNav.setButtonNavigation(MouseEvent.BUTTON1_MASK,
                              NavigationState.FLY_STATE);
groundNav.setButtonNavigation(MouseEvent.BUTTON2_MASK,
                              NavigationState.TILT_STATE);
groundNav.setButtonNavigation(MouseEvent.BUTTON3_MASK,
                              NavigationState.PAN_STATE);
```

14

INTEGRATING THE
JAVA MEDIA APIS

LISTING 14.8   Continued

```java
        NavigationStateManager gnd_nav_mgr =
            new NavigationStateManager(navCanvas);
        gnd_nav_mgr.setMouseHandler(groundNav);

        topDownNav = new MouseViewHandler();
        topDownNav.setCanvas(topDownCanvas);
        topDownNav.setButtonNavigation(MouseEvent.BUTTON1_MASK,
                                       NavigationState.PAN_STATE);

        NavigationStateManager top_nav_mgr =
            new NavigationStateManager(topDownCanvas);
        top_nav_mgr.setMouseHandler(topDownNav);

        buildScene();

        viewFrustum = new ViewFrustum(navCanvas);

        // Now set up the material and appearance handling for the generator
        material = new Material();
        material.setLightingEnable(true);

        polyAttr = new PolygonAttributes();
        polyAttr.setCapability(PolygonAttributes.ALLOW_MODE_WRITE);
        polyAttr.setCullFace(PolygonAttributes.CULL_NONE);
        polyAttr.setBackFaceNormalFlip(true);

        heightRamp = new ColorInterpolator(ColorInterpolator.HSV_SPACE);
        heightRamp.addRGBKeyFrame(-20,  0,    0,    1,    0);
        heightRamp.addRGBKeyFrame(0,    0,    0.7f, 0.95f, 0);
        heightRamp.addRGBKeyFrame(5,    1,    1,    0,    0);
        heightRamp.addRGBKeyFrame(10,   0,    0.6f, 0,    0);
        heightRamp.addRGBKeyFrame(100,  0,    1,    0,    0);
        heightRamp.addRGBKeyFrame(1000, 0.6f, 0.7f, 0,    0);
        heightRamp.addRGBKeyFrame(1500, 0.5f, 0.5f, 0.3f, 0);
        heightRamp.addRGBKeyFrame(2500, 1,    1,    1,    0);
    }

    //-------------------------------
    // Methods required by ItemListener
    //-------------------------------

    /**
     * Process the change of state request from the colour selector panel.
     *
     * @param evt The event that caused this method to be called
     */
```

LISTING 14.8   Continued

```java
public void itemStateChanged(ItemEvent evt)
{
    if(evt.getStateChange() != ItemEvent.SELECTED)
        return;

    Object src = evt.getSource();

    if(textureFilesMap.containsKey(src))
    {
        // map change request
        String terrain = (String)terrainFilesMap.get(src);
        String texture = (String)textureFilesMap.get(src);

        loadTerrain(terrain, texture);
    }
    else
    {
        Integer mode_int = (Integer)polyModeMap.get(src);
        polyAttr.setPolygonMode(mode_int.intValue());
    }
}


//------------------------------
// Methods required by AppearanceGenerator
//------------------------------

/**
 * Create a new appearance instance. We set them all up with different
 * appearance instances, but share the material information.
 *
 * @return The new appearance instance to use
 */
public Appearance createAppearance()
{
    Appearance app = new Appearance();
    app.setMaterial(material);
    app.setPolygonAttributes(polyAttr);

    return app;
}


//------------------------------
// Internal convenience methods
//------------------------------
```

LISTING 14.8   Continued

```
/**
 * Build the scenegraph for the canvas
 */
private void buildScene()
{
    Color3f ambientBlue = new Color3f(0.0f, 0.02f, 0.5f);
    Color3f white = new Color3f(1, 1, 1);
    Color3f black = new Color3f(0.0f, 0.0f, 0.0f);
    Color3f blue = new Color3f(0.00f, 0.20f, 0.80f);
    Color3f specular = new Color3f(0.7f, 0.7f, 0.7f);

    VirtualUniverse universe = new VirtualUniverse();
    Locale locale = new Locale(universe);

    BranchGroup view_group = new BranchGroup();
    BranchGroup world_object_group = new BranchGroup();

    PhysicalBody body = new PhysicalBody();
    PhysicalEnvironment env = new PhysicalEnvironment();

    Point3d origin = new Point3d(0, 0, 0);
    BoundingSphere light_bounds =
        new BoundingSphere(origin, BACK_CLIP_DISTANCE);
    DirectionalLight headlight = new DirectionalLight();
    headlight.setColor(white);
    headlight.setInfluencingBounds(light_bounds);
    headlight.setEnable(true);

    //
    // View group for the ground navigation system that the
    // roam code will apply to.
    //

    ViewPlatform gnd_camera = new ViewPlatform();

    Transform3D angle = new Transform3D();

    gndViewTransform = new TransformGroup();
    gndViewTransform.setCapability(TransformGroup.ALLOW_TRANSFORM_READ);
    gndViewTransform.setCapability(TransformGroup.ALLOW_TRANSFORM_WRITE);

    gndViewTransform.addChild(gnd_camera);
    gndViewTransform.addChild(headlight);
//      gndViewTransform.addChild(new Box(10, 10, 10));
```

LISTING 14.8   Continued

```
        View gnd_view = new View();
        gnd_view.setBackClipDistance(BACK_CLIP_DISTANCE);
        gnd_view.setFrontClipDistance(FRONT_CLIP_DISTANCE);
        gnd_view.setPhysicalBody(body);
        gnd_view.setPhysicalEnvironment(env);
        gnd_view.addCanvas3D(navCanvas);
        gnd_view.attachViewPlatform(gnd_camera);

        groundNav.setViewInfo(gnd_view, gndViewTransform);
        groundNav.setNavigationSpeed(50.0f);

        view_group.addChild(gndViewTransform);
        view_group.addChild(groundNav.getTimerBehavior());

        //
        // View transform group for the system that looks in a top-down view
        // of the entire scene graph.
        //

        ViewPlatform god_camera = new ViewPlatform();
        god_camera.setCapability(TransformGroup.ALLOW_LOCAL_TO_VWORLD_READ);

        angle = new Transform3D();
        angle.setTranslation(new Vector3d(0, 0, 50));

        topViewTransform = new TransformGroup(angle);
        topViewTransform.setCapability(TransformGroup.ALLOW_TRANSFORM_READ);
        topViewTransform.setCapability(TransformGroup.ALLOW_TRANSFORM_WRITE);
        topViewTransform.setCapability(TransformGroup.ALLOW_LOCAL_TO_
➥VWORLD_READ);

        topViewTransform.addChild(god_camera);
//        topViewTransform.addChild(headlight.cloneNode(false));

        angle = new Transform3D();
        angle.rotX(-Math.PI / 2);

        TransformGroup god_view_tg = new TransformGroup(angle);
        god_view_tg.setCapability(TransformGroup.ALLOW_LOCAL_TO_VWORLD_READ);
        god_view_tg.setCapability(TransformGroup.ALLOW_TRANSFORM_READ);
        god_view_tg.addChild(topViewTransform);

        View god_view = new View();
        god_view.setBackClipDistance(3*BACK_CLIP_DISTANCE);
        god_view.setFrontClipDistance(FRONT_CLIP_DISTANCE);
```

LISTING 14.8 Continued

```
            god_view.setPhysicalBody(body);
            god_view.setPhysicalEnvironment(env);
            god_view.addCanvas3D(topDownCanvas);
            god_view.attachViewPlatform(god_camera);

            topDownNav.setViewInfo(god_view, topViewTransform);
            topDownNav.setNavigationSpeed(500);

            view_group.addChild(god_view_tg);
            view_group.addChild(topDownNav.getTimerBehavior());

            // Just an axis for reference
//          world_object_group.addChild(new Axis());

            // Create a new branchgroup that is for the geometry. Initially starts
            // with a null child at position zero so that we only need to write the
            // child and not extend. One less capability to set is good.
            terrainGroup = new BranchGroup();
            terrainGroup.setCapability(Group.ALLOW_CHILDREN_WRITE);
            terrainGroup.setCapability(Group.ALLOW_CHILDREN_EXTEND);
//          terrainGroup.addChild(null);

            world_object_group.addChild(terrainGroup);

            Material mat = new Material(ambientBlue, ambientBlue, blue, specular, 0);
            Appearance app = new Appearance();
            app.setMaterial(mat);
            Box box = new Box(50, 50, 1000, app);


            angle.set(new Vector3f(0, 0, -500));
            TransformGroup tg = new TransformGroup(angle);
            tg.addChild(box);

            gndViewTransform.addChild(tg);

            // Add everything to the locale
            locale.addBranchGraph(view_group);
            locale.addBranchGraph(world_object_group);
        }

    /**
     * Load the terrain and get it read to roll. If the texture file is not
     * specified then no texture will be loaded and colour information is
     * used instead.
     *
```

LISTING 14.8   Continued

```java
 * @param filename The name of the terrain file
 * @param textureName The name of the texture file, or null
 */
private void loadTerrain(String filename, String textureName)
{
    BTParser ldr = new BTParser();
    File bt_file = new File(filename);

    View v = navCanvas.getView();
    v.stopView();

    try
    {
        if(landscape != null)
        {
            landscape.setAppearanceGenerator(null);
            landscape.detach();
            landscape = null;
        }

        System.gc();

        System.out.println("Loading terrain file. Please wait");

        ldr.reset(new FileInputStream(bt_file));
        ldr.parse();

        TerrainData terrain = null;

        BTHeader header = ldr.getHeader();

        SimpleTiledTerrainData t = new SimpleTiledTerrainData(ldr);
        terrain = t;

        System.out.println("Terrain loading complete");

        // Use a tiled texture
        TextureTileGenerator myGen = new CachedTextureTileGenerator
➥("numgrid.jpg");
            ((AbstractTiledTerrainData)terrain).setTextureTileGenerator(myGen);

            System.out.println("Finished texture");
        System.out.println("Building landscape");

        landscape = new SplitMergeLandscape(viewFrustum, terrain);
        landscape.setCapability(BranchGroup.ALLOW_DETACH);
        landscape.setAppearanceGenerator(this);
```

14

INTEGRATING THE
JAVA MEDIA APIS

LISTING 14.8 Continued

```
float[] origin = new float[3];
terrain.getCoordinate(origin, 1, 1);

Transform3D angle = new Transform3D();

// setup the top view by just raising it some amount and we want
Vector3f pos = new Vector3f();
pos.z += 15000;
pos.x = origin[0];
pos.y = origin[2];
angle.setTranslation(pos);

topViewTransform.setTransform(angle);

// the initial view to be some way off the ground too and rotate at
// 45 deg to look into the "middle" of the terrain.
terrain.getCoordinate(origin, 0, 0);
pos.set(origin);
pos.y += 100;
pos.x -= 100;
pos.z -= 100;
angle.rotY(Math.PI * -0.25); // 45 deg looking into the terrain
angle.setTranslation(pos);

gndViewTransform.setTransform(angle);


// Force a single render so that the view transform is updated
// and the projection matrix is correct for the view frustum.
v.renderOnce();

viewFrustum.viewingPlatformMoved();

Matrix3f mtx = new Matrix3f();
Vector3f orient = new Vector3f(0, 0, -1);

angle.get(mtx, pos);
mtx.transform(orient);

landscape.initialize(pos, orient);

groundNav.setFrameUpdateListener(landscape);

terrainGroup.removeAllChildren();
terrainGroup.addChild(landscape);
```

LISTING 14.8 Continued

```
            // Set the nav speed to be one grid square per second
            groundNav.setNavigationSpeed((float)terrain.getGridXStep());


            v.startView();

            System.out.println("Ready for rendering");
        }
        catch(IOException ioe)
        {
            System.out.println("I/O Error " + ioe);
            ioe.printStackTrace();
        }
    }

    public static void main(String[] argv)
    {
        TiledCullingDemo demo = new TiledCullingDemo();
        demo.setSize(600, 400);
        demo.setVisible(true);
    }
}
```

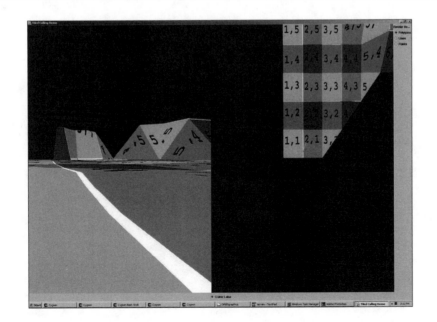

FIGURE 14.3

Screen shot from TiledCullingDemo, *showing a simple numbered texture.*

Summary

The Java Media APIs are intended to work together to deliver multimedia content. Integrating these packages can be challenging because few developers have experience in multiple domains of the APIs. The key to developing an application that takes advantage of multiple APIs is to analyze where the connection should be made.

Duchaineau M, Wolinsky, M., Sigeti, D.E., Miller, M.C., Aldrich, C., Mineev-Weinstein, M.B. IEEE Visualization (pp 81-88), 1997.

INDEX

NUMBERS

X-Z

W

Your Guide
to Computer
Technology

www.informit.com

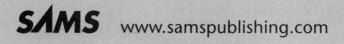

Other Related Titles

Developing Java Servlets, Second Edition
Jim Goodwill and Bryan Morgan
0-672-32107-6
$39.99 US/$59.95 CAN

XML Internationalization and Localization
Yves Savourel
0-672-32096-7
$49.99 US/$74.95 CAN

XML Development with Java 2
Michael Daconta and Al Saganich
0-672-31653-6
$49.99 US/$74.95 CAN

Voice Application Development with VoiceXML
Rick Beasley, Kenneth Michael Farley, John O'Reilly and Leon Squire
0-672-32138-6
$49.99 US/$74.95 CAN

Java Security Handbook
Jamie Jaworski and Paul Perrone
0-672-31602-1
$49.99 US/$74.95 CAN

Java GUI Development
Vartan Piroumian
0-672-31546-7
$34.99 US/$52.95 CAN

Wireless Java Programming with Java 2 Micro Edition
Yu Feng and Dr. Jun Zhu
0-672-32135-1
$49.99 US/$74.95 CAN

Java Deployment
Mauro Marinilli
0-672-32182-3
$39.99 US/$59.95 CAN

SAMS

www.samspublishing.com

All prices are subject to change.